MAGNA CARTA
AND THE
RULE OF LAW

**Foreword by Former Justice
Sandra Day O'Connor**

**Daniel Barstow Magraw, Andrea Martinez,
and Roy E. Brownell II**

Cover by Andrew Alcala/ABA Publishing.

The materials contained herein represent the opinions of the authors and editors, and should not be construed to be the views or opinions of the law firms or companies with whom such persons are in partnership with, associated with, or employed by, nor of the American Bar Association or the Section of International Law unless adopted pursuant to the bylaws of the Association.

Nothing contained in this book is to be considered as the rendering of legal advice for specific cases, and readers are responsible for obtaining such advice from their own legal counsel. This book is intended for educational and informational purposes only.

Printed in the United States of America.

18 17 16 15 5 4

Library of Congress Cataloging-in-Publication Data

Magna Carta and the rule of law / edited by Daniel B. Magraw, Andrea Martinez, Roy E. Brownell II—First edition.
    p. cm.
Includes bibliographical references.
    ISBN 978-1-62722-697-4 (print : alk. paper)
    1. Magna Carta. 2. Constitutional history—England. 3. Rule of law. I. Magraw, Daniel Barstow, editor. II. Martinez, Andrea, editor. III. Brownell, Roy E., editor. IV. Title.
    KD3946.M33 2014
    323.44—dc23

                                                                          2014020768

This book is dedicated to
"The Magraw Boys": Jack, Dick, Dan, and Chuck;
Peg Downey, Liza Schaeffer, and Claudia Moriel;
Sandra Adams and Eleanor Elliott Brownell;
and to the memory of Dr. Edmund Begole Brownell

The American Bar Association and the ABA Fund for Justice and Education would like to thank the following donors for their generous contributions to restore the ABA Memorial to Magna Carta located in Runnymede, England.

Boies Schiller & Flexner, LLP
and
Charles Brower

Contents

Chapter 5
Magna Carta in Supreme Court Jurisprudence   111
Stephen J. Wermiel

Chapter 6
Magna Carta and Executive Power   141
Louis Fisher

Foreword

Sandra Day O'Connor

"No free man shall be taken or imprisoned or disseised or outlawed or exiled or in any way ruined, nor will we go or send against him, except by the lawful judgment of his peers or by the law of the land."[1] Much has been said and written about those fateful words thrust upon King John at Runnymede 800 years ago. Forming chapter 39 of Magna Carta, they embraced the revolutionary idea that no one, including the king, is above the law, and that government must be administered according to the law. As Winston Churchill put it, the "fundamental principle" that united the barons in their quest for Magna Carta was that "[g]overnment must henceforward mean something more than the arbitrary rule of any man, and custom and the law must stand even above the King."[2] And as the Supreme Court of the United States put it, chapter 39 was "intended to secure the individual from the arbitrary exercise of the powers of government, unrestrained by the established principles of private rights and distributive justice."[3] Today, we call the principle underlying chapter 39 "the rule of law." It is a principle that has shaped, and continues to shape, our constitutional development, as well as that of countless countries around the world.

When King John acceded to Magna Carta in 1215, few would have guessed that it would be one of the most important events in English legal history. John was an unlikely king. As the youngest son of King Henry II of England and Eleanor of Aquitaine, he was not expected to inherit much land. Indeed, John earned the nickname "Lackland" in anticipation of his paltry inheritance. But when John's three older brothers rose up against their father, John suddenly, but perhaps unsurprisingly, found himself the favorite son. Shortly thereafter, two of his older brothers met their untimely deaths, and John's future began to look quite different than expected. Following Henry II's death in 1189, John's only remaining brother, Richard I, ascended to the English throne. When Richard I died in 1199, John took his place.

---

1. The translation of Magna Carta used in this foreword is *Magna Carta 1215, Appendix IV, in* J.C. HOLT, MAGNA CARTA 317–37 (1965).
2. 1 WINSTON S. CHURCHILL, THE BIRTH OF BRITAIN 253 (1956).
3. Bank of Columbia v. Okely, 17 U.S. (4 Wheat.) 235, 244 (1819).

From the start, John did not have an easy time being king. As was often the case in medieval Europe, his claim to the throne was not undisputed. Accordingly, John had to spend considerable time and resources fighting off his rival and his rival's allies before his crown was secure. From there, things only got worse. John lost the Duchy of Normandy to King Philip II of France in 1204. That loss would define the rest of his reign. John was determined to recapture Normandy and devoted vast sums of money to trying to do so. The money, as well as the manpower for fighting Philip II's forces, had to come from somewhere. To finance his campaign, John imposed heavy economic burdens on the barons, the noblemen of his realm. And he also demanded military service. In return, John gave the barons little; he encroached on their traditional feudal rights and did not bring peace or stability to the kingdom. As one scholar put it, "the Crown, while it exacted the fullest measure of services legally exigible, curtailed those rights and privileges which had originally balanced the obligations."[4] In other words, "[t]he barons were compelled to give more, while they received less."[5]

By 1215, some of the barons were done putting up with the status quo. John had just suffered yet another loss at the Battle of Bouvines, in what would prove his last attempt at retaking Normandy. Rebellion spread among the ranks of the barons. A group of them renounced their feudal ties to John and took up arms against the Crown. The rebel army marched on London, taking the capital, as well as other English cities. In the hopes of avoiding a civil war, John agreed to meet with the barons on the great meadow at Runnymede alongside the Thames. And there, in June 1215, he acquiesced to the barons' demands for a written accord, acceding to Magna Carta.

The barons who impelled John to come to Runnymede were by no means "disinterested protectors of the common good."[6] They were mostly self-interested men who had a long list of specific grievances against John, such as dissatisfaction with the amount of military service they owed the king, the amount of "scutage" they had to pay to avoid military service, and the amount of "relief" they had to pay to inherit property. Indeed, some of the barons' grievances were quite mundane. Chapter 23 of Magna Carta provides that "[n]o vill or man shall be forced to build bridges at river banks, except those who ought to do so by custom and law." And chapter 33 specifies that "[h]enceforth all fish-weirs shall be completely removed from the Thames and the Medway and throughout all England, except on the sea coast." (A fish-weir is an obstruction placed across a river to block or to redirect the passage of fish.) At bottom, Magna Carta is a practical

---

4. WILLIAM SHARP MCKECHNIE, MAGNA CARTA: A COMMENTARY ON THE GREAT CHARTER OF KING JOHN 49 (2d ed. 1958).

5. *Id.*

6. A.E. DICK HOWARD, THE ROAD FROM RUNNYMEDE: MAGNA CARTA AND CONSTITUTIONALISM IN AMERICA 7 (1968).

document, spelling out, one by one, tangible remedies for the barons' grievances against the king. It is also a document tailored to the particular problems of feudal times, defining certain rights and obligations accompanying
the relationship between the king and his subjects. As Alexander Hamilton
later put it in arguing that our country had no need for a bill of rights:
"[B]ills of rights are, in their origin, stipulations between kings and their
subjects, abridgments of prerogative in favor of privilege, reservations of
rights not surrendered to the prince. Such was Magna Charta, obtained by
the barons, sword in hand, from King John."[7]

The barons' demands, however, had implications for other Englishmen
as well. A number of the abuses of John's reign affected many elements
of English society. In securing remedies against the abuses for themselves,
the barons also secured them for their brethren. For example, chapter 17
of Magna Carta provides that "[c]ommon pleas shall not follow our court
but shall be held in some fixed place." That provision required lawsuits
in which the Crown did not have a special interest to take place in a set
location, rather than following the king from place to place. And chapter
40 specifies that "[t]o no one will we sell, to no one will we deny or delay
right or justice," targeting the king's practice of charging high fees for various writs. Provision was also made for the merchant class. Chapter 41 of
Magna Carta stipulates that "[a]ll merchants are to be safe and secure in
leaving and entering England, and in staying and travelling in England, both
by land and by water." And chapter 35 sets out weights and measures for
wine, ale, corn, and cloth. Even women received some rudimentary rights.
Chapter 7 of Magna Carta provides that "[a]fter her husband's death, a
widow shall have her marriage portion and her inheritance at once and
without any hindrance." And chapter 8 specifies that "[n]o widow shall be
compelled to marry so long as she wishes to live without a husband." As one
scholar put it, "One of the first great stages in the emancipation of women
is to be traced in the emergence of the proffer that they should not be distrained to marry for a second time without their consent."[8] Magna Carta
thus transcended the barons' parochial concerns, incorporating provisions
vindicating the rights of many in England.

The barons' success at Runnymede was short lived. Ten weeks later,
John persuaded Pope Innocent III to nullify Magna Carta and to threaten
to excommunicate anyone who observed or tried to enforce its provisions.
England plunged into a civil war.

Magna Carta might well have been relegated to the ash heap of history,
but John, "a notorious glutton," died of dysentery in 1216.[9] His successor,

---

7. THE FEDERALIST No. 84, at 512–13 (Alexander Hamilton) (Clinton Rossiter ed.,
1961) (capitalization omitted).

8. HOLT, *supra* note 1, at 46.

9. KATE NORGATE, JOHN LACKLAND 281 (1902).

King Henry III, was only nine years old. The young king's guardians and the pope's legate reissued the Charter, albeit without some of its original provisions, in an effort to appease the rebellion and to rally support around Henry III. Additional reissues followed in 1217 and 1225. In 1297, King Edward I reissued the Charter once again and put it on the English statute books for the first time.

Since then, Magna Carta has risen above its uncertain beginnings. It has been a crucial influence on the development of the rule of law, first in England and then around the world. The Charter was key in Parliament's enactment of the Petition of Right in 1628, which condemned taxation without Parliament's consent, imprisonment without a showing of cause, and abuse of martial law. It also inspired the 1689 English Bill of Rights, which prohibited excessive bail and cruel and unusual punishment, secured the right to petition the government for redress of grievances, and forbade royal interference in parliamentary elections.

As the principles animating Magna Carta gained momentum, they also spread beyond England. The American colonists brought them to the New World, where the rights first extracted "at the point of the sword" from an unwilling king were incorporated into the colonial governments that would ultimately break free from the Crown.[10] And appeal to Magna Carta became part of the rallying cry for American independence, as the colonists invoked the Charter in their case for replacing arbitrary government by England with self-rule.

Magna Carta was likewise a central inspiration to our founding fathers in framing our Constitution, which is itself one of the greatest embodiments of the rule of law. The influence is most felt in the Bill of Rights. It is in those first ten Amendments that "we find the bridge between Magna Carta in England and the Charter's legacy in America."[11] Two examples are especially noteworthy. First, the Due Process Clause of the Fifth Amendment, a provision as vital as any to American constitutionalism, finds its roots in chapter 39 of Magna Carta. As you will recall, chapter 39 assured that "[n]o free man shall be taken or imprisoned or disseised or outlawed or exiled or in any way ruined, nor will we go or send against him, except by the lawful judgment of his peers or by the law of the land." The Due Process Clause echoes those auspicious words, providing that no person shall "be deprived of life, liberty, or property, without due process of law." In the years since the adoption of that guarantee, the Supreme Court has made clear that "[t]he words, 'due process of law,' were undoubtedly intended to convey the same meaning as the words, 'by the law of the land,' in Magna Charta."[12] Magna Carta was

---

10. Davidson v. New Orleans, 96 U.S. 97, 102 (1878).

11. HOWARD, *supra* note 6, at 239–40.

12. Murray's Lessee v. Hoboken Land & Improvement Co., 59 U.S. (18 How.) 272, 276 (1856) (italicization omitted).

thus the inspiration for the provision of our Constitution that ensures no less than "the right to notice and a meaningful opportunity to be heard"[13] and "the fundamental elements of fairness in a criminal trial."[14]

A second example of Magna Carta's impact on the Bill of Rights is found in the Speedy Trial Clause of the Sixth Amendment. That clause provides that "[i]n all criminal prosecutions, the accused shall enjoy the right to a speedy and public trial." As Chief Justice Earl Warren wrote for the Supreme Court in *Klopfer v. North Carolina*,[15] it "has its roots at the very foundation of our English law heritage."[16] The clause's "first articulation in modern jurisprudence appears to have been made in Magna Carta (1215), wherein it was written, 'We will sell to no man, we will not deny or defer to any man either justice or right.'"[17] Accordingly, Magna Carta gave rise to the constitutional provision "designed to minimize the possibility of lengthy incarceration prior to trial, to reduce the lesser, but nevertheless substantial, impairment of liberty imposed on an accused while released on bail, and to shorten the disruption of life caused by arrest and the presence of unresolved criminal charges."[18] It is the basis for a right "as fundamental as any of the rights secured by the Sixth Amendment."[19]

The influence of Magna Carta on our constitutional development did not end at the founding. The Great Charter has proven its durability. It has had an enduring significance for the identification and the elaboration of our constitutional rights. The Supreme Court has invoked Magna Carta frequently, citing it in numerous opinions from the early days of our nation to the present. And the Court has done so in important decisions concerning, for example, the requirement that a jury trial be afforded in state criminal prosecutions,[20] the framework for determining whether a punishment violates the Eighth Amendment,[21] and the access of indigent defendants to appellate review of criminal convictions.[22]

Three cases from the past decade showcase especially well Magna Carta's continuing relevance. In *Hosanna-Tabor Evangelical Lutheran Church and School v. EEOC*,[23] the Supreme Court considered whether the Establishment Clause and the Free Exercise Clause of the First Amendment bar employment discrimination suits when the employer is a religious group and

---

13. Lachance v. Erickson, 522 U.S. 262, 266 (1998).
14. Spencer v. Texas, 385 U.S. 554, 563–64 (1967).
15. 386 U.S. 213 (1967).
16. *Id.* at 223.
17. *Id.*
18. United States v. MacDonald, 456 U.S. 1, 8 (1982).
19. *Klopfer*, 386 U.S. at 223.
20. Duncan v. Louisiana, 391 U.S. 145, 151 (1968).
21. Trop v. Dulles, 356 U.S. 86, 100 (1958).
22. Griffin v. Illinois, 351 U.S. 12, 16–17 (1956).
23. 132 S. Ct. 694 (2012).

the employee is one of its ministers. The Court answered that question in the affirmative, holding that there is a "ministerial exception" to employment discrimination laws. That exception, grounded in the First Amendment religion clauses, precludes the application of employment discrimination laws to claims concerning the employment relationship between a religious group and its ministers. In upholding religious groups' right to select their ministers free from government interference, the Court began at Magna Carta. It explained that "[c]ontroversy between church and state over religious offices is hardly new" and invoked "the very first clause of Magna Carta" in which "King John agreed that 'the English church shall be free, and shall have its rights undiminished and its liberties unimpaired.'"[24] Magna Carta thus played a role in the contemporary affirmation of "a religious group's right to shape its own faith and mission through its appointments."[25]

A year earlier, in *Borough of Duryea v. Guarnieri*,[26] the Supreme Court addressed whether a government employee must show that he petitioned the government as a citizen on a matter of public concern to state a claim against his employer under the Petition Clause of the First Amendment. The Court concluded that the public concern test applies to the Petition Clause, as it does to the Speech Clause of the First Amendment. To reach that conclusion, the Court identified "the historic and fundamental principles that led to the enumeration of the right to petition in the First Amendment."[27] The Court started with Magna Carta here as well. As it explained, "The right to petition traces its origins to Magna Carta, which confirmed the right of barons to petition the King."[28] Indeed, "Magna Carta itself was King John's answer to a petition from the barons."[29] The Court, therefore, looked to the historical example of Magna Carta to delineate the bounds of the right that "allows citizens to express their ideas, hopes, and concerns to their government," a right "integral to the democratic process" itself.[30]

Rounding out the trio of cases, in *Boumediene v. Bush*,[31] the Supreme Court considered whether aliens designated as enemy combatants and detained at Guantánamo Bay, Cuba, are protected by the writ of habeas corpus and the Suspension Clause. The Court held that such aliens "may invoke the fundamental procedural protections of habeas corpus" to challenge the legality of their detention and that their right to do so may be withdrawn only in accordance with the Suspension Clause.[32] In so holding,

24. *Id.* at 702.
25. *Id.* at 706.
26. 131 S. Ct. 2488 (2011).
27. *Id.* at 2498.
28. *Id.* at 2499.
29. *Id.*
30. *Id.* at 2495.
31. 553 U.S. 723 (2008).
32. *Id.* at 798.

the Court traced the history and the origins of the writ, beginning once again at Magna Carta. Citing chapter 39 of the Charter, the Court noted that "Magna Carta decreed that no man would be imprisoned contrary to the law of the land."[33] And it explained that although "the Barons at Runnymede prescribed no specific legal process to enforce it," "the writ of habeas corpus became the means by which the promise of Magna Carta was fulfilled."[34] Even in considering our "present, urgent concerns" relating to national security, the Court harkened back to Magna Carta to preserve the "freedom from arbitrary and unlawful restraint and the personal liberty that is secured by adherence to the separation of powers."[35]

In the 800 years since King John acceded to Magna Carta, therefore, the Great Charter has proven its "capacity for growth and adaptation."[36] To this day, it continues to serve as a reminder of why countries around the world moved away from systems defined by the arbitrary exercise of government power. It continues to serve as a beacon for those committed to the rule of law, a testament to government limited by "the law of the land." Over the past several decades, more and more countries have established governments embracing the principle underlying chapter 39 of Magna Carta. But many people still live under governments that fall short of that ideal. At least until all people may be secure in the promise that no one is above the law and that government must be administered according to the law, Magna Carta will continue to have a role to play.

---

33. *Id.* at 740.
34. *Id.*
35. *Id.* at 797.
36. Hurtado v. California, 110 U.S. 516, 530 (1884).

Acknowledgments

As with any book of this magnitude, the editors are indebted to many people who assisted during the course of its preparation.

The authors would like to express their sincere gratitude to Sir Robert Worcester KBE DL of the Magna Carta 2015 800th Anniversary Commemoration Committee, Claire Breay of the British Library, Robin Griffith-Jones of Temple Church, Olivia Nelson of The National Trust, Emm Johnstone of Royal Holloway, University of London, Robert Newlen of the Library of Congress, and Phil Hamlyn Williams (formerly of Lincoln Cathedral) for graciously sharing their knowledge and enthusiasm about Magna Carta throughout this project. Some of these people also helped in other ways, including gaining permission to reprint translations and reproduce images. They have been immensely helpful.

The same is true of Richard Paszkiet, Amanda Wilander, Leanne Pfautz, Katy Englehart, and Marina Jacks, all at the American Bar Association. The book would not have been produced without their hard work and support. We are deeply grateful.

For their assistance in securing permission for reproduction of images that appear in this volume, the authors would like to thank Darlene McClurkin of the U.S. National Archives and Records Administration; Emma Butterfield of the National Portrait Gallery (UK); Lori Sullivan, Tom Blazej, and Jeff Surette of the Massachusetts Secretary of State's Office; Nathan Dorn of the Law Library of Congress; Steve Petteway and Rebekah-Anne Gebler of the Office of the Curator of the Supreme Court of the United States; Jovita Calleung of the British Library; and Michael O'Connor. We are also grateful to David Rubenstein for ensuring that an exemplification of Magna Carta remains in the United States and is available to the public.

Similarly, we wish to thank Jenny Gelman of Johns Hopkins University's School of Advanced International Studies for her invaluable assistance in locating English-language versions of historical texts relating to Magna Carta. We also wish to thank Dirk Van Tuerenhout from the Houston Museum of Natural Science, Connie Robertson and Anne-Marie Hansen from Oxford University Press, and Rosemary Bavister from Taylor & Francis Books (UK) with respect to English-language translations.

We are also grateful to those who have granted us permission to use copyrighted material: the British Library for the images of King John Hunting Venison, the Articles of the Barons, the great seal of King John that originally was attached to the Articles of the Barons, Pope Innocent III's papal bull declaring the 1215 Magna Carta null and void, and the 1225 Magna Carta; Lincoln Cathedral for the images of the 1215 Magna Carta and the 1217 Carta de Foresta; the Library of Congress for the images of the Miniature Magna Carta for use by a judge in medieval England and the title page of the book *A Conference Desired by the Lords and HAD by a Committee of both Houses, Concerning the Rights and Privileges of the Subjects*; David Rubenstein for the image of the 1297 Magna Carta; the National Portrait Gallery (UK) for the image of the portrait of Sir Edward Coke (1592); the Commonwealth of Massachusetts for the image of the 1775 seal of the colony of Massachusetts; the Office of the Curator of the Supreme Court of the United States for the image from the door panel of the Supreme Court (on the back cover of this book); Professor Nicholas Robinson of Pace University for the translation of Carta de Foresta; Professor Daniel Power of Swansea University (UK) for the translation of the King's Writ; Taylor & Francis Books (UK) for the translations of the 1216 Magna Carta, the 1217 Magna Carta, the 1225 Magna Carta, and the Confirmatio Cartarum; and the National Archives for the U.S. Constitution and Bill of Rights. Finally, we are grateful to Dr. Henry Summerson for the translations of the 1215 Magna Carta and the Articles of the Barons, which were prepared by him for the AHRC Magna Carta Project.

A different type of thanks goes to the authors of the chapters in this volume. They worked extremely hard to produce original and interesting scholarship in a field that has been plowed by historians, lawyers, and others for hundreds of years. They succeeded, for which we are truly grateful. We are also very grateful to Nga Kit "Christy" Tang for her excellent assistance in preparing the appendices to this book.

We add a special expression of gratitude to Justice Sandra Day O'Connor, not only for authoring the Foreword to this volume but also for being a source of inspiration to so many women and men who believe in the rule of law for which Magna Carta stands. We all owe her a deep debt of gratitude.

Finally, the editors wish to thank their families, who supported their work on this project even when the hours were long.

List of Illustrations

King John Hunting Venison (from the British Library)

Articles of the Barons (June 1215) (from the British Library)

Seal of King John originally attached to the Articles of the Barons (June 1215)

1215 Magna Carta (from the Lincoln Cathedral)

Papal Bull declaring that Magna Carta is null and void (August 24, 1215) (from the British Library)

1217 Carta de Foresta (Charter of the Forest) (from the Lincoln Cathedral)

1225 Magna Carta (from the British Library)

1297 Magna Carta (from the U.S. National Archives)

Miniature Magna Carta for use by a judge in medieval England (from the Library of Congress)

Portrait of Sir Edward Coke (1592) (from the National Portrait Gallery (UK))

Title page of book titled *A Conference Desired by the Lords and HAD by a Committee of both Houses, Concerning the Rights and Privileges of the Subjects*, including discourses by Edward Coke and John Selden praising Magna Carta as the foundational instrument of English liberties (1642) (from the Library of Congress)

Seal of the colony of Massachusetts with a patriot holding Magna Carta and sword (1775)

About the Authors

Roy E. Brownell II is an attorney residing in Washington, D.C.

David Clark is a professor of law at Flinders University, South Australia.

Michael Dillon is chair and professor of political science at La Salle University in Philadelphia, where he teaches constitutional law, environmental law, and political philosophy.

Danieli Evans is a law clerk to Senior Judge Harry T. Edwards, U.S. Court of Appeals for the D.C. Circuit. She formerly served as a law clerk to Chief Judge Diane P. Wood. She earned her law degree from Yale Law School in 2012.

Louis Fisher is a scholar in residence at the Constitution Project and a visiting professor at the William and Mary Law School. From 1970 to 2010 he served as senior specialist in separation of powers at the Congressional Research Service and as a specialist in constitutional law at the Law Library of Congress.

Tore Lindholm is professor emeritus at the Norwegian Centre for Human Rights, University of Oslo. His field is the philosophy of human rights.

Daniel Barstow Magraw is a Senior Fellow at the Foreign Policy Institute, and a professorial lecturer at Johns Hopkins University School of Advanced International Studies; and he is President Emeritus of the Center for International Environmental Law.

Andrea Martinez is an Associate with the International Justice Initiative at the Foreign Policy Institute at Johns Hopkins University School of Advanced International Studies.

Larry May is the W. Alton Jones Professor of Philosophy, a professor of law, and a professor of political science at Vanderbilt University.

Thomas J. McSweeney is an assistant professor of law at the William and Mary Law School and holds a J.D. and a Ph.D. in medieval history from Cornell University.

Sandra Day O'Connor is a retired Associate Justice of the Supreme Court of the United States.

Nicholas A. Robinson is University Professor for the Environment at Pace University in New York and an adjunct professor at Yale University School of Forestry & Environmental Studies in Connecticut.

Ralph V. Turner is a professor of history, emeritus, at the Florida State University in Tallahassee, where he was named Distinguished Research Professor in 1994. His research on the Angevin kings, their officials, their administration of justice, and the common law has led to his writing a number of articles and books.

Stephen J. Wermiel is a professor of practice at American University Washington College of Law. He was the *Wall Street Journal* Supreme Court correspondent from 1979 to 1991.

Justin Wert is the Associates Second Century Presidential Professor and an associate professor of political science at the University of Oklahoma.

Diane P. Wood is Chief Judge of the U.S. Court of Appeals for the Seventh Circuit and a senior lecturer in law at the University of Chicago School of Law.

Chapter 1

Introduction: Magna Carta and the Rule of Law

Daniel B. Magraw, Andrea Martinez,
and Roy E. Brownell II

I. Introduction

Magna Carta has left a profound and multifaceted legacy for law and culture around the world. Indeed, it is difficult to think of a legal document that exceeds it in historical importance and breadth of legacy. It has been called "England's greatest export" because of its worldwide influence,[1] and it is inscribed in the Memory of the World Register of the United Nations Educational, Scientific and Cultural Organization (UNESCO).[2] It has even entered into the English-language lexicon as a term meaning a foundational document or law guaranteeing basic rights or liberties.[3]

The English barons who brought King John (r. 1199–1216) to heel at Runnymede almost assuredly did not see themselves as the founding fathers of some new and enlightened constitutional order.[4] (For an image depicting King John hunting venison, see Illustration No. 1.) But the agreement they forced upon the monarch to satisfy their own immediate grievances would over time germinate into a legal document, the impact of which is still felt to this day across the globe. A sense of Magna Carta's impact is evident in

---

1. *E.g.*, Robert Worcester, The Relevance of Magna Carta in the 21st Century, Magna Carta 800th (Sept. 27, 2013), http://magnacarta800th.com/speeches/the-relevance-of-magna-carta-in-the-21st-century/.

2. Magna Carta, Issued in 1215, Memory of the World, UNESCO, http://www.unesco.org/new/en/communication-and-information/flagship-project-activities/memory-of-the-world/register/full-list-of-registered-heritage/registered-heritage-page-5/magna-carta-issued-in-1215/ (last visited May 7, 2014).

3. *E.g.*, Costas Pitas, *Web Founder Berners-Lee Calls for Online 'Magna Carta' to Protect Users*, REUTERS (May 17, 2014), http://www.reuters.com/article/2014/03/13/us-internet-bernerslee-idUSBREA2B0PC20140313.

4. *See, e.g.*, CLAIRE BREAY, MAGNA CARTA: MANUSCRIPTS AND MYTHS 28 (2002).

Winston Churchill's historic Fulton, Missouri, speech in which he unveiled the expression "Iron Curtain." In his address, he characterized Magna Carta as one of the "title deeds of freedom."[5]

Magna Carta's impact has occurred in spite of the fact that it was not a statement of principles but rather a "practical solution to a political crisis"[6] arising out of a set of specific grievances. Magna Carta contained specific resolutions to those problems, some of which were quite mundane. Nevertheless, many uncertainties remain regarding the negotiating history of Magna Carta. Some of its provisions had been previously included in the 1100 Coronation Charter of Henry I (r. 1100–1135), which Henry promptly disregarded.[7] But the sources of other ideas and the roles of individuals who might have been the drafters of Magna Carta, such as Stephen Langton, are not clear.[8]

Moreover, very little is known about what actually happened in June 1215. For example, it is not clear exactly where King John and the barons met at Runnymede: Was it on the meadow on which the memorial to Magna Carta erected by the American Bar Association in 1957 stands (as depicted on the front cover), or was it across the River Thames at Ankerwycke?[9] The identity of the true location is lost in the mists of time.

It is not even clear what document, if any, actually was sealed on June 15, 1215.[10] It is possible that there was a master agreement sealed on June 15 that contained the terms actually agreed to and was the basis for the exemplifications that were made thereafter. There is no record of such an agreement, however.[11] The four existing exemplifications of Magna Carta from 1215 are dated June 15.[12] But in keeping with the custom of the times, each exemplification of Magna Carta is in the form of a description of what was

---

5. Winston Churchill, Former Prime Minister U.K., Sinews of Peace at Westminster College, Fulton, Missouri (Mar. 5, 1946) *in The Sinews of Peace, The Churchill Centre*, WINSTON CHURCHILL, https://www.winstonchurchill.org/learn/speeches/speeches -of-winston-churchill/120-the-sinews-of-peace (last visited May 7, 2014).

6. BREAY, *supra* note 4, at 7.

7. *See, e.g.*, NICHOLAS VINCENT, MAGNA CARTA: A VERY SHORT INTRODUCTION 10, 65–66, 77, 102 (2012); J.C. HOLT, MAGNA CARTA 38 (2d ed. 1992). An English-language translation of Henry I's Coronation Charter is contained in appendix A.

8. VINCENT, *supra* note 7, at 49, 64–65; BREAY, *supra* note 4, at 25. There is a version of the Great Charter carrying the date June 15, 1215, and the location of Windsor, which is held currently at the Huntington Library in San Marino, California. The manuscript was likely assembled by chancery clerks for the two parties to agree to at the Runnymede gathering. RALPH V. TURNER, MAGNA CARTA THROUGH THE AGES 63 (2003); HOLT, *supra* note 7, at 445–46.

9. *Fascination of Plants, Ankerwycke, Surrey,* NATIONAL TRUST, http://www .nationaltrust.org.uk/article-1356400643565/ (last visited May 7, 2014).

10. *See, e.g.*, TURNER, *supra* note 8, at 63–64; BREAY, *supra* note 4, at 25–27, 34.

11. TURNER, *supra* note 8, at 63–64; BREAY, *supra* note 4, at 34.

12. *See, e.g.*, BREAY, *supra* note 4, at 27. *See* appendix C, "1215 Magna Carta."

agreed to, akin to minutes of a meeting, not in the form of an actual agreement; and each has the date the agreement was made, not the date when the
document was actually written.[13] These exemplifications of Magna Carta
thus must have been written and sealed after the agreement was reached
on June 15, and King John therefore could not have had his seal affixed to
them on June 15.[14]

Chapter 62 of the 1215 Magna Carta refers to "letters patent" that
were issued over the seals of certain named individuals "testifying" to the
concessions in the preceding chapters. Sadly, this document is nowhere
to be found.[15] It is also possible that on June 15, King John sealed the
so-called Articles of the Barons, a list of demands now in the collection of
the British Library together with King John's seal, which became detached
in the ensuing centuries.[16] (The Articles of the Barons is reproduced as
Illustration No. 2 and an image of the seal of King John that was attached
to the Articles of the Barons is reproduced as Illustration No. 3.) But that
is not entirely certain; some scholars believe the Articles were sealed on
June 10 (or in any event before June 15), to indicate that King John was
accepting the basic contents to be negotiated.[17] Moreover, even among
those who believe the Articles were sealed by King John on June 15, there
is disagreement about whether the Articles were brought to Runnymede
already finalized as the result of the previous negotiations between King
John and the barons, or whether they were drafted at Runnymede or finalized at Runnymede on the basis of a fairly complete draft.[18]

---

13. BREAY, *supra* note 4, at 27.

14. *See id.*, at 34; *cf.* TURNER, *supra* note 8, at 63.

15. *E.g.*, BREAY, *supra* note 4, at 33.

16. *Id.* at 39.

17. *See, e.g.*, TURNER, *supra* note 8, at 62 (the Articles were "[a] product of weeks
of negotiations, its text was copied by a clerk . . . before a meeting with John, and the
king likely set his seal to it as a sign that he accepted its provisions on 10 June."). An
English-language translation of the Articles of the Barons is included as appendix B.
Claire Breay writes: "[I]t is possible that the Articles predated the meeting by the
Thames, and that they were sealed by the king in advance to demonstrate his agreement
to their basic demands, in order to bring the opposing parties together for a final settlement." BREAY, *supra* note 4, at 27.

18. J.C. Holt notes that traditionally there have been two theories regarding the
Articles: "first, that they were presented by the barons on 15 June and conceded by the
king forthwith." HOLT, *supra* note 7, at 429. Bishop William Stubbs, Sidney Painter, and
Charles McIlwain are advocates of this position. *Id.* at n.5. The second is "that they were
not drawn up until the 15th itself in the first general discussions between the two parties
at Runnymede." *Id.* at 429. William Blackstone and William McKechnie are supporters
of this theory. *Id.* at n.6. Holt dismisses both as "[un]satisfactory." *Id.* at 429. Ultimately,
he concludes, "the Articles must have been prepared in some form before the first plenary
meeting of 15 June." *Id.* at 431. Holt himself concedes that this "leaves the sealing of such
a peculiar document inadequately explained." *Id.* He concludes that "[t]he issue depends

Finally, it is possible that nothing was actually sealed on June 15, 1215.[19] The barons did not swear their fealty to King John until June 19, and it can be argued that the king would not have sealed anything until they had done so.[20]

Nor is it clear how many copies of Magna Carta were made or distributed in 1215 (or thereafter). Several exemplifications of Magna Carta were created by officials from the royal chancery before June 24, 1215: seven exemplifications were "delivered for distribution" on June 24, and at least six more were issued thereafter; but how many others were distributed "in 1215 is obscure."[21] Nicholas Vincent estimates there could have been up to 40.[22] Four exemplifications are known to exist from that year (two in the British Library and one each in Lincoln Cathedral and Salisbury Cathedral (the Lincoln exemplification, which was stored in Fort Knox for safekeeping during World War II, is reproduced as Illustration No. 4).[23] But it is not unreasonable to assume that a copy was sent to each shire,[24] which would mean roughly 40 copies were made of the 1215 Magna Carta.[25] Each of the exemplifications was equally authentic, though because they were hand-copied they contain minor inconsistencies.[26] The exemplifications have been described as "working documents," written in Latin and rather plain looking without any ornate lettering as found in medieval illustrated manuscripts, as is evident from the reproduction of the so-called Lincoln Magna Carta in this volume.[27] There also was a French-language translation in conjunction with a letter dated June 27, 1215, indicating a desire that persons not fluent in Latin would know Magna Carta's contents.[28]

King John issued the so-called King's Writ on June 20, 1215, to the Sheriff of Gloucester, alerting him to the fact that Magna Carta was coming and

---

on a reconstruction of the circumstances which led to the sealing of the document; [and] there is no direct evidence to determine it either way." *Id.*

Nicholas Vincent writes that "the 'Articles of the Barons' . . . [were] a sealed draft of the eventual treaty, almost certainly produced at Runnymede prior to the final rearrangements and revisions that produced Magna Carta on 15 June." VINCENT, *supra* note 7, at 103.

19. *See* BREAY, *supra* note 4, at 34.
20. TURNER, *supra* note 8, at 63.
21. BREAY, *supra* note 4, at 34–35.
22. VINCENT, *supra* note 7, at 72, 102.
23. *Id.* at 102–04; BREAY, *supra* note 4, at 35. Appendix C contains an English-language translation of the 1215 Magna Carta.
24. TURNER, *supra* note 8, at 64.
25. *See* VINCENT, *supra* note 7, at 72, 102; *see also* BREAY, *supra* note 4, at 35.
26. TURNER, *supra* note 8, at 64; BREAY, *supra* note 4, at 37.
27. TURNER, *supra* note 8, at 64.
28. *See id.*

directing that it be implemented.[29] It is not clear whether this was a unique document or if a similar letter was sent to each sheriff, but there is no reason to conclude that it was sealed on June 15.

It seems very clear that June 15, 1215, is not the date that the documents now known as Magna Carta were sealed.[30] It was rather the date on which an agreement apparently was reached that resolved (at least temporarily) hostilities between King John and the barons and led to the reproduction and actual sealing of Magna Carta exemplifications sometime between June 19 and June 24.[31] June 15 thus has both historical and symbolic significance. As is demonstrated in this book, that is entirely appropriate, because Magna Carta's influence in recent centuries is largely based on myth.

The profound impact of Magna Carta occurred in spite of the facts that the 1215 Magna Carta was declared invalid by Pope Innocent III (r. 1198–1216) only ten weeks after it was agreed to (an English-language translation of this papal bull is contained in appendix E) and that it demonstrably failed to bring peace between King John and the barons. Nevertheless, over the following centuries, English kings repeatedly issued new versions of Magna Carta or confirmed the version that then existed. New versions were issued in 1216, 1217 (when the Charter of the Forest, which is the subject of chapter 12 of this volume and is depicted in Illustration No. 6, was spun off as a separate charter), and 1225, with the last-mentioned version being essentially reissued in 1297 and given statutory status (Illustration No. 8), and finally in 1300 using the same text. Many confirmations of Magna Carta and of the Charter of the Forest have occurred over the centuries since 1217. However, many of the same kings—including Henry III (r. 1216–1272), who issued the 1225 Magna Carta—acted in ways that ignored or evaded Magna Carta and its close relation, the Charter of the Forest, when it suited their purposes.[32] Nevertheless, from the 13th century on, litigants, barons, and judges have resorted to Magna Carta, as is indicated by the image of a 14th-century mini-Magna Carta, presumably for use by a traveling judge, reproduced as Illustration No. 9.

Perhaps most importantly, judges, politicians, and commentators in England (most prominently Edward Coke in the 17th century; Illustration No. 10 reproduces a portrait of Coke, and Illustration No. 11 reproduces the title page of a book containing "discourses" by Coke and John Selden promoting Magna Carta) and elsewhere (especially in the American colonies) often used Magna Carta for their own ends, arguing forcefully for

---

29. The only existing copy of the King's Writ is in the collection of the Hereford Cathedral. An English-language translation of the King's Writ is provided in appendix D to this volume.

30. See BREAY, *supra* note 4, at 34.

31. See TURNER, *supra* note 8, at 63.

32. See, e.g., *id.* at 89–91; VINCENT, *supra* note 7, at 84, 86.

principles they asserted were embodied in Magna Carta.[33] In fact, the story of Magna Carta's impact is the story of advocacy of what turned out to be powerful ideas (such as the requirement of a trial by jury and due process of law), regardless of whether those ideas were precisely embodied in, or originated with, the text of Magna Carta, while at the same time ignoring less noble concepts that are reflected in the text of some versions of Magna Carta (such as the implicit embrace of trial by battle in chapter 54 of the 1215 Magna Carta[34] and the unfavorable treatment of loans owed to Jews in chapter 10 of the 1215 Magna Carta).[35]

The year 2015 will mark the 800th anniversary of the adoption of this venerable text. As part of the commemoration of this historic event, we have assembled a distinguished group of scholars to take a fresh look at Magna Carta and its impact on various aspects of the law. Over the course of many generations, Magna Carta has been analyzed from numerous perspectives, including through important works of history and political science. Nonetheless, it is hoped that this book will be of value to those interested in contemporary legal issues related to this ancient document.

Chapter 2 of this book provides historical context for the 1215 Magna Carta and describes the subsequent transmogrification of Magna Carta from a failed peace treaty to an iconic document. Chapters 3 through 12 each explore a different aspect of Magna Carta and its legacy. Following those chapters are appendices that provide the texts of several documents with an important connection to Magna Carta's history. The final appendix provides a chronology of Magna Carta and related events. It is followed by a glossary and a subject index.[36]

Section II of this chapter explains various points that will be helpful in reading this book. Following that, Section III briefly describes chapters

---

33. *See generally* ANNE PALLISTER, MAGNA CARTA: THE HERITAGE OF LIBERTY (1994 ed.); A.E. DICK HOWARD, THE ROAD FROM RUNNYMEDE: MAGNA CARTA AND CONSTITUTIONALISM IN AMERICA (1968).

34. This provision was included because a woman who asserted this could hire a strong champion to fight for her in a trial by battle, whereas the accused had to fight for himself. *See* WILLIAM SHARP MCKECHNIE, MAGNA CARTA: A COMMENTARY ON THE GREAT CHARTER OF KING JOHN 451 (2d ed. 1914); appendix C, "1215 Magna Carta." *See also id.*, at ch. 36 (discussing a writ relating to trial by combat).

35. *See* 1215 Magna Carta, chapter 10 (providing unfavorable treatment regarding loans owed to Jews but not to other persons). In contrast, chapter 11 of the 1215 Magna Carta provides equal treatment to loans owed to all persons. These chapters were not included in subsequent versions of Magna Carta.

36. Appendixes to this book are as follows: A. Coronation Charter of Henry I; B. Articles of the Barons; C. 1215 Magna Carta; D. King's Writ; E. Pope Innocent III: Papal Bull Declaring that Magna Carta is Null & Void; F. 1216 Magna Carta; G. 1217 Magna Carta; H. 1217 Carta de Foresta (Charter of the Forest); I. 1225 Magna Carta; J. Confirmatio Cartarum 1297 (Confirmation of the Charters); K. United States Constitution; L. United States Bill of Rights; and M. Chronology of Magna Carta & Related Events.

2 through 12. Section IV of this chapter then identifies themes that run throughout this work.

II. Explanation of Terminology and Translations

A. Use of Numbers and "Chapter" for Parts of Magna Carta

The different versions of Magna Carta were written by scribes in abbreviated Latin,[37] without any numbers denoting its constituent parts.[38] A standard numbering system has evolved over the years, however, and it is used in this book. It is common to refer to the parts of Magna Carta as "chapters," a convention that is also adopted in this book.

B. Identification of Different Versions of Magna Carta

Because the various versions of Magna Carta differ in content, it is important to identify which version is being analyzed or referred to. Specific versions of Magna Carta are identified herein by date if it is not otherwise clear from the context, e.g., "1225 Magna Carta."

For the same reason, the number for a particular chapter can change over time. For example, chapter 39 of the 1215 Magna Carta corresponds to chapter 29 of the 1225 Magna Carta. Chapter numbers herein normally relate to the 1215 Magna Carta; when a chapter number is from a different version, that version will be specified unless the context already makes it clear.

As noted above, different exemplifications of the same version of Magna Carta also differ slightly, presumably due to the fact that the texts were inscribed by hand. In addition to the four exemplifications of the 1215 Magna Carta identified above, there is one exemplification of the 1216 Magna Carta, and several exemplifications each of the 1217, 1225, 1297, and 1300 versions of Magna Carta.[39] Because any inconsistencies between

---

37. BREAY, *supra* note 4, at 38.
38. *E.g.*, A.E. DICK HOWARD, MAGNA CARTA: TEXT & COMMENTARY 9 (1998 rev. ed.).
39. The four 1215 Magna Cartas are in Lincoln Cathedral (reproduced as Illustration 4), Salisbury Cathedral, and the British Library, which has two exemplifications; the British Library also has a 1225 exemplification and a 1300 exemplification. The only 1216 exemplification is in Durham Cathedral, which also has a 1225 exemplification and 1300 exemplification. Three 1217 exemplifications are in Oxford University's Bodleian Library, and one is in Hereford Cathedral. One 1297 exemplification is in the National Archives in Washington, D.C. (reproduced as Illustration No. 6), and one is in the National Library of Australia. Two 1217 exemplifications of Carta de Foresta survive, in Durham Cathedral and Lincoln Cathedral (reproduced as Illustration No. 8). English-language translations of the 1215, 1216, and 1225 Magna Cartas are contained

the exemplifications of a particular version of Magna Carta are thought to be insignificant, this book makes no distinction among them.

C.   Use of Different Translations

English-language translations of Magna Carta vary, and the authors in this book have used different ones. The translation used in the Foreword and in each chapter thus is identified the first time Magna Carta is quoted.

There is one translation issue that at least theoretically could be significant. The famous chapter 39 of the 1215 Magna Carta (which as noted above has the number 29 in the 1225 Magna Carta) uses the word "vel" between the references to judgment by one's peers and law of the land. "Vel," as described by the noted Magna Carta scholar William McKechnie, "introduced an unfortunate element of ambiguity" into the text, because "vel" can mean either "or" or "and."[40] Some translators have taken the view that it means "or," some "and," and some both.[41] Many modern authors have tended to use "or" as the appropriate translation.[42] McKechnie, who appeared to prefer "and,"[43] translated the chapter as:

> No freeman shall be taken or [and] imprisoned or disseised or exiled or in any way destroyed, nor will we go upon him nor send upon him, except by the lawful judgment of his peers or [and] by the law of the land.[44]

If "vel" means "or" it seems clear that the harms listed in the chapter can be imposed without a jury trial as long as the imposition is according to the law of the land. Indeed, in chapter 11 of this book, "Magna Carta, Civil Law, and Canon Law," Thomas McSweeney relies partly on a translation of "vel" in chapter 39 as "or" to conclude that the "origins of the criminal jury have nothing to do with Magna Carta."[45] In contrast, if "vel" means "and," the argument that Magna Carta forms the basis for the right to a trial by jury is strengthened.

---

in appendices F, G, and I, respectively. An English-language translation of the Charter of the Forest is contained in appendix H.

40. McKECHNIE, *supra* note 34, at 381.

41. *See id.* at 381 n.3.

42. *See, e.g.*, HOLT, *supra* note 7, at 461 (providing translation); British Library, *Treasures in Full: Magna Carta, Translation,* http://www.bl.uk/treasures/magnacarta /translation/mc_trans.html (last visited May 7, 2014).

43. *See* McKECHNIE, *supra* note 34, at 381–82.

44. *Id.* at 375.

45. *See also* chapter 4, "Magna Carta and the United States Constitution: An Exercise in Building Fences."

D. Name and Spelling of Magna Carta

The name and spelling of the Great Charter have changed over time, just as its content and interpretation have. Originally referred to as the "Charter of Liberties," it became "Magna Carta" (i.e., Great Charter) in 1217 to differentiate it from the shorter Carta de Foresta (Charter of the Forest), which spun off from Magna Carta that year. During earlier periods, the spelling "Magna Charta," rather than "Magna Carta," was in wider use. In part because so many people mispronounced the name by using a "ch" sound instead of a hard "k" sound, Magna Carta is now the more common usage.[46] Some of the quotations contained in this book use the spelling "Magna Charta," and we have retained that spelling in those quotations. Otherwise, we use the spelling "Magna Carta." We use "Magna Carta," "Great Charter," and "Charter" interchangeably.

The Carta de Foresta is referred to herein by that term, by the English-language translation "Charter of the Forest," and by "Forest Charter." Carta de Foresta is a formidable instrument in its own right and is the subject of chapter 12 of this book.

III.   The Chapters in This Book

A.   Chapter 2: "The Making of Magna Carta:
The Historical Background"

Professor Ralph Turner begins his analysis by providing a brief history of the context leading to Magna Carta and the events surrounding it, and its subsequent evolution in English history. Among other things, Turner describes how Coke, the great common law jurist, and others in late-16th-century and early-17th-century England recast the meaning and historical importance of Magna Carta, giving rise to its iconic status. Turner also briefly describes how the mythic Magna Carta spread to English colonies and was further reinterpreted in that context. The 1775 seal of Massachusetts, reproduced as Illustration No. 12, shows a patriot brandishing a sword in one hand and Magna Carta clutched in the other, indicating the importance of Magna Carta in the American colonies. This chapter forms the basis for those that follow, though the perspectives of some authors differ from Turner's.

---

46. A.E. Dick Howard, *Magna Carta Celebrates Its 750th Year*, 51 A.B.A. J. 529, 530 (1965) (Editor's Note).

B. Chapter 3: "Magna Carta and Sovereign Immunity: Strained Bedfellows"

Chief Judge Diane Wood and Dr. Danieli Evans address the apparent inconsistency between Magna Carta's promise that everyone is under the rule of law, even the king, and current U.S. law on sovereign immunity, which provides extensive immunity to federal, state, and foreign governments and Native American tribes. Wood and Evans argue that U.S. Supreme Court jurisprudence establishing such extensive immunity is based on a misunderstanding of English law regarding bringing a suit against the king at the time the United States Constitution was ratified. They further argue that the time is ripe to reexamine the historical record and bring U.S. sovereign immunity law into line with Magna Carta's promise, thus in the words of Wood and Evans giving effect to "the propositions that no person is above the law, that governments must be held to be accountable to their citizens, and that effective remedies are essential," even vis-à-vis governments.

C. Chapter 4: "Magna Carta and the United States Constitution: An Exercise in Building Fences"

Magna Carta and its reissues constitute a pivotal point in the development of the unwritten English Constitution. Professor Michael Dillon asserts that a side-by-side review of Magna Carta and the original United States Constitution demonstrates that the Magna Carta that had an impact on the 1789 Constitution was neither the Magna Carta of 1215 nor the Magna Carta of 1225. It was instead the *mythic* Magna Carta, in large part the product of the late 16th and early 17th centuries, particularly the work of Coke as interwoven with John Locke's social contract theory. It was this reconstituted Magna Carta that was conveyed to the American colonies by William Blackstone, that influenced the original Constitution, and that has been greatly influential around the world. While Dillon argues that there are essentially no equivalent segments of the 1215 or the 1225 versions of Magna Carta in the text of the original U.S. Constitution, there are comparable passages between these two versions of the Great Charter and the Bill of Rights, in particular elements of the Fifth, Seventh, and Eighth Amendments. That said, Dillon contends that those parallels may well originate with Coke and Blackstone "rather than directly from Magna Carta."

D. Chapter 5: "Magna Carta in Supreme Court Jurisprudence"

Magna Carta not only contributed to the creation of the United States Constitution, as amended, but also to its subsequent interpretation in the courts. The Supreme Court has frequently utilized Magna Carta to highlight key legal principles. Professor Stephen Wermiel examines the High Court's jurisprudence in this vein. He finds that the U.S. Reports make mention of the Great Charter in more than 170 Supreme Court cases. Professor Wermiel concludes that historically the use of Magna Carta in Supreme Court jurisprudence has been "largely symbolic." For Supreme Court justices, and the advocates who appear before them, Magna Carta is a venerable document cited to establish the pedigree and legitimacy of their assertions. Justices have clearly indicated, however, that Magna Carta is not positive law in the United States, because it antedates the 1789 Constitution. Nevertheless, Professor Wermiel concludes that Magna Carta does have an impact on the legal reasoning and historical analysis of Supreme Court justices—an influence that has increased as the Court has adopted a broader view of individual rights and liberties originating in the second half of the last century.

E.   Chapter 6: "Magna Carta and Executive Power"

This chapter entails a discussion by Dr. Louis Fisher about Magna Carta and its influence on the development and limitation of executive authority throughout English and early American history. Fisher points out that modern American claims of inherent power by presidents and their defenders are "reminiscent" of the views of King John regarding royal power. Likewise, parallels can be found between legislative and judicial branch measures to check the president's claims of inherent powers and the barons' efforts to counter the king's potentially limitless claims of authority. While the framers did not draw directly upon Magna Carta in fashioning a presidency bound by law, notions of the mythic Great Charter's role in defending individual rights in England against overweening executive power were transplanted onto, and took root in, American soil.

F.   Chapter 7: "Magna Carta and Habeas Corpus"

Professor Justin Wert compares the respective evolutions of Magna Carta and habeas corpus over the past 800 years. His analysis reveals that just as Magna Carta's significance has waxed, waned, and ultimately been transformed to its current mythic status, so too the writ of habeas corpus has evolved in reaction to its use for a variety of legal purposes serving the political interests of those using it, ultimately becoming the guarantor of freedom from arbitrary confinement that it now represents. Habeas corpus was used for a range of purposes, for example, to ensure that a person appeared in court at the time of the 1215 Magna Carta and to determine who owned slaves in the antebellum South in the United States. These applications of habeas corpus are a far cry from today's usage.

G. Chapter 8: "Magna Carta and Religious Freedom"

Freedom of worship is a bedrock principle in most modern democracies and is firmly embedded in the First Amendment to the United States Constitution. Professor Tore Lindholm examines Magna Carta in light of the current concept of freedom of religion as embodied in the 1948 Universal Declaration of Human Rights and concludes that it has no roots in Magna Carta. That conception of religious freedom (found in historical antecedents as far back as the third century B.C.E. in the edicts of Emperor Ashoka) requires that each person has the right to freedom of thought, freedom of conscience, and freedom of religion. This encompasses the right to change religion or belief, the freedom— alone or with others—to practice that religion or belief, as well as the freedom to practice no religion at all. Lindholm concludes that this concept appears nowhere in Magna Carta, which focused on the freedom of one religion from interference by the government, not contemporary notions of the principle.

H. Chapter 9: "Magna Carta and International Law"

Professor Larry May inaugurates this segment by looking at the experience of Magna Carta for insight into how international law today should be viewed and how the international legal system can be strengthened. May examines the rights laid out in the Great Charter and ties them to international law rights, as well as the concept of the rule of law in Magna Carta serving as a template for the international rule of law in the 21st century. He also analyzes the pivotal role of fair trials in establishing a legitimate political system, and how the Great Charter's role in merging different sources of law and courts into a unified order can serve as a template for the continued advancement of international tribunals. Finally, he articulates a notion of international due process accompanied by an independent judiciary, citing the evolution of the latter in England from 1215 until the 17th century.

I. Chapter 10: "Magna Carta Unchained: The Great Charter in Modern Commonwealth Law"

As the British Empire expanded to the far reaches of the globe, it carried with it notions of English law as colonists understood that their rights as Englishmen would go with them. Precepts embodied in Magna Carta as envisioned by Coke and other 17th-century political theorists thus spread and currently can be found in the 53 countries of the Commonwealth of Nations, and even beyond. Professor David Clark discusses the global reach of Magna Carta's legacy and analyzes it with respect to specific legal doctrines in various Commonwealth countries. Again, we see that Magna Carta's influence is one that "broke free of its medieval roots," as Clark puts it. Clark examines various ways Magna Carta entered the law of Commonwealth countries, including express incorporation by statute and judicial opinion.

J. Chapter 11: "Magna Carta, Civil Law, and Canon Law"

Professor Thomas McSweeney asserts that elements of the *ius commune*—a legal system composed of canon law and Roman law that is the precursor to today's civil law—which found their way into Magna Carta, were inserted not to influence the early development of the common law, as many scholars have assumed, but rather to attract the support of Pope Innocent III. According to Professor McSweeney, both King John and the barons knew that the pope could be a powerful ally and they used *ius commune* to bring their local dispute into the broader politics of Western Christendom. Professor McSweeney identifies different ways that *ius commune* could have influenced Magna Carta and also discusses the impact on common law of the Fourth Lateran Council, which he refers to as "the forgotten event of 1215."

K. Chapter 12: "The Charter of the Forest: Evolving Human Rights in Nature"

Professor Nicholas Robinson addresses Carta de Foresta, an important charter in its own right, and its relationship to Magna Carta. Carta de Foresta was issued as a stand-alone charter in 1217 when Magna Carta was reissued that same year, and it includes and expands on several chapters of the 1215 Magna Carta. Also referred to as the Charter of the Common Man because of its beneficial impact on the lives not just of freemen (who constituted about half of the population of England at that time) but also all others in England, the Charter of the Forest helped effectuate Magna Carta with respect to important issues relating to the use of forests. Robinson concludes that the Forest Charter consciously developed novel legal approaches to promoting justice and sustaining relations between citizens and the natural resources of the time, and that in this way in Robinson's words "it became a foundation for an intergenerational struggle toward defining a rule of law for nature."

IV. Themes Running Through This Book

A. Everyone Is Subject to the Law and Can Be Made So by Virtue of a Written Instrument

The primary principle of Magna Carta is that everyone, even the king or head of state, is subject to the law and that this can be established via a written instrument. This is the essence of constitutionalism and is inherent in Magna Carta from 1215 onward. That King John immediately sought to have Magna Carta invalidated by Pope Innocent III on the ground of duress (and that the pope agreed) demonstrates that in this respect King John took Magna Carta seriously and recognized the validity of this principle; the many reissues, demands for reconfirmation by various elements of society, and reconfirmations in the ensuing centuries illustrate the same.[47] This principle, unlike other aspects of Magna Carta, has not changed for 800 years.

B.   Dynamism and Adaptability

Magna Carta has been dynamic throughout its existence. As mentioned above, Magna Carta's actual content changed from 1215 to 1216 (elimination of some chapters and postponement of others for further consideration), 1216 to 1217 (e.g., spin-off of the forest chapters into Carta de Foresta), and 1217 to 1225 (i.e., further revisions).[48] Its status also changed, first being included in an English statute book in 1297[49] and, starting in the 19th century, gradually being repealed. Now only three and a half provisions from the 1297 Magna Carta remain good law in England.[50] Perhaps most significantly from a historical perspective, the contents *attributed* to Magna Carta have changed dramatically over the centuries, and particularly in the late 16th and early 17th centuries in England and later in the American colonies.

Magna Carta has thus been a dynamic, not a static, document. It has also been an adaptable document in the sense that it has been capable of being used as support for a range of specific political and legal arguments over the past several centuries. Indeed, Magna Carta influenced legal developments in England and the law of the English colonies—including the colonies in America and the laws in Commonwealth and other countries—such as the United States where it has continued to influence the jurisprudence of the United States Supreme Court.

---

47. *See* chapter 3, "Magna Carta and Sovereign Immunity: Strained Bedfellows," 49–50.

48. *See, e.g.,* BREAY, *supra* note 4, at 43–44; VINCENT, *supra* note 7, at 84. The 1297 Magna Carta contains a minor change from the 1225 version in chapter 2 (introducing a distinction between what an earl and a baron had to pay to inherit). VINCENT, *supra* note 7, at 87. The 1300 Magna Carta, which introduced no changes, was the last formal issuance. *Id.* at 88. There were more than 40 confirmations of Magna Carta over the ensuing two centuries. *Id.* at 88.

49. *See* TURNER, *supra* note 8, at 105; BREAY, *supra* note 4, at 44.

50. 1297 Magna Carta, chapters 1, 9, 29, and part of 37. VINCENT, *supra* note 7, at 102. *See also* chapter 10, "Magna Carta Unchained: The Great Charter in Modern Commonwealth Law."

C. Mythic Magna Carta

Apart from the primary principle described above, it is clear that the Magna Carta often invoked in recent centuries bears little or no resemblance to the 1215 Magna Carta or subsequent versions. Earlier commentators have reached the same conclusion.[51] More specifically, it is argued in this book, for example, that sometimes-heard claims that Magna Carta established the rights to trial by jury, religious freedom, and habeas corpus are simply wrong. These concepts developed separately, sometimes with a legitimate though distant connection to Magna Carta (e.g., due process of law) and sometimes with virtually no connection (e.g., habeas corpus as we now know it). For most purposes, in fact, the relevant period for analyzing the impact of Magna Carta is in recent centuries, not in the 13th century.

Another indication that Magna Carta as now conceptualized is mythic is that we now ignore aspects of it that we recognize as repugnant. Prime examples are the references to "free men" in Magna Carta and Carta de Foresta,[52] which implicitly recognize the legitimacy of the feudal system then prevalent in England and that excluded roughly half the English population from the benefits of Magna Carta and from some of the benefits of Carta de Foresta.[53] Another example is the discriminatory treatment of Jews contained in chapter 10 of the 1215 Magna Carta, described above. A further instance is the implicit recognition of trial by combat in chapter 54, which provides that no person shall be arrested or imprisoned as a result of a charge by a woman for the death of any person other than her husband. At that time, the standard in criminal trials (such as those covered by chapter 54) was trial by battle, in which the parties themselves had to fight. However, "[w]omen, men over sixty, and men with physical disabilities were allowed to fight by proxy."[54]

---

51. *See, e.g.,* HOLT, *supra* note 7, at 378–405; HOWARD, *supra* note 35, at 369 ("[T]he Magna Carta of the seventeenth century was not the Magna Carta of the days of King John."); *see also* VINCENT, *supra* note 7, at 92 ("The charter as totem and as artefact").

52. *E.g.,* appendix B, "1215 Magna Carta," ch. 1: "And we have also granted to all the free men of our kingdom, for ourselves and our heirs in perpetuity, all the following liberties, for them and their heirs to have and to hold of us and our heirs"; Carta de Foresta, chapters 9, 12, and 13. However, chapter 17 of Carta de Foresta declares that that Charter applies to "everyone" (chapters 9, 12, and 13 presumably are exceptions to that). *See* appendix H, "1217 Carta de Foresta (Charter of the Forest)."

53. *See* BREAY, *supra* note 4, at 32.

54. Helena F. Normanton, *Magna Carta and Women,* THE ENGLISHWOMAN 129, 140 (1915), *microformed on* History of Women reel 937 No. 8201. *See* MCKECHNIE, *supra* note 34, at 451.

A woman therefore could hire a strong champion to fight on her behalf—a practice that put the respondent in a sometimes difficult, even fatal, position.[55]

The iconic view of Magna Carta as an unblemished symbol of freedom ignores such provisions.

D.   Resilience in the Face of Vacillating Treatment

Magna Carta has persisted and even thrived in spite of repeated royal actions that violated or attempted to evade its provisions. This is also the case with respect to certain topics covered in Magna Carta, as well as with Carta de Foresta.[56] Although it did not provide for equal rights of women, for example, Magna Carta did provide some protection to women in chapters 6, 7, 8, 11, and 26.[57] These provisions, among other things, prohibited the king from forcing widows to marry without their permission and protected some aspects of inheritance.[58] Women lost some of these rights under English law in subsequent centuries,[59] though women's rights substantially improved in the 20th century.

E.   Rule of Law and Enduring Relevance and Persuasiveness of Magna Carta

A final theme running through the chapters of this book is the enduring nature of the Great Charter's contribution to the rule of law. Each of the authors concludes in his or her own way that Magna Carta is highly relevant today and each acknowledges Magna Carta's fundamental teaching that both "the governor and the governed" should be subject to prescribed rules of behavior applied in accordance with law.[60]

---

55. See Normanton, *supra* note 54, at 140. The rule had been that a man accused by a woman could select trial by ordeal instead of trial by battle, but the church came to oppose the former. *Id.*

56. See, *e.g.*, McKechnie, *supra* note 34, at 139–59; Breay, *supra* note 4, at 32; Turner, *supra* note 8, at 82–88.

57. Normanton, *supra* note 54, at 136.

58. *Id.* at 136–40. See *generally* Janet S. Loengard, *What Did Magna Carta Mean to Widows? in* Magna Carta and the England of King John 134 (Janet S. Loengard ed., 2010).

59. Normanton, *supra* note 54, at 134, 142.

60. William C. Koch, Jr., *Reopening Tennessee's Open Courts Clause: A Historical Reconsideration of Article i, Section 17 of the Tennessee Constitution*, 27 U. Mem. L. Rev. 333, 356–57 (1997).

Chapter 2
The Making of Magna Carta: The Historical Background

Ralph V. Turner

Throughout the English-speaking world, Magna Carta is still celebrated 800 years after King John (r. 1199–1216) agreed to it in 1215 as the first attempt to impose limitations on a monarch's power and to guarantee fundamental rights to his subjects. Multitudes of Americans, and indeed multitudes around the world, are aware that it has some connection with the civil liberties that they enjoy today as citizens. King John's opponents were familiar with doctrines of the supremacy of the law, but no effective means of subjecting a tyrannical ruler to the law had been devised. The English barons' problem of defining and limiting what later became known as the royal prerogative lies at the heart of their rebellion of 1215–1217, and Magna Carta would become periodically the focus of struggles against despotic rulers in England and later in 18th-century North America. Obviously, much myth surrounds a document still hallowed after eight centuries, and grasping its meaning requires placing it in its historical context.

I. Tyrannical Angevin Monarchy

The baronial rebels in 1215 held not only King John but also his Angevin predecessors, Henry II (r. 1154–1189) and Richard I (the Lionheart) (r. 1189–1199), responsible for debasing the good old law of Edward the Confessor (r. 1042–1066) and Henry I (r. 1100–1135). A contemporary chronicler wrote that John's opponents demanded an end to the "evil customs which the father and brother of the king had created . . . along with those abuses which the king himself had added."[1] England's unique history in the 12th century as the one European kingdom where the king could control his most powerful subjects—his earls, barons, and bishops—gave rise to demands for a charter of liberties. Post-Conquest England retained a base

---

1. RADULPHI DE COGGESHALL, CHRONICON ANGLICANUM 170 (London, Her Majesty's Stationery Office, J. Stevenson ed., Roll Series 66, 1875).

of old English law and government, but building on the Anglo-Saxon base were late Roman and Frankish patterns of governance that had survived in Normandy and Anjou and had been imported as a result of the Norman Conquest. Unlike other regions on the Continent, public authority had not collapsed and fallen into private hands, with local strong men forcing weaker neighbors to submit to their lordship. While continental monarchs could not control their magnates, the Norman and Angevin kings, combining their lordship over the baronage with surviving public agencies, such as the office of sheriff, exercised effective coercive power over all their subjects, even the earls. The king's clerks enhanced his supremacy with expansive views of kingship derived from the Old Testament and Roman traditions despite the Church's continued attacks on rulers' sacred character.[2]

On attaining the English crown in 1154, Henry II moved to curb the power of barons who had taken advantage of civil war following the disputed succession of his predecessor, King Stephen (r. 1135–1154). During this period, the barons defied royal agents and consolidated control over their lordships. Henry II was "determined to be not merely king, but just such a king as his grandfather [Henry I] had been."[3] Henry II's legal innovations rested on old doctrines of the king's overriding responsibility for suppressing crime and remedying failures of justice, and they extended the reach of royal justice, threatening lords' judicial rights over their free tenants.[4] His expansion of royal jurisdiction and ever-increasing financial demands revived and expanded the "administrative monarchy" initiated by the Anglo-Norman kings.[5] Aristocrats murmured against upstart "new men" staffing royal government, whom they saw usurping their proper role as the king's counselors. The barons also saw their social and economic superiority challenged as career royal servants competed with them for disputed inheritances, lucrative custodies, and marriages for their sons and retainers.[6]

Henry II's need for funds to defend Normandy's borders against the Capetian kings of France and to crush rebellious nobles in his queen Eleanor's lands in Aquitaine forced him to exploit his new kingdom as a vast treasure trove. Henry and his sons Richard I and John regularly went to war with the French rulers Louis VII (r. 1137–1180) and his son Philip II (Philip

---

2. R.V. Turner, *King John's Concept of Royal Authority*, 17 HIST. POL. THOUGHT 157–78 (1996).

3. W.L. WARREN, HENRY II 59 (1973).

4. Joseph Biancalana, *For Want of Justice: Legal Reforms of Henry II*, 88 COLUM. L. REV. 433–536 (1988).

5. C.W. Hollister & J.W. Baldwin, *The Rise of Administrative Kingship: Henry I and Philip Augustus*, 83 AM. HIST. REV. 867, 905 (1978).

6. R.V. Turner, *Changing Perceptions of the New Administrative Class in Anglo-Norman & Angevin England: The Curiales and Their Conservative Critics*, in JUDGES, ADMINISTRATORS AND THE COMMON LAW IN ANGEVIN ENGLAND 225, 241–43 (R.V. Turner ed., 1994), *originally printed in* 29 J. BRIT. STUD. 93, 117 (1990).

Augustus) (r. 1180–1223), who were in theory lords of their French lands: Normandy, greater Anjou, and Aquitaine. As incessant wars required more and more resources, the Angevins loaded ever-heavier military and fiscal burdens onto their earls and barons, just as these lords were burdening their own knights with onerous obligations. Each generation made more excessive demands on the English baronage, and John's reign differed only in degree from his two predecessors' authoritarian rule.[7]

Accusations that Henry II and his sons ruled as tyrants began with John of Salisbury in his *Policraticus*.[8] Later, an unremitting critic of the Angevins, Gerald of Wales, compared the king to "a robber permanently on the prowl, always probing, always searching for the weak spot where there is something for him to steal."[9] Weaker subjects of medieval monarchs were often willing to overlook occasional despotic, harsh, and violent deeds necessary for keeping the peace; for peace was all-important in a disorderly age, especially to churchmen and the peasantry. Yet even the Angevins' subjects came to see them as predatory monarchs, irresistible forces whose wrath aroused terror. Unlike modern historians, they gave Henry little credit for his legal reforms that expanded royal protection of property rights. Henry appeared to them as an oppressor, and his oppression of the English church condemned him as a sinner, complicit in archbishop Thomas Becket's murder.[10] Henry was not alone in his inability to win his subjects' hearts; both his sons aroused widespread fear and anger, although Richard Lionheart much less so than his brother John. As king, John lacked his father's and his brother's ability to manage the baronage in part because in dealing with them he rejected their chivalric standards of courtliness. John appeared to them as resentful, mercurial, and treacherous; he mistrusted them, and they in turn mistrusted him.[11]

All three Angevin kings' anger could erupt into acts of outright cruelty. Both Henry II and Richard Lionheart ordered enemies imprisoned under

---

7. J.E.A. JOLLIFFE, ANGEVIN KINGSHIP 349 (2d ed. 1963).

8. JOHN OF SALISBURY, POLICRATICUS 28 (Cary J. Nederman ed. & trans., 1990).

9. GERALD OF WALES, 8 GIRALDI CAMBRENSIS OPERA: DE PRINCIPIS INSTRUCTIONE LIBER 316 (London, Her Majesty's Stationery Office, G.F. Warner ed., Roll Series 1891).

10. Nicholas Vincent, *Introduction: Henry II & the Historians*, in HENRY II: NEW INTERPRETATIONS 1, 9, 19–21 (Christopher Harper-Bill & Nicholas Vincent eds., 2007) [hereinafter HENRY II]; ANNE DUGGAN, THOMAS BECKET 266, 268 (2004); Bjorn Weiler, *Bishops and Kings in England, c. 1066–1215*, in RELIGION AND POLITICS IN THE MIDDLE AGES: GERMANY & ENGLAND BY COMPARISON 157, 193 (Ludger Körnten & Dominik Wassenhoven eds., 2012).

11. David Crouch, *Baronial Paranoia in King John's Reign*, in MAGNA CARTA AND THE ENGLAND OF KING JOHN 45, 49, 51 (Janet S. Loengard ed., 2010) [hereinafter MAGNA CARTA].

such harsh conditions that death resulted.[12] Best known, however, are John's punishments, such as ordering one of his clerks so weighed down with a coat of iron or lead that he died. John marred his most noteworthy military success, the rescue of his mother at Mirebeau Castle in 1202, by his shameful treatment of the prisoners that were taken, 22 of whom perished from their cruel incarceration. The most important of these prisoners, his nephew Arthur of Brittany, soon disappeared, almost certainly murdered at John's command.[13] Equally monstrous was John's hounding of William de Briouze and his family to exile and death. When this former royal favorite could not pay a debt of over £13,000, John applied to Briouze the full force of the law of the exchequer, imprisoning and starving his wife and son and forcing him to flight and death in exile.[14] The Briouze family's fate was a lesson to other barons that John's notion of lawful procedure bore little resemblance to their concept of lawful judgment.

Henry II spent his last years in incessant warfare against Philip II of France, who exploited his nobles' insurrectionist tendencies and his uncommonly difficult relations with his quarrelsome sons. Conflict with Philip continued under Richard Lionheart after his return from crusade in 1194, when the French king resolved to enforce his lordship over the Angevin king's lands in western France and to expel him from the Continent. Richard's exploitation of England for Normandy's defense had attained unprecedented levels by the time of his death in 1199. A chronicler wrote shortly afterward, "No age can remember or history tell of any king, even one who ruled for a long time, who demanded and took so much money from his kingdom as this king extorted and amassed within five years after his return from captivity."[15]

II.   King John

It was John's bad luck to succeed his brother Richard, whose chivalric courtesy, leadership, and military valor on crusade had aroused his subjects' admiration such that it offset their anger and fear engendered by his explosive personality and harsh exploitation of England. A combination of

---

12. ROGER OF HOVEDEN, 3 CHRONICA ROGERI DE HOUVEDENE, 239, 287 (London, Her Majesty's Stationery Office, William Stubbs ed., Roll Series, 1868–71); D.E. Desborough, *Politics and Prelacy in the Late Twelfth Century: The Career of Hugh de Nonant, Bishop of Coventry, 1188–98*, 64 HIST. RES. 1, 6 (1991).

13. R.V. Turner, *England in 1215: An Authoritarian Angevin Dynasty Facing Multiple Threats*, in MAGNA CARTA, *supra* note 11, at 10–26.

14. David Crouch, *The Complaint of King John against William de Briouze*, in MAGNA CARTA, *supra* note 11, at 168–79.

15. COGGESHALL, *supra* note 1, at 92–93; JOHN GILLINGHAM, RICHARD THE LIONHEART 303 & notes to ch. 13 (1978).

circumstances during King John's reign would bring together a coalition of interests determined to impose limitations on his royal power. By the time of the Lionheart's death in 1199, the French king posed a greater threat than ever to the Angevins' continental lands. Philip's resources were increasing steadily, and by 1203–1204 his fiscal position had reached parity with King John's. Despite raising enormous sums, John could not match the Capetian king's growing wealth, which after 1204 included revenues from his newly conquered duchy of Normandy.[16]

Competition with the French monarch forced first Richard and then John to organize England as a "war economy," burdening their subjects with heavy financial and military obligations.[17] The Angevin kings' expansion of royal authority threatened the magnates' power but had not yet broken their might. In the early 13th century, earls and barons still claimed a place in royal governance as the king's counselors, military commanders, and heads of their own courts sitting in judgment of their men. They controlled a considerable share of the kingdom's resources; and many magnates, especially on the Welsh borders and in northern England, continued to construct castles, keep large armed bands, and hold liberties or franchises beyond royal officials' reach. With their resources and loyal followers in the counties, the baronage could hope to maintain its privileges through armed revolt if necessary. Nonetheless, many lived in fear of royal wrath, knowing that John would not shrink from tangling with them either in the law courts or outside the law altogether. Their high position in the kingdom afforded no safety against John's intimidation and violence in his frenzy to collect funds and compel services.

King John, more than his father and brother, engaged in a gigantic shakedown of great landholders. He arbitrarily seized their lands as a means of disciplining them, sometimes cloaking his extralegal pursuit of victims with the law of the exchequer, tightening or loosening pressure for repayment of their debts as he saw fit. John also exploited his courts, encouraging lawsuits to threaten those who lost his favor. Any flaw in their title allowed the king to recruit a claimant to challenge their right to inheritances in his court. John made disseizin "by the king's will"[18] into a common disciplinary

---

16. J.W. Baldwin, The Government of Philip Augustus: Foundations of French Royal Power in the Middle Ages 153–75 (1986); J.C. Holt, *The Loss of Normandy and Royal Finance, in* War and Government in the Middle Ages 92, 97–105 (J.C. Holt & John Gillingham eds., 1984); Nick Barrett, *The Revenues of John and Philip Augustus Revisited, in* King John: New Interpretations 75, 80–99 (Stephen D. Church ed., 1999). *See also* Nick Barratt, *The English Revenue of Richard I*, 116 Engl. Hist. Rev. 635, 644–56 (2001).

17. J.O. Prestwich, *War and Finance in the Anglo-Norman State, in* Anglo-Norman Warfare (Matthew Strickland ed., 1992), *reprinted from* 4 Transactions Royal Hist. Soc'y 19, 20 (5th ser., 1954).

18. *Per voluntatem regis, in* royal letters found in Jolliffe, *supra* note 7, at 52–65.

measure that did not require a court's prior judgment, and his writs refer routinely to disseizin "by the king's command."[19] English barons could see that their own tenants enjoyed access to royal writs against them, claiming that their property had been taken "unjustly and without judgment;" yet no such writs were available to them when the king took their property.[20] At the very time when the barons' tenants were finding protection for their property in the royal courts, John was arbitrarily closing his court to them and revoking their cases for hearing in his presence.

With the loss of Normandy in 1203–1204, John became a resident ruler in England unlike his mostly absentee predecessors, and he proved to be very much a hands-on monarch, deeply involved in the details of governing. Constantly present in his kingdom, he could not push blame for his arbitrary acts onto officials acting in his stead, as had his often absent father and brother. The contrast between Richard's chivalry and John's greedy, boorish behavior, coupled with his own suspicion, dislike, and even contempt for his barons, was so great that he could never win their respect.[21] Yet a basic change in England's government, the growth of administrative monarchy, perhaps was a greater source of baronial discontent. Many barons felt their local authority slipping into the hands of royal agents, often foreigners or men on the margins of the knightly class. Even in warfare, John's recruitment of mercenary captains reduced his dependence on his magnates. By the midpoint of his reign, his arbitrary demands on his English subjects had surpassed those of his father and brother, and he appeared to them as "a suspicious ruler, keeping his subjects in hand through fear."[22]

In 1205, following the Archbishop of Canterbury's death, the process of naming a new head of the English Church led to a new crisis over the proper role of secular princes in the spiritual sphere. Pope Innocent III (r. 1198–1216) took advantage of a disputed election for the primate of England to consecrate his own candidate in 1206, Stephen Langton. King John, like previous English monarchs, felt that he had a right to a major role in selecting the new archbishop, also a significant secular lord. He complained that Langton was a man unknown to him, an English cleric who had spent many years in the capital of his archenemy, the French king. John refused to allow Langton to enter England to take up his duties, and the pope used all his weapons to bring him to heel, first imposing an interdict on England in 1208, and then following with the excommunication of

---

19. *Per preceptum regis,* in *royal letters found in* RALPH V. TURNER, MAGNA CARTA THROUGH THE AGES 205–07 (2003).

20. John Hudson, *Magna Carta, the Ius Commune, and English Common Law,* in MAGNA CARTA, *supra* note 11, at 112.

21. Crouch, *supra* note 11, at 51.

22. DORIS M. STENTON, ENGLISH JUSTICE BETWEEN THE NORMAN CONQUEST AND THE GREAT CHARTER 101 (1964).

the king.[23] English clerics saw John's insistence on keeping Langton from assuming his duties as Archbishop of Canterbury, from 1206 to 1213, as part of a long ideological struggle reaching back to St. Anselm's quarrels with William II (r. 1087–1100) and Henry I and Becket's fatal battle with Henry II.[24] Once consecrated, Langton's own actions as archbishop illustrated his strong identification with Becket and his struggle for the English Church's liberties.[25]

When King John suddenly turned against three of his closest confidantes and counselors among the baronage in 1207, fear mounted among others that the king was likely to turn on them as well.[26] Rumblings of wider discontent in 1208 and 1209 gave evidence of the barons' disquiet with John's rule. John had reason to feel insecure about their loyalty, especially along his frontiers, where nobles holding great liberties or franchises had potential for successful opposition. One source of John's concern was the strength of marcher lords of South Wales, who also controlled substantial lands in Ireland. Another worry was the almost autonomous position of barons in the North of England, who resented John's attempts to bring them under closer royal control. If King John's persecution of great aristocrats was making them more conscious of issues of law and right, the knights of the counties and merchants in the towns were not far behind. Many knights busied themselves acting as semiprofessionals in local government, where they learned practical lessons in governance from their attendance at shire courts, serving on local commissions and juries, and holding offices as bailiffs or coroners. Knights first surfaced as a politically significant group in 1212 and 1213, when John summoned representatives of the knights of the counties to "speak with us about the affairs of our kingdom."[27] Yet he failed to win them to his cause, for they too resented the arbitrary and exploitative nature of Angevin government. Many knights would fight in the baronial movement against John, and not always simply because they were following their lords. Although personal loyalty or ties of kinship to their lords doubtless drove some, others with personal experience of John's tyranny joined the rebel ranks even when their lords stood with the king.

The commercial activity of town dwellers set them apart from the rural gentry of the medieval countryside. Towns' abnormal situation in a largely agrarian society impelled them to seek rights to govern themselves, and on

---

23. Nicholas Vincent, *Stephen Langton, Archbishop of Canterbury, in* ETIÈNNE LANGTON: PRÉDICATEUR, BIBLISTE, THÉOLOGIEN, 9 BIBLIOTHÈQUE D'HISTOIRE CULTURELLE DU MÔYEN ÂGE 51, 77–97 (Louis-Jacques Bataillon et al. eds., 2010).

24. Weiler, *supra* note 10, at 160, 169, 194.

25. Vincent, *supra* note 23, at 67–73.

26. Crouch, *supra* note 11, at 51–52.

27. SELECT CHARTERS AND OTHER ILLUSTRATIONS OF ENGLISH CONSTITUTIONAL HISTORY 282 (William Stubbs ed., 9th ed. 1913).

the Continent townspeople formed revolutionary communes, associations of citizens bound together by oath to seize self-government by force from their lords. English towns gained varying measures of autonomy by purchasing charters from their lords or the king. Citizens took part in governing towns through election to offices, gaining experience in governance comparable to that of the knights of the counties. Most eager for rights of self-government and most aggressive in seeking them were the Londoners, who gained the right to choose their own sheriffs in the time of Henry I.

By the mid-12th century, London merchants mingled with members of the royal household and dominated the city's government, holding office as sheriffs and aldermen; and winning their support would be crucial for any group opposing the English monarch. Like the elites of lesser towns, they invested in land in the countryside and developed close ties with knights of the counties, serving together on commissions, engaging in business, and even marrying into one another's families. Londoners, just as other towns-people and knights did, experienced John's thirst for funds as he demanded tallages and "fines," supposedly voluntary offerings. Complaints of knights and townspeople would force negotiators framing Magna Carta to think in terms of more generalized remedies, and this had an impact on the Charter, incorporating general political principles applicable to all free men.

By the last quarter of John's reign, baronial unrest was rising, first revealed in 1212 before a summer military expedition to Wales, when a handful of barons hatched a conspiracy to murder the king. Two barons suspected of being parties to the plot—FitzWalter and Eustace de Vescy—soon took flight, FitzWalter to Paris and Vescy, a northern lord, to Scotland. FitzWalter was a powerful East Anglian baron with ties to clerics at St. Paul's, London, several of whom joined him in exile. At Paris, FitzWalter met clerical dissidents descended from the murdered Becket's circle, living there during the interdict imposed after King John's refusal to accept Langton as Archbishop of Canterbury. Depicting himself as a fugitive from an ungodly ruler, he took advantage of the settlement of the Canterbury crisis to return to England with Langton and other English exiles.[28]

Once King John learned of the 1212 plot against him, he moved quickly to seize the plotters' castles and to outlaw them. Nonetheless, the conspiracy led to a crucial loss of political initiative, pushing him to adopt contradictory policies. Early in 1213 and in 1214 John tried conciliation, moderating some of his harsh policies in the North. Around the same time, however, he moved to bring his great men under tighter control, demanding custody of their castles, hostages for their good behavior, and charters pledging their

---

28. Matthew Strickland, *Fitzwalter, Robert (d. 1235)*, *in* 19 OXFORD DICTIONARY OF NATIONAL BIOGRAPHY (H.C.G. Matthew & Brian Harrison eds., 2004) (on file with author).

fidelity. Such repressive steps, along with his continued fierce money-raising for his projected campaign in France, counteracted his conciliatory gestures.

King John's most important conciliatory gesture was settling his long quarrel with the pope over the archbishopric of Canterbury and finally acknowledging Langton as archbishop. It seems likely that by February, Pope Innocent III was preparing to declare his deposition. Since the interdict on England imposed by the pope in 1208 followed by the king's excommunication had failed to bring him to heel, the logical next step was a papal decree deposing him. By 1213, John saw his vulnerability and knew that he must forestall an alliance between Innocent III and Philip II that could result in a "holy war" on England proclaimed by the pontiff and fought by the French. John surrendered to Innocent, doing homage and fealty and acknowledging that he held England as a papal fief, and by doing this, he won powerful papal support. In John's last three years, his new friend would give him consistent backing. As a contemporary chronicler wrote, "From the moment [John] put himself under apostolic protection and made his kingdom part of St. Peter's Patrimony, there was no prince in the Roman world who would dare attack him or invade his lands to the damage of the Apostolic See."[29]

John had good reason to be wary of his new Archbishop of Canterbury, who early in their long struggle had urged English knights to support his position militarily against the king. In a 1207 letter to the knights, Langton had pointed out that fealty to their monarch was secondary to their "loyalty to the superior Lord, the eternal king who is king of kings and lord of lords. Hence whatever service is rendered to the temporal king to the prejudice of the eternal king is undoubtedly an act of treachery."[30] Almost as soon as Langton arrived in England in 1213, he sought ways to ingratiate himself with the baronage. At the ceremony absolving John from excommunication in July 1213, he obliged the king to swear to abolish all evil laws and restore good ones, and also to judge all men by the just sentences of his court.[31]

Langton had belonged to the school of Peter the Chanter at Paris, center of an "antimonarchical" movement that influenced his views on kingship. Langton's disputations, biblical commentaries, and sermons from his Paris years stress the sinful nature of royal government and its predatory nature.[32]

---

29. WALTER OF COVENTRY, 2 MEMORIALE FRATRIS WALTERI DE COVENTRIA 210 (London, Her Majesty's Stationery Office, William Stubbs ed. & trans., Roll Series, 1873); C.R. CHENEY, INNOCENT III AND ENGLAND 339 (1979).

30. FREDERICK MAURICE POWICKE, STEPHEN LANGTON 94–97 (1928), *citing* 2 GERVASE OF CANTERBURY, at xxxii (William Stubbs ed., 1880).

31. John W. Baldwin, *Master Stephen Langton, Future Archbishop of Canterbury: The Paris Schools and Magna Carta*, 123 ENGL. HIST. REV. 811, 829–31 (2008).

32. *Id.* at 813; David d'Avray, *Magna Carta: Its Background in Stephen Langton's Academic Biblical Exegesis and its Episcopal Reception, in* 38 STUDI MEDIEVALI 423–32 (3d ser., 1997).

In Langton's writings, he set forth three ideas that were important for his political stance once in England after 1213. First, he noted in his treatment of the founding of the Israelite monarchy that once the Hebrews acclaimed their first king, God ordered the prophet Samuel "to reduce the laws of the kingdom to writing."[33] The book of laws set forth not only the people's obligations to the king, but also imposed limits on what the king could exact from them.[34] Second, Langton taught that to protect God's sovereignty, his people have the right to resist an evil ruler if he commanded them to commit a mortal sin, and also if he issued an unjust order without the judgment of his court.[35] Third, Langton placed limits on the monarch's financial exactions; he wrote that kings act contrary to God's teaching when they "collect treasure not in order [that] they may sustain necessity, but to satiate their cupidity."[36] Kings, in taxing their subjects, must not go "beyond the measure of necessity,"[37] for to do so is evil and a sin.[38] Unlike Roman and canon lawyers' use of necessity as a justification for arbitrary acts by rulers, Langton interpreted it as imposing limitations on them. Later he would agree with disaffected English barons that King John's financial exactions failed to qualify as a necessity.[39]

In the year of Langton's arrival in England, King John planned a massive military campaign in Poitou to regain his lost lands in France, and his demand for military service created new discord with his barons. They had little enthusiasm for fighting in France or sending their knights, and the king had to abandon campaigns planned for 1205 and 1212. When summoned again for service in Poitou in 1213, barons in the north of England raised an outcry, insisting that they and their knights owed service only in John's lost duchy of Normandy. The king marched northward with a mercenary force to punish the recalcitrant barons, but the new archbishop of Canterbury insisted that he proceed against them only after a judgment of his court.[40] Langton's action is early evidence for a combination of baronial rebels and radical churchmen uniting in opposition to King John.[41] When John's Poitevin expedition finally got under way early in 1214, a powerful group of northern opponents stayed behind and refused to send their knights.

---

33. Baldwin, *supra* note 31, at 823.
34. *Id.* at 813.
35. *Id.* at 815–20, 824–25.
36. *Id.* at 823.
37. *Id.* at 813.
38. d'Avray, *supra* note 32, at 425–27, 431, Appendix, Extract 3, 437.
39. *Id.* at 431.
40. J.C. Holt, *The Origins of Magna Carta, in* MAGNA CARTA AND MEDIEVAL GOVERNMENT 220 (1985).
41. NICHOLAS VINCENT, MAGNA CARTA: A VERY SHORT INTRODUCTION 55, 58 (2012).

III.   Framing a Baronial Reform Program

A baronial reform program began to take shape as early as 1213. Vital to the process was a revived interest in the "good old law" predating Henry II that both discontented laymen and embittered clerics found to contrast with unjust Angevin innovations. Formerly the rebel barons were denigrated as illiterate "feudal reactionaries," pursuing only their own selfish goals and incapable of intellectual depth. Yet they profited from practical lessons in governance, presiding over their own tribunals and participating in shire courts. Under John's harsh rule, they became politically conscious in "the school of bitter experience."[42] Although formerly assumed to have been illiterate, many early 13th-century barons and knights had achieved some level of literacy.[43] Medieval literature affords numerous examples of the *miles literatus*, who was not simply a "literate knight," but a "learned knight," able to read Latin. Numerous 12th-century knights not counted as "learned" could read French, and a large body of writing in Anglo-Norman French was accessible to them. Indeed, when vernacular French emerged in England it was barely beginning in mainland France; "an unusually large percentage"[44] of early French vernacular manuscripts are of English origin, among them translations of early English laws.[45]

English barons and knights, armed with their literacy, could turn to collections of Anglo-Saxon and Anglo-Norman laws and coronation charters compiled during the quarrel between Becket and Henry II as part of the church's effort to preserve its independence. When Henry represented his Constitutions of Clarendon as a statement of ancient custom, Becket's clerical supporters turned to the old law in order to refute his claim.[46] The Canterbury succession conflict revived clerical hostility against the Angevin dynasty, and clerics defending Langton turned once more to law books for ammunition against the king. By the early 13th century, legal collections dating from the Becket conflict were circulating in Anglo-Norman French translations.[47] Barons with access to such translations were not dependent

---

42. H.G. Richardson & George Osborne Sayles, The Governance of Mediaeval England from the Conquest to Magna Carta 368–69 (1963).

43. Martin Aurell, Le Chevalier Lettré: Savoir Et Conduite De L'aristocratie Aux Xii Et Xiii Siècles 82–91 (2011); Michael T. Clanchy, From Memory to Written Record: England 1066–1307, 18–19, 246–52 (2d ed. 2006).

44. Ian Short, *Patrons and Polyglots: French Literature in Twelfth-Century England*, *in* 14 Anglo-Norman Studies 229, 245 (1992).

45. Ian Short, *Literary Culture at the Court of Henry II*, *in* Henry II, *supra* note 10, at 350.

46. Bruce O'Brien, God's Peace and King's Peace: The Laws of Edward the Confessor 117 (1999).

47. *E.g.*, British Library MS/manuscript Harley 458; Crouch, *supra* note 11, at 61; Vincent, *supra* note 23, at 93.

on Langton or the canons of St. Paul's Cathedral; yet clerical intellectuals were pleased to point out to them the support that these collections lent to subjecting King John to the law.[48]

One influential legal compilation was the work of an anonymous cleric, known as the London Collector, writing in London in the years just before and after Magna Carta.[49] He organized old English law codes and Anglo-Norman coronation charters in chronological order, ending with the law book *Glanvill* from Henry II's reign, and he also inserted numerous interpolations.[50] Most useful for King John's clerical and baronial opponents were the Laws of Edward the Confessor and the Laws of Henry I. One of the London Collector's insertions was a forged letter purportedly from a second-century pope to a legendary king of the Britons, setting forth rules of good conduct and imposing limits on the king. The papal letter rejected rule by unrestrained royal power, declaring, "Right and justice ought to reign in the kingdom rather than [the king']s perverse will; law is always what does right; for will and force and violence are not right."[51] The Pope placed the monarch under God's law: "[T]he king ought to fear and love God above all things and keep his commandments throughout all his kingdom."[52] He added that the king "ought to set up good laws and approved customs . . . . He ought to make righteous judgment . . . and maintain justice through the advice of the nobles of his kingdom."[53] This forged letter represents an early expression of principles underlying the Articles of the Barons and Magna Carta.[54]

The London Collector's interpolations borrowed heavily from Geoffrey of Monmouth's *History of the Kings of Britain*. This pseudo-history, written in Latin and translated into French by 1155, introduced the legends of King Arthur and his knights of the round table to the medieval nobility. The

---

48. J.C. Holt, *Book Review*, 118 ENGL. HIST. REV. 478–79 (2003) (reviewing NATALIE FRYDE, WHY MAGNA CARTA? ANGEVIN ENGLAND REVISITED).

49. The London Collection survives in two parts. One is located at the British Library. Add. MS/manuscript 14252, *published in* FELIX LIEBERMANN, DIE GESETZE DER ANGEL-SACHSEN 3 vols. (Max Miemayer ed., 1903–1916). Another is located in Manchester. John Rylands Library, Latin MS/manuscript 155, *in* Felix Liebermann, *A Contemporary Manuscript of the* Leges Anglicorum Collectae, 28 ENGL. HIST. REV. 732–45 (1913).

50. LIEBERMANN, 1 GESETZE, *supra* note 49, at 636–37 (1903); O'BRIEN, *supra* note 46, at 118–19.

51. Derek Keene, *Text, Visualisation and Politics: London, 1150–1250*, 18 TRANSACTIONS ROYAL HIST. SOC'Y 69, 80–83 (6th ser., 2008); John Gillingham, *Stupor Mundi: 1204 Et Un Obituaire de Richard Coeur de Lion Depuis Longtemps Tombé Dans L'oubli*, *in* PLANTAGENÊTS ET CAPÉTIENS: CONFRONTATIONS ET HÉRITAGES 397–411 (Martin Aurell & Noel-Yves Tonnerre eds., 2006).

52. LIEBERMANN, 1 GESETZE, *supra* note 49, at 636–37; translation by O'BRIEN, *supra* note 46, at 118.

53. *Id.*

54. *Id.* at 636–37, 653.

book depicts Arthur, legendary king of the Britons, defying the Romans, yet taking time from fighting to make laws and hand down justice. Arthurian romances inspired by Geoffrey of Monmouth had an enormous influence on vernacular literature, contributing to the cult of chivalry, but also influencing the views of King John's baronage on good government.[55] The English aristocracy looked back longingly to ages before the Angevin kings, when they imagined England to have been a truly feudal society. From experiences in presiding over their own courts and from Arthurian literature, they constructed an idealized vision of King Arthur's "consultative kingship," taking counsel with his faithful men gathered at his round table in contrast to the Angevins' arbitrary rule.[56] The baronage thought of itself as the king's natural counselors, yet they witnessed the reality of "household" or "secret" government, of low-born and foreign professionals holding powerful posts in the royal household and advising the king.[57]

A reform program that could generate wide support among the dissident barons was taking shape before autumn 1213, and playing a role in formulating it was the newly arrived Stephen Langton, Archbishop of Canterbury, who would act as a mediator between King John and the opposition.[58] At the core of concerns of both disaffected churchmen and barons was finding a means for subjecting King John to the law. England's past provided them with ample precedent for curbing his excesses in charters of liberties recorded in the law books circulating among them, whether discovered for themselves, or pointed out by Langton or by others. At the least, his teachings and the barons' own views coincided; both were convinced that no one should be dispossessed of goods or lands except by legal process.[59]

Most important as a precedent was the coronation charter of Henry I, granted in 1100, as a set of promises by the new king to correct wrongs done by his older brother King William II to the English Church and his earls and barons. One clause promises to take only just and lawful reliefs, payments to the king required of heirs when they succeeded to their fathers' lands; they were no longer to be arbitrary "as in the time of my brother."[60]

---

55. Keene, *supra* note 51, at 83, 87; Holt, *supra* note 40, at 56; O'BRIEN, *supra* note 46, at 118–19; *see also* Bruce O'Brien, *Forgers of Law and Their Readers*, 43 PS: POLITICAL SCIENCE AND POLITICS 467–70 (2010).

56. O'Brien, *supra* note 55, at 470–72.

57. J.W. Baldwin, *The Capetian Court at Work under Philip II, in* THE MEDIEVAL COURT IN EUROPE 71, 80–81 (E.R. Haymes ed., 1986); Turner, *supra* note 6, at 247–49.

58. J.C. HOLT, MAGNA CARTA 280 (2d ed. 1992).

59. Baldwin, *supra* note 31, at 836. *See also* David A. Carpenter, *Archbishop Langton and Magna Carta: His Contribution, His Doubts and His Hypocrisy* 1041, 1042–50, 126 ENGL. HIST. REV. (2011).

60. Coronation Charter of Henry I, art. 4, *found in* 2 ENGLISH HISTORICAL DOCUMENTS 1042–1189, 400, 401 (David Douglas & George W. Greenaway eds., 1968) [hereinafter 2 EHD].

Other clauses promised to end William's abuses of his rights of wardship and marriage over a baron's widow and his minor children. Only a few clauses in Henry I's charter gave remedies to lesser-ranking people, and it includes only one statement of general principle, his promise to restore "the law of King Edward together with such emendations to it as my father made with the counsel of his barons."[61]

Roger of Wendover—a chronicler widely regarded by historians as unreliable—described two meetings as early as 1213 and 1214, where dissident barons discussed Henry I's coronation charter. First, he reports a meeting at St. Paul's cathedral, London, in late summer 1213, where Langton was rumored to have met secretly with a group of barons and told them, "Now we have found a certain Charter of King Henry I through which . . . you can recover those liberties which you have long since lost."[62] Second, Wendover writes that in November 1214, after the King's return in defeat from Poitou, barons gathered at the abbey of Bury St. Edmunds. There they pledged to press for reforms, grounding their proposals on Henry I's coronation charter, as suggested earlier by the archbishop. They jointly swore that if King John refused to grant the "liberties and laws of St. Edward . . . and also certain liberties which Henry I had added,"[63] they would "make war on him and break off their fealty, until he would confirm their demands by a Charter under his seal."[64] Historians have long questioned Langton's central role in revealing Henry I's coronation charter to the rebels because of their suspicion of Roger of Wendover's truthfulness. Certainly the barons could easily have encountered exemplars of Henry I's coronation charter elsewhere, but it is plausible that meetings between Langton and the barons took place.[65] Whatever the truth about the two meetings, dissatisfied barons were turning to Henry I's coronation charter before 1215, possibly influenced by Langton.[66]

Another document, the so-called Unknown Charter of Liberties, is the first evidence of rebel barons' efforts to set forth specific demands to present

---

61. *Id.* at art. 13.

62. ROGER OF WENDOVER, CHRONICA 263–64 (London, H.O. Coxe ed. & trans., 1841–44); J.A.P. JONES, KING JOHN AND MAGNA CARTA 131 (1971).

63. WENDOVER, *supra* note 62.

64. *Id.* at 263–64.

65. Baldwin, *supra* note 31, at 830–31; M.T. CLANCHY, ENGLAND AND ITS RULERS 1066–1272: FOREIGN LORDSHIP AND NATIONAL IDENTITY 193–94 (1983); Vincent, *supra* note 23, at 92, 93; R.M. Thompson, *The Meeting of the Rebel Barons at St. Edmunds, Nov. 1214, in* THE CHRONICLE OF THE ELECTION OF HUGH ABBOT BURY ST. EDMUNDS AND LATER BISHOP OF ELY, App. IV, 189–92 (R.M. Thompson ed. & trans., 1974).

66. VIVIAN HUNTER GALBRAITH, 4 KINGS AND CHRONICLERS: ESSAYS IN ENGLISH MEDIEVAL HISTORY 227–28 (Hambledon Press, 1982); HOLT, *supra* note 58, at 225–26; WARREN, *supra* note 3, at 11–13, 227–28.

to King John.[67] The document is not in fact a charter, but a copy of Henry I's coronation charter with a list of baronial demands added to it. The Unknown Charter survives in a single copy discovered in the French archives at Paris only in the late 19th century, and its date is uncertain, perhaps autumn 1214 or early 1215. Its demand for a limitation on barons' overseas military service to the Anglo-Norman kings' former holdings, however, suggests a date before John's 1214 expedition to Poitou.[68] The first clause foreshadows the core of Magna Carta, chapters 39 and 40. Other demands are more radical than any provisions in the Great Charter, for example, a demand for a drastic reduction in the area of royal forests that would have rolled back their boundaries to the beginning of Henry II's reign.[69]

IV. The Road to Runnymede

The destruction of the army of King John's allies at the battle of Bouvines in July 1214 left his grand strategy for defeating the Capetian monarch in ruins. Not only had he suffered the loss of all the Angevins' French lands north of the Loire River plus parts of Poitou, but his treasury was empty after squandering vast sums in vain. By October 1214, when he returned from Poitou, he tried to force barons who had refused to send their knights to fight in France to pay scutage, a money payment in lieu of service. Open opposition to John had already flared in summer 1213, when some northern barons had rejected an earlier demand for their knights' military service in Poitou, insisting that their overseas service was obligatory only in his lost duchy of Normandy. Now he encountered wider opposition to the 1214 scutage from those who had refused to send their quotas of knights. His military humiliation coupled with his failed fundraising effort completed the barons' estrangement from him, and enfeebled as he was, they no longer feared him. John's path to Runnymede meadow ran straight and swift from Bouvines.

Elements of the baronage would move actively toward rebellion against King John during the autumn and winter of 1214–1215. First to act were barons in the North of England, who had refused to send knights for his proposed 1213 Poitevin expedition or for his 1214 campaign. In addition to grievances over military service abroad, a number felt personally wronged by the king; they were convinced that he had unlawfully withheld from them lands, castles, or other privileges that they saw as rightfully theirs.

---

67. 3 ENGLISH HISTORICAL DOCUMENTS 1189–1327, at 310–11 (Harry Rothwell ed., 1975) [hereinafter 3 EHD].

68. HOLT, *supra* note 58, at app. 4, 420–23.

69. Chapter 47 of Magna Carta disafforested some lands, but only to the beginning of King John's reign. *1215 Magna Carta ch. 47, in* 3 EHD, *supra* note 67, at 321.

Others felt that he had demanded too high a price for their lawful inheritances, leaving them deeply in debt to the crown or the Jews. As Sir James Holt wrote, "It was a rebellion of the king's debtors."[70] Since contemporaries considered the Northerners the core of baronial opposition, they applied that label to all rebels, even after a group of barons in Essex and East Anglia and another rather ill-defined group in the west country joined the rebellion. Indeed, the primary figure in the rebellion was the East Anglian baron, Fitz-Walter, who had shown a tendency to reject legal processes and the courts in favor of force and violence in disputes with his neighbors. To his contemporaries, he appeared to be "quarrelsome and impetuous, swift to resort to violence in support of his claims."[71]

By the beginning of 1215, the disaffected barons had joined together in a sworn association or *conjuratio*, bound by a common oath to seek redress from King John. Familiarity with such corporations as communes and chartered boroughs allowed them to make the leap from their subversive association to conceptualizing the baronage as a corporate body and later, the kingdom of England as a commune, comprising all the king's subjects and possessing certain liberties. The rebellious barons came with their clerical allies to the king's great council at London in January "to petition the king about their grievances."[72] John postponed his answer until another council was scheduled to meet at Northampton a week after Easter, April 26. The Northerners claimed that John at the London council had "not only scorned to grant them their ancient and customary liberties but wanted them to promise in writing that they would never again demand such liberties."[73] The London council made clear the breadth of the rift between the king and his discontented barons. The king continued to make proposals for pacifying them with proposals for arbitration, primarily to present an appearance of seeking a peaceful solution, and he appealed to Innocent III, his new friend in Rome, to condemn the barons.

In Holy Week 1215, the barons mustered at Stamford in Lincolnshire to march together in arms south for the post-Easter council at Northampton. When the barons arrived there, attended by their men at arms, they were prepared to present a list of nonnegotiable demands to the king. On his failure to appear, they sent their demands to him at his nearby castle of Wallingford. On May 5, 1215, the rebels formally "defied" King John or renounced their fealty to him, possibly in a belief that an openly announced revolt that

---

70. J.C. HOLT, THE NORTHERNERS: A STUDY IN THE REIGN OF KING JOHN 34 (1992).

71. Strickland, *supra* note 28.

72. ROTULI LITTERARUM PATENTIUM 126b (T.D. Hardy ed., London 1835) [hereinafter RLP].

73. CHENEY, *supra* note 29, at 268.

threatened the king's authority, but not his life, did not constitute treason.[74] The rebels chose as their commander John's longtime foe FitzWalter, who took the bombastic title "Marshal of the Host of God and Holy Church."[75] When armed rebellion began in early May, John missed his opportunity to crush the rebels quickly.

He suffered a major blow when the Londoners opened the city gates to the rebels in mid-May. Great London merchants were incensed by King John's arbitrary demands for funds, for example, his tallage of over £1,500 in 1214.[76] The barons' possession of London was an inducement for John to come to terms. London's citizens were a source of new political ideas with their periodic experiments in self-government.[77] In 1191, they had won the right to organize themselves into a commune, though it was soon suppressed; and not long afterward the new office of mayor appeared. In early May 1215, hoping to forestall an alliance of Londoners and rebels, John had granted the city of London a confirmation of their ancient liberties, but it failed to win them over to his side.

After the fall of London, King John sought discussions with the baronial rebels, and meetings by royal emissaries with rebel representatives resulted in the drafting of the Articles of the Barons. Chief among intermediaries during negotiations between the king and the rebel barons over the content of the Articles and later over Magna Carta was the respected warrior William Marshal, Earl of Pembroke.[78] Bearing the heading, "These are the articles that the barons ask for and the lord king grants,"[79] its 49 articles outline a preliminary agreement. The Articles are undated but belong to a late stage in negotiations. The text was drafted by clerks of the royal chancery and sealed with the royal seal as a sign of John's acceptance of its provisions.[80] When final talks began at Runnymede by June 10, 1215, the Articles of the Barons, a somewhat more moderate document than the Unknown Charter, would provide the basis for final discussions. Magna Carta is little more than the Articles, "carefully worked over by highly intelligent men with a

---

74. Daniel Power, *La Rage Méchant des Traîtres Prit Feu': Le Discours Sur la Revolt Sous les Rois Plantagenêt (1133–1224)*, *in* LA TRAHISON AU MOYEN AGE 53, 57 (Maïté Billoré & Myriam Soria eds., 2009).

75. HOLT, *supra* note 58, at 295–96.

76. FRANK BARLOW, THE FEUDAL KINGDOM OF ENGLAND 1042–1216 265–66 (4th ed. 1988).

77. RICHARD MORTIMER, ANGEVIN ENGLAND 181 (1994).

78. DAVID CROUCH, WILLIAM MARSHAL: COURT, CAREER AND CHIVALRY IN THE ANGEVIN EMPIRE 1147–1219 112 (1990).

79. 3 EHD, *supra* note 67, at 311; *see also The Magna Carta Project, The Articles of the Barons*, MAGNACARTA.CMP.UEA.AC.UK, http://magnacarta.cmp.uea.ac.uk/read/articles _of_barons/Introduction__Articles_of_the_Barons_1215 (last visited May 9, 2014).

80. V.H. Galbraith, *Runnymede Revisited*, 110 PROC. AM. PHIL SOC. 307, 309–10 (1966).

thorough knowledge of English government."[81] Thirteen of its provisions reappear in the final version with little change, but others incorporate more detailed language for greater legal precision.

V. Magna Carta 1215

Final negotiations to settle the dispute between King John and his rebellious barons began by June 10, 1215, at Runnymede meadow between Windsor Castle and the rebels' camp at Staines. The two parties spent several days in hard bargaining and they reached agreement by June 19. The rebels and the king made a "firm peace" to signify agreement; a two-part indenture recorded it, and it was symbolized by exchanges of the kiss of peace and renewal of the barons' homage. To ensure that John made restitution to all those with claims against him, the document specified that the barons' occupation of London and Langton's custody of the Tower of London should continue until mid-August. The likely date of the Great Charter is June 19, although it is dated June 15, probably the day that a draft was sealed.[82]

Those who hammered out the Charter's text were "a mixed bag of rebels, royalists, and moderates."[83] Clear-eyed royalist bishops and barons, capable of admitting King John's shortcomings and counseling moderation, worked alongside experienced royal administrators to draft first the Articles of the Barons and then Magna Carta. Twenty-six names appear in the preamble of Magna Carta to acknowledge their role in counseling the king during negotiations; listed are the names of prelates, earls, barons, and royal officials. First on the list is the Archbishop of Canterbury, Langton. Even though John suspected him of being too hostile to be trusted, Langton nonetheless served as a mediator between the contending parties during the June negotiations at Runnymede.[84] Eight other prelates' names follow, including four bishops who had served the excommunicate king throughout his quarrel with Langton, and another cleric, the papal legate Pandulf. Four loyal earls are listed, headed by Earl William Marshal. Three names listed are men labeled by chroniclers as "evil counselors" of the king: Peter des Roches, bishop of Winchester; Earl William of Salisbury, John's half-brother; and Thomas Basset II, a longtime royal servant. No rebels are named in the preamble.[85]

Making and sealing official copies of Magna Carta with the great seal would have required several days or even weeks, probably taking place at

---

81. SIDNEY PAINTER, THE REIGN OF KING JOHN 316 (1949).
82. Galbraith, *supra* note 80, at 309–12.
83. CHENEY, *supra* note 29, at 376.
84. Galbraith, *supra* note 80, at 312; HOLT, *supra* note 58, at 244.
85. 3 EHD, *supra* note 67, at 316–24, *Translation with comments at Magna Carta Project*, THE 1215 MAGNA CARTA (on file with author).

Windsor Castle.[86] The drafters were clerks of the royal chancery, who followed the chancery's templates.[87] Some of the clerks must have been familiar with Roman and canon law, since some words in various chapters of the Charter are correctly used in the technical legal sense of the law, but only a few indicate direct influence of Roman or canon law.[88] Copies were sent throughout the kingdom to the sheriffs and bishops, along with royal letters ordering that it "should be publicly read throughout your whole bailiwick and firmly held."[89] Of more than 40 copies sent to the shires, only four survive today.[90]

The 1215 Charter consists of 63 chapters remedying specific grievances ranging over a variety of topics from promises of fundamental rights of all free men to specific matters of merely local or temporary interest. The Charter's first chapter records John's grant to God of the freedom to the English Church, and the king confirms his earlier charter guaranteeing to the Church free elections of its prelates. Inclusion of this provision ensured that English clerics in succeeding centuries would treasure Magna Carta as a protector of the Church's liberty.[91] Then King John granted "to all free men of our kingdom all the liberties written below." Unlike earlier English charters of liberties, the remedies granted in Magna Carta were not to be restricted to the great men of the kingdom. Six chapters (15, 20, 27, 30, 34, and 39) refer to "free man/men," a term that in 1215 defined not only barons and knights, but also smaller landholders who held land "freely" of a lord, about half of the population of England in 1215.[92] The free man in medieval England had privileges denied to those of unfree status such as serfs: the right to bear arms, freedom from capricious work assignments by their lords, and freedom from humiliating corporal punishments.[93] Chapter 1 also stands out from others for guaranteeing that the English Church "shall be free, and shall have its rights undiminished and its liberties unimpaired." (This is repeated in chapter 63.)

The Charter's other chapters follow in no particular order, with the first 15 addressing the rebel barons' complaints about King John's abuses of the "feudal" obligations that his tenants-in-chief owed him in his capacity as

---

86. Galbraith, *supra* note 80, at 311 & n.13.

87. Holt, *supra* note 40, at 25.

88. Hudson, *supra* note 20, at 103, 104, 114.

89. RLP, *supra* note 72, at 180b.

90. London, British Library MS/Manuscript Cotton Charter xiii.31a; British Library MS/Manuscript Cotton Augustus ii.106; Lincoln Cathedral Archives (A1/1/45); Salisbury Cathedral Archives (Press IV, C2: Royal Charters/39).

91. Carpenter, *supra* note 59, at 1057.

92. DANNY DANZIGER & JOHN GILLINGHAM, 1215: THE YEAR OF MAGNA CARTA 41 (2003).

93. Sidney Painter, *Magna Carta, in* FEUDALISM AND LIBERTY: ARTICLES AND ADDRESSES OF SIDNEY PAINTER 246–48 (Fred A. Cazel, Jr. ed., 1961).

their lord. They set specific limits on their financial responsibilities, restoring what they held to be the "good old law" preceding Henry II's reign. Chapter 2 sets a limit of £100 as suitable "relief," a payment on an heir's succession to a barony, and 100 shillings (£5) when succeeding to a knight's fee. Chapter 3 bans relief payments by youths whose estates had been held by the king during their wardship. Widows gained protection of their marriage portions or dower right and their inheritances in chapter 7, and chapter 8 prohibited the king or other lords from forcing them to remarry. The chapters treating widows and daughters in the king's wardship are the only ones that afford protection to women. Other chapters remedy abuses of royal rights to wardship and marriage, such as excessive exploitation of royal wards' lands (chapters 4 and 5) or forcing them to marry beneath their social rank (chapter 6).

Two chapters on financial obligations of royal tenants-in-chief are significant for their requirement that the king take counsel with his baronage before imposing scutages or aids on them. Chapter 12 declares that no scutage or aid "shall be imposed in our kingdom unless by common counsel of our kingdom," except the traditional three aids for ransoming a captive king, the knighting of his eldest son, and the marrying of his eldest daughter. Chapter 14 describes the method for obtaining "the common counsel of the kingdom." The king must summon "the archbishops, bishops, abbots, earls and greater barons, individually by our letters," and his lesser tenants of knightly rank were to receive a general summons sent to the sheriff of each county. This seems at best a partial recognition of the demands for governance "by counsel" voiced by Langton and the rebels.

Chapter 60 of the Charter extends these remedies granted to royal tenants-in-chief to their own tenants, free landholders not holding directly from the king. It required all lords in the kingdom to make available to their free men the same customs and liberties that the king was granting to them. Another restriction on lords' financial dominance over their tenants is the limitation in chapter 15 of aids that tenants were obliged to pay to the traditional three "feudal" aids. Such chapters continue a tendency of the Angevin kings to curb their magnates' ability to dictate to their free tenants with impunity and to claim royal responsibility for all free men, undermining traditional ties of lordship and strengthening the direct ruler-subject relationship.

A second group of chapters treats various administrative topics, most dealing with payments owed to the monarch. Chapter 25 eliminates increases or "increments" to the traditional fixed rents or "farms" paid annually by sheriffs and other local officials. Other chapters (28, 30, and 31) limit the king's right of prise or purveyance, regulating a common royal practice of requisitioning food supplies, horses, carts, and other goods for the king's household without adequate reimbursement. Chapters 9 to 11 define proper methods for collecting debts to the crown or to Jewish moneylenders (10 and 11), and two chapters (26 and 27) ease terms for widows and heirs of men who died with such debts unpaid. Chapters concerning collection of debts to Jews reflect the discrimination that they endured in England until their expulsion in 1290. An early law book declares, "Jews and all their property are the king's."[94] The king allowed them to lend money, and he ensured that debtors paid off their loans. In return, however, he periodically wrung out of them massive sums for the privilege of plying their trade in England.

Among other chapters dealing with administrative subjects are four concerning royal forests (44, 47, 48, and 53), a constant cause of complaint, for wide swaths of territory and the animals roaming over them were subject to arbitrary forest law enforced by a host of royal foresters. Periodic forest eyres added to royal income, producing profitable fines for violations of forest law; the "savage" forest eyre of 1212 accounted for over 11 percent of that year's revenues.[95] These chapters call for disafforestation of all lands annexed to the royal forests by King John, similar treatment of river banks that had been restricted by King John, and inquiries into "evil customs" enforced by royal foresters.

A third group of chapters treats the courts and justice, and several chapters centering on the effective functioning of the common law courts acknowledge the popularity of these tribunals. Chapter 17, requiring that common pleas be heard at some fixed place, represents a criticism of John's suspension of the court of common pleas at Westminster after 1209, forcing litigants to follow his erratic movements about the kingdom. Two other chapters (18 and 19) mandate more frequent circuits of the counties by itinerant justices to hear the assizes, provisions that benefited many modest landholders. These two chapters make clear the growing role of the knights of the counties in England's local government, as they were assigned duties as jurors or assisted itinerant justices in other ways, and also served as jurors in forest inquiries (chapter 48).

Three of the chapters dealing with justice treat criminal proceedings. Chapter 24 bars sheriffs or other local royal officers from hearing pleas of the crown, reserving such serious criminal cases for royal justices. Chapter 36 makes writs "of life and limb" freely available. Such writs were popular because they enabled suspected criminals to escape the ordeal by allowing the accused to seek a jury that would determine whether the prosecution was malicious, and if the jurors confirmed his accuser's malice, then

---

94. ROBERT BARTLETT, ENGLAND UNDER THE NORMAN AND ANGEVIN KINGS 1075–1225 351–52 (2000), *citing* 1 LIEBERMAN, at 650.

95. David Crook, *The Forest Eyre in the Reign of John, in* MAGNA CARTA, *supra* note 11, at 45, 49, 51.

the accused went free. Other chapters limit the king's profits from justice. Chapter 32 reaffirms the custom that the king can hold the lands of convicted felons for no more than a year and a day. Two chapters (20 and 22) ban amercements, or fines, from taking away offenders' means of making a living, and another (chapter 21) provides that amercements of earls and barons must be assessed by their "peers," that is, not by low-born royal officials. Chapter 20 is the only one in Magna Carta giving a guarantee to the unfree, a significant portion of the rural population; it protected them from such heavy amercements that they would be deprived of their means of earning a living. Chapter 54, one of the few concerning women, reaffirms limits on their right to initiate prosecutions for homicide, allowing them to do so only when their husband was the victim.

A fourth set of chapters gives concessions to townspeople and traders, a group fitting uncomfortably within the largely rural English population. Chapter 13, reflecting Londoners' contribution to the rebel success, confirms to the city "all its ancient liberties and free customs" and confers similar rights on all other cities and towns. Chapter 41 promises merchants free movement in and out of the kingdom without being subjected to evil tolls; and chapter 42 extends this right of free entry and exit to all English subjects. Chapter 33 calls for removal of fish weirs from major rivers, an advantage for maritime trade because the weirs created barriers to ships' passage to ports upriver. Chapter 35 simplified tradespeople's work by setting up a single standard for weights and measures of ale, wine, grain, and cloth throughout the kingdom.

A fifth category of chapters seeks to guarantee that King John would carry out his promises, remedying his wrongs and restoring properties unlawfully taken. In chapter 49, he promised to release hostages and return charters of fidelity earlier demanded of those whom he distrusted. Chapters 52 and 55 echo the barons' call for proceeding by judgment, providing for immediate restoration of lands, castles, or franchises that were taken "without the legal judgment of his peers" and for remission of all fines or amercements levied "unjustly and against the law of the land." Chapters 56 to 58 restore the rights of John's Welsh subjects, promising them justice in accordance with the law of Wales. The next chapter (59) commits him to treat the Scottish king as he would his English barons, releasing the hostages he had taken, and submitting disputed matters to "the judgment of his peers in our court." Other chapters deal with foreign soldiers brought to England by John whose appointment as sheriffs and constables of castles had provoked much resentment. Chapters 50 and 51 require the king to remove several mentioned by name from office, and require the withdrawal of all foreign mercenaries from the kingdom.

Chapter 61, the security chapter, creates a committee of 25 barons to see that King John observed the Charter's terms, and in case of his failure in that regard, to coerce him into doing so. Calling for the barons to choose the committee members, who were to reprimand John for violations of the Charter's terms and to threaten renewed war if he refused to correct them, is "surely the most fantastic surrender of any English king to his subjects."[96] If the king failed to correct an offense within 40 days of a warning from a subcommittee of four barons, then the 25 "together with the community of the whole land shall distrain and distress [him] in every way they can, namely, by seizing castles, lands, possessions, and in such other ways as they can."[97] The author of a classic work on medieval kingship notes that this chapter first "incorporated the right of resistance in the written public law of a nation" and that the committee formed for its enforcement furnished "the vitality necessary for institutional development."[98] Although cloaked in the language of the common law, this chapter had the purpose of protecting the barons from the forfeiture of their lands for making war on an anointed king. With the legal vocabulary of "distraint and distress,"[99] terms for temporary seizure of a suspect's land to force his appearance in court, the rebel barons hoped to place their threat of force against their king within the letter of the law.

Chapter 61 concludes with King John's assurance that he would not seek a discharge from his commitments from anyone, a provision added because the rebel barons expected him to petition his new ally, Pope Innocent III, to release him from his promises in the Charter. In the next chapter (62), John pronounced his full pardon for all, clerical or lay, who had incurred his "ill-will, indignation and rancour" since the beginning of his conflict with the barons. Although John was infamous for breaking oaths, the barons deemed it necessary that he swear yet another one. A final chapter (63) declares that both he and the barons had sworn to observe "in good faith and without evil disposition" all the promises in the earlier chapter.

Magna Carta, drafted hastily to correct specific complaints, was not framed to establish permanent political principles, yet some chapters set forth precepts of lasting importance that still shape our views on law and government. The mere fact of King John's submission to written promises to his subjects in a written document, although couched in the language of a freely given grant, suggests limits to royal authority.[100] With the king's renunciation of his arbitrary acts and his promise to rule in accordance

---

96. Galbraith, *supra* note 80, at 308.

97. 3 EHD, *supra* note 67, at 323–24.

98. FRITZ KERN, KINGSHIP AND LAW IN THE MIDDLE AGES 127–29 (S.B. Chrimes trans., 1956).

99. For more on *districtio* or distraint, see JOLLIFFE, *supra* note 7, at 51–53.

100. R.V. TURNER, KING JOHN 246–47 (1994). Royal authority in the 13th century encompassed elements of what later theorists would term executive, legislative, and judicial power.

with the law, the Charter accomplished goals shared by both the barons and Langton of reinstating governance "by judgment" and "by counsel."

Chapter 39, the most frequently cited provision in the 1215 Charter, marks a giant step toward achieving the reformers' goal of governance "by judgment" or by what is termed today "due process of law." It recognizes the fundamental right of justice under the law, "No free man shall be taken or imprisoned or disseised [i.e., dispossessed] or outlawed or exiled or in any way victimized, nor will we [the king] attack him or send anyone to attack him, except by the lawful judgments of his peers or by the law of the land."[101] In 1215, judgment by peers meant neither the common law inquest by 12 neighbors nor a modern jury trial. Rebel barons understood it as promising them a hearing before a panel of their social equals, similar to their own courts where knights gathered together to settle disputes with each other or with their lord, not a process before professional royal officials in the common law courts or the exchequer. Chapter 39's final phrase, "law of the land," likewise had no specialized meaning in 1215. For many of John's contemporaries, it meant the ancient custom of the realm upheld by William the Conqueror and his sons and enshrined in popular memory as the laws of Edward the Confessor. Indeed, royal justices read "law of the land" as meaning the traditional proceedings in shire courts that they contrasted with the newer processes by writ and jury. Yet the phrase would prove to be "magically elastic" over the centuries.[102] Immediately preceding and following chapter 39 are two chapters that strengthened due process in the courts. Chapter 38 provides that no one should be put on trial simply by the word of a local official, "without reliable witnesses produced for this purpose." Also restating the king's subjection to due process is chapter 40, "To no one will we sell, to no one will we deny or delay right or justice." Of course, in the early 13th century none of these protections applied to the unfree, who continued to be subject to their lords' arbitrary authority.

A second principle featuring prominently among the rebel barons' demands was governance "by counsel," the king's obligation to seek the advice of his great men. The rebels feared John's penchant for relying on the advice of his intimate advisers, lowborn or foreign royal appointees. Chapters 12 and 14 of the Charter mark a step in this direction, demanding that the king levy no aids or scutages without "the common counsel of the kingdom." Appearing in another chapter (61) is a similar phrase, "the community of the whole land," implying that all those living in the kingdom formed a single community or commune. The idea that all English free men formed a community, a single body representing all ranks and classes within the kingdom, would resound throughout the 13th century. No monarch would

101. *1215 Magna Carta, in* 3 EHD, *supra* note 67, at 320.
102. FAITH THOMPSON, MAGNA CARTA: ITS ROLE IN THE MAKING OF THE ENGLISH CONSTITUTION 1300–1629 87 (1948).

be willing to recognize a community of his subjects that was "self-governing without him,"[103] yet John's notorious misdeeds aroused even conservative aristocrats and clerics to collective action on behalf of the kingdom.

Chapter 14 attempts to devise a means for the king to take counsel with the free men of the kingdom on scutages and aids. Earls and barons, bishops and abbots were to be summoned by individual writs to meet at a fixed date and place for a specified issue, and sheriffs and bailiffs would receive a general summons for lesser-ranking royal tenants. Chapters 12 and 14 make clear that the baronage not only felt that the king must take counsel with them on certain tax measures, but that "a regular institutional mechanism" was necessary in order for the whole kingdom to be heard.[104] No doubt, the baronage considered itself qualified to speak to the king on behalf of the "community of the whole land," for chapter 14 specified that not all those summoned needed to be present. No effective means for taking council with other groups in the kingdom, whose interests differed from those of the baronage, took shape until the 14th-century parliaments that regularly included knights of the counties and members of urban elites.

The charter granted by John at Runnymede remained in effect for only a few weeks. The king had hardly negotiated in good faith; in Sidney Painter's 1949 study of his reign, he wrote, "Even when he sealed Magna Carta, John had not the slightest intention of giving in or permanently abandoning the powers which the Angevin kings had come to enjoy."[105] Even the most moderate royalists saw the committee of 25's power as an unacceptable limitation on monarchical authority. The rebel barons suspected the king of duplicity, and his appeal in late June or early July to Pope Innocent III for release from any concessions restricting his royal authority strengthened their suspicions. The barons went ahead with the selection of the 25, however. Almost all those designated for the committee came from dedicated foes of the king; among them were FitzWalter, Vescy, and others who had been conspirators against the king in 1212. Not one of the respected moderates listed in the Charter's preamble as royal advisers, not even Langton, was selected.[106]

By mid-August, each side saw the other failing to live up to its commitments to implement Magna Carta, and both rebels and royalists mobilized for war. Fighting broke out by September 1215 when news reached England that the pope had excommunicated the rebels, and baronial forces occupied the royal castle at Rochester. In spring 1216, the heir to the French throne, Prince Louis (the future Louis VIII), landed in England at the invitation of the 25 with 1,200 knights to wrest the throne from John. After Louis arrived

103. SUSAN REYNOLDS, KINGDOMS AND COMMUNITIES IN WESTERN EUROPE 900–1300 269 (2d ed. 1997).

104. BARTLETT, *supra* note 94, at 147.

105. PAINTER, *supra* note 81, at 340.

106. Strickland, *supra* note 28.

with a large army, the beleaguered English king's forces scurried about in a confusing contest of royalist barons and foreign mercenaries against rebel barons and their French allies. John controlled the west of the kingdom, and foreign mercenaries loyal to him held out in isolated strongholds elsewhere, while the rebels and the French were confined to London, the southeast, and some scattered northern outposts. King John fell ill and died in October 1216, leaving the situation stalemated.[107]

VI.   Subsequent Issues of Magna Carta

The true significance of Magna Carta, apparently dead by late summer 1215, lies in the early years of King John's successor, his nine-year-old son Henry III (r. 1216–1272). The royalist barons, officials in his late father's administration, almost the entire episcopate, and a new papal legate Gualo all gave the boy-king their loyalty. The authority of this council governing in Henry's name depended on the support of assemblies of great men and high-ranking officials, and the governance by counsel that the rebel barons had sought approached reality during his minority. The situation was so desperate in autumn 1216, with the rebels still holding out and Prince Louis of France still in the kingdom fighting on their behalf, that young Henry's counselors had to take dramatic action. Along with the papal legate, they ignored both John's and Pope Innocent III's repudiation of Magna Carta, and reissued it in November, appropriating the rebels' own cause.[108]

Both William Marshall, Henry III's regent, and the pope's legate, sealed the 1216 Magna Carta. Several chapters deemed "important yet doubtful" (10, 11, 12, 14, 15, 25, 27, 42, 45, 48–53, and 55) were deferred "until we have fuller counsel, when we will . . . do what is for the common good."[109] All the original Charter's enforcement provisions (chapters 61–63) were omitted, and they would be excluded from all subsequent issues. Although the 1216 Magna Carta was "an interim assertion of policy made in the middle of a civil war within a month of John's death,"[110] considerable thought had gone into it.[111] It was a promise of good government aimed at winning over rebel barons whose quarrel was with King John, not with his innocent son or with the monarchy as an institution. Innocent III's successor as the young king's overlord, Honorius III (r. 1216–1227), was urged to support the second Charter by his legate in England; and he sanctioned it, giving it respectability, and papal policy favored Magna Carta's "permanence and survival."[112]

---

107. PAINTER, *supra* note 81, at 349–77.
108. BARTLETT, *supra* note 94, at 66–67.
109. 3 EHD, *supra* note 67, at 327–32.
110. HOLT, *supra* note 58, at 381–82.
111. *Id.* at 382.
112. Galbraith, *supra* note 80, at 316.

Within a year, the young king's adherents had achieved military success with startling victories over rebel forces on land at Lincoln in spring 1217 and at sea off Sandwich in late summer, destroying a fleet bringing reinforcements from France. Following Prince Louis's departure from England in September 1217, there was a second reissue of Magna Charter—again designed to convince the barons and others that Henry III would be a good king, omitting almost all the chapters deemed "important yet doubtful" in 1216.[113] Issued along with this third version was the first Charter of the Forest, restricting the king's arbitrary authority over royal forests and their boundaries.[114] Now there were two charters, Magna Carta or the Great Charter and the shorter Forest Charter; when later generations called for confirmations, they would speak in the plural of "the Charters." For a full account of the Charter of the Forest, see chapter 12.

In 1225, King Henry III issued versions of both charters that became definitive; with the exception of very minor changes in the 1297 version of Magna Carta issued by King Edward I (r. 1272–1307), later monarchs did not issue their own versions, but merely ratified the two 1225 Charters. Magna Carta 1225, with only 37 chapters, differs substantially from earlier ones. It is the first to declare that the king granted it on his own initiative, "out [of his] own spontaneous goodwill;"[115] and the last chapter (37) states that in return for his grant of liberties, his people had granted the king "a fifteenth part of all their moveables."[116] Although chapter 12 of the first Charter—King John's promise to levy aids or scutages only with "the common counsel of the kingdom"—was missing from all later issues, Henry's statement asserts "in the most practical way the necessity of a general consent to all new taxation,"[117] and he continued to seek great councils' or Parliaments' consent before new taxation. At the end of the 13th century during Edward I's reign, the 1225 Charters would be enrolled as the first of England's statutes.

After Henry assumed personal power by 1230, he initiated a short-lived experiment in "household government," but a baronial reaction followed in 1234 to end it. A passage in the law book *Bracton*, written shortly after the crisis, sums up Magna Carta's underlying principle, "The king has a superior, namely God. Also the law by which he is made king. Also his *curia*, namely the earls and barons, because if he is without law, they ought to put the bridle on him."[118]

Other 13th-century crises preserved the Great Charter as a potent protection against royal tyranny, as continued royal violations of custom and law

113. 3 EHD, *supra* note 67, at 332–37.
114. *Id.* at 337–40.
115. *Id.* at 341.
116. *Id.* at 332–37, 341–46.
117. Galbraith, *supra* note 80, at 316.
118. HENRY DE BRACTON, 2 BRACTON DE LEGIBUS ET CONSUETUDINIBUS ANGLIAE 110 (G.E. Woodbine ed., Samuel E. Thorne trans., 1968–77).

aroused reactions that resulted in confirmations by Henry III in 1259 and by his son Edward I (r. 1272–1307) in 1297.

VII.   Magna Carta in Early Modern England and North America

Late medieval monarchs confirmed Magna Carta at least 30 times, the last occurring under Henry V (r. 1413–1422),[119] but its prominence waned in English political life in the 15th and 16th centuries. Tudor propaganda restored King John to favor, but in that same period antiquarians and printers were making copies of early law codes, and half-forgotten royal charters were widely available, chief among them Magna Carta.[120] Lawyers and parliamentarians found in these works useful ammunition for their struggle against royal tyranny in the reigns of the first two Stuart kings, James I (r. 1603–1625) and his son Charles I (r. 1625–1649). They treasured the Charter as a key element of England's "ancient constitution," a body of laws and customs existing since "time immemorial" that imposed limits on the king's power over his subjects.[121]

A champion of this doctrine was the 17th-century antiquarian and jurist, Sir Edward Coke, who viewed the Charter as a reaffirmation of ancient English liberties. He and other lawyers in the common law courts anachronistically and uncritically found in Magna Carta's chapters confirmation of such rights as trial by jury, the right of habeas corpus, and even parliamentary dominance. Coke viewed the Great Charter's promises as still binding because of its many royal confirmations, and he urged Parliament to demand a new confirmation. The civil war of 1642–1648 ignited by the Charter's revival had more extreme consequences than the 1215–1216 rebellion, resulting in the beheading of Charles I and a short-lived republic or commonwealth. Yet competition between the king and Parliament continued until James II's (r. 1685–1688) deposition, and the Glorious Revolution of 1688–1689 settled the issue in favor of Parliament. Many saw the events of 1688–1689 as a repetition of the 1215 baronial rebellion, and under William III (r. 1689–1702) and Mary II (r. 1689–1694) Parliament enacted the Declaration of Rights as a new Magna Carta.[122]

---

119. WILLIAM SHARP MCKECHNIE, MAGNA CARTA: A COMMENTARY ON THE GREAT CHARTER OF KING JOHN 159 (1914).

120. TURNER, *supra* note 19, at 134–41.

121. J.G.A. POCOCK, THE ANCIENT AND THE FEUDAL LAW: A STUDY OF ENGLISH HISTORICAL THOUGHT IN THE SEVENTEENTH CENTURY 16, 18–46 (1957).

122. English Bill of Rights (1689), *available at* http://avalon.law.yale.edu/17th_century/england.asp; Bill of Rights, (1689), *available at* http://www.parliament.uk/about/living-heritage/evolutionofparliament/parliamentaryauthority/revolution/collections/billofrights/.

The Charter's revival by opponents of Stuart tyranny coincided with the beginnings of the British Empire, and while the indigenous population in the colonies remained under their tribal customs, English settlers retained their rights under English law, including Magna Carta. As a result, it came to be that the sun never sets on Magna Carta. For a fuller description, see chapter 11. Nowhere was Magna Carta's principle of the rule of law held in more reverence than in the 13 colonies established along North America's eastern seaboard. Since the settlers of New England were religious dissenters motivated to migrate by a search for religious freedom, they saw the 17th-century struggle against the Stuart kings as part of their own history, guaranteeing that the Charter's 17th-century significance would endure in American political thought.

The first charter for an English colony in the New World was granted by King James I to the Virginia Company in 1606. It stated that the colonists "shall have and enjoy all liberties, franchises, and immunities . . . as if they had been abiding and born, within this our realm of England, or any other of our said dominions."[123] Later the 1629 Charter of the Massachusetts Bay Colony made the same commitment with a similar statement, and the founding charters of most other colonies also included such language.[124] When the Massachusetts colonists considered drafting a law code, they agreed "that some men should be appointed to frame a body of grounds of law, in resemblance to Magna Carta, which . . . should be received for fundamental laws."[125]

As John Adams said, no people were "more strongly attached to their natural and constitutional rights and liberties than the British Colonists of the American Continent."[126] As early as 1647, officials in Massachusetts ordered from England two copies of Edward Coke's writings on the Charter.[127] Virginia's legislative assembly in 1666 ordered a number of law books from England.[128] In Philadelphia in 1687, William Penn published the first text of the Charter printed on this side of the Atlantic.[129] William

---

123. The First Charter of Virginia (Apr. 10, 1606), *available at* http://avalon.law.yale.edu/17th_century/va01.asp.

124. The Charter of Massachusetts Bay (1629), *available at* http://avalon.law.yale.edu/17th_century/mass03.asp; A.E. Dick Howard, *Rights in Passage: English Liberties in Early America*, 3, 3–4, *in* PATRICK T. CONLEY & JOHN P. KAMINSKI, THE BILL OF RIGHTS AND THE STATES: THE COLONIAL AND REVOLUTIONARY ORIGINS OF AMERICAN LIBERTIES (1992).

125. GEOFFREY HINDLEY, THE BOOK OF THE MAGNA CARTA 194 (1990).

126. WILLIAM F. SWINDLER, MAGNA CARTA, LEGEND AND LEGACY 217 (1965).

127. GEOFFREY HINDLEY, A BRIEF HISTORY OF THE MAGNA CARTA 288 (2008).

128. A.E. DICK HOWARD, THE ROAD FROM RUNNYMEDE: MAGNA CARTA AND AMERICAN CONSTITUTIONALISM 30 (1968).

129. Nathan Dorn, *From Magna Carta on Trial to the Holy Experiment*, LIBRARY OF CONGRESS, BLOGS.LOC.GOV (Feb. 19, 2013), http://blogs.loc.gov/law/2013/02/from-magna-carta-on-trial-to-the-holy-experiment/.

Blackstone's *Commentaries on the Laws of England* appeared in the 1760s, just as Britain's heavier financial demands and unfamiliar new regulations imposed on the North American colonies were fueling discontent. Blackstone traced three fundamental rights to Magna Carta, the rights to personal security, individual liberty, and private property.[130] His *Commentaries* soon became the standard text for apprentice lawyers in the colonies, where it was published in 1770.[131]

While the Great Charter's relevance was receding in England after the Glorious Revolution of 1688–1689 established parliamentary sovereignty, its reputation remained powerful among 18th-century American colonists. For them Magna Carta continued to be fundamental law, standing above both king and Parliament and unalterable by statute. By the 1760s, as Britain was tightening its control over the 13 colonies, rebellious acts by the Americans and British reprisals multiplied, and full-scale warfare broke out in 1775. Colonial lawyers and pamphleteers turned to Magna Carta for support against parliamentary tyranny, interpreting Magna Carta's chapters anachronistically as supporting their cries of "no taxation without representation."[132]

After declaring independence in July 1776, the colonies considered themselves free and independent states. They drafted state constitutions to replace their royal charters and in 1787 drafted a federal Constitution. Nearly all the new states included in their constitutions declarations of rights with chapters much like chapter 29/39 of Magna Carta.[133] Added to the federal Constitution in 1791 were the first ten amendments, the Bill of Rights. Among them is the fifth amendment promising that no person shall be "deprived of life, liberty, or property without due process of law," paraphrasing chapter 29/39, and the following amendments spell out proper procedures for ensuring "due process of law."[134]

---

130. ANNE PALLISTER, MAGNA CARTA: THE HERITAGE OF LIBERTY 58 (1971); S.F.C. Milsom, The Nature of Blackstone's Achievement, 4 Selden Society Lecture 1980 (London, 1981).

131. MICHAEL H. HOEFLICH, LEGAL PUBLISHING IN ANTEBELLUM AMERICA 26 (2010).

132. Philip B. Kirkland, *Magna Carta and Constitutionalism in the United States: "The Noble Lie,"* 54, *in* SAMUEL E. THORNE, THE GREAT CHARTER: FOUR ESSAYS (New York, 1965).

133. CONSTITUTION OF MARYLAND, art. 21, Nov. 11, 1776, *available at* http://avalon.law.yale.edu/17th_century/ma02.asp; VIRGINIA DECLARATION OF RIGHTS, 1776, § 8, *available at* http://www.constitution.org/bcp/virg_dor.htm.

134. U.S. CONST. amends. I–X.

Further Reading

Church, Stephen D. (ed.) (1999), *King John: New Interpretations*, Woodbridge, Suffolk: Boydell Press. Papers by experts on John and his times.

Holt, J.C. (1992), *Magna Carta*, 2d ed., Cambridge: Cambridge University Press. The standard work.

Jolliffe, J.E.A. (1963), *Angevin Kingship*, 2d ed., London: A.&C. Black. The despotic nature of England's governance under Henry II, Richard I, and John.

Loengard, Janet S. (ed.) (2010), *Magna Carta and the England of King John*, Woodbridge, Suffolk: The Boydell Press. Recent views on John's reign and aspects of Magna Carta.

O'Brien, Bruce, (2010), "Forgers of Law and Their Readers: The Crafting of English Political Identities between the Norman Conquest and the Magna Carta," 43 *PS: Political Science and Politics* 470–72. The role of collections of Old English law and Arthurian legend in the making of Magna Carta.

Pallister, Anne (1971), *Magna Carta: The Heritage of Liberty*, Oxford: Oxford University Press. Excellent account of the Charter from the 17th century forward.

Rothwell, Harry (ed.) (1975), *English Historical Documents, vol. 3: 1187–1327*, London: Eyre & Spottiswoode. English translations of the 1216, 1217, and 1225 Charters, as well as the "Unknown Charter" and the "Articles of the Barons."

Turner, Ralph V. (2003), *Magna Carta through the Ages*, Harlow, Essex: Pearson Longman. On both the changing role of the Charter in law and politics and on the actual documents.

Vincent, Nicholas (2010), "Stephen Langton, Archbishop of Canterbury," *in* Louis-Jacques Bataillon et al. (eds.), *Etienne Langton: Predicateur, Bibliste, Theologien, 9 Bibliotheque D'histoire Culturelle Du Moyen Age*, 77–97, Turnhout, Brepols. The most recent survey of Langton's career and his impact on the Charter.

Warren, W.L. (1978), *King John*, 2d ed. Berkeley and Los Angeles: University of California Press. A readable and generally reliable biography in need of updating.

Chapter 3
Magna Carta and Sovereign Immunity: Strained Bedfellows

Diane P. Wood and Danieli Evans

One of the most distinguished legal historians of our time, Professor Richard Helmholz, once commented that "writing about Magna Carta at all requires a measure of presumption. Certainly it does if the writer pretends to have something new to say about the topic."[1] We are acutely aware of that warning. Much indeed has been written on both sides of the Atlantic on the history and influence of the Great Charter. That body of scholarship leaves no doubt that Magna Carta has made its mark on American law, just as it has on its native soil. Our goal in this chapter is a modest one: we do not pretend to reveal any new *historical* facts about the document or even about its influence in the United States. Rather, building on what is known of Magna Carta, we have narrowed our focus to the United States and to the values in Magna Carta to question the historical justification for the peculiar form that the U.S. law of sovereign immunity has taken. As the doctrine governing the sovereign's right not to be sued either civilly or criminally, sovereign immunity lives uneasily with the principle of accountability reflected in Magna Carta. The scope and exact content of the doctrine, such as who has immunity and how far it reaches, varies among jurisdictions.

In this chapter, we consider whether U.S. law regarding sovereign immunity has remained true to the Charter's basic principles. Not entirely, we conclude. United States law of sovereign immunity (or perhaps we should say immunity of sovereigns, plural, since U.S. law recognizes immunity of foreign governments, the U.S. federal government, state governments, and Indian tribes) is in considerable tension with the fundamental principles reflected in Magna Carta, as elaborated in English and early American law. Magna Carta was a revolutionary assertion of individual rights, devised to restrain the sovereign's lawless conduct: at its most basic level, it guaranteed individuals a *right* to a *remedy* for violations of their rights.

The notion that no one—not even the sovereign—is above the law is a powerful one. In Magna Carta, the barons succeeded in extracting from

---

1. R.H. Helmholz, *Magna Carta and the Ius Commune*, 66 U. Chi. L. Rev. 297, 297 (1999).

the king the acknowledgement that he too was accountable under the law. (Indeed, the fact that King John (r. 1199–1216) tried so quickly to repudiate the 1215 charter is a testament to how seriously he took its language.) The primacy of law, even over the sovereign, was a central principle of Magna Carta and of the developments that followed first in English law and then, across the ocean, in the nascent United States.

The contemporary doctrine of sovereign immunity in the United States appears at first glance (and maybe even later) to run in the opposite direction. With respect to the 50 states, the doctrine prohibits suits against the states (in any capacity, either sovereign or proprietary) in either federal courts or federal agencies.[2] It even bans suits against states based on federal law in *state* court,[3] unless the state has expressly consented to being sued on the claim. The federal government has equivalent protection unless Congress has waived immunity from the claim. Immunity of foreign governments is governed by the Foreign Sovereign Immunities Act,[4] which confers only a restrictive immunity that excludes commercial acts, torts, and a few other matters.

Why, one might ask, should tension between the principles of sovereign *accountability* in Magna Carta and our modern doctrine of sovereign *immunity* be of any concern to anyone? One reason is that the U.S. Supreme Court has invited our attention to the English roots of our law. The Court has justified the contemporary conception of sovereign immunity as something based on the understanding that "[w]hen the Constitution was ratified, it was well established in English law that the Crown could not be sued without consent in its courts."[5] Looking back at the English law that developed in elaboration of Magna Carta, however, we discover a much more complicated situation. Indeed, the Court's statement clashes with one of the central principles of Magna Carta—a

---

2. Blatchford v. Native Vill. of Noatak, 501 U.S. 775, 779 (1991) (holding that states are immune from federal court suits by Indian tribes); Monaco v. Mississippi, 292 U.S. 313 (1934) (holding that states are immune from federal court suits by foreign nations); *Ex parte* New York, 256 U.S. 490 (1921) (holding that states are immune from admiralty proceedings); Hans v. Louisiana, 134 U.S. 1 (1890) (holding that states are immune from federal question suits brought by their own citizens); Fed. Mar. Comm'n v. S.C. State Ports Auth., 122 S. Ct. 1864 (2002) (holding that states are immune from Federal Maritime Commission adjudicative proceedings); Alden v. Maine, 527 U.S. 706 (1999) (holding that sovereign immunity shields states from private suits in state courts pursuant to federal causes of action).

3. The most notable exception is that Congress may abrogate the states' immunity from suit in legislation enforcing the Fourteenth Amendment. Fitzpatrick v. Bitzer, 427 U.S. 445 (1976). In addition, in the field of bankruptcy the Supreme Court has held that the states acquiesced in the subordination of their sovereign immunity to federal authority when they joined the Union. Central Va. Comm. College v. Katz, 546 U.S. 356 (2006).

4. 28 U.S.C. §§ 1330, 1602–11.

5. *Alden*, 527 U.S. at 717.

principle that was, for the most part, adopted into English law: individual persons have a *right* (not just a privilege) to petition the sovereign for violations of individual rights and the law of the land.

This chapter begins by describing the sovereign's accountability to the law in England before Magna Carta. This discussion sheds light on how Magna Carta was intended to remedy the recurring problem of the king's failure to adhere to the law. Magna Carta revolutionized the legal regime by introducing the concept that the sovereign was bound to follow the law and was under a duty to redress violations of individual legal rights. The discussion then turns to a review of how English common law during the period following Magna Carta, up through the time of the American Revolution, provided citizens with a right to petition for relief against the sovereign. Staying with America at that point, we move to the question of how the right to petition for redress from the sovereign's allegedly illegal actions was recognized in colonial law, state constitutions, and early Supreme Court decisions. Finally, the chapter concludes by arguing that, based on this history, Supreme Court decisions finding that the current scope of government immunity was a part of the law at the time of the founding of the United States have been based on a misguided or incomplete analysis of the English and colonial law and the Eleventh Amendment to the U.S. Constitution.

As we have noted, the broad scope of immunity enjoyed by the states and the federal government today is in tension with a central theme of the colonies and the early Republic: popular restraint on the sovereign. Insofar as a degree of immunity is founded in Magna Carta and the English origins of American law, this immunity derives from legislative power over appropriations. But the latter immunity would not be nearly as broad as the immunity enjoyed by governments in the United States today. Immunity derived from legislative control over appropriations addresses only whether a plaintiff is able to collect a monetary judgment. This is considerably narrower than the current conception of sovereign immunity, because it would not prevent courts from assessing liability, ordering declaratory or injunctive relief, or ordering monetary damages that the legislature would have a choice to satisfy. This chapter shows that sovereign *accountability*, as opposed to *immunity*, has been seen as essential to the rule of law since Magna Carta. It is time to reevaluate whether the U.S. concept of sovereign immunity is supported by the historical sources on which it purports to rely.

I.   English Law before Magna Carta

In the period leading up to Magna Carta, arbitrariness appeared to be the rule, not the exception, in the various layers of law that prevailed in England. Feudal lords were responsible for most of the governance in their own estates, and each one was entitled to, and did, set the rules for those subject to his power. Before the Norman Conquest in 1066, the king of England had not yet assumed the power and ability to administer laws throughout the country as a whole. Instead, the feudal lords held court and provided some form of dispute resolution for those who were under that lord's domain.[6] These local courts competed with each other to expand their spheres of influence and to increase their fees. After 1066, William the Conqueror (r. 1066–1087) took steps to create a stronger, more centralized monarchy by establishing a king's court that followed him from place to place as he traveled through the country.[7] But, to use modern parlance, the king's court was a tribunal of limited jurisdiction. It was just one among many feudal courts that would hear cases pertaining to the king's tenants, and it was not designed to administer justice to the entire nation. Attaining redress in the king's court was slow, costly, and unavailable to most, since petitioners or litigants were required to follow the king's court from place to place.[8] Nonetheless, it slowly evolved into a competitor of the feudal courts. Predictably, strife developed between the king's rule and the local autonomy of the landowners, who jealously guarded their own mechanisms for enforcing the law.[9]

Henry II (r. 1154–1189) furthered the establishment of a central judicial system by opening the royal courts to ordinary freeholders who could pay for a royal writ, as well as by converting county courts to royal courts. One needed permission to use the royal courts, and this was accomplished by the writ system. A litigant could gain access to the king's courts by obtaining a writ from the chancellor; only certain types of cases fell within royal jurisdiction, and each individual crime or civil proceeding had its own writ. Royal justice did not come free: people had to pay in order to obtain a specific writ. The prices for the writs were sometimes fixed, but other times the king would manipulate them depending on the facts of the case. In time, the king's courts came to replace the baronial courts, and as they did, there was a permanent shift in the balance of judicial power from local barons to the king. The barons opposed this change because it meant a loss in revenue from the fees they had previously collected in their own courts. Equally unpopular was the idea that the barons themselves would be subject to enforcement of the law in the king's courts if they committed a crime.[10]

---

6. William C. Koch, Jr., *Reopening Tennessee's Open Courts Clause: A Historical Reconsideration of Article i, Section 17 of the Tennessee Constitution*, 27 U. Mem. L. Rev. 333, 351 (1997).

7. *Id.* at 351–52.

8. *Id.* at 352.

9. *Id.* at 351.

10. *Id.* at 353.

Before Runnymede, King John had notoriously abused the royal court system without regard for any form of reliability, consistency, or uniformity in the law. He threatened to place his personal and political rivals under arrest before judgment, and he ignored the feudal tradition providing that persons were to be judged by their equals. Instead, as part of a broader, seemingly insatiable need for revenue, he used the royal tribunals to exile his enemies and deprive them of their estates and money. He used royal writs as a source of revenue and frequently increased the price of the writ in proportion to the value of the claim or the wealth of the person seeking the writ.[11]

These and other abuses prompted the barons to press for something that would restrain the king and force him to respect the legal process and their rights. That *something* turned out to be Magna Carta; it represented the barons' effort to prevent the king from using the royal courts to transfer their land, money, and rights to the monarchy, "to prevent him from taking the law into his own hands."[12] It "was the first manifestation of the fundamental principle that both the governor and the governed are subject to the rule of law."[13]

Chapter 40 of the original Magna Carta (later folded into chapter 29) was, in substance, a right-to-remedy clause; it promised that, "To no one will we sell, to no one will we refuse or delay, right or justice."[14] But the Charter did not stop with the recognition of the right to a remedy, or the right to petition for redress from the king if he or his officials committed a violation of rights. Nor did it rely solely on the hope or fiction that the king would keep his word. Instead, in chapter 61 the Charter attempted to set up an enforcement mechanism, in the form of a body of 25 elected barons. Here is what chapter 61 said:

> [T]he barons shall choose any twenty-five barons of the realm they wish, who with all their might are to observe, maintain and cause to be observed the peace and liberties which we have granted and confirmed to them by this our present charter; so that if we or our

---

11. *Id.*
12. *Id.*
13. *Id.* at 356–57 (citing WILLIAM S. MCKECHNIE, MAGNA CARTA, A COMMENTARY ON THE GREAT CHARTER OF KING JOHN 123–24 (2d ed. 1914); WILLIAM F. SWINDLER, MAGNA CARTA, LEGEND AND LEGACY 226 (1965)); *see also* Edward E. Kallgren, *Our Essential Heritage*, 10 EXPERIENCE 3, 25 (Summer 2000) ("[T]he most dramatic and enduring principle epitomized by Magna Carta is the then-revolutionary underlying notion that the sovereign was subject to the law—that in certain important respects he was not free to act as his whim or fancy dictated, but must conform to established procedures and had to respect and defer to certain rights of the people.").
14. WILLIAM S. MCKECHNIE, MAGNA CARTA, A COMMENTARY ON THE GREAT CHARTER OF KING JOHN 395 (2d ed. 1914).

justiciar or our bailiffs or any of our servants offend against anyone in any way, or transgress any of the articles of peace or security, and the offence is indicated to four of the aforesaid twenty-five barons, those four barons shall come to us or our justiciar, if we are out of the kingdom, and shall bring it to our notice and ask that we have it redressed without delay.[15]

This is quite extraordinary—in fact, it was so forward-thinking that the group of 25 never got off the ground and the concept was not included in the versions of Magna Carta issued in 1216 and thereafter. But the idea had seen the light of day, and it is the ideas expressed in Magna Carta that have survived and expanded for nearly 800 years, not the details, and not the particular implementation efforts.

II.   English Law in the Wake of Magna Carta

At first it seemed that Magna Carta might be short-lived. King John attempted almost immediately to repudiate it; and he succeeded in persuading Pope Innocent III (r. 1198–1216) to declare it null and void ten weeks after Runnymede. Moreover, it failed in its mission of bringing peace between the barons and King John, as the future King Louis VIII of France (r. 1223–1226) invaded England thereafter. But John died only a year and a half after Runnymede, in 1216, leaving behind the nine-year-old Henry III (r. 1216–1272) to succeed to the throne. In an effort to secure legitimacy, Henry's regent William Marshall and the papal legate Guala Bicchieri issued a shortened version of the Charter in 1216 and then again in 1217. It took a more or less permanent form in the version that appeared in 1225 over Henry III's seal; in the years and centuries that followed, it was repeatedly reaffirmed at varying levels of generality.

During the reign of Edward I (r. 1272–1307) in the latter part of the 13th century (from 1274), several forms of action developed that would enable subjects to bring a claim against the king before the Royal courts of Exchequer, Chancery, or King's Bench.[16] These courts were not independent from the Crown, as "[m]odern notions of separation of powers did not yet exist, and the judicial power was not yet perceived as something separate

---

15. *1215 Magna Carta ch. 61*, translated and reprinted, *in* J.C. Holt, Magna Carta 333–35 (1965).

16. Ludwik Erhlich, *Proceedings against the Crown* (1216–1377), *in* 6 Oxford Studies in Social and Legal History (Paul Vinogradoff ed., 1974); James E. Pfander, *Sovereign Immunity and the Right to Petition: Toward a First Amendment Right to Pursue Judicial Claims against the Government*, 91 Nw. U. L. Rev. 899, 909 (1997).

and distinct."[17] Instead, "[t]hese principal courts . . . were adjuncts of the executive, except that the highest court was Parliament itself, with the King presiding."[18]

The original action that enabled a subject to press a claim against the sovereign was the petition of right, which required the Crown's consent. In a petition of right, the complaining party would assert that his interests had been injured in such a way that, had the action involved a private defendant rather than the Crown, the petitioner would have had a legal claim. The petition of right asked the Crown to submit itself to the laws that applied to private persons. Although the petitions technically appealed to the king's grace, in practice he usually endorsed such petitions, and in time the concept of grace seems to have faded into a legal fiction.[19]

In the 14th century, Parliament created the remedies of *monstrans de droit* and traverse of office as alternative methods of obtaining possession or restitution of real or personal property from the Crown. These had the interesting feature of the *lack* of any requirement to request consent from the king.[20] Although they developed at a time when most disputes involved title to real property, over time they became available in disputes over personal and intangible property as well. Any time the Crown sought to establish its title to property and chose to proceed by inquest of office, individual persons were entitled to assert claims to the property by way of *monstrans* and traverse. This meant not only that the owner of the property could defend against the Crown's claim of entitlement, but also that other interested parties (such as competing creditors or mortgagees) could set up their own title in litigation against the Crown. As in other cases to which the *monstrans* and traverse applied, these third-party claims went forward on a petition without any requirement of the king's prior consent. Although obtaining permission to sue the Crown was never as routine as obtaining a writ to sue a private party, suits against the Crown were unremarkable.[21]

---

17. Larry D. Kramer, *The Supreme Court 2000 Term Foreword: We the Court*, 115 HARV. L. REV. 4, 25 (2001).

18. *Id.* These courts had jurisdiction over different types of claims: The Court of Common Pleas had jurisdiction chiefly over cases between subject and subject; King's Bench consisted mostly of cases touching the king's interest and encompassed criminal and civil cases and supervision over various state officials; Exchequer had jurisdiction over revenue matters, as well as some equitable and common law jurisdiction; and Chancery was the principal court of equity. Roger W. Kirst, *Administrative Penalties and the Civil Jury: The Supreme Court's Assault on the Seventh Amendment*, 126 U. PA. L. REV. 1281, 1314–15 (1978).

19. Erhlich, *supra* note 16.

20. Pfander, *supra* note 16, at 912.

21. Paul F. Figley & Jay Tidmarsh, *The Appropriations Power and Sovereign Immunity*, 107 MICH. L. REV. 1207, 1212–13 (2009).

Similarly, suits against officers or agencies of the Crown were possible, and in some circumstances they too could proceed without consent. The Statute of Westminster I 1275[22] (enacted under the reign of Edward I) provided for the writ of disseisin against the king or king's officers, if the plaintiff had been deprived or dispossessed of his property. The Statute of Westminster II 1285[23] provided that the king's officers were liable if they imprisoned somebody for a felony without indictment.[24] In addition to being able to bring claims for damages sounding in tort, individuals were entitled to bring petitions for what were called the "high prerogative writs": mandamus, prohibition, certiorari, habeas corpus, and quo warranto. In issuing the writ of mandamus, the King's Bench directed inferior courts and administrative officials to take nondiscretionary action clearly required of them by law. The writ of habeas corpus directed the jailer to bring an inmate before the court for an adjudication of the sufficiency of the reasons for his confinement. Prohibition directed a lower court to refrain from exercising authority over a matter beyond its jurisdiction. Certiorari effected the removal of a judicial record or cause (often an indictment) from a lower court over to the King's Bench for trial (or other disposition). Quo warranto tested the title of an individual to royal office and supplied the means of ousting those who held office unlawfully, though it also sometimes had the effect of upholding the individual's rights vis-à-vis a claim by the Crown.

These writs were issued by the king's court, after it reviewed the sufficiency of the petition and supporting affidavits; critically for present purposes, if the court found a showing of cause for the writ, it could be issued without the king's consent. The prerogative writs were seen as a supplemental "means of substantial justice"—they provided a special remedy to which a subject could turn when remedies at law were not available.[25] They were extraordinary remedies, enforceable through contempt sanctions and not subject to appeal.[26] In a 1762 decision, Lord Coke explained that the writ of mandamus "was introduced . . . to prevent disorder from a failure of justice, and defect of police. Therefore it ought to be used upon all occasions where the law has established no specific remedy, and where in justice and good government there ought to be one."[27]

The King's Privy Council played the role of screening petitions of right brought against the king. It also oversaw writs challenging official action. In each case, it would determine the likely merit of a petition and whether the king would consent to the claim. As English law developed, the king

---

22. 3 Edw. ch. 15 (Eng.).
23. 13 Edw. ch. 34 (Eng.).
24. LOUIS JAFFE, JUDICIAL CONTROL OF ADMINISTRATIVE ACTION 204 (1965).
25. Pfander, *supra* note 16, at 919–20.
26. *Id.* at 920.
27. JAFFE, *supra* note 24, at 211 (internal quotations omitted).

himself was said to bear no personal legal responsibility for officers' tortious invasions of the rights of his subjects. Instead, the fiction strengthened the principle that the inferior officers had acted faithlessly; English law thus required individuals to bring their tort claims directly against the king's subordinate officers.[28] Louis Jaffe explains that

> [f]rom the reign of Edward I on, there was a continuous parallel development of both types of action. We can conclude on the basis of this history that the King, or the Government, or the State, as you will, has been suable throughout the whole range of the law, sometimes with its consent, sometimes without, and that whether consent was necessary was determined by expediency rather than by abstract theory as to whether the action was really against the state.[29]

Occasionally, the Privy Council would protect Crown officials from an action. For instance, it once passed an order forbidding judicial interference with sewer commissioners against whom actions had been brought for taking property in order to satisfy a sewer assessment. This is noteworthy because it illustrates the opposite presumption from the one that prevails in modern American law: the fact that the King's Council needed to specify by a special order that the sewer commissioners' actions were *not* subject to challenge indicates that the background assumption was that they ordinarily *would be* subject to challenge. In the United States today, the background assumption is that actions directly against a primary governmental entity are not subject to challenge unless the legislature specifies that they are;[30] for officials, however, immunity remains an affirmative defense.[31]

At least in the pre-Stuart era (i.e., before 1603), the requirement of consent was "not based on a view that the king was above the law."[32] To the contrary, the general notion was that he "could not refuse to redress wrongs when petitioned to do so by his subjects."[33] Rather, the consent requirement emerged from the structural fact that the courts were not an independent branch of government. They were part of the king, and "it seemed an anomaly to issue a writ against oneself."[34] In other words, because the king was in charge of the court system, it was inevitably his decision to hold proceedings against himself; any time the king's court held proceedings, the king must have consented to suit because there was no branch empowered

---

28. Pfander, *supra* note 16, at 920–21.
29. JAFFE, *supra* note 24, at 198.
30. See sources cited *supra* note 2.
31. *See* Harlow v. Fitzgerald, 457 U.S. 800, 817–18 (1982).
32. JAFFE, *supra* note 24, at 199.
33. *Id.* (quotations omitted).
34. *Id.*

to hold proceedings without his authorization. While no independent body could force liability on the sovereign, it was widely understood that the king was obliged to consent to a petition if it stated a valid claim of illegal action: The expression "[t]he King can do no wrong" meant "'that the King was not allowed, not entitled to do wrong.'"[35] The king's power, it was said, was derived from acting as a vicar of God, and in order to maintain that status he was bound not to do wrong. If he acted illegally, he lost his special status and was equal to everyone else.[36] "[T]he King was bound not to infringe rights; it was the King's duty to redress wrongs done by himself or on his behalf; and it was the King's duty to discharge all other obligations arising for him as they would arise for a private person."[37] The king's dignity, however, prevented him from paying damages beyond restitution or being subject to physical or corporal punishment.[38]

It is important to recognize that the requirement of the king's consent was distinct from the king's liability for illegal conduct. In other words, the requirement of the king's consent was structural: the king logically had to consent to suit in order to hold proceedings against himself, since he sat at the top of the court system. But, counterintuitive as it may seem to modern eyes, the consent requirement was not understood as something that immunized the king's unlawful conduct or that served as an acceptable ground for denying a remedy for a valid claim. Hence, when it was required (as with the petition of right), the king routinely gave his consent; and, as the writs of *monstrans de droit* and traverse illustrate, consent was not always required. The law thus assumed that the king acknowledged an *obligation* to redress any wrongdoing committed by himself personally or by his officers.

In 1668, the Court of Exchequer affirmed this principle when it held the King liable under a petition brought without consent by a mortgagor seeking to redeem the property of a mortgagee, after the property had escheated to the Crown as a result of the mortgagee's conviction for treason.[39] In finding that the Crown owed the mortgagor payment for the mortgagee's escheated property, the court explained that as "fountain and head of justice and equity; it shall not be presumed, that [the King] will be defective in either."[40]

The effectiveness of remedies against the Crown eventually became ensnarled with the struggle for power between Parliament and the king; one can see this most clearly in a number of disputes over the power to raise

---

35. *Id.* (quoting Ehrlich, No. XII: *Proceedings against the Crown* (1216–1377) in 6 Oxford Studies in Social and Legal History 42 (1921)).

36. Ehrlich, No. XII: *Proceedings against the Crown* (1216–1377), *in* 6 Oxford Studies in Social and Legal History 42 (1921).

37. *Id.* at 43.

38. *Id.* at 43–44.

39. Pfander, *supra* note 16, at 914 (citing Pawlett v. Attorney General, Hardres 465, 145 Eng. Rep. 550 (1668)).

40. Jaffe, *supra* note 24, at 202.

and appropriate revenue. Until the 18th century, the king had been expected to provide certain financial support, including for his royal household and navy. He did so principally by relying on hereditary revenue in the form of rents from his land and other family income, inherited by each successor to the monarchy; if the king required supplemental funding, he could turn to taxes.[41] Under King John, however, taxes had spiraled out of control. Magna Carta restricted the king's power unilaterally to increase taxes by requiring approval of various impositions designed to raise revenue for the Crown. "[T]axes were intended as exceptional grants to meet the extraordinary necessities of the crown."[42] Over time, the approval power shifted to Parliament, and its chief source of power became the ability to approve or disapprove the king's increasingly frequent applications for funding.

When the Stuarts came to power with James I (r. 1603–1625), the Crown was deeply in debt, and so it began to seek funding from Parliament more often. Parliament, for its part, began to attach conditions to its grants of funding, limiting the way the king spent money and prescribing the king's actions. In 1628, Parliament forced Charles I (r. 1625–1649) (James I's successor) to accept the petition of right (distinct from the cause of action described above), which precluded the king from compelling anyone to make a gift, loan, benevolence, or tax without Parliament's approval. This measure effectively prevented the Crown from raising its own revenues outside of its hereditary revenue.[43]

Charles I responded by refusing to call another Parliament for 11 years, during which period he made efforts to finance the Crown through private loans from bankers and fees that were legally questionable. For instance, he reinstituted compulsory knighthood for certain landowners and then demanded fees from the recipients; he resurrected ancient forest rights and fined those who could not prove title; and he extended the collection of ship taxes, traditionally levied against seaports, to inland counties.[44]

In 1640, when the Scots threatened to attack England because Charles I was unable to pay his debts, Parliament reconvened for the "long Parliament," which lasted from 1640 until 1660 and resulted in Parliament's seizure of nearly exclusive control over revenues and spending. In 1641, Parliament ordered the publication of Sir Edward Coke's Second *Institute*,[45] which lauded chapter 29 (the number by which it was then referenced; in 1215 it was chapter 39) of Magna Carta (the "right-to-a-remedy" clause) as

---

41. Figley & Tidmarsh, *supra* note 21, at 1217–20.
42. *Id.* at 1218 (internal quotation omitted).
43. *Id.* at 1220–22.
44. *Id.* at 1222.
45. Coke's *Institutes* were widely understood as the most authoritative commentary on the laws of England, so much so that Charles I had seized Coke's manuscripts out of fear that he was becoming too great of an oracle. Koch, *supra* note 6, at 358.

a "roote" from which "many fruitfull [sic] branches of the law of England have sprung." Coke reworded the clause as follows:

> [E]very subject of this realm, for injury done to him in goods, lands, or person, by any other subject, be he ecclesiastical, or temporall, . . . or any other without exception, may take his remedy by the course of the law, and have justice, and right for the injury done to him, freely without sale, fully without any deniall, and speedily without delay.[46]

Coke's interpretation of Magna Carta is now widely recognized as something that "expound[s] on the law as it stood in the early seventeenth century rather than to explain the law as it stood in the early thirteenth century."[47] Nevertheless, it is interesting precisely because it formed the basis for the understanding and continued salience of the Charter during that period, especially in Colonial America.[48]

By the time Charles II (r. 1660–1685) assumed the throne, Parliament controlled all revenue beyond the king's hereditary revenue, and it soon abolished the last of the king's feudal estates, replacing this source of hereditary revenue with a grant of excise duties bestowed upon the Crown. Charles, however, failed to live within that (still generous) budget; he supplemented his revenue with loans from bankers.[49] This struggle between the Stuarts and Parliament gave rise to the *Bankers' Case*, often cited to demonstrate that the Crown was liable to suit in the immediate post-Stuart period (1697–1700).[50] When Charles II fell behind on payments to the bankers for the loans he had taken out to finance the monarchy, the bankers brought an action in the Court of Exchequer without first obtaining the king's consent. They sought a writ ordering the barons of the Exchequer to pay the amounts due on the annuities. The House of Lords ultimately concluded that the plaintiffs had proceeded properly by seeking a remedy in the Court of Exchequer. Lord Chief Justice Holt found that a *monstrans de droit* did not require the king's prior consent, and observed that it was unnecessary to obtain the king's consent even where the plaintiff proceeded by petition of right.[51] "We are all agreed that they [the King's creditors] have a right; and

---

46. Thomas R. Phillips, *The Constitutional Right to a Remedy*, 78 N.Y.U. L. REV. 1309, 1320–21 (2003).

47. Koch, *supra* note 6, at 361.

48. *Id.*

49. Figley & Tidmarsh, *supra* note 21, at 1223–26.

50. Susan Randall, *Sovereign Immunity and the Uses of History*, 81 NEB. L. REV. 1, 29 & n.146 (2002).

51. The Case of the Bankers in the Court of Exchequer, 1700, 2 W. & M., 12 Will. 3, *reprinted in* THOMAS BAYLY HOWELL, 14 A COMPLETE COLLECTION OF STATE TRIALS 1–114, 34 (1812).

if so, then they must have some remedy to come at it too."[52] Lord Somers argued that the only appropriate remedy was a petition of right addressed to the king; in his view, control of the government's resources was a public policy decision properly left to political rather than judicial control.[53] Lord Somers acknowledged, however, that not all petitions required the king's consent.[54] Lord Somers's argument prevailed in the Exchequer Chamber, but it was rejected by the House of Lords.[55]

The House of Lords' reasoning in the *Bankers' Case* is strikingly similar to Chief Justice John Marshall's reasoning in *Marbury v. Madison*,[56] in which the great chief justice famously affirmed the "general and indisputable rule, that where there is a legal right, there is also a legal remedy by suit or action at law, whenever that right is invaded."[57] Under English law this statement meant that the sovereign must be accountable to suit for violating private contractual right. In the United States, the same statement has been used instead to justify the supremacy of the judicial branch; it has not been understood, as it was in England, as a guarantee to seek a remedy against the sovereign.

While the *Bankers' Case* is often cited as authority "that sovereign immunity did not exist in England in the years before the American Revolution,"[58] prevailing on the writ against the king did not in the end provide the bankers with an effective remedy against the Crown.[59] By the time the *Bankers' Case* was decided, Parliament had seized control of the king's hereditary revenue and had substituted lifetime and annual grants to the king. In 1700, Parliament appropriated none of the king's revenue to repay the bankers. In 1705, it passed legislation to repay the bankers, but at half the interest rate and principal.[60] In the end, the bankers were repaid only part of what they were owed on the face of the notes.[61] This point, however, relates more to the relation between the judicial and legislative authorities within a government than it does to the relation between the judiciary and the highest executive power. Inevitably, legislative power comes into play in determining whether an effective remedy has actually been provided against the sovereign. (In America, we recall President Andrew Jackson's alleged reaction to a Supreme Court decision vacating the conviction of Samuel Worchester in the course of upholding the rights of the Cherokee Nation:

---

52. *Id.*
53. *Id.* at 103, 105.
54. *Id.* at 83–84.
55. *Id.* at 111.
56. 5 U.S. (1 Cranch) 137 (1803).
57. *Id.* at 163.
58. Figley & Tidmarsh, *supra* note 21, at 1234.
59. *Id.*
60. *Id.* at 1235 & n.236.
61. *Id.* at 1235 & n.237.

"John Marshall has made his decision; now let him enforce it!"[62]) While the sovereign may be available for suit, the judgment secured is potentially of little value if the legislature has discretion not to appropriate the funds to satisfy it.

This prompted the King's Bench, in a decision following the *Bankers' Case*, to observe that while a petition of right would be available against the Crown, it would be futile because it was up to Parliament to determine whether to appropriate money to redress the damages. The court suggested that the petition should properly be brought before the legislature:

> According to the tenor of Lord Somers's argument in the *Bankers['] Case*, though a petition of right would lie, yet it would probably produce no effect. No benefit was ever derived from it in the *Bankers['] Case*; and Parliament was afterwards obliged to provide a particular fund towards the payment of those debts. Whether however this alteration in the mode of distributing the supplies had made any difference in the law upon this subject, it was unnecessary to determine; at any rate, if there were a recovery against the Crown, application must be made to Parliament, and it would come under the head of supplies for the year.[63]

It is noteworthy that the King's Bench does not suggest that the sovereign is immune from being asked to redress the damages; the issue is instead where to bring the petition in order to make it effective. At the time, in the absence of an independent judiciary,[64] the King's Bench thought that the petitioners would have the best chance of obtaining redress by asking the legislature to remedy their dispute with the king. The King's Bench presumed that, pursuant to the *Bankers' Case*, individuals have a right to petition the government for redress.

The struggle for power between the Stuart regime and Parliament sets the backdrop for the struggle for power between general assemblies and the executive in the colonies. It also shows that de facto immunity resulting from legislative control over appropriations reflected the spirit of democratic

---

62. For one account of the story, *see* Jeffrey Rosen, *The Supreme Court: The First Hundred Years Court History PBS*, PBS.ORG, http://www.pbs.org/wnet/supremecourt/antebellum/history2.html (last visited May 9, 2014).

63. Figley & Tidmarsh, *supra* note 21, at 1237 (quoting MacBeath v. Haldimand, 99 Eng. Rep. 1036, 1038 (K.B. 1786) (opinion of Lord Mansfield)).

64. Judicial independence did not emerge in the United Kingdom until the Act of Settlement in 1701. *See* Judiciary of England and Wales, *Judges, Tribunals and Magistrates, Judicial Accountability & Independence*, JUDICIARY.GOV.UK, http://www.judiciary.gov.uk/about-the-judiciary/the-judiciary-in-detail/jud-acc-ind/independence (last visited May 9, 2014).

control over the king's actions; it did not imply any effort to insulate the king from accountability.

Blackstone's *Commentaries on the Laws of England*, published between 1765 and 1769, further elaborated on English law following Magna Carta. Blackstone was widely cited in early U.S. judicial decisions as an authoritative source on English law. He notoriously stated that "no suit or action can be brought against the king, even in civil matters, because no court can have jurisdiction over him,"[65] but that statement has been over-read. To begin with, Blackstone explained that this immunity resulted from the structure of government.[66] Because the legislature and the king were the only two branches in England, there were no independent courts that could judge the acts of either branch. This meant that any judicial action was subordinate to the king's will; the king necessarily consented to suit in order to facilitate proceedings against himself in his own courts. Moreover Blackstone qualified his seemingly blanket statement about immunity in a critical way: he recognized that the prerogative writs and petitions of right were extraordinary remedies that lie outside the ordinary judicial process:

> That the king can do no wrong, is a necessary and fundamental principle of the English constitution: meaning only, . . . that in the first place, whatever may be amiss in the conduct of public affairs is not chargeable personally on the king . . . ; and, secondly, that the prerogative of the crown extends not to do any injury. . . . Whenever therefore it happens, that, by misinformation or inadvertence, the crown hath been induced to invade the private rights of any of its subjects, though no action will lie against the sovereign, . . . *yet the law hath furnished the subject with a decent and respectful mode of removing that invasion, by informing the king of the true state of the matter in dispute: and, as it presumes that to know of an injury and to redress it are inseparable in the royal breast, it then issues as of course, in the king's own name, his orders to his judges to do justice to the party aggrieved.*[67]

The latter part of this passage refers to the alternative right to address the king's wrongdoing by way of petition, rather than with a common-law writ such as trespass on the case. Courts entertaining these petitions were "administering the prerogative of the king for the benefit of his subjects rather than entertaining suits or proceedings against the Crown."[68]

---

65. 3 WILLIAM BLACKSTONE, COMMENTARIES ON THE LAWS OF ENGLAND 242 (St. George Tucker ed., 1803).

66. Pfander, *supra* note 16, at 921–23.

67. BLACKSTONE, *supra* note 65, at 254–55 (emphasis added).

68. Pfander, *supra* note 16, at 923.

Blackstone viewed the availability of these alternative remedies against the Crown as an absolute individual right:

> If there should happen any uncommon injury, or infringement of the rights before-mentioned, which the ordinary course of law is too defective to reach, there still remains a fourth subordinate right, appertaining to every individual, namely, the right of petitioning the king, or either house of parliament, for the redress of grievances.[69]

Professor James Pfander summarizes Blackstone's position as follows:

> [Blackstone] carefully preserved the fiction of sovereign immunity by reaffirming the Crown's immunity from the ordinary course of the law and by treating Crown practice as a collection of extraordinary remedies available only upon petition. Yet he recognized the existence of the subject's absolute right to seek judicial relief from government misconduct, both in his definition of the right to petition for redress of grievances and in his subsequent discussion of the petition of right and the prerogative writs. For Blackstone, then, the Crown's sovereign immunity remained theoretically intact but yielded as a practical matter to the subject's right to petition the courts of justice for redress of royal invasions of life, liberty, and property.[70]

The development of the ideas in Magna Carta that had occurred by the time of the American Revolution caused Professor Jaffe to conclude that in *English* law during that period, "the so-called doctrine of sovereign immunity was largely an abstract idea without determinative impact on the subject's right to relief against government illegality."[71] It is notable that the English common law had nothing akin to modern public-law litigation, which holds the government accountable for broad constitutional violations. To sue the Crown successfully, a person needed to point to some immediate action of the Crown that caused a wrong cognizable within the then-extant forms of action (principally torts and contracts).[72] But it was widely recognized that each individual had a right to seek redress against the sovereign if he (or rarely she) could demonstrate that the sovereign violated the law in a way that fell under one of the recognized private causes of action that would be available against any other citizen. In sum, "in England, what our system has termed 'sovereign immunity' did not bar relief against the Crown, but specified how such relief could be obtained, channeling actions against the

---

69. BLACKSTONE, *supra* note 65, at 143.
70. Pfander, *supra* note 16, at 926.
71. JAFFE, *supra* note 24, at 212.
72. Figley & Tidmarsh, *supra* note 21, at 1267.

sovereign through a system of mandatory writs which existed alongside other forms of action."[73]

III. Remedies against the Sovereign in the Colonies and the Early Republic

The U.S. Supreme Court has justified sovereign immunity on the ground that "[w]hen the Constitution was ratified, it was well established in English law that the Crown could not be sued without consent in its courts."[74] The Court's account, however, fails to take account of the forms of petitioning that were available and used in the early colonies. It also overlooks state constitutional provisions suggesting that the states intended to preserve Magna Carta's guarantee of a right to petition the sovereign for redress. In addition, it does not explain why the colonies would adopt English law only partially, by embracing the notion that the king's consent is required, while at the same time eschewing the alternative remedies (clearly recognized by Blackstone) for redressing illegal actions by the sovereign. Moreover, colonial emphasis on the power of legislatures has been misconstrued as proof that government had a privilege to put itself beyond the practical reach of the law. During the colonial era, legislatures were the all-purpose organ of government.

A closer look at law in the colonies, state constitutions, and early Supreme Court decisions thus calls into question the assertion that our 20th-to-21st-century view of sovereign immunity was a part of the law at the time of the founding. Indeed, the claim that the early American Republic embraced broad governmental immunity is somewhat ironic, given that the founders of the Republic were ideologically inclined to restrain executive abuses of power, as one can see in their effort to create a sophisticated system of checks and balances among all three branches of government.

A. Colonial Law

Eighteenth-century America replayed the struggle for power between the Stuarts (the executive) and Parliament (the general assemblies) that occurred in 17th-century England. In particular, colonists sought to move their own constitutions "toward increasing limitations upon prerogative power and

---

73. Randall, *supra* note 50, at 30.

74. Alden v. Maine, 527 U.S. 706, 715 (1999) (holding that sovereign immunity shields states from suits brought in state court pursuant to federal causes of action); *see also* Seminole Tribe of Florida v. Florida, 517 U.S. 44, 54 (1996) ("It is inherent in the nature of sovereignty not to be amenable to the suit of an individual without its consent.").

greater security for individual and corporate rights under the protection of a strong legislature."[75] Following Parliament's lead, colonial legislatures succeeded in gaining power over appropriations that were designed to fund the governors or corporations that represented the Crown. This control over the purse carried with it the power to issue paper currency; to set salaries and fees; to appoint revenue officials, treasurers, and other public officers; to control public works projects; to provide input on military and Indian affairs; to create courts; and to establish terms of office for judges. Assemblies pushed "their authority well beyond that of the British House of Commons . . . and in many cases obtained a significant share of the traditional powers of the executive."[76]

It appears that the colonies did adopt remedies against the Crown akin to the petition of right and the prerogative writs. Even though the causes of action that allowed claims against the Crown—petition of right, traverse of office, and *monstrans de droit*—were not introduced into colonial law by the same terms, the colonies provided for equivalent remedies by legislative petition.[77] That the colonists did not refer to these actions in terms of the same categories of writs that were described in the king's courts likely follows from the fact that the colonists were too far removed (physically) to bring claims in the king's courts.[78] Cases affecting the colonists generally pertained to the king's officers stationed as governors or commissioners in the colonies. This required the colonies to develop methods of holding the king's officers accountable outside of the king's courts. Without a king's court, the general assembly initially was the only body that could entertain petitions for redress against the king's officers; later, as the general assemblies created courts and appointed judges, those courts also afforded remedies against the Crown.

It was not only common for subjects to submit petitions signed by many people on matters of public interest; it was also routine for subjects to petition on a strictly individual claim, seeking such relief as a government pension, payment of a public claim, legislative relief from the misconduct of a neighbor, or the grant or denial of a new trial or other equitable relief from judicial decisions.[79] Legislatures had power to award judicial-type remedies.

---

75. Figley & Tidmarsh, *supra* note 21, at 1242 (quotations omitted).

76. *Id.* at 1245–46 (quotations omitted).

77. *Id.* at 1239 (citing United States v. Lee, 106 U.S. 196, 238–39 (1882) (Gray, J. dissenting)).

78. *Id.* at 1238 & n.252 (observing that no monarch ever directly injured a colonist nor to the authors' knowledge, did any English monarch ever enter into, and then breach, a contract with a colonist).

79. Pfander, *supra* note 16, at 930–31 (citing *Judicial Action by the Provincial Legislature of Massachusetts Bay*, 15 HARV. L. REV. 208 (1901)) (reproducing orders issued by the Massachusetts Bay legislative body on individual claimants' appeals from local court decisions).

In addition, "[t]raditions of legislative prerogative empowered committees of the assembly to utilize many of the investigative tools we now associate with judicial dispute resolution. Such powers included that to subpoena witnesses and documents, to take testimony, and to punish the recalcitrant through contempt sanctions."[80] Some colonies allowed legislatures to make case-by-case decisions about divorce proceedings, debtors' relief from creditors, applications for naturalization, and money claims against the government. Notably, the right to petition the legislature that was employed in the colonies was designed so as *not* to require any consent from the king. It was meant to check sovereign power:

> [t]he governor and the courts of justice in the colonies were appointed by the Crown; distrust of these royal officials (and dissatisfaction with the results of royal justice) led many individuals to seek redress from the assembly. Assemblies responded by working to defend their access to petitions in order to broaden their power vis-à-vis the Crown. Part of the early American reluctance to establish courts of equity reflects a preference for the determination of claims for extraordinary relief by the popular branch of government. Similarly, colonial reliance on the legislative petition in the determination of money claims against the government was a part of what has been aptly characterized as their "quest" for control over the machinery of the fisc.[81]

Furthermore, while declarations of the constitutional right to petition in American constitutions focused on submissions to the legislature, early American statutes reveal evidence of reliance upon British-style judicial modes for asserting claims against the government as an entity:

> [M]ost of the states that directed the forfeiture of loyalist property during the Revolutionary War also authorized the judicial determination of claims to post-forfeiture assets held by the state through the adoption of proceedings such as the monstrans and traverse. Courts determined claims to the forfeited property of British loyalists in Virginia, New York, Pennsylvania, Georgia, Delaware, New Jersey, and New Hampshire; legislation in those states specifically protected the rights of third parties to assert judicial claims to property that had been forfeited into the hands of the government. New Jersey went further than Georgia and Delaware in making the favorable decision of its courts of common pleas a sufficient warrant for the payment of money to the creditors of forfeited estates. New Hampshire briefly

---

80. *Id.* at 931 n.109.
81. *Id.* at 933–34 (citations omitted).

followed a similar course. Even in the Carolinas, Maryland, and New England, where the tradition of legislative control remained largely intact throughout the period, courts were given some modest responsibility for overseeing claims against forfeited estates.

In addition to these widespread but rather specialized provisions relating to forfeited estates, at least three different states—New York, Pennsylvania, and Virginia—adopted statutes that more generally authorized individuals to carry their claims against the government into state court.[82]

These statutes reflected growing concern about legislative tyranny. They also represented an effort to allow state courts to entertain the equivalent of petitions of right against the state. In sum, far from allowing the sovereign to be immune from redress in the colonies, general assemblies served the function of courts hearing petitions for redress against the sovereign; later they supported judicial awards of redress against the sovereign. By entertaining individual petitions against the sovereign and later designating courts to do so, the colonial legislatures were operating to provide redress for sovereign wrongdoing in the absence of access to the king's courts. Their prerogative to adjudicate disputes against the sovereign should not be equated to a prerogative to restrict remedies against the sovereign.

B.   State Constitutions

Further evidence that the founders of the early American Republic intended to preserve the right to petition the sovereign for redress in cases of governmental wrongdoing is the fact that 40 states eventually included "right to a remedy" clauses in their constitutions. These provisions were consciously modeled after chapter 29 of Magna Carta.[83] One typical expression of the principle is as follows:

> That every person for every injury done him in his goods, land or person, ought to have remedy by the course of the law of the land and ought to have justice and right for the injury done to him freely without sale, fully without any denial, and speedily without delay, according to the law of the land.[84]

---

82. *Id.* at 939.

83. Phillips, *supra* note 46, at 1310–13 (citing the constitutions listed *infra*, notes 84 & 85).

84. Phillips provides this sample language as a composite of clauses in the following state constitutions: Arkansas, Illinois, Indiana, Maine, Maryland, Massachusetts, Minnesota, New Hampshire, Rhode Island, Vermont, and Wisconsin. *Id.* at 1311 & n.8.

Other states are more concise, saying simply "[t]hat all courts shall be open, and every person, for an injury done him in his person, property or reputation, shall have remedy by the due course of the law."[85]

State supreme courts have read these clauses to limit the extent to which the legislature may declare government immune from suit. For instance, the South Dakota Supreme Court explained that its constitutional provision along these lines amounts to "a guarantee that . . . where a cause of action is implied or exists at common law without statutory abrogation, a plaintiff has a right to litigate and the courts will fashion a remedy."[86] The court struck down legislation granting immunity to municipalities for lawsuits arising out of their actions in constructing, maintaining, and operating parks, playgrounds, and pools, because these were traditionally proprietary functions subject to a cause of action for negligence.[87] And the Utah Supreme Court found unconstitutional an amendment to the state's Governmental Immunity Act that would define a municipality's decisions regarding height and insulation of power lines as discretionary governmental functions from which the state was immune from suit.[88] The court found that this amended definition would cut off a previously existing cause of action without providing an adequate alternative remedy.[89] Subsequent decisions characterized the rule under the open courts clause of the Utah Constitution as follows:

When a remedy has been abrogated, we must first determine whether the legislature has provided a reasonable alternative remedy by due course of law for vindication of [a plaintiff's] constitutional interests. In order to suffice, the substitute benefit must be substantially equal in value or other benefit to the remedy abrogated in providing essentially comparable substantive protection to one's person, property, or reputation, although the form of the substitute remedy may be different.[90]

---

85. Phillips offers this language as a composite of 27 state constitutional clauses: Alabama, Arizona, Colorado, Connecticut, Delaware, Florida, Idaho, Indiana, Kentucky, Louisiana, Mississippi, Missouri, Montana, Nebraska, North Carolina, North Dakota, Ohio, Oklahoma, Oregon, Pennsylvania, South Dakota, Tennessee, Texas, Utah, Washington, West Virginia, and Wyoming. *Id.* at 1311 & n.9.

86. Oien v. City of Sioux Falls, 393 N.W.2d 286, 290 (S.D. 1986).

87. *Id.* at 291 ("[C]onstruction, maintenance, and operation of parks, playgrounds and pools have traditionally been held to be a proprietary function, the park immunity statutes which attempt to expand sovereign immunity to municipalities acting in a proprietary capacity and to thereby defeat a cause of action for negligent acts committed in that capacity clearly violates the constitutional limitations of article VI, § 20 of the South Dakota Constitution.").

88. Laney v. Fairview City, 57 P.3d 1007, 1027 (Utah 2002).

89. *Id.*

90. Jenkins v. Jordan Valley Water Conservancy Dist., 283 P.3d 1009, 1038, *rev'd on other grounds*, 321 P.3d 1049 (Utah 2013) (quotations omitted).

This is evidence that the colonies and states embraced the right to petition the Crown for redress and intended to preserve that right against their own governments. Interestingly, the U.S. Supreme Court came to the opposite conclusion in a famous Eleventh Amendment case, *Hans v. Louisiana*, in which it concluded that suits against a state by the state's own citizens were categorically barred in federal court.[91]

C. Early Constitutional Law

In light of this history, some have argued that two provisions of the Constitution guarantee citizens the right to challenge actions of their sovereign governments. First, by creating Article III courts, the Constitution eliminated the structural basis for requiring the king's consent that existed in England—the "anomaly" of the king issuing a writ against himself. The framers accomplished this by the simple yet elegant solution of establishing the judiciary as a third, independent branch of government. Unlike the king's courts, Article III courts were not agents of the executive. If they are agents of anyone, they are agents of "We the People," just as the executive and the legislative branches of government are. Without a theory of executive supremacy, the anomaly disappears.

Second, in light of the history of the petition of right, the colonial practice of petitioning the general assembly, and the state statutes granting the right to bring petitions akin to the prerogative writs, some have urged that the right to pursue claims against the government lies in the Petition Clause of the First Amendment, which guarantees the "right to petition the government for redress."[92] Specifying the right to petition the *government for redress* suggests more than an abstract right to speech. The clause is not written as a ban on punishing those who petition government; it is an affirmative guarantee of a meaningful opportunity to request redress from the government.[93]

Early Supreme Court decisions suggest that Americans understood English law and the American Constitution (quickly amended by the Bill of Rights) as providing a right to seek redress when the government allegedly invaded the right of a citizen. In *Chisholm v. Georgia*,[94] a majority of four justices allowed a South Carolina citizen to bring suit against the state of Georgia in order to recover payments allegedly due to him from the state. Justices Jay, Blair, and Cushing based their judgment on the constitutional

---

91. Hans v. Louisiana, 134 U.S. 1, 12–16 (1890).

92. Pfander, *supra* note 16, at 902 ("[a]s originally understood, in short, the Petition Clause appears to establish a constitutional right to pursue judicial claims against the government and its officers.").

93. *Id.*

94. Chisholm v. Georgia, 2 U.S. 419 (1793).

grant of jurisdiction over controversies between a "State and a citizen of another State." Justice Wilson addressed and rejected Georgia's defense of sovereign immunity:

> The only reason, I believe, why a free man is bound by human laws, is, *that he binds himself*. Upon the same principles, upon which he becomes bound *by the laws*, he becomes amenable to the *Courts of Justice*. . . . If one free man, an original sovereign, may do all this; why may not an aggregate of free men, a collection of original sovereigns, do this likewise?[95]

And Wilson pointed out that under English law, the sovereign's misconduct could be addressed by prerogative writs. He believed that it followed that citizens were likewise entitled to petition the state governments for redress:

> Under [the Saxon] Government, as we are informed by the Mirror of Justice, a book said, by Sir Edward Coke, to have been written, in part, at least, before the conquest; under that Government it was ordained, that the King's Court should be open to all Plaintiffs, by which, without delay, they should have remedial writs, as well against the King or against the Queen, as against any other of the people. The law continued to be the same for some centuries after the conquest. Until the time of Edward I the King might have been sued as a common person. The form of the process was even imperative. . . . Bracton, who wrote in the time of Henry III, uses these very remarkable expressions concerning the King . . . 'in receiving justice, he should be placed on a level with the meanest person in the Kingdom.' True it is, that now in England the King must be sued in his Courts by petition, but even now, the difference is only in the form, not in the thing.[96]

Justice Iredell's dissent also acknowledged that the appropriate remedy in a case like this under English law would have been a petition of right, which required the King's assent. He described at length the petition of right under English law and the *Bankers' Case*, and explained that:

> If however any such cases were similar to those which would entitle a party to relief by petition to the King in England, that Petition being only presentable to him as he is the sovereign of the Kingdom, so far as analogy is to take place, such Petition in a State could only be presented to the sovereign power, which surely the Governor is not.

---

95. *Id.* at 456 (Wilson, J.).
96. *Id.* at 460.

The only constituted authority to which such an application could with any propriety be made, must undoubtedly be the Legislature, whose express consent, upon the principle of analogy, would be necessary to any further proceeding. So that this brings us (though by a different route) to the same goal; The discretion and good faith of the Legislative body.[97]

In light of the history of colonial legislatures adjudicating individual claims for damages against the sovereign, this passage from the *Chisolm* dissent seems to suggest that an individual damages remedy might be available against the state, but the proper venue for bringing such a claim would be a petition to the legislature. Thus, Justice's Iredell's dissent in *Chisolm*, by common account adopted by the Eleventh Amendment to the Constitution, is consistent with the notion that there is an individual right to petition for a remedy from the sovereign's wrongdoing. Within the context of the dissent's argument for redress by petition of right to the legislature, the Eleventh Amendment could be understood as suggesting that the proper way of redressing a dispute between a state and a foreign citizen is by legislative petition. But it would be a special kind of petition—one that would require the legislature to assent to the claim, since under English law the sovereign assented to every petition that showed cause for a claim of illegal conduct. In other words, the secondary issue is about which branch of government should adjudicate individual petitions against the sovereign; the primary issue is whether such petitions or suits can be brought in the first place.

Further evidence that the Eleventh Amendment was not understood as precluding a petition for redress against government misconduct lies in *Marbury v. Madison*.[98] The Supreme Court did not consider sovereign immunity as a basis for refusing to issue a writ of mandamus to compel Secretary of State James Madison to deliver William Marbury's commission; instead it found that it did not have original jurisdiction over the dispute. *Marbury*'s reasoning is wholly consistent with recognizing a right to petition to redress the government's violation of the law. Nine years after the Eleventh Amendment was adopted, Chief Justice Marshall observed "[i]n Great Britain the king himself is sued in the respectful form of a petition, and he never fails to comply with the judgment of his court," and he quoted Blackstone for the proposition that "it is a settled and invariable principle in the laws of England, that every right, when withheld, must have a remedy, and every injury its proper redress."[99] Marshall went out of his way to observe that, according to Blackstone, this principle applied to the sovereign:

---

97. *Id.* at 446 (Iredell, J.).
98. *See* Marbury v. Madison, 5 U.S. 137 (1803).
99. *Id.* at 163 (quotations omitted).

After stating that personal injury from the king to a subject is presumed to be impossible, Blackstone, Vol. III p. 255, says, "but injuries to the rights of property can scarcely be committed by the crown without the intervention of its officers; for whom, the law, in matters of right, entertains no respect or delicacy; but furnishes various methods of detecting the errors and misconduct of those agents, by whom the king has been deceived and induced to do a temporary injustice."[100]

Others have observed that *Marbury* is in tension with the current doctrine of sovereign immunity:

[I]n *Marbury v. Madison*, Chief Justice John Marshall explained that the central purpose of the Constitution is to limit the actions of government and government officers. In other words, the government is accountable for its actions. In *Marbury*, the Court emphasized the need for accountability and redress in its declaration that "[t]he very essence of civil liberty certainly consists in the right of every individual to claim the protection of the laws, whenever he receives an injury."[101]

Nearly a century later, the Court continued to recognize the historic availability of a right to petition the sovereign for redress. In *United States v. Lee*,[102] officers of the federal government purchased the estate of Robert E. Lee's wife for an alleged default in taxes, over Mrs. Lee's objection. The Lees had sent an agent to pay the taxes owed, but the government refused to accept the payment under a rule requiring overdue taxes to be paid by the owner in person. This rule was later declared unlawful, and the Lees challenged the government's compelled purchase of their estate on the ground that they should have been allowed to pay their taxes and prevent the sale. Four dissenting justices argued that there was no right to sue the sovereign—under English law a petition of right would have required consent. They argued that the United States similarly could not lawfully be sued without its consent in any case.

In allowing the suit to go forward, the majority reasoned that remedies for a similar situation would be available using a petition of right against the king under English law; they could see no reason why there would not be such a remedy against the U.S. sovereign, since the United States does not have the problem of holding the king accountable in the king's own courts. The Court elaborated at length on the development of sovereign immunity in the states, relating it to English law:

---

100. *Id.* at 165.

101. Erwin Chemerinsky, *Against Sovereign Immunity*, 53 STAN. L. REV. 1201, 1213 (2001).

102. United States v. Lee, 106 U.S. 196 (1882).

It is believed that this petition of right, as it has been practiced and observed in the administration of justice in England, has been as efficient in securing the rights of suitors against the crown in all cases appropriate to judicial proceedings, as that which the law affords in legal controversies between the subjects of the King among themselves. If the mode of proceeding to enforce it be formal and ceremonious, it is, nevertheless, a practical and efficient remedy for the invasion by the sovereign power of individual rights.

There is in this country, however, no such thing as the petition of right, as there is no such thing as a Kingly head to the nation, or to any of the states which compose it. There is vested in no officer or body the authority to consent that the state shall be sued except in the law-making power, which may give such consent on the terms it may choose to impose. Congress has created a court in which it has authorized suits to be brought against the United States, but has limited such suits to those arising on contract, with a few unimportant exceptions.

What were the reasons which forbid that the King should be sued in his own court, and how do these reasons apply to the political body corporate which we call the United States of America? As regards the King, one reason given by the old judges was the absurdity of the King's sending a writ to himself to command the King to appear in the King's court. No such reason exists in our government, as process runs in the name of the president and may be served on the attorney general, as was done in the case of *Chisholm* v. *State of Georgia*. Nor can it be said that the dignity of the government is degraded by appearing as a defendant in the courts of its own creation, because it is constantly appearing as a party in such courts, and submitting its rights as against the citizens to their judgment. . . . As we have no person in this government who exercises supreme executive power or performs the public duties of a sovereign, it is difficult to see on what solid foundation of principle the exemption from liability to suit rests. It seems most probable that it has been adopted in our courts as a part of the general doctrine of publicists, that the supreme power in every state, wherever it may reside, shall not be compelled, by process of courts of its own creation, to defend itself from assaults in those courts.

. . .

Under our system the *people*, who are there called *subjects*, are the sovereign. Their rights, whether collective or individual, are not bound to give way to a sentiment of loyalty to the person of the monarch. The citizen here knows no person, however near to those in power, or however powerful himself, to whom he need yield the rights which the law secures to him when it is well administered. When he, in one of the courts of competent jurisdiction, has established his right to property, there is no reason why deference to any person, natural or artificial, not even the United States, should prevent him from using the means which the law gives him for the protection and enforcement of that right.[103]

This excerpt from *Lee* shows a majority of the Court recognizing that the structure of U.S. government eliminated the justification for the requirement for the king's consent to suit—the "anomaly" of the king issuing a writ against himself. It also illustrates that the sentiment in the early republic was to hold government accountable to the law and to resist royal prerogatives.[104]

IV.   The Emergence of Contemporary Sovereign Immunity

The U.S. doctrine fundamentally shifted course just eight years after *Lee*, in *Hans v. Louisiana*,[105] where the Court held that a federal court could not entertain a suit brought by a citizen against his own State. The Court relied heavily on the Eleventh Amendment and the reasoning of members of the constitutional conventions who opposed a version of Article III that would have extended the judicial power to "controversies between a state and citizens of another state." The *Hans* Court recounted Hamilton's statement that,

[i]t has been suggested that an assignment of the public securities of one state to the citizens of another would enable them to prosecute that state in the federal courts for the amount of those securities, a suggestion which the following considerations prove to be without foundation: It is inherent in the nature of sovereignty not to be amenable to the suit of an individual without its consent.[106]

The Court pointed out that Chief Justice Marshall had stated "[w]ith respect to disputes between a state and the citizens of another state, its jurisdiction has been decried with unusual vehemence."[107] It concluded that the same reasoning must apply to suits brought against a state by its own

---

103. *Id.* at 204–09.

104. Chemerinsky, *supra* note 101, at 1214 ("[I]f there is any universally agreed upon interpretation of the American Constitution, it is its rejection of a monarchy and royal prerogatives.").

105. Hans v. Louisiana, 134 U.S. 1 (1890).

106. *Id.* at 12–13 (internal quotations omitted).

107. *Id.* at 14.

citizens: "Can we suppose that, when the eleventh amendment was adopted, it was understood to be left open for citizens of a state to sue their own state in the federal courts, while the idea of suits by citizens of other states, or of foreign states, was indignantly repelled?"[108] The Court reasoned that it would be illogical to prohibit suits against a state by foreign citizens, but not by its own citizens. Further, the Court said:

> The truth is that the cognizance of suits and actions unknown to the law, and forbidden by the law, was not contemplated by the constitution when establishing the judicial power of the United States.
>
> . . .
>
> The suability of a state, without its consent, was a thing unknown to the law. This has been so often laid down and acknowledged by courts and jurists that it is hardly necessary to be formally asserted. It was fully shown by an exhaustive examination of the old law by Mr. Justice IREDELL in his opinion in *Chisholm v. Georgia*.[109]

While *Hans* relies heavily on Justice Iredell's dissent in *Chisolm*, it skips over the fact that Justice Iredell acknowledged that there was, in fact, a known remedy under the laws of England. A petition of right would have been the proper remedy in England; because there was no king in the United States to consent to the suit, the analogous petition against a state should be brought to the legislature. Nor does *Hans* acknowledge that many colonies allowed for similar remedies by either a petition to the general assembly or claims similar to *monstrans* and traverse for repayment of property forfeited during the Revolution. Despite the language in *Lee* quoted above, suggesting that a remedy should lie against the U.S. government in the same manner as it would against any other citizen, the *Hans* Court distinguished *Lee* as a suit against an individual. It stated that had suits like *Lee* been brought "against either the state or the United States, they could not be maintained."[110] But the United States was clearly the named defendant in *Lee*. And this distinction does not hold up because any suit against a government entity is necessarily challenging the actions of individuals who carry out illegal conduct on behalf of the government.

Furthermore, *Hans* neglects to consider the differences between suits against a state by a *foreign* citizen and suits against a state by its own citizens. *Hans* dedicates no discussion to what seems to be an obvious and inevitable question: If Article III and the Eleventh Amendment were meant

---

108. *Id.* at 15.
109. *Id.* at 15–16.
110. *Id.* at 16.

to hold states immune from suits brought by their own citizens, why does it speak only about "Citizens of *another* State" or "Citizens or Subjects of any *Foreign* State"?[111] Those words ("other," "foreign") appear in every statement that is quoted from the debate over Article III judicial power. It would have been simpler and more straightforward to speak about states being immune from suits brought by citizens, period, if this is what was meant. There must be a reason that the amendment and the debates pertaining to Article III specify "foreign" or "other" states, rather than simply referring to suits against states. An individual's right to petition for redress from a government to which he owes no allegiance, and which has no responsibility for him, is different from a citizen's right to petition his own sovereign for redress of illegal conduct. English law guaranteed subjects a right to petition their sovereign, the Crown, for redress in the king's courts. It did not, and because the petition of right depended on the king's (albeit routine and expected) consent, it could not guarantee English subjects the right to petition a foreign sovereign, such as the king of France, for redress in English courts. Given that a majority of the American states imported Magna Carta's right to a remedy clause, and that they provided for actions against the state that were similar to petition of right and the prerogative writs, the emphasis on suits by "foreign" citizens could reflect that the states essentially imported the English law notion that citizens have the right to petition their own sovereigns (their state or the federal government) for redress of the sovereign's wrongdoing. A citizen of New York had the right to seek redress from illegal actions of the New York government, in both state court and federal court. He was also entitled to seek redress against the U.S. government in federal court. What he lacked, after the passage of the Eleventh Amendment and before the enactment of the Foreign Sovereign Immunities Act, was the right to seek redress against a foreign power—that is, the Virginia government or the French government—in U.S. courts.

The legislative prerogative to control spending may be considered an alternative basis for sovereign immunity, and is perhaps better rooted in the history of Magna Carta, English law, and early American law. For instance, in *Reeside v. Walker*,[112] the U.S. Supreme Court refused to authorize a writ of mandamus ordering the secretary of the treasury to pay a judgment on a counterclaim against the United States because of the "well-known constitutional provision, that no money can be taken or drawn from the Treasury except under an appropriation by Congress."[113] The Court stated

---

111. The Eleventh Amendment reads, in its entirety, as follows: "The Judicial power of the United States shall not be construed to extend to any suit in law or equity, commenced or prosecuted against one of the United States by Citizens of another State, or by Citizens or Subjects of any Foreign State."

112. 52 U.S. (11 How.) 272 (1850).

113. *Id.* at 291.

that "the petitioner should have presented her claim on the United States to Congress, and prayed for an appropriation to pay it."[114] In this view, "legislative supremacy over appropriations was not simply a limit on remedy, but also a limit on the very authority to hear the claim."[115]

But this view equates justiciability (whether the claim is redressable by a favorable outcome) with constitutional limits on federal court jurisdiction and congressional power to subject states to suit. The power-of-the-purse rationale rests on a limit on the government's ability to satisfy a judgment, not on the ability of a court to entertain a case or enter a judgment. These are two distinct stages of a case. If Congress's power over appropriations were the basis for sovereign immunity, federal courts could hear claims against state and federal governments, enter judgments in favor of the plaintiff, and, if part or all of the relief were monetary, send the plaintiff to the legislature in order to petition to collect his judgment. (Note that the appropriations rationale has no bearing on declaratory or injunctive relief.) It would be Congress's decision, case-by-case, to decide whether a petitioner receives a monetary remedy, *after* the executive's conduct has already been declared unlawful by the court (as occurred in the *Bankers' Case*). This would be consistent with the individual right to petition for redress of government wrongdoing. Moreover, if the federal Constitution's Appropriations Clause were the basis for immunity, such immunity would affect only damage actions against the federal sovereign. It would provide no support for limits on injunctive claims that require no appropriations from the Treasury, claims against states, damages or injunctive suits against federal officers for which the officers are personally responsible, or suits against state officers.[116]

V. Conclusion

Magna Carta has largely disappeared as a direct source of positive law, but its broader principles have never been more important. And, when all is said and done, perhaps the core principle that motivated those barons in 1215 to squeeze promises from King John was the idea that even the king should be

---

114. *Id.*; *see also* Figley & Tidmarsh, *supra* note 21, at 1262–64 & n.433 (citing McCarty v. McCarty, 453 U.S. 210 (1981); United States v. MacCollom, 426 U.S. 317 (1976); Cincinnati Soap Co. v. United States, 301 U.S. 308 (1937); Hart v. United States, 118 U.S. 62 (1886); Knote v. United States, 95 U.S. 149 (1877); and Buchanan v. Alexander, 45 U.S. (4 How.) 20 (1846)). *See also* Dep't of the Army v. Blue Fox Inc., 525 U.S. 255, 264 (1999) ("[S]overeign immunity bars creditors from attaching or garnishing funds in the Treasury.").

115. *Figley & Tidmarsh, supra* note 21, at 1262.

116. *Id.* at 1265.

subject to the law. It makes no difference whether the promises designed to achieve that goal were realized back in the 13th century. What does matter is that this idea has gained worldwide acceptance. The rule of law is based on the propositions that no person is above the law, that governments must be held accountable to their citizens, and that effective remedies are essential. It is our duty to ensure, each of us within our own legal systems and countries, that we can implement these fundamental principles in our day-to-day administration of justice.

One area in the United States where critical assessment and reform is needed, we have suggested, is that of the law of domestic sovereign immunity. First Magna Carta, and then English and colonial law, embody the notion of sovereign accountability to the rule of law, not immunity from it. Our brief consideration of this complex history persuades us that the modern U.S. law of sovereign immunity has strayed from the history on which the Supreme Court relies. Fidelity to the past would involve the creation of mechanisms to hold government accountable that could be invoked by aggrieved litigants as a matter of right. There would be nothing inconsistent with history if these mechanisms were in the nature of extraordinary remedies. Nor would it be a problem if the judicial determination of rights was sometimes only the first step toward monetary compensation. But the idea that absolute sovereign immunity can insulate government from all legal responsibility cannot coexist with the basic message of Magna Carta: no person, and no institution, is above the law.

Chapter 4

Magna Carta and the United States Constitution: An Exercise in Building Fences

Michael Dillon*

This chapter argues that a side-by-side comparison of Magna Carta and the Constitution of 1789 will show that the Magna Carta that influenced the United States Constitution was neither the 1215 Magna Carta (or Great Charter)[1] of King John (r. 1199–1216) nor the 1225 Magna Carta of his son King Henry III (r. 1216–72). Rather it was the "mythic" Magna Carta,[2] created largely in the late 16th and early 17th century by the great common law jurist Sir Edward Coke,[3] which was commingled with John Locke's social contract theory[4] for transmission to Britain's American colonies by William Blackstone[5] that influenced the Constitution of 1789. This discussion of Magna Carta proceeds in five steps. The first step discusses the English/Angevin foundations, the second considers the contemporary opinions linking Magna Carta and the U.S. Constitution, the third provides a more detailed comparison of the two documents, the fourth focuses on Coke's creation of the "mythic" Magna Carta, and the fifth addresses America's use of the Great Charter. In closing, the chapter argues that Blackstone's melding of Coke's "mythic" Magna Carta with John Locke's natural rights theory provided the

---

*The author gratefully acknowledges the comments on his chapter provided by Professor Michael Boyle, Professor Miguel Glatzer, and Steven Johnston as well as the many former and current students posing thoughtful questions regarding Magna Carta in POL 319 Courts, Judges and Judging: An Introduction to Anglo-American Jurisprudence.
    1. The definitive study of Magna Cart is J.C. HOLT, MAGNA CARTA (2d ed. 1992). Also useful are the following: GEOFFREY HINDLEY, A BRIEF HISTORY OF THE MAGNA CARTA: THE STORY OF THE ORIGINS OF LIBERTY (2008); A.E. DICK HOWARD, MAGNA CARTA: TEXT AND COMMENTARY (rev. ed. 1998); NICHOLAS VINCENT, MAGNA CARTA: A VERY SHORT INTRODUCTION (2012).
    2. HOLT, *supra* note 1, at n.403; HINDLEY, *supra* note 1, at n.277.
    3. EDWARD COKE, 1 THE SELECTED WRITINGS OF SIR EDWARD COKE (Steve Sheppard ed., 2003). A portrait of Edward Coke is reproduced as Illustration No. 10.
    4. JOHN LOCKE, TWO TREATISES OF CIVIL GOVERNMENT (Peter Lassett ed., 1960).
    5. WILLIAM BLACKSTONE, THE COMMENTARIES OF SIR WILLIAM BLACKSTONE ON THE LAWS AND CONSTITUTION OF ENGLAND (2005).

American founders with flexible tools useful to oppose and resist government excesses as well as to forge stable and responsive representative government.

I. English Foundations

Any attempted comparison of Magna Carta 1215 or 1225 and the U.S. Constitution of 1789 and its Amendments from 1791 to today is necessarily also a comparison of Old England with its feudal, land-based, loyalty-infused social-political structures and the American colonies, especially New England, with their self-reliance, independence, and initially unlimited land. A typically New England poem by Robert Frost, *Mending Wall*, reflects upon the traditional New England spring work of mending stone walls separating parcels of land whenever the walls have fallen into disrepair with gaps and breaches over the seasons. Referring to the "gaps" Frost writes:

> No one has seen them made or heard them made,
> But at spring mending-time we find them there.
> I let my neighbor know beyond the hill,
> And on a day we meet to walk the line
> And set the wall between us once again.
> . . .
> Before I built a wall I'd ask to know
> What I was walling in or walling out,
> And to whom I was like to give offense
> . . .
> He will not go beyond his father's saying
> And he likes having thought of it so well
> He says again, "Good fences make good neighbors."[6]

Frost's image of wall or fence building provides a useful metaphor with which to begin to compare Magna Carta and the U.S. Constitution. Magna Carta 1215 can be seen as an effort by the barons to "fence in" the prerogative and power of the king, the sovereign, in Old England, while the U.S. Constitution of 1789 can be seen as a more complex effort to expand the national government, thereby repairing the gaps and defects of the Articles of Confederation (e.g., no taxing power, no commerce power, no federal judiciary), while simultaneously fencing in these newly expanded

---

6. ROBERT FROST, THE POETRY OF ROBERT FROST: COMPLETE AND UNABRIDGED 33 (Edward Connery Latham ed., 1969).

national powers.[7] Magna Carta also evolves, but often in the direction of restoring power to the sovereign rather than in repairing gaps in the original instrument.

Similarly, the various constitutional amendments from the Bill of Rights in 1791 to the Civil Rights Amendments of the 1860s and beyond can be seen as the wall-mending exercises necessary to patch up the gaps and breaches that either could not be addressed by the original Constitution (slavery and voting rights for blacks and women immediately come to mind) or that appeared over time (e.g., changing to direct election of senators and setting limits upon presidential reelection).

Moreover, understanding what both the barons at Runnymede in 1215 and the representatives at Congress Hall in Philadelphia in 1787 were seeking to "wall in" and "wall out" can prove important to our understanding of the relationship between these two documents. Nearly 600 years separate the participants, and we should not be surprised if their goals and ambitions differed greatly.

Land and liege loyalty were integral to the hierarchical feudal order in England. Technically all land in the realm was ultimately in the possession of the monarch. Following the Norman Conquest and the Battle of Hastings in 1066, the Doomsday Book detailed all land holdings throughout England, thereby greatly facilitating taxation by the king. The king granted large tracts of land to his tenants-in-chief (earls, barons, archbishops) who in turn granted smaller holdings to lesser nobles, abbots, and freemen. The large class of serfs and villeins held no land but worked small portions of the lands held by others and paid rent often in the form of days of service or a percentage of the produce grown. This hierarchical system required that members of each level of society pay taxes, fees, and services to the lord above them to whom they owed loyalty.

From the Norman Conquest in 1066 to 1300, the Angevin descendents of William I (r. 1066–1087) battled for control of southwestern France and of England, Scotland, and Wales. Often they battled with rebellious Anglo-Saxon barons and equally as often they battled with French and even family challengers. This almost constant warfare had to be paid for and the monarchs assessed taxes in the form of "scutage"[8] (a payment in lieu of military service) to pay for the crusades and the military forays. Moreover, the entire feudal structure was periodically required to pay "aid,"[9] another form of tax to, at a minimum, ransom a king captured by a foreign power,

---

7. Merrill Jensen, The Articles of Confederation: An Interpretation of the Social-Constitutional History of the American Revolution, 1774–1781 (1959).

8. Black's Law Dictionary 1589 (3d ed. 1944).

9. Id. at 86.

marry the king's first daughter, or have the king's first son knighted. Historical Chart 4.1 details key figures of Angevin rule and describes important developments of Magna Carta.

Historical Chart 4.1 Key Figures Angevin Rule and Magna Carta

- William I (1066–1087), William the Conqueror, Norman Conquest 1066.
- William II (1087–1100), son of the Conqueror.
- Henry I (1100–1135), fourth son of William the Conqueror, issued a Coronation Charter of Liberties to appease the earls, barons, and clergy, with many provisions similar to those in Magna Carta, but he did not fulfill its terms.
- Henry II (1154–1189), father of King Richard and King John, expanded the extent and power of the king's administrators, bailiffs, sheriffs, foresters, and justiciaries; and he was king at the time of the murder of Thomas Beckett, Archbishop of Canterbury.
- Richard I (1189–1199), denied his younger brother John rule in Aquitaine, heavily taxed nobles to pay for his crusade to retake Jerusalem, and was captured and ransomed for 150,000 German marks after failing to take Jerusalem.
- John (1199–1216), continued the abusive taxation of his brother, battled with the barons, was pressed into negotiations, and issued Magna Carta on or around June 15, 1215. Magna Carta was rendered null and void by Pope Innocent III after three months. John died following renewed battling with the barons in 1216.
- Henry III (1216–1272), John's nine-year-old son ascends to the throne. His supporters reissue much shortened versions of Magna Carta in 1216 and 1217, which Henry reissues with some changes in his own name although still not of age, i.e., Magna Carta 1225.
- Edward I (1272–1307), reissues Magna Carta of 1225 in 1297, placing it for the first time into the Statute Books of England; Edward subdues and incorporates Wales into England.

In the period up to Magna Carta and beyond, Angevin kings levied a constant stream of ever-greater assessments to support not only military exploits but also the building of monuments to each king's reign. The successors of William the Conqueror built castles, cathedrals, and churches with the chattels, services, and taxation of the English people. King Richard's (r. 1189–1199) leadership of the Third Crusade against the forces of Saladin, and his subsequent rescue at the cost of 150,000 marks, as well as King John's extravagances, ruthlessness at home, and costly military failures abroad, paved the road to Runnymede by pushing many English barons into resistance and ultimately outright denial of aid to King John.[10]

In addition to excessive taxation and the building of monuments, the Angevin monarchs also played favorites among the powerful and thereby created enemies among the nobility and the clergy. These kings rewarded and increased the power and property of loyal barons and archbishops while mercilessly punishing and imprisoning, not only the barons, but also the wives and children of those who resisted the monarch's demands for more and more scutage or aid.

---

10. HOLT, *supra* note 1, at 235.

Like the American colonists 500 years later petitioning King George III (r. 1760–1820), the barons first petitioned King John. He ignored them. Some of the barons then refused to pay, organized themselves into an opposition army, and thereby set up a confrontation, which would ultimately lead to Magna Carta.[11] The king set out with his loyal armed supporters to make an example of the rebellious barons. After a few skirmishes, King John took refuge in London, but the rebellious barons entered the city and took control of the Tower of London, bringing King John to the negotiations that took ultimately place along the Thames at Runnymede in May of 1215.[12]

The original Magna Carta sealed with King John's seal on or around June 15, 1215, was thus essentially a peace treaty between King John and the rebellious barons.[13] The peace treaty, written in Latin, contained provisions that were later numbered and are referred to herein as chapters. Specific chapters limited interference with and excessive taxes on inheritance,[14] protected widows and orphans,[15] and required the convening of common counsel[16] prior to imposing scutage. The sole—but radical—enforcement mechanism in the document was a provision for a committee of 25 barons who could return to the "self-help" of warfare to harass the king's lands and castles to correct any further or ongoing abuses of the king's power.[17]

Perhaps neither side was acting in good faith; the rebellious barons neither disbanded nor disarmed, and King John immediately requested that Pope Innocent III (r. 1198–1216) proclaim Magna Carta to be null, void, and executed under duress. On August 24, 1215, in exchange for promises to the Catholic Church in England, the Pope nullified Magna Carta. Magna Carta 1215 thus lasted a mere ten weeks from official sealing to nullification. It established no new institutions and did not end the king's battles with the barons.

The Magna Cartas in 1216 and 1217 reissued on behalf of nine-year-old King Henry III and the "voluntary" reissue of 1225 in King Henry III's own name contain neither the requirement for common counsel to assess

---

11. *Compare id.* at 58 (the opposition referred to itself as an "Army of God") *with* VINCENT, *supra* note 1, at 57 (calling the resistance a "tax strike").

12. HOLT, *supra* note 1, at 241–42; HINDLEY, *supra* note 1 at 291; VINCENT, *supra* note 1 at 61.

13. VINCENT, *supra* note 1, at 71 ("Magna Carta was first and foremost a peace treaty. As a peace treaty it entirely failed.").

14. *See Magna Carta 1215 chs. 2, 4, 7, in* HOWARD *supra* note, 1 at 35–54 (preserved intact in Magna Carta 1225); *as well as* British Library, *Treasures in Full: Magna Carta, Translation,* BL.UK, http://www.bl.uk/treasures/magnacarta/translation/mc_trans .html (last visited May 9, 2014).

15. *Id.* at ch. 12 (deleted in 1225 and subsequent reissues).

16. *Id.* at chs. 3, 7, 8, and 11 (preserved in subsequent reissues).

17. *Id.* at chs. 52, 55, and 61 (deleted in 1225 and subsequent reissues).

scutage[18] or aid nor the self-help enforcement mechanism to harass the king that were found in the original Charter. Thus, those who suggest that the "respect for property" in chapter 12 of Magna Carta is "an anticipation of one of the great principles of the American Revolution, 'No taxation without representation'"[19] appear at best to be overstating the case. As Holt makes clear, King Henry employed the same heavy-handed taxation schemes that had been employed by his father and his Angevin supporters.[20] The history of Magna Carta 1215's impact on the great issues of "taxation" and "representation" appears vastly different, even futile, when compared to the history of the Constitution of 1789 on these same issues. But a fuller comparison is obviously required.

II.   Common Opinions and Initial Comparison

The commonly held opinion about Magna Carta today in the United States, from a distance of 800 years, appears to be that Magna Carta, usually without identifying any particular chapter or language, is the "fountainhead" from which the U.S. Constitution sprang. The bronze doors to the Supreme Court building in Washington, D.C. contain a panel depicting King John in negotiations with the barons at Runnymede.[21] In 2012, the National Endowment for the Humanities prepared and circulated a high school course outline titled "Magna Carta: Cornerstone of the U.S. Constitution."[22] Professor A. E. Dick Howard asserts that the American colonists "were to write into their new Constitution a guarantee of 'due process of law,' an ideal traceable to Magna Carta's promise that none would be proceeded against save by the 'law of the land.'"[23] Howard further suggests that King Edward III (r. 1327–1377) treated Magna Carta as a "super statute" in 1326:

> The declaration that statutes contrary to Magna Carta are null and void carries the obvious similarity to the language of the American Constitution that it and the laws "made in Pursuance thereof" shall be

---

18. *Id.* at ch. 12 (deleted in 1225).

19. GEORGE ANASTAPLO, REFLECTIONS ON CONSTITUTIONAL LAW 12 (2006).

20. HOLT, *supra* note 1, at 385–87 (see entire chapter 11 entitled "The Re-Issues and the Beginning of the Myth").

21. *See* Office of the Curator, *The Bronze Doors: Information Sheet*, SUPREME COURT OF THE UNITED STATES, May 4, 2010, http://www.supremecourt.gov/about /bronzedoors.pdf.

22. National Endowment for the Humanities, *Magna Carta: Cornerstone of the U.S. Constitution*, EDSITEMENT.NEH.GOV, http://edsitement.neh.gov/lesson-plan/magna -carta-cornerstone-us-constitution (last visited May 9, 2014).

23. HOWARD, *supra* note 1, at 4.

"the supreme law of the land" and to the doctrine of judicial review by which Acts of Congress or of State legislatures are held invalid if they are found to conflict with the Constitution.[24]

Similarly, in 2013 Professor Ellis Sandoz contended that chapter 39 of Magna Carta 1215 and "related passages" form "the cornerstone of individual liberty in the Anglo-American constitutional tradition of rule of law with jury trial as an essential validating and enforcement mechanism."[25]

Finally, Francis Fukuyama in his monumental *The Origins of Political Order: From Prehuman Times to the French Revolution* accepts the core of the mythic Magna Carta, stating that the growth of "liberty, prosperity and representative government" "is enshrined early on in Magna Carta" and "then spread to the rest of the world via Britain's colonization of North America."[26] Fukuyama even argues that the barons at Runnymede were "speaking in the name of the entire realm" "on behalf of the whole national community, including the church and ordinary Englishmen, and demanded constitutional protection for their rights."[27]

As if to link the two countries through Magna Carta, the American Bar Association erected a memorial to Magna Carta in the field at Runnymede in 1957,[28] and there existed proposals that Queen Elizabeth II (r. 1952–present) loan or give a copy of the Great Charter to the United States to celebrate America's bicentennial in 1976.

If today's commonly held opinion that Magna Carta is the cornerstone of American Constitutionalism were true, it should be a simple matter to set Magna Carta and the U.S. Constitution side-by-side and immediately observe the weight, input, and impact of this great cornerstone. But the task is not so simple.

In fact, attempting a side-by-side comparison immediately raises a series of four important questions. (1) Which particular documents are we to compare? (2) Are the documents placed side-by-side actually comparable or commensurate? (3) What are we to think if the evidence of cornerstone impact is substantially weaker than the common opinion presumes? (4) And where outside the words of the Constitution can we look for additional supporting evidence of input or impact from Magna Carta?

---

24. *Id.* at 25.

25. Ellis Sandoz, Give Me Liberty: Studies in Constitutionalism and Philosophy 7 (2013).

26. Francis Fukuyama, The Origins of Political Order: From Pre-human Times to the French Revolution 326 (2011).

27. *Id.* at 378, 529 n.1.

28. Vincent, *supra* note 1, at 107–08.

The first problem to be faced is which Magna Carta will be compared with the Constitution. There are multiple options for our comparison. The first Magna Carta written in Latin and sealed by King John is generally dated June 15, 1215 (though it is not entirely clear what was sealed that day). But different versions of Magna Carta were reissued by English monarchs multiple times during the 13th century including in 1216 and 1217 by the king's regent and the pope's legate on behalf of deceased King John's nine-year-old son Henry, in 1225 by King Henry III himself, and in 1297 by King Edward I (r. 1272–1307).[29] The 1297 reissue of Magna Carta was placed in the Statute Books for the realm making it clear that this is statutory law, not a written constitution. Sir Edward Coke claims Magna Carta was reissued over 30 times.[30]

Magna Carta 1215 and Magna Carta 1225 immediately appear as perhaps the most likely choices for comparison with the Constitution because they were transmitted to the American colonists, including the many lawyers at the Constitutional Convention in 1787, through the works of William Blackstone.[31] Magna Carta 1215 and 1225 are, therefore, likely to have been the most influential versions of the Great Charter available in the United States during the writing of the U.S. Constitution.

There is room to disagree with the use of Magna Carta 1215 and Magna Carta 1225. For example, George Anastapolo argues that the English translation of Magna Carta closest in time to the American founding would most accurately reflect the thinking of the day in America. For Anastapolo, this would be the English translation of Magna Carta in 1829, only 30 years removed from the ratification of the Constitution.[32] And contemporary debates in the British Parliament generally refer to Magna Carta as the three parts of Magna Carta 1297, which still remain on the Statute Books.[33] Nonetheless, Magna Carta 1215 and 1225 permit the fullest comparison with the U.S. Constitution. The only third competing option would be Magna Carta 1297, which is a restatement of 1225.

---

29. *Id.* at 87–88 (identifying reissues in 1216, 1217, 1225, 1265, 1297, and 1300 ("the final reissue") and COKE *supra* note 3 holds the Charter "was confirmed more than forty times during the course of the next two hundred years").

30. COKE, *supra* note 3, at 134 (when holding an action "against the Statute of Magna Carta . . . which Act hath been confirmed over 30 times").

31. BLACKSTONE, *supra* note 5, at 9 (treating "the famous *magna carta*" as the oldest written law of the kingdom).

32. ANASTAPOLO, *supra* note 19, at 9.

33. *See Magna Carta Today: Magna Carta Trust 800th Anniversary—Celebrating 800 Years of Democracy*, MAGNACARTA800TH.COM, http://magnacarta800th.com/magna -carta-today/ (last visited May 9, 2014).

The second question to be addressed is whether the documents we seek to compare are actually comparable or commensurate. Some obvious differences jump out.

Magna Carta 1215, as noted above, is much more a peace treaty than a constitutional or founding document. While Magna Carta 1215 does require the court of common pleas to be held in a set place,[34] the only institution established by the document is the committee of 25 barons whose duty is to "secure the peace" (chapters 52 and 61). But these chapters, which only seem to perpetuate self-help by the barons, were deleted in the 1216 version and never reappeared in any of the subsequent reissues of Magna Carta.

Unlike the Constitution of 1789, which recognizes popular sovereignty,[35] limited government, and checks and balances between the three branches,[36] Magna Carta 1215 seeks to limit or fence in arbitrary or excessive action of a unitary government by extracting promises from a ruler or ruling family. The immediate reissues of Magna Carta (1216, 1217, and 1225) not only eliminate many of those key promises extracted to limit the king's action but also add provisions increasing the potential for unitary, if not arbitrary, action by the monarch.[37] There is in Magna Carta no underlying federal structure, no separation of powers, and no emphasis on the document as a compact or a consensual act. These critical elements of the Constitution of 1789 will be found in almost all founding-era documents in the United States, such as the Mayflower Compact, Fundamental Orders of Connecticut, the Articles of Confederation, or the Constitution of 1789. Instead, Magna Carta 1225 specifically describes itself as a one-sided document, issued "spontaneously" by the king.

Numerous other differences appear on the surface and in the structure of Magna Carta and the U.S. Constitution. Three at least are noteworthy.

First, where the promises in Magna Carta are often made to specific institutions (the Church of England) or even specific persons (e.g., archbishops, earls, barons, Welshmen, hostages), who are often individually

---

34. *Magna Carta 1215 ch. 17, in* Howard *supra* note, 1 at 35–54.

35. U.S. Const. pmble. ("We the people of the United States, in order to . . . secure the Blessings of Liberty to ourselves and our Posterity, do ordain and establish this CONSTITUTION of the United States of America.").

36. *Id. Compare* art. I, § 1, art. II. § 1, cl. 1, art. III, § 1, *compare as well* art. I, § 8, art. II, § 2, cl. 2, art. III, § 2, cl. 2.

37. *Magna Carta 1225 chs. 32, 35, 36, 37, and the final chapter compelling 1/15 of all movable property in exchange for the Charter, in 1225 Magna Carta—The Full Text, Magna Carta Libertatum The Third Great Charter of Henry III,* bsswebsite.me.uk, http://www.bsswebsite.me.uk/History/MagnaCarta/magnacarta-1225.htm (Richard Thomson trans., Barry Sharples explanation, 1829).

identified by name, the Constitution addresses classes of individuals but never specific individuals.

Second, the centrality of "land" in Magna Carta also distinguishes it from the Constitution. In 1215 all land "escheated" or reverted back to the king, who legally owned and controlled the entire realm. Where Magna Carta addresses inheritance, minors, widows, wards, and intestacy, by the time of the adoption of the Constitution of 1789 these property issues are all being addressed in the United States by the common law of the 13 individual states and appear nowhere in the Constitution. Indeed the only discussions of property in the Constitution focus upon what will become the District of Columbia (Article I, Section 8, Clause 17) and upon the acquisition of new territory beyond the boundaries of the original 13 states (Article IV, Section 3, Clause 2).

A third significant difference appears between what today we might call "statutory law" and "constitutional law," a distinction unknown at the time of Magna Carta. Magna Carta of 1215 and of 1225 could be changed or at least selectively enforced at the will of the king. Even after it was entered into the Statute Books in 1297 and accorded what Howard refers to as "super-statute" status, it could and would be changed by simply enacting a new statute. Today, the Magna Carta of the Statute Books based upon the 1297 reissue contains only three of the provisions from 1225—chapter 1 guaranteeing the freedom of the Church of England, chapter 13 confirming the City of London's ancient liberties, and chapter 29 (which combines chapters 39 and 40 of the 1215 Charter) with guarantees not to sell, deny, or delay justice or to prosecute anyone "except by the lawful judgment of his peers and by the law of the land." Every other provision has been eliminated or replaced.

Holt recognizes that the phrase "law of the land" was vague and ambiguous in 1215 and that it would take centuries to flesh out its interpretation in England. Yet it certainly seems strained to give the phrase too modern an interpretation when the Angevin monarchs for another century would claim to rule "by the grace of God." In the United States, on the other hand, the Constitution of 1789 contains a "supremacy" clause, Article VI, Section 2, clearly stating that the Constitution is the "supreme Law of the Land" unchangeable by ordinary statute but rather changeable only by an amending process in Article V. The American approach emphasizes popular sovereignty and mandates supermajorities of two-thirds of each house of Congress and three-fourths of the states respectively during the proposal and ratification process.

These differences raise serious doubts about whether either Magna Carta 1215 or Magna Carta 1225 is actually comparable or commensurate with the U.S. Constitution of 1789. But a closer comparison of the detailed provisions of the documents is required.

III.   More Detailed Comparison

The third question regarding the evidence supporting the claim that Magna Carta is the cornerstone of the U.S. Constitution moves us directly to the comparison of our documents. Magna Carta 1215, negotiated between King John and the barons, contained a preface and 63 chapters as numbered by Blackstone, for a total of 64 provisions. Magna Carta 1225 claims it is "voluntarily" given by King Henry III, not negotiated, and it contained only 37 chapters. Magna Carta 1225 combined a few chapters from the 1215 Charter, most notably 39 and 40, and deleted 23 provisions entirely,[38] while adding five new chapters,[39] including the unnumbered final chapter. Provisions regarding the king's forests were deleted and moved into a new document called the Charter of the Forest in 1217, which is discussed in detail in chapter 12 of this book.[40]

A significant number of the chapters deleted from Magna Carta 1215 cut to the very heart of the original Magna Carta. For example, chapters 12, 14, and 15 limiting scutage and aid and requiring the convening of "common counsel" to impose such demands for support were all deleted, as were chapters 52 and 61, which invoked the 25 barons as the sole enforcement mechanism of the peace treaty.

Moreover, the chapters added by King Henry III to his "voluntary" reissue in 1225 all increased the power of the king, from reestablishing tithing and increasing the powers of the king's sheriffs (chapter 35) to limiting collusion on land rental between clergy and barons (chapter 36), to specifically reestablishing scutage without common counsel (chapter 37), to commanding one-fifteenth of all movable property from clergy, earls, and barons in the unnumbered final chapter. This payment was alleged to be in exchange for the reissue of the guarantees in the charter.

A detailed comparison of Magna Carta 1215 and 1225 to the U.S. Constitution reveals that 56 chapters of Magna Carta 1215's 64 chapters, or 90 percent of the chapters, have no equivalent in the body of the Constitution of 1789. Of the eight potential comparisons between Magna Carta 1215 and the Constitution, that is, the preface and chapters 1, 6, 12, 14, 35, 39, and 40, only the last two even begin to provide support for the idea of cornerstone influence.

---

38. The deleted chapters are 10, 11, 12, 14, 15, 25, 27, 40 (this was combined with original chapter 39 to form new chapter 29), 42, 44, 45, 47, 48, 50, 51, 52, 53, 55, 56, 57, 58, 59, and 61.

39. The added chapters are 32, 35, 36, 37, and a final chapter left unnumbered by Coke.

40. *See* chapter 12 of this book, "The Charter of the Forest: Evolving Human Rights in Nature."

Both documents begin with a preface, but Magna Carta's preface provides greetings and promises from a monarch ruling "by the grace of god" to multiple orders of nobles both lay and clerical, while the Constitution's preface is from "We the people."[41] Moreover, the Constitution specifically prohibits both the federal government and the states from conferring any titles of nobility.[42] Thus, to the extent that both documents speak of rights, in Magna Carta the rights, or privileges, come from the king, while in the Constitution they come from the people.

As to chapter 1, some have argued that both documents preserve religious liberty, but Magna Carta guarantees only the freedom of a specific church, the Catholic Church, while the Constitution forbids any religious test for the holding of public office,[43] and the subsequently adopted First Amendment prohibits any "establishment" of religion and provides for the "free exercise" of religion regardless of faiths. This is further discussed in chapter 8 of this book, "Magna Carta and Religious Freedom."

While both documents speak about freedom to contract, Magna Carta's freedom of heirs to contract marriage in chapter 6 hardly seems comparable to the Constitution's outright prohibition on infringement of the right of contract in Article I,[44] which would appear to owe more to 17th- and 18th-century economic theory than to Magna Carta.

In a similar vein, while the provisions in chapter 35 for "one measure" of wine, ale, corn, and dyed cloth seem comparable to Article I,[45] empowering Congress to set "one standard" for weights and measures, the multiplicity of those measures in 13 different states and the interstate conflict this created under the Articles of Confederation seems a more likely source for this constitutional language.[46]

Some have suggested that the language in chapters 12 and 14 of Magna Carta's attempt to limit the king's taxing power by requiring "common counsel" prefigures "no taxation without representation," which was such an important slogan during the Revolutionary War.[47] Certainly the Constitution does fence in the taxing power by requiring that "all bills for raising revenue shall originate in the House of Representatives,"[48] that all

---

41. *See* A.E. DICK HOWARD, THE ROAD FROM RUNNYMEDE: MAGNA CARTA AND CONSTITUTIONALISM IN AMERICA 237–38 (1968) [hereinafter THE ROAD FROM RUNNY-MEDE].

42. U.S. CONST. art. I, § 9, cl. 8 and art. I, § 10, cl. 1.

43. *Id.* at art. IV, § 1.

44. *Id.* at art. I, § 10, cl. 1.

45. *Id.* at art. I, § 8, cl. 5.

46. JENSEN, *supra* note 7.

47. HOWARD, *supra* note 1, at 11 (even Howard warns against "too strong" and "too modern" an analysis).

48. U.S. CONST. art. I, § 7, cl. 1.

"duties, imposts and excises be uniform,"[49] and that no direct tax shall be laid unless in proportion to the census.[50] But these constitutional provisions seem to flow more from the colonial resistance to oppressive parliamentary taxes on paper, tea, and other household goods than to a provision of Magna Carta that survived for only ten weeks in the summer of 1215.[51]

And the requirement in chapter 14 for notice and a fixed time and place for the meeting of the king with "common counsel" is hardly likely to have been the source of the fixed time and place for each yearly meeting of Congress in Article I.[52] The efforts of colonial governors appointed by King George to limit the meetings and power of colonial legislatures seems a far more likely source.[53]

This leaves the evidence for a "cornerstone" argument solely to chapters 39 and 40. Chapter 39 reads in its entirety that "No freeman shall be taken, imprisoned, disseised, outlawed, banished, or in any way destroyed, nor *will We proceed against or prosecute him, except by the lawful judgment of his peers and by the law of the land.*"[54] Some suggest this is comparable to the Constitution's prohibition on the suspension of the writ of habeas corpus in Article I, Section 9, but a more likely source for this section of the Constitution on the great writ was the common law inheritance of the colonists.[55] Moreover, the "law of the land" language in Magna Carta in chapter 39 cannot be fairly compared to the "supreme Law of the Land" language in Article VI, Clause 2, of the Supremacy Clause of the Constitution. In 1215, the king ruled "by the grace of God," not as a representative of the people of the realm. His will and word were the law (at least in theory), which is why the barons in rebellion needed his seal on the document.

And it is worth noting that the king's promise in chapter 40, "To no one will We sell, to none will We deny or delay, right or justice," is not exactly a promise of fair trial and justice in any modern sense. Justiciaries were all still appointees of and loyal to the king.[56] Under Magna Carta they served with knights of the county to hold trials, which collected fees and services due. In the same general section of Magna Carta in a parallel chapter 36, the king

---

49. *Id.* at art. I, § 8, cl. 1.

50. *Id.* at art. I, § 9, cl. 4.

51. THE ROAD FROM RUNNYMEDE, *supra* note 41, at 188–200.

52. U.S. CONST. art. I, § 4, cl. 2.

53. THE DECLARATION OF INDEPENDENCE para. 2 (U.S. 1776) (list of "injuries and usurpations" including "forbidding Governors to pass Laws" and "dissolved Representative Houses repeatedly").

54. *Magna Carta 1215 ch.* 39, *in* HOWARD, *supra* note, 1 at 45 (emphasis added). A.E. Dick Howard points out a long-running scholarly conflict over whether the Latin "vel" should be translated as "or" or as "and;" Howard's Magna Carta translation from *Magna Carta: Text and Commentary* uses "and."

55. *See* PAUL D. HALLIDAY, HABEAS CORPUS: FROM ENGLAND TO EMPIRE (2010).

56. HOLT, *supra* note 1, at 126–27.

promises to freely give and not deny the "writ of inquisition upon life or limbs," reminding us that trials were often by inquisition and/or by combat in 1215. Thus the evidence that Magna Carta 1215 is the cornerstone of the Constitution of 1789 is thin at best.

A comparison with Henry III's Magna Carta 1225 is actually less compelling. The new preface compounds the problem by asserting that the charter is given "spontaneously and of our own free will," as if it were not a negotiated document. Chapters 1, 6, and 35 (on the freedom of the Church of England, the right of heirs to contract marriage, and standard units of weight and measure) remain intact but, as we saw, they create no cornerstone.

Chapters 12 and 14 on the need for consultation and common counsel for taxation, which carried some promise, were deleted from the 1225 reissue of Magna Carta, never to reappear. We are left solely with chapter 29 (now combining old chapters 39 and 40) and, as set forth in the further detailed comparisons to come, that appears insufficient to carry the claim.

As a final effort to measure Magna Carta's impact on the American experiment of 1789, we need to compare Magna Carta 1215 and 1225 to the Bill of Rights and the Fourteenth Amendment to the U.S. Constitution.[57] There are 11 chapters of Magna Carta 1215 to consider for this comparison: chapters 1, 16, 19, 20, 21, 28, 30, 31, 38, 39, and 40. While chapter 1 and the issue of freedom of religion was addressed and dismissed earlier, here a combination of chapters appear to be close to a number of the rights protected in the Bill of Rights in 1791 and in the Fourteenth Amendment adopted in 1868.

Chapter 16 (and the identical chapter 10 in Magna Carta 1225), limiting required service to no more *than is due* from the landholding, along with chapter 40 of Magna Carta 1215 (combined into chapter 29 of 1225), in which the king promises, "To no one will We sell, to none will We deny or delay, right or justice," has been argued to be a primitive form of Fifth and Fourteenth Amendment requirements. They provide that *"no person . . . be deprived of life, liberty or property without due process of law."*

Chapters 18 and 19 of Magna Carta 1215 (fundamentally identical to combined chapter 12 of Magna Carta 1225), addressing when and where courts of common pleas will be held, appear close to the Sixth Amendment's command in criminal prosecutions of "the right to a speedy and public trial, by an impartial jury of the State and district" where the crime was committed. However, that "fixed place" is not named in Magna Carta and when the king does decide, the court is held in Westminster, not the place where the crime was committed.

---

57. *See* The Road from Runnymede, *supra* note 41, at 239–40.

Chapters 20 and 21 of Magna Carta 1215 (combined into chapter 14 of Magna Carta 1225) assert that "amercements,"[58] or fines, are to be based "in proportion to the measure of the offense" and to be determined by "peers" or by "oath of honest men of the neighborhood." Again this appears close to the Eighth Amendment's prohibition on the imposition of "excessive fines." But Holt reminds us that terms such as "in proportion to the offense" and "peers" are vague and indeterminate and if determined by the king or the king's bailiffs or sheriffs, they may not appear so fair.[59]

Chapters 28, 29, and 31 of Magna Carta 1215 (essentially combined into chapters 19 and 21 of Magna Carta 1225) prohibit the king or his agents from taking corn or other chattel, horses, carts, or wood without payment or without the owner's consent. They have a clear parallel in the Fifth Amendment's wording that "nor shall private property be taken for public use, without just compensation." The 1225 reissue actually defines rates of compensation for the use of carts and horses (chapter 21) but also reduces the wall- and fence-building impact of Magna Carta 1215 by allowing the taking of corn and chattels if the person is a resident of the town where the castle needing to be fed or fortified is located (chapter 19).

Collectively then these chapters of Magna Carta do seem comparable to a portion of the Bill of Rights even though there is no actual discussion of "rights" in the former. In Magna Carta, there is only the king's prerogative and privileges granted. Finally, as noted above, chapters 39 and 40 of Magna Carta 1215 (combined into chapter 29 of Magna Carta 1225) provide perhaps the strongest comparison with the Constitution and must carry the burden of proving a cornerstone impact.

In summary, chapter 39 reads "No free man shall be taken, imprisoned, disseised, outlawed, banished, or in any way destroyed, nor will We proceed against or prosecute him, except by the lawful judgment of his peers or by the law of the land." The related chapter 40 reads, "To no one will We sell, to none will We deny or delay, right or justice." Both are combined in chapter 29 of Magna Carta 1225 and are commonly argued to be the fountainhead for the Seventh Amendment's right to trial by jury and the Fifth and Fourteenth Amendment's right to due process of law.

But other key components of the 1791 Bill of Rights raise serious doubts about Magna Carta serving as a cornerstone. First and foremost, there is nothing in any issue of Magna Carta even close to the protection of freedom of religion, freedom of speech, freedom of the press, freedom to assemble, and freedom to petition the government so prominently placed in the First Amendment. Failure to specifically protect these key political rights

---

58. BLACK'S LAW DICTIONARY, *supra* note 8, at 104.

59. HOLT, *supra* note 1, at 6–8 (recognizing the vagueness of many key terms in the Charter).

was one of the main contentions against the Constitution of 1789 by the Anti-Federalists.

And there is nothing remotely like the Tenth Amendment's assertion, "The powers not delegated to the United States by the Constitution, nor prohibited by it to the States, are reserved to the States respectively or to the people." Matching the preamble's statement of "We the people," the Tenth Amendment sees the people, not royalty or monarchy, not prerogative or privilege, as the source of order and liberty. In contrast, it is instructive to recall that chapter 40 of Magna Carta uses the capitalized royal "We" to underscore that right or justice was dispensed or denied by the king, not by the law.

In conclusion, there is scant evidence of Magna Carta having a cornerstone or fountainhead impact on the U.S. Constitution as it emerged from the Constitutional Convention in 1787. There is more evidence of the impact of Magna Carta 1215 and 1225 on the content of the Fifth, Seventh, and Eighth Amendments but still not enough to accept the claim that Magna Carta is the cornerstone of the U.S. Constitution.

The fourth and final question posed by this comparison is where outside the Constitution we should look for supporting "evidence" of input or impact from Magna Carta that would bolster the claim of its being a cornerstone of the U.S. Constitution. One might expect that the debates in the Constitutional Convention and/or the debates over ratification that occurred in the states from 1787 to 1789 would have witnessed multiple appeals to Magna Carta if it were in fact a cornerstone of the Constitution. That is to say we could look to (a) Madison's *Journal of the Federal Convention*, (b) *The Federalist*, and (c) the state ratification debates.

Strikingly, James Madison's *Journal*[60] maintained throughout the summer of 1787 in Philadelphia makes no reference to Magna Carta at all, which seems strange if it was indeed a cornerstone of the Constitution of 1789.

The newspaper editorials attributed to Publius (Hamilton, Madison, and Jay) and now printed as *The Federalist*[61] are largely silent on Magna Carta. *Federalist* No. 52 by Madison, published February 8, 1788, focuses upon the House of Representatives and the election of representatives by the people every two years. In a comparison with England, Madison writes that the specific practices of the House of Commons are "too obscure to yield instruction" prior to Magna Carta.[62] And after Magna Carta, Madison asserts that the Parliaments were to sit once a year, not to be elected each year, but that "these annual sessions were left so much at the discretion

---

60. James Madison, Journal of the Federal Convention (E.H. Scott ed., 1893) (even in the final days of the 1787 convention when debating and rejecting proposals for a bill of rights Magna Carta was never mentioned).

61. The Federalist No. 52 (Madison).

62. *Id.* at 356.

of the monarch" that "very long and dangerous intermissions" occurred.[63]
Thus Madison knew of and could appeal to Magna Carta as a model if he
so chose. But he did not.

The second and last reference to Magna Carta in the *Federalist* occurs
in *Federalist* No. 84 by Alexander Hamilton, responding to the Anti-
Federalist objection that the Constitution needed a "bill of rights" prior to
any ratification.

> It has been several times truly remarked, that bills of rights are in their
> origins, stipulations between kings and their subjects, abridgements of
> prerogative in favor of privilege, reservations of rights not surrendered
> to the prince. Such was MAGNA CHARTA, obtained by the Barons,
> sword in hand, from king John.[64]

Thus Hamilton as well as Madison knew Magna Carta.

Perhaps explaining why neither he nor Madison looked to the Great
Charter to defend the Constitution, Hamilton continues by saying such bills
of rights "*have no application to constitutions professedly founded upon the
power of the people*, and executed by their immediate representatives and
servants."[65] Hamilton continues "Here, in strictness, the people surrender
nothing, and as they retain everything, they have no need of particular
reservations."[66] In addition to having no application, Hamilton declares
"bills of rights, in the sense and in the extent in which they are contended
for, [i.e., akin to Magna Carta] are not only unnecessary in the proposed
constitution, but would even be dangerous."[67]

A final opportunity to find support for the claim that Magna Carta is
the cornerstone of the Constitution would appear to be in the ratification
debates that occurred in the several states between 1787 and 1789. Pauline
Maier recently published a comprehensive history of those debates, relying
upon letters, memoranda, and other documents found in private, state, and
local collections.[68] Yet she cites no instance where Magna Carta played any
role, much less a defining role, in the debate over the ratification of the
Constitution of 1789.

---

63. *Id.*
64. THE FEDERALIST No. 84, at 578 (Hamilton) (Jacob E. Cooke ed., 1961).
65. *Id.* (emphasis added).
66. *Id.*
67. *Id.* at 579
68. PAULINE MAIER, RATIFICATION: THE PEOPLE DEBATE THE CONSTITUTION
1787–1788 (2010).

IV.   Creating the Myth of Magna Carta

J. C. Holt in chapter 11 of his classic treatment on the subject identifies how in the 13th century there was already the start of the "myth" that the Charter of 1225 had been a "statement of good and lawful custom," when all parties involved knew differently.[69] The concluding two chapters of Goeffrey Hindley's *A Brief History of Magna Carta* emphasize "the persistence of the Magna Carta legend,"[70] and describe a document that between 1650 and 1750 had "acquired an almost mystic incantatory quality."[71]

In 1621 a member of Parliament and former chief justice of the Court of Common Pleas, Sir Edward Coke, turned to Magna Carta to fence in the prerogative of King James I (r. 1603–1625). As Hindley phrases it, Coke took "recourse to a fictional past" to redress an imbalance between the king and Parliament in the present.[72] And the effort earned Coke seven months in the Tower of London charged with treason.[73]

From 1215 and John's original Magna Carta to Coke's imprisonment in 1621 was a span of over 400 years during which the Great Charter failed to restrain or fence in royal prerogative, much less advance popular sovereignty or individual rights. For example, past the year 1600 the King's Bench continued to assert supervisory jurisdiction over all inferior criminal courts in the realm, even when the king was not physically present to hear the plea.[74] Yet from 1621 to 1688, a span of only 67 years, everything changed. From the execution of Charles I (r. 1625–1649) in 1649 to the Glorious Revolution in 1688, England experienced the establishment of parliamentary sovereignty. And the primary voice creating the myth or legend of Magna Carta as the great underpinning for the events taking place in the 17th century was Coke.

Hindley correctly argues that "for American history, the influence of Magna Carta lay not in the encounter of King John and the barons at Runnymede but in Coke's colorful if essentially inaccurate version of it and his exalted conception of the common law."[75]

But Coke did not act alone. The main players in this drama or reconstruction in the history of ideas were Coke; his political rival for royal favor, Francis Bacon; his chief philosophic detractor, Thomas Hobbes, who likely thought

---

69. HOLT, *supra* note 1, at n.403 (see all of chapter 11).

70. HINDLEY, *supra* note 1 at 274.

71. *Id.* at 289.

72. *Id.* at 284.

73. *Id.* at 280.

74. *Court of the King's Bench 1200-1600, The National Archives,* NATIONAL ARCHIVES.GOV.UK, http://www.nationalarchives.gov.uk/records/research-guides/kings-bench -1200-1600.htm (last visited May 9, 2014).

75. HINDLEY, *supra* note 1, at 288.

the charge of treason well pleaded against Coke; another supporter of parliamentary sovereignty, John Locke; and Coke's main publicist, William Blackstone. (Historical Chart 4.2 describes each of these participants in the myth-making of Magna Carta.) Ultimately, it was Coke transmitted through Blackstone that brought the "mythic" Magna Carta and Coke's "exalted conception of the common law"[76] to the colonies in America.

Historical Chart 4.2 Participants in the Myth-Making

- Edward Coke (1552–1634), member of Parliament, Speaker of the House of Commons, and Chief Justice of the Court of Common Pleas, published a four-volume *Institutes of the Laws of England* and 13 volumes of case *Reports* from 1600 to 1611 and 1650 to 1659.
- Francis Bacon (1561–1626), philosopher, member of Parliament, and Coke's greatest rival, had Coke removed as chief justice of the Court of Common Pleas.
- Thomas Hobbes (1588–1679), philosopher and defender of monarchy, published *Leviathan* and *Dialogue between a Philosopher and a Student of the Common Laws of England*, and he saw Coke's ideas as dangerous, perhaps even treasonous.
- John Locke (1632–1704), philosopher and defender of Parliament, property, and the right to revolution, published *Second Treatise of Civil Government*.
- William Blackstone (1723–1780), professor of common law at Oxford, published a four-volume *Commentaries on the Laws of England*, beginning in 1761. A member of Parliament, he was read and studied widely in the American colonies.

Coke's voice had power both because he was widely published and because he wrote to educate. His four-volume *Institutes of the Laws of England*, published between 1628 and 1644, was at least partly in English, not solely Latin, thereby making statutes, court practices, and common law rulings much more accessible. The 13 volumes of his case *Reports* each begin with a preface in which Coke talks directly to his readers, trying to educate them about his views, especially his views about Magna Carta, courts, trials, and the excellence of the common law. Liberty Fund currently makes available almost 60 cases from Coke's *Reports*, annotated and with all the remaining Latin translated in the footnotes.[77]

As early in the *Reports* as the preface to the second part, Coke opens by telling his readers to do their duty to God, to the sovereign, and to their parents, and to give "reverence and obedience to the Common Laws of England."[78] Coke then asserts that Queen Elizabeth (r. 1558–1603) charged her justices that no matter what is commanded, even by the sovereign, "the Justices of her Laws should not therefore cease to do right in any point."[79]

---

76. *Id.* (the language is Hindley's).
77. COKE, *supra* note 3.
78. *Id.* at 39.
79. *Id.* at 40.

Coke's only support for this amazing assertion in 1602 that justices may overrule commands under seal, or writs, or letters of the sovereign is chapter 40 of Magna Carta 1215, namely "To no one will We sell, to none will We deny or delay, right or justice."

In the preface to the third part of the *Reports*, also published in 1602, Coke takes a different tack to "exalt" the common law. There he proclaims that "God is the fountain and founder of all good laws and constitutions,"[80] establishing a higher law dimension without having to define a "good law." He then asserts that the "Common Law of England" had been in existence "before the Conquest" and was not "altered or changed" by William the Conqueror.[81] Not satisfied yet, Coke turns to Greek and Roman authorities to finally announce that "the lawes of England are of much greater antiquity than they are reported to be," older even than any constitutions or laws of Roman Emperors.[82]

Having initiated his recreation of English history, in the preface to the fifth part of the *Reports* in 1605, Coke announces to the reader, "The ancient & excellent Lawes of England are the birth-right and most ancient and best inheritance that the subjects of this realm have."[83] Both *Clark's Case* and *Semayne's Case* are reported and both are important in beginning to establish individual rights arising from Coke's recast Magna Carta.

Clark's Case (1596)[84] in the Court of Common Pleas addressed a claim for false imprisonment under an ordinance issued by the town of St. Albans. Coke's *Report* asserts that the town had no authority to imprison the defendant because the ordinance was "against the Statute of Magna Charta," citing solely chapter 29.[85]

Also in the fifth part of the *Reports* is *Semayne's Case* (1604)[86] in the Court of King's Bench. Here Coke considers the case of a man who locked himself in his house to avoid service of a writ by a sheriff to seize goods to repay a debt. Coke's analysis of the issue elevates the common law to fence in and limit the king's lesser officers, moving far beyond Magna Carta to assert both that experience teaches that "the King's Writs are executed by Bailiffs, persons of little or no value"[87] and that "the house of every one is to him as his Castle and Fortress," which cannot be broken into except for arrest and even then not at night.[88] Even the King's Writ is limited by common law.

---

80. *Id.* at 60.
81. *Id.* at 63.
82. *Id.* at 66.
83. *Id.* at 127.
84. *See id.* at 134.
85. *Id.*
86. *See id.* at 135.
87. *Id.* at 140.
88. *Id.* at 137.

The seventh part of Coke's *Reports* was published in 1608, 80 years prior to the Glorious Revolution, and contains a lengthy report on *Calvin's Case* (1608)[89] in the Court of King's Bench. The editor of *The Selected Writings of Sir Edward Coke, Volume 1*, asserts that this case was of great importance both to Great Britain's relationship "with her new colonies" and in determining "the role of the courts, the Parliament and the King."[90] The issue focused upon whether Robert Calvin, born in Scotland, was an "alien" unable to hold land in England. The case was argued multiple times in King's Bench, in the Exchequer, and finally by "all the Judges of England,"[91] including Coke as chief justice of Common Pleas, Bacon as solicitor general, and Hobart as attorney general. Ultimately the court ruled that "the Plaintiff [Calvin] was no alien, and consequently that he ought to be answered in this Assise [trial] by the Defendant,"[92] who was asserting a claim to Calvin's land.

But to get to this result, Coke goes out of his way to discuss not only citizenship by birth and by blood, what today we refer to as *jus soli* and *jus sanguine*, but also "the Law of Nature," which is "immutable and cannot be changed."[93] This introduction of what Edward Corwin will later refer to as "the higher law background of American Constitutional Law"[94] allows Coke to assert:

> First, the ligeance or faith of the Subject is due unto the King by the Law of Nature: Secondly, That the Law of Nature is part of the Law of England; Thirdly, That the Law of Nature was before any Judicial or Municipal Law: Fourthly, That the Law of Nature is Immutable.
>
> The Law of Nature is that which God at the time of creation of the nature of man infused into his heart, for his preservation and direction: and this is *lex aeterna*, the Moral Law, called also the Law of Nature.[95]

By invoking the Law of Nature found nowhere in Magna Carta, Coke is able to place the king himself under law. Coke argues that the symbol of the Crown signifies that the king "is, to do Justice and Judgment, to maintain the Peace of the Land, & to separate right from wrong, and the good from the ill."[96] Coke's formulation here appears closer to Thomas Aquinas and 13th-century Paris than it is to Magna Carta and 13th-century England.

---

89. *See id.* at 166.

90. *Id.* at 161 (editor's note).

91. *Id.* at 169.

92. *Id.* at 172.

93. *Id.* at 175.

94. EDWARD CORWIN, THE "HIGHER LAW" BACKGROUND OF AMERICAN CONSTITUTIONALISM 22–32 (2008) (originally published, 42 HARV. L. REV. 149 (1928)).

95. COKE, *supra* note 3, at 195.

96. *Id.* at 193.

Aquinas's definition of Natural Law as the participation of the rational creature (man) in the Eternal Law (God), requires that all human or positive law be directed to the "common good,"[97] as Coke would prefer.

Coke's effort to place the king under the rule of law and establish parliamentary supremacy begun in 1602 continues in the seventh part of the *Reports* with a letter from all the Justices of England to the Crown contesting a grant from Queen Elizabeth releasing specified persons from penal statutes before they had been tried and convicted. The case is listed in Coke's *Reports* simply as *Penal Statutes* (1605).[98] Coke asserts that "when a Statute is made by Parliament for the good of the Commonwealth, the King cannot give the penalty, benefit and dispensation of such Act to any subject; Or give power to any subject to dispense with it."[99] The letter from the justices concludes that "the penalty of an Act of Parliament" cannot be waived by the king, nor can any penal Statute be "executed by his Majesty's grant, in other manner or order of proceeding, than by the Act itself is provided."[100] More than 80 years before the Glorious Revolution, Coke seems to be announcing parliamentary supremacy.

In the preface to the eighth part of the *Reports* published in 1611 Coke again reasserts all the key components of his revised mythic view of English history. First, the grounds of the common law are so ancient as to be "beyond memory."[101] Second, William the Conqueror swore to uphold the laws of England, which were in substance that which is found in Magna Carta. Third, the Court of Common Pleas was not a result of Magna Carta, but as Coke claimed in the preface to the third part, was more ancient still. Fourth, trial by a jury of 12 men existed long before the Norman Conquest. And, fifth, there are no human laws as honorable, ancient, and excellent as the laws of England.[102] The myth of Magna Carta is almost complete.

The famous *Dr. Bonham's Case* (1610)[103] in the Court of Common Pleas was decided by Coke and reported in the eighth part. The case addresses an act of Parliament that granted an exclusive right to license those who would practice medicine in London to its College of Physicians. Bonham, who had been educated at Cambridge, was denied a license and the College of Physicians sought to fine and imprison him. This time Coke sought to extend the reach of the common law to control or fence in the power of Parliament. Ultimately, Coke writes:

---

97. THOMAS AQUINAS, TREATISE ON LAW 10–11 (Ralph McInerny ed., 1956) (law "is nothing else than an ordinance of reason, for the common good, made by him who has the care of the community, and promulgated.").

98. COKE, *supra* note 3, at 241.

99. *Id.* at 241.

100. *Id.* at 243.

101. *Id.* at 245 (Coke's preface to part eight).

102. *Id.* at 252.

103. *Id.* at 264 (Dr. Bonham's case).

It appeareth in our Books, that in many Cases, the Common Law doth controll Acts of Parliament, and sometimes shall adjudge them to be void: for when an Act of Parliament is against Common right and reason, or repugnant, or impossible to be performed, the Common Law will control it, and adjudge such Act to be void.[104]

Apparently, the well-trained common law judge will determine not what is old, ancient, or customary but what is "against Common right and reason" and on that basis declare laws of Parliament "void." One suspects that Chief Justice John Marshall would be impressed by Coke's arguments, but perhaps this is where Marshall learned them.[105]

In the preface to the ninth part, Coke reemphasizes his educational mission by claiming that a "substantial and compendious Report of a Case" should produce three good effects upon the student or reader:

1. It openeth the Understanding of the Reader and Hearer; 2. It breaketh through difficulties; and 3. It bringeth home to the hand of the studious, variety of pleasure and profit: I say it doth set open the Windows of the Law to let in that gladsom Light whereby the right reason of the Rule (the Beauty of the Law) may be clearly discerned.[106]

Having elevated the Common Law and reconfigured English history, Coke attacks specific issues in parts ten, eleven, and twelve of his *Reports*. In the *Case of the Isle of Ely* (1609),[107] the commissioners had decided that a new seven-mile long river needed to be cut through the island and they imposed a general tax upon 15 towns. The King's Privy Council referred the case to Coke as chief judge of Common Pleas. To avoid the tax, Coke read the duties of the commissioners narrowly and found that they were limited to reparation and repair of old gutters, walls, and sewers but could not order new walls, gutters, or sewers to be made. Coke's legal support goes to Magna Carta 1225 and King Edward I's reissue of Magna Carta. Coke warns "sometimes when a public good is pretended, a private benefit is intended,"[108] and he asserts that any new tax on the towns could be imposed only by an Act of Parliament.

James Bagg's Case (1615) in part eleven addresses an individual's right to speak his mind. Bagg was one of 12 burgesses or magistrates of his town. He

---

104. *Id.* at 273.

105. *Compare* Marshall's argument for judicial review *with* Coke's argument in Dr. Bonham's case, Marbury v. Madison, 5 U.S. 137 (1803) declaring the expansion of the Supreme Court's original jurisdiction in the Judiciary Act of 1789 to be unconstitutional.

106. COKE, *supra* note 3, at 307 (preface to part nine).

107. *Id.* at 378.

108. *Id.* at 382.

publicly disparaged his fellow magistrates and the mayor and opposed the mayor's policies. The mayor and other magistrates voted to remove him from office and he sued in King's Bench. The court found that "there was not any just cause to remove him" and ordered the town "to restore him." The court did not stop there but rather went on to hold that King's Bench had authority:

> Not only to correct errors in judicial proceedings, but other errors and misdemeanors extra-judicial, tending to the breach of peace, or oppression of subjects, or to the raising of faction, controversy, debate or to any manner of misgovernment; so that no wrong or injury, either public or private, can be done but that the same shall be reformed or punished by the due course of Law.[109]

For support the court turned to chapter 29 of Magna Carta 1225, saying "he ought to be convicted by course of law before he can be removed."

And finally in part twelve in *Prohibitions del Roy* (1607),[110] although a statute of Queen Elizabeth stated that "Judges are but delegates of the King" so that the king may take and decide a case "in his Royal person," because "such Authority belongs to the King by the Word of God in the Scriptures,"[111] Coke answered that all judgments in England are given per curiam, by the court. Coke then continued that even with the Great Seal the "King cannot take any cause out of any of his Courts, and give Judgment upon it himself."[112] Citing to Magna Carta chapter 29 a final time, Coke asserts, "Judgments given in the king's courts shall not be annulled (elsewhere), but a judgment shall stand in its force until [it is annulled] by judgment of the king's courts as erroneous."

Coke died in 1634 shortly after his personal papers were seized by the king and almost a decade after being imprisoned at age 70 in the Tower of London by King James I. Nonetheless, a few decades later, Thomas Hobbes, the English political philosopher and staunch defender of monarchy and royal prerogative, chose to attack Coke both in his masterpiece *Leviathan* (1651)[113] and in a lesser-known *Dialogue Between a Philosopher and a Student of the Common Law of England* (1662).[114] It appears that Hobbes saw Coke as a real threat to monarchy, peace, and stability in the 17th century.

---

109. *See id.* at 413.

110. *Id.* at 478.

111. *See id.* at 479.

112. *See id.* at 480.

113. THOMAS HOBBES, LEVIATHAN, OR THE MATTER, FORME AND POWER OF A COMMONWEALTH ECCLESIASTICAL AND CIVIL 176 (Michael Oakeshott ed., 1960).

114. THOMAS HOBBES, A DIALOGUE BETWEEN A PHILOSOPHER AND A STUDENT OF THE COMMON LAWS OF ENGLAND (Joseph Cropsey ed., 1997).

In the pivotal section of the *Dialogue*, a chapter titled "On Courts," Hobbes challenges Coke's underlying claims and asserts both that the king can decide any case in King's Bench[115] and that there is no historic record of any Court of Common Pleas prior to Magna Carta.[116] Hobbes also recognizes that court precedents can vary widely, "judgments one contrary to another," and suggests that Coke selectively placed in his *Reports* only those court outcomes that supported his opinions.[117] As if prefiguring our own litigious society, Hobbes concludes that this variety and conflict in precedent leads men to read their preferences into statutes and court opinions and to seek victory when they have no chance.[118]

In his monumental *Magna Carta*, Holt recognizes that Hobbes and Locke "were the real enemies of legal precedent. . . . [T]here was no room for ancient law in the monolithic structure of the *Leviathan* or in the *Second Treatise of Civil Government*. Coke and his work were outmoded, irrelevant, and of antiquarian rather than political interest."[119] However, as explained in detail below, Holt emphasizes that Coke and Magna Carta continued to be relevant in the American colonies because of the way in which Blackstone accepted and transmitted both Coke and Locke to the New World.

V.   America's Use of Magna Carta

While Coke's defense and elevation of the common law could not be reconciled with the natural rights theories of Hobbes and Locke in England, Holt does not place enough emphasis upon Blackstone's melding of Locke and Coke in his four-volume *Commentaries on the Laws of England*, published between 1765 and 1769. This melding made Coke's "mythic" Magna Carta a useful tool of resistance during the prerevolutionary and Revolutionary War period in the United States.

While the present chapter contends that Magna Carta 1215 and 1225 had little impact on the nature of the U.S. Constitution, no one can deny that Coke's mythic Magna Carta and his rewriting of English history exerted great influence during the prerevolutionary struggle with parliamentary authority in the American colonies. Historical Chart 4.3 lays side by side a series of critical events in both English and American political history in an effort to visualize how significant Blackstone's linking of Coke and Locke was to the American founding.

---

115. *Id.* at 88–89.
116. *Id.* at 82.
117. *Id.* at 90
118. *Id.* at 84.
119. HOLT, *supra* note 1, at 16.

Historical Chart 4.3 English and Colonial Resistance:
The Persistence of Magna Carta

• Elizabeth I, 1558–1603	1606 Colonial Charter Virginia
• James I, 1603–1625	1607 Founding of Jamestown
• Thirty Years War, 1618–1648	1620 Mayflower Compact
• Charles I, 1625–1649 (beheaded)	1629 Colonial Charter Massachusetts
• Petition of Right, 1628 (Coke)	1639 Fundamental Orders of Connecticut
• 1649–1658 reign of Oliver Cromwell	
• Charles II, 1660–1685	1669 Constitutions of the Carolinas (Locke)
• James II, 1685–1688	1681 Colonial Charter Pennsylvania
• Glorious Revolution 1688	
• William III and Mary II, 1689–1702	
• English Bill of Rights 1689	1776 Virginia Declaration of Rights
• George III, 1760–1820	1775 Great Seal of Massachusetts

The colonial foundings at Plymouth and at Jamestown coincide precisely with Coke's efforts to limit the prerogative of the king and to elevate the common law. Littleton and Coke would likely have been among the first law books available in the colonies.

And when Coke in the 1628 Petition of Right sought to limit the ability of King Charles I (r. 1625–1649) to tax without parliamentary approval, to imprison anyone arbitrarily, or to force the billeting of soldiers in private homes, the colonists surely took notice.

By the time of the Glorious Revolution in 1688 establishing parliamentary sovereignty, finally achieving the resisting barons' goal of fencing in the king at Runnymede, essentially all the colonial charters had been issued. William Penn, the founder of Pennsylvania, was put on trial in England in 1670 for preaching his Quaker faith. Penn later wrote a report of his trial and following Coke appealed numerous times to Magna Carta.[120] The entire trial is described in A. E. Dick Howard's *The Road from Runnymede: Magna Carta and Constitutionalism in America*.[121] Penn also published his own commentary on Magna Carta titled *The Excellent Priviledge of Liberty and Property*, again commingling Coke and Locke in ways that never happened in England. From the beginning at Plymouth and the Mayflower Compact, the American colonists depended upon written agreements and contracts to secure both their political rights (à la Coke) and their property (à la Locke).

---

120. THE ROAD FROM RUNNYMEDE, *supra* note 41, at 78.
121. *Id.* at 78–98.

In 1765, Parliament passed the Stamp Act,[122] in part to cover a massive debt created by the Seven Years' War.[123] The colonial response created the first Congress across all the colonies, the Stamp Act Congress in New York City with its rallying cry of "no taxation without representation."[124] As Howard notes, Pennsylvania's John Dickinson, who had studied law in England, and James Otis of Massachusetts both appealed to Magna Carta in rejecting the validity of the Stamp Act. And judges in Virginia resigned their office rather than enforce the Act, noting that chapter 40 of Magna Carta was the motto on their county seal.[125]

Colonial resistance to the Stamp Act and the tea tax grew rapidly; at the same time more and more British troops were required to protect the colonists. The Crown and Parliament needed tax revenue from the colonies to defer the costs of their protection. The parallel to the barons' unanswered petitions prior to taking up arms against King John were obvious to the colonists. By 1775, ten years after the Stamp Act, Massachusetts adopted a new Great Seal depicting an American dressed as an Englishman holding a drawn sword in his right hand and Magna Carta in his left.[126] (Massachusetts' Great Seal of 1775 is reproduced as Illustration No. 12.)

Despite these numerous appeals to Magna Carta during the colonial resistance to parliamentary excesses, in the final run up to the Continental Congress and the Declaration of Independence in 1776, appeals to Magna Carta essentially disappear. George Mason's *Virginia Declaration of Rights*, drafted less than a month before the Declaration of Independence, draws upon Locke's *Second Treatise*, not upon Magna Carta.

Section 1 of *Virginia's Declaration* follows Locke in declaring that "all men are by nature equally free and independent and have certain inherent rights . . . namely, the enjoyment of life and liberty, with the means of acquiring and possessing property, and pursuing and obtaining happiness and safety."[127] This is followed by the Lockean right to revolution in Section 3 of Mason's *Declaration* declaring that

> government is, or ought to be instituted for the common benefit, protection, and security of the people. . . . And that when any government shall be found inadequate or contrary to these purposes, a majority of the community has an indubitable, inalienable, and indefeasible right to reform, alter or abolish it.[128]

---

122. *See* BERNARD BAYLIN, THE IDEOLOGICAL ORIGINS OF THE AMERICAN REVOLUTION (1967).
123. *Id.*
124. THE ROAD FROM RUNNYMEDE, *supra* note 41, at 189.
125. *Id.* at 144–46.
126. *Id.* at 174–75.
127. LOCKE, *supra* note 4, at 307, 311.
128. *Id.* at 367.

The following month there was once again no reference to Magna Carta in Thomas Jefferson's Declaration of Independence. Modeled on Mason's document, it added a long string of specific abuses, including many identical to Coke's *Petition of Right*, such as "imposing Taxes on us without our Consent," "depriving us in many cases, of the benefits of Trial by Jury," and "Quartering large bodies of armed troops amongst us."[129]

As we saw in the side-by-side comparison earlier in this chapter, there are effectively no corresponding passages of Magna Carta 1215 or 1225 in the body of the U.S. Constitution as ratified in 1789. While there are some corresponding passages between Magna Carta 1215 or 1225 and the Bill of Rights, especially in parts of the Fifth, Seventh, and Eighth Amendments, those similarities may well derive from Coke and Blackstone rather than directly from Magna Carta.

Between 1765 and 1769, at the precise time of the Stamp Act and the run up to the revolution, Blackstone's *Commentaries on the Laws of England* was published in four volumes (*I. Of the Rights of Persons, II. Of the Rights of Things, III. Of Private Wrongs*, and *IV. Of Public Wrongs*). The Lockean influence in Blackstone's language of rights is evident. Indeed, the opening two paragraphs of book I, chapter 1, titled "Of the Absolute Rights of Individuals" assert

> The absolute rights of man . . . are usually summed up in one general appellation, and denominated the natural liberty of mankind. This natural liberty consists properly in a power of acting as one thinks fit, without any restraint or control, unless by the law of nature. . . . And these rights may be reduced to three principle or primary articles: the right of personal security, the right of personal liberty, and the right of private property.[130]

These passages are readily attributable to John Locke in the *Second Treatise*.[131]

Yet Blackstone's "Introduction" to Book 1 follows Coke and begins by announcing that the law of England is divided into two kinds: the unwritten or common law and written or statute law. The common law is "communicated from the former ages to the present solely by word of mouth" and "receive their binding power, and the force of laws, by long and immemorial usage."[132] These customs must be "reasonable" to be law, "[w]hich is not always, as Sir Edward Coke says, to be understood by every

---

129. THE DECLARATION OF INDEPENDENCE para. 2 (U.S. 1776) (among the listed "injuries and usurpations").

130. BLACKSTONE, *supra* note 5, at 13.

131. LOCKE, *supra* note 4, at 311–12.

132. BLACKSTONE, *supra* note 5, at 1.

unlearned man's reason, but of artificial and legal reason, warranted by authority of law."[133]

Only 75 years after the Glorious Revolution, this commingling of John Locke and Edward Coke allowed Blackstone to link "representative government" to absolute individual rights. Thus, in chapter 2, "Of the Parliament," Blackstone asserts, "In a free state every man, who is supposed a free agent, ought to be in some measure his own governor: and therefore a branch at least of the legislative power should reside in the whole body of the people."[134]

This amalgam of Coke and Locke must have appeared very powerful and attractive to the American colonists preparing to take up arms against Great Britain. Blackstone's transmission of Coke and his mythic Magna Carta provided a historic English foundation for resisting government oppression. Blackstone's transmission of Locke mixed with Coke and the common law provided even more—a theoretical basis for individual rights and popular sovereignty not available in the history of Magna Carta and its reissues.

Magna Carta as transmitted by Coke and Blackstone could be resorted to both when walls and fences were needed against taxation and oppression and when self-help became inevitable. Locke and Coke's common law provided a theory of individual rights, representative government, and the role of courts, which could be turned to when institutional development was needed. Thus we should not be surprised to find the American founders turning to Locke and the common law and not Magna Carta when drafting the Constitution of 1789. Hamilton, therefore, can declare "bills of rights, in the sense and in the extent in which they are contended for, [i.e., Magna Carta] are not only unnecessary in the proposed constitution, but would even be dangerous."[135]

VI.   Epilogue: The 21st Century

In 1787, the founders had enough experience to worry about legislative and executive abuses of power. Checks and balances, fences and walls, were built into their Lockean institutions to protect Coke's and Locke's vision of individual rights, but the federal court system received much less attention. Justice Antonin Scalia reminds us the common law "is not really customary law or the reflection of the people's practices but is rather law developed by judges."[136] He suggests that the reason the first year of law school with

---

133. *Id.* at 5.

134. *Id.* at 20.

135. THE FEDERALIST No. 84 (Hamilton), *supra* note 64, at 579.

136. ANTONIN SCALIA, A MATTER OF INTERPRETATION: FEDERAL COURTS AND THE LAW 4 (1997).

all its common law courses is exhilarating is "because it consists of playing common-law judge, which in turn consists of playing king—devising out of the brilliance of one's own mind, those laws that ought to govern mankind."[137]

The Supreme Court itself has played an important fence-building role against both executive and legislative excesses and state-level abuses. In various eras, the Court has limited executive removal power,[138] limited executive seizure power,[139] prevented the commerce power from being used as a general federal police power,[140] and prevented the establishment of a line-item veto power.[141] The Court has also used the Fourteenth Amendment to pull down state-built walls of inequality by nationalizing the Bill of Rights under the due process clause and assuring equal protection of the laws in education.[142]

Nonetheless, today Justice Scalia worries that the common law approach in federal court decision making is dangerous to the individual rights Coke and Blackstone set out to protect. In the Supreme Court, the notions of a "living constitution" that must keep up with the changing times and technology and "evolving standards of decency that mark the progress of a maturing society"[143] create rights not found in the words of the Bill of Rights but emanating from multiple provisions like halos, allow private homes to be turned over to a corporation for private development, and reduce the Fourth Amendment to a shadow of itself in the United States Foreign Intelligence Surveillance Act court.[144]

Although the Supreme Court held there was no General Federal Common Law in *Erie Railroad v. Tompkins*, justices and judges of both the right and the left still behave like common law judges "playing king" and "devising out of their own mind the laws that ought to govern."[145] On this 800th anniversary of Magna Carta it would be ironic if the next great invocation of Magna Carta in America is to build stronger fences or walls around the federal judiciary.

---

137. *Id.* at 7.
138. *See* Humphrey's Ex'r v. United States, 295 U.S. 602 (1935).
139. *See* Youngstown Sheet & Tube Co. v. Sawyer, 343 U.S. 579 (1952).
140. *See* United States v. Lopez, 514 U.S. 549 (1995); United States v. Morrison, 529 U.S. 598 (2000).
141. *See* Clinton v. N.Y.C., 524 U.S. 417 (1998).
142. *See* Gitlow v. N.Y., 268 U.S. 652 (1925); Brown v. Bd. of Educ., 449 U.S. 483 (1954).
143. Trop v. Dulles, 356 U.S. 86 (1958); *see also* SCALIA, *supra* note 136, at 40 (discussing "dynamic constitutional construction").
144. Griswald v. Connecticut, 381 U.S. 479 (1965); Kelo v. City of New London, 545 U.S. 469 (2005).
145. SCALIA, *supra* note 136, at 7.

Chapter 5
Magna Carta in Supreme Court Jurisprudence

Stephen J. Wermiel*

There is no doubt that Magna Carta has influenced conceptions of rights and power in the United States[1] and elsewhere and has shaped the evolution of the common law. But what happens when you drill down beyond general precepts into the actual decision making of the U.S. Supreme Court? What influence has Magna Carta had on the jurisprudence of the Supreme Court?

I. Overview

In its 224 years of operation,[2] the U.S. Reports of the Supreme Court's decisions refer to Magna Carta in more than 170 cases.[3] There is a common theme that spans two centuries: the role of Magna Carta is largely symbolic. For Supreme Court justices, and the lawyers who argue before them, Magna Carta is venerable historical evidence invoked to establish the pedigree of a claim that a particular right exists or to determine what that right means. Many examples are explored below. As justices have made clear in speeches and decisions, however, Magna Carta is not and cannot be positive law in the Supreme Court, since it far predates the writing of the U.S. Constitution, which created the Supreme Court.

---

*The author would like to acknowledge the help and support of Christopher Rogers, a second-year law student, and Amy Taylor, a librarian, both at American University Washington College of Law.

1. For an earlier discussion of federal and state case law and Magna Carta, *see* A.E. DICK HOWARD, ROAD FROM RUNNYMEDE: MAGNA CARTA AND CONSTITUTIONALISM IN AMERICA 289–91, 295–367 (1968). *See also* BERNARD H. SIEGAN, PROPERTY RIGHTS: FROM MAGNA CARTA TO THE FOURTEENTH AMENDMENT (2001); PETER LINEBAUGH, THE MAGNA CARTA MANIFESTO: LIBERTIES AND COMMONS FOR ALL 170–91 (2008).

2. The Supreme Court of the United States first sat in New York City in February 1790.

3. This number is based on a search on Westlaw for reference to "Magna Carta" and "Magna Charta" and the "Great Charter" in the U.S. Reports, the official reports of Supreme Court decisions.

There is no question, however, that Magna Carta can and does influence the thinking and historical analysis of justices. That influence has grown over time, increasing significantly as the Supreme Court has taken a more expansive view of individual rights and liberties for much of the last half of the 20th century.

The expansion of rights, and of resort to Magna Carta, may be seen in the contrast between two speeches delivered some 50 years apart.

Benjamin Cardozo discussed Magna Carta in December 1931, at an annual dinner of the New York County Lawyers Association.[4] This was about three months before the highly regarded judge on the New York Court of Appeals took a seat on the U.S. Supreme Court,[5] where as a justice it appears that he never personally cited Magna Carta. Discussing the power of myths in one portion of his speech, Cardozo turned to the myth of Magna Carta:

> Take Magna Charta for example. Today it is not what is written in the charter—if the words are read in the sense in which they were understood by those who wrote them—that has any commanding interest, any throbbing and vital meaning, for those who walk the earth. What lives in the charter today is the myth that has gathered around it—the things that it has come to stand for in the thought of successive generations—not the pristine core within, but the incrustations that have formed without.[6]

Cardozo then drew analogy from this view of the symbolism of Magna Carta to the role of the Constitution and Bill of Rights:

> Now, what is true of Magna Charta is true, I think of our own constitution in many of its provisions; true, for example, of the bill of rights, which is much more important for the spirit it enshrines than for this or the other privilege or immunity which it professes to secure. Some of them have a vital meaning even to this day, others are reminiscent of battles long ago. The myth that has enveloped them has become greater than the reality, or rather in a sense the genuine reality.[7]

---

4. Benjamin N. Cardozo, *Faith and a Doubting World*, Dec. 17, 1931, *reprinted in* SELECTED WRITINGS OF BENJAMIN NATHAN CARDOZO 99 (1947), downloaded from HeinOnline (http://heinonline.org).

5. Cardozo sat on the New York Court of Appeals for 18 years until he was sworn in to the U.S. Supreme Court in March 1932. He cited Magna Carta (using its old spelling of Magna Charta) once on the New York Court of Appeals. Techt v. Hughes, 229 N.Y. 222, 230 (1920).

6. Cardozo, *supra* note 4, at 104.

7. *Id.* at 105.

Justice William J. Brennan Jr. provided a considerably more positive view of the role of Magna Carta in judicial decision making in a speech at Runnymede, England, in July 1985, when the American Bar Association rededicated its memorial to Magna Carta.[8] "Throughout the . . . history of the Supreme Court of the United States, the bedrock principles of Magna Carta have had and continue to have, a profound influence over the Justices' deliberations," said Brennan,[9] who cited Magna Carta in four opinions.

It is important to remember that Brennan was speaking when the Supreme Court was well launched on the rights revolution that brought depth and breadth of meaning to the provisions of the Bill of Rights and to the notions of due process and equal protection in the Fourteenth Amendment.[10] Cardozo, in contrast, was speaking when the first sparks of the rights revolution had scarcely begun to illuminate the path that lay ahead and before he was even nominated to the Supreme Court, where he would more directly face issues for which Magna Carta might be relevant.

Thus, Brennan could attribute more influence to Magna Carta and did in the 1985 speech. "Two themes emerge from the Court's opinions that explicitly address Magna Carta,"[11] Brennan said:

> The first is that the Magna Carta was both a substantive and symbolic contribution to the ongoing development and refinement of principles that protect the fundamental rights and liberties of the individual; it set forth certain specific guarantees that are cornerstones of our modern concepts of liberty. . . .
>
> The second theme emerging from our opinions emphasizes the significance of our decision in the United States to entrench these safeguards in a written constitution.[12]

Brennan underscored one additional very important way that Magna Carta influences the justices of the Supreme Court—an ever-present visual reminder that captures the importance of the document and its principles, at least for those justices who have occupied the Supreme Court building since

---

8. William J. Brennan, Jr., *Rededication Address: The American Bar Association's Memorial to the Magna Carta*, speech delivered at Runnymede on July 13, 1985, *reprinted in* 19 LOY. L.A. L. REV. 55 (1985).

9. *Id.* at 56.

10. While there is no fixed definition of the Supreme Court's rights revolution, many commentators identify the proliferation of rights as having reached its peak in the 1960s during the Warren Court led by Chief Justice Earl Warren. The Warren Court lasted from 1953 to 1969. But the expansion of civil rights and liberties continued, albeit perhaps at a slower pace, in the 1970s in the Burger Court which lasted from 1969 to 1986.

11. Brennan, *supra* note 8.

12. *Id.* at 56, 57.

it opened in 1935. There are depictions of Magna Carta on the bronze front door of the Supreme Court building and in the marble relief around the top of the courtroom. Said Brennan:

> Thus, it is not mere symbolism that accounts for the depiction on the bronze door entering the Supreme Court building of King John sealing Magna Carta and the depiction on the marble frieze around our courtroom (seen by each of us Justices on every argument day) of King John in chain mail armor holding Magna Carta in his arms. The first eight amendments to our Federal Constitution, our explicit Bill of Rights, owes its parentage to Magna Carta; and, Americans regard the enforcement of those amendments as the Supreme Court's most important and demanding responsibility.[13]

Reference to Magna Carta spans most of the Supreme Court's history in different forms.[14] The first reference to Magna Carta in the U.S. Reports appears to be in the summary of oral arguments by the very first Supreme Court reporter of decisions, Alexander J. Dallas. In the official report of *State of Georgia v. Brailsford*,[15] Dallas wrote in 1794 that lawyers for the defendant, Brailsford, a British citizen who lived in Great Britain, referred to Magna Carta in their argument in a string of authorities.[16] But according to Dallas, Chief Justice John Jay did not refer to Magna Carta in his opinion in the case, which involved the question of whether the state or original creditors had the right to sue to recover a debt.[17]

The first reference to Magna Carta in a justice's opinion appears to be by Justice Joseph Story in a dissenting opinion from the majority ruling of Chief Justice John Marshall in 1814 in the case of *Brown v. United States*.[18] The case from a Massachusetts court was a lawsuit over the ownership of timber. Armitz Brown, a U.S. citizen, claimed the timber was rightfully his, but the federal government claimed to own it as forfeited enemy property. Chief Justice Marshall ruled that Congress had not authorized the seizure of enemy property that was in the United States and held that the property belonged to Brown. Justice Story had written the opinion for the circuit court of Massachusetts and cited Magna Carta several times there. In his

---

13. *Id.* at 58.
14. Quotations from Magna Carta in this chapter are taken directly from U.S. Supreme Court decisions and use the versions of Magna Carta referenced in and cited in those opinions.
15. Georgia v. Brailsford, 3 U.S. (3 Dall.) 1 (1794).
16. *Id.* at 3.
17. *Id.* at 3–5.
18. Brown v. United States, 12 U.S. (8 Cranch) 110 (1814).

Supreme Court dissent, he repeated his own words from the circuit court, reiterating his references to Magna Carta.[19]

At the other end of the span of centuries, the Supreme Court most recently resorted twice in 2012 to Magna Carta. In *Hosanna-Tabor Evangelical Lutheran Church v. Equal Employment Opportunity Commission,*[20] Chief Justice John Roberts concluded that the church autonomy guaranteed by the religion clauses of the First Amendment precludes a minister from suing her church for employment discrimination. Setting the historical context for the issues raised by the case, Roberts wrote in January 2012:

> Controversy between church and state over religious offices is hardly new. In 1215, the issue was addressed in the very first clause of Magna Carta. There King John agreed that "the English church shall be free, and shall have its rights undiminished and its liberties unimpaired." The King in particular accepted the "freedom of elections," a right "thought to be of the greatest necessity and importance to the English church." J. Holt, Magna Carta App. IV, p. 317, cl.1 (1965).[21]

In *Southern Union Co. v. United States,*[22] Justice Stephen Breyer referred to Magna Carta in a June 2012 dissenting opinion that was joined by Justices Anthony Kennedy and Samuel Alito. The court's majority, in an opinion by Justice Sonia Sotomayor, ruled that the Sixth Amendment[23] requires that juries, not judges, determine any relevant facts that increase the amount of a criminal fine.[24] Justice Breyer argued that enhanced criminal fines, unlike sentences of imprisonment, could be based on factual determinations by judges.[25] Breyer noted that any limitations on the power of judges in imposing fines were historically included in Magna Carta.[26]

As a final preliminary matter before examining the ways Magna Carta has been used, it is instructive to examine the frequency of references in different periods and by different justices. An informal examination of

---

19. *Id.* at 142–44 (Story, J., dissenting).

20. Hosanna-Tabor Evangelical Lutheran Church v. Equal Employment Opportunity Comm'n, 132 S. Ct. 694 (2012).

21. *Id.* at 702.

22. S. Union Co. v. United States, 132 S. Ct. 2344 (2012).

23. The Sixth Amendment, among other guarantees, provides for trial by "an impartial jury."

24. *S. Union Co.,* 132 S. Ct. at 2357. The majority extended the Court's earlier ruling in Apprendi v. New Jersey, 530 U.S. 466 (2000) (holding that the jury must determine any facts that might lead to a longer prison sentence).

25. *S. Union Co.,* 132 S. Ct. at 2357.

26. *Id.* at 2362.

references to Magna Carta, Magna Charta, and Great Charter[27] produced the following statistics:

- 19th century—56 references
- 20th century—103 references
- 21st century—13 references

The spread of usage in the 20th century tends to support the idea that Magna Carta was used most often in a period in which the Supreme Court was taking an expansive view of civil rights and liberties. Prior to 1950, there were 24 references to Magna Carta in the 20th century. There were eight more references between 1950 and 1959. But from 1960 to the end of the 20th century, Supreme Court justices referred to Magna Carta 71 times, more than in the entire 19th century.

Roughly half of the references to Magna Carta have been in majority opinions. For the other half, about three-quarters of the references have been in dissenting opinions and about one quarter in concurring opinions. The most frequent users of Magna Carta have been justices of relatively recent vintage. Here are the most frequent users of Magna Carta among Supreme Court Justices:

- John Paul Stevens (1975–2010) —16 cases;
- Hugo Black (1937–1971) —14 cases;
- John M. Harlan (1877–1911) —11 cases;
- William O. Douglas (1939–1975) —9 cases.

Although these leaders in usage of Magna Carta are largely progressive justices, resort to Magna Carta does not seem to be purely ideological. Justice Felix Frankfurter, who took a narrow view of the Court's role, referred to Magna Carta in six cases; Justice Antonin Scalia, who says the Constitution must be read according to its language and the intent of its authors, has referred to Magna Carta in seven cases.

II. Using Magna Carta for Philosophical and Historical Reflection

Parsing the frequency and statistical analysis of Supreme Court references to Magna Carta does not capture the true sense of how justices use the importance of the document. Only examination of specific cases can illuminate that picture with sufficient detail and depth.

---

27. These statistics are based on a Westlaw search for the term "Magna Carta," or "Magna Charta," as it was used in earlier periods.

It is logical to begin with some big picture cases in which Supreme Court justices reflect on Magna Carta in philosophical and historical terms. These references involve issues like the origins of judicial impartiality, expanding the accountability in Magna Carta to the legislative branch, and using Magna Carta as a starting point for thinking about rights and governmental power.

A. General Philosophical and Historical Discussion

In a number of instances, Supreme Court justices used Magna Carta to establish benchmark perceptions of the origins of and importance of rights. For example, Justice Henry Baldwin wrote in an 1837 opinion,[28] "From the beginning of the revolution, the people of the colonies clung to magna charta, and their charters from the crown; their violation was a continued subject of complaint."

More than a century later, Justice Felix Frankfurter articulated another principle when he observed, "The administration of justice by an impartial judiciary has been basic to our conception of freedom ever since Magna Carta."[29]

Justice Hugo Black had another, similar take on the fundamental influence of Magna Carta to promote fairness in the judiciary, especially in the criminal justice system. Writing in 1956 in *Griffin v. Illinois*,[30] Black wrote:

> Providing equal justice for poor and rich, weak and powerful alike is an age-old problem. People have never ceased to hope and strive to move closer to that goal. This hope, at least in part, brought about in 1215 the royal concessions of Magna Charta: "To no one will we sell, to no one will we refuse, or delay, right or justice. . . . No free man shall be taken or imprisoned, or disseised, or outlawed, or exiled, or anywise destroyed; nor shall we go upon him nor send upon him, but by the lawful judgment of his peers or by the law of the land." These pledges were unquestionably steps toward a fairer and more nearly equal application of criminal justice. In this tradition, our own constitutional guaranties of due process and equal protection both call for procedures in criminal trials which allow no invidious discriminations between persons and different groups of persons. [31]

---

28. Proprietors of Charles River Bridge v. Proprietors of Warren Bridge, 36 U.S. 420 (1837).

29. Bridges v. California, 314 U.S. 252, 282 (1941) (Frankfurter, J., dissenting).

30. Griffin v. Illinois, 351 U.S. 12 (1956).

31. *Id.* at 16–17.

One of the more extensive discussions of how to think about and use the influence of Magna Carta was written by Justice Stanley Matthews in 1884 in his majority opinion in *Hurtado v. California*.[32] Matthews warned that Magna Carta should not limit the flexibility of the nation and its citizens to respond to new events and developments and that it should be viewed as an inspiration capable of embracing new ideas. Matthews wrote:

> The constitution of the United States was ordained, it is true, by descendants of Englishmen, who inherited the traditions of the English law and history; but it was made for an undefined and expanding future, and for a people gathered, and to be gathered, from many nations and of many tongues; and while we take just pride in the principles and institutions of the common law, we are not to forget that in lands where other systems of jurisprudence prevail, the ideas and processes of civil justice are also not unknown. Due process of law, in spite of the absolutism of continental governments, is not alien to that Code which survived the Roman empire as the foundation of modern civilization in Europe, and which has given us that fundamental maxim of distributive justice, suum cuique tribuere. There is nothing in Magna Charta, rightly construed as a broad charter of public right and law, which ought to exclude the best ideas of all systems and of every age; and as it was the characteristic principle of the common law to draw its inspiration from every fountain of justice, we are not to assume that the sources of its supply have been exhausted. On the contrary, we should expect that the new and various experiences of our own situation and system will mould and shape it into new and not less useful forms.[33]

B.   Limiting Government Power

One of the important contributions of Magna Carta was the concept of government agreeing in a written document to limit its own powers. In sealing Magna Carta, King John agreed to a list of principles that curtailed the power of the English monarch.

This idea of written limitations on government was a critical influence in the formation of the constitutions of the colonies before the formation of the United States and in the choice to create a written constitution for the country. But there were differences between what was recorded in Magna

---

32. Hurtado v. California, 110 U.S. 516 (1884).
33. *Id.* at 530–31.

Carta and in the scope and role of written constitutions in the United States. One of the more extensive discussions of these differences and their importance is found in the majority opinion of Justice Stanley Matthews in 1884 in *Hurtado*.[34] Justice Matthews discussed not only the significance of the written constitution but also how the novel development of extending restrictions on government power to all three branches of government may require different approaches to interpretation and the role of the judiciary. Matthews wrote:

> The concessions of Magna Charta were wrung from the king as guaranties against the oppressions and usurpations of his prerogative. It did not enter into the minds of the barons to provide security against their own body or in favor of the commons by limiting the power of parliament; so that bills of attainder, ex post facto laws, laws declaring forfeitures of estates, and other arbitrary acts of legislation which occur so frequently in English history, were never regarded as inconsistent with the law of the land . . . . The actual and practical security for English liberty against legislative tyranny was the power of a free public opinion represented by the commons.
>
> In this country written constitutions were deemed essential to protect the rights and liberties of the people against the encroachments of power delegated to their governments, and the provisions of Magna Charta were incorporated into bills of rights, [sic] They were limitations upon all the powers of government, legislative as well as executive and judicial. It necessarily happened, therefore, that as these broad and general maxims of liberty and justice hald [sic] in our system a different place and performed a different function from their position and office in English constitutional history and law, they would receive and justify a corresponding and more comprehensive interpretation. Applied in England only as guards against executive usurpation and tyranny, here they have become bulwarks also against arbitrary legislation; but in that application, as it would be incongruous to measure and restrict them by the ancient customary English law, they must be held to guaranty, not particular forms of procedure, but the very substance of individual rights to life, liberty, and property. Restraints that could be fastened upon executive authority with precision and detail, might prove obstructive and injurious when imposed on the just and necessary discretion of legislative power; and while, in every instance, laws that violated express and specific injunctions and prohibitions might without embarrassment be judicially declared to be void, yet

---

34. *Id.*

any general principle or maxim founded on the essential nature of law, as a just and reasonable expression of the public will, and of government as instituted by popular consent and for the general good, can only be applied to cases coming clearly within the scope of its spirit and purpose, and not to legislative provisions merely establishing forms and modes of attainment.[35]

The theme of the importance of committing guarantees to a written constitution and of extending limitations on government power is discussed by other justices as well and runs through other opinions. This discussion by Matthews appears to have become the gold standard for consideration of this issue, subsequently quoted by others. For example, when Justice William Day made similar points in 1917 in a dissent in *Wilson v. New*,[36] he quoted Matthews.[37] Justice William Brennan, too, quoted from this passage by Matthews in his 1985 speech.[38]

Justice Matthews' discourse was not the first discussion of the change brought about by the Constitution that made the legislature subject to judicial review. Chief Justice Roger Taney made several notable observations in 1864. In *Gordon v. United States*,[39] Taney wrote:

The position and rank, therefore, assigned to this Court in the Government of the United States, differ from that of the highest judicial power in England, which is subordinate to the legislative power, and bound to obey any law that Parliament may pass, although it may, in the opinion of the court, be in conflict with the principles of Magna Charta or the Petition of Rights. . . .

For whether an act of Congress is within the limits of its delegated power or not is a judicial question, to be decided by the courts, the Constitution having, in express terms, declared that the judicial power shall extend to all cases arising under the Constitution.

This power over legislative acts is not possessed by the English courts. They cannot declare an act of Parliament void, because in the opinion of the court it is inconsistent with the principles of Magna

---

35. *Id*. at 531–32.

36. Wilson v. New, 243 U.S. 332 (1917).

37. *Id*. at 366 (Day, J., dissenting). For other opinions citing *Hurtado,* see Louisiana *ex rel*. Francis v. Resweber, 329 U.S. 459, 467 (1947) (Frankfurter, J., concurring) (referring to the "classic language" of Hurtado); Albright v. Oliver, 510 U.S. 266, 292 (1994) (Stevens, J., dissenting); Poe v. Ullman, 367 U.S. 497, 541 (1961) (Harlan, J., dissenting).

38. Brennan, *supra* note 8, at 58.

39. Gordon v. United States, 117 U.S. 697 (1864). Chief Justice Roger Taney wrote this opinion in the spring of 1864 in anticipation of the case being argued in December 1864. Taney died before the argument, but the other justices retrieved the opinion and issued it as one of the last pieces of writing by Taney.

Charta or the Petition of Rights. They are bound to obey it and carry it into execution. Yet, in that country, the independence of the Judiciary is invariably respected and upheld by the King and the Parliament as well as by the courts; and the courts are never required to pass judgment in a suit where they cannot carry it into execution, and where it is inoperative and of no value, unless sanctioned by a future act of Parliament. The judicial power is carefully and effectually separated from the executive and legislative departments.[40]

Clearly then, to the justices, Magna Carta was a major step forward in creating some degree of accountability and redress within government, but there seems to be universal agreement that the Constitution improved on this development by making the legislative branch equally accountable.

III. Turning to the Cases

At the heart of analyzing the Supreme Court's use of Magna Carta must be the cases that focus on specific rights and other issues.

Magna Carta references occur in a wide range of cases. There are antitrust cases, tax disputes, and property battles. There are also struggles over due process, trial by jury, the right to travel, excessive fines, the right to petition government, speedy trials, habeas corpus, cruel and unusual punishment, separation of church and state, and more.

A. Due Process

Perhaps no effect of Magna Carta is more significant than the historical support the document provides for the concept of "due process of law."

The precise phrase "due process of law" does not appear in Magna Carta but rather appeared later in England. It was adopted by the authors of the Bill of Rights as part of the Fifth Amendment and took effect when the amendments were ratified in 1791. The second reference to "due process of law" in the U.S. Constitution took effect as part of the Fourteenth Amendment, ratified in 1868. The Fifth Amendment phrase served as a limitation on the power of the federal government, while the Fourteenth Amendment guarantee curbs the authority of state governments.[41]

---

40. *Id.* at 699, 705–06.
41. Through a process called incorporation, the Supreme Court between 1925 and 2010 defined liberty protected by due process in the Fourteenth Amendment to include most of the provisions of the Bill of Rights as checks on the power of state governments.

Faced on numerous occasions with the question of what "due process" means, Supreme Court justices have frequently turned to Magna Carta—and to Sir Edward Coke's influential commentary[42] on its meaning several hundred years after Runnymede. Consider the opinion of Justice Benjamin Curtis in 1855,[43] one of the earliest and most significant of many examples that rely on Coke for the proposition that the phrase "due process of law" means the same thing as "the law of the land" in Chapter 39 of the original Magna Carta. Curtis wrote:

> The words, "due process of law," were undoubtedly intended to convey the same meaning as the words, "by the law of the land," in Magna Charta. Lord Coke, in his commentary on those words, (2 Inst. 50,) says they mean due process of law. The constitutions which had been adopted by the several States before the formation of the federal constitution, following the language of the great charter more closely, generally contained the words, "but by the judgment of his peers, or the law of the land." The ordinance of congress of July 13, 1787, for the government of the territory of the United States northwest of the River Ohio, used the same words.
>
> The constitution of the United States, as adopted, contained the provision, that "the trial of all crimes, except in cases of impeachment, shall be by jury." When the fifth article of amendment containing the words now in question was made, the trial by jury in criminal cases had thus already been provided for. By the sixth and seventh articles of amendment, further special provisions were separately made for that mode of trial in civil and criminal cases. To have followed, as in the state constitutions, and in the ordinance of 1787, the words of Magna Charta, and declared that no person shall be deprived of his life, liberty, or property but by the judgment of his peers or the law of the land, would have been in part superfluous and inappropriate. To have taken the clause, "law of the land," without its immediate context, might possibly have given rise to doubts, which would be effectually dispelled by using those words which the great commentator on Magna Charta had declared to be the true meaning of the phrase, "law of the land," in that instrument, and which were undoubtedly then received as their true meaning.[44]

---

42. Edward Coke, The Second Part of the Institutes of the Laws of England (1628).

43. Murray's Lessee v. Hoboken Land & Improvement Co., 59 U.S. 272 (1855).

44. Id. at 276.

Reference to Magna Carta to define and bolster the meaning of due process is far and away the most frequent usage among Supreme Court justices and arises in a wide variety of different cases. Due process issues are about 28 percent of the references to Magna Carta. Trial by jury cases represent 13 percent of the total; cases generally evaluating the influence of Magna Carta on the Constitution account for 8 percent; those raising antitrust issues, and those raising habeas corpus issues each totaled about 6 percent; other civil rights and liberties were about 5 percent of the total; and cruel and unusual punishment and excessive fines each represented about 4 percent.

In the Court's early years, well before ratification of the Fourteenth Amendment imposed the requirements of due process on the states, Justice William Johnson articulated a concept like due process—being free from arbitrary government action—found in the Maryland state constitution and based on Magna Carta. In *Bank of Columbia v. Okely*,[45] Johnson wrote in 1819:

> As to the words from Magna Charta, incorporated into the constitution of Maryland, after volumes spoken and written with a view to their exposition, the good sense of mankind has at length settled down to this: that they were intended to secure the individual from the arbitrary exercise of the powers of government, unrestrained by the established principles of private rights and distributive justice.[46]

Fast-forward more than 170 years. In their joint, lead opinion on abortion rights in *Planned Parenthood of Southeastern Pennsylvania v. Casey*,[47] Justices Sandra Day O'Connor, Anthony Kennedy, and David Souter referred to Magna Carta to make the point that while due process applied in the form of the "law of the land" clause to limit "tyranny" by the executive branch, under the Constitution due process also protected against the actions of the legislative branch.[48]

A year earlier, Justice Antonin Scalia engaged in a lengthy analysis of the meaning of due process and whether it imposed limits on the award of punitive damages. Arguing that due process imposed no limits on punitive damages, Scalia's dissenting opinion in 1991 in *Pacific Mutual Life Insurance Co. v. Haslip*[49] discussed the relationship between due process and Magna Carta in some detail. Scalia wrote:

---

45. Bank of Columbia v. Okely, 17 U.S. (4 Wheat.) 235 (1819).
46. *Id.* at 244.
47. Planned Parenthood of Se. Pa. v. Casey, 505 U.S. 833 (1992).
48. *Id.* at 847.
49. Pac. Mut. Life Ins. Co. v. Haslip, 499 U.S. 1 (1991).

Determining whether common-law procedures for awarding punitive damages can deny "due process of law" requires some inquiry into the meaning of that majestic phrase. Its first prominent use appears to have been in an English statute of 1354: "[N]o man of what estate or condition that he be, shall be put out of land or tenement, nor taken nor imprisoned, nor disinherited, nor put to death, without being brought in answer by due process of the law." 28 Edw. III, ch. 3. Although historical evidence suggests that the word "process" in this provision referred to specific writs employed in the English courts (a usage retained in the phrase "service of process") . . . Sir Edward Coke had a different view. In the second part of his Institutes, see 2 Institutes 50 (5th ed. 1797), Coke equated the phrase "due process of the law" in the 1354 statute with the phrase "Law of the Land" in Chapter 29 of Magna Charta (Chapter 39 of the original Magna Charta signed by King John at Runnymede in 1215), which provides: "No Freeman shall be taken, or imprisoned, or be disseised of his Freehold, or Liberties, or free Customs, or be outlawed, or exiled, or any otherwise destroyed; nor will we not pass upon him, nor condemn him, but by lawful Judgment of his Peers, or by the Law of the Land." 9 Hen. III, ch. 29 (1225). In Coke's view, the phrase "due process of law" referred to the customary procedures to which freemen were entitled by "the old law of England," 2 Institutes 50.

The American colonists were intimately familiar with Coke . . . and when, in their Constitutions, they widely adopted Magna Charta's "law of the land" guarantee, see, e.g., N.C. Const., Art. XII (1776) ("[N]o freeman ought to be taken, imprisoned, or disseized of his freehold, liberties or privileges, or outlawed, or exiled, or in any manner destroyed, or deprived of his life, liberty, or property, but by the law of the land"); Mass. Const., Art. XII (1780) ("[N]o subject shall be arrested, imprisoned, despoiled, or deprived of his property, immunities, or privileges, put out of the protection of the law, exiled or deprived of his life, liberty, or estate, but by the judgment of his peers, or the law of the land"), they almost certainly understood it as Coke did. It was thus as a supposed affirmation of Magna Charta according to Coke that the First Congress (without recorded debate on the issue) included in the proposed Fifth Amendment to the Federal Constitution the provision that "[n]o person shall be . . . deprived of life, liberty, or property, without due process of law." Early commentaries confirm this. See, e.g., 2 W. Blackstone, Commentaries 133, nn. 11, 12 (S. Tucker ed. 1803); 2 J. Kent, Commentaries on American Law 10 (1827); 3 J. Story, Commentaries on the Constitution of the United States 661 (1833).[50]

---

50. *Id.* at 28–29.

There are many other cases that refer to Magna Carta in passing, sometimes noting that the goal of both Magna Carta and due process was to prevent arbitrary government action. Others simply note the relationship suggested by Coke between the "law of the land" passage of Magna Carta and "due process" in the Fifth and Fourteenth Amendments.

These references and the longer passages already cited provide the classic examples of Supreme Court reliance on Magna Carta. Justices across a broad spectrum of years and ideologies seem to have been reassured by the venerability of the basic due process ideals—freedom from arbitrary decisions and access to impartial justice. That these ideals date back hundreds of years seems to enhance their legitimacy and their staying power. How could anyone doubt the importance of a nation committing to freedom from arbitrary power when the pedigree of that principle is Magna Carta?

At times this reverence leads to anomalous usage. When Justice Felix Frankfurter suggested in a 1941 dissent discussed above[51] that "an impartial judiciary has been basic to our conception of freedom ever since Magna Carta,"[52] about whom is he speaking? Since 13th-century courts were hardly independent of the king and judicial independence in England did not occur until the Act of Settlement of 1701, since the colonies that eventually would become the United States did not exist for some 400 or more years after King John agreed to Magna Carta in 1215, and since the Constitution was not written for 572 years after 1215, the statement actually makes little sense. Presumably Frankfurter was talking about Western civilization and English-speaking peoples who existed between 1215 and the creation of the "new world." But the hyperbole adds to the mythic quality of resort to Magna Carta by Supreme Court justices in their opinions.

B. Trial by Jury

After due process, the right of trial by jury is one of the subjects on which justices turn to Magna Carta most often for historical support, roughly in 13 percent of the cases. The root of the right to trial by jury has the same origin in Magna Carta as due process.[53] In chapter 39 of the original Magna Carta, an individual is guaranteed that he will not be imprisoned, exiled, or deprived of his property without the "lawful judgment of his peers." This is the phrase that immediately precedes "the law of the land" in the alternative. So as promulgated in 1215, chapter 39[54] read, "No freemen shall be

---

51. Bridges v. California, 314 U.S. 252, 282 (1941) (Frankfurter, J., dissenting).

52. *Id.*

53. For a discussion of the relationship between Magna Carta, civil and canon law, and the right to a jury trial, see chapter 11 of this volume.

54. In the reissued version of Magna Carta subscribed to by King Edward I (r. 1272–1307) in 1297, the original chapter 39 became chapter 29.

taken or imprisoned or disseised or exiled or in any way destroyed, nor will we go upon him nor send upon him, except by the lawful judgment of his peers or by the law of the land."[55]

The recognition of the importance of "judgment of his peers" has produced a number of discussions of trial by jury in Supreme Court decisions. A good example is the majority opinion of Justice Frank Murphy in 1942 in *Glasser v. United States*[56] that overturned a criminal conviction for one defendant while upholding the convictions of two others. Justice Murphy wrote:

> Since it was first recognized in Magna Carta, trial by jury has been a prized shield against oppression, but while proclaiming trial by jury as "the glory of the English law," Blackstone was careful to note that it was but a "privilege." Commentaries, Book 3, p. 379. Our Constitution transforms that privilege into a right in criminal proceedings in a federal court. This was recognized by Justice Story: "When our more immediate ancestors removed to America, they brought this great privilege (trial by jury in criminal cases) with them, as their birthright and inheritance, as a part of that admirable common law which had fenced round and interposed barriers on every side against the approaches of arbitrary power. It is now incorporated into all our state constitutions as a fundamental right, and the Constitution of the United States would have been justly obnoxious to the most conclusive objection if it had not recognized and confirmed it in the most solemn terms." 2 Story, Const. sec. 1779.[57]

The first Justice John Harlan wrestled with the question of what a right to trial by jury meant in 1898 in *Thompson v. Utah*.[58] In particular the issue was whether trial by jury meant 12 jurors for a felony tried in Utah when it was still a territory and before it became a state. Justice Harlan analyzed the issue at some length, including a discussion of the meaning of Magna Carta:

> Assuming, then, that the provisions of the constitution relating to trials for crimes and to criminal prosecutions apply to the territories of the United States, the next inquiry is whether the jury referred to in the original constitution and in the sixth amendment is a jury constituted, as it was at common law, of twelve persons, neither more

---

55. There are numerous online sources for reading the text of Magna Carta. One helpful source is *Treasure in Full: Magna Carta, Translation*, BL.UK, http://www.bl.uk /treasures/magnacarta/translation/mc_trans.html (last visited May 9, 2014).

56. Glasser v. United States, 315 U.S. 60 (1942).

57. *Id.* at 84–85.

58. Thompson v. Utah, 170 U.S. 343 (1898).

nor less. . . . This question must be answered in the affirmative. When Magna Charta declared that no freeman should be deprived of life, etc., "but by the judgment of his peers or by the law of the land," it referred to a trial by twelve jurors. Those who emigrated to this country from England brought with them this great privilege "as their birthright and inheritance, as a part of that admirable common law which had fenced around and interposed barriers on every side against the approaches of arbitrary power." 2 Story, Const. § 1779. . . . So, in 1 Hale, P. C. 33: "The law of England hath afforded the best method of trial that is possible of this and all other matters of fact, namely, by a jury of twelve men all concurring in the same judgment, by the testimony of witnesses viva voce in the presence of the judge and jury, and by the inspection and direction of the judge." It must consequently be taken that the word "jury" and the words "trial by jury" were placed in the constitution of the United States with reference to the meaning affixed to them in the law as it was in this country and in England at the time of the adoption of that instrument; and that when Thompson committed the offense of grand larceny in the territory of Utah—which was under the complete jurisdiction of the United States for all purposes of government and legislation—the supreme law of the land required that he should be tried by a jury composed of not less than twelve persons.[59]

The question of when trial by jury is required has preoccupied the justices on occasion and led to more references to Magna Carta. In *Duncan v. Louisiana*[60] in 1968, Justice Byron White, writing for the majority, and Justice Hugo Black, concurring, both resorted to Magna Carta for support. White's decision held that Louisiana had to provide jury trials for offenses like battery, which although it was classified as a misdemeanor, carried a possible sentence of two years in prison. Justice White wrote:

The history of trial by jury in criminal cases has been frequently told. It is sufficient for present purposes to say that by the time our Constitution was written, jury trial in criminal cases had been in existence in England for several centuries and carried impressive credentials traced by many to Magna Carta. Its preservation and proper operation as a protection against arbitrary rule were among the major objectives of the revolutionary settlement which was expressed in the Declaration and Bill of Rights of 1689. . . .

---

59. *Id.* at 349–50.
60. Duncan v. Louisiana, 391 U.S. 145 (1968).

Jury trial came to America with English colonists, and received strong support from them. Royal interference with the jury trial was deeply resented.[61]

In the same case, Justice Hugo Black wrote a separate concurring opinion. Black was responding to a dissent in the case by Justice John Harlan. Harlan, reopening a debate on incorporation of the Bill of Rights to apply to the states through the Fourteenth Amendment, suggested that the question of whether the Sixth Amendment guarantee of a jury trial in criminal cases should apply to the states rather than just to the federal government should be one of basic fairness. Justice Black turned to Magna Carta to help establish the fundamental, historical importance of the jury trial and to negate Justice Harlan's suggestion of a case-by-case, right-by-right determination of what is fair. Discussing both due process and the right to fair trials and referring to Chapter 39 of Magna Carta, Black wrote:

Thus the origin of this clause was an attempt by those who wrote Magna Carta to do away with the so-called trials of that period where people were liable to sudden arrest and summary conviction in courts and by judicial commissions with no sure and definite procedural protections and under laws that might have been improvised to try their particular cases. Chapter 39 of Magna Carta was a guarantee that the government would take neither life, liberty, nor property without a trial in accord with the law of the land that already existed at the time the alleged offense was committed. This means that the Due Process Clause gives all Americans, whoever they are and wherever they happen to be, the right to be tried by independent and unprejudiced courts using established procedures and applying valid pre-existing laws. There is not one word of legal history that justifies making the term "due process of law" mean a guarantee of a trial free from laws and conduct which the courts deem at the time to be "arbitrary," "unreasonable," "unfair," or "contrary to civilized standards." The due process of law standard for a trial is one in accordance with the Bill of Rights and laws passed pursuant to constitutional power, guaranteeing to all alike a trial under the general law of the land.[62]

Perhaps it is not surprising that Magna Carta made at least a cameo appearance when the Supreme Court in 2005 confronted the question of whether federal judges were in effect usurping the role of the jury under federal sentencing guidelines.[63] The Court ruled that standards for jury trials

---

61. *Id.* at 151, 152 (citations omitted).
62. *Id.* at 169–70 (Black, J., concurring).
63. United States v. Booker, 543 U.S. 220 (2005).

under the Sixth Amendment did apply to the federal sentencing guidelines and that the mandatory nature of the guidelines needed to be modified. Justice John Paul Stevens wrote one of two lead opinions and observed about Sixth Amendment principles:

> Those principles are unquestionably applicable to the Guidelines. They are not the product of recent innovations in our jurisprudence, but rather have their genesis in the ideals our constitutional tradition assimilated from the common law. . . . The Framers of the Constitution understood the threat of "judicial despotism" that could arise from "arbitrary punishments upon arbitrary convictions" without the benefit of a jury in criminal cases. . . . The Founders presumably carried this concern from England, in which the right to a jury trial had been enshrined since the Magna Carta.[64]

Stevens then cited the Court's earlier decision in *Apprendi v. New Jersey*,[65] in which he also wrote the majority opinion. Although *Apprendi* did not specifically mention Magna Carta, Stevens wrote from *Apprendi*:

> [T]he historical foundation for our recognition of these principles extends down centuries into the common law. "[T]o guard against a spirit of oppression and tyranny on the part of rulers," and "as the great bulwark of [our] civil and political liberties," trial by jury has been understood to require that "the truth of every accusation, whether preferred in the shape of indictment, information, or appeal, should afterwards be confirmed by the unanimous suffrage of twelve of [the defendant's] equals and neighbours."[66]

C. Speedy Trial

Along with the right to trial by jury, the Supreme Court referred to Magna Carta at some length to establish the pedigree of a right to a speedy trial. The most extended discussion of this right is by Chief Justice Earl Warren in 1967 in *Klopfer v. North Carolina*.[67] Covering some of the same ground used to analyze the right to trial by jury, Warren wrote for a unanimous court:

---

64. *Id*. at 238–39.
65. Apprendi v. New Jersey, 530 U.S. 466 (2000).
66. *Id*. at 477, *quoted in United States v. Booker*, 543 U.S. at 239.
67. Klopfer v. N.C., 386 U.S. 213 (1967).

We hold here that the right to a speedy trial is as fundamental as any of the rights secured by the Sixth Amendment. That right has its roots at the very foundation of our English law heritage. Its first articulation in modern jurisprudence appears to have been made in Magna Carta (1215), wherein it was written, "We will sell to no man, we will not deny or defer to any man either justice or right"; . . . but evidence of recognition of the right to speedy justice in even earlier times is found in the Assize of Clarendon (1166). . . . By the late thirteenth century, justices, armed with commissions of gaol delivery and/or oyer and ter-miner . . . were visiting the countryside three times a year. . . . These justices, Sir Edward Coke wrote in Part II of his Institutes, "have not suffered the prisoner to be long detained, but at their next coming have given the prisoner full and speedy justice . . . without detaining him long in prison." . . . To Coke, prolonged detention without trial would have been contrary to the law and custom of England; . . . but he also believed that the delay in trial, by itself, would be an improper denial of justice. In his explication of Chapter 29 of the Magna Carta, he wrote that the words "We will sell to no man, we will not deny or defer to any man either justice or right" had the following effect:

> "And therefore, every subject of this realme, for injury done to him in bonis terris, vel persona, by any other subject, be he eccle-siasticall, or temporall, free, or bond, man, or woman, old, or young, or be he outlawed, excommunicated, or any other with-out exception, may take his remedy by the course of the law, and have justice, and right for the injury done to him, freely without sale, fully without any deniall, and speedily without delay. . . ."

Coke's Institutes were read in the American Colonies by virtually every student of the law . . . . Indeed, Thomas Jefferson wrote that at the time he studied law (1762-1767), "Coke Lyttleton was the universal elemen-tary book of law students." . . . And to John Rutledge of South Caro-lina, the Institutes seemed "to be almost the foundation of our law." . . . To Coke, in turn, Magna Carta was one of the fundamental bases of English liberty. . . . Thus, it is not surprising that when George Mason drafted the first of the colonial bills of rights, . . . he set forth a principle of Magna Carta, using phraseology similar to that of Coke's explication: "[I]n all capital or criminal prosecutions," the Virginia Declaration of Rights of 1776 provided, "a man hath a right . . . to a speedy trial . . . ." That this right was considered fundamental at this early period in our history is evidenced by its guarantee in the constitutions of several of the States of the new nation, . . . as well as by its prominent position in the

Sixth Amendment. Today, each of the 50 States guarantees the right to a speedy trial to its citizens.

The history of the right to a speedy trial and its reception in this country clearly establish that it is one of the most basic rights preserved by our Constitution.[68]

More than most Supreme Court references to Magna Carta, Chief Justice Warren's discussion is interesting and somewhat unique in that he really uses the history, including Magna Carta and Coke's commentaries, to establish the importance and legitimacy of the right. He seems to put more emphasis than some other discussions on the substantial influence of Magna Carta.

D. Habeas Corpus

The right to habeas corpus does not appear directly in Magna Carta. But Supreme Court justices have referred to Magna Carta in cases involving habeas corpus as a way of connecting the dots between the expectation of fair and impartial trials and habeas corpus as the means of vindicating that expectation. Justice William Brennan said as much in 1963 in *Fay v. Noia*.[69] Noting that a habeas corpus bill was proposed in the British House of Commons in 1593, Brennan wrote, "Although it was not enacted, this bill accurately prefigured the union of the right to due process drawn from Magna Charta and the remedy of habeas corpus accomplished in the next century."[70]

Indeed, habeas corpus became the law in Great Britain in 1679, and Supreme Court justices would later observe the importance of this development. Justice Antonin Scalia, dissenting when the Supreme Court reviewed detention procedures in the war on terror in *Hamdi v. Rumsfeld*,[71] observed, "The struggle between subject and Crown continued, and culminated in the Habeas Corpus Act of 1679 . . . described by Blackstone as a 'second magna carta, and stable bulwark of our liberties.'"[72]

Historical pedigree seemed to be a repeat theme in the Supreme Court's war on terror decisions. In *Boumediene v. Bush*,[73] Justice Anthony Kennedy used Magna Carta to help establish the historical importance of habeas corpus and, of greater significance to the development of the law, to demon-

---

68. *Id.* at 223–26 (footnotes omitted).
69. Fay v. Noia, 372 U.S. 391 (1963).
70. *Id.* at 402.
71. Hamdi v. Rumsfeld, 542 U.S. 507 (2004).
72. *Id.* at 557, citing 1 Blackstone 133 (Scalia, J., dissenting).
73. Boumediene v. Bush, 553 U.S. 723 (2008).

strate its application to restrain the actions of the crown or the executive. Justice Anthony Kennedy wrote:

> Magna Carta decreed that no man would be imprisoned contrary to the law of the land. . . . Important as the principle was, the Barons at Runnymede prescribed no specific legal process to enforce it. Holdsworth tells us, however, that gradually the writ of habeas corpus became the means by which the promise of Magna Carta was fulfilled. 9 W. Holdsworth, A History of English Law 112 (1926) (hereinafter Holdsworth).
>
> The development was painstaking, even by the centuries-long measures of English constitutional history. The writ was known and used in some form at least as early as the reign of Edward I. Id., at 108–125. Yet at the outset it was used to protect not the rights of citizens but those of the King and his courts. The early courts were considered agents of the Crown, designed to assist the King in the exercise of his power. . . . Thus the writ, while it would become part of the foundation of liberty for the King's subjects, was in its earliest use a mechanism for securing compliance with the King's laws. . . . Over time it became clear that by issuing the writ of habeas corpus common-law courts sought to enforce the King's prerogative to inquire into the authority of a jailer to hold a prisoner. . . . [74]
>
> Even so, from an early date it was understood that the King, too, was subject to the law. As the writers said of Magna Carta, "it means this, that the king is and shall be below the law." 1 F. Pollock & F. Maitland, History of English Law 173 (2d ed. 1909). . . . And, by the 1600's, the writ was deemed less an instrument of the King's power and more a restraint upon it. [75]

Justice Kennedy's accurate description of the development of habeas corpus into an instrument of due process and liberty in England as "painstaking" applies also to its development in the United States, as is described in detail in chapter 7 of this volume.

E. Right to Travel

The freedom to travel within the country or abroad is a right that has been recognized by the Supreme Court. It is also one that has been traced to Magna Carta. In *Kent v. Dulles*,[76] Justice William O. Douglas, denying the

---

74. *Id.* at 740.
75. *Id.* at 741 (some citations from Supreme Court opinion omitted).
76. Kent v. Dulles, 357 U.S. 116 (1958).

authority of the U.S. Department of State to refuse to issue passports to avowed Communists, relied on Magna Carta to underscore the freedom of movement of individuals. Justice Douglas wrote, "The right to travel is a part of the 'liberty' of which the citizen cannot be deprived without the due process of law under the Fifth Amendment. So much is conceded by the Solicitor General. In Anglo-Saxon law that right was emerging at least as early as the Magna Carta."[77] To support the idea, Douglas relied on chapter 42 of Magna Carta, which establishes the freedom of individuals to leave and return to England.[78]

F. Right to Bear Arms

In finding that the Second Amendment confers an individual right to bear arms in 2008,[79] Justice Antonin Scalia did not rely directly on Magna Carta. But he quoted favorably a Georgia Supreme Court ruling from 1846 that traced the historical origins of the right to bear arms and then likened the U.S. Constitution to Magna Carta. Scalia wrote in *District of Columbia v. Heller*:

> In *Nunn v. State*, 1 Ga. 243, 251 (1846), the Georgia Supreme Court construed the Second Amendment as protecting the "natural right of self-defence" and therefore struck down a ban on carrying pistols openly. Its opinion perfectly captured the way in which the operative clause of the Second Amendment furthers the purpose announced in the prefatory clause, in continuity with the English right:
>
> > "The right of the whole people, old and young, men, women and boys, and not militia only, to keep and bear arms of every description, and not such merely as are used by the militia, shall not be infringed, curtailed, or broken in upon, in the smallest degree; and all this for the important end to be attained: the rearing up and qualifying a well-regulated militia, so vitally necessary to the security of a free State. Our opinion is, that any law, State or Federal, is repugnant to the Constitution, and void, which contravenes this right, originally belonging to our forefathers, trampled under foot by Charles I and his two wicked sons and successors, re-established by the revolution of 1688, conveyed to this land of liberty by the colonists, and finally incorporated conspicuously in our own Magna Charta!"[80]

---

77. *Id.* at 125.
78. *Id.*
79. District of Columbia v. Heller, 554 U.S. 570 (2008).
80. *Id.* at 612–13.

G. Cruel and Unusual Punishment

The Eighth Amendment protects against "cruel and unusual punishment," an oft-analyzed and oft-debated phrase. Some justices have looked to Magna Carta to find the origin of this right and to help explain its meaning.

One such case was *Trop v. Dulles*,[81] in which the Court said that Congress could not authorize that a citizen be stripped of citizenship because of desertion from the military during wartime. Chief Justice Earl Warren examined the history of the phrase:

> The exact scope of the constitutional phrase "cruel and unusual" has not been detailed by this Court. . . . But the basic policy reflected in these words is firmly established in the Anglo-American tradition of criminal justice. The phrase in our Constitution was taken directly from the English Declaration of Rights of 1688 . . . and the principle it represents can be traced back to the Magna Carta. . . . The basic concept underlying the Eighth Amendment is nothing less than the dignity of man. While the State has the power to punish, the Amendment stands to assure that this power be exercised within the limits of civilized standards. Fines, imprisonment and even execution may be imposed depending upon the enormity of the crime, but any technique outside the bounds of these traditional penalties is constitutionally suspect.[82]

H. Excessive Fines

The Eighth Amendment to the Constitution also prohibits government from levying excessive fines. In *Browning-Ferris Industries of Vermont v. Kelco Disposal, Inc.*,[83] the Supreme Court ruled in 1989 that the term "excessive fines" applied to criminal penalties and was not applicable to the award of punitive damages in civil cases. In arguments made in the case, lawyers for Browning-Ferris relied on Magna Carta, among other sources, to suggest that excessive fines historically meant monetary penalties, both criminal and civil.

Writing for the Court, Justice Harry Blackmun discussed Magna Carta at some length. Ultimately, he concluded that the history of fines levied by the king, called amercements, did not establish that the excessive fines clause applied to punitive damages. Blackmun relied very heavily on practice at the time of Magna Carta and differences as the law evolved under the U.S. Constitution. Blackmun observed:

---

81. Trop v. Dulles, 356 U.S. 86 (1958).
82. *Id.* at 99–100 (footnotes omitted).
83. Browning-Ferris Indus. of Vt. v. Kelco Disposal, Inc., 492 U.S. 257 (1989).

Amercements were payments to the Crown, and were required of individuals who were "in the King's mercy," because of some act offensive to the Crown. Those acts ranged from what we today would consider minor criminal offenses, such as breach of the King's peace with force and arms, to "civil" wrongs against the King, such as infringing "a final concord" made in the King's court. . . . Amercements were an "all-purpose" royal penalty. . . . [84]

In response to the frequent, and occasionally abusive, use of amercements by the King, Magna Carta included several provisions placing limits on the circumstances under which a person could be amerced, and the amount of the amercement. . . . The barons who forced John to agree to Magna Carta sought to reduce arbitrary royal power, and in particular to limit the King's use of amercements as a source of royal revenue, and as a weapon against enemies of the Crown. . . . The Amercements Clause of Magna Carta limited these abuses in four ways: by requiring that one be amerced only for some genuine harm to the Crown; by requiring that the amount of the amercement be proportioned to the wrong; by requiring that the amercement not be so large as to deprive him of his livelihood; and by requiring that the amount of the amercement be fixed by one's peers, sworn to amerce only in a proportionate amount. . . .

Petitioners, and some commentators . . . find in this history a basis for concluding that the Excessive Fines Clause operates to limit the ability of a civil jury to award punitive damages. We do not agree. Whatever uncertainties surround the use of amercements prior to Magna Carta, the compact signed at Runnymede was aimed at putting limits on the power of the King, on the "tyrannical extortions, under the name of amercements, with which John had oppressed his people," T. Taswell-Langmead, English Constitutional History 83 (T. Plucknett 10th ed. 1946), whether that power be exercised for purposes of oppressing political opponents, for raising revenue in unfair ways, or for any other improper use. . . . These concerns are clearly inapposite in a case where a private party receives exemplary damages from another party, and the government has no share in the recovery. . . .

Petitioners ultimately rely on little more than the fact that the distinction between civil and criminal law was cloudy (and perhaps nonexistent) at the time of Magna Carta. But any overlap between civil and criminal procedure at that time does nothing to support petitioners' case, when all the indications are that English courts never have understood the amercements clauses to be relevant to private

---

84. *Id.* at 269.

damages of any kind, either then or at any later time. . . . It is difficult to understand how Magna Carta, or the English Bill of Rights as viewed through the lens of Magna Carta, compels us to read our Eighth Amendment's Excessive Fines Clause as applying to punitive damages when those documents themselves were never so applied. [85]

Browning-Ferris represents one of the rare occasions in which the justices actually argue among themselves over what lessons may be drawn from the experience and history of Magna Carta. Justice Sandra Day O'Connor, in an opinion concurring in part and dissenting in part, disputed Justice Blackmun's lessons from the history of Magna Carta. For example, Justice O'Connor wrote:

The Court argues that Chapter 20 of Magna Carta and Article 10 of the English Bill of Rights were concerned only with limiting governmental abuses of power. Because amercements and fines were paid to the Crown, the Court assumes that governmental abuses can only take place when the sovereign itself exacts a penalty. That assumption, however, simply recalls the historical accident that, prior to the mid-18th century, monetary sanctions filled the coffers of the King and his barons.[86]

O'Connor also disputed Blackmun's analysis of the history when she observed, "The link between the gradual disappearance of the amercement and the emergence of punitive damages provides strong historical support for applying the Excessive Fines Clause to awards of punitive damages."[87]

I. The Right to Petition the Government

The First Amendment includes, among other provisions, the right to "petition the government for a redress of grievances." In *Adderly v. Florida*,[88] the majority found that the conviction of student protesters on jail grounds did not violate their First Amendment rights. Justice William O. Douglas in dissent argued for the historic origins of the right to petition government to be heard. Citing chapter 61 of Magna Carta,[89] Douglas said, "The historical

---

85. *Id.* at 270–73 (some citations in Supreme Court opinion omitted).
86. *Id.* at 291–92 (O'Connor, J., concurring in part and dissenting in part).
87. *Id.* at 292.
88. 385 U.S. 39 (1966).
89. 385 U.S. at 49 (Douglas, J., dissenting) ("'[T]hat if we or our justiciar, or our bailiffs, or any of our servants shall have done wrong in any way toward any one, or shall have transgressed any of the articles of peace or security and the wrong shall have been shown to four barons of the aforesaid twenty-five barons, let those four barons come to

antecedents of the right to petition for the redress of grievances run deep, and strike to the heart of the democratic philosophy."[90]

Justice Anthony Kennedy also looked to Magna Carta for historical pedigree in 2011 in *Borough of Duryea, Pa. v. Guarnieri*.[91] Writing for the majority in rejecting a claim under the petition clause, Kennedy said:

> The right to petition traces its origins to Magna Carta, which confirmed the right of barons to petition the King. W. McKechnie, Magna Carta: A Commentary on the Great Charter of King John 467 (rev. 2d ed. 1958). The Magna Carta itself was King John's answer to a petition from the barons.[92]

J.   Land Ownership and Navigable Waters Control

No discussion of the use of Magna Carta in the Supreme Court would be complete without some consideration of cases involving ownership of property and waterways.

In *Appleby v. City of New York*,[93] for example, Chief Justice William Howard Taft, writing for the court in 1926, cited an earlier ruling by a New York court that observed, "By Magna Charta, and many subsequent statutes, the powers of the king are limited, and he cannot now deprive his subjects of these rights by granting the public navigable waters to individuals."[94]

Almost 100 years earlier, Chief Justice Roger Taney also considered Magna Carta in a case involving land in Perth Amboy, New Jersey, that was rich with oyster beds under a portion of the Raritan River.[95] The claim of ownership apparently dated back to a land grant by the King of England, but Chief Justice Taney considered whether after Magna Carta, the king could grant land that was covered by navigable waters.[96] In holding that control of the land under the river passed to the state of New Jersey as a public trust, Chief Justice Taney said that "the question must be regarded

---

us or to our justiciar, if we are out of the kingdom, laying before us the transgression, and let them ask that we cause that transgression to be corrected without delay.' Sources of Our Liberties 21 (Perry ed. 1959).").

90. *Id.*

91. Borough of Duryea, Pa. v. Guarnieri, 131 S. Ct. 2488 (2011).

92. *Id.* at 2499.

93. Appleby v. N.Y.C., 271 U.S. 364 (1926).

94. *Id.* at 382, citing Lansing v. Smith, 4 Wend. (N.Y.) 9 (1829) (Supreme Court of Errors of New York).

95. Martin v. Waddell's Lessee, 41 U.S. 367 (1842).

96. *Id.* at 410.

as settled in England, against the right of the king, since Magna Charta, to make such a grant."[97]

IV.   Other References to Magna Carta

Besides the rights already considered, there are a small number of other references to Magna Carta in different contexts.

A.   Antitrust

One of the most frequent references to Magna Carta is through metaphorical usage, exalting another provision of law by comparing it to Magna Carta. Justice Thurgood Marshall, reflecting on the importance of antitrust laws in a 1972 opinion,[98] observed, "Antitrust laws in general, and the Sherman Act in particular, are the Magna Carta of free enterprise."[99]

Justice Marshall's line was repeated by other justices in a half dozen opinions over the ensuing 30 years.[100]

B.   Church and State

References to Magna Carta have been relatively scarce in the context of the religion clauses of the First Amendment. The clearest example is one discussed earlier in this chapter, when Chief Justice John Roberts wrote in 2012:

> Controversy between church and state over religious offices is hardly new. In 1215, the issue was addressed in the very first clause of Magna Carta. There King John agreed that "the English church shall be free, and shall have its rights undiminished and its liberties unimpaired." The King in particular accepted the "freedom of elections," a right "thought to be of the greatest necessity and importance to the English church." J. Holt, Magna Carta App. IV, p. 317, cl. 1 (1965).[101]

Perhaps the paucity of references to Magna Carta regarding religious freedom should not be surprising. As described in chapter 8 of this book,

---

97. *Id.*

98. United States v. Topco Assoc., Inc., 405 U.S. 596 (1972).

99. *Id.* at 610.

100. *See, e.g.,* Verizon Communications Inc. v. Law Offices of Curtis v. Trinko, LLP, 540 U.S. 398 (2004) (Scalia, J.) ("The Sherman Act is indeed 'the Magna Carta of free enterprise.'").

101. Hosanna-Tabor Evangelical Lutheran Church v. Equal Emp't Opportunity Comm'n, 565 U.S. ___ (2012).

none of the versions of Magna Carta contained the idea of freedom of religion as that is now conceptualized, that is, to include a person's right to choose and change his or her religion and to exercise that belief either alone or with others free from discrimination.

V. Distinguishing Magna Carta: Freedom of Speech

There is one significant set of rights for which Supreme Court justices have made clear that Magna Carta does *not* provide the benchmark for constitutional development. When it comes to freedom of speech, the First Amendment and the Supreme Court have followed an entirely different path, according to the leading opinions.

In *Bridges v. California*,[102] Justice Hugo Black discussed the evolution of free speech as following an entirely different path from what developed under Magna Carta. Black said:

> In any event it need not detain us, for to assume that English common law in this field became ours is to deny the generally accepted historical belief that "one of the objects of the Revolution was to get rid of the English common law on liberty of speech and of the press." 7 Schofield, Freedom of the Press in the United States. 9 Publications Amer. Sociol. Soc., 67, 76.
>
> More specifically, it is to forget the environment in which the First Amendment was ratified. In presenting the proposals which were later embodied in the Bill of Rights, James Madison, the leader in the preparation of the First Amendment, said: "Although I know whenever the great rights, the trial by jury, freedom of the press, or liberty of conscience, come in question in that body (Parliament), the invasion of them is resisted by able advocates, yet their Magna Charta does not contain any one provision for the security of those rights, respecting which the people of America are most alarmed. The freedom of the press and rights of conscience, those choicest privileges of the people, are unguarded in the British Constitution." 1 Annals of Congress 1789-1790, 434. And Madison elsewhere wrote that "the state of the press . . . under the common law, cannot . . . be the standard of its freedom in the United States." VI Writings of James Madison 1790-1802, 387.[103]

---

102. *Bridges*, 314 U.S. at 282.
103. *Id.* at 264.

For freedom of speech, therefore, Magna Carta is not the iconic fountain of liberty that it has become in regard to other issues.

VI.   Conclusion

There is no question that Magna Carta has influenced decisions by the justices of the Supreme Court. The venerable text and rich history of Magna Carta do not have the force of law per se in Supreme Court jurisprudence, since the document predates the formation of the United States. But the principles articulated on a field in Runnymede in 1215 and reiterated and recast on numerous occasions thereafter clearly have played an important part in the evolution of thinking about rights and government authority; concepts of critical importance to Supreme Court justices and Supreme Court jurisprudence.

As the many cases and opinions make clear, it is hard to top the pedigree of being able to trace a right back to Magna Carta or of attributing particular meaning to development at the time of Magna Carta. Perhaps this is not surprising in a judicial system that relies so heavily on precedent and that defines rights implicit in the Constitution based on history and tradition.

Resort to Magna Carta to define the dimensions of a right has the unique ability to transcend ideological differences among the justices. Reliance on Magna Carta to clarify our understanding of the Constitution and its origins has been used by liberal and conservative justices alike.

After 800 years, the tradition of justices turning to Magna Carta remains strong, and Magna Carta will undoubtedly be resorted to by justices in the future as an iconic fountain of liberty.

Chapter 6
Magna Carta and Executive Power

Louis Fisher

The decision by King John (r. 1199–1216) at Runnymede in 1215 to agree to Magna Carta has sparked many claims about its relationship to executive power. Anne Pallister writes that the Great Charter "was regarded as fundamental and inalienable law, limiting upon and superior to the crown, and repeated confirmations in the thirteenth and fourteenth centuries further enhanced its position as higher law."[1] She claimed that William Blackstone, in his influential *Commentaries on the Laws of England*, argued there must be in all governments a supreme authority, and that the sovereign power in England resides in Parliament "whose authority is omnipotent and boundless."[2] Blackstone concluded that what Parliament "doth, no authority upon earth can undo." On the basis of such remarks, Pallister said that modern lawyers "have tended to regard Blackstone's *Commentaries* as an authoritative statement of the modern doctrine of parliamentary sovereignty."[3] At the same time, Blackstone regarded the rights protected in chapter 39 of Magna Carta as fundamental rights in England:

> To bereave a man of life, or by violence to confiscate his estate, without accusation or trial, would be so gross and notorious an act of despotism, as must at once convey the alarm of tyranny throughout the whole kingdom. But confinement of the person, by secretly hurrying him to gaol, where his sufferings are unknown and forgotten; is a less public, a less striking and therefore a more dangerous engine of arbitrary government.[4]

---

1. ANNE PALLISTER, MAGNA CARTA: THE HERITAGE OF LIBERTY 2 (1971).
2. *Id*. at 57.
3. *Id*. at 57–58.
4. 1 WILLIAM BLACKSTONE, COMMENTARIES ON THE LAWS OF ENGLAND 131–32 (1765).

I. Blackstone's Prerogative

Whatever encouragement Blackstone might have given to parliamentary supremacy and whatever importance he might have attributed to Magna Carta's chapter 39, he is also known for promoting broad and exclusive powers for the king in external affairs. He defined the king's prerogative as "those rights and capacities which the king enjoys alone."[5] Some of those powers were *direct*, that is, powers that are "rooted in and spring from the king's political person," including the right to send and receive ambassadors and the power "of making war or peace."[6] By placing in the king the sole power to make war, individuals who entered society and accepted the laws of government necessarily surrendered any private right to make war: "It would indeed be extremely improper, that any number of subjects should have the power of binding the supreme magistrate, and putting him against his will in a state of war."[7] If private citizens could not encroach upon this royal prerogative, neither could Parliament.

Blackstone recognized other exclusive foreign policy powers for the executive. The king could make "a treaty with a foreign state, which shall irrevocably bind the nation."[8] He could issue letters of marque (authorizing private citizens to use their ships and other possessions to undertake military actions) and reprisal (retaliatory military actions short of war). As he explained, that power was "nearly related to, and plainly derived from, that other of making war."[9] Blackstone regarded the king as "the generalissimo, or the first in military command," who had the "sole power of raising and regulating fleets and armies."[10] When the king exercised those powers, he "is and ought to be absolute; that is, so far absolute, that there is no legal authority that can either delay or resist him."[11]

Article I, Section 8 of the U.S. Constitution vests in Congress the authority to raise and support armies, provide and maintain a navy, and make regulations for the land and naval forces. The implications of Blackstone's position—that the king possesses certain powers that may not be limited by any legal authority, including the legislative branch—has become known as "inherent powers." Several administrations, starting with Harry Truman, advanced that view of presidential power. The existence of inherent power, rooted in the British prerogative model, was rejected by the framers and has been consistently repudiated by Congress and federal courts. Unfortunately,

---

5. *Id.* at 232.
6. *Id.* at 232–33 (emphasis in original).
7. *Id.* at 249.
8. *Id.* at 244.
9. *Id.* at 250.
10. *Id.* at 254.
11. *Id.* at 243.

lawmakers, federal judges, and scholars continue to treat "implied" and "inherent" as synonymous. They are fundamentally different concepts. Implied powers must be drawn reasonably from enumerated powers and are subject to checks from other branches. Inherent powers, as the term indicates, are vested exclusively in a particular person or office and may not, in theory, be responsive to the system of checks and balances.[12] Before discussing inherent powers, it is important to understand how the framers viewed the British model of government. At the same time, it is necessary to clear up some confusion about the national government in the United States being one of enumerated powers.

II. Breaking with the British Model

The American framers studied the prevailing models of government in ancient times and in contemporary Europe. They knew that foreign policy in England was largely placed with the executive. It was their decision, after personal experience and extended debate, to vest a substantial part of that power in the legislative branch. Their judgment drew heavily from a political commitment to self-government. In a republic, the sovereign power rests with citizens and the individuals they select to represent them in Congress. Some powers of foreign affairs belong solely to the president, such as receiving ambassadors, but they are few.

English colonists carried their rights as British nationals, including those deriving from Magna Carta, when they came to North America (as will be described later).[13] Perhaps for that reason, a number of federal courts and scholars have drawn presidential power from English sources. In a state secrets privilege case in 1953, *United States v. Reynolds*, the Supreme Court noted that the experience of English courts with this privilege "has been more extensive" than in the United States "but still relatively slight compared with other evidentiary privileges."[14] The Court cited language from a British case of 1942 for guidance.[15] When the Third Circuit decided this case two years earlier, it rejected the government's reliance on the British case, explaining that the plans of the submarine *Thetis* "were obviously military secrets," the suit was between private parties (*Reynolds* involved a private suit against the government), and the British case should not be "controlling

---

12. LOUIS FISHER, THE LAW OF THE EXECUTIVE BRANCH: PRESIDENTIAL POWER 58–62, 68–73 (2014).

13. A.E. DICK HOWARD, THE ROAD FROM RUNNYMEDE: MAGNA CARTA AND CONSTITUTIONALISM IN AMERICA xi, 88 (1968).

14. United States v. Reynolds, 345 U.S. 1, 7 (1953).

15. *Id.* at 8, n.20 (citing Duncan v. Cammell, Laird & Co., [1942] A.C. 624, 638).

in any event."[16] The basic reason: "For whatever may be true in Great Britain the Government of the United States is one of checks and balances."[17]

In 2001, an article by Saikrishna Prakash and Michael Ramsey advocated a "residual" presidential power that incorporates broad executive prerogatives developed by John Locke and William Blackstone from British practice.[18] Although they acknowledge that the president "had a greatly diminished foreign affairs power as compared to the English monarchy,"[19] they looked to Locke, Blackstone, and other British writers of the 18th century to treat "foreign affairs as an aspect of executive power."[20] Claims of "residual" authority open the door to relying on British precedents to define broadly the authority of the U.S. president. In a separate study published in 2001, Ramsey rejected the notion that the president possesses "inherent powers in foreign affairs."[21] The concept of inherent power will be examined closely in a subsequent section.

A study by Prakash in 2003 developed the theory of executive branch "essentialism" (powers essential in carrying out the duties of a president). According to this theory, "even if the Constitution did not vest the American executive with all of the English crown's executive powers, it still might have codified the executive's essential power."[22] John Yoo, in a lengthy article in 1996, argued that the U.S. Constitution "did not break with the tradition of their English, state, and revolutionary predecessors, but instead followed in their footsteps."[23] He concluded that "the war powers provisions of the Constitution are best understood as an adoption, rather than a rejection, of the traditional British approach to war powers."[24] This is a curious argument. Blackstone vested all external affairs with the king. Most of those royal prerogatives appear in Article I of the U.S. Constitution, setting forth the powers of Congress.

A number of scholars reject this dependence on British precedents. Writing in 1989, Louis Henkin observed that the framers "turned their backs on Locke and Montesquieu, on British and European practice."[25] More recent

---

16. Reynolds v. United States, 192 F.2d 987, 997 (3d Cir. 1951).

17. Id.

18. Saikrishna B. Prakash & Michael D. Ramsey, *The Executive Power over Foreign Affairs*, 111 Yale L.J. 231, 234–36 (2001).

19. Id. at 254.

20. Id. at 272.

21. Michael D. Ramsey, *The Myth of Extraconstitutional Foreign Affairs Power*, 42 Wm. & Mary L. Rev. 379, 442 (2001).

22. Saikrishna Prakash, *The Essential Meaning of Executive Power*, 2003 U. Ill. L. Rev. 701, 810 (2003).

23. John C. Yoo, *The Continuation of Politics by Other Means: The Original Understanding of War Powers*, 84 Cal. L. Rev. 167, 197 (1996).

24. Id. at 242.

25. Louis Henkin, *Treaties in a Constitutional Democracy*, 10 Mich. J. Int'l L. 406, 409 (1989).

evaluations conclude that the framers "self-conscious[ly] discarded the British model of government."[26] Other scholars agree that Yoo "relies too much on the English experience, without recognizing ways the Framers sought to depart from that experience."[27] Writing in 2007, David Gray Adler concluded that the framers "rejected the British model—the monarchical model, a design that emphasized executive unilateralism."[28]

A study in 2009 reviewed British history to demonstrate that the framers dismissed royal prerogatives and limited the president to a combination of enumerated and implied powers.[29] In 2011, I offered this assessment: "The American framers could not have been more explicit in rejecting the British model of an executive who possesses exclusive control over external affairs."[30] An article in 2012 noted that the framers "made it clear that they consciously and deliberately rejected the British constitutional model, particularly with respect to the powers of war and foreign affairs."[31]

III. Creating a Republic in America

Unlike England, with its history of monarchy over which Parliament gradually gained some control, particularly through the power of the purse, America as a national government began with a legislative branch and no other. After America declared its independence from England, all national powers (including executive) were vested in a Continental Congress.[32] By the time delegates assembled at the Philadelphia Convention in 1787 to draft the Constitution, it was understood that the new government would have three separate branches to handle executive, legislative, and judicial duties.

Charles Pinckney said he was for "a vigorous Executive but was afraid the Executive powers of [the existing] Congress might extend to peace & war which would render the Executive a Monarchy, of the worst kind, towit

---

26. Curtis A. Bradley & Martin S. Flaherty, *Executive Branch Essentialism and Foreign Affairs*, 102 MICH. L. REV. 545, 552 (2004).

27. Michael D. Ramsey, *Toward a Rule of Law in Foreign Affairs*, 106 COLUM. L. REV. 1450, 1458 (2006).

28. David Gray Adler, *George W. Bush and the Abuse of History: The Constitution and Presidential Power in Foreign Affairs*, 12 UCLA J. INT'L L. & FOREIGN AFFAIRS 75, 76 (2007).

29. Robert J. Reinstein, *The Limits of Executive Power*, 59 AM. U. L. REV. 259 (2009).

30. Louis Fisher, *John Yoo and the Republic*, 41 PRESIDENTIAL STUD. Q. 177, 183 (2011).

31. Janet Cooper Alexander, *John Yoo's War Powers: The Law Review and the World*, 100 CAL. L. REV. 101, 120 (2012).

32. EDMUND CODY BURNETT, THE CONTINENTAL CONGRESS 118–21 (1964 ed.).

[sic] an elective one."[33] John Rutledge wanted the executive power placed in a single person, "tho' he was not for giving him the power of war and peace."[34] James Wilson supported a single executive but "did not consider the Prerogatives of the British Monarch as a proper guide in defining the Executive powers. Some of these prerogatives were of a Legislative nature. Among others that of war & peace &c."[35] Edmund Randolph worried about executive power, calling it "the fœtus of monarchy."[36] The delegates at the convention, he said, had "no motive to be governed by the British Governmt. as our prototype." If the United States had no other choice it might adopt the British model, but "the fixt genius of the people of America required a different form of Government."[37] Wilson agreed that the British model "was inapplicable to the situation of this Country; the extent of which was so great, and the manners so republican, that nothing but a great confederated Republic would do for it."[38]

In a lengthy speech at the Philadelphia Convention, Alexander Hamilton shared with his colleagues that in his "private opinion he had no scruple in declaring . . . that the British Govt. was the best in the world."[39] Having announced his personal preference, he admitted that the models of Locke and Blackstone had no application to America and its commitment to republican government.[40] Hamilton's draft constitution required the executive to seek the Senate's approval for treaties and ambassadors. The Senate would have "the sole power of declaring war."[41] In *Federalist* No. 69, Hamilton detailed the vast difference between the war powers vested in the British king and the "inferior" powers granted to the president.[42]

On August 17, 1787, the delegates debated language to give Congress the power to "make war." Charles Pinckney objected that legislative proceedings "were too slow" for the safety of the country in an emergency.[43] He anticipated that Congress would meet "but once a year."[44] Also, members of the House of Representatives would be "too numerous for such

---

33. 1 The Records of the Federal Convention of 1787 at 64–65 (Max Farrand ed., 1966).

34. *Id.* at 65.

35. *Id.* at 65–66.

36. *Id.* at 66.

37. *Id.*

38. *Id.*

39. *Id.* at 288.

40. *Id.* at 291.

41. *Id.* at 292.

42. The Federalist No. 69, 446 (Hamilton) (Benjamin F. Wright ed., 2002).

43. 2 The Records of the Federal Convention of 1787 at 318 (Max Farrand ed., 1966).

44. *Id.*

deliberations."[45] The Senate would be "the best depository, being more acquainted with foreign affairs, and most capable of proper resolutions."[46]

Pierce Butler announced he was "for vesting the [war] power in the President, who will have all the requisite qualities, and will not make war but when the Nation will support it."[47] No delegate offered any support for that position. James Madison and Elbridge Gerry moved to change the draft language from to "make war" to "declare war," thereby "leaving to the Executive the power to repel sudden attacks."[48] The president could take certain defensive actions, particularly when Congress was not in session. Roger Sherman expressed his approval: the president "shd. be able to repel and not to commence war."[49] Gerry expressed astonishment at Butler's proposal. He "never expected to hear in a republic a motion to empower the Executive alone to declare war."[50] Mason was "agst giving the power of war to the Executive, because not <safely> to be trusted with it; or to the Senate, because not so constructed as to be entitled to it."[51] He was for "clogging rather than facilitating war; but for facilitating peace."[52] The motion to strike "make" and insert "declare" carried, seven states to two.[53]

The balance struck by the framers with respect to providing war-making authority to the executive is reminiscent of that struck in Magna Carta to resolve the barons' anger at the increasing scutage (taxes) levied by King John to support his foreign wars. Magna Carta restricts the imposition of scutage in chapter 14, but does not directly curtail the king's power to enter into foreign wars. However, there is no evidence that the framers explicitly relied on Magna Carta for their constitutional principles.

IV. Enumerated and Implied Powers

In *McCulloch v. Maryland*, Chief Justice John Marshall made this claim: "This government is acknowledged by all, to be one of enumerated powers. The principle, that it can exercise only the powers granted to it . . . is now universally admitted."[54] He spoke grandly but carelessly. Someone could have asked him: "If government is one of enumerated powers, where did the Supreme Court get its power of judicial review? It is not expressly

---

45. *Id.*
46. *Id.*
47. *Id.*
48. *Id.*
49. *Id.*
50. *Id.*
51. *Id.* at 319.
52. *Id.*
53. *Id.*
54. McCulloch v. Maryland, 17 U.S. (4 Wheat.) 316, 404 (1819).

provided." As Marshall moved more deeply into his opinion, he had to correct his overbroad statement about enumerated powers. He now reasoned: "[T]here is no phrase in the instrument which, like the articles of confederation, excludes incidental or implied powers; and which requires that everything granted shall be expressly and minutely described."[55]

Marshall benefited from principles developed by the framers, who fully understood the need for implied powers. Madison wrote in *Federalist* No. 44: "No axiom is more clearly established in law, or in reason, than that wherever the end is required, the means are authorized; wherever a general power to do a thing is given, every particular power necessary for doing it is included."[56] During the First Congress, Madison successfully defeated an effort to limit the national government to powers expressly delegated. The Articles of Confederation, which took effect in 1781, gave protection to the states. They retained all powers except those "expressly delegated" to the national government.[57]

In debating the Bill of Rights, someone proposed that the Tenth Amendment include the words "expressly delegated." It would have read: "The powers not expressly delegated to the United States by the Constitution, nor prohibited by it to the States, are reserved to the States respectively, or to the people."[58] Madison objected to the word "expressly" because the functions and duties of the federal government could not be delineated with such precision. It was impossible, he said, to confine a government to the exercise of express or enumerated powers, for there "must necessarily be admitted powers by implication, unless the Constitution descended to recount every minutiae."[59] Madison prevailed. The word "expressly" was deleted.

One of the first implied powers recognized for the president concerned the authority to remove executive officials. The Constitution does not mention that power. From May 19 through June 24, 1789, members of Congress debated the existence of a removal power for the president.[60] Key to the discussion was the president's express duty under Article II to "take Care that the Laws be faithfully executed." What would happen if the head of an executive department could not, or would not, carry out a law? Could the president remove that person? Madison led the debate and both houses of Congress agreed that the president possesses an implied power to remove department heads.

---

55. *Id.*

56. The Federalist No. 44 at 322 (Madison) (Benjamin F. Wright ed., 2002).

57. Art. of Confed., art. II (1781).

58. 1 Annals of Cong. 761 (Aug. 18, 1789).

59. *Id.*

60. A summary of the congressional debate on the president's removal powers appears in Louis Fisher, Constitutional Conflicts between Congress and the President 48–52 (5th ed., 2007).

Congress has a range of implied powers. From the express power to legislate, it necessarily has the power to investigate in order to ensure that it legislates in an informed manner. From the implied power to investigate comes the implied power to issue subpoenas. If someone receives a subpoena to testify and does not appear, or receives a subpoena to provide documents and fails to do so, there is the implied power of Congress to hold that individual in contempt. As the Supreme Court noted in 1821, if Congress lacked the power of contempt it would be "exposed to every indignity and interruption that rudeness, caprice, or even conspiracy, may meditate against it."[61]

The existence of implied powers for the three branches of the national government is regularly acknowledged by federal courts.[62] Nonetheless, the Supreme Court continues to promote the fiction of government confined to enumerated powers. In 1995, while striking down a congressional effort to regulate guns in schoolyards, the Court confidently announced: "We start with first principles. The Constitution creates a Federal Government of enumerated powers."[63] It is not a first principle. In 1997, the Court again stated: "Under our Constitution, the Federal Government is one of enumerated powers."[64] In supporting the Affordable Care Act in 2012, Chief Justice Roberts made this claim: "If no enumerated power authorizes Congress to pass a certain law, that Law may not be enacted."[65] Congressional power has never been defined or restricted in that manner. Some powers are enumerated, but the federal government is more than that. All three branches have numerous implied powers, provided they are reasonably drawn from enumerated powers.

Why would the Supreme Court repeatedly make statements about the federal government being one of enumerated powers when any reasonably educated high school student would know that is false? Is it to impress the public that the federal government is subject to limits and the Court is available to police the boundaries? Wouldn't that objective be better satisfied by saying the federal government is one of limited powers, which is surely the case? However, in making false assertions about enumerated powers, the Court runs the risk of deliberately misleading the public by making simplistic and erroneous comments about fundamental principles of constitutional government.

---

61. Anderson v. Dunn, 19 U.S. (6 Wheat.) 204, 225 (1821).
62. *E.g.*, United States v. Midwest Oil Co., 236 U.S. 459, 475 (1915); Inland Waterways Corp. v. Young, 309 U.S. 517, 525 (1940).
63. United States v. Lopez, 514 U.S. 549, 552 (1995).
64. Boerne v. Flores, 521 U.S. 507, 516 (1997).
65. Nat'l Fed'n Indep. Bus. v Sebelius, 567 U.S. __ (2012).

V.   Inherent Powers

Scholars at times refer to "inherent" presidential power when the more accurate word is *implied*. For example, in a study on treaties and international agreements, Oona Hathaway stated that the president "has the power to make international agreements entirely on his own inherent constitutional authority. Yet that power is not unlimited."[66] The limits, she explained, are not supplied by international law but by domestic law, and in the United States "the central source to which we must turn is the U.S. Constitution, which is the source of both the President's unilateral international lawmaking authority and the limits thereon."[67] In other words, the authority is a mix of express and implied powers, not inherent ones, which as invoked by presidents and their advisers means powers not subject to checks by the legislative and judicial branches.

An express commitment to inherent presidential power comes from Yoo, who during his service in the Justice Department supported "inherent executive powers that are unenumerated in the Constitution."[68] Some scholars treat implied powers and inherent powers as the same.[69] They are markedly different. Implied powers are drawn reasonably from express powers. They are therefore anchored in the Constitution. Inherent powers, by definition, are not drawn from express powers. As the word suggests, these powers "inhere" in a person or an office, as Blackstone had argued for the king. *Black's Law Dictionary* has defined inherent powers in this manner: "An authority possessed without its being derived from another. . . . [P]owers over and beyond those explicitly granted in the Constitution or reasonably to be implied from express grants."[70]

The Constitution is protected when the three branches operate under express and implied powers. It is in danger when they claim inherent powers. Yoo consistently treats inherent powers as so central to presidential power and national security that they cannot be limited by statutes or treaties. According to his analysis, any power "that is executive in nature" must be vested solely in the executive branch.[71] The president, he argues, possesses "complete discretion in exercising the Commander-in-Chief power."[72] Congress's power to declare war "does not constrain the President's independent

---

66. Oona A. Hathaway, *Presidential Power over International Law: Restoring the Balance*, 119 YALE L.J. 140, 210 (2009).

67. *Id.* at 210–11.

68. Memorandum opinion from John C. Yoo, Deputy Assistant Attorney General, to Timothy Flanagan, Deputy Counsel to the President, Sept. 24, 2001, at 4.

69. *E.g.*, STEVEN G. CALABRESI & CHRISTOPHER S. YOO, THE UNITARY EXECUTIVE: PRESIDENTIAL POWER FROM WASHINGTON TO BUSH 20, 430 (2008).

70. BLACK'S LAW DICTIONARY 703 (5th ed., 1979).

71. Yoo, *supra* note 68, at 4.

72. *Id.* at 2.

and plenary constitutional authority over the use of military force."[73] The president exercises "plenary authority in foreign affairs."[74] Congress may not by statute "place any limits on the President's determinations as to any terrorist threat, the amount of military force to be used in response, or the method, timing, and nature of the response. These decisions, under our Constitution, are for the President alone to make."[75]

For reasons to be given, Yoo's description of presidential power has no basis in the Constitution or in the practice of American government from 1789 to the present. His analysis resembles what Blackstone wrote about the prerogatives available to the king. A constitution safeguards individual rights and liberties by specifying and limiting government. Express and implied powers serve that purpose. Inherent powers invite claims of authority that have no limits, other than those voluntarily accepted by the president. What "inheres" in the president? The word "inherent" is sometimes cross-referenced to "intrinsic," which can be something "belonging to the essential nature or construction of a thing."[76] What is in the "nature" of a political office? Nebulous words and concepts invite political abuse and unconstitutional actions. They threaten individual liberties. Presidents who assert inherent powers move the nation from one of limited powers to boundless and ill-defined authority, undermining republican government, the doctrine of separation of powers, and the system of checks and balances.[77] When this type of authority is asserted, as Madison noted in his *Helvidius* article, "no citizen could any longer guess at the character of the government under which he lives; the most penetrating jurist would be unable to scan the extent of constructive prerogative."[78]

Several presidents have claimed the right to exercise inherent powers. On each occasion they were rebuffed by Congress, the courts, or both: Truman trying to seize steel mills in 1952 to prosecute the war in Korea, Nixon impounding appropriated funds, Nixon conducting warrantless domestic surveillance, and George W. Bush in November 2001 creating military tribunals without first obtaining authority from Congress. By reviewing these examples, it will be clear how the American system differs fundamentally from the British model and the prerogatives that Blackstone placed with the king.

---

73. *Id.* at 3.
74. *Id.* at 5.
75. *Id.* at 16.
76. Merriam-Webster's Collegiate Dictionary 614 (10th ed., 1965).
77. Louis Fisher, *The Unitary Executive and Inherent Executive Power*, 12 U. Pa. J. Const. L. 569, 586–80 (2010); Louis Fisher, *Invoking Inherent Powers: A Primer*, 37 Presidential Stud. Q. 1 (2007).
78. 6 The Writings of James Madison 152 (Gaillard Hunt ed., 1900–10).

VI.   Inherent Powers Rejected

On April 8, 1952, President Truman issued Executive Order 10340, authorizing and directing the secretary of commerce to take possession "of all
or such of the [steel] plants, facilities, and other property of the companies
named in the list attached hereto, or any part thereof, as he may deem necessary in the interests of national defense."[79] Eighty-seven companies were
included on the list. Truman felt compelled to act to avert a nationwide strike
of steel companies. His executive order referred to "American fighting men
and fighting men of other nations of the United Nations . . . now engaged in
deadly combat with the forces of aggression in Korea."[80] Weapons of other
materials needed by the armed forces "are produced to a great extent in this
country, and steel is an indispensable component of substantially all of such
weapons and materials."[81] He identified his legal and constitutional authority: "NOW, THEREFORE, by virtue of the authority vested in me by the
Constitution and laws of the United States, and as President of the United
States and Commander in Chief of the armed forces of the United States."[82]

Several steel companies took the dispute to federal district court. Holmes
Baldridge of the Justice Department defended the steel seizure as "a legal
taking under the inherent executive powers of the President."[83] Over the
course of oral argument, he used the word "inherent" 11 times.[84] To Judge
David A. Pine, Baldridge pressed this claim: "Our position is that there is no
power in the Courts to restrain the President and, as I say, [Commerce] Secretary Sawyer is the alter ego of the President and not subject to injunctive
order of the Court."[85] Baldridge agreed with Judge Pine that the government
was not asserting any statutory authority. Instead, the president's power was
based on Sections 1, 2, and 3 of Article II "and whatever inherent, implied
or residual powers may flow therefrom."[86] He argued that the president
"has the power to take such action as is necessary to meet the emergency,"
subject to only two limitations: "One is the ballot box and the other is
impeachment."[87]

---

79. 17 Fed. Reg. 3139, 3142 (1952).
80. *Id.* at 3139.
81. *Id.*
82. *Id.* at 3142.
83. *The Steel Seizure Case*, H. Doc. No. 534 (Part I), 82d Cong., 2d Sess. 253
(1952). This document contains proceedings and oral argument in district court and the
D.C. Circuit.
84. *Id.* at 253, 254, 371, 386–89, 426, 427. Baldridge makes 11 references. Additional references to "inherent" powers are by other attorneys.
85. *Id.* at 362.
86. *Id.* at 371.
87. *Id.*

On April 29, 19 days after he first heard the case, Judge Pine issued a blistering opinion that repudiated the arguments that defended Truman's action in seizing the plants. He found no express or implied constitutional authority for the seizure. No "residuum of power" or "inherent" power existed to justify this exercise of presidential power.[88] To Pine, the scope of executive power described by Baldridge "spells a form of government alien to our Constitutional government of limited power."[89] He acknowledged that his ruling might precipitate the heavy costs that Baldridge warned of, such as "the contemplated strike, if it came, with all its awful results."[90] Yet such a consequence

> would be less injurious to the public than the injury which would flow from a timorous judicial recognition that there is some basis for this claim to unlimited and unrestrained Executive power, which would be implicit in a failure to grant the injunction. Such recognition would undermine public confidence in the very edifice of government as it is known under the Constitution.[91]

Judge Pine's rejection of unrestricted inherent executive power, though not expressly based on Magna Carta, has parallels to Magna Carta's restrictions on the exercise of authority by King John that he considered to be his sovereign prerogative.

The Supreme Court granted certiorari and heard oral argument on May 12, 1952. Solicitor General Philip Perlman presented the case for the executive branch. He did not once use the words regularly promoted by Baldridge: "inherent" presidential power. On June 2, by a 6–3 vote, the Supreme Court invalidated Truman's executive order.[92] All six justices in the majority rejected the claim of inherent presidential power.

Two more attempts to invoke inherent presidential power came in the Nixon administration. During a news conference on January 31, 1973, President Nixon asserted that the "constitutional right for the President to impound funds—and that is not to spend money, when the spending of money would mean either increasing prices or increasing taxes for all the people—that right is absolutely clear."[93] In the past, presidents on numerous occasions had declined to spend appropriated funds, provoking heated political battles but no litigation. The disputes were settled through

---

88. Youngstown Sheet & Tube Co. v. Sawyer, 103 F. Supp. 569, 573 (D.D.C. 1952).
89. *Id.* at 576.
90. *Id.* at 577.
91. *Id.*
92. Youngstown Co. v. Sawyer, 343 U.S. 579 (1952).
93. PUBLIC PAPERS OF THE PRESIDENTS OF THE UNITED STATES, RICHARD M. NIXON 1973 62 (1975).

accommodations by the elected branches. Nixon's extreme position led to legislative action, dozens of court rulings against him, and eventually a statute that curbed his power and those of presidents to follow.[94]

Deputy Attorney General Joseph Sneed doubted that Congress could legislate against impoundment even in the domestic area: "To admit the existence of such power deprives the President of a substantial portion of the 'executive power' vested in him by the Constitution."[95] As to national defense and foreign relations, he argued that the president's constitutional power to impound funds had their source not only in the Take Care Clause and his "express status as Commander-in-Chief" but as the "sole organ of the Nation in the conduct of its foreign affairs."[96]

The sole-organ doctrine, based on a total misrepresentation by Justice George Sutherland in *United States v. Curtiss-Wright Export Corp.*,[97] largely recreates Blackstone's theory of exclusive monarchical control over external affairs. Sutherland's assertion that the president is the "sole organ" of foreign affairs appears to come with impressive credentials. It relies on a speech in 1800 by John Marshall when he served in the House of Representatives. A year later he would be chief justice of the Supreme Court. However, Marshall never took the position that Sutherland attributed to him. In fact, he took the direct opposite.

The issue before the Supreme Court in *Curtiss-Wright* concerned only *legislative* power, not presidential power. How much could Congress delegate *its* power to the president in the field of international affairs? In upholding the delegation, Sutherland added pages of extraneous material entirely irrelevant to the issue before the Court. He claimed that the principle that the federal government is limited to enumerated and implied powers "is categorically true only in respect to our internal affairs."[98] In arguing for independent, exclusive, inherent, and plenary powers for the president in the field of foreign affairs, he proceeded to distort Marshall's speech.

Some members of the House of Representatives wanted to censure or impeach President John Adams for turning over to Great Britain a British subject charged with murder. Marshall took the floor to explain why there were no grounds to criticize or punish Adams. The Jay Treaty provided for extradition in cases involving the charge of murder.[99] Adams had not acted on the basis of any plenary or inherent presidential power but on

---

94. 88 Stat. 297 (1974); Fisher, *supra* note 12, at 237–42.

95. *Impoundment of Appropriated Funds by the President*, joint hearings before the Senate Committee on Government Operations and the Senate Committee on the Judiciary, 93d Cong., 1st Sess. 369 (1973).

96. *Id.*

97. United States v. Curtiss-Wright Export Corp., 299 U.S. 304 (1936).

98. *Id.* at 315.

99. *Treaty of Amity, Commerce, and Navigation*, 1796, art. 27.

express language in a treaty, with treaties under Article VI of the Constitution included as part of the "supreme Law of the Land." Adams was not independently creating law; he was carrying it out. Marshall's floor presentation was so tightly reasoned that critics of John Adams did not attempt a rebuttal.[100]

President Nixon claimed the constitutional right to use impoundment to cut programs in half or eliminate them altogether. The severity of those reductions prompted about 80 lawsuits, with the administration losing almost all of them, including one decided by the Supreme Court.[101] In addition, Congress passed legislation in 1974 to severely restrict all presidents in their efforts to impound funds. Lawmakers agreed to prohibit presidents from canceling a program ("rescinding" funds) unless Congress specifically approves by statute. If a president wants to delay ("defer") spending on a program, either chamber could disapprove by a one-house veto.[102] When the Supreme Court in *INS v. Chadha* struck down the legislative veto, including the one-house variety, the D.C. Circuit determined that the one-house veto was tied inextricably to the deferral authority. If one fell, so did the other. The president's authority to make policy deferrals thus disappeared. Only routine, nonpolicy deferrals were permitted. Congress promptly converted the judicial ruling into statutory policy.[103]

In another effort to exercise inherent powers, President Nixon on June 5, 1970, met with the heads of several intelligence agencies, including the National Security Agency (NSA), to initiate a program designed to monitor individuals and groups in the United States that the administration considered radical, particularly those opposed to the war in Vietnam. Joining others at the meeting was Tom Charles Huston, a young White House attorney. He drafted a 43-page, top-secret memorandum that became known as the Huston Plan. He put the matter bluntly to Nixon: "Use of this technique is clearly illegal; it amounts to burglary."[104] Huston's plan directed the NSA to use its technological capacity to intercept—without judicial

---

100. For greater detail on the context of Marshall's speech and the misrepresentation by Justice Sutherland *see* Louis Fisher, *Judicial Errors That Magnify Presidential Power*, 61 FED. L. 66 (Jan/Feb 2014); Louis Fisher, *The Law: Presidential Inherent Power: The "Sole-Organ" Doctrine*, 37 PRESIDENTIAL STUD. Q. 139 (2007); Louis Fisher, *The "Sole Organ" Doctrine*, L. LIBR. CONG. 1 (Aug. 28, 2006), http://www.loufisher.org/docs/pip/441.pdf.

101. Train v. N.Y.C., 420 U.S. 35 (1975). For impoundment cases in lower courts, *see* LOUIS FISHER, PRESIDENTIAL SPENDING POWER 175–201 (1975).

102. 88 Stat. 297, 334–35, § 1013 (1974).

103. City of New Haven v. United States, 809 F.2d 900 (D.C. Cir. 1987); 101 Stat. 785, § 206 (1987).

104. KEITH W. OLSON, WATERGATE: THE PRESIDENTIAL SCANDAL THAT SHOOK AMERICA 16 (2003).

warrant—the communications of U.S. citizens using international phone calls or telegrams.[105]

Although Nixon, under pressure from Federal Bureau of Investigation (FBI) Director J. Edgar Hoover, withdrew the Huston Plan, NSA had been targeting domestic groups for several years and continued to do so. Huston's blueprint, kept in a White House safe, became public in 1973, after Congress investigated the Watergate affair, and it provided documentary evidence that Nixon ordered NSA to illegally monitor American citizens. To conduct its surveillance operations, NSA entered into agreement with U.S. companies, including Western Union and RCA Global. U.S. citizens, assuming their telegrams would be handled with utmost privacy, learned that American companies had been turning over telegrams to NSA.[106]

In 1971, a federal district court expressly dismissed the claim of a broad "inherent" presidential power to conduct domestic surveillance without a warrant.[107] The Sixth Circuit affirmed, unimpressed by the government's sweeping argument that the power at issue "is the inherent power of the President to safeguard the security of the nation."[108] Unanimously, the Supreme Court affirmed the Sixth Circuit and held that the Fourth Amendment required prior judicial approval for surveillance of domestic organizations and individuals.[109]

Congress then passed legislation to provide statutory guidelines for the president's power to conduct surveillance over foreign powers. The result was the Foreign Intelligence Surveillance Act (FISA) of 1978.[110] The claim of independent and inherent presidential power would be replaced by a judicial check. FISA established a special court, the Foreign Intelligence Surveillance Court, to ensure outside supervision over the exercise of this type of executive power. FISA specifically eliminated the claim of inherent presidential power by making clear that the statutory procedures for electronic surveillance within the United States for intelligence purposes "shall be the exclusive means" for conducting such surveillance.[111]

Nonetheless, on December 16, 2005, the *New York Times* reported that President George W. Bush, in the period immediately following the 9/11 attacks, had secretly authorized the NSA to listen to Americans and others inside the United States without a court-approved warrant. The administration decided that the exclusive framework of FISA was not legally binding

---

105. James Bamford, Body of Secrets: Anatomy of the Ultra-Secret National Security Agency 430 (2002).

106. *Id.* at 431–39.

107. United States v. Sinclair, 321 F. Supp. 1074, 1077 (E.D. Mich. 1971).

108. United States v. United States Dist. Ct. for E.D. of Mich., 444 F.2d 651, 658 (6th Cir. 1971).

109. United States v. United States Dist. Ct., 407 U.S. 297 (1972).

110. Foreign Intelligence Surveillance Act, 92 Stat. 1788 (1978).

111. *Id.* at 1797, § 201(f).

and proceeded to follow a purely executive-made process.[112] In a weekly radio address a day later, Bush conceded that he had authorized the NSA, "consistent with U.S. law and the Constitution, to intercept the international communications of people with known links to Al Qaeda and related terrorist organizations."[113] On December 19, Attorney General Alberto Gonzales claimed that "the President has the inherent authority under the Constitution, as Commander-in-Chief, to engage in this kind of activity."[114]

The formal legal defense was issued on January 19, 2006, when the Office of Legal Counsel produced a 42-page "white paper" defending the legality of warrantless surveillance.[115] It offered two arguments: one statutory (the Authorization for Use of Military Force, or AUMF), the other constitutional (Article II powers of the president). The AUMF did not amend FISA and remove the judicial check. Amendments to statutory law are not made by implication, with members of Congress unaware of what they are voting on and what they might be changing. Congress is always at liberty to pass a future statute that modifies an earlier one, but when it acts it does so expressly, consciously, and not by vague and unspoken implications.

As for Article II, the Office of Legal Counsel said that NSA's activities "are supported by the President's well-recognized inherent constitutional authority as Commander in Chief and sole organ for the Nation in foreign affairs to conduct warrantless surveillance of enemy forces for intelligence purposes to detect and disrupt armed attacks on the United States."[116] The sole-organ doctrine, of course, is a Justice Sutherland fabrication, no matter how often it is repeated. Some attorneys within the Justice Department may believe that the president's power to conduct warrantless surveillance is "well-recognized," but there is no such general agreement by federal courts, members of Congress, or the academic community. The phrase "well-recognized" is often used by the executive branch to suggest that a particular claim is so obvious on its face that it need not be argued or supported by evidence. There is nothing obvious about inherent presidential power. The notion of "inherent" power is a claim or assertion, not a fact, and opens the door to illegal, unconstitutional, and extraconstitutional actions, regularly rejected in the past by the legislative and judicial branches. Another judicial rejection of inherent presidential power that occurred in 2006 is described next.

---

112. James Risen & Eric Lichtblau, *Bush Lets U.S. Spy on Callers without Courts,* N.Y. TIMES, Dec. 16, 2005, at A1.

113. *Bush on the Patriot Act and Eavesdropping,* N.Y. TIMES, Dec. 18, 2005, at 30.

114. Press briefing by Attorney General Alberto Gonzales and General Michael Hayden, Principal Deputy Director for National Intelligence, December 19, 2005.

115. *Legal Authorities Supporting the Activities of the National Security Agency Described by the President,* Office of Legal Counsel, U.S. Department of Justice, Jan. 19, 2006.

116. *Id.* at 1.

On November 13, 2001, President Bush issued an order to create military tribunals to try individuals who gave assistance to the terrorist attacks of 9/11.[117] Instead of going to Congress for statutory authority (as it eventually had to do), the administration justified the order by referring to the availability of inherent presidential power. As with previous claims by Presidents Truman and Nixon to justify their action in seizing steel mills, impounding funds, and ordering warrantless domestic surveillance, Bush's claim of inherent power would similarly misfire.

The constitutionality of Bush's military order reached the Supreme Court in the 2006 decision *Hamdan v. Rumsfeld*. The Court held that the military order violated both the Uniform Code of Military Justice (UCMJ) and the Geneva Conventions. Congress had enacted the UCMJ and it was the president's duty to comply with it. No inherent presidential authority existed to circumvent the statutory policy. In its briefs, the Bush administration claimed that the founding-era history supported presidential establishment of military tribunals: "It was well established [again!] when the Constitution was written and ratified that one of the powers inherent in military command was the authority to institute tribunals for punishing enemy violations of the laws of war," and that General George Washington had appointed a Board of General Officers in 1780 to try British Major John André as a spy.[118] The Justice Department argued that there was no provision in the American Articles of war providing for the jurisdiction in a court-martial to try an enemy for the offense of spying.[119]

Three amicus briefs I filed in *Hamdan* (when the case was in the D.C. Circuit, when a motion was filed for certiorari, and after the Supreme Court granted certiorari), explained why these arguments by the administration were false.[120] The Continental Congress adopted a resolution in 1776 expressly providing that enemy spies "shall suffer death . . . by sentence of a court martial, or such other punishment as such court martial shall direct," and ordered that the resolution "be printed at the end of the rules and articles of war."[121] The previous year, Congress had made it punishable by court-martial for members of the Continental Congress to "hold

117. 66 Fed. Reg. 57,833 (2001).

118. *Brief for Appellants*, Hamdan v. Rumsfeld, No. 04-5393 (D.C. Cir. Dec. 8, 2004), at 58.

119. *Id.*

120. *Brief* Amicus Curiae *of Louis Fisher in Support of Petitioner-Appellee Urging Affirmance*, Hamdan v. Rumsfeld, No. 04-5393, D.C. Cir., Dec, 29, 2004; *Brief* Amicus Curiae *of Louis Fisher in Support of Petitioner*, Hamdan v. Rumsfeld, No. 05-184, on petition for writ of certiorari, Sept. 7, 2005; *Brief* Amicus Curiae *of Louis Fisher in Support of Petitioner [Commissions—History]*, Hamdan v. Rumsfeld, No. 05-184, on writ of certiorari, Jan. 6, 2006.

121. 5 Journals of the Continental Congress, 1774–1789 at 693 (1906).

correspondence with" or "give intelligence to" the enemy.[122] It was a conceptual and historical mistake for the Bush administration to rely on the John André trial of 1780. There was no president at that time. There was no separate executive branch. There was only one branch of government: the Continental Congress. In convening Major André's trial, Washington did not act unilaterally as an executive possessing inherent or independent power but as a general carrying out procedures set forth by Congress. Moreover, other military tribunals created after 1789 raised important questions about presidential power and judgment.[123]

VII.   Limits on Executive Power

It was unclear the degree to which Magna Carta limited royal power. At King John's request (and as discussed further later), Pope Innocent III (r. 1198–1216) annulled the charter on August 24, 1215—that is, ten weeks after it was agreed to—on the ground it had been granted under duress.[124] In the 17th century, Sir Edward Coke, attorney general to Elizabeth I (r. 1558–1603) and James I (r. 1603–1625), and later chief justice of Common Pleas and King's Bench and a member of Parliament, interpreted Magna Carta as a limit to the absolutist doctrines of the Stuarts.[125] To Coke, the principles of the charter had been reconfirmed by one English ruler to the next, making it a weapon to limit the royal prerogative.[126] His scholarship has been questioned. Ralph Turner concludes that Coke "reinterpreted or misinterpreted Magna Carta to give it relevance, misconstruing its clauses anachronistically and uncritically."[127] Yet, Turner states that Coke "and his fellow lawyers grasped Magna Carta's essential meaning, that the king must be under the law."[128]

Turner faults Coke and his followers with creating "a mythical view of Parliament's origin that surpassed their anachronistic interpretations of Magna Carta."[129] Coke and his colleagues imagined representative bodies in England "from time immemorial," with some tracing representative government to the Goths, a term for Anglo-Saxon settlers.[130] The myth of

---

122. American Articles of War of 1775, art. 28, *reprinted in* William Winthrop, Military Law and Precedents 966 (2d ed. 1920).

123. Louis Fisher, Military Tribunals and Presidential Power: American Revolution to the War on Terrorism 168–70 (2005).

124. J.C. Holt, Magna Carta 255, 261 (2d ed. 1992).

125. Ralph V. Turner, Magna Carta through the Ages 147 (2003).

126. *Id.* at 148.

127. *Id.*

128. *Id.* at 149.

129. *Id.*

130. *Id.*

Parliament's antiquity allowed parliamentarians to maintain that the Stuart kings were "absolutist innovators, while parliamentarians were simply seeking to preserve an ancient tradition of shared authority by king, Lords and Commons, with sovereign power belonging to 'the king in Parliament.'"[131] Whatever the merits of his scholarship, Coke's advocacy led to his being committed to the Tower in 1621.[132]

VIII.   Procedural Safeguards

An important check on executive power comes from the right of due process invoked by individuals at trial. In 1670, William Penn was brought before Old Bailey in London after he was arrested for giving a speech. The indictment: "disturbance of the peace of the said Lord the King."[133] Penn stood his ground, insisting that the court "let me know by what law it is you prosecute me, and upon what you ground my indictment,"[134] and arguing that his trial violated the "Great Charter."[135] The jury, similarly uncertain about what wrong he had committed, returned with this verdict: "Guilty of speaking in Grace-churchstreet."[136] The court insisted on something stronger, but the jury would not waver from its initial judgment, despite threats from the court.[137]

Penn succeeded on two fronts: the right of a defendant to know precisely what law he is being charged with violating, and having a jury that preserves its independent authority to reach a fair judgment. He regarded the court's conduct at his trial as a violation of basic tenets in Magna Carta and he brought those principles to America where they were established in Pennsylvania.[138] Other colonies in America relied on Magna Carta to defend individual rights against authority "in all its forms, whether legislative, executive, or judicial."[139] For example, the Virginia Bill of Rights of 1776 provided: "all men are by nature equally free and independent, and have certain inherent rights . . . namely the enjoyment of life and liberty, with the means of acquiring and possessing property, and pursuing and obtaining happiness

---

131. *Id.*
132. *Id.*
133. HOWARD, *supra* note 13, at 78.
134. *Id.* at 79.
135. 6 A COMPLETE COLLECTION OF STATE TRIALS (T.B. Howell ed., 1816) (6 How. 951).
136. HOWARD, *supra* note 13, at 80.
137. *Id.* at 80–82
138. *Id.* at 83–98.
139. HOLT, *supra* note 124, at 17.

and safety." No man could be deprived of his liberty "except by the law of the land or the judgement of peers."[140]

Although Magna Carta was influential in America, the colonists developed their own understanding through individual initiative and constant practice on how to structure political power and move toward self-government. Each colony had its own experiences in contending with rival factions. When the delegates reached Philadelphia to begin debate on a draft Constitution, there were no references to Magna Carta. Of the Federalist Papers, only Alexander Hamilton in *Federalist* No. 84 made brief mention of Magna Carta in discussing the origin of individual rights.[141] The Anti-Federalist Papers do not appear to refer to Magna Carta.

Often we think of procedural safeguards being protected by the courts, but the record demonstrates that the judiciary can fail to defend basic rights of due process. Instead, a private individual may require the assistance of Congress and the press. Examples in the following section explain that judicial failures frequently occur either in time of war or in periods when the nation feels threatened by outside forces and decides to ferret out the *loyal* from the *disloyal*. At such times, the executive and judicial branches are inclined to violate the rights of citizens and aliens, even withholding from them evidence needed to clear their name. Judicial failings appear in many fields, such as the Japanese-American cases of 1943 and 1944.[142]

IX. Deportation and Exclusion Proceedings

Executive abuse of procedural safeguards, acquiesced in by the Supreme Court, appears in the case of Ellen Knauff. She was held on Ellis Island from 1948 to 1951 as a security risk and regularly threatened with deportation. The Truman administration justified its action on the basis of "confidential information" it refused to show to Knauff, to her attorney, and even to federal courts. She was born in Germany and lived in Prague. Her mother, father, and other Jewish relatives perished in the Nazi camps. She managed to escape to England where she worked during World War II. After the war, she returned to Germany to assist the American military government. On February 28, 1948, she married Kurt Knauff, a U.S. citizen and veteran who had been honorably discharged. Intent on becoming a U.S. citizen, she

---

140. *Id.* at 18.
141. THE FEDERALIST No. 84 at 534 (Hamilton) (Benjamin F. Wright ed., 2002).
142. Hirabayashi v. United States, 320 U.S. 81 (1943); Korematsu v. United States, 323 U.S. 214 (1944).

booked a ship to America and arrived in New York Harbor on August 14, 1948.[143]

Instead of being allowed to land, she was taken to Ellis Island and held for weeks while being questioned without access to visitors or legal counsel. On October 6, 1948, an immigration official recommended that she be permanently excluded from America. She was not given a hearing nor advised on what information the government was acting. The official justified exclusion because her admission would be "prejudicial" to the United States. No other reasons were given. The official's decision was not subject to an appeals process. On that same day, Attorney General Tom Clark entered a final order of exclusion.[144]

After obtaining legal assistance, Knauff filed a habeas corpus petition with a district court. It dismissed the petition, as did the Second Circuit.[145] Neither court offered any objection to an exclusion order based on confidential information that she, her attorney, and federal judges were not permitted to see. The judges were willing to defer wholly to unsupported and uncorroborated claims by executive officials. On January 16, 1950, the Supreme Court decided 4–3 in support of the Truman administration.[146] Two years earlier, Justice Robert Jackson had warned that the war power and associated concerns of national security lead to governmental decisions that are hasty and careless of constitutional rights. Worst of all, he said, these actions are "interpreted by judges under the influence of the same passions and pressures."[147]

In the Ellen Knauff case, Justice Jackson issued a powerful dissent. He found no evidence that Congress had authorized "an abrupt and brutal exclusion of the wife of an American citizen without a hearing."[148] The advice from the administration to the judiciary was that "not even a court can find out why the girl is excluded."[149] To Jackson, the claim that evidence of guilt "must be secret is abhorrent to free men, because it provides a cloak for the malevolent, the misinformed, the meddlesome, and the corrupt to play the role of informer undetected and uncorrected."[150] His pointed reminder: "Security is like liberty in that many are the crimes committed in its name."[151]

---

143. For details on her arrival in New York City and subsequent detention on Ellis Island, see ELLEN RAPHAEL KNAUFF, THE ELLEN KNAUFF STORY (1952).

144. *Id.* at 78.

145. United States *ex rel.* Knauff v. Watkins, 173 F.2d 599 (2d Cir. 1949).

146. Knauff v. Shaughnessy, 338 U.S. 537 (1950).

147. Woods v. Miller Co., 333 U.S. 138, 148 (1948) (Jackson, J., concurring).

148. Knauff v. Shaughnessy, 338 U.S. 537, 550 (Jackson, J., dissenting).

149. *Id.* at 551.

150. *Id.*

151. *Id.*

With the executive and judicial branches joined against Ellen Knauff, several newspapers came to her defense, as did Representative Francis Walter.[152] The House Judiciary Committee unanimously supported a private bill to permit her to enter the country. The committee report included a letter from the Justice Department that the president and the attorney general had sole authority to deny her entry for "security reasons." Knauff had "to stand the test of security" and "she failed to meet that test."[153] Confidentiality prevented lawmakers and judges from knowing on what ground she was being excluded. They did not know what the test was or how she had failed to meet it. The private bill reached the House floor on May 2, 1950, and passed unanimously.[154] Legislation was introduced in the Senate but no further action was taken.

On March 26, 1951, after the Supreme Court had ruled in her case, the Immigration Service finally held a hearing. Three witnesses selected by the administration testified that Ellen Knauff was a security risk. Although their statements relied entirely on hearsay, with no personal knowledge about her, the immigration board found the information sufficient.[155] An immigration appeals board on August 29, 1951, however, regarded the evidence submitted by the witnesses inadequate to justify her exclusion. Hearsay in an administrative hearing might be admissible if corroborated by direct evidence, but "all we have in this case is hearsay."[156] The appeals board ordered Knauff admitted for permanent residence. On November 2, 1951, Attorney General J. Howard McGrath approved the decision of the appeals board and Ellen Knauff left Ellis Island to begin her life in America.[157]

Ellen Knauff entered the United States because her case did not depend on the world of shadows, secrets, and confidentiality embraced by both the executive branch and federal courts. Her cause moved into the public arena, to be assisted by the press and members of Congress. Statements by the three witnesses could be monitored and analyzed by those who knew them, including individuals following the case from Europe. Citizens and aliens should not be condemned by informers who rely on speculation, secondhand conjectures, and perhaps malice. Although these factors are not specifically mentioned in chapter 39 of Magna Carta, the treatment of Ellen Knauff is clearly inconsistent with the basic thrust of that chapter, which reads: "No free man shall be taken or imprisoned or disseised or outlawed

---

152. For further details on the assistance of the press and Congress, Louis Fisher, *Truman's National Security Policy: Constitutional Issues, in* 7 CONGRESS AND HARRY S. TRUMAN: A CONFLICTED LEGACY (Donald A. Ritchie ed., 2011).

153. *Mrs. Ellen Knauff*, H. Rep. No. 1940, 81st Cong., 2d Sess. 4 (1950).

154. 96 CONG. REC. 6174 (1950).

155. KNAUFF, *supra* note 143, at 194–201.

156. *Id.* at app. 16.

157. *See* Charles D. Weisselberg, *The Exclusion and Detention of Aliens: Lessons from the Lives of Ellen Knauff and Ignatz Mezei*, 143 U. PA. L. REV. 933 (1995).

or exiled or in any way ruined, nor will we go or send against him, except by the lawful judgment of his peers or by the law of the land."[158]

In 1953, the Supreme Court upheld the right of the attorney general to exclude Ignatz Mezei.[159] Pending inquiry, he was temporarily excluded and kept on Ellis Island. The attorney general then ordered the temporary exclusion made permanent without a hearing before a board of special inquiry, on the "basis of information of a confidential nature, the disclosure of which would be prejudicial to the public interest."[160] That sounds very much like the treatment of Ellen Knauff. Jackson, joined by Frankfurter, dissented, insisting that Mezei was entitled by procedural due process to be informed of the grounds for exclusion and have "a fair chance" of overcoming the government's decision.[161] It was "inconceivable" to Jackson that "this measure of simple justice and fair dealing would menace the security of this country. No one can make me believe that we are that far gone."[162] Justice Jackson makes no specific reference to Magna Carta, but his appeal to basic notions of due process again recalls the principles established in chapter 39 of Magna Carta.

In 1954, the Court split 5–4 on the case of an individual, born in Italy of Italian parents, subject to deportation proceedings in 1947. The attorney general announced at a press conference that he planned to deport certain "unsavory characters" and prepared a confidential list that included the petitioner.[163] Did issuance of the list amount to public prejudgment by the attorney general, making fair consideration of his case by the Board of Immigration Appeals impossible? The board, appointed by the attorney general, served at his pleasure. Yet the board was required "to exercise its own judgment when considering appeals."[164] The Court held that if the petitioner could prove his allegation that the attorney general's announcement prejudged his application to have his deportation suspended, he should receive a new hearing to convince the board that he was entitled to suspension.[165]

Justice Jackson, joined by Justices Reed, Burton, and Minton, dissented. To Jackson, the petitioner was in the country illegally and had no grounds to challenge his deportation.[166] He said the power and discretion vested in the attorney general was analogous to the power of pardon or commutation of

---

158. This translation of the 1215 version of Magna Carta is from *Appendix IV* to J.C. Holt, Magna Carta 317–37 (1965).
159. Shaughnessy v. Mezei, 345 U.S. 206 (1953).
160. *Id.* at 208.
161. *Id.* at 227.
162. *Id.* at 228. Justices Black and Douglas wrote a separate dissent.
163. Accardi v. Shaughnessy, 347 U.S. 260, 262 (1954).
164. *Id.* at 266.
165. *Id.* at 268.
166. *Id.* at 269.

a sentence, "which we trust no one thinks is subject to judicial control."[167] The pardon power, including commutation, is vested in the president by the Constitution. The decision to deport is not. Jackson denied that courts have any role in reviewing "a discretionary and purely executive function."[168] He did not explain why in other cases, such as Knauff and Mezei, he believed the judiciary had a right to independently review executive judgments about deportation and exclusion.

X. Executive Concessions

J.C. Holt explains that the issuance of Magna Carta "was invalid if issued under duress" and that King John "was certainly under strong compulsion when he issued the Charter."[169] Pope Innocent III annulled it "partly on the grounds that it had been granted under duress."[170] United States presidents frequently make concessions when pressured, but there is no basis to regard those accommodations as invalid. Under certain conditions, presidents decide it is in their interest to cede ground in an effort to preserve their political standing. On March 2, 1973, President Nixon objected to allowing White House Counsel John Dean to testify at congressional hearings. Nixon offered several reasons, under the doctrine of separation of powers, for refusing any White House aide to testify. Yet, under heavy political pressure with the Watergate scandal and with impeachment in the House of Representatives looming, Nixon gradually retreated, eventually agreeing to allow White House aides to testify before the Senate Select Committee on Presidential Campaign Activities. To underscore the exceptional nature of allowing these individuals to testify, he attempted to set forth certain conditions.

Given his political circumstances, Nixon found it necessary to relax his own conditions, such as waiving executive privilege if possible criminal conduct was involved. With that understanding, many White House aides testified before the Senate committee, including John Dean, former Special Assistant Jeb Magruder, former Deputy Assistant Alexander Butterfield, former Chief Domestic Adviser John Ehrlichman, former White House Aide H.R. Haldeman, former Consultant Patrick Buchanan, and former Staff Coordinator General Alexander M. Haig Jr.[171] Many of those individuals were convicted and served prison terms.

Confidentiality is highly valued for White House aides who provide legal counsel to the president. Nevertheless, under the conditions of Watergate,

---

167. *Id.*
168. *Id.* at 272.
169. HOLT, *supra* note 124, at 261.
170. *Id.*
171. LOUIS FISHER, THE POLITICS OF EXECUTIVE PRIVILEGE 200 (2004).

Nixon agreed to permit even these aides to testify: personal attorney Herbert W. Kalmbach, Special Counsel Richard A. Moore, Counsel Leonard Garment, former Special Counsel Fred C. LaRue, Special Counsel J. Frederick Buzhardt, and Counsel Thomas H. Wakefield. Other White House aides who testified during the Watergate period included Bruce A. Kehrli, Hugh W. Sloan Jr., Herbert L. Porter, Gordon Strachen, Clark McGregor, William H. Maramoto, L.J. Evans Jr., and Rose Marie Woods, who served as personal secretary to Nixon.[172] Following the Watergate hearings conducted by Senator Sam Ervin, the House Judiciary Committee held hearings on the impeachment of Nixon. White House aides who testified at those hearings included Butterfield, Dean, Kalmbach, and Charles W. Colson.[173] White House aides have been called to a number of other congressional committees.[174]

Nixon hoped that by cooperating with the congressional investigation he could avoid impeachment. Senate hearings revealed the existence of listening and recording devices in the Oval Office. After much legal maneuvering, some of the tapes wound up in the hands of District Judge John Sirica, exposing unmistakable evidence of a cover-up. For example, at a March 22, 1973, meeting, Nixon remarked: "And, uh, for that reason, I am perfectly willing to—I don't give a shit what happens, I want you to stonewall it, let them plead the Fifth Amendment, cover-up or anything else, if it'll save the plan."[175] Other tapes, released as a result of the Supreme Court's decision in *United States v. Nixon*,[176] demonstrated that Nixon had agreed that the Central Intelligence Agency should put a halt to the FBI investigation.[177] With the release of the tape, Nixon was forced to leave office, announcing his resignation on August 8, 1974, effective the next day.

Presidents often invoke "executive privilege" to withhold documents from Congress and deny the right of committees to require certain executive officials to testify.[178] Under certain pressures, as with Watergate, they will be forced to make unusual concessions. Such was the case with the Iran-Contra scandal that began in November 1986 when Congress learned that the Reagan administration had sent funds to Contra rebels in Nicaragua in violation of statutory restrictions, and had sold arms to Iran contrary to its own publicly stated policy to remain neutral in the war between Iran

---

172. *Id. See also* Louis Fisher, *White House Aides Testifying before Congress*, 27 PRESIDENTIAL STUD. Q. 139, 141–42 (1997).

173. *Testimony of Witnesses*, Hearings before the House Committee on the Judiciary, 93d Cong., 2d Sess. (1974).

174. FISHER, *supra* note 171, at 199–227.

175. JOHN J. SIRICA, TO SET THE RECORD STRAIGHT 162 (1979).

176. United States v. Nixon, 418 U.S. 683 (1974).

177. H. Rep. No. 93-1305, 93d Cong., 2d Sess. 53 (1974).

178. MARK J. ROZELL, EXECUTIVE PRIVILEGE: PRESIDENTIAL POWER, SECRECY, AND ACCOUNTABILITY (3d ed. 2010).

and Iraq. Especially grave, constitutionally, was the violation of the funding restriction in the Boland Amendment, which prohibited United States assistance to the Contra rebels for the purpose of overthrowing the Nicaraguan government, while allowing assistance for other purposes.[179]

Officials in the Reagan administration understood from Watergate that sometimes a cover-up is more damaging politically than the initial, underlying issue. Attorney General Edwin Meese III concluded that the merging of assistance to the Contras with the sale of arms to Iran could cause the possible "toppling" of Reagan, unless the administration made facts publicly available and got them "out the door first."[180] Because Reagan made documents and executive officials available to Congress and waived executive privilege in its entirety, members of Congress never took seriously the thought of impeaching him.[181] Reagan permitted former National Security Advisers Robert McFarlane and John Poindexter to testify before Congress,[182] and allowed his Cabinet officials, including Secretary of State George Schulz and Secretary of Defense Caspar Weinberger, to discuss with Congress their conversations with the President.[183]

A final example of a President having to release confidential documents and allow White House officials to publicly testify comes from the 9/11 Commission created by Congress to investigate the terrorist hijackings of four planes, two that crashed into the World Trade Center, one that hit the Pentagon, and one that crashed into a field in Pennsylvania while en route to Washington, D.C. Among documents sought by the commission were the Presidential Daily Briefings (PDBs) that were given each morning to the president by intelligence officials. The documents were so sensitive that the House and Senate Intelligence Committees had never seen them.[184]

After the White House refused any access to the documents, a compromise was reached to allow three of the commissioners and one staffer to review selected PDBs.[185] A PDB of great interest was one dated August 6, 2001, informing President Bush that Osama bin Ladin planned to strike in the United States using hijacked airplanes. National Security Adviser Condoleezza Rice regarded the document as providing merely "historical" information, but others viewed it as a specific warning of a planned operation.[186] Eventually it was publicly released. It stated:

---

179. *See, e.g,*. P.L. 98-473, 98 Stat. 1935–1937.

180. Theodore Draper, A Very Thin Line: The Iran-Contra Affairs 521 (1991).

181. William S. Cohen & George J. Mitchell, Men of Zeal: A Candid Inside Story of the Iran-Contra Hearings 45–50 (1988).

182. Draper, *supra* note 180, at 498.

183. *Id.* at 540.

184. *See* Philip Shenon, The Commission: An Uncensored History of the 9/11 Investigation 73 (2008).

185. *Id.* at 211–25.

186. *Id.* at 237–38.

Clandestine, foreign government, and media reports indicate Bin Ladin since 1997 has wanted to conduct terrorist attacks in the US. . . . We have not been able to corroborate some of the more sensational threat reporting, such as that from a . . . service in 1998 saying that Bin Ladin wanted to hijack a US aircraft to gain the release of "Blind Shaykh" 'Umar 'Abd al-Rahman and other US-held extremists.[187]

Another controversy involved the request of the 9/11 Commission to have National Security Adviser Rice testify. White House Counsel Alberto Gonzales refused to make her available, but her willingness to appear on the morning news programs of ABC, CBS, NBC, and CNN, to be later interviewed by Sean Hannity of Fox News, undermined the position that she was not permitted to speak publicly.[188] Gonzales was forced to reverse his decision, announcing that she could testify as "a matter of comity."[189] Rice appeared before the commission, in public and under oath, and responded to questions.[190]

XI.   Habeas Corpus

When King John agreed to Magna Carta, he established the principle in chapter 39 that no man shall be "taken or imprisoned or dispossessed, or outlawed or banished . . . except by the legal judgment of his peers or by the law of the land." In the 14th century, Edward III affirmed in Statute 25 "that detention required indictment or a common law writ."[191] It is generally understood that the writ did not provide a reliable remedy to free improperly detained prisoners until much later,[192] and there were periods when England suspended the writ.

From 1593 to the 1670s, England made a number of efforts to legislate on the right of habeas corpus.[193] Throughout this period, Parliament regarded itself as empowered to pass imprisonment orders. Habeas corpus sent some defendants to arraignment, trial, and execution, while others were

---

187. The 9/11 Investigations: Staff Reports of the 9/11 Commission, app. D (Steven Strasser ed., 2004).

188. Shenon, *supra* note 184, at 291.

189. Louis Fisher, *Talking About Secrets*, Legal Times, April 19, 2004, at 66–67.

190. Shenon, *supra* note 184, at 293–302.

191. Anthony Gregory, The Power of Habeas Corpus in America: From the King's Prerogative to the War on Terror 13 (2013).

192. *Id.* For a more complete discussion of this, see chapter 7 of this book, "Magna Carta and Habeas Corpus."

193. Paul D. Halliday, Habeas Corpus: From England to Empire 220–37 (2012 ed.).

released to return home.[194] Parliament passed the Habeas Corpus Act in 1679 to deal with obstacles to issuing the writ.[195] During the 17th century, kings also considered themselves empowered to imprison individuals without charging them or bringing them to trial. Following such actions by Charles I (r. 1625–1649), Attorney General Robert Heath argued that it was the king's prerogative to imprison by his "special command" for "a matter of state," and that judges should defer to the king's judgment about the methods necessary to protect the country from threatened dangers.[196] Habeas corpus was suspended in England in 1689 and also from 1777 to 1783, 1794 to 1795, and 1798 to 1801.[197]

In April 1861, at the outset of the Civil War and with Congress in recess, President Abraham Lincoln issued proclamations calling forth the state militia, suspending the writ of habeas corpus, and placing a blockade on the rebellious states. Article I, Section 9 of the United States Constitution states that the privilege of the writ of habeas corpus "shall not be suspended unless when in Case of Rebellion or Invasion the public Service may require it." Although it appears in Article I defining the powers of Congress, the language does not specify which branch may suspend the writ. Lincoln did not lay claim to an exclusive power over suspension. His attorney general, Edward Bates, advised him in 1861 that he had a limited emergency authority to suspend habeas corpus. He said that if the language in the Constitution meant "a repeal of all power to issue the writ, then I freely admit that none but Congress can do it."[198] The president's power in time of emergency was "temporary and exceptional."[199]

Bates went beyond the position of Lincoln, who never argued that his decision to take emergency actions after Fort Sumter was unquestionably constitutional and that he had no need to share power with other branches. When Congress assembled in special session on July 4, 1861, Lincoln explained the actions he had taken with the outbreak of the Civil War. His measures, he said, "whether strictly legal or not, were ventured upon under what appeared to be a popular demand and a public necessity, trusting then, as now, that Congress would readily ratify them."[200] Through that language he made it clear that he had no inherent power to do what he did. Lincoln believed that "nothing has been done beyond the constitutional competency of Congress."[201]

---

194. *Id.* at 237–38.
195. *Id.* at 239.
196. JONATHAN HAFETZ, HABEAS CORPUS AFTER 9/11 81 (2011).
197. HALLIDAY, *supra* note 193, at 247–53.
198. 10 OP. ATT'Y GEN. 74, 90 (1861).
199. *Id.*
200. 7 A COMPILATION OF THE MESSAGES AND PAPERS OF THE PRESIDENTS 3225 (James D. Richardson ed., 1925).
201. *Id.*

Through those unambiguous words he admitted to exercising not only his Article II powers but the Article I powers of Congress. For that reason, the only means through which his actions could be brought into harmony with the Constitution was for Congress to pass legislation stating that his independent actions were retroactively authorized. Congress passed that bill with lawmakers understanding that Lincoln's acts, standing alone, were illegal.[202] The superior lawmaking body was Congress, not the president. Two years later, Lincoln and Bates acknowledged congressional power to pass legislation that defines when and how a president may suspend the writ of habeas corpus during a rebellion. On March 3, 1863, Congress enacted a bill authorizing the president, during the rebellion, to suspend the privilege of the writ of habeas corpus, subject to the terms and procedures set forth in the statute.[203]

Although Lincoln recognized the constitutional necessity to work jointly with Congress, he did not accept the authority of Chief Justice Roger Taney, sitting as circuit judge, to issue a writ of habeas corpus directing the commandant at Fort McHenry in Baltimore to bring John Merryman to the circuit courtroom. Military authorities had arrested Merryman as someone suspected of being the captain of a secession troop determined to destroy railroads and bridges to prevent the ability of federal troops from the North to reach Washington, D.C. The commandant, acting under Lincoln's orders, refused to produce Merryman. Although Taney issued an opinion stating that Merryman was entitled to be free,[204] Taney was not the federal officer responsible for preserving the Union. He had neither the authority nor the capacity. His decision in *Dred Scott* in 1857 had helped propel the country toward civil war. In May 1861, Lincoln faced a different choice. Having lost Virginia south of Washington, D.C., he could not afford to lose Maryland to the North and have the nation's capital encircled. At that moment in time, it was Lincoln's constitutional call, not Taney's.

The terrorist attacks of 9/11 provoked new issues of access by U.S. citizens and aliens to habeas corpus petitions. One case involved a U.S. citizen, Yaser Esam Hamdi, considered by the Bush administration to be an "enemy combatant." He was held without charges in a naval brig in Charleston, South Carolina. On June 28, 2004, eight justices rejected the government's central argument that his detention was quintessentially a presidential decision, not to be reevaluated and second-guessed by the courts. Four members of the plurality, joined by Justices Souter and Ginsburg, held that a U.S. citizen classified as an enemy combatant must "be given a meaningful opportunity to contest the factual basis

---

202. 12 Stat. 326 (1861). *See* remarks by Senator Breckinridge at CONG. GLOBE, 37th Cong., 1st Sess. 137–42 (1861) and Senator Howe; *id.* at 393.

203. 12 Stat. 755 (1863).

204. *Ex parte* Merryman, 17 F. Cas. 144, 147 (C.C.D. Md. 1861) (No. 9,487).

for that detention before a neutral decisionmaker."[205] A dissent by Justices Scalia and Stevens cited this language by Blackstone: "To bereave a man of life, or by violence to confiscate his estate, without accusation or trial, would be so gross and notorious an act of despotism, as must at once convey the alarm of tyranny throughout the whole kingdom."[206] Instead of trying Hamdi through some type of military tribunal, the government decided to transfer him to Saudi Arabia in October 2004. On the same day that the Court decided *Hamdi*, it reviewed the government's argument that detainees held at the U.S. naval base in Guantánamo lay beyond the jurisdiction of federal courts to grant habeas relief. A 6–3 decision rejected that position, identifying a number of differences between detainees held at the base and a Court ruling in 1950 relied on by the administration.[207] Among basic distinctions, the individuals in the earlier case had been charged, tried, and convicted in China. Detainees at the naval base had not been charged and were held on territory within the sovereign control of the United States.

Following the Court ruling in *Hamdan v. Rumsfeld* that Bush lacked inherent authority to create military tribunals,[208] Congress passed the Military Commissions Act (MCA), providing statutory support for the tribunals for the first time. On June 12, 2008, the Court in *Boumediene v. Bush* held that both the MCA and the Detainee Treatment Act of 2005 operated as an unconstitutional suspension of the writ.[209] Responding to *Boumediene*, federal district courts began granting habeas corpus relief to a number of Guantánamo detainees. On a regular basis, however, the federal Court of Appeals for the D.C. Circuit reversed and the Supreme Court declined to grant certiorari. In all of these certiorari denials, not a single justice dissented.[210]

XII. Conclusions

Individual rights in America have never been reliably protected by any of the three branches. At various times courts, lawmakers, and executive officials fail in their duty to see that constitutional liberties are defended and basic

---

205. Hamdi v. Rumsfeld, 542 U.S. 507, 509 (2004) (plurality of O'Connor, Rehnquist, Kennedy, and Breyer, JJ.), 553 (Souter and Ginsburg, JJ., concurring).

206. *Id.* at 555 (Scalia and Stevens, JJ., dissenting).

207. Rasul v. Bush, 542 U.S. 467 (2004); Johnson v. Eisentrager, 339 U.S. 763 (1950).

208. 548 U.S. 557 (2006).

209. Boumediene v. Bush, 553 U.S. 723, 771–92 (2008).

210. Erwin Chemerinsky, *Losing Interest: Since the Supreme Court's Latest Ruling Guaranteeing Habeas Corpus Rights to Guantánamo Detainees, in 2008, It Has Refused to Hear a Single Detainee Case*, NAT'L L. J., 34 (June 24, 2012).

procedural safeguards respected. The record underscores the importance of the system of checks and balances, which is regularly assisted by outside forces, including the press, citizens, aliens, and private organizations willing to press for justice, as well as fundamental principles of due process now viewed as enshrined in Magna Carta.

Chapter 7
Magna Carta and Habeas Corpus

Justin Wert

At the beginning of the 20th century, Charles McIlwain observed that the new histories of Magna Carta were portraying the Charter as a *document of reaction* that could fulfill its purported greatness only "when men [were] no longer able to understand its real meaning."[1] Characteristic of these early-20th-century writers was Edward Jenks, who, in his 1904 article, *The Myth of Magna Carta*, came to the conclusion that real beneficiaries of the document—the *liber homo* of chapter 39—were not "the people"[2] we traditionally imagine, but rather an "aristocratic class . . . who can no more be ranked amongst the people, than the country gentleman of to-day."[3] Although Jenks's position is often criticized as extreme, it is nevertheless the case that virtually all of Magna Carta's modern commentators recognize vast historical inaccuracies in the Whiggish accounts of the Charter's development up until the late 19th century.[4] What these new revisionist histories suggested was that Magna Carta's greatest provisions—due process and trial by jury—only became great when, forgetting or ignoring the Charter's seemingly lackluster beginnings, generations subsequent to 1215 gave them new meaning—a process that is described in chapters 1 and 2.

But despite Magna Carta's admittedly feudal origins, we continue to regard the Charter as the foundational expression of modern constitutionalism. What this suggests, then, is that as we attempt to make sense of Magna Carta, we should not begin *at* Runnymede, but *after it*, accounting along the way for other political and legal developments that helped facilitate the Charter's transformation into its elevated position in the Western

---

1. C.H. McIlwain, *Due Process of Law in Magna Carta*, 14 Colum. L. Rev. 27, 46 (1914).

2. Edward Jenks, *the Myth of Magna Carta*, 4 Indep. Rev. 260, 269 (1904).

3. Max Radin, *The Myth of Magna Carta*, 60 Harv. L. Rev. 1060 (1947).

4. *Id.*; *see also* John Phillip Reid, 4 *The Jurisprudence of Liberty: The Ancient Constitution in the Legal Historiography of the Seventeenth and Eighteenth Centuries*, *in* The Roots of Liberty: Magna Carta, Ancient Constitution, and the Anglo-American Tradition of the Rule of Law (Ellis Sandoz ed., 1993); *see also* Paul Halliday, Habeas Corpus: From England to Empire (2010); *see also* Herbert Butterfield, The Whig Interpretation of History (1931) (putting forward the notion of "Whig" history).

legal tradition. When we do, we quickly discover that the uses of Magna Carta's seemingly liberty-regarding provisions did not develop through time in one unilinear direction toward ever-increasing freedom. We also see that Magna Carta became linked to other developing procedural legal mechanisms—like habeas corpus—that tracked similarly uneven and oftentimes oppressive routes.

As I argue in this chapter, habeas corpus and Magna Carta remain rhetorical partners because political actors can repair to their idealized forms and use them strategically to enforce their own normative conceptions of constitutional governance.

The first section of this chapter traces the separate developments of Magna Carta and habeas corpus, discusses how the early uses of habeas corpus in England were very different from the use of the writ to protect individual liberty, and shows how and why Magna Carta and habeas corpus became linked during the 17th century in England through notions of due process. We see that their link was in no way preordained, and that legal elites had to rewrite the histories of both to link them together. The next section examines in detail the development of habeas corpus in the New World and particularly in the United States, touching briefly on the 17th and 18th centuries and then turning to the antebellum period, particularly with respect to slave law. We see the attendant troubles with the due process link in the application of habeas corpus during the antebellum period, which also reveals very different approaches to habeas corpus among states and between the states and the federal government. The chapter then discusses habeas corpus development in the post–Civil War period and then briefly turns to developments in the 20th century. Like others before, legal elites had to rewrite the history of habeas corpus in the 20th century as they expanded the writ's reach, a project that relied heavily upon similarly Whiggish histories of habeas corpus and Magna Carta during the 17th century. Finally, the chapter concludes by arguing that the shifting conceptions of due process that ultimately form the basis of Magna Carta and habeas corpus, actually provide more room for more humane understandings of each, even if that means that less noble ones could sometimes gain the upper hand.

I.   Habeas Corpus and Magna Carta: Linkages

One of the most effective tools used to enforce subsequent reinterpretations of the core of Magna Carta's procedural provisions after Runnymede was the simultaneous, but initially wholly separate, development of the writ of habeas corpus. This writ has been so intertwined with our understanding of Magna Carta that in both Coke's *Institutes* and Blackstone's *Commentaries*, it is portrayed in the same lofty terms as the Charter itself, as "the great and efficacious writ"[5] that serves to free those who may be "taken, or committed to prison *contra legem terrae*, against the Law of the land."[6] Reborn together in the early 17th century during the battles between the Common Law and Chancery courts of James I (r. 1603–1625), habeas corpus henceforth served as the preferred legal mechanism to enforce substantive readings of Magna Carta's *legem terrae*—now read as the *due process*—provision of chapter 39.[7] By the 18th century, Blackstone felt confident enough to assert that habeas corpus was now "another Magna Carta."[8]

But like the Great Charter that it came to enforce, the origins of habeas corpus suggest that the writ was not always deserving of its modern encomiums. The first recorded appearance of habeas corpus was, in fact, in 1199, predating Magna Carta by 16 years.[9] Originally part of the *mesne* process of early legal adjudication, the writ was widely used to ensure the presence of parties in court.[10]

In the 15th century, a distant variant of modern habeas corpus appeared as the King's Chancery courts began to use habeas corpus, along with writs of certiorari, to remove cases from inferior courts into their own. Hardly concerned with the vindication of individual rights or issues of due process as we understand them today, this *cum causa* version of habeas corpus served to enforce the privilege of certain classes, such as "clergy, members of Parliament, ministers of the King, and officers of superior courts,"[11] to enjoy legal proceedings in more sympathetic jurisdictions. Moreover, some early commentators, like Coke, evidently mistook Magna Carta's chapter 36 for habeas corpus, which states that "Nothing in future shall be given or taken for a writ of inquisition of life or limbs, but freely it shall be granted, and never denied,"[12] for habeas corpus.

Permutations of habeas corpus developed throughout the 16th century that allowed the writ to be used in criminal matters to discharge prisoners if they were held unlawfully. And with the constitutional crises of the early

---

5. EDWARD COKE, THE SECOND PART OF THE INSTITUTES OF THE LAWS OF ENGLAND 55 (1797); 4 WILLIAM BLACKSTONE & ST. GEORGE TUCKER, BLACKSTONE'S COMMENTARIES: WITH NOTES OF REFERENCE TO THE CONSTITUTION AND LAWS OF THE FEDERAL GOVERNMENT OF THE UNITED STATES AND OF THE COMMONWEALTH OF VIRGINIA 290 (William Young Birch & Abraham Small 1803).

6. BLACKSTONE, *supra* note 5, at 131.

7. *See* WILLIAM DUKER, A CONSTITUTIONAL HISTORY OF HABEAS CORPUS 44–45 (1980); HALLIDAY, *supra* note 4, at 15–16.

8. BLACKSTONE, *supra* note 5, at 131.

9. DANIEL MEADOR, HABEAS CORPUS AND MAGNA CARTA: DUALISM OF POWER AND LIBERTY 8 (1966).

10. *Id.* at 9.

11. MEADOR, *supra* note 9, at 11.

12. *Magna Carta 1215 ch. 36, in* WILLIAM SHARP McKECHNIE, MAGNA CARTA: A COMMENTARY ON THE GREAT CHARTER OF KING JOHN 359 (2d ed. 1914).

17th century, prior use of habeas corpus both as a tool in jurisdictional conflicts and as a developing legal challenge to unlawful imprisonment quickly set it against monarchical power.

In *Darnel's Case* (1627),[13] for example, Magna Carta and habeas corpus were partially reinvented, with habeas corpus now explicitly enforcing a more capacious reading of Magna Carta's *legem tarrae* (chapter 39).[14] Imprisoned by the Privy Council for failure to pay the king's tax through forced loans, Darnel petitioned the King's Bench for a writ of habeas corpus challenging the jurisdiction of the Council to hold him. The Crown's response to the writ, however, stated that Darnel was being held *per speciale mandatum Domini Regis*, and not as the result of indictment or other established common law legal processes. Darnel argued that habeas corpus served to "return the cause of the imprisonment, that it may be examined in this court."[15] Although a return was made and a cause provided, substantively, there was "no cause at all expressed in it."[16] John Selden, one of Darnel's counsels, contended further that the king's return violated chapter 39's *per legem terrae* provision by imprisoning subjects without "presentment or by indictment."[17] He then went on to argue that if "*per special mandatum* be within the meaning of these words . . . then this act has done nothing."[18]

In response, Sir Robert Heath, who argued the Crown's position in the case, agreed that the "fundamental grounds of argument upon this case begins with Magna Carta,"[19] but he argued that the substantive meaning of the *legem terrae* provision certainly encompassed any command of the king. The king's cause, while not *expressed*, was simply not yet *ripe*, and the "judicature have ever rested satisfied therewith . . . if a man be committed by the commandment of the king, he is not to be delivered by a Habeas Corpus in this court, for we know not the cause of the commitment."[20] Although Darnel was ultimately successful, the very suggestion that habeas corpus was the natural guarantor of Magna Carta's *legem terrae* provision, along with the increasingly popular assertion that the king's prerogative was no part of the *legem terrae*, were salient developments.[21]

The next year, in 1628, Parliament passed the Petition of Right. In the Commons, a version of the Petition was put forward that specifically allowed habeas corpus to challenge detentions (especially by the Crown)

---

13. Darnel's Case (The Five Knights case), 3 How. St. Tr. 1 (K.B. 1627).

14. *See* HALLIDAY, *supra* note 4, at 137–39.

15. WILLIAM COBBETT ET AL., A COMPLETE COLLECTION OF STATE TRIALS & PROCEEDINGS FOR HIGH TREASON AND OTHER CRIMES AND MISDEMEANORS 6–7 (London, 1809), *available at* https://archive.org/details/acompletecollec03cobbgoog.

16. *Id.* at 30.

17. *Id.* at 15.

18. *Id.*

19. *Id.* at 38.

20. *Id.* at 57.

21. MEADOR, *supra* note 9, at 13–15.

that lacked a specific cause of commitment, thus attacking the *Darnel* decision directly. Leading the debate in Parliament was Sir Edward Coke, who, at the same time, was completing his *Institutes on the Law of England.* Coke's section on chapter 39—*Nisi per legem terrae*—not only read it as "without due process of law,"[22] but further asserted that due process simply meant the "Common Law."[23] Tellingly, he then asked, "what remedy hath a party grieved"[24] under due process to rectify false imprisonment? Coke's answer, in two chapters in this section, was "habeas corpus."[25]

With habeas corpus's role as the preferred enforcement mechanism for Magna Carta's *legem terrae* provision asserted by Coke, the writ received further imprimatur in the Habeas Corpus Act of 1679.[26] The 1679 Act, however, was not the palladium of liberties that some, like Blackstone, would later assert. Although the Act decreased time limitations in returns to the writ, allowed individual judges—not just full courts—to issue the writ during vacation, and sought to prohibit transfers of prisoners out of the realm to avoid the writ's reach, it also contained limitations to the writ that seem inimical to modern sensibilities. Significantly, although the Act was limited to criminal detentions, it excepted from its protections those people detained for "felony if ordered by justices of the peace"[27] and it did not allow the release of prisoners completely unless the writ challenged the timeliness of an indictment.[28] What the Act did suggest, though, was that the substantive content of the *legem terrae*, now enforced through habeas corpus, was primarily aimed at correcting the arbitrary nature of royal prerogative, and not providing a wider set of personal rights.

II.   Habeas Corpus and Magna Carta in the New World

The fusion of Magna Carta's *legem terrae* and the writ of habeas corpus would, of course, make its way into the nascent American colonies, initially through Coke and then primarily through Blackstone, who, in his *Commentaries*, proclaimed that the Habeas Corpus Act of 1679 was "another *Magna Carta*."[29] Blackstone asserted that the "glory of the English law consists in

---

22. COKE, *supra* note 5, at 50.

23. *Id.*

24. *Id.* at 54.

25. MEADOR, *supra* note 9, at 16–17; *see also* HALLIDAY, *supra* note 4, at 137–39.

26. On the legislative history of the 1679 Habeas Corpus Act, *see* Helen Nutting, *The Most Wholesome Law—The Habeas Corpus Act of 1679*, 65 AM. HIST. REV. 527 (1960).

27. Nutting, *supra* note 26, at 541.

28. HALLIDAY, *supra* note 4, at 242.

29. BLACKSTONE, *supra* note 5, at 135; *see also* JAMES R. STONER, COMMON LAW AND LIBERAL THEORY: COKE, HOBBES AND THE ORIGINS OF AMERICAN CONSTITUTIONALISM 21 (1992).

clearly defining the times, the causes, and the extent when, wherefore, and to what degree, the imprisonment of the subject may be lawful."[30] As a "natural inherent right"[31] that is "established on the firmest basis by the provisions of *magna carta*,"[32] it is best supported and defended by "habeas corpus."[33] But even before Blackstone, and as early as the 1680s, Massachusetts, New York, and Pennsylvania attempted to guarantee the writ modeled on the provisions of the 1679 Act, but these measures were summarily annulled by the Privy Council. In the first few decades of the 18th century, royal governors in Virginia, North Carolina, and South Carolina provided for the writ through proclamation, not statute.[34]

But in *Federalist* No. 84,[35] Alexander Hamilton seemed to suggest that habeas corpus, now enumerated in the proposed Constitution, brought within its protection our most fundamental rights, and did so in a more effective manner than would a Bill of Rights, or even Magna Carta itself.[36] For Hamilton, the protection of fundamental rights was already secured more fully in the Constitution as it stood with no amendments than if specific rights were enumerated. Along with the prohibitions against ex post facto laws, bills of attainder, and grants of nobility, Hamilton proposed that the habeas corpus clause in Article 1 was the primary defense against arbitrary arrests and imprisonments, which in his words, were the "favorite and most formidable instruments of tyranny."[37] Mere parchment barriers, according to Hamilton, such as those that would eventually be enumerated in the first eight amendments, could never be as powerful in guaranteeing individual liberty as the simple protection of habeas corpus. Hamilton then went on to distinguish the rights guaranteed in the unamended Constitution from "bills of rights" more generally, which he considered to be simply "stipulations between kings and their subjects, abridgements of prerogative in favor of privilege, reservations of rights not surrendered to the prince. Such was MAGNA CHARTA, obtained by the barons, sword in hand, from king John."[38] Here, then, habeas corpus further assumed the burden of Magna Carta's *legem terrae* provision through a Whiggish fiction that allowed the Great Writ of Liberty to become a fundamental guarantor of due process in the Constitution.

---

30. BLACKSTONE, *supra* note 5, at 135.
31. *Id.*
32. *Id.*
33. *Id.*
34. Dallin H. Oaks, *Habeas Corpus in the States—1776–1865*, 32 U. CHI. L. REV. 243, 251 (1965).
35. THE FEDERALIST No. 84 (Alexander Hamilton) (Bantam Dell ed., 2003).
36. "The privilege of the writ of habeas corpus shall not be suspended, unless when in cases of rebellion or invasion the public safety may require it." (Alexander Hamilton commenting on Article I, § 9, Clause 2 of the United States Constitution). *Id.* at 523.
37. *Id.* at 522.
38. *Id.* at 523.

To be sure, our modern notion of habeas corpus as a remedy that, in the words of Justice Oliver Wendell Holmes, can "cut through all forms and go . . . to the very tissue"[39] of unconstitutional detention, never crossed the minds of Selden, Coke, or Blackstone. Important limitations, modeled on the 1679 Act, would continue to constrain both the procedural reach of habeas corpus and the set of substantive rights that the writ was now imagined to protect in the United States. Like Magna Carta before it, habeas corpus's power was only ever as large and far-reaching as contemporary notions of due process allowed.[40] Like the Privy Council's acceptance of the King's *speciale mandatum* as consistent with the *legem terrae*, habeas corpus would also reflect the limits of substantive rights and legitimate governmental processes.

III.   Habeas Corpus in Antebellum America

In antebellum America, for example, habeas corpus was used to enforce substantive rights and limit governmental procedural abuses on both the state and national levels, but what exactly constituted due process was widely divergent. Moreover, procedural limitations to the writ all but prevented national courts from removing cases from state jurisdictions into their own.[41] These limitations in part spurred the development of habeas corpus, as this concept was used in some southern states to vindicate asserted due process rights of slaveholders when their *property* was absconded or stolen.[42] Some northern states, on the other hand, advanced a more capacious notion of due process and aggressively used habeas corpus to thwart the enforcement of the fugitive slave clause of the Constitution.[43]

Before the Civil War and Reconstruction, habeas corpus developed on two different tracks in the United States, one state and one federal. Section 14 of The Judiciary Act of 1789[44] stated that:

All the before mentioned courts of the United States, shall have the power to issue writs of *scire facias, habeas corpus,* and all other writs not specifically provided for by statute, which may be necessary for the exercise of their respective jurisdictions, and agreeable to the principles and usages of law. And either of the justices of the Supreme

---

39. Frank v. Mangum, 237 U.S. 309, 346 (1915).

40. Justin Wert, Habeas Corpus in America: The Politics of Individual Rights 199 (2011).

41. For example, Section 14 of the Judiciary Act of 1789 did not provide for the hearing of state habeas corpus cases by federal courts. 1 Stat. 73 (1789).

42. *See* cases discussed in Wert, *supra* note 40, at ch. 2.

43. *Id.*

44. Judiciary Act of 1789, 1 Stat. 73 (1789).

Court, as well as judges of the district courts, shall have the power to grant writs of *habeas corpus* for the purpose of an inquiry into the cause of commitment.—*Provided*, That writs of *habeas corpus* shall in no case extend to prisoners in gaol, unless where they are in custody, under or by colour of the authority of the United States, or are committed for trial before some court of the same, or are necessary to be brought into court to testify.

This effectively precluded federal habeas corpus review for state prisoners in the antebellum period.

On the state level, though, habeas corpus developed in protean ways, sometimes vindicating idealized due process rights, but sometimes serving the very opposite.[45] State variation in the use of habeas corpus to adjudicate slavery law tracked the sectional and geographic divisions before the Civil War. Northern states often employed habeas corpus on the state level to protect their free black populations from kidnappings even though they often acquiesced to southern state demands to recover fugitive slaves.[46] This meant that there were sharp differences in the use and development of habeas corpus on the state level during the antebellum period. Some states, like Mississippi, explicitly provided statutory habeas corpus remedies for slaveholders to recover their slaves when they were stolen.[47] Mississippi's habeas corpus provisions provided for the use of the writ to deliver up a slave to inquire into cases of contested legal ownership. In part, the Mississippi law provided that habeas corpus could be issued to determine whether "any slave or slaves for life shall be taken or seduced out of the possession of the master, owner, overseers of such slaves, by force, stratagem or fraud."[48] In the 1824 case of *Scudder v. Seals*, for example, a habeas corpus petition was issued to bring before the Supreme Court of Mississippi the bodies of two slaves, Dicey and Daniel, to inquire into the legality of their current owner's title.[49] The court determined that Dicey and Daniel, who had been willed to their former owner's daughter, were effectively stolen from her. The habeas corpus proceeding then returned the slaves to the owner.

Issues of state sovereignty also crosscut state habeas corpus in the South. In *Nations v. Alvis*, the Supreme Court of Mississippi refused to release a slave on habeas corpus to her original owner because the theft

---

45. Wert, *supra* note 40, at ch. 2.

46. *Id.*

47. *Id.*

48. 1 Miss. Code Ann. § 11; Oaks, *supra* note 34, at 243, 278; *see also* Wert, *supra* note 40, at 52 (for a more detailed list of antebellum slave law cases in the states).

49. Scudder v. Seals, 1 Miss. 154 (1824); *see also* Hardy v. Smith, 11 Miss. 316 (1844) (where a similar course of events plays out).

had occurred in Tennessee, not Mississippi, where the slave was held.[50] The court ruled that although the use of habeas corpus to recover stolen slaves was a "prompt and effectual remedy,"[51] the notion of state sovereignty "cannot, by any inherent authority, claim respect beyond the jurisdiction of the state which enacts them."[52] The use of habeas corpus to retrieve or recover property was limited to that inquiry only, not only in Mississippi, but in other southern states as well. Legitimate questions concerning the actual freedom of African-Americans sometimes arose in cases involving their disputed ownership, and most southern states increasingly determined that jury trials, not habeas corpus proceedings, were the most appropriate legal mechanisms for decisions involving fundamental rights of property.[53] Because most states simply required a return to a habeas corpus writ that could show some legitimate justification for detention, though, the ubiquitous presumption in slave states that blackness implied servitude significantly limited the utility of the writ for more libertarian causes.

In northern states, habeas corpus laws were enacted in the late 18th and early 19th centuries as part of Revolutionary-inspired slavery prohibitions and manumissions and also in reaction to fugitive slave problems, especially kidnapping. Here, too, there were important variations. Border states such as Pennsylvania were more likely to be conciliatory toward their slave state neighbors with respect to early fugitive slave issues, while New England states such as Massachusetts explicitly linked habeas corpus to its kidnapping statutes as early as 1785.[54]

Even as some states were moving toward gradual abolition, states such as New Jersey routinely allowed habeas corpus to issue in order to resolve disputed claims of title to slaves. In *The State v. Anderson*, for example, the Supreme Court of New Jersey issued a writ of habeas corpus to inquire into the detention of a slave child named Silas.[55] Silas's mother, Betsy, was sold pursuant to her owner's will, which stated that she was to remain a slave for only 15 years after his death. However, during her tenure as a slave for her new owner, she gave birth to a child. The owner then claimed the child as a slave for life, arguing that his property was damaged because she had given birth. The court ultimately ruled that the child was free, and Betsy was also to be free after her 15 years of servitude.

---

50. Nations v. Alvis, 13 Miss. 338, 345 (1845).

51. *Id.* at 345.

52. *Id.*

53. *See, e.g.*, Thornton v. Demoss, 13 Miss. 609 (1846); Weddington v. Sam Sloan (of color), 54 Ky. 147 (1854); Ruddle's Ex'or v. Ben, 37 Va. 467 (1839).

54. *See* Thomas D. Morris, Free Men All: The Personal Liberty Laws of the North 1780–1861, at 11 (1974).

55. State v. Anderson, 1 N.J.L. 41, 43 (1790).

In the same year, another case came to the Supreme Court of New Jersey that presented a similar probate question.[56] After the death of his master, a slave, Tom, was sold to a man named Bloomfield, along with the original owner's other slaves. Evidence was presented to the court that argued that Tom's owner had always wished him to be free at his death: at times he was heard to have stated that "they had sucked the same breasts, and that he should never serve another master."[57] The court then issued a writ of habeas corpus. Bloomfield's counsel argued that for a slave to be free, his master must do more than "mention it to a third party."[58] The court, relying again on the owner's complete power over his property, ruled that his verbal intention was enough, and Tom was discharged with his freedom. Just four years later, however, the same court ruled that a verbal intention to free a slave upon an owner's death was not enough for freedom. In the words of the court, the slaves in question "must go with the other property, and legally belong to the defendant."[59] Although the habeas corpus petition failed to free the slaves, the court nevertheless refused to hold those who filed the writ liable for court costs and damages to the defendant. The court justified its position by saying that "they would not in any case compel the prosecutors of these writs to pay costs; it was a laudable and humane thing in any man or set of men to bring up the claims of these unfortunate people before the court for consideration."[60]

On the state level in the antebellum period, then, while habeas corpus did have a due process component, it was often in no way concerned with freedom.

Nevertheless, there were two important antebellum congressional modifications in habeas corpus jurisdiction for federal courts. In 1833, Congress modified federal court habeas corpus jurisdiction to include habeas corpus petitions from those who might be detained by state authorities when enforcing federal law.[61] In 1842, Congress again expanded federal court habeas corpus authority for foreign nationals detained by state governments.[62] The 1833 Act was used to remove from state to federal courts cases in which federal marshals were arrested by state authorities for enforcing the fugitive slave provisions of the Compromise of 1850.[63] This unintended consequence—which was recognized as such by federal court judges at the time—nevertheless fueled significant backlash from states that were actively

---

56. State v. Adm'rs of Prall, 1 N.J.L. 4 (1790).
57. Id.
58. Id.
59. State v. Frees, 1 N.J.L. 299, 300 (1794).
60. Id.
61. Force Bill, 4 Stat. 632 (1833).
62. 5 Stat. 539 (1842).
63. CONG. GLOBE, 31st Cong., 1st Sess. 1502–1837 (1850).

using their own newly improved state habeas corpus powers to thwart federal fugitive slave legislation and protect their free black populations from kidnappings. The Jacksonian regime's habeas corpus expansion might not have been needed after the passage of the Force Bill,[64] but the provision nevertheless remained law, buttressing both the enforcement of the Democratic Party's vision of constitutional governance with respect to the maintenance of slavery as well as state-level Republican backlash during the 1850s.[65] What is most interesting about the 1833 Act is that it was never used for its original purpose, which was to provide a legal mechanism for the removal of cases involving federal revenue officers who might be arrested by state authorities.[66]

The 1842 Act resulted from the McCleod Affair. On December 30, 1837, the American steamboat *Caroline* was destroyed by British troops as it lay moored in Schlosser, New York. Canadian insurgents, who had recently engaged British troops in Ontario, hoped that the *Caroline* would bring much-needed provisions to their resistance efforts. That day, however, British troops sacked the ship, burned it, and sent it over Niagara Falls, killing two people. The administration of U.S. President Martin Van Buren directed Secretary of State John Forsyth to protest the British actions. His protests were met with the response that the United States had failed to quell its citizens' involvement in British and Canadian affairs.[67]

Alexander McCleod, a Canadian, was subsequently arrested by New York authorities for his suspected involvement in the assault on the ship. Angered, the British government demanded that McCleod be released because he was acting on orders directly from the British Crown. His actions, according to the British government, were public, not private, and were simply the extension of a sovereign nation. Importantly, in Secretary Forsyth's reply, he not only disagreed with the characterization of McCleod's actions as public, which might have precluded his prosecution by the state of New York, but he also stated that the federal government did not have the power to reach into the criminal proceedings of the states.[68]

When John Tyler assumed the presidency, his secretary of state, Daniel Webster, reversed the United States' previous position on McCleod's actions but still maintained that the federal government did not have the ability to reach into the domain of state criminal law to free McCleod. Convinced that the government was powerless, but sympathetic to Britain's position, Webster even went so far as to enlist the help of Attorney General John

---

64. Force Bill, *supra* note 61.
65. WERT, *supra* note 40, at 46–48.
66. *Id.* at 63.
67. David J. Bederman, *Cautionary Tale of Alexander Mcleod: Superior Orders and the American Writ of Habeas Corpus*, 41 EMORY L. J. 515, 517 (1992).
68. *Id.* at 518.

Crittenden to aid in McCleod's defense in New York courts. With little subsequent fanfare, McCleod was held over for trial and then subsequently acquitted.[69]

In March 1842, just a few months after McCleod's acquittal, another participant in the raid on the *Caroline* was arrested. In order to avert another international incident, and well aware of similar situations in which foreign nationals were detained by state authorities, President Tyler proposed that Congress remedy this problem through appropriate habeas corpus legislation. As would be expected, the initial wording of the bill from the Senate Judiciary Committee, which provided for the removal of cases from state to federal courts via habeas corpus for "any act done . . . under the law of nations . . . or authority of any foreign State or sovereignty,"[70] met with spirited resistance, particularly from Democrats. Not only did these habeas corpus provisions potentially threaten the traditional criminal justice domain of state courts, but in the minds of some Southern members of Congress, they might inspire foreigners to incite slave revolts in states, only to have their cases removed to federal court and dismissed.[71] The final bill, which equally divided Whigs and Democrats, provided that federal habeas corpus authority would extend to

> all cases of any prisoner or prisoners in jail or confinement, where he, she, or they, being subjects or citizens of a foreign State, and domiciled therein, shall be committed or confined, or in custody, under or by authority of law, or process founded thereon, of the United States or any one of them; for or on account of any act done or omitted under any alleged right, title, authority, privilege, protection, or exemption, set up or claimed under the commission, or order, or sanction, of any foreign State or sovereignty, the validity and effect whereof depend upon the law of nations, or under color thereof.[72]

What is important to understand about the two antebellum changes to federal habeas corpus court jurisdiction is the overtly political origins of those changes and their federalism dimensions. Like previous English changes to habeas corpus, both the 1833 and 1842 acts were engineered by political regimes to meet critical challenges to their ability to govern. For Andrew Jackson, habeas corpus changes were necessary to enforce a core regime principle in the form of a centrist federalism that, while deferential to states' rights as a political proposition, was nevertheless unyielding on the basic enforcement powers of the national government. For the Tyler

69. *Id.* at 526.
70. *Id.* at 527.
71. *Id.* at 528.
72. Act of 29 August 1842, 5 Stat. 539.

administration, as for others before it, the ability of the federal government to operate with legitimacy and authority on the international stage required habeas corpus changes to remove state cases against foreign nationals to federal courts.

These changes also directly implicated issues of federalism and states' rights, and criticisms of both changes in this regard were swift.[73] Both acts are often cited by contemporary critics in support of broad arguments about the inevitability of increased federal habeas corpus court supervision of state criminal trials. But there is nothing in the history of these two acts that suggests that they were initiated for reasons other than the enforcement and maintenance of core regime principles of Jacksonian Democrats in the early 1830s and Whigs in the early 1840s.

Moreover, the regime principles that were enforced through these changes to habeas corpus were never conceived as having anything remotely to do with the individual rights of the potential petitioners in the ways with which we are familiar today. The removal of state cases to federal habeas corpus courts for federal revenue officers or foreign nationals was a far cry from the use of habeas corpus to vindicate the rights of minority criminal defendants in southern state courts during the height of Jim Crow. If anything, these changes were solicitous of majorities, not minorities.

The unintended use of the 1833 Act described above began soon after the passage and implementation of the Compromise of 1850, which in part strengthened fugitive slave laws. The essential parts of the Fugitive Slave Act in the Compromise of 1850 provided that the Act's provisions were to be carried out by commissioners appointed by United States circuit courts who would have authority to issue certificates of removal for fugitive slaves. If United States marshals refused to carry out their duties in reclaiming slaves, they were to be fined $1,000. Marshals were also to be held liable for the value of slaves in their custody. Slave owners had two options in reclaiming their property. In the first, the Act reaffirmed slave owners' common law right of reception, which would allow them to seize physically their property anywhere, in any state, at any time, and in any way. After the seizure, they could then bring the slave to a United States commissioner, who would issue a certificate of removal. Alternatively, slave owners could first apply for a certificate of removal and then, with the aid of United States marshals, who could call forth a *posse commitatus*, physically recover their property. Hearings for certificates before the commissioners could not involve any testimony from slaves themselves. Just as important, the Act also prohibited any interference in the rendition of fugitive slaves "by any process issued by any court, judge, magistrate, or other person whomsoever."[74] Effectively

---

73. *See, e.g.*, Justice Brennan's opinion in Fay v. Noia, 372 U.S. 391, 401 at n.9 (1963).

74. Fugitive Slave Act, 9 Stat. 462 § 6 (1850).

gutting any meaningfully substantive review of a suspected fugitive's status through habeas corpus, a writ of habeas corpus could still theoretically be issued, but a certificate of removal was all that was needed to answer the writ.[75]

Before signing the bill into law, President Millard Fillmore first requested that his attorney general, John Crittenden, advise him on the constitutionality of the bill with respect to its effect on habeas corpus, specifically the very real possibility of the Act's de facto suspension of the writ in its prohibitions against legal "molestations."[76] Crittenden's response was that the bill did not jeopardize habeas corpus "in any manner."[77] At issue, of course, was the larger problem of conflicting habeas corpus writs between states and the federal government, as well as the extent to which habeas corpus could be used (on either level) to inquire into the substantive issues associated with detention. The Compromise of 1850 seemed to preclude any use of the writ by states to frustrate the return of fugitive slaves. Moreover, suspecting that collisions between state and federal power were imminent immediately after the Compromise was signed into law, Supreme Court Justice Robert Grier and Circuit Court Judge John Kane personally requested that President Fillmore use federal troops in the enforcement of the law. Not wanting to foment uneasiness in the North concerning this issue, Fillmore agreed to provide troops only in emergencies. Nevertheless, the president remained committed "to bring[ing] the whole force of the government to sustain the law."[78]

These habeas corpus issues would come to implicate the 1833 Act in early 1853 in *Ex parte Jenkins* when four slave catchers were arrested for trespass in Pennsylvania during a violent seizure of a slave named Thomas.[79] The marshals then filed a habeas corpus writ in federal circuit court arguing that their detention was unconstitutional. Justice Grier and circuit court justice Kane ruled that the 1833 Habeas Corpus Act allowed the writ to issue from federal to state courts, and the marshals were discharged. The unintended consequence of the 1833 Act's use in these types of cases did not escape either judge; in fact, their use of it suggests that they thought that the 1833 Act's application to these types of cases was only a natural application of the Act's general propositions and intent.[80]

---

75. STANLEY W. CAMPBELL, THE SLAVE CATCHERS: ENFORCEMENT OF THE FUGITIVE SLAVE LAW 1850–1860, at 24–25 (2011).

76. *Id.* at n. 77.

77. *Id.* at 96–97.

78. *Id.* at 98.

79. *Ex parte* Jenkins, 13 F. Cas. 445 (1853).

80. Judge Kane argued, "the phraseology of the [1833] statute is unequivocal in its import, and entirely consonant with its apparent object. It applies in broad and general terms to all officers of the United States, by whatever law or authority confined." *Id.* at 445, 451.

It was just this type of state interference with federal law that originally prompted Congress to provide federal habeas corpus relief for tariff officers should they be detained by South Carolina authorities during the nullification crisis. With respect to similar state-level interference with the fugitive slave provisions of the Compromise of 1850, Justice Grier proclaimed, "The extreme advocate of state rights would scarcely contend that in such cases the courts of the United States should be wholly unable to protect themselves or their officers."[81] Here again, habeas corpus became a central tool in the larger political process of sustaining and enforcing core constitutional principles during the antebellum period.

Of course, backlash against this coalition and its use of habeas corpus was already brewing. No case better exemplifies these tensions, especially with respect to the use of habeas corpus to serve competing jurisdictional and political regimes, than *Ableman v. Booth*.[82] Here, Chief Justice Roger Taney faced head-on the dual track development of state and federal habeas corpus during the antebellum period as he was forced to resolve the question of whether an affirmative grant of a state habeas corpus writ by Wisconsin state courts should be obeyed by federal courts. The scenario was a familiar one: Sherman Booth, an abolitionist editor, was arrested by U.S. Marshall Stephen Ableman for helping a fugitive slave named Joshua Glover escape his jail cell and flee to Canada.[83]

For Taney, the practical problem with Wisconsin's position—particularly its use of habeas corpus—was that it effectively precluded any kind of national enforcement, prosecution, and judicial resolution of national criminal law. If states exercised this supposed authority to use habeas corpus to free those detained, indicted, and prosecuted within their states' territorial jurisdiction, they would quickly undermine any national legislative and judicial power. The result would be that "because State courts would not always agree . . . it would often happen, that an act which was admitted to be an offence, and justly punished, in one State, would be regarded as innocent, and indeed praiseworthy, in another."[84]

Taney's argument then moved to one of the strongest assertions of national power that the Court had as yet made. Without specific authority to issue habeas corpus for federal prisoners either from its own state constitution or from the national one, it was forever to be understood that "no

---

81. *Id.* at 448. Other antebellum cases in which the 1833 Act was used to discharge federal officers involved in fugitive slave renditions include *Ex parte* Robinson, 30 F. Cas. 965 (1856) and *Ex parte* Sifford, 22 F. Cas. 105 (1857).

82. Ableman v. Booth, 62 U.S. 506 (1859).

83. For a detailed account of the case *see* H. ROBERT BAKER, THE RESCUE OF JOSHUA GLOVER: A FUGITIVE SLAVE, THE CONSTITUTION, AND THE COMING OF THE CIVIL WAR (2006).

84. *Id.* at 515.

State can authorize one of its judges or courts to exercise judicial power, by *habeas corpus* or otherwise, within the jurisdiction of another independent government."[85] Although both the state and national governments will inevitably exercise their jurisdictional powers within the same territorial limits, Taney forcefully asserted that these powers are derived from:

> separate and distinct sovereignties, acting separately and independently of each other, within their respective spheres. And the sphere of action appropriated to the United States is as far beyond the reach of the judicial processes issued by a State judge or State court, as if the line of division was traced by landmarks and monuments visible to the eye.[86]

Importantly, toward the end of the opinion, Taney nevertheless held that states were not prohibited from issuing the great writ for those held within their jurisdictions. What they could not do, however, was go beyond an answer to the writ when it was determined that a prisoner was held by authority of the United States. Thus there could not be any substantive inquiry into the constitutionality of the law by which a prisoner was held—this power was reserved to the Supreme Court alone.[87] As it had so often, then, habeas corpus—and the substantive rights it would protect, including Magna Carta's due process ideals—would yield to *procedural* adjustments to those substantive rights by political elites.

IV.   Civil War, Reconstruction, and the Gilded Age

Certainly, the Republican regime during the Civil War and Reconstruction would redefine some substantive fundamental rights, and, as would be expected, habeas corpus was similarly redefined, both in its procedural reach and in its substantive application, to enforce these rights. During this time, the substantive rights that habeas corpus sought to protect—due process and equal protection rights for newly freed slaves—were borne out, but only temporarily. The substantive and procedural changes to the writ by political regimes during the Civil War and Reconstruction ultimately led to decreased substantive protections by the end of the 19th century.[88]

The major habeas corpus developments in this period—Lincoln's suspension and Taney's response; Congress's legislation that retroactively gave an imprimatur to executive suspension; the Habeas Corpus Act of 1867 and its subsequent repeal; and the Supreme Court's own judicially created habeas

---

85. *Ableman*, 62 U.S. at 515–516.
86. BAKER, *supra* note 83, at 515.
87. *Id.* at 522.
88. WERT, *supra* note 40, at 116.

corpus rules for review of state habeas corpus cases in the 1880s—tracked a pattern of increased use of habeas corpus by federal courts for state prisoners initially predicated on new substantive rights. But the use of habeas corpus to enforce these new rights soon gave way to a decreased commitment for those particular rights and new commitments for a different set of substantive rights that habeas corpus did not reach, specifically substantive due process rights of property and contract during the Gilded Age.[89]

Significantly, after Reconstruction, some members of Congress felt that the provisions for the removal of state cases to federal courts were an insult to state courts. With decreased support throughout the country for aggressive national supervision of the kinds of fundamental due process rights that had been pushed for during the height of Reconstruction, Congress reinstated the Court's appellate power to hear habeas corpus cases under the 1867 Habeas Act,[90] and explicitly invited the Court to set its own rules for these cases. Not surprisingly, in the first case to come before them, *Ex parte Royall*,[91] the Court announced what would become to be known as the "exhaustion requirement,"[92] which required that habeas corpus petitioners first exhaust all state appellate avenues before even the lowest federal court could entertain the writ.[93]

V. 20th Century and Beyond

Beginning in the first half of the 20th century, habeas corpus slowly developed into a legal remedy for almost any due process violation, coming as close as any time in its history to reflecting the idealized due process ideals in the 17th-century rewriting of habeas corpus and Magna Carta. Covering a catalogue of fundamental rights wider than Magna Carta ever promised, the esteemed law professor Zechariah Chafee proclaimed that the substantive reach of habeas corpus now included:

> [T]he right to be accused by a grand jury, to be immune from double jeopardy, not to be deprived of liberty without due process of law, to a speedy and public trial by a jury of the vicinage, to be informed of the nature of the accusation, to be confronted with the witnesses against him, to call his own witnesses and have his own lawyer.[94]

---

89. *Id.* at ch. 3.
90. *Id.* at 111–13.
91. *Ex parte* Royall, 117 U.S. 241 (1886).
92. *See* DUKER, *supra* note 7, at 181.
93. *Ex parte* Royall, 117 U.S. at 251.
94. Zechariah Chafee Jr., *The Most Important Human Right in the Constitution*, 32 B.U. L. REV. 143, 144 (1952).

In *Fay v. Noia* (1963), which came at the apex of the Supreme Court's liberalization of habeas corpus during the 1960s, Justice Brennan said of modern encomiums for the writ:

> These are not extravagant expressions. Behind them may be discerned the unceasing contest between personal liberty and government oppression. It is no accident that habeas corpus has time and again played a central role in national crises, wherein the claims of order and of liberty clash most acutely, not only in England in the seventeenth century, but also America from our very beginnings, and today. Although in form the Great Writ is simply a mode of procedure, its history is inextricably intertwined with the growth of fundamental rights of personal liberty. For its function has been to provide a prompt and efficacious remedy for whatever society deems to be intolerable restraints.[95]

Perpetuating the myth of habeas corpus's progressive development as much as anyone before him, Brennan then asserted that as early as the 16th century, habeas corpus simply "prefigured the union of the right to due process drawn from Magna Charta."[96] Brennan's encomiums to Magna Carta are replete within his habeas corpus opinions. In fact, *Fay v. Noia* was one-third of the "habeas trilogy"[97] cases that the Court handed down in 1963, effectively widening federal habeas corpus access for state prisoners more than at any other point before or since in American history.[98]

VI.   Conclusion

What, then, are we to make of the historically inaccurate accounts of Magna Carta and habeas corpus? One profitable way might be to treat Blackstone's assertion of habeas corpus as another Magna Carta not as an account of origins for either Magna Carta or habeas corpus, but rather as an account of their capacity to develop and change over time. Blackstone's attribution of the new role of habeas corpus as successor to Magna Carta could easily be questioned and then summarily rejected as nothing more than what Alfred Kelly called "law office history," whereby lawyers pick and choose facts that construct a supposedly inevitable narrative purely in the service of their own position.[99]

---

95. Fay v. Noia, 372 U.S. 391, 400–01 (1963).

96. *Id.* at 402.

97. *Id.* at 404, 426.

98. *See* the trilogy cases: *Fay*, 372 U.S. at 391; Sanders v. United States, 373 U.S. 1 (1963); and Townsend v. Sain, 372 U.S. 293 (1963).

99. Alfred Kelly, *Clio and the Court: An Illicit Love Affair*, 1965 Sup. Ct. Rev. 119, 122 (1965).

Certainly accounts of both Magna Carta and habeas corpus fall prey to this vice as the substantive rights of the barons that the Great Charter most likely sought to protect at the time—like the substantive "rights" of slave owners that habeas corpus was used to protect—are too often ignored or forgotten.

Another profitable way to understand the link between habeas corpus and Magna Carta would be to see habeas corpus as a repository for Magna Carta's due process ideals. Here, though, we have to pay more attention to the attendant *political* context of habeas corpus development. If due process is a murky and changing notion in Magna Carta, it is for habeas corpus too. Like Magna Carta, habeas corpus is simply not the counter-majoritarian check against executives or political majorities that we tend to assume. Because habeas corpus and the Whiggish ideals of Magna Carta are often tools of political regimes, they often serve powerful interests first. This is certainly true of habeas corpus *and* the revisionist histories of Magna Carta that relied so heavily on a critique founded on the feudal character of the barons. We can understand their link better, then, if we understand both as procedural more than substantive rights. Their real power is in their procedural ability to change substantive rights. This means that both have the potential to enforce conceptions of rights that are consistent with our best ideals. But it also means that they have the potential to enforce our worst ideals, too. This was certainly the case in the slave law of antebellum America. Both habeas corpus and Magna Carta, then, are procedural repositories—markers if you will—for changing notions of what we mean by due process.

Nevertheless, the very fact that the substantive and procedural due process rights that Magna Carta and habeas corpus have protected through the centuries have varied considerably, even in negative directions, is proof enough of their liberty-yielding potential. In this sense, our acceptance of less–than-accurate histories is, at the very least, testament to our normative preference for more capacious notions of personal rights and liberties.

In McIlwain's 1914 article critiquing Whiggish accounts of Magna Carta, he came to the conclusion that while some modern rights, like trial by jury, were never implied in Magna Carta in the way that we imagine today,[100] "we may still hold, as our fathers did, that the law of the land is there."[101] Intentional or not, then, the wisdom of the barons who managed to secure feudal rights at Runnymede was present in the framing of procedural rights like *legem terrae* that were specific enough to protect their most immediate substantive concerns but, fortuitously, general enough to remind us that there is still work left to be done.

---

100. For a discussion of this, please see chapter 11, "Magna Carta, Civil Law, and Canon Law."

101. McIlwain, *supra* note 1, at 51.

Chapter 8
Magna Carta and Religious Freedom

Tore Lindholm

I. Introduction: The Notion of Religious Freedom

Readers may know much about the celebrated Great Charter of Liberty: the real-world political agreement struck between King John Lackland of England (r. 1199–1216) and his barons, sealed at Runnymede in June 1215. They may know about Magna Carta's several reissues in the course of the 13th century and the at-times significant changes to its contents, interpretations, and legal status. Readers may also be familiar with Magna Carta's astonishing success in later centuries, once it had become a potent semi-mythic entity in the hands of Sir Edward Coke in the 17th century and Whig-minded historians in 18th-century Britain. And many readers may appreciate the Charter's high standing, when reinterpreted and constructively memorialized, once more, by prominent actors and their constituencies in North America, before, during, and after the American Revolution, up until the present time.

But not all readers may have contemplated the specific subject matter to be addressed in this chapter: religious freedom. They may not have reflected on what the term "religious freedom" reasonably may be said to refer to, nor have considered where, when, under what circumstances, and to what extent such liberty has been embodied in real-world law or practices, nor have thought about possible unintended and perhaps unwelcome implications of its use. Now, deciding upon the most suitable interpretation of the term "religious freedom" is not beyond reasonable dispute—far from it. So, this chapter utilizes a particular and widely favored contemporary understanding.

A basic notion of religious freedom was spelled out, with considerable international legal and political authority, in the 1948 Universal Declaration of Human Rights,[1] Article 18, and more meticulously in Article 18 of the

---

1. *See* Universal Declaration of Human Rights, G.A. Res. 217A (III), U.N. Doc. A/RES/217(III) (Dec. 10, 1948), http://www.ohchr.org/EN/UDHR/Documents/UDHR _Translations/eng.pdf.

1966 International Covenant on Civil and Political Rights.[2] Similar notions
of religious freedom are standard in other modern human rights documents,
in domestic legal orders, and in international political discourse,[3] including
that engaged in by the United States.[4] This contemporary notion of religious
freedom has after 1948 been fleshed out in a large body of international
jurisprudence.[5] Crucially, it includes the concept that no person is to be dis-
criminated against on the grounds of religion. But the basic idea, conceived
in response to the fact and the perceived legitimacy of religious diversity
and disagreement in the polity, is not a modern invention. It is a notion of
religious freedom in line with a venerable albeit interrupted politico-legal
tradition pioneered by, and unmistakably manifested and made public by,
Indian Emperor Ashoka (r. 302–232 B.C.E.).[6]

Emperor Ashoka, a devoted and learned Buddhist, had his famous Rock
Edicts carved into smooth rock surfaces for general public accessibility in
a large number of places in his Mauryan empire. These were made public
around 259–258 B.C.E. Most significant for religious freedom are Edict 7
and Edict 12.[7] Emperor Ashoka's Edict 7, in a translation rendered by Ven

---

2. Article 18 of the International Covenant on Civil and Political Rights provides:

   1. Everyone shall have the right to freedom of thought, conscience and religion.
      This right shall include freedom to have or to adopt a religion or belief of his
      choice, and freedom, either individually or in community with others and in
      public or private, to manifest his religion or belief in worship, observance,
      practice and teaching.
   2. No one shall be subject to coercion which would impair his freedom to have
      or to adopt a religion or belief of his choice.
   3. Freedom to manifest one's religion or beliefs may be subject only to such
      limitations as are prescribed by law and are necessary to protect public safety,
      order, health, or morals or the fundamental rights and freedoms of others.
   4. The States Parties to the present Covenant undertake to have respect for the
      liberty of parents and, when applicable, legal guardians to ensure the religious
      and moral education of their children in conformity with their own convictions.

See International Covenant on Civil and Political Rights, Dec. 19, 1966, UN Doc.
A/6316(1966), 999 UNTS 171, 1155 UTS 331, https://treaties.un.org/doc/Publication
/UNTS/Volume%20999/volume-999-I-14668-English.pdf.

3. See FACILITATING FREEDOM OF RELIGION OR BELIEF: A DESKBOOK 873–918
(Tore Lindholm et al. eds., 2004) [hereinafter FACILITATING FREEDOM].

4. See U.S. Department of State, Religious Freedom, STATE.GOV, http://www.state
.gov/j/drl/irf/ (last visited May 17, 2014).

5. See W. COLE DURHAM JR. & BRETT G. SCHARFFS, LAW AND RELIGION: NATIONAL,
INTERNATIONAL, AND COMPARATIVE PERSPECTIVES 77–111 (2010).

6. Amulya Chandra Sen, Encyclopedia Britannica: Ashoka (emperor of India),
BRITANNICA.COM, available at http://www.britannica.com/EBchecked/topic/38797/Ashoka.

7. See Ven. S. Dhammika, King Ashoka: His Edicts and His Times, The Fourteen
Rock Edicts, CS.COLOSTATE.EDU, http://www.cs.colostate.edu/~malaiya/ashoka.html#
FOURTEEN (last visited May 17, 2014). For a recent study of Emperor Ashoka's Rock
Edicts, see CHARLES ALLEN, ASHOKA: THE SEARCH FOR INDIA'S LOST EMPEROR 383–85,
405–16 (2012).

S. Dhammika, begins: "Beloved-of-the-Gods, King Piyadasi [this is Emperor Ashoka's self-presentation], *desires that all religions should reside everywhere*, for all of them desire self-control and purity of heart."[8]

Emperor Ashoka's Edict 12 continues:

> But Beloved-of-the-Gods, King Piyadasi, does not value gifts and honors as much as he values this—that *there should be growth in the essentials of all religions*. Growth in essentials can be done in different ways, but all of them have as their root restraint in speech, that is, not praising one's own religion, or condemning the religion of others without good cause. And if there is cause for criticism, it should be done in a mild way. But it is better to honor other religions for this reason. By so doing, one's own religion benefits, and so do other religions, while doing otherwise harms one's own religion and the religions of others. Whoever praises his own religion, due to excessive devotion, and condemns others with the thought "Let me glorify my own religion," only harms his own religion. Therefore contact (between religions) is good. One should listen to and respect the doctrines professed by others. Beloved-of-the-Gods, King Piyadasi, desires that all should be well-learned in the good doctrines of other religions.[9]

Article 18 of the 1948 Universal Declaration of Human Rights similarly facilitates religious diversity and reciprocal respect. It provides: "Everyone has the right to freedom of thought, conscience and religion; *this right includes freedom to change his religion or belief*, and freedom, either alone or in community with others and in public or private, to manifest his religion or belief in teaching, practice, worship and observance."[10]

An Ashoka/Universal Declaration approach to religious freedom is based on principled mutual respect across substantive religious divides. But when it was introduced in many great empires of antiquity, from the Persian King Cyrus in the sixth century B.C.E. to the Roman Empire until the advent of Christians, religious freedom was, admittedly, often a political expedient in the wake of major imperial conquests.[11]

A different, and on the face of it, outdated—while *partisan*—interpretation of religious freedom leaning toward "freedom of the church" has flourished in North America, at least since the 1760s. In Section III of this chapter, I shall argue that a focus stemming from "freedom of the church" may, once it is transformed and pruned to cope with the legitimate diversity of religions and worldviews in the modern era, help offset reduction of

---

8. Dhammika, *supra* note 7, at Edict 7 (emphasis added).

9. *Id.* at Edict 12 (emphasis added).

10. *See* Universal Declaration of Human Rights, *supra* note 1, at art. 18 (emphasis added).

11. *See* Facilitating Freedom, *supra* note 3, at 25, 30–31.

religious freedom to the nonpublic spheres of society and shield unimpeded exercise of conscientious commitment for all human beings, whether they are religious or not.

However, now referring to the first-mentioned authorities and sources, I submit that government-protected religious freedom should be conceptualized as: protection of people's freedom to embrace mutually divergent faiths and rivaling conscientious commitments; protection of their freedom to uphold, revise, or change their religious or nonreligious fundamental convictions; and protection of people's freedom, restricted only by proper legal regulation, to engage in corresponding faith-based practices. If such a concept of religious freedom—an interpretation in line, so to speak, with Emperor Ashoka's Rock Edicts and the Universal Declaration—is adopted, then it inescapably follows that Magna Carta did not provide for religious freedom. Nor was protection of religious freedom, conceived as shielding religious diversity and change, detectably anticipated by King John or by any coauthor of Magna Carta in 1215.

Had it been the case that the text of Magna Carta, particularly in the most "pro-religious" parts of the document—the Greeting, the Preamble, and chapter 1—could arguably be said to provide for religious freedom, then of course a reasonable point of departure for this chapter would have been to spell out and discuss the way and the extent to which it did so provide. However, I shall argue that there is, upon close examination, not even a trace of religious freedom provisions in the Great Charter of Liberty.

Scholars who decline to recognize "that religious freedom was the *first* freedom guaranteed by Magna Carta" have, for this their alleged mistake, been scolded for "historical revisionism" and worse.[12] To defend the proposition that Magna Carta does not provide for religious freedom is of course not to discredit the Great Charter. To the contrary, the argument that Magna Carta does not provide for religious freedom is based straightforwardly on the relevant historical facts: first on the text of Magna Carta itself and then on the relevant institutional and political circumstances of John's Angevin England.

Section I presents the evidence for this view and initiates the argument. Section II deals with reinterpretations and creative uses of Magna Carta, first by Sir Edward Coke and then by Whig historians and then by later Britons until the arrival of post–World War II human rights. The question throughout is: Was Magna Carta reinterpreted, or made use of, so as to provide for or facilitate religious freedom? Section III turns to creative reinterpretations of Magna Carta by prominent American actors and institutions and addresses more normative issues: the question here concerns the context, and the manner, in which recourse to a distant Magna Carta today may benefit the noble cause of government protection for freedom of

---

12. *See, e.g.,* Bojidar Marinov, *The Forgotten Clauses of the Magna Carta,* AMERICANVISION.ORG (Sept. 22, 2010), http://americanvision.org/3524/the-forgotten -clauses-of-the-magna-carta/#sthash.laCAiWlG.dpbs.

religion and conscientious nonreligious commitment. At stake is, perhaps, whether and how America's unique religious freedom–contribution to the world, with its remote roots in Magna Carta and "the rights and liberties of all Englishmen" can survive contemporary conflicts between belligerent adherents of conservative religion and equally belligerent secularists. Finally, Section IV addresses ramifications for public civility of our competing faith-based knowledge claims in a pluralist democracy.

II. Whether the Original Magna Carta of June 1215 Protected Religious Freedom

The first three parts of the original 1215 version of Magna Carta, sealed in June 1215, are clearly the parts of the document most pertinent to matters of religion. Comprising a scant one-twelfth of the entire text, the first three parts run as follows:[13]

[Greeting:]

JOHN, by the grace of God King of England, Lord of Ireland, Duke of Normandy and Aquitaine, and Count of Anjou, to his archbishops, bishops, abbots, earls, barons, justices, foresters, sheriffs, stewards, servants, and to all his officials and loyal subjects, Greeting.

[Preamble:]

KNOW THAT BEFORE GOD, for the health of our soul and those of our ancestors and heirs, to the honor of God, the exaltation of the holy Church, and the better ordering of our kingdom, at the advice of our reverend fathers Stephen, archbishop of Canterbury, primate of all England, and cardinal of the holy Roman Church, Henry archbishop of Dublin, William bishop of London, Peter bishop of Winchester, Jocelin bishop of Bath and Glastonbury, Hugh bishop of Lincoln, Walter bishop of Worcester, William bishop of Coventry, Benedict bishop of Rochester, Master Pandulf subdeacon and member of the papal household, Brother Aymeric master of the knighthood of the Temple in England, William Marshal earl of Pembroke, William earl of Salisbury, William earl of Warren, William earl of Arundel, Alan de Galloway constable of Scotland, Warin Fitz Gerald, Peter Fitz Herbert, Hubert

---

13. British Library, *Treasures in Full: Magna Carta, Translation*, BL.UK, http://www .bl.uk/treasures/magnacarta/translation/mc_trans.html (last visited May 17, 2014). The British Library translation of the 1215 text of Magna Carta "sets out to convey the sense rather than the precise wording of the original Latin." *Id.*

de Burgh seneschal of Poitou, Hugh de Neville, Matthew Fitz Herbert, Thomas Basset, Alan Basset, Philip Daubeny, Robert de Roppeley, John Marshal, John Fitz Hugh, and other loyal subjects:

[Chapter 1, first part]:

FIRST, THAT WE HAVE GRANTED TO GOD, and by this present charter have confirmed for us and our heirs in perpetuity, that the English Church shall be free, and shall have its rights undiminished, and its liberties unimpaired. That we wish this so to be observed, appears from the fact that of our own free will, before the outbreak of the present dispute between us and our barons, we granted and confirmed by charter the freedom of the Church's elections—a right reckoned to be of the greatest necessity and importance to it—and caused this to be confirmed by Pope Innocent III. This freedom we shall observe ourselves, and desire to be observed in good faith by our heirs in perpetuity.

Lest there be any doubt, the last chapter—chapter 63—expressly reiterates that the English Church shall be free: "IT IS ACCORDINGLY OUR WISH AND COMMAND that the English Church shall be free."[14]

Thus there can be no doubt that King John explicitly in the "Greeting," "Preamble," "chapter 1," and chapter 63 of Magna Carta, and implicitly in the entire document, acknowledges the unquestioned legitimacy and authority of one particular religious body, the Roman Church, and its supreme head, Pope Innocent III (r. 1198–1216). And there can be no denying that King John does grant and confirm "for us and our heirs in perpetuity" that the English Church (*ecclesia Anglicana*, i.e., the Roman Church in John's realm) "shall be free, and shall have its rights undiminished" nor that King John, stressing what had earlier been "granted and confirmed by charter" also reaffirms "the freedom of the Church's elections—a right reckoned to be of the greatest necessity and importance to it [i.e., the freedom of the Church to elect its clerics]."[15]

However, our question is whether the freedom that King John in the very first chapter of Magna Carta is granting "to God" and confirming "for us and our heirs in perpetuity" does amount to religious freedom: Does it provide for people's freedom to embrace mutually divergent faiths or rivaling religious commitments? Does it facilitate religious change? If it does not amount to providing for religious freedom, does it at least indicate an opening in that direction in Angevin England?

Clearly, the text of Magna Carta does not protect religious freedom along the lines of the Ashoka/Universal Declaration notion of religious freedom.

14. *Id.*
15. *Id.*

But in order better to grasp Magna Carta as it relates to religious freedom we must turn to the institutional and political context of John's England, in particular to the historical background in the "Papal Revolution"[16] initiated by Pope Gregory VII (r. 1073–1085) and the investiture conflict between the pope, the spiritual lord of Christendom, and Christendom's temporal lords, over supremacy in matters of church appointments and church control.

Pope Gregory VII had in 1075 published his revolutionary *Dictatus Papae*, consisting of 27 terse propositions, including the following:

1. That the Roman Church is founded by the Lord alone.
2. That the Roman bishop alone is by right called universal.
3. That he alone may depose and reinstate bishops. . . .
9. That the pope alone is the one whose feet are to be kissed by all princes. . . .
11. That he may depose emperors. . . .
27. That he may absolve subjects of unjust men from their [oath of] fealty.[17]

Gregory's Papal Manifesto soon triggered his struggle with Holy Roman Emperor Henry IV (r. 1084–1105), a struggle that climaxed in January 1077 with the deposed Henry's journey to Canossa as a humble penitent. When Henry, absolved and reinstalled as emperor, opposed Gregory's exclusive control of investing and deposing bishops in 1078, the Wars of Investiture in continental Europe erupted.

In England, the investiture struggle had first peaked with Anselm, archbishop of Canterbury, and his struggle against the intrusion in church matters by the king and nobility. This conflict came to an uneasy and preliminary termination with a concordat in 1106–07, only to be reopened with the contest between Pope Innocent III and King John from 1205 to 1213, after which it was laid to rest for some centuries.

William the Conqueror (r. 1066–1087), the first Norman king of England, and his two successors William II (r. 1087–1100) and Henry I (r. 1100–1135) in the main succeeded in opposing papal claims to supremacy over the church in their realm. During the following chaotic reign of King Stephen (r. 1135–1154), the papal party in England made important gains in prestige and power. But King Henry II (r. 1154–1189) reasserted royal supremacy over the church, at first efficaciously. However, the king's titanic conflict with his old friend Thomas Becket, whom in 1162 he had appointed archbishop of Canterbury, culminated with the 1170 murder of Becket in the cathedral. The king was widely held culpable. The upshot was that Henry II's 1164 Constitutions of Clarendon, a set of royal decrees

---

16. HAROLD J. BERMAN, LAW AND REVOLUTION: THE FORMATION OF THE WESTERN LEGAL TRADITION 255–64 (1983). Berman's volume is a main source of the information used in the eight paragraphs that follow.

17. *Id.* at 96 (quoting the *Dictatus Papae*).

challenging vital provisions of canon law (church laws and regulations), to a large extent had to be retracted. Provisions offensive to the jurisdictional claims of the papacy were rescinded in 1172.

Henry II's successor, King Richard I Lionheart (r. 1189–1199), mostly spent his reign abroad, engaged in waging war. He won fame, and earned papal favor, organizing and leading, with French king Philip Augustus (r. 1180–1223) and German emperor Frederick Barbarossa (r. 1155–1190), the Third Crusade, which took place from 1188 to 1192.

Toward the end of Richard's reign, his exploitation of England for defense of his possessions in France had attained unprecedented levels. Yet relations with the Roman Church were not unfavorable when his younger brother John Lackland mounted the Angevin throne in 1199. Relations with the papacy soon soured, however.

During the early part of his reign, John lost most of his inherited French possessions. Those losses discredited him and led to a constant need for ever-more money to pay for new, costly military expeditions. Excessive and arbitrary royal demands for scutage and other fines and taxes to be extracted from John's magnates triggered fierce baronial opposition. Any sign of resistance was followed by royal attacks on a baronial castle or a royal demand for a baron's son as hostage. The king's heavy exploitation of his barons also included exploitation of the realm's churchmen, the spiritual magnates.

King and Church in Angevin England were again struggling, head-on, over the proper authority to nominate, select, appoint, control, tax, and (if need be) depose church officials, in particular archbishops, bishops, and abbots. Such church officials were in John's England also often wealthy and powerful magnates. Hence, royal control of the appointment of and the power to tax archbishops, bishops, and abbots were of major interest to King John, always in desperate need of revenue for the purpose of waging his (as it turned out, mostly unsuccessful) wars seeking to regain lost territory in France.

In 1205, John disputed Pope Innocent III's choice of English-born Stephen Langton, a cardinal of the Roman see, as the new archbishop of Canterbury. John refused Langton access to the realm. In response, the pope placed England under *papal interdict* in 1208, suspending all religious services, including baptisms, marriages, and burials. John retaliated by seizing church revenues. In 1209, John was then *excommunicated* from the church and by 1212 Innocent III was even preparing his *deposition* and negotiating with John's enemy, King Philip of France, about a *crusade* against England. Each of these papal steps (in italics) was a politically potent measure, due to the unquestioned spiritual authority of the Church and its immense practical significance for underwriting well-nigh all legitimate societal bonds and transactions. John saw his vulnerability coming to a head, and eventually submitted to the pope, accepted Stephen Langton, the papal nominee, as archbishop of Canterbury, and agreed to hold his Angevin kingdom as a fief of the papacy and even to pay an annual monetary tribute to the pope.[18]

After his submission to the papacy in 1213, John was, however, unswervingly supported by Innocent III, a support further reinforced by John's promising in early 1215 to go on a crusade (a promise perhaps not seriously intended). To Pope Innocent III, crusades were a major preoccupation, whether directed against Muslims in the Holy Land or in Spain, against heretics within Christendom (e.g., the Albigensian Crusade), or against insubordinate Christian princes (e.g., the threat of a crusade against John himself before his submission to Innocent III).

Thus, King John could know he was backed by the pope in his struggle with his revolting barons during the first half of 1215, a conflict that terminated, temporarily as we know, with John's acceptance of Magna Carta in June. We shall discover that such submission was not inconsequential with respect to the prospects for religious freedom in John's kingdom.

I do not, of course, dispute that King John in Magna Carta, when granting the "holy Church" freedom in the important matter of clerical appointments, was submitting to the pope and leaving to Rome control over the hierarchy of the Roman Church in England. The point is, rather, that granting freedom to the head of and to the organs of the one supremely dominant religion of England in the matter of selecting its officials and managing its own affairs does not institute, nor even anticipate, religious freedom in the realm. In short: providing the Roman Church in Angevin England with a significant degree of autonomy is not providing for religious freedom in England, nor does it anticipate religious freedom in the future.

No other religious body, whether Christian or non-Christian, was accorded similar autonomy or freedom of any kind, nor were John's "loyal subjects" granted religious freedom as individual "free men." The last part of chapter 1 "runs as follows: . . . TO ALL FREE MEN OF OUR KINGDOM we have also granted, for us and our heirs for ever, all the liberties written below to have and to keep for them and their heirs, of us and our heirs."[19]

This concluding introductory statement is then followed by the long, multifarious, and deservedly famous list of specific liberties "granted to all free men," a Magna Carta counterpart to a modern catalogue of "civil, political, and economic rights." But included in the numerous freedoms granted by Magna Carta, there is no freedom for any of the king's subjects to modify their authorized religious belief, no freedom to revise their religious practices, no freedom to alter their religious allegiances. The Great Charter of Liberty assumes without argument that there is but one pertinent religion in the Angevin realm: the religion of the Roman Church.

18. *Id.* at 262.
19. *See* British Library, *supra* note 13.

Did other religious options, other feasible religious alternatives, exist in the world of King John and his revolting barons? One exception to the religious monopoly of the Roman Church should be noted. The Charter does tacitly recognize the legitimate presence in the realm of a small class of people known to belong to a different religion: the presence of Jews.

In 1201, John had issued a Charter of Liberties stating that Jews may "have all their liberties and customs as well and peaceably and honorably as they had in the time of aforesaid King Henry our father's grandfather"[20] (i.e., King Henry I). But, by 1215, the situation for Angevin Jews had gravely worsened. And neither king nor barons were intent on safeguarding their lot.

Magna Carta, rather than introducing specific freedoms for Jews, provides for circumscribed benefits or freedoms to people (always non-Jews) who have borrowed money from Jews. But by this detour the Charter nevertheless acknowledges the presence of Jews in the Angevin realm. Chapters 10 and 11 of Magna Carta regulate the situation that arises if a man who has borrowed a sum of money from Jews dies before the debt has been repaid: In such a case his "heir shall pay no interest as long as he remains under age"[21] and, similarly, "his wife may have her dower and pay nothing towards the debt from it."[22]

So, Magna Carta does not spell out liberties for Jews, only exemptions for others from the regular obligations owed to Jews, by heirs or by widows of men who have borrowed money from Jews. By 1215, the presence of Jews and their peculiar and specialized social role as moneylenders to Christians could still be taken for granted.

Angevin Jews had under earlier Plantagenet kings enjoyed a somewhat privileged position as moneylenders to king and magnates, being the only category of people permitted by Church regulations to engage in money lending and to this end allowed to travel in the realm without paying tolls or customs and permitted even to settle reasonably freely. Their right to exist was recognized by the Roman Church.[23] But there were always special exemptions: Jews were prohibited from bearing arms under the 1181 Assize of Arms. Being aliens in faith ("enemies of Christ")[24] and nationality

20. JEWS IN MEDIEVAL BRITAIN: HISTORICAL, LITERARY AND ARCHEOLOGICAL PERSPECTIVES 17–18 (Patricia Skinner ed., 2012).

21. Id.

22. Id.

23. Sicut Judaeis was a papal bull issued by Pope Callixtus II (r. 1119–1124) in 1120. The bull was intended to protect Jews in Christendom. It was prompted by the massacres of Jews during the First Crusade and was later reaffirmed by several popes, including by Pope Innocent III in 1199, who, however, added ominous conditionals and warnings to the text. See John Tolan, Of Milk and Blood: Innocent III and the Jews, Revisited, in JEWS AND CHRISTIANS IN THIRTEENTH CENTURY EUROPE (Michael A. Signer & John Van Engen eds., 2001), available at https://www.academia.edu/1896777/Of_Milk_and_Blood_Innocent_III_and_the_Jews_revisited.

24. See Tolan, supra note 23.

(unable to take Christian oaths),[25] Jews were socially excluded, were often distrusted and disliked, were frequently envied for their amassing of riches, and were repeatedly subjected to inordinately high taxes (aids, reliefs, fines, amercements) by the Crown. With the growing crusading fervor in England under Richard I, anti-Jewish sentiments became stronger, triggering violence and several massacres of Jews (the most malignant of which occurred at York, March 16–17, 1190).[26]

Under King John, the situation for Angevin Jews deteriorated further, particularly after 1206 when John lost the last remnants of his possessions in Normandy, thereby cutting off Angevin Jews' vital intellectual, cultural, and financial bonds to Jews living in Normandy. John's subsequent endeavor to recover Normandy led him to weigh down harshly on Jews with arbitrary and excessive taxes (of which the most devastating was the "Bristol tallage" of 1210), inflicting upon them, when in arrears—as was largely inevitable—imprisonment, torture, and executions.[27]

As noted above, King John by 1213 had agreed to hold his kingdom as a fief of the papacy by submitting to Pope Innocent III, the most powerful of medieval popes. Innocent III has been identified as one of the key sources for the rising anti-Jewish prejudice in medieval Western Christendom.[28] If all money lending with interest counts as "usurious," Innocent III's letters banning usury would make the very existence of Jews, excluded from most other livelihoods, virtually impossible, given that they were denied access to land. In November 1215, the Fourth Lateran Council of the Roman Church, convoked in 1213 and forcefully directed by Innocent III, decreed that princes should block any "contagious" commerce of Christians with Jews. Canons 67, 68, 69, and 70, respectively, do the following: ban usury ("The more the [C]hristian religion is restrained from usurious practices, so much the more does the perfidy of the Jews grow in these matters . . ."); decree that Jews (and Muslims) "in every [C]hristian province and at all times, are to be distinguished in public from other people by the character of their dress . . ."; forbid Jews "to be appointed to public office"; and decree that Jews who have converted to Christianity "shall be wholly prevented by prelates of churches from observing their old rite."[29] Because Innocent III's treatment of Jews was so harsh, King John's submission to

---

25. *See* CHRISTIANS AND JEWS IN ANGEVIN ENGLAND: THE YORK MASSACRE OF 1190, NARRATIVES AND CONTEXTS 125 ff (Sarah Rees Jones et al. eds., 2013) [hereinafter CHRISTIANS AND JEWS].

26. *Id.* An earlier and incisive source is *Chapter 2: The Beginning of Persecution and the Organization of Jewry 1189–1216, in* CECILE ROTH, A HISTORY OF THE JEWS IN ENGLAND (1964).

27. *See* JEWS IN MEDIEVAL BRITAIN, *supra* note 20; *see also* CHRISTIANS AND JEWS, *supra* note 25.

28. *See* Tolan, *supra* note 23, at 2.

29. 1 DECREES OF THE ECUMENICAL COUNCILS 265–67 (Norman P. Tanner ed., 1990).

the papacy and his vow to take the cross were hardly conducive to religious freedom in his realm.

Moreover, Innocent III used even more forceful language against heretics. In one of the first of the canons adopted by the Lateran Council, Innocent III promised that "[C]atholics who take the cross and gird themselves up for the expulsion of heretics shall enjoy the same indulgence and be strengthened by the same holy privilege, as is granted to those who get to the aid of the holy Land."[30]

Canon 3 of the altogether 71 canons adopted by the Fourth Lateran Council deals with heresy. It leaves no room for religious freedom in John's kingdom, taking into account that John's kingdom is held as a fief of the papacy:

> We excommunicate and anathematize every heresy raising itself up against this holy, orthodox and catholic faith which we have expounded above. We condemn all heretics, whatever names they may go under. They have different faces indeed but their tails are tied together inasmuch as they are alike in their pride. Let those condemned be handed over to secular authorities present, or to their bailiffs, for due punishment. . . . Let secular authorities, whatever offices they may be discharging, be advised, and urged and if necessary be compelled by ecclesiastical censure, if they wish to be reputed and held to be faithful, to take publicly an oath for the defense of the faith to the effect that they will seek, as far as they can, to expel from the lands subject to their jurisdiction all heretics designated by the church on good faith.[31]

Although the Fourth Lateran Council adopted these canons several months after King John had agreed to Magna Carta, they were drafted by, or under the supervision of, Innocent III and reflected his long-held beliefs.

Given the Ashoka/Universal Declaration notion of religious freedom described and adopted above—a notion of religious freedom requiring that religious diversity, religious disagreement, and religious change are protected and not prohibited or made impossible by government regulations and policies—one must conclude that Magna Carta, in its original 1215 version, did not provide for religious freedom. This conclusion is based straightforwardly on the relevant historical facts. The text of the Great Charter of Liberty is clear. It accords to the Roman Church internal autonomy and status as the one and only legitimate and authoritative religious body of the realm. By John's submitting his kingdom as a fief of the papacy under Innocent III, no *other* religious doctrine, commitment, or practice is to be tolerated. No religious diversity, nor religious disagreement, nor

---

30. *Id.* at 234.
31. *Id.* at 233.

religious change, is to be facilitated in the Angevin realm, nor to be protected by the royal power.

But were there in Angevin England relevant religious "others" to whom religious freedom could conceivably be accorded and for whom religious freedom could have made an important difference? Within the Roman Church in England all theological strife and discord were of course not fully eliminated, although we do not know the extent or character of internal religious diversity within *Ecclesia Anglicana* around 1215. Then there were the Jews in the Angevin realm, as alluded to above; but conversion to Judaism was treason according to the Church as well as the king. Moreover, the Roman Church had toward the end of the 12th century discovered within Christendom allegedly dangerous heretical religious movements, including the Waldensians and the Cathars. By 1199, Innocent III pronounced Cathars to be enemies of the Church and he declared armed military crusade against them in March 1208.[32] Cathars, with their high moral standards, their purportedly dualist doctrine, and their pungent criticisms of debauched Church practices, were particularly successful in Southern France and Italy. Innocent III's Albigensian Crusade (1209–1229) against Cathars in Languedoc included massacres of Cathars as well as Catholics, the most grievous being the slaughtering of the population of Bézier in July 1209.[33] Christian criticism of, opposition to, and disagreement with the Roman Church were surely not unknown in Angevin England of 1215.[34]

The absence of religious freedom provisions—indeed the tacit barring of religious freedom—in the Great Charter of Freedom, and the lack of detectable anticipation of religious freedom among its authors, thus cannot be due to the paucity of religious alternatives intelligible to political and religious leaders in Angevin England around 1215.

Understanding Magna Carta in light of the Ashoka/Universal Declaration notion of religious freedom reflects, admittedly, the current concept of human rights. But that is not the same as *judging* a medieval past by the

---

32. Stephen Haliczer, *Secret Titles of the Inquisition*, PBS.ORG/INQUISITION/, *The Cathar Heresy*, http://www-tc.pbs.org/inquisition/pdf/TheCatharHeresy.pdf (last visited May 17, 2014); THE CATHARS AND THE ALBIGENSIAN CRUSADES: A SOURCEBOOK 1–20 (Catherine Léglu et al. eds., 2014).

33. *See* R.I. MOORE, THE WAR ON HERESY: FAITH AND POWER IN MEDIEVAL EUROPE (2012) (regarding the struggle by the Roman Church against heretics in the high Middle Ages).

34. The Crusades against Cathars and other heretics were soon to be followed by the Roman Church's establishing ecclesiastical tribunals of inquisition instituted to try heretics, as exemplified by Pope Gregory IX's (r. 1227–1241) 1233 "rescript" to the bishops of Southern France and the priors of the Dominican Order. *See* JOSEPH BLÖTZER, 8 THE CATHOLIC ENCYCLOPEDIA *"Inquisition"* (Kevin Knight ed., Matt Dean transcriptionist, 1910), http://www.newadvent.org/cathen/08026a.htm; *see also* ANDREW MEEHAN, 12 THE CATHOLIC ENCYCLOPEDIA "Papal Rescripts" (Kevin Knight ed., Douglas J. Potter transcriptionist, 1911), http://www.newadvent.org/cathen/12783b.htm.

standards of the present. And such an understanding may protect today's readers against erroneously and perhaps unthinkingly presuming that people in Angevin England of 1215 were ignorant of, and had no interest in, significant and even radical religious diversity.

III.   Magna Carta and Religious Freedom in England from 1215 to 1948

The United Kingdom in 1948 voted in the General Assembly of the United Nations to adopt the Universal Declaration of Human Rights. In 1950, the United Kingdom ratified the European Convention on Human Rights and Fundamental Freedoms, which came into force in 1953. By 1966, the United Kingdom had granted "individual petition," which is the right of citizens and residents of the United Kingdom to take a case to the European Court of Human Rights in Strasbourg, France. Freedom of religion, spelled out in Article 9 of the European Convention of Human Rights, is thus after 1966 reasonably well protected in England, though there are still unresolved controversies in this field. These include the recent case, *Eweida and Others v. United Kingdom*,[35] which deals with employees' freedom to wear religious symbols in the workplace (e.g., wearing Christian crosses around the neck), and employees' dismissal for refusing to carry out duties they consider at odds with their religion (e.g., failing to condone homosexuality). The United Kingdom has no constitutional clause guaranteeing religious freedom but is bound by her ratifications of international covenants and conventions providing for protection of religious freedom. Moreover, human rights protection in the United Kingdom has been reinforced since 1998 by the hotly debated Human Rights Act.

Assessing Magna Carta's significance for Britain's perhaps somewhat hesitant embrace of post–World War II international human rights precepts is beyond the scope of this chapter. The task is to elucidate, by brief descriptions of some significant and representative cases, whether and how invoking Magna Carta may have influenced the fortunes of religious freedom in England between 1215 and 1948.

Magna Carta's numerous reissues and reconfirmations in the course of the 13th and 14th centuries brought some generally significant changes to its contents, interpretations, and legal status, as discussed in chapter 1 of this volume. None of these changes was of much consequence to the protection of religious freedom in England. Twenty-one chapters of the original 1215 version of Magna Carta, including the two chapters (10 and 11) regulating relief from debt owed to Jews, were removed in the 1216 reissue. Several reissues followed, the two most significant being that of 1225, giving

---

35. [2013] Eur. Ct. H.R. 37.

the definitive and for centuries the only version generally known, and that of 1297 (same wording as in 1225), turning Magna Carta into statutory law. Magna Carta is still in the Statute Book of England, but most chapters are now repealed. Three of the 1215 chapters are still in force.[36] Of these, two chapters might conceivably be invoked to safeguard religious freedom: chapter 1, providing for the freedom of the English Church, and chapter 39 (chapter 29 in the 1225 and later reissues), which in the 17th century and onward was reinterpreted so as to provide for the right to due process of law, as discussed later in this chapter.

A. The Case of Jews

Magna Carta was surely not invoked when on July 18, 1290, King Edward I (r. 1272–1307) issued his Edict of Expulsion, expelling all Jews from his realm. This made England the first European country to do so, though Edward had in 1287 expelled all Jews from Gascony, seizing their property and all debts payable to them.[37]

Between the year of expulsion 1290 and the year 1664, when residence for Jews in England was officially reauthorized,[38] Jews had never been totally absent from England. Notwithstanding their expulsion, Jews in subsequent centuries trickled into the country—unnoticed, disregarded, under various disguises, or because the king might need a good physician.[39] Even before 1664 a small synagogue was operative in London. Anglo-Jews were predominantly Marranos, refugees from persecution in Spain or Portugal. Some were successful in business but none was safe against sudden and nasty shifts in popular goodwill. Jews were for a very long time burdened by a variety of legal, religious, guild, and other professional disabilities, the removal of which required tenacious and persistent efforts by English Jews and non-Jew supporters of their cause. Only in July 1858 was the last barrier for Jews to equal political citizenship removed. Both Houses of Parliament adopted a bill, "the fourteenth of that wearisome series that had occupied the attention of Parliament for more than a quarter of a century," finally recognizing "an English Jew . . . as an equal citizen of his native land."[40]

Were Magna Carta, or any of its provisions, ever evoked during the 374 years of official expulsion of Jews or, after 1664, by any significant actors engaged during the two centuries of struggle for the emancipation of the Jewish minority population of England? I have not been able to discover any

---

36. British Library, *supra* note 13.
37. MICHAEL PRESWICH, EDWARD I 306, 343–46 (1997).
38. ROTH, *supra* note 26, at ch. 7.
39. *See* Ariel Hessayon, *JCR-UK: Jews in England: From Expulsion (1290) to Readmission (1656)*, JEWISHGEN.ORG (July 5, 2009), *reformatted* Dec. 15, 2011), http://www.jewishgen.org/jcr-uk/england_articles/1290_to_1656.htm.
40. ROTH, *supra* note 26, at ch. 11.

evidence of a visible role for Magna Carta in the endeavors for readmission and emancipation of Jews to England.

B. The Case of Catholics

The Roman Church in England was the official religion until the reign of King Henry VIII (r. 1509–47). Henry broke with the papacy and often violated his subjects' rights thereafter by enforcing conformity with his new church regime. The Act of Supremacy issued in 1534 declared the king to be "the only supreme head on earth of the Church of England," in place of the Roman pope.[41] Some very prominent Catholics, including Archbishop Warham in 1532 and Sir Thomas More in 1534, claimed protection under Magna Carta's chapter 1 promising freedom for the English Church, "but most turned to the theology of universal papal authority for arguments against Henry's supremacy over the Church of England."[42] During Henry's reign many Catholics were executed under English law, since denial of royal supremacy "was made a treasonable offense effective February 1, 1535."[43] The *Act of Supremacy* was repealed in 1554 by Henry's devoutly Catholic daughter Queen Mary I (r. 1553–1558) who reinstituted the Roman Church as England's state religion. Again, many were sentenced and executed for their religious adherence, but now Anglicans and Protestants were at risk. The statutory penalty in England for high treason by men was, from 1351 and for several centuries, to be hanged, drawn, and quartered, whereas, for reasons of "public decency," women were to be burned at the stake.

Under Queen Elizabeth I (r. 1558–1603) the number of people—now Catholics—sentenced and executed for their faith first abated, only to rise after 1570 when Pope Pius V issued the bull Regnans in Excelsis declaring "Elizabeth, the pretended Queen of England and the servant of crime" to be an excommunicate and a heretic, releasing all her subjects from any allegiance to her and threatening Catholics who obeyed her orders with excommunication. Sixty-three Catholic martyrs in England were recognized already during the papacy of pope Gregory XIII (r. 1572–85).[44]

Persecution of "recusants" (i.e., Catholics refusing to attend Church of England services) peaked after the attempted invasion by the Spanish Armada in 1588. Persecution slowly subsided as threats to English external

---

41. David Ross, *The Act of Supremacy*, BRITAIN EXPRESS, http://www.britain express.com/History/tudor/act-of-supremacy.htm (last visited May 17, 2014).

42. RALPH V. TURNER, MAGNA CARTA THROUGH THE AGES 135 (2003) (referring to FAITH THOMPSON, MAGNA CARTA: ITS ROLE IN THE MAKING OF THE ENGLISH CONSTITUTION 1300–1629 142–43 (1948)).

43. BRAD S. GREGORY, SALVATION AT STAKE: CHRISTIAN MARTYRDOM IN EARLY MODERN EUROPE 255 (2001).

44. WILLIAM LILLY, 5 THE CATHOLIC ENCYCLOPEDIA *"England (Since the Reformation)"* (Kevin Knight ed., Douglas J. Potter transcriptionist, 1909), http://www.new advent.org/cathen/05445a.htm.

power waned in the 17th and 18th centuries. But the plight of English Catholics was markedly eased only toward the end of the 18th century, beginning with the 1778 Catholic Relief Act[45] and culminating with Parliament passing the 1829 Catholic Emancipation Act.[46]

If the question is, What was the extent to which Catholics in England invoked Magna Carta during the several centuries of their struggle for religious freedom?, the answer is in a sense doubly awkward: Magna Carta does not shield religious freedom, and Catholics in England could not base a struggle for religious freedom on Church doctrine, since principled Catholic embrace of religious freedom occurred only at Vatican II in 1965, with the adoption of the Declaration on Religious Freedom (Dignitatis Humanae Personae).[47] This Catholic "Magna Carta" of religious freedom was not available to Catholics at the time of the political and legislative breakthroughs in England toward full religious, civil, and political rights.

The only known invocation of Magna Carta by English Catholics in their struggle against religious persecution and discrimination following Henry VIII's Act of Supremacy is that by a few prominent leaders, including Archbishop Warham and Sir Thomas More. Both claimed protection under Magna Carta's chapter 1 providing for freedom for the English Church.[48]

C. The Case of Puritans and Other Non-Anglican Protestants

Ralph Turner has written that "[b]y Elizabeth I's last years Puritans presented a greater threat to royal supremacy than Catholic supporters of papal sovereignty. . . . Protestants found that Magna Carta, with its first article confirming the English Church's liberties, afforded them no advantage in the struggle to end papal authority over England."[49] Nevertheless, some early Puritans invoked chapter 1 in defense of their separatist conception of the "right and liberty of the Church of Christ; which the great charter of England granteth shall be free, and have her whole rights and liberty inviolable, &c."[50] These words are lifted from a ten-point letter of January 8, 1594, addressed to the lord treasurer by a Puritan pastor, Francis Johnson, in prison for violating the Act of Uniformity,[51] asking his release. Faith Thomson, in her 1948 volume *Magna Carta—Its Role in the Making of the English Constitution 1300–1629*, devotes an entire chapter to "Puritans and Magna Carta" and reports in detail on Puritans' uses of several parts of Magna Carta for a variety of other Puritan purposes—but there is little,

45. Catholic Relief Act, 1778, 18 Geo. 3, c. 60.
46. Catholic Emancipation Act, 1829, 10 Geo. 4, c. 7.
47. 2 Decrees of the Ecumenical Councils 1001–1011 (Norman P. Tanner ed., 1990).
48. Thompson, *supra* note 42, at 138.
49. Turner, *supra* note 42, at 136, 138.
50. Thompson, *supra* note 42, at 225.
51. Act of Uniformity, 1559, 1 Eliz. c. 2.

beyond what is mentioned previously, on Puritans invoking Magna Carta in defense of religious freedom.

D. Sir Edward Coke (1552–1634) and Oliver Cromwell (1599–1658)

Magna Carta during the 14th century had been held almost sacrosanct, but it was then rebutted by a 1387 judgment confirming the supremacy of the Royal Prerogative.[52] It had lost public and legal standing during the 15th and 16th centuries, but regained a central role in the 17th-century conflict between king and Parliament as "common lawyers and parliamentarians turned to a mythical 'ancient constitution' as a defense against Stuart kings' assertion of the royal prerogative."[53] The key figure in the rediscovery and the creative reinvention of England's medieval constitutional past was Sir Edward Coke, attorney-general to Elizabeth I and James I and later chief justice of Common Pleas and member of Parliament. His two chief contributions to his contemporaries' new appreciation of Magna Carta were, first, taking Magna Carta to be a link in a chain of royal reconfirmations of fundamental law stretching back to, and beyond, Edward the Confessor and, second, misinterpreting its chapter 39 (chapter 29 in the 1225 and later versions) anachronistically so as to imply due process of the common law and the "perpetual rights of the English people to *habeas corpus* and trial by jury."[54]

Although Coke embraced conventional religious beliefs, he did much for religious toleration. As chief justice, he worked to keep many cases out of Elizabeth I's ecclesiastical courts that foreseeably would have sentenced religious dissenters to be tortured, imprisoned, or burned. And he hired an independent-minded secretary named Roger Williams, who later went on to establish Rhode Island as a sanctuary for religious freedom. But Coke did not himself apply creatively reinterpreted Magna Carta provisions in defense of religious liberty.

Oliver Cromwell (1599–1658) was of course instrumental in widening the leeway for religious toleration in England. But in his revolutionary endeavors he did not rely on a revived tradition of reverence for Magna Carta. Cromwell's approach to Magna Carta was the opposite of that of Coke. Once Cromwell had become lord protector he was contemptuous of Magna Carta to redress grievances. For Cromwell, it was not Magna Carta but "Magna Farta." "Such a boorish dismissal of Magna Carta was even more unjustified than Coke's claims for it," writes Baron Wolf, lord chief justice of England and Wales. [55]

---

52. TURNER, *supra* note 42, at 127.

53. Ralph V. Turner, *The Meaning of Magna Carta since 1215*, 53 HIST. TODAY (Sept. 2003), http://www.historytoday.com/ralph-v-turner/meaning-magna-carta-1215.

54. TURNER, *supra* note 42, at 148.

55. Lord Woolf, *Judges, Tribunals & Magistrates, Media Speeches 2005, Magna Carta: A Precedent for Recent Constitutional Change*, JUDICIARY.GOV.UK (June 15, 2005) (on file with author).

E. William Penn (1644–1718)

An early Quaker, a learned philosopher, a preacher-publicist, a real estate entrepreneur, and the founder of the Province of Pennsylvania, William Penn certainly made diligent and effective use of Coke's upgraded Magna Carta in defense of religious freedom. A brilliant early example is found in Penn's procedural performance at his trial when arrested, at age 26, for preaching his Quaker faith in public—an action made illegal by the Conventicle Act of 1664,[56] a piece of legislation Penn wanted to challenge, based on Magna Carta chapter 39 as explained by Coke. The source of the report reproduced below is Penn's own 1670 publication, *The peoples ancient and just liberties asserted, in the tryal of William Penn, and William Mead, at the sessions held at the Old-Baily in London, the first, third, fourth and fifth of Sept. 70, against the most arbitrary procedure of that court*:

Penn.   I affirm I have broken no law, nor am I Guilty of the indictment that is laid to my charge; and to the end the bench, the
jury, and myself, with these that hear us, may have a more
direct understanding of this procedure, I desire you would let
me know by what law it is you prosecute me, and upon what
law you ground my indictment.

Rec.   Upon the common-law.

Penn.   Where is that common-law?

Rec.   You must not think that I am able to run up so many years,
and over so many adjudged cases, which we call common-law,
to answer your curiosity.

Penn.   This answer I am sure is very short of my question, for if it be
common, it should not be so hard to produce.

Rec.   Sir, will you plead to your indictment?

Penn.   Shall I plead to an Indictment that hath no foundation in law?
If it contain that law you say I have broken, why should you
decline to produce that law, since it will be impossible for the
jury to determine, or agree to bring in their verdict, who have
not the law produced, by which they should measure the truth
of this indictment, and the guilt, or contrary of my fact?

Rec.   You are a saucy fellow, speak to the Indictment.

Penn.   I say, it is my place to speak to matter of law; I am arraigned a
prisoner; my liberty, which is next to life itself, is now concerned: you are many mouths and ears against me, and if I
must not be allowed to make the best of my case, it is hard,
I say again, unless you shew me, and the people, the law you
ground your indictment upon, I shall take it for granted your
proceedings are merely arbitrary.

---

56. Conventicle Act, 1664, 16 Charles 2, c. 4.

Obser.	At this time several upon the Bench urged hard upon the Prisoner to bear him down.
Rec.	The question is, whether you are Guilty of this Indictment?
Penn.	The question is not, whether I am Guilty of this Indictment, but whether this Indictment be legal. It is too general and imperfect an answer, to say it is the common-law, unless we knew both where and what it is. For where there is no law, there is no transgression; and that law which is not in being, is so far from being common, that it is no law at all.
Rec.	You are an impertinent fellow, will you teach the court what law is? It is "Lex non scripta," that which many have studied 30 or 40 years to know, and would you have me to tell you in a moment?
Penn.	Certainly, if the common law be so hard to be understood, it is far from being very common; but if the lord Coke in his Institutes be of any consideration, he tells us, That Common-Law is common right, and that Common Right is the Great Charter-Privileges: confirmed 9 Hen. 3, 29, 25 Edw. 1, 12 Ed. 3, 8 Coke Instit. 2 p, 56.[57]
Rec.	Sir, you are a troublesome fellow, and it is not for the honour of the court to suffer you to go on.
Penn.	I have asked but one question, and you have not answered me; though the rights and privileges of every Englishman be concerned in it.
Rec.	If I should suffer you to ask questions till to-morrow morning, you would be never the wiser.
Penn.	That is according as the answers are.
Rec.	Sir, we must not stand to hear you talk all night.
Penn.	I design no affront to the court, but to be heard in my just plea: and I must plainly tell you, that if you will deny me Oyer of that law, which you suggest I have broken, you do at once deny me an acknowledged right, and evidence to the whole world your resolution to sacrifice the privileges of Englishmen to your sinister and arbitrary designs.
Rec.	Take him away. My lord, if you take not some course with this pestilent fellow, to stop his mouth, we shall not be able to do any thing to night.
Mayor.	Take him away, take him away, turn him into the bale-dock.
Penn.	These are but so many vain exclamations; is this justice or true judgment? Must I therefore be taken away because I plead for the fundamental laws of England? However, this I

---

57. These references are to reconfirmations of the 1297 version of Magna Carta, hence "29" for chapter 39 in the 1215 version.

leave upon your consciences, who are of the jury (and my sole judges,) that if these ancient fundamental laws, which relate to liberty and property, (and are not limited to particular persuasions in matters of religion) must not be indispensably maintained and observed, who can say he hath right to the coat upon his back? Certainly our liberties are openly to be invaded, our wives to be ravished, our children slaved, our families ruined, and our estates led away in triumph, by every sturdy beggar and malicious informer, as their trophies, but our (pretended) forfeits for conscience sake. The Lord of Heaven and Earth will be judge between us in this matter.

Rec.   Be silent there.[58]

The trial of Penn was "most arbitrarily" administered by Sir Samuel Sterling, lord mayor of London. But the young Penn triumphed in court, winning in the end the right for English juries to be free from the control of judges.[59] And it became important for future American law (e.g., jury nullification and habeas corpus).[60]

Penn was a well-off gentleman. He was respected for his intelligence and integrity, but he was also highly controversial because of his strong Quaker commitments. The persecution of Quakers in England accelerated, and after years of Quaker missionary work traveling in Germany and Holland, Penn in 1677 with some Quaker friends started planning a massive emigration of English Quakers to the English colonies in North America. As repayment of a large debt owed by King Charles II (r. 1660–1685) to Penn's admiral father, King Charles granted Penn a huge area of colonial land in 1681, named by the king Pennsylvania (in honor of Penn's father). Penn drafted a charter of liberties for the settlements (Pennsylvania and Delaware, which initially was included in the royal grant), guaranteeing free and fair trial by jury, freedom from unjust imprisonment, free elections, and religious freedom (at least for everybody believing in God). Soon English, Welsh, German, and Dutch Quakers settled in the colony, followed by French Huguenots and German Mennonites, Amish, and Lutherans arriving from Catholic German states,

58. Nathan Dorn, *From Magna Carta on Trial to the Holy Experiment, In Custodia Legis: Law Librarians of Congress,* BLOGS.LOC.GOV (Feb. 19, 2013), http://blogs.loc.gov /law/2013/02/from-magna-carta-on-trial-to-the-holy-experiment/ (reporting a representative exchange between Penn and the Court's administrator).

59. For Chief Justice Vaughan's 1670 report on the case of imprisonment of Edward Bushell for alleged misconduct as juryman in the case against Penn and Mead. *See Bushell's Case,* CONSTITUTION.ORG, http://www.constitution.org/trials/bushell/bushell.htm#64 (last visited May 17, 2014). For a modern assessment, see Kevin Crosby, *Bushell's Case and the Juror's Soul,* 33 J. LEGAL HIST. 251 (2012).

60. JEFFREY B. ABRAMSON, WE, THE JURY: THE JURY SYSTEM AND THE IDEAL OF DEMOCRACY 68–72 (1994).

as well as by Catholics, Jews, and Muslims (albeit the three latter groups were without voting rights in Penn's Pennsylvania).

In 1687, as part of a tract authored by Penn titled *The Excellent Priviledge of Liberty and Property: Being the Birth-Right of the Free-Born Subjects of England*, the 1225 version of Magna Carta was printed for the first time on American soil.[61] Coke's interpretation of the Charter became important for many politically influential Americans. Subscribing to Coke's anachronistic views, they held it to be the guarantor of their ancient English liberties, including rights to trial by jury and the writ of habeas corpus. They saw the 17th-century struggle against the Stuart kings as part of their own history, and they accepted the Great Charter as part of the "ancient constitution," providing them with the same protections enjoyed by their cousins in the mother country. In the decade before the outbreak of the American Revolution in 1775, colonial lawyers and pamphleteers turned to Magna Carta for support against the government across the Atlantic. This platform became vital also for the good fortunes of a comprehensive religious freedom in America.

F. Religious Freedom in 18th- and 19th-Century England

The Glorious Revolution of 1688–1689, culminating in the deposition of King James II (r. 1685–1688) and the establishment of Parliament's supremacy, seemed a repetition of the baronial rebellion against King John. The settlement following William III (r. 1689–1702) and Mary II's (r. 1689–1694) accession included a Declaration of Rights, enacted in 1689 by Parliament as a new Magna Carta: the Bill of Rights. Like Magna Carta, the Bill of Rights did not facilitate religious freedom. But Coke's portrayal of England's past was now fashioned into the "Whig interpretation" of history, with a triumphalist, self-congratulatory view of liberty's ceaseless advance in England. However, Tories and royalist writers tended to dismiss Magna Carta as a feudal document with little long-term relevance, and in fact royalist historians such as Robert Brady (d. 1700) painted a more accurate picture of the medieval past than Coke. Nonetheless, the Whig interpretation triumphed in the 18th century.

Resistance in England was strong and stubborn against full equality across religious and worldview divides. The advance of religious freedom was slow. Not only was the shine of Magna Carta eclipsed, but its relevance as inspiration and legitimization for the drawn-out struggles for religious freedom and equality turned out to be limited, in part for reasons we have already encountered.

A study published in 2011 by the British Equality and Human Rights Commission noted that:

---

61. Turner, *supra* note 42, at 210.

[F]or much of British history, there were attempts, in England and Wales, and in Scotland, to impose varying degrees of uniformity in the public profession of belief and in participation in religious worship in which the law was itself the medium and instrument of religious discrimination (see Robilliard, 1984).

The amelioration and eventual removal of most of the civil disabilities associated with this occurred only gradually (Jordan, 1932, 1936). For most of the 19th century, issues concerned with the civil and political rights and disabilities of Nonconformist (Larsen, 1999) and Roman Catholic Christians (Norman, 1968), Jews (Salbstein, 1982), Atheists, Humanists, Freethinkers and other groups outside the established religious traditions were at the forefront of social, religious and political debate. The removal in the 19th century of the majority of legally entrenched inequalities for religious minorities and non-believers came about in response to organised struggle and campaigning on the part of those who were affected by them (Larsen, 1999). Numerous bodies were formed which engaged in campaigning against religious privilege and civil disabilities. The legal academic St John Robilliard (1984: ix) identified the origins of the 19th-century movement for religious equality as being grounded initially in the "struggle for existence" of those religious groups that were concerned with "establishing an identity of their own," and then passing into the next phase of a "struggle for equality."[62]

The references to Timothy Larsen's work are crucial.[63] Larsen demonstrates that, during the middle decades of the 19th century, the English Nonconformist community (i.e., late 17th-century Protestants who did not conform to the governance of the established Church of England) *developed a coherent theologically grounded political philosophy of its own, of which a central tenet was the principle of religious equality* (in contrast to the stereotype of Evangelical Dissenters). The dissenting community (i.e., Protestants who had separated from the Church of England in the 16th, 17th, and 18th centuries) fought for the civil rights of Roman Catholics, non-Christians, and even atheists, on a principle that had its flowering in the enthusiastic and undivided support that Nonconformity gave to the campaign for Jewish emancipation. Larsen's study examines the political efforts and ideas of Nonconformists during the period, covering the whole range

---

62. Paul Weller, *Religious Discrimination in Britain: A Review of Research Evidence 2000–10*, 73 Eq. & Hum. Rts. Comm'n. 1, 23–24 (2011), http://www.equalityhuman rights.com/uploaded_files/research/research_report_73_religious_discrimination.pdf.

63. Timothy Larsen, Friends of Religious Equality: Nonconformist Politics in Mid-Victorian England (2008). Professor Larsen's main thesis is argued in chapter 4, pages 110 to 136.

of national issues raised, from state education to the Crimean War. It offers a case study of a theologically conservative group *defending religious pluralism and religious freedom in the civic sphere, including for the heterodox and the nonreligious*, showing that the concept of religious and worldview equality was a grand vision at the center of the political philosophy of the Dissenters. Their theologically grounded vision, however, is not held by a movement devoted to or inspired by Magna Carta.

Invocations of Magna Carta, it turns out, were not important in English struggles for religious freedom during the 18th, the 19th, and the first half of the 20th century. There is, surprisingly, not a single reference to the Great Charter of Liberty in the literature referred to in the quotation provided above from the Equality and Human Rights Commission's study.

IV. Freedom of the Church: Tweaking Magna Carta in America

Our examination of Magna Carta and religious freedom started with a presentation of the notion of religious freedom laid down in the 1948 Universal Declaration of Human Rights and subsequently elaborated in international human rights agreements. As with Emperor Ashoka's Rock Edicts welcoming religious freedom and religious plurality some 2,400 years ago, the modern, by now standard, notion of religious freedom is conceived in response to the fact and perceived legitimacy of religious diversity and disagreement in the polity. This notion of religious freedom includes the idea that governments shall protect persons against discrimination on grounds of their respective religion or conscientious nonreligious commitment and shall protect people's freedom to practice their religion or worldview by commission and omission, restricted only by proper legal regulation. Examining the original Magna Carta for provisions protecting religious freedom and, thereafter, probing the history of its applications in English history until 1948 for cases where invocation of Magna Carta has made a difference for religious freedom, our findings among English authorities are rather meager, albeit with some auspicious exceptions.

Turning now to the creative usages of Magna Carta and "the rights and liberties of all Englishmen" by actors and constituencies in England's North American colonies, it is thus gratifying to discover an emerging world of more generous religious freedom. Here, Penn, drawing on Coke, is one vital transitional figure; and so is, most of all, Coke's onetime secretary, Williams. As noted earlier, Williams was Penn's predecessor in instituting comprehensive religious freedom by founding another North American colony, Rhode Island.

Firmly based in his own heterodox but deeply held religious convictions, Williams proclaimed a principle of comprehensive religious freedom:

Sixthly, it is the will and command of God that (since the coming of his Son the Lord Jesus) a permission of the most paganish, Jewish, Turkish, or antichristian consciences and worships, be granted to all men in all nations and countries; and they are only to be fought against with that sword which is only (in soul matters) able to conquer, to wit, the sword of God's Spirit, the Word of God.[64]

A survey of the vast range of evolving doctrines and disputes on religious freedom in America, before, during, and after the American Revolution, up until the present time, would far exceed the space available. Instead, I shall outline a normative argument, to the effect that a religious freedom focus on "freedom of the church," as inherited from Magna Carta chapter 1 and still upheld in America, should, once irreversible and legitimate religious diversity is generally acknowledged, be matched first by a focus on "the freedom of each believer." And, second, the scope of the legal concept of religion should be conceived, as by Williams, to include traditional and new and foreign religions as well as nonreligious conscientious commitments.[65] I am not sure whether these two arguments amount to a tweaking of Magna Carta's American turn. But I submit that both steps are in line with James Madison's creative application of the tradition originating from chapter 1 and chapter 39, and brought to him through Coke, Rogers, and Penn and shared with other illustrious fathers of the American Constitution.

The discussion begins with an examination of James Madison's views on the absolute freedom of religious conscience. It then moves to two recent religious freedom cases brought before the United States Supreme Court, *Hosanna-Tabor v. E.E.O.C.* decided January 11, 2012, and *Sebelius v. Hobby Lobby Stores, Inc.*, foreseeably to be decided in June 2014. And it concludes with a brief look at the peculiar public ramifications of religious belief or, to be specific, of *faith-based knowledge claims* that ground people's religious as well as nonreligious conscientious commitments and the *political implications* of such knowledge claims for proper legal regulation of matters of religion or conscience in a constitutional democracy dedicated to "liberty for all."

James Madison stands out among the founding fathers for the depth of his contribution to constitutional protection of religious freedom. Madison, himself an Episcopalian (i.e., American Anglican), feared political tyranny, including tyranny of even benign democratic majorities, and responded with abhorrence against religious oppression, at times triggered by the

---

64. ROGER WILLIAMS, THE BLOUDY TENENT OF PERSECUTION 3–4 (Providence, Narragansett Club, 1867).

65. Also, Douglas Laycock understands Williams to embrace such an inclusive notion of the constituency of religious freedom. *See* Douglas Laycock, *"Nonpreferential" Aid to Religion: A False Claim about Original Intent*, 27 WM. & MARY L. REV., 875, 898 (1986). For the scope of religion, *see* DURHAM & SCHARFFS, *supra* note 5, at 40–57.

contentious religious diversity prevalent in pre-Revolutionary America. Moved by finding Baptist preachers imprisoned in Virginia for practicing their heterodox faith, he wrote *A Memorial and Remonstrance against Religious Assessments, On the Religious Rights of Man*, written in 1784–1785 at the request of the Religious Society of Baptists in Virginia. In this work, one key passage stands out:

> Before any man can be considered as a member of civil society, he must be considered as a subject of the Governour of the Universe; and if a member of civil society, who enters into any subordinate association, must always do it with a reservation to his duty to the general authority, much more must every man who becomes a member of any particular civil society do it *with a saving of his allegiance to the Universal Sovereign*. We maintain, therefore, that *in matters of religion, no man's right is abridged by the institution of civil society*; and that religion is wholly exempt from its cognizance.[66]

The basic normative point Madison makes when protesting against the government of Virginia's making "provisions for teachers of the Christian religion" is, I submit, that the freedom of religious conscience is not to be subjected to any political or legal restriction; the conscientious and free commitment of the individual human being is accorded absolute sovereignty vis-à-vis government.

Madison was at first reluctant to embrace the need for a Bill of Rights to be added to the U.S. Constitution. But having for good political reasons changed his mind, in 1789 he helped draft the celebrated first ten amendments. Religious freedom is addressed in the First Amendment: "Congress shall make no law respecting an establishment of religion, or prohibiting the free exercise thereof." Perhaps only fortuitously in line with a Madisonian fear of even benign majority decisions, the Bill of Rights was in 1868 supplemented by the Fourteenth Amendment providing, "No State shall make or enforce any law which shall abridge the privileges or immunities of citizens of the United States." Thus, "*in matters of religion*," the Constitution provides special benefits to religion: "no law prohibiting free exercise," and special restrictions on religion: "no law respecting establishment." The peculiar benefits to and restrictions on religion provided by the First Amendment are, in my view, innovative American boughs of a tradition rooted, however remotely, in Magna Carta chapter 1 and chapter 39.

---

66. James Madison, *Religious Freedom Page, Memorial and Remonstrance Against Religious Assessments*, RELIGIOUSFREEDOM.LIB.VIRGINIA.EDU, 1785 at para. 1, http://religiousfreedom.lib.virginia.edu/sacred/madison_m&r_1785.html (last visited May 17, 2014) (emphasis added).

Madison's framework of constitutional thought was theist but nonde-nominational, not excluding deism. This was reasonable in a cultural and political world in which protestant denominations were hegemonic, ranging from Episcopalians to Unitarians. Today, irreversible religious diversity and worldview plurality is widely politically acknowledged as fully legitimate in America. Hence, I submit that today a reasonable application of Madison's central insight in laying the foundation of religious freedom is that a human being's ultimate conscientious commitment cannot be *"abridged by the institution of civil society."* Therefore the legitimate grounds for conscientious commitment ought not be restricted today to a metaphysical framework that is theist, deist, or religious, however broadly conceived. The constitutional framework for interpreting the First Amendment providing for religious freedom today should be egalitarian and inclusive across the divides of religious and nonreligious conscientiously held worldviews.

American philosophers and jurists have recently produced a large quantity of books and papers addressing the dilemmas of religious freedom. At the time of this writing, scholarly conferences on the topic abound. One good book by jurists on the problem of religious freedom is Christopher L. Eisgruber and Lawrence G. Sager's *Religious Freedom and the Constitution*.[67] The authors develop an equal liberty theory that aims at *excluding* special benefits for, and special restrictions on, religion provided for by the First Amendment. In my view they have not succeeded in reducing the First Amendment religion advantages and constraints to a general liberal-egalitarian framework.[68] But their effort is laudably instructive and shall serve as my point of departure for maintaining a Madisonian taboo on governmental restrictions on conscience, or the doctrine "that *in matters of religion, no man's right is abridged by the institution of civil society."*[69] I hold that Madison transformed but he did not discard a historically transmitted religious freedom focus on "freedom of the church." Today, this tree, only remotely rooted in Magna Carta's references to the freedom of the English Church, needs pruning or perhaps grafting in order to accommodate the legitimate diversity of religions and worldviews in contemporary America. Today, freedom of religion or belief cannot exclude the conscientious commitment of human beings who are not religious.

---

67. CHRISTOPHER L. EISGRUBER & LAWRENCE G. SAGER, RELIGIOUS FREEDOM AND THE CONSTITUTION (2007).

68. *See* Cecile Laborde, *Equal Liberty, Non-Establishment and Religious Freedom*, J. LEGAL THEORY 25–26 (2012), *available at* http://ssrn.com/abstract=2160896. Laborde concludes that "the special treatment afforded religion *qua* religion in the law has lost any purchase in contemporary society." *Id*. In Section IV of the present chapter, when discussing salvific knowledge, I propose that a Madisonian special status for religious conscience be universalized to include also a nonreligious conscientious commitment.

69. Madison, *supra* note 66.

The need for constitutional parity between religious and nonreligious citizens is widely perceived. Perhaps some aid can be found in operative international legal provisions for freedom of religion or belief to which American contributions have been crucial.[70] Article 18 is the religious freedom provision of the 1948 Universal Declaration of Human Rights. It is the model for Article 9 of the 1950 European Convention for the Protection of Human Rights and Fundamental Freedoms. The European Convention has for some 20 years served as a legal basis for binding international jurisprudence. *Kokkinakis v. Greece*,[71] a 1993 landmark decision by the European Court of Human Rights, affirms that

> freedom of thought, conscience and religion is one of the foundations of a "democratic society" . . . . It is, in its religious dimension, one of the most vital elements that go to make up the identity of believers and their conception of life, but it is also a precious asset for atheists, agnostics, skeptics and the unconcerned. The pluralism indissociable from a democratic society, which has been dearly won over the centuries, depends on it.

The idea here is that *every human being* under the jurisdiction of the Court is imputed absolute sovereignty vis-à-vis government, with respect to his or her thinking, conscience, belief, or conscientious conviction (the internal forum). But in the exercise of his or her belief, however, a person is subject to legal regulation that is required if necessary to protect the fundamental rights and equal dignity and freedom of others.[72]

Pruning or grafting is not axing: In order to explain how the exercise of religious faith and conscientious commitment necessarily have to be restricted by proper legal regulation but without reducing religious freedom to a general liberal-egalitarian framework, this chapter proceeds with a discussion of two recent cases brought before the United States Supreme Court.

A.   Hosanna-Tabor v. E.E.O.C.

This volume's chapter 5, "Magna Carta in Supreme Court Jurisprudence," by Stephen J. Wermiel, discusses, as one of the clearest examples of references

---

70. Mary Ann Glendon, A World Made New: Eleanor Roosevelt and the Universal Declaration of Human Rights 57, passim (2001).

71. Kokkinakis v. Greece, 14307/88 Eur. Ct. H.R. para. 31 (May 25, 1993), http://hudoc.echr.coe.int/sites/eng/pages/search.aspx?i=001-57827.

72. *See* Facilitating Freedom, *supra* note 3, at xxxvii–xxxix; Javier Martínez-Torrón & Rafael Navarro-Valls, *The Protection of Religious Freedom in the System of the Council of Europe, in id.* at 239–54; United Nations Human Rights Committee CCPR General Comment No. 22: Article 18 (Freedom of Thought, Conscience or Religion), *in id.* at 911–14, *available at* http://refworld.org/docid/453883fb22.html.

to Magna Carta in Supreme Court jurisprudence, the unanimous opinion of the Court in the 2012 case *Hosanna-Tabor Evangelical Lutheran Church and School v. Equal Employment Opportunity Commission et al.* The opinion is authored by Chief Justice Roberts:

> Controversy between church and state over religious offices is hardly new. In 1215, the issue was addressed in the very first clause of Magna Carta. There, King John agreed that "the English church shall be free, and shall have its rights undiminished and its liberties unimpaired." The King in particular accepted the "freedom of elections," a right "thought to be of the greatest necessity and importance to the English church." J. Holt, *Magna Carta* App. IV, p. 317, cl. 1 (1965).[73]

In his opinion, Roberts elaborates on American developments of religious freedom jurisprudence rooted in the Magna Carta heritage, emphasizing Madison's contributions. In particular, he quotes Madison on what has become the "ministerial exception": The "scrupulous policy of the Constitution in guarding against a political interference with religious affairs," Madison explained, prevented the government from rendering an opinion on the "selection of ecclesiastical individuals."[74]

Summing up, Roberts draws a general conclusion:

> Until today, we have not had occasion to consider whether this freedom of a religious organization to select its ministers is implicated by a suit alleging discrimination in employment. . . . the Courts of Appeals have uniformly recognized the existence of a "ministerial exception," grounded in the First Amendment, that precludes application of such legislation to claims concerning the employment relationship between a religious institution and its ministers.
>
> *We agree that there is such a ministerial exception.* The members of a religious group put their faith in the hands of their ministers. Requiring a church to accept or retain an unwanted minister, or punishing a church for failing to do so, intrudes upon more than a mere employment decision. Such action interferes with the internal governance of the church, depriving the church of control over the selection of those who will personify its beliefs. By imposing an unwanted minister, the state infringes the Free Exercise Clause, which protects a religious group's right to shape its own faith and mission through its appointments. According the state the power to determine which individuals will minister to the faithful also violates the Establishment

---

73. Hosanna-Tabor Evangelical Lutheran Church and School v. Equal Employment Opportunity Commission, 565 U.S. __ (2012).

74. *Id.*

Clause, which prohibits government involvement in such ecclesiastical decisions.[75]

Arguing from a Madisonian taboo on governmental restrictions on conscience preventing government from rendering an opinion on "the selection of ecclesiastical individuals" this outcome can hardly be disputed.[76] Thus, based on the First Amendment, respondent Cheryl Perich cannot prevail in her claim for reinstatement in her former position as "called minister." But, even so, it seems unfounded and harsh that the Court failed to award her front pay, back pay, or some other form of compensatory relief.[77]

But, arguing from the Madisonian doctrine that *in matters of religion, no man's right is abridged by the institution of civil society*, my objection to Roberts's opinion concerns his cavalier dismissal of the relevance of the 1990 case, *Employment Division v. Smith*, denying two members of the Native American Church state unemployment benefits after they had been fired from their jobs for ingesting peyote as part of exercising a sacrament of their church:

> We held that this did not violate the Free Exercise Clause, even though the peyote had been ingested for sacramental purposes, because the "right of free exercise does not relieve an individual of the obligation to comply with a valid and neutral law of general applicability on the ground that the law proscribes (or prescribes) conduct that his religion prescribes (or proscribes)." *Id.*, at 879, 110 S.Ct. 1595 (internal quotation marks omitted). It is true that the [Americans with Disabilities Act] ADA's prohibition on retaliation, like Oregon's prohibition on peyote use, is a valid and neutral law of general applicability. But a church's selection of its ministers is unlike an individual's ingestion of peyote. *Smith* involved *government regulation of only outward physical acts*. The present case, in contrast, concerns government interference with an internal church decision that affects the faith and mission of the church itself. *See id.*, at 877, 110 S.Ct. 1595 (distinguishing the government's regulation of "physical acts" from its "lend[ing] its power to one or the other side in controversies over religious authority or dogma").[78]

---

75. *Id.* (emphasis added).

76. *Id.*

77. Being myself a member of the Evangelical-Lutheran Church of Norway, I also fail to see on what grounds Cheryl Perich was not offered such compensation by her church in the first place.

78. *Hosanna-Tabor Evangelical Lutheran Church and School*, 565 U.S. __ (emphasis added).

Now, such a top-down governmental differentiation of internal religious authority and significance is clearly at odds with a Madisonian taboo on governmental restrictions on conscience. And, of course, during Prohibition the Catholic Church served wine even to minors in the sacrament of communion. This would never have been interfered with by the Court on the grounds marshaled in *Employment Division v. Smith*. In my view, Roberts here salvages consistency of the Supreme Court at the price of disclosing the Court's discrimination against a minority religion. And referring to sacramental practice as involving "only outward physical acts" seems arrogant.

I realize *Smith* is said to follow from Supreme Court doctrines on compelling government interest and strict scrutiny, developed since the 1950s. That is the worse for these doctrines.

B. Sebelius v. Hobby Lobby Stores, Inc.

On March 25, 2014, the Becket Fund for Religious Liberty ran a one-page Internet text: "Supreme Court Hears Landmark Hobby Lobby Case." It states,

> The Supreme Court heard oral arguments today in the landmark case *Sebelius v Hobby Lobby*, determining whether individuals lose their religious freedom when they open a family business.
>
> At issue is the Health and Human Services (HHS) Mandate which requires David and Barbara Green and their family business Hobby Lobby to provide and facilitate four potential life-terminating drugs and devices in their health insurance plan, against their religious convictions, or pay severe fines to the IRS (*see video*).[79]

The Becket Fund has also collected and made available on the Internet all amicus curiae briefs in support of Hobby Lobby and in support of the government. There are 59 "Briefs in Support" (i.e., siding with the Green family) and 23 "Briefs in Opposition" (i.e., siding with Sebelius). An impressive array of think tanks, law firms, civic organizations, law professors, senators, religious and worldview organizations, and others have made great efforts in this litigation.[80] The Becket Fund does not hide its partisan position. Twice, on its Hobby Lobby page, the Fund requests readers to "[s]upport Hobby Lobby: Send a thank you note to the Greens letting them know you're standing by their side."[81] I have not found a similar organized effort

---

79. *Supreme Court Hears Landmark Hobby Lobby Case*, BECKETFUND.ORG (Mar. 25, 2014), http://www.becketfund.org/schearshobbylobbypr/. Immediately before this book went to press, the Supreme Court ruled 5–4 in favor of Hobby Lobby in this litigation.

80. *Hobby Lobby Supreme Court Amicus Briefs*, BECKETFUND.ORG, http://www .becketfund.org/hobbylobbyamicus/ (last visited May 17, 2014).

81. *Support Hobby Lobby: Send a Thank You Note to the Green Family*, BECKET FUND.ORG, http://www.becketfund.org/support-hobby-lobby-send-a-thank-you-note-to-the -green-family/ (last visited May 17, 2014).

in support of Sebelius, but there may be some. At the time of this writing, there are numerous Internet sites, conferences, and seminars in the United States addressing the case. A word-for-word, 104-page report on the oral arguments presented in Court was available on the Internet the next day.[82] Such rich and wide-ranging scholarly and not-so-scholarly information and debate on an upcoming case before the Supreme Court is remarkable and to be envied from outside the United States!

The Supreme Court is expected to decide *Sebelius v. Hobby Lobby* in June 2014. What is the likely outcome and what ought the outcome to be? I do not have the competence to say what the outcome should be according to U.S. constitutional and federal law. Putting aside many of the constitutionally contested elements of the *Hobby Lobby* case, however, I shall address a mostly ignored aspect that is morally vital and of profound religious significance: the interpersonal relationship between employers, the Green family owning Hobby Lobby, and employees working in the corporation owned by the Greens, more than 13,000 women and men spending their working days in the Hobby Lobby facilities spread around the United States. It is curious that there is, in the above-mentioned rich and wide-raging debates and analyses, relatively little said about the values and interests of Hobby Lobby employees and next to nothing about their identity and their respective religions or worldviews or conscientious commitments. Very much is written about the Green family and their religious beliefs, which are said to be threatened if they, or their corporation, are coerced to comply with the HHS mandate. What seems lacking in the prevailing American discourse is a discussion of the need for mutually respectful relationships between employers and employees, in particular how the religious beliefs of employers relate to the religious beliefs of employees from the perspective of freedom of religion. Such matters, of course, were never a concern to Magna Carta's drafters.

The First Amendment protects against governmental restrictions on conscience, for employees as well as for employers. But in *Hobby Lobby*, due to elementary health insurance for employees being organized and financed as a tax to be paid by their employers, there is an irresoluble and tragic conflict, since there is no possible happy outcome, no resolution that does not burden the interests, values, beliefs, or conscientious commitments of one of the parties. I find it curious, and somewhat shocking, if employers who advertise their earnest Christian belief, do not include among what is required by their belief a concern for the religious beliefs and conscientious commitments of their employees, most of whom do not share their particular religion.

---

82. Transcript of Oral Argument, Sebelius v Hobby Lobby, S. Ct. Mar. 31, 2014 (No. 13-356), http://www.supremecourt.gov/oral_arguments/argument_transcripts/13-354_5436 .pdf.

As far as I can see, *Hobby Lobby*, by giving rise to a prospective tragic conflict between adherents of conservative religion and their secularist adversaries, is no exceptional affair. It is just one case in a category of several unavoidable conflicts over matters of religion or conviction in which we are now entangled, and which were far from the minds of Magna Carta's drafters. That brings me to the concluding topic of this chapter.

V. The Character of Salvific Knowledge and Its Public Ramifications in a Pluralist Democracy

Let me indicate some much simplified basic dilemmas of living civilly together in a scientifically advanced, religiously pluralist, and increasingly divisive constitutional democracy. Assume, for the sake of argument, that serious adherents of most religious or worldview traditions hold their particular heartland doctrines—their *salvific knowledge*—to be the truth and their peculiar faith and/or practice to be the path to salvation; or to paradise; or to extinction of suffering; or to an autonomous and illusion-free human life. On this assumption, if a person endorses a constitutional entitlement of all to freedom of religious belief and nonreligious commitment, then she has to respect doctrines of others that claim to capture the truth—even when, as far as she can understand, they do not; and she has to respect practices of others that claim to lead to salvation or nonsuffering or autonomy or freedom from illusions—even when, as far as she can understand, they do not.

Our *salvific knowledge*—if we have it—is knowledge of highest importance to us. Yet living in a scientifically mature society we realize that salvific knowledge is not *societally warranted knowledge*. Our salvific knowledge is not shared across society's religious and worldview divides; as a society we are divided by our salvific knowledge. Our societally warranted and generally sharable knowledge includes scientific, technological, and a lot of commonsense knowledge and perhaps much more. In a scientifically advanced, religiously pluralist constitutional democracy we also share that we are expected to comply with and be loyal to society's *basic institutions*: the constitution, democratic governance, rule of law, and heed of the equal dignity and freedom of every human being—including those whose religion or worldview differs from and is incompatible with ours.

A public ramification of foundational but mutually incompatible salvific knowledge is that it breeds potential conflict, once we cannot avoid becoming increasingly entangled with others or more dependent on them. We all have religious freedom, our constitutionally backed right to be protected from government interference in matters of our religion or our worldview.

But at present the diversity of our incompatible religious and worldview commitments is increasing and so is the bulk of our inescapable entanglement with others: same-sex marriage, contraception, abortion, circumcision, euthanasia, employer-employee relationships, and physician-patient relationships. These are becoming matters that can give rise to shrill conflicts over religious freedom claims.

Calling for more tolerance across religious and worldview divides is hardly helpful. Showing we are willing to put up with other beliefs is not much. Rather, mutual respect for and keen interest in others, including in their salvific knowledge and practices, is conducive to civil living together. Knowing that our *salvific knowledge* is not *societally warranted knowledge*, we may strive to discover, clarify, and strengthen the ground in our heartland doctrine for embracing society's *basic institutions*: constitutional and democratic governance, rule of law, and heed of the equal dignity and freedom across divides. Thus, we also strengthen our capability to exercise our constitutional freedom to disseminate and critique salvific knowledge publicly, and publicly ground our political arguments and choices on such knowledge, to the extent we find that respectful of other citizens.

We may expect more and more religious freedom conflicts in the above-mentioned matters. And no one-size-fits-all solution is available for resolving the jurisprudential and legislative battles ahead on religious freedom issues. In many cases, conflicting parties cannot both have their preferred practices, sincerely motivated by religion or worldview, fully honored. Compromises must be found. Belligerent adherents of conservative religion and equally belligerent secularists should acknowledge that civility requires that each should respect and attempt to understand, and even learn from (as advocated by Ashoka), the salvific knowledge of the other.

Proper legal regulation of potentially tragic conflicts over matters of religion or worldview should maintain a Madison-inspired doctrine that in matters of religion or conscientious commitment, no person's right is abridged by the institution of civil society. Only in tragic conflicts where no happy outcome is possible, legislators, judges, and the parties at odds in matters of religion or worldview must look for the least unfavorable outcomes. That is the best they can do, knowing that unimpeded exercise of conscientious commitment for everyone, religious or not, may not be abridged so much by the institutions of civil society as by lack of respectful civility across religious and worldview divides.

Unfortunately, Magna Carta does not provide guidance with respect to how to avoid these conflicts, how to resolve them, or how to find wise and fair compromises.

Chapter 9
Magna Carta and International Law

Larry May

Many important legal developments have become associated with Magna Carta, including these four: (a) a set of fundamental rights was protected; (b) the rule of law was established; (c) a system of law was formed out of a highly disparate collection of courts and lawmaking bodies; and (d) a constitutional order was founded. Those who work in international law can learn quite a lot from Magna Carta, both what was actually agreed to as well as how it has been interpreted and applied over the past 800 years. Today, in many ways, international law is in its infancy, very similarly to the way that English law was in its infancy at the time of Magna Carta.

For English law in 1215, no clear representative lawmaking body existed, and yet there were courts applying the law. Significantly, the same is true of international law today. In 1215, there was considerable controversy about what the law was and what it should be, as well as considerable controversy about what the role of the courts was and what it should be. In addition, there was a significant disagreement about how much of the old system of individual sovereign domains could be interfered with by a central authority. All of these are similar to international law today.

This chapter will look to the successes and failures of Magna Carta for insight into how international law today should be viewed. The chapter will particularly examine the development of tribunals at the international level, in light of how Magna Carta was perceived and interpreted in the 17th century, especially by Edward Coke, who is often seen as the greatest exponent of the idea of judicial independence in England, and the chapter will look at how a common law emerged from very disparate sources of law. The discussion will draw on Coke since he was well known for linking the independent judiciary, as a protector of the fundamental rights of citizens, with Magna Carta.

The chapter will proceed as follows. The first section will discuss the rights that were articulated in Magna Carta, especially in the famous chapter 39, and it will link these rights to the rights that are, or should be, most significant in international law today. The second section will discuss the idea of the rule of law that is articulated in Magna Carta as a model for the international rule of law today. The third section will discuss the idea of the importance of fair trials for a legitimate political order. The fourth section will discuss how Magna Carta was instrumental in melding the disparate sources of law and courts into a single system of law and courts as a model for how to see the development of international tribunals like the International Criminal Court. The final section will set out and defend a conception of an international due process with an independent judiciary, again referring to the development of this idea from Magna Carta onward to the 17th century in England.

I.   Fundamental Rights and Jus Cogens Norms

In chapter 39 of Magna Carta 1215 (chapter 29 of subsequent versions of Magna Carta), a set of basic rights is articulated and a mechanism is identified for defending those rights, as follows: "No freeman shall be taken or imprisoned or desseised or exiled or in any way destroyed, nor will we go upon him nor send upon him, except by the lawful judgment of his peers or by the law of the land [*per legem terrae*]."[1]

Here we have, or it was said over the centuries that one could infer, a fundamental set of rights: the right not to be imprisoned, exiled, or dispossessed of land, without a lawful judgment of one's peers in some kind of judicial proceeding.

Indeed, it was common to say that the right of habeas corpus received its first significant protection here in Magna Carta. Habeas corpus, as it is now viewed, is the right of a person who is imprisoned to be brought out of prison and have his or her jailer publicly declare the charges against him or her that have justified this imprisonment. This right, which can be traced at least to 1199, is often said to be the foundation of all of the rights of citizens against their government. Indeed, this is the only right that is mentioned in the main body of the United States Constitution, perhaps giving it pride of place over the rights listed in the amendments to the United States Constitution, including the rights to free speech, religion, and the press.

In commenting on chapter 39 (29) of Magna Carta in the second part of his *Institutes of the Laws of England*, Edward Coke said:

> That no man be taken or imprisoned, but *per legem terrae*, that is by the common law, statute law, or custom of England; for these words *per legem terrae*, being towards the end of this chapter, do refer to all precedent matters in this chapter, and this hath the first place, because the liberty of a man's person is more precious to him, then all the rest

---

1. *1215 Magna Carta ch. 39, in* WILLIAM SHARP MCKECHNIE, MAGNA CARTA: A COMMENTARY ON THE GREAT CHARTER OF KING JOHN 375 (2d ed. 1914).

that follow, and therefore it is great reason, that he should by law be relieved therein, if he be wronged, as hereafter shall be showed.[2]

We shall later examine more fully the role of courts in Magna Carta. Note here though that Coke sees the rights mentioned in chapter 39 (29) as the most precious and in need of protection. And Coke reads Magna Carta as providing a remedy for the deprivation of any of these basic freedoms through the legal system.

William Blackstone, writing in the 18th century, put the rights of chapter 39 (29) at the top of the most fundamental of rights in England:

To bereave a man of life, or by violence to confiscate his estate, without accusation or trial, would be so gross and notorious an act of despotism, as must at once convey the alarm of tyranny throughout the whole kingdom. But confinement of the person, by secretly hurrying him to gaol, where his sufferings are unknown and forgotten; is a less public, a less striking and therefore a more dangerous engine of arbitrary government.[3]

Blackstone thus joins Coke (the two greatest commentators on the laws of England) as seeing the rights of chapter 39 (29) of Magna Carta as the most fundamental and the most in need of preserving against interference by the state.

Historians have seen Magna Carta's rights of chapter 39 (29) as forming the basis for an ancient constitution. J. G. A. Pocock has said: "In this way there grew up—or rather, there was intensified and renewed—a habit in many counties of appealing to 'the ancient constitution,' of seeking to prove that the rights it was desired to defend were immemorial and therefore beyond the king's power to alter or annul."[4] And it is most often Edward Coke who is cited as having done the most to establish Magna Carta as the touchstone for the fundamental rights of Englishmen that the king could not abrogate. Indeed, Coke sees chapter 39 (29) as standing for the proposition that: "the law is the surest sanctuary, that a man can take, and the strongest fortress to protect the weakest of all."[5]

The idea that there are fundamental rights that predate the statutes of any monarch or other secular lawmaker and that draw their support from

---

2. EDWARD COKE, THE SECOND PART OF THE INSTITUTES OF THE LAWS OF ENGLAND: CONTAINING THE EXPOSITION OF MANY ANCIENT AND OTHER STATUTES 45 (1974) (1797).

3. 1 WILLIAM BLACKSTONE, COMMENTARIES ON THE LAWS OF ENGLAND 131–32 (1979) (1765).

4. J.G.A. POCOCK, THE ANCIENT CONSTITUTION AND THE FEUDAL LAW 16 (1957).

5. COKE, *supra* note 2, at 55.

the morally foundational character of these rights is similar to the idea of *jus cogens* norms in contemporary international law. *Jus cogens* norms are norms of international law that no state can derogate from by treaty or other means. Under this category we find rights against slavery, apartheid, genocide, aggression, and crimes against humanity. These *jus cogens* norms are sometimes referred to as the international bill of rights. Like the United States Bill of Rights, these rights are said to emanate from a strongly moral source—making them quite similar to the inalienable rights spoken of by the founding fathers in the Declaration of Independence.

In trying to understand the nature of *jus cogens* rights, it is important to see in what sense they are fundamental or foundational, and here Magna Carta and the debates about it can provide guidance for international law advocates and scholars. As Coke tells us, fundamental rights protect especially the "weakest of all." Fundamental rights are guarantees that the legal system will be fair to all parties, especially to those who can least defend themselves. In this sense, fundamental rights provide a system of law with a moral grounding. These rights protect citizens against the oppression of their government. And this is accomplished with the recognition of both substantive rights and procedural rights. Indeed, Magna Carta, at least in chapter 39 (29), seems to be mainly focused on basic procedural rights to due process.

International law has focused more on substantive *jus cogens* rights than on procedural ones, but given the model of Magna Carta, that may be the wrong emphasis. We will explore this topic more in the next section. At the moment it should be pointed out that foundational rights such as the right to life and liberty come in two kinds. There is the recognition of what the state must not do to its citizens, the substance of the right. But there is also the recognition of what process protects citizens from having basic substantive rights violated. In addition, there are procedures that allow for the recognition and protection of rights that are not yet recognized. Here basic procedural rights are gap fillers as well. And so in two senses, procedural rights are more important or prior to substantive rights: they give substantive rights teeth, and they allow for the recognition of new substantive rights.

The idea of *jus cogens* norms or rights as prior to any acts of lawmakers has troubled many international law scholars. International law is sometimes characterized as simply concerned with consensual rights and duties, that is, those rights and duties that states have agreed to regard as binding. And Magna Carta is also seen as an agreement between the king and the barons for what are binding duties and rights in England. But the reception of Magna Carta over the centuries has emphasized that the rights and duties recognized in 1215 were not created then by the agreement. Rather, the rights and duties are recognized as already existing and as having existed from time immemorial. Similarly the rights and duties in treaties such as the International Covenant on Civil and Political Rights were not created by the consent of the State-Parties to this convention, but the convention gave them legal recognition.

It would thus behoove those interested in strengthening international law to focus much more than they have on basic procedural rights such as habeas corpus rights that are established to protect basic substantive rights. Already there are some rights, such as the right of nonrefoulement (the right of a refugee not to be returned to a country where his or her basic rights to life or liberty will be jeopardized), that have achieved a de facto status as fundamental procedural rights, and there is the beginning of a recognition that habeas corpus rights should be afforded the same *jus cogens* status. International law advocates should recognize the lessons of Magna Carta and continue to press for the recognition of more procedural rights to protect the fundamental substantive rights of people against their governments.

II. The Domestic and International Rule of Law

In chapter 38 (28) of Magna Carta, one of the most important components of the rule of law is enunciated: "No bailiff [*balivus*] for the future, shall upon his own unsupported complaint, put anyone to his 'law,' without credible witnesses brought for this purpose." Most commentators agree with Coke that "*balivus*" here refers to all officials of a government: "[U]nder this word *balivus*, in this act is comprehended every justice, minister of the king, steward and bailiff."[6]

Chapter 38 (28) contains a strong statement that no person of whatever office shall be able to make of himself "the law." As the phrase is normally used, it refers to the principle that we should have a system of laws not of men. The rule of law is understood to be opposed by the rule of men. And chapter 38 (28) also makes it clear that the king "was no longer to take the law into his own hands: the deliberate judgment of a court of law must precede any punitive measures to be taken by the king against freemen of his realm."[7]

In chapter 40 of Magna Carta, another of the main pillars of the rule of law is declared: "To no one will we sell, to no one will we refuse or delay, right or justice." This refers to the component of the rule of law where justice is not supposed to be administered on the basis of who is the wealthiest or who can bribe the most officials. The rule of law also encompasses the idea

---

6. COKE, *supra* note 2, at 44.
7. MCKECHNIE, *supra* note 1, at 381.

that justice cannot be bought, and no one can get a favorable treatment before the law merely because of his or her wealth. In combination with the other dimension of the rule of law, that there must be rule by law and not by men, we get the strong requirement that the law is blind to who it is who comes before it. Whether the person who stands before the law is a ruler or is the poorest citizen does not matter.

In my view, William McKechnie somewhat undervalues this chapter of Magna Carta when he says: "It is evident that Magna Carta did not put down the practice of charging heavy fees for writs."[8] While fees continued to be charged, which still occurs today in the Anglo-American legal system where the highest-priced lawyer often wins the day, the abuse that is ruled out is the actual buying of a judgment or the granting of a judgment simply because of one's economic status. It is important to point out that all fees have not been eliminated, and the poor still have a harder time getting justice than the rich. But at the time of King John (r. 1199–1216), things were much worse and Magna Carta seemingly put a stop to the worst abuses concerning the selling of justice. And today we should recognize that we are not living up to the ideal of Magna Carta when there are significant financial barriers to obtaining justice.

McKechnie is correct, though, to point out that there is something more important at stake here than the selling of writs.

> Yet this chapter, although frequently misunderstood and exaggerated, is still of considerable importance. It marks for one thing a stage in the process by which the King's courts outdistanced all rivals. In certain provinces, at least, royal justice was left in undisputed possession. In these the grievance was not that there was too much royal justice, but that it was sometimes delayed or denied.[9]

The rule of law was put on the firm foundation that justice was not to be delayed or denied merely because of who the parties are.

International law has faced just this problem concerning the early failure to put heads of state and former ministers on trial. The first case before the Yugoslav Tribunal and many subsequent cases were criticized for prosecuting "small fries" and leaving unprosecuted the political and military leaders who are the architects of genocide and crimes against humanity. And it is often said that what gave the trials subsequent to the Nuremberg Trial their legitimacy was that in the first Nuremberg trial the very top civilian and military leaders of the Third Reich were prosecuted.

---

8. *Id.* at 397.
9. *Id.* at 398.

King John Hunting Venison (from the British Library)

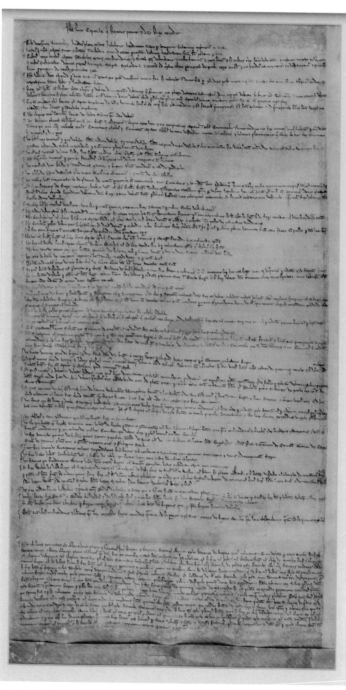

Articles of the Barons (June 1215) (from the British Library)

Seal of King John
originally attached
to the Articles of the
Barons (June 1215)

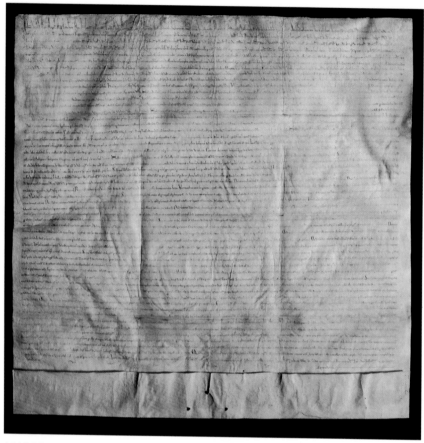

1215 Magna Carta (from the Lincoln Cathedral)

Papal Bull declaring that Magna Carta is null and void (August 24, 1215) (from the British Library)

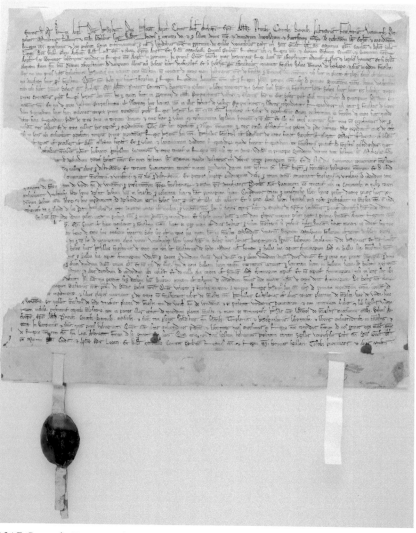

1217 Carta de Foresta (Charter of the Forest) (from Lincoln Cathedral)

1225 Magna
Carta (from the
British Library)

1297 Magna Carta (from the U.S. National Archives)

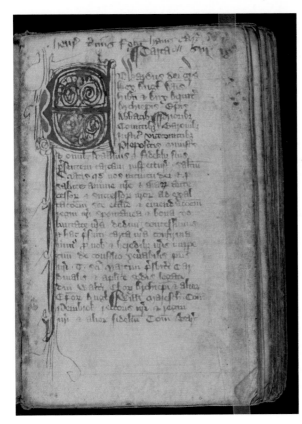

Miniature Magna Carta
for use by a judge in
medieval England (from
the Library of Congress)

Edward Coke Esqr. Speaker, 1592.
From an Original picture at the Speakers House.

Portrait of Sir Edward Coke (1592) (from the National Portrait Gallery (UK))

A
CONFERENCE
DESIRED BY THE
LORDS AND HAD
by a Committee of both
Houfes,

CONCERNING

THE *RIGHTS* AND *PRIVILEGES*
of the *Subjects*.

Difcourfed by

Sir DUDLEY DIGGES.
Sir EDWARD LITTLETON Knight,
now Lord Keeper.
Mafter SELDEN.
Sir EDWARD COOKE.

With the *Objections* by Sir *Robert Heath* Knight
then Attorney Generall, and the *Anfwers*.

3°.*Apr.* 4.*Car.* 1628.

LONDON,
Printed by *A.N.* for *Mathew Walbancke*, and *Richard
Beft*, and are to be fold at their fhops at
Graies-Inne Gate. 1642.

Title page of book titled *A Conference Desired by the Lords and HAD by
a Committee of both Houses, Concerning the Rights and Privileges of the
Subjects,* including discourses by Edward Coke and John Selden praising
Magna Carta as the foundational instrument of English liberties (1642)
(from the Library of Congress)

Seal of the colony of Massachusetts with a
patriot holding Magna Carta and sword (1775)

There remains a significant problem of legitimacy in international criminal law today in that the International Criminal Court (ICC) has not prosecuted or even indicted any leader from Western or other powerful countries in the world. And certain powerful states (e.g., the United States) have not ratified the Rome Statute, thus relieving their leaders of having to face justice at the ICC. As Magna Carta recognized, the king could not get citizens of England to conform to his dictates unless he was seen as not standing above the law. Indeed, that is perhaps the greatest lesson from Magna Carta—that political legitimacy is granted only when justice is seen to sweep to leaders and citizens, rich and poor, equally.

Another issue concerning the rule of law has to do with access to justice by those who do not have substantial economic resources. Magna Carta spoke to this point specifically in chapter 40. One way in which this has been an especially troubling aspect of international law concerns the fact that most international trials take place in The Hague, in the Netherlands, which is very far from where most of the cases originate. It is prohibitively costly for victims and their relatives to go to The Hague and hence many do not feel that they have access to the criminal justice that The Hague is mandated to mete out.

Some victims' advocates have proposed that the trials be held in several parts of the world, and others have proposed that the preliminary hearings be conducted in situ so that the people who were affected by the purported criminal acts will be able to participate and tell their stories or at least be present to make sure that the stories that are told are accurate. Such changes, especially the latter one, would be quite in keeping with the general idea behind chapter 40 of Magna Carta and would go some way toward making the world's population more receptive to the idea that the ICC is a legitimate court.

In some sense the leaders of the states of the world are like the barons who worried that if they gave too much power to the central authority of the monarch they would risk a significant loss of liberty. The concerns about legitimacy are intensified with the realization that the barons are also like the individual people of the world who worry that international tribunals will put their liberties at risk. There are really two constituencies today in the international arena: states, who, like the barons, are skeptical of accepting centralized power arrangements, and individuals, who are organized into nongovernmental organizations and business corporations, among other collective entities.

The international rule of law, like the domestic one, also focuses on the idea that justice not be overly delayed. This has been a chronic problem at the international tribunals. The trial of Slobodan Milosevic took several years, and Milosevic died before a judgment could be rendered. The trials at the ad hoc tribunals for Rwanda and Yugoslavia took much, much longer than initially anticipated. And in the Kenya case, now before the ICC, delays have resulted from witnesses refusing to testify and from the African Union's lobbying efforts. In many cases ten years or more passed from the time of the alleged mass atrocity to the time judgments were issued. These delays have adversely affected the courts' legitimacy and also the likelihood that deterrence will follow from these verdicts.

The international rule of law is also hampered by the lack of a representative legislature that makes the laws that the international tribunals and courts apply. This was also true at the time of Magna Carta when in England there was no representative legislature either. There was a lawmaking authority, the monarch, and many levels of courts. In the international arena today there is a lawmaking authority of sorts, the Security Council of the United Nations, and there are many different international judicial and arbitral bodies as well. Today, there is no political body that is representative of the people or of the states that make up the international society.

A representative system of government grew up only after there was a consolidated centralized system of courts in England, and one can look to this legacy of Magna Carta for hope that the nearly free-standing courts (especially the International Court of Justice (ICJ), the ICC, and the many ad hoc tribunals) will also spawn a demand or hunger for a representative political body to oversee and place limits on these courts. The people in charge of these courts now should definitely not try to stop such movements and should do all they can to facilitate the transition from the free-standing court structure to a truly integrated set of political institutions at the world level that offer the checks and balances now sorely lacking.

III.   A System of Law through Trials

To understand why Magna Carta has for so long stood for the idea that every English citizen is guaranteed a trial by jury, we need to return to chapter 39 (29), which enunciates three important components of trial by jury, even though they do not add up to a robust trial by jury system. Recall that chapter 39 (29) said: "No freeman shall be taken or imprisoned or desseised or exiled or in any way destroyed, nor will we go upon him nor send upon him, except by the lawful judgment of his peers or by the law of the land [*per legem terrae*]." Here we have three elements: (a) lawful judgment, (b) by one's peers, (c) according to the law of the land. I will refer to these elements as: (a) the priority requirement; (b) the equal status requirement; and (c) the legality requirement.

The priority requirement is the requirement that probably seems to be the least important today, but it was and continues to be of supreme importance. The idea is that no adverse action can be taken against a citizen until a judgment has been rendered. What is ruled out is the practice of having a sentence administered before the trial, which was an especially pernicious practice in the Middle Ages. But in addition, the idea is that there must be some kind of proceeding before adverse action is taken. This issue is of the utmost importance today, as we will see later in this section, in the controversy about drone strikes, where the president of the United States is said to have the authority to order a drone strike as long as some kind of hearing is held later to show that it was justified. The priority requirement says that the hearing, or other court proceedings, must take place prior to any issuing of sentence or adverse action against a citizen.

The equal status requirement also initially may not seem all that important today. The requirement that one be tried only by one's peers, or at least not by those who are less than one's peers, is not terribly important in societies that, unlike Medieval England, are not rigidly class-divided. Again, though, there is the reaffirmation that some sort of trial must take place. It seems likely that trial by jury was not the only type of trial countenanced at the time of Magna Carta, but that there also had to be a trial involving judgment by those who knew what it was like to experience the world in the same way as the accused. Indeed, in military justice the idea that an officer cannot be tried except by his equals or superiors is still considered very important for ruling out jurors who would be envious of the position of the person who is accused. Today the closest thing, outside of the military context, is that a person must not be forced to be judged by a group in which none of the members are of his or her race or gender.[10]

The equal status requirement and the priority requirement establish firmly that there must be some kind of trial—today we would say hearing—before any adverse action can be taken against a citizen. This makes Magna Carta primarily about procedural rather than substantive rights, a topic that will be revisited at the end of this chapter. And when we add the third requirement we begin to get a fairly sophisticated set of procedural rules governing the kind of hearing that must precede judgment.

The legality requirement has at least three parts. The first is that a hearing must be held according to law, which reinforces the idea that there cannot be a hearing in which the whim of the judge rules. Second, the judgment must be based on laws that are already in existence—hence no ex post facto judgments. And third, the judgment must be based on the law of one's own land, not the law of a jurisdiction that is not proper for this kind of case and this kind of party. Combined, these three legality requirements set the stage for a system of law in England that operates through courts with common procedural standards.

---

10. I am referring to the rules that concern who may be struck from a jury, including the Batson rule.

We can also consider again chapter 40: "To no one will we sell, to no one will we refuse or delay, right or justice." Even though McKechnie was skeptical of how extensively it applied, he makes an important point by saying: "It marks for one thing a stage in the process by which the King's courts outdistanced all rivals."[11] Magna Carta began a process whereby the courts of England were consolidated. Prior to Magna Carta, there were many often-conflicting sources of legal authority with overlapping jurisdictions. This situation did not change overnight but one can easily mark the sealing of Magna Carta as the beginning of this change. And the change was accomplished by first setting a common set of procedures for guaranteeing the basic rights of English citizens.

One thing to say today is that the ICC is supported by the idea from Magna Carta that trials in formal court proceedings are needed for the rule of law at the international level. And the judgments of these courts must be respected by the community that the courts serve. This respect comes in part from a recognition that the procedures are fair—not favoring any side or type of litigant. But in another sense the fairness of the courts comes from a recognition that the courts, even though free-standing, are indeed inspired by the undergirding moral concepts that make any legal system one deserving of respect.

One fascinating question that in a sense is addressed by Magna Carta is how a system of courts can gain legitimacy independently of the legitimacy of the lawmaker or sovereign. This is at least how Edward Coke often approaches Magna Carta's legacy. The courts must be able to tap into deep-seated values that are easily recognizable by the population at large. Coke calls this the common law, which he believes is itself enmeshed in the practices and ideas of the people in a given society. Indeed, Coke invokes the idea of "ancient and fundamental law" in explaining why certain acts of Parliament should not be allowed to overrule the judgments of justices.[12] In Coke's view, the common law, as interpreted and administered through the courts, has more legitimacy than the king in Parliament insofar as the courts are able to tap into the common law and sentiment of the citizens.

In international law, the same kind of idea can be seen when international courts try valiantly to appeal to as many sources of law as possible in giving reasons to support a particular judgment. The constant references to customary norms in international law is meant to function in a similar way to that of the common law appeals by Coke and the great English jurists who so often invoke Magna Carta. And here is where the analogy may break down between the consolidation and centralization of English courts and that at the international level. For one thing, it is unclear that there is

---

11. McKechnie, *supra* note 1, at 398.
12. Coke, *supra* note 2, at 50.

a common law of peoples and societies, given that peoples are as different from each other as those globally today.

One question to pose here is why a system of courts that was unconnected to a representative legislature could gain democratic legitimacy. Here Magna Carta may provide a model, not in terms of Coke's common law, but in terms of what is considered a *fair* mechanism for resolving disputes and for punishing those who commit atrocities. We thus return to the way that Magna Carta, in my view, was able to gain credibility through its advocacy of procedural rights that were seen by all to be capable of protecting life and liberty, especially to secure life and liberty of individuals from the oppression of governments and other organized groups.

Democratic legitimacy can come from a community that has a civil society where rigorous debate informs the electorate. But democratic legitimacy can also come from a population's sense that the rules are fairly interpreted and applied even if the body that interprets and applies the rules is not itself democratically elected. Courts generally gain legitimacy by being fair in the sense that those who are least powerful are given protection. This is what Coke meant in talking about how Magna Carta provided "the surest sanctuary, that a man can take, and the strongest fortress to protect the weakest of all."[13] If a system of courts is able to provide such a sanctuary, then the populace over which those courts have jurisdiction will come to regard the courts and tribunals as legitimate. This is another of the lessons that Magna Carta offers to international law today.

IV. Ancient Liberties and Centralized Courts

In several chapters of Magna Carta, reference is made to ancient liberties and customs.[14] What is important is not only that the liberties were seen as having existed from time immemorial as we have already seen in earlier sections, but also that these liberties were best preserved in centralized courts, not in the disparate courts of the counties and shires. In this respect, reference is often made to chapter 24: "No sheriff, constable, coroner, or others of our bailiffs, shall hold pleas of our Crown." Pleas of the crown meant those that the king had a special interest in, namely criminal cases.[15] According to this provision in Magna Carta, criminal matters were to be tried before the king's judges. What is being ruled out is the practice that was ripe for abuse of having local officials try murder cases in particular. As McKechnie has argued, the idea was that there was a "condemnation of

---

13. *Id.* at 55.

14. *See, e.g., 1215 Magna Carta chs. 2,13, in* McKechnie, *supra* note 1, at 196–203 & 241–48.

15. *See* McKechnie, *supra* note 1, 305–09.

local administration of justice"[16] and the affirmation of "the comparative purity of the justice dispensed by the King's own judges."[17]

We can add to this once again the famous provisions of chapter 39 (29) where imprisonment of the accused was disallowed unless it followed from "the lawful judgment of his peers or by the law of the land." In part this chapter also gives the clear impression that the law that was to be used in criminal cases was the "law of the land" or in other words the law of England, not merely the law of the individual county or region. Indeed, this is also the clear intent of chapter 38: "No bailiff for the future shall upon his own unsupported complaint, put anyone to his 'law,' without credible witnesses brought for this purpose." While not eliminating the use of the "law" of a bailiff or other non-state official, since this was probably primarily about civil matters, there is here a clear preference against the use of local laws as a basis for denial of important rights, such as debt matters.

In addition, we can see that chapter 45 also is probably aimed at a consolidation of justice throughout England: "We will appoint as justices, constables, sheriffs, or bailiffs, only such as know the law of the realm and mean to observe it well." Once again this is aimed at eliminating the abuses of those officers who would be administering justice not on the basis of the laws of England but on the basis of some kind of *rough justice* or purely local laws.

Finally, we should note that at the end of Magna Carta, the idea of a legal judgment of one's peers surfaces again but for a wider array of plaintiffs, and the idea that a person should be judged according to the laws of his land also surfaces. Concerning the former, in chapter 52 a remedy is provided for any person who has been dispossessed: "If any one has been dispossessed or removed by us, without the legal judgment of his peers, from his lands, castles, franchises, or from his right, we will immediately restore them to him." And concerning the latter, we have this from chapter 56: "If we have disseised or removed any Welshmen from lands or liberties, or other things without the legal judgment of their peers in England or Wales, they shall be immediately restored to them." Then in chapter 61 the execution of the Charter is given a constitutional form insofar as the barons provide procedures for enforcing any of the other chapters. And the more general idea of ancient liberties also is given clear protection in these final chapters of Magna Carta.

Magna Carta stands for the idea that a centralized system of justice, especially criminal justice, will produce the fairest results for defendants. One of the rationales for this is that criminal matters are most properly thought of as affronts to the whole of the English society. And as far as the

16. *Id.* at 305.
17. *Id.*

ancient liberties are concerned, it appears that these are best protected by such a centralized system of justice through trials where other procedural rights will also be protected in a manner that conforms to ancient customs. Criminal punishment was singled out here because the consequences were so grave for those who suffered at the hands of those who would abuse the courts; indeed this was surely one of the most notorious abuses that Magna Carta aimed to stop.

In international law over the past 60 years, there has been a movement toward seeing certain kinds of criminal matters as best prosecuted by international tribunals rather than by state courts, similar to the way that criminal matters were taken over by the king's judges in England from the time of Magna Carta. One rather direct point of comparison concerns the fact that the ICC has claimed for itself universal jurisdiction on the grounds that it is better placed to be the court for this jurisdiction than was true of the prosecutors from various states who would claim universal jurisdiction as they sought to indict foreign heads of state.

What has set international criminal law apart from the rest of international law is the idea that the crimes committed are in some sense "against humanity,"[18] similar to the idea that crimes committed in England are in some sense against England, making them properly prosecutable only in courts of the king. Crimes committed against humanity are thought to be properly prosecutable in courts of humanity—international courts or tribunals—not in merely domestic courts.

The complication in international criminal law is the principle of complementarity, which arguably at the moment makes it less likely that a centralized court system can develop internationally. This principle holds that cases are to be tried at the ICC only if the relevant state has proved unable or unwilling to prosecute the crime, under international law, in its domestic criminal courts. But if the crime is committed against humanity in the sense that the crime itself was perpetrated by a state against its own people, as is characteristic of the crime of genocide or of some other crimes against humanity, it does not seem appropriate for such crimes to be prosecuted by the very same entities that perpetrated the crimes. The kind of abuse that Magna Carta worried about looks like it is highly relevant for international criminal law today.

Complementarity was a kind of concession to the states that worried that the ICC would usurp the historical prerogative of states to have exclusive jurisdiction over crimes committed within the borders of these states. There

---

18. I here use the term "crimes committed against humanity" in a broader way than just to refer to the category of "crimes against humanity." I use the term "crimes committed against humanity" to refer to genocide, war crimes, and aggression, as well as "crimes against humanity." See LARRY MAY, CRIMES AGAINST HUMANITY: A NORMATIVE APPROACH (2005).

is also the practical concern that the ICC will simply never have sufficient resources to prosecute all of the international crimes committed in the world. But those who support the ICC need to think more carefully about whether the pursuit of complementarity does not in principle, and in practice so far, open the door for forum shopping.

Centralization of courts also offers the ability to have consistency of interpretation of the law, which is not as easily had when autonomous or semiautonomous courts operate independently of one another. The development of the common law in England could not have occurred, at least in the opinion of jurists like Coke and Blackstone, if it were not for the centralization of courts that Magna Carta initiated.

In addition to consistency of interpretation, Magna Carta also offers the lesson that centralization is needed for the protection of liberties, especially ancient basic liberties, which must be protected for the legitimacy of the system of law to be maintained. Ancient liberties can become the basis of an unwritten constitution, as was true in England after Magna Carta. But with such an unwritten constitution, it is crucial that all judges and courts view the ancient liberties as encompassing the same principles and give them the same weight.

In international law, there are various large multilateral treaties on rights, such as the Covenant on Civil and Political Rights and the Covenant on Economic, Social, and Cultural Rights.[19] These treaties were established to enforce the Universal Declaration of Rights that was adopted a few years after the founding of the United Nations. So, there is some written text on which to base claims concerning rights violations. But like all treaties, they bind only those who have ratified them. There is also a substantial, although controversial, body of customary international law that supports some rights as well. Courts are left with the task of making sure that these rights are given a consistent interpretation and protection in the absence of a written constitution that binds all states in the same way.

The ICC also has some of the same problems as the international covenants in that the ICC is grounded on a multilateral treaty, the Rome Statute, which does not encompass all states. But over time the ICC has the potential to affect jurisprudence and enforcement of international criminal law by the sheer force of its authoritative decisions, which are already being cited by high courts in many countries including some that have not ratified the Rome Statute.

In my view, the courts of England, especially the King's Bench and common law courts, created their own authority by the persuasiveness and common sense of their rulings. This is at least part of what is meant by Coke's support

---

19. *See* International Covenant on Economic, Social, and Cultural Rights, Dec. 16, 1966, UN Doc. A/6316 (1966), 993 UNTS 3, 6 ILM 368 (1967), http://www.ohchr.org /Documents/ProfessionalInterest/cescr.pdf.

of the common law—it tapped into the common sentiments of the members of society, especially concerning the most fundamental rights in society.

V. Due Process in International Law

This final section will now examine a lynchpin in the international rule of law, the idea of due process of law, again drawing on Magna Carta for support. There has been a controversy about whether at the time of the drafting of Magna Carta the king and barons really had a conception of due process like that of modern times. Much of Magna Carta is indeed taken up with procedural matters, as we have seen. In chapter 39 (29) we find the phrase "by the law of the land." Commenting on this phrase, Coke says:

> Now here it is to be known, in what cases a man by law of the land, may be taken, arrested, or imprisoned in case of treason or felony, before presentment, indictment, etc. Wherein it is to be understood, that process of law is two fold, namely, by the king's writ, or by due proceeding.[20]

Coke is probably as much responsible as anyone for seeing Magna Carta as standing for due process of law.

We might also consider chapter 18, which seems to be solely about procedure and is quite clear in what it requires:

> Inquests of *novel disseisin*, of *mort d'ancestor*, and of *darrein present-ment*, shall not be held elsewhere than in their own county courts, and that in manner following—We, or, if we should be out of the realm, our chief justiciar will send two justiciars through every county four times a year, who shall, along with four knights of the county chosen by the county, hold the said assizes in the county court, on the day and in the place of meeting of that court.[21]

The exact number of times that itinerant judges would come through each county is one of the very few specific processes of Magna Carta. And it is highly significant that it was a procedure that received such clear specificity.

In addition we should again consider chapter 36 of Magna Carta, which also speaks straightforwardly to procedural rights: "Nothing in future shall be given or taken for a writ of inquisition of life or limbs, but freely it shall be granted, and never denied." Here there is specific attention to a particular

---

20. COKE, *supra* note 2, at 51.
21. *1215 Magna Carta ch. 18, in* MCKECHNIE, *supra* note 1, at 269–70.

writ and a very clear requirement that this writ be both "freely granted" and also "never denied." Due process here would have to conform to these requirements.

Chapter 52 includes two mentions of the legal or lawful "judgment of his peers." The many references to what is legal or lawful, as well as the reference to who shall judge whether or not the law does pertain, surely set the stage for the idea of due process even if they are not quite the same as what we would mean by due process today. Magna Carta provides many such procedural requirements and references to following the procedures that are required by law. And as many commentators have pointed out, all of these references to procedures were meant to curb the arbitrary exercise of power by the king and the king's ministers.

Magna Carta is a kind of treaty or pact, but it does not rely on this agreement primarily for its authority. There is a persuasiveness that is overwhelming due to the reasonableness of the procedures set out. At a time when even the king's word was being challenged as truly authoritative, Magna Carta achieved support both by the way it reminded people of the longstanding customary procedures and by the highly reasonable character of the new procedures that were announced. This is also how the common law gained authority over time.

Due process in effect creates its own authority in the sense that if procedures are followed that seem to the average person to be those that are due, then what follows is rendered acceptable even in the absence of a written constitution with a bill of rights spelling out the rights of citizens. International criminal law can follow the good sense of Coke's understanding of Magna Carta and by the clear-cut fairness of its proceedings gain legitimacy, where before it was unclear on what precisely the legitimacy of international tribunals rested.

One of the most important ideas associated with the rule of law is that all are subject to the same rules and that these rules act to provide a minimally fair basis for treating each other with respect in terms of the effective protection of their rights. Some of this is clearly enunciated in Magna Carta, but since it was written in feudal times, the idea of equality is not the same as today. Nonetheless, the idea that procedures should guarantee fairness to citizens is the part of the rule of law that is most significant for international law today.

Yet, one of the problems is that basic procedural rights, such as that a person will have the opportunity to challenge the terms of his or her incarceration or that a person should not be sent out of the country without a proper hearing, are not fully recognized and protected in international law. The continuing abuses of process at Guantánamo are in many ways just the tip of the iceberg. The millions of people who are currently in refugee camps are generally denied the most basic due process rights. Not only are they not equal before the law, but it is often unclear whether any law is recognized as a stop to arbitrary treatment at all.

Strong states that do not recognize international law as applicable to their own practices, or rogue states that do not recognize even basic domestic law protections for their own people, have made the idea of international due process nearly unworkable. Yet, there is no lack of instruments that could make for an international rule of law. What is needed is the will of the international community to support those instruments with more than just lip service.

Chapter 39 (29) of Magna Carta includes arguably four due process rights, all of them at least procedurally focused, and each having a direct connection to the international domain: (a) the right not to be imprisoned without due process of law; (b) the right not to be exiled without due process of law; (c) the right not to be outlawed without due process of law; and (d) the right to a trial of one's peers. As mentioned earlier, the first of these rights is similar to the right of habeas corpus. The second right is similar to what is today called the right of nonrefoulement. The third is a right not to be forced outside the protection of the law. And the fourth is a right to have a certain kind of trial before one's life or liberties can be taken away. Each of these has an effect on debates in international law today, and will be discussed in turn next.

First, something like an international right to habeas corpus, similar to that of the guarantees of chapter 39 (29) of Magna Carta, needs to be enforced internationally. This right is indeed a part of several significant conventions, including the International Covenant on Civil and Political Rights and various regional human rights councils and courts. What we do not have is a uniform set of procedures by which a prisoner can challenge his or her incarceration in an international tribunal. The prisoners (or detainees, as the United States calls them) at Guantánamo for a while fell through the cracks that exist in the international system of rights protection.

As mentioned earlier, the right of habeas corpus is considered to be so important that it is the only right specified in the main body of the United States Constitution. From Magna Carta, this right was recognized as one of the most significant for protecting a host of substantive rights that could be abridged by simply throwing someone in prison. Protecting the right of habeas corpus thus encompassed a larger value of protecting many other rights as well. These included such things as the right not to be tortured— where the right to be brought out of prison and to confront one's jailer also had the advantage that any marks on the body of the prisoner inflicted by torture would come to light.

Second, another largely procedural right is the right of a refugee not to be returned to a country that is likely to harm him or her. Again, while various instruments address this right, such as the Refugee Convention,[22]

---

22. *See* Convention Relating to the Status of Refugees, Jul. 28, 1951,189 UNTS 150, UST 6223, https://treaties.un.org/doc/Publication/UNTS/Volume%20189/volume-189-I-2545-English.pdf.

there is no widespread protection of this right largely because there is no clear international procedure with a specific court that has jurisdiction to hear cases of denial of nonrefoulement. The Refugee Convention attempted to close this gap; but even though many states have ratified this convention, today there are many renditions and deportations to countries where the person has justifiable fears for life or liberty.

The threat to deport someone can act similarly to the threat to throw someone in prison. And the right not to be deported, except to a non-hostile state, thereby also protects other rights—for example, the right to seek asylum and its corresponding right to flee a hostile situation that could jeopardize life and liberty. The refugee who has not secured another home state where his or her rights can be protected is virtually without rights for all practical purposes, as can be seen in the horrible conditions of most refugee camps.

Third is the right not to be forced outside of the protections of the law. Here again we can start by thinking of those who are incarcerated at Guantánamo. In addition there are significant debates about the right not to be rendered stateless. One theorist declared that the prisoners at Guantánamo were in "a legal black hole."[23] Before the issue was addressed by the United States Supreme Court,[24] the United States government declared that United States domestic law did not apply because Guantánamo was outside the jurisdiction of the United States and that international law did not apply because the people held at Guantánamo were enemy combatants and not covered by the Geneva Conventions in international law.

In the time of Magna Carta, one of the most serious abuses to be corrected was that the king could force a person outside of the towns and into the forests where that person was outside the protection of the law. International law needs to have a set of protections similar to those offered by Magna Carta to curtail the abuse of rendering a person an outlaw in the international arena. Like the refugee without a home state, the person who has been forced outside the protections of the law is in a very precarious and vulnerable position. This person needs to be protected by international law.

Fourth, a further right is the right to a trial or hearing by impartial persons. Magna Carta did not address the impartiality of the peers who were to judge the defendant. Indeed, one of the ideas behind calling for a trial by one's peers is that those people would be more sympathetic than people who are not one's peers. Today the practicality of having people who are one's peers has transformed this idea into the idea that the trial should be by people who are impartial, since the greatest worry is that they would be partial to the government and the prosecutor.

---

23. Silvia Borelli, *Casting Light on the Legal Black Hole: International Law and Detentions Abroad in the "War on Terror,"* 87 INT'L REV. RED CROSS, 39, 55 (2005).

24. *See* Hamdan v. Rumsfeld, 548 U.S. 557 (2006).

In addition, it should be noted that none of the international courts and tribunals currently operating employ juries in any event. Panels of judges or arbitrators are the most common form of judicial fact and law determiners. This does not mean that a person is gravely disadvantaged, but it should make us alert to the possibility that when a jury of one's peers is not provided, something else needs to take its place that would equally protect the person who has been forced to defend himself or herself.

VI. Final Thoughts

I wish to end with just a few words on the importance of the Chancery Court in England after Magna Carta as a model for an international court of equity that could be the court that hears cases of denial of the four Magna Carta–era procedural rights and others that are of equal importance. At the moment we have an International Court of Justice that is mainly focused on disputes between states. This court lacks compulsory jurisdiction even for those states that ratified its charter. Its decisions are binding only when both parties agree in advance to be bound by the ruling; otherwise the decision is merely advisory. We also have the ICC, which has compulsory jurisdiction, but only for those states that have ratified its charter and at least at the moment, it has a very specific jurisdiction that concerns only genocide, crimes against humanity, war crimes, and aggression (although this last is not yet fully under its jurisdiction). There are no major international courts or tribunals focused on the abuses of the kind of procedural rights discussed in the previous section.

What is needed is an international court of equity that has compulsory jurisdiction. This court could operate, as was true of the Chancery Court, as the conscience of the international community handling cases dealing with fairness that would otherwise slip through the cracks of the existing international courts and tribunals. In my other writings on this topic, I have made the full case for such a court.[25] Let me end this chapter by once again calling for a new international court that would be able to provide the guarantee against abuse and oppression that was the hallmark of Magna Carta and the courts that were to develop in England over the centuries after the seminal event at Runnymede in 1215. International lawyers can learn many lessons from the model of Magna Carta for how to aid in the development of the protection of rights at the international level, and for the creation of an effective international system of law.

---

25. *See* Larry May, Global Justice and Due Process (2011). Chapter 9 builds on and expands the ideas developed in this book.

Chapter 10

Magna Carta Unchained: The Great Charter in Modern Commonwealth Law

David Clark

I. Introduction

As the world approaches the 800th anniversary of the conclusion of Magna Carta in June 2015, the literature on the Charter continues to be dominated by historians on the subject of the context leading to the creation of Magna Carta. But the Charter broke free of its medieval roots a long time ago. Even after a statutory form of the Charter was established in 1297, changes continued to be made to Magna Carta when the phrase "law of the land"[1] in the 1215 version became "due process of law" in statutes passed in 1354 and 1368.[2] One feature of the post 13th-century history of Magna Carta then has been change either through modification of the language of the various versions and revisions, or by the attribution of new meanings in the contexts in which it operated during its long history, both as a document and as an idea. While historians are largely preoccupied with situating the Charter in its 13th-century context, they also acknowledge that Magna Carta has had a dynamic subsequent history during which it came to be seen in a different light and in the course of which it was put to new uses.[3]

Note: All non-American case law is cited according to the BLUEBOOK, 19th edition, part T2.2 Australia.

1 1215 *Magna Carta chs. 39 and 55, Appendix 6* to J.C. HOLT, MAGNA CARTA 461, 467 (2d ed., 1992).

2. Liberty of the Subject Act 1354, 28 Edw. III c. III; 1 Statutes of the Realm 345; Due Process of Law Act 1368, 42 Edw. III c. III; 1 Statutes of the Realm 388. This was a change widely noted. *See Curr v R* [1972] S.C.R. 889, 898 (SCC); *Adler v Dist. Court of New South Wales* (1990) 19 NSWLR 317, 345–48 (CA); *Jaroo v Attorney Gen. Trin. & Tobago* [2002] 1 AC 871, 881 [24] (PC); *Special Reference Pursuant to Constitution Section 19,* [1995] PGSC 482 [18] (Papua N.G. SC); *McVeagh v Attorney Gen.* [2002] 1 NZLR 808, 817 (CA); *Punjab v Dalbir Singh* [2012] INSC 84 [92]–[93] (Indian SC).

3. FAITH THOMPSON, MAGNA CARTA: ITS ROLE IN THE MAKING OF THE ENGLISH CONSTITUTION 1300–1629 (1948).

Although lawyers and judges are not historians, they are interested in the past, as citations of older cases and even medieval statutes attest. But they are not normally concerned with the past for its own sake, but in the *presentness* of the past.[4] They are drawn to the past either because the law of the past is still current, or because, although obsolete in the formal sense, the law of the past is a starting point to scaffold a modern argument.[5] This may arise because lawyers wish to highlight the changes made by current law, in which case they stress discontinuities, or because they wish to underscore the continuity of an idea even if the details have changed. To take one example of this practical attitude to the history of the Charter, the Supreme Court of Bermuda traced the roots of judicial review back to Magna Carta in a recent case.[6] In fact, judicial review of administrative action is a creature of the late 17th century[7] and there is no trace of it in Magna Carta, even if some of the remedies commonly sought, such as certiorari, did emerge late in the 13th century.[8]

Attitudes toward Magna Carta in Commonwealth countries have veered between the adulatory and the dismissive. Older citations suggest an attitude of reverence. An Australian judge pointed out in 1925 that the principles "are inscribed in that great confirmatory instrument, seven hundred years old, which is the groundwork of all our Constitutions."[9] Modern attitudes, on the other hand are more skeptical. A 1973 law reform commission report in Australia, for example, considered Magna Carta to be chiefly sentimental.[10] One Australian judge thought of it less as law than the expression of a political ideal,[11] a view shared by a Canadian court that concluded that while Magna Carta was an "inspirational document it is incorrect to say that it has literal application."[12] The language of the Charter has also been

---

4. 1 FREDERIC W. MAITLAND, THE COLLECTED PAPERS OF FREDERIC WILLIAM MAITLAND: WHY THE HISTORY OF ENGLISH LAW IS NOT WRITTEN 491 (Herbert A. Laurens Fisher ed., 1911).

5. *Roberts v Swangrove Estates Ltd.* [2008] ch. 439, 451 [38] (Eng. CA); *Moore v British Waterways Bd.* [2012] 1 WLR 3289, 3295–96 [27] (Eng. Ch. D).

6. *In the Matter of an Application for Judicial Review* [2012] SC (Bda) 39 Civ. 1 [25].

7. EDITH HENDERSON, FOUNDATIONS OF ENGLISH ADMINISTRATIVE LAW: CERTIORARI AND MANDAMUS IN THE SEVENTEENTH CENTURY (1963).

8. S.A. DE SMITH, JUDICIAL REVIEW OF ADMINISTRATIVE ACTION 587–88 (J.M. Evans ed., 4th ed. 1980).

9. *Ex parte Walsh & Johnson, In re Yates* (1925) 37 CLR 36, 79 (HCA).

10. LAW REFORM COMMISSION OF THE AUSTRALIAN CAPITAL TERRITORY, REPORT ON IMPERIAL ACTS IN FORCE IN THE AUSTRALIAN CAPITAL TERRITORY 7 (1973).

11. Justice McHugh argument in *Essenberg v The Queen* [2000] High Ct. of Austl., trans. 385 at 7.

12. *R v Ahmad* (2008) 256 CCC (3d) 552, 566 [31] (Ont. SCJ).

criticized as vague,[13] and though this has proved to be a defect for its lack of precision, it has also provided an opening for judicial creativity. One indication of the changes that the Charter has wrought by those into whose hands it has fallen has been to ground a tradition of constitutionalism. Thus, judges have noted that the Charter was one of the first steps taken to curtail the absolute powers of the Crown and that it forms part of a tradition of constitutional development leading to a modern constitutional state based on the rule of law and liberty.[14]

Often citations of Magna Carta are dismissed as simply irrelevant to the argument before the court.[15] In some cases resort to the Charter verges on the delusional such as when an Australian litigant sought to use the Charter to invalidate all courts in the country.[16] On the other hand, during wartime and other emergencies, official attitudes have asserted, though not without criticism,[17] that a war cannot be carried on according to the principles of Magna Carta.[18] Even more recently in a terrorism matter, the Charter proved to be of no avail.[19] Although the courts have sometimes expanded the scope of the Charter by reinterpreting its language, they have also on occasion refused to extend the meaning or reach of the Charter, such as when the High Court in England did not allow Magna Carta to be the foundation of a new tort of exile,[20] while another court dismissed the Charter as a basis for the illegality of torture.[21] Often the link between the Charter and contemporary law is so tenuous that while it may be a ringing affirmation of due process, it does not necessarily replace existing statute

---

13. *Adler v Dist. Court of New South Wales* (1990) 19 NSWLR 317, 348F (NSW CA).

14. *Elia v Police* (1980) 2 CLR 118, 122 (Cyprus SC); *R v Sec'y of State for the Home Dep't, ex parte Muboyayi* [1992] QB 244, 254G (Eng. CA); *Khadr v Can. (Prime Minister)* [2010] 4 FCR 36, 64 [59] (Can. Fed. Ct.); *Qarase v Bainimarama* [2008] FJHC 241 (79) (Fiji HC); *Antunovic v Dawson* (2010) 30 VR 355, 363[42] (Vict. SC); *TTM v London Borough of Hackney* [2011] EWCA Civ. 4 [33] (Eng. CA); *McAteer et al. v Attorney Gen. of Canada* [2013] ONSC 5895[16].

15. *Police v Casino Bar (No 9)* [2013] NZHC 44[68].

16. *Wilson v Condon* [2013] FCA 184 [1], [4] (Austl. Fed. Ct.).

17. Commonwealth of Australia, PARLIAMENTARY DEBATES, HOUSE OF REPRESENTATIVES 6863 (Sept. 9, 1915).

18. *Ronnfeldt v Phillips* (1918) 35 TLR 46, 47 (Eng. CA); *Malaysia v Mahan Singh* [1975] 2 MLJ 155, 164 [75] (Malaysian Fed. CA). This sentiment was criticized in *Kol Ha'am Co. Ltd. v Minister of the Interior* (1953). 1 Selected Judgments of the Supreme Court of Israel 90, 100 (Israeli SC).

19. *R (Mohammed) v Sec'y of State for Foreign & Commonwealth Affairs (No 2)* [2011] QB 218 (Eng. CA).

20. *Chagos Islanders v Attorney Gen. of HM British Indian Ocean Territory Comm'r* [2003] EWHC 2222 (Eng. QB) [117], [373].

21. *A v Sec'y of State for the Home Dep't (No 2)* [2006] 2 AC 221, 246 [11] (HL(E)).

law.[22] In short, the argument is that since 1215, Magna Carta has been extended beyond matters conceived of in the 13th century by abandoning medieval concerns, by reconceptualizing medieval ideas through the work of subsequent generations, and lastly by extending the ideas implicit in the Charter into new areas altogether.

Despite claims to the contrary, Magna Carta was not a statement of human rights[23] or a plan for a democratic system of government,[24] nor did it lay down a written constitution.[25] The 13th century did not know of the separation of powers, judicial review, judicial independence, bills of rights, a written constitution, or freedom of speech, let alone democratically elected governments on the basis of a universal adult franchise via the secret ballot, parliamentary government,[26] or international human rights conventions. These elements of the rule of law are accretions added subsequently to the history of the Charter to construct political and legal arguments in later centuries. Many of these arrangements arose as devices to legitimate arguments about the limits to royal power in the 17th century in particular, much influenced by the writings and speeches of Sir Edward Coke.[27] In short the Charter was a start, not an ending, for, as Coke wrote in the 17th century of chapter 39 of Magna Carta, "Upon this chapter, as out of a roote, many fruitfull branches of the law of England have sprung."[28] For a modern lawyer, then, the Charter matters less for what it said or meant in the 13th century than for what has been made of it by later generations.

This chapter considers the Charter in modern Commonwealth law where it continues to have a modest but significant role to play in judicial decisions. The Commonwealth as an organization is a free association of independent states and in this chapter the term Commonwealth is not to be confused with the Commonwealth of Australia, or American commonwealths such

---

22. *Westco Lagan Ltd. v Attorney Gen.* [2001] 1 NZLR 40, 52 [43] (HC) (Magna Carta not an early public works compensation scheme).

23. *Victoria v Australian Bldg. Constr. Emp. & Builder Labourers' Fed'n* (1982) 152 CLR 25, 109 (HCA).

24. *Reference Re Secession of Que.* [1998] 2 S.C.R. 217, 253–54 (SCC). *Cf.* Legislative Assembly of Ontario, OFFICIAL REPORT OF DEBATES (HANSARD) 609 (Feb. 23, 2012), http://www.ontla.on.ca/house-proceedings/transcripts/files_pdf/23-FEB-2012_L015.pdf.

25. *MacDonald v Cnty Court of Victoria* [2013] VSC 109 [37].

26. *Raja Ram Pal v Speaker, Lok Sabha* [2007] INSC 24 [11] (Indian SC).

27. *See, e.g.*, EDWARD COKE, THE SECOND PART OF THE INSTITUTES OF THE LAWS OF ENGLAND: CONTAINING THE EXPOSITION OF MANY ANCIENT AND OTHER STATUTES 1–78 (W. Clarke, 1817) (1797); Paul Christianson, *Ancient Constitutions in the Age of Sir Edward Coke and John Selden, in* THE ROOTS OF LIBERTY: MAGNA CARTA, ANCIENT CONSTITUTION AND THE ANGLO-AMERICAN TRADITION OF THE RULE OF LAW 89–146 (Ellis Sandoz ed., 1993).

28. EDWARD COKE, THE SECOND PART OF THE INSTITUTES OF THE LAWS OF ENGLAND: CONTAINING THE EXPOSITION OF MANY ANCIENT AND OTHER STATUTES 45 (W. Clarke, 1817) (1797).

as those in Virginia, Massachusetts, Pennsylvania, and Kentucky. The term British Commonwealth was first used in 1922[29] and was repeated in 1931.[30] After World War II, the members agreed in 1949 to henceforth use the term Commonwealth,[31] and this was written into law in 1953[32] and again in 1966.[33] With a total population of over two billion, the Commonwealth comprises 53 independent countries, 32 of which are republics, while 16 recognize Queen Elizabeth as their head of state, and five have their own monarchs. All the states of the Commonwealth outside the United Kingdom are former British territories except Mozambique (Portugal), Rwanda (Belgium), and Cameroon (France).[34] In a number of declarations, and then by a Charter—a term itself an echo of 1215—they have expressed their adherence to the rule of law, among other important principles. The Singapore Declaration of Commonwealth Principles in 1971, for instance, provided:

> We believe in the liberty of the individual, in equal rights for all citizens regardless of race, color, creed or political belief, and in their inalienable right to participate by means of free and democratic political processes in framing the society in which they live. We therefore strive to promote in each of our countries those representative institutions and guarantees for personal freedom under the law that are our common heritage.[35]

In the Charter of the Commonwealth dated December 14, 2012, the member states reaffirmed their adherence to democracy, human rights, tolerance, freedom of expression, the separation of powers, and the rule of law as key Commonwealth values.[36]

Given the number of jurisdictions in the Commonwealth, the emphasis here is on the law in England, Canada, and the Commonwealth Caribbean, and the jurisdictions bordering the Indian and Pacific Oceans, namely Australia,

---

29. Constitution of the Irish Free State Act 1922 (Ireland) First Schedule, art I.

30. Statute of Westminster 1931, 22 Geo. V, c. 4 (UK) preamble.

31. H. DUNCAN HALL, COMMONWEALTH: A HISTORY OF THE BRITISH COMMONWEALTH OF NATIONS, SECTION: THE DECLARATION OF LONDON—APRIL 27, 1949, at 982–83 (1971).

32. Royal Style & Title Act 1953 (UK) Preamble.

33. Commonwealth Secretariat Act 1966 (UK).

34. Commonwealth Act 2002 (UK) § 2 and sch. 2; BBC News, RWANDA BECOMES A MEMBER OF THE COMMONWEALTH (Nov. 29, 2009 12:49 GMT), http://news.bbc.co .uk/2/hi/8384930.stm.

35. Commonwealth Secretariat, *Singapore Declaration of Commonwealth Principles 1971*, THE COMMONWEALTH SECRETARIAT (2004), http://secretariat.thecommon wealth.org/shared_asp_files/GFSR.asp?NodeID=141097 (last visited May 19, 2014).

36. *Our Charter*, THECOMMONWEALTH.ORG, Charter of the Commonwealth Dec. 14, 2012, http://thecommonwealth.org/our-charter (last visited May 19, 2014).

New Zealand, India, Malaysia, Mauritius, and the Commonwealth states in the South Pacific such as Papua New Guinea, Fiji, and Samoa. Also included in this study are territories that are either not independent, such as the Cayman Islands, Bermuda, the British Indian Ocean Territory (Chagos), and Pitcairn Island, or that have left the Commonwealth, such as Hong Kong, which reverted to China in 1997,[37] but where Magna Carta has also been cited. One cautionary note is that the laws of the various Commonwealth jurisdictions have diverged from each other and in each case the common law is the common law of the country itself, not a law in common for the Commonwealth as a whole. The best example of this is the United Kingdom, which has incorporated the European Convention on Human Rights into its domestic law, and although some of these rights are said to have begun with Magna Carta, it is the Strasbourg, France, jurisprudence and contemporary British legislation that govern discussions of legal rights.[38]

The legal material cited in this chapter is available free online via the *worldlii legal website*[39] or the *commonlii website*.[40] The latter website lists all Commonwealth states and includes sub-libraries for states such as Britain, Australia, Canada, the Pacific Islands, and New Zealand. It also includes the Law Reports Commonwealth (LRC) published on behalf of the Commonwealth Secretariat. All report cases are in English except those in Quebec, which are in French (although these are often in bilingual reports), Cyprus, which switched to Greek, and Malta, which uses Maltese in its law reports.

The risk to be avoided in considering the contemporary significance of Magna Carta is a tunnel view of the history of Magna Carta that suggests that the Charter was the only influence on subsequent constitutional development, or worse, that all subsequent legal development arose out of the Charter. Some Commonwealth jurisdictions, after all, such as Mauritius, have French and Roman law elements in their law and have sourced rights in both French and international human rights instruments.[41] Others, such as South Africa and Sri Lanka, were originally Dutch colonies and Roman-Dutch law remains an influence there. As the Supreme Court of Ceylon pointed out in 1965, the "Great Charter of Liberty has not been attracted to our Constitution, though some of its terms find a place in our Statute book."[42] The influence of international human rights instruments

---

37. Hong Kong Act 1985 (UK) § 1(1).

38. Human Rights Act 1998 (UK), Schedule; *B v Sec'y of State for Justice* [2012] 1 WLR 2043, 2063 [53] (Eng. CA).

39. *World Legal Information Institute*, WORLDLII.ORG, http://www.worldlii.org (last visited May 19, 2014).

40. *Commonwealth Legal Information Institute*, COMMONLII.ORG, http://www.commonlii.org (last visited May 19, 2014).

41. *Matadeen v Pointu* [1999] 1 AC 98, 113–116 (PC).

42. *R v Abeysinghe* (1965) 68 NLR 386, 398 (Ceylon SC).

such as the European Convention for the Protection of Human Rights and Fundamental Freedoms 1950 is also particularly noticeable in the constitutions of Commonwealth Caribbean states and Mauritius, as the courts have explained on more than one occasion.[43]

II.   Status in Britain

Generally speaking, references to Magna Carta are most often made to the version of 1215 but that document was in the nature of an agreement, not a statute.[44] As Fredric Maitland warned, it is important to distinguish between the various versions of the Charter, especially as the text varies between the different versions and the judges sometimes cite them incorrectly.[45] The Charter was concluded in June 1215, only to be annulled by Pope Innocent III (r. 1198–1216) ten weeks later on August 24, 1215.[46] The pope was able to do this as he had acquired temporal power in England when, in May 1213 by Letters Patent, John (r. 1199–1216) placed his kingdom under the protection of Innocent III.[47] The Charter was subsequently reissued in a modified form in November 1216 and again in 1217, before being enacted as statute in 1225[48] and in 1297.[49] By the end of the reign of Henry V (r. 1413–1422), it had been confirmed, as the rolls of parliament show, 37 times.[50] The early version actually underwent changes from the 63 chapters of 1215 to 42 in 1216, to 47 in 1217, and to 37 in 1225 and in 1297.[51] As will be seen later, the language of 1297 is not identical to that of 1215.

---

43. *Attorney Gen. v Antigua Times Ltd.* [1976] AC 16, 24–25 (PC); *Sabapathee v State* [1999] 1 WLR 1836, 1842 (PC); *Hurnam v Mauritius* [2006] 1 WLR 857, 860F (PC); A. W. Brian Simpson, Human Rights and the End of Empire (2001).

44. *Perlman v Piché & Attorney Gen. of Canada* (1918) 41 DLR 147, 150 (Que. Superior Ct).

45. F.W. Maitland, The Constitutional History of England 15 (1926). *See also In R (Lumba) v Sec'y of State for the Home Dep't* [2012] 1 AC 245, 315 [219] (SC(E)) (Lord Collins cites chapter 39 of 1215, but wrongly attributes it to the version of 1225).

46. Selected Letters of Pope Innocent III concerning England (1198–1216) 212–19 (C.R. Cheney & W.H. Semple eds., 1953).

47. 1 Catholic Church, Calendar of Entries in the Papal Registers relating to Great Britain and Ireland 1198–1304, at 38 (W.H. Bliss ed., HMSO 1893).

48. 9 Hen. III c. 1(1225); 1 Statutes at Large 1–10.

49. 25 Edw. I c. 1(1297); 1 Statutes of the Realm 114–19.

50. Faith Thompson, *Parliamentary Confirmations of the Great Charter*, 38 Am. Hist. Rev. 659, 661 (1933).

51. William F Swindler, *Runnymede Revisited: Bicentennial Reflections on the 750th Anniversary*, 41 Mo. L. Rev. 153, 163–164 (1976); Michael Evans & R. Ian Jack, Sources of English Legal and Constitutional History 55–56 (1984) (for charts tracing the changes to the various versions of Magna Carta).

It is the 1297 version that will be referred to in this chapter, as parts of it remain on the English statute book.[52] Both of the 13th-century statutes were, of course, acts of the English Parliament, and Magna Carta is therefore not part of the law of Scotland.[53] Nevertheless, Magna Carta's influence of ideas has found its way into Scottish law both as a result of Scottish legislation, such as the Wrongous Imprisonments Act 1701, which was enacted to prevent undue delays in trials,[54] and by virtue of the United Kingdom's Human Rights Act 1998, which applies to Scotland as well as to the other parts of the United Kingdom. The position in Ireland was different from that in England and Scotland, for a separate Magna Carta Hiberniae was issued in 1216, most chapters of which mirrored several of the chapters of the 1216 version, but which also referred to Irish barons and Irish land problems. The Hiberniae version is still part of Irish law.[55] The 1297 Act was also part of the law of Ireland and remained an Irish enactment even after Ireland left the Commonwealth in 1949,[56] only being partially removed from the Irish statute book in 2005 and 2007.[57]

Although the Charter continued to be referred to in subsequent centuries and is still revered in legal and political circles, the Parliament at Westminster was less sentimental, for in 1863 it repealed most of the 1297 version; the process of repeal continued until 1969.[58] What remains current in the 21st century are the substantive chapters 1, 9, and 29 and the ratifying and approving chapter 37 of the 1297 version.[59] The substantive chapters provide as follows:

---

52. 1 Statutes of the Realm 117; *Attorney-General's Reference (No 1 of 1990)* [1992] 1 QB 630, 640 D (Eng. CA).

53. JAMES STAIR, THE INSTITUTIONS OF THE LAW OF SCOTLAND 411 (1693) (1981); Law Society of Scotland, *Memorandum of the Scottish Law Society*, PARLIAMENT.UK, http://www.publications.parliament.uk/pa/jt200708/jtselect/jtrights/memo/britishbill /ucm1502.htm (last visited May 19, 2014).

54. THE SCOTTISH GOVERNMENT, THE ACTS OF THE PARLIAMENTS OF SCOTLAND 1424–1707, at 274–77 (1908).

55. 1 HENRY F. BERRY, STATUTES AND ORDINANCES OF IRELAND 5–19 (1907); MAGNA CHARTA HIBERNIAE 1216 (GREAT CHARTER OF IRELAND), 5–19, http://ua _tuathal.tripod.com/magna.html (last visited May 19, 2014).

56. Ireland Act 1949 (UK).

57. Statute Law Revision (Pre-1922) Act 2005 (Ireland) Schedule, pt. 2 removing chapters 1, 9, 10, 18, 22, 23, 25, 35, and 37 of *Magna Carta 1297*; Statute Law Revision Act 2007 (Ireland) sch. 1, pt. 2, which retains chapters 8, 15, 16, 29, and 30 of *Magna Carta 1297*.

58. Statute Law Revision Act 1863 (UK) 26 & 27 Vict. c. 125, § 1 and Schedule; ANNE PALLISTER, MAGNA CARTA: THE HERITAGE OF LIBERTY 89–107 (1971).

59. 1297 *Magna Carta*, 25 Edw. 1 c. 9, *available at* http://www.bailii.org/uk/legis /num_act/1297/1517519.html (details the repeal legislation between 1863 and 1969); *Mayor, Commonality, & Citizens of London v. Samede*, [2012] 2 All ER 1039, 1049 [30] (Eng. CA).

I. FIRST, We have granted to God, and by this our present Charter have confirmed, for Us and our Heirs for ever, that the Church of England shall be free, and shall have all her whole Rights and Liberties inviolable. We have granted also, and given to all the Freemen of our Realm, for Us and our Heirs for ever, these Liberties under-written, to have and to hold to them and their Heirs, of Us and our Heirs for ever.

. . .

IX. THE City of London shall have all the old Liberties and Customs [which it hath been used to have]. Moreover We will and grant, that all other Cities, Boroughs, Towns, and the Barons of the Five Ports, and all other Ports, shall have all their Liberties and free Customs.

XXIX. NO Freeman shall be taken or imprisoned, or be disseised of his Freehold, or Liberties, or free Customs, or be outlawed, or exiled, or any other wise destroyed; nor will We not pass upon him, nor [condemn him] but by the lawful judgment of his Peers, or by the Law of the Land. We will sell to no man, we will not deny or defer to any man either Justice or Right.

III.   As a Statute in Commonwealth Countries

Magna Carta was not a statute that applied as such to the British Empire but it was said to "follow the flag"[60] in that as the British expanded their colonial possessions, in theory they took English law with them as a part of an Englishman's birthright.[61] In practice settled colonies were sometimes denied the full benefit of English law. In 1803, for example, Jeremy Bentham criticized the legal system of New South Wales on the grounds that it conflicted with Magna Carta.[62] English law included the common law and the statutes affirming common law, such as Magna Carta.[63] In several colonies legislation was passed to import English law, usually by the simple expedient

---

60. *Calder v Attorney Gen. of British Columbia* [1973] S.C.R. 313, 395 (SCC).

61. *Ex parte Nichols* [1839] NSW Sup. C. 76, at 5; *Keilley v Carson* (1842) 4 Moo PC 63, 84–85; 13 ER 225, 233 (PC); *Li Hong Mi v Attorney Gen.* (1918) 18 HKLR 6, 40 (SC); *Calder v Attorney Gen. of British Columbia* [1973] S.C.R. 313, 395 (SCC); *Raja Ram Pal v Speaker, Lok Sabha* [2007] INSC 24, at 17 (Indian SC); *R (Bancoult) v Foreign Sec'y (No 2)* [2009] 1 AC 453, 495 [83] (HL(E)).

62. 1 LIBRARY COMMITTEE OF THE COMMONWEALTH PARLIAMENT, HISTORICAL RECORDS OF AUSTRALIA, 1788–1796: PLEA FOR A CONSTITUTION 896–97 (Series IV 1922).

63. *Ordinance Establishing Civil Courts 1764, in* 1 DOCUMENTS RELATING TO THE CONSTITUTIONAL HISTORY OF CANADA 1759–1791, at 207 (Adam Shortt & Arthur C Doughty eds., 1907); *Borton v Howe* [1875] 3 NZCA 5, 13; *Belilios v Ng Li Shi* (1893) reported in [1969] HKLR 202, 204 (HK SC); *Delohery v Permanent Trustee Co. of New South Wales* (1904) 1 CLR 283, 313 (HCA).

of laying down the rule that all English and British legislation in existence at a certain date, usually the date of foundation, automatically became the law of the colony subject to any necessary adaptions to local circumstances.[64] Since Magna Carta preceded the foundation of these territories, it therefore became part of the received statute law of the jurisdiction. Magna Carta was in consequence included both as a text and in lists of applicable imperial statutes in 19th-century colonial compilations of enactments.[65]

Later, in several jurisdictions, statutes were passed to identify which parts of the English and British statutes were applicable in the jurisdiction. Ontario undertook this in 1897 and thereby adopted chapter 29 of Magna Carta 1297 as part of the law of the province.[66] Similarly, in 1922 the Victorian parliament passed an Imperial Acts Application Act[67] that adopted chapter 29 of Magna Carta 1297 as part of the statute law of the state.[68] In most of the Commonwealth, however, Magna Carta either does not exist as a local statute or has been severely pared back. One reason for this is that many of the chapters, including two of the chapters retained in current English law, simply do not apply in a Commonwealth country. Thus, chapter 1 does not apply in Australia, for example, as the country never had an established church,[69] and chapter 9 applies only to English cities. Despite this, and the conclusion that would seem to flow from it—that the Charter is increasingly irrelevant in a practical sense—it is surprising to learn that it has been cited in the Commonwealth courts more often in the past 20 years than in the previous two centuries.[70]

---

64. Declaratory Act 1799 (Bahamas Consolidated Acts Cap 4) § 2; *Bahamas Entm't Ltd. v Kroll* [1996] 2 LRC 45, 57 (Bah. SC); Northwest Territories Act 1886 (Can.) § 22 (1) in RSC 1985, ch. N-27; English Laws Act 1888 (BC) § 2 (Revised Statutes of British Columbia 1897 vol. II, 1239); *Re Immigration Act and Munshi Singh* (1914) 6 WWR 1347, 1371 (BC CA); *Falkner v Gisborne Dist. Council* [1995] 3 NZLR 622, 626 (HC); Michael Blakeney, *The Reception of Magna Carta in New South Wales*, 65 J. ROYAL AUS- TL'N HIST. SOC'Y 128, 128–39 (1979).

65. 1 BRITISH COLUMBIA, REVISED STATUTES OF BRITISH COLUMBIA xvii–xxviii (1897); IMPERIAL STATUTES IN FORCE IN NEW SOUTH WALES 56, 58 (H.B. Bignold ed., 1913).

66. An Act respecting Certain Rights and Liberties of the People, R.S.O. 1897, ch. 322 *reprinted in* RSO 1980 vol. 9, 1; *Wright v Wright* [1951] S.C.R. 728, 730 (SCC).

67. This legislation listed the British (i.e., Imperial) statutes that apply in the juris- diction.

68. Imperial Acts Application Act 1922 (Vic.) div. 13.

69. Commonwealth Constitution (Austl.) § 116; Parliament of New South Wales, REPORT OF THE LAW REFORM COMMISSION ON THE APPLICATION OF IMPERIAL ACTS 62 (Nov. 1967).

70. A search of the term Magna Carta on Commonlii on February 25, 2014, located 504 hits for cases alone, and 1167 hits for all collections in this database.

Chapter 29 of Magna Carta 1297 continues to exist as a statute in New Zealand;[71] in half of the Australian states (New South Wales,[72] Victoria,[73] and Queensland[74]) by virtue of Imperial Acts legislation; and in the remaining three states by virtue of the rule that English and British acts in existence at the foundation of the jurisdiction are part of the law of the state subject to any appropriate adaptions to local circumstances;[75] in the Australian Capital Territory;[76] and in the Canadian province of Ontario. It follows from the above that as chapter 29 of Magna Carta 1297 is the only part of the English legislation on the Charter in force in these jurisdictions, no other parts of the 1297 Act apply, nor do any of the previous versions of Magna Carta have any place in the formal law of these Commonwealth jurisdictions, a proposition that also applies to the United Kingdom itself. Moreover, since the 1215 version is not a statute, it does not formally apply in these jurisdictions at all.

IV. Legal Myths

Not all judicial references to the Charter are well grounded historically though many judges have recognized the considerable body of myth that has grown up around the Charter.[77] One common misconception is that King John (r. 1199–1216) actually signed the charter,[78] which the evidence shows he did not, for the king had others attach his seal to such documents as a token of his assent, as the surviving copies show;[79] and in any event, while

---

71. Imperial Acts Application Act 1988 (NZ) First Schedule.

72. Imperial Acts Application Act 1969 (NSW) sch. 2, pt. 1; *Prisoners A-XX v New South Wales* (1995) 38 NSWLR 622, 633–34 (CA).

73. Imperial Acts Application Act 1980 (Vic) Schedule; *Antunovic v Dawson* (2010) 30 VR 355, 362–63[25]–[28] (Victorian SC); *Waddington v Dandenong Magistrates' Court* [2014] VSCA 12[24].

74. Imperial Acts Application Act 1984 (Qld) First Schedule.

75. LAW REFORM COMMITTEE OF SOUTH AUSTRALIA, RELATING TO INHERITED IMPERIAL LAW 61st. Report, at 3 (1980); LAW REFORM COMMISSION OF WESTERN AUSTRALIA, REPORT ON UNITED KINGDOM STATUTES IN FORCE IN WESTERN AUSTRALIA, Project No 75, at 24 (1994).

76. Legislation Act 2001 (ACT) § 17 (2) and sch. 1, pt. 1.1.

77. *Westco Lagan Ltd. v Attorney Gen.* [2001] 1 NZLR 40, 51 [42] (HC).

78. Evelyn Ellis, *Sources of Law and Hierarchy of Norms, in* ENGLISH PUBLIC LAW 45 (David Feldman ed., 2004); *cf. Re Chettiar* [1938] 1 MLJ 233 [21] (Malayan SC) (a judge noted that the Charter was sealed not signed; *see also Leung Kwok Hong v HKSAR* (2005) 3 HKLRD 164, 220C (HK Ct of Final Appeal) and *Central Inland Water Transp. Corp. Ltd. v Brojo Nath Ganguly* [1986] INSC 64 [22] (Indian SC).

79. John C Fox, *The Originals of the Great Charter,* 39 ENG. HIST. REV. 321, 321–36 (1924); A.J. Collins, *The Documents of the Great Charter of 1215,* 34 PROC. BRIT. ACAD. 233, 270–73 (1948).

it is known that he could read, there is some doubt as to whether he could write.[80] One Canadian judge offered the dramatic scenario of King John signing the Great Charter "with dagger at his throat,"[81] while Alexander Hamilton also thought that the Charter had been extorted by the barons "sword in hand."[82] Other myths surrounding the Charter are that it was the origin of trial by jury, habeas corpus, the principle of no taxation without representation, and the right to apply for bail.[83] (For more on Magna Carta and habeas corpus, see chapter 7). None of these claims is accurate and the work of historians in the 20th century has exploded these myths, though these myths sometimes find their way into judicial opinions. But then judges and litigants are not historians and when they turn their hand to history, they sometimes make historical mistakes. One use to which Magna Carta has been put is as a foundational document and this manifests itself in references to other documents as a "Magna Carta" either of a jurisdiction or of a field of law. Thus, a decision of the Privy Council[84] on appeal from Cyprus referred to a Turkish Magna Carta;[85] Canadian and New Zealand courts have referred to treaties with indigenous peoples as the Magna Carta of Indian or Maori[86] matters respectively; and Article 21 of the Constitution of India has been described as the procedural Magna Carta protective of life and liberty.[87]

V.   Trial by Jury

The historical evidence shows that Magna Carta did not institute or guarantee trial by jury.[88] The term "jury" does not appear in any version of

---

80. Claire Breay, Magna Carta: Manuscripts and Myths 38 (2010).

81. *Blanshay v Piché* (1918) 32 CCC 151, 158 (Que. Sup. Ct).

82. The Federalist No. 84 (Alexander Hamilton) at 475 (Isaac Kramnick ed. 1987).

83. Ernest Scott, *The Myth of Magna Carta*, The Argus (Melbourne), Nov. 27, 1920, at 6; *R v Spilsbury* [1898] 2 QB 615, 622 (QBD); *R v Adam* [1924] SASR 252, 253 (S. Austl. SC).

84. The Judicial Committee of the Privy Council, normally just called the Privy Council (PC), hears appeals from some Commonwealth states in the Caribbean as well as Mauritius. In the 19th century from 1833 on the Privy Council heard appeals from all British colonies and still does for the 14 remaining British overseas territories. Canada abolished such appeals in 1951, Australia in 1986 and New Zealand in 1999.

85. *Parapano v Happaz* [1894] AC 165, 171 (PC).

86. *R v Marshall* [2005] 2 S.C.R. 220, 257[86] (SCC); Paul McHugh, The Maori Magna Carta (1991).

87. *P S R Sadhanantham v Arunachalam* AIR 1980 SC 856, 858 (Indian SC).

88. *R v Wong King Chau* [1964] DCLR 94, 108 (HK District Ct); *Kingswell v R* (1985) 159 CLR 264, 299 (HCA); *R v Bryant* (1984) 15 DLR (4th) 66, 76–81 (Ont. CA);

the Charter and the term "judgment of his peers"[89] does not refer to trial by jury either.[90] It seems that when juries did emerge, they were actually witnesses to the offense and only later became judges of fact in the modern sense.[91] Litigants who have sought to rely on Magna Carta as guaranteeing a trial by jury have had to point to the general language in chapter 29 in support of their argument.[92] This was a peculiar feature of early Australian law, since trials were conducted by military juries during the penal colony period and lawyers sought the aid of the Charter in pressing for the right to civilian juries.[93] Although the arguments mounted were an example of bad history enlisted in aid of a contemporary constitutional struggle, they eventually prevailed with the institution of civilian juries in 1832.[94] Trials by jury in Commonwealth countries are now regulated by local enactments and in some cases by the Constitution of the country.[95] The courts have repeatedly stated that there is no common law right to a trial by jury because jury trials are regulated exclusively by statute.[96] In practice civil juries have largely disappeared[97] and juries in criminal cases are limited to trials for serious offenses. The lower courts do not use them.[98] Even where a right to a trial by jury exists, a party may elect to be tried by a judge alone.[99] It follows in any case that whatever may be made of Magna Carta, it does not displace local statutes and it is clear in this area, as in many others where the

---

R v Sheratt [1991] 1 S.C.R. 509, 522 (SCC); R v Genest (1990) 61 CCC (3d) 251, 255–56 (Que. CA); R v J. SM [2013] SASCFC 96[41] (S. Austl. Sup. Ct., Full Court).

89. *1215 Magna Carta ch. 39, supra* note 1, at 461.

90. *Smart v Australian* & *New Zealand Banking Grp. Ltd.* [2002] VSCA 111 [9] (Vict. CA).

91. *Munday v Gill* (1930) 44 CLR 38, 52 (HCA).

92. *R v Magistrates of Sydney* [1824] NSW Sup. Ct. 20; *R v SB* (1982) 142 DLR (3d) 339, 350 (BC SC); *R v Kenny* (1991) 68 CCC (3d) 36, 55 (Nfld. SC); *R v Gargan* [2010] NWTCA 11 [6] (NWT CA).

93. *Kingswell v R* (1985) 159 CLR 264, 298–99 (HCA).

94. Jury Trials Act 1832 (NSW) (2 Will. IV No 3) § 1.

95. Constitution of Australia, § 80; Canadian Charter of Rights and Freedoms 1982, § 11(f) (Part 1 of The Constitution Act, 1982, being Schedule B to the Canada Act 1982 (UK), 1982, c. 11), *available at* http://www.canlii.org/en/ca/laws/stat/schedule-b-to-the-canada-act-1982-uk-1982-c-11/latest/schedule-b-to-the-canada-act-1982-uk-1982-c-11.html; *R (Misick) v Sec'y of State for Foreign & Commonwealth Affairs* [2009] EWHC 1039 (Admin) [22]–[26] (Eng. HC).

96. *R. W. Miller & Co. v Wilson* (1932) 32 SR (NSW) 466, 475 (NSW SC); *In re David Lam Shu-Tsang* [1977] HKLR 393, 398 (HK FC); *R v Cornelius* [1994] 2 NZLR 74, 81–82 (CA).

97. *Nat'l Australia Bank v Walter* [2004] VSC [222] (Vict. SC); *Gregory v Gollan* [2007] NZHC 606 [13]–[14]; *Attorney Gen. of New S. Wales v Wilson* [2010] NSWSC 1008 [35], [55].

98. *Dreziolis v Wellington Dist. Court* [1994] 2 NZLR 198, 200 (HC).

99. *R v D. WD* (2013) 116 SASR 99 (South Austl. CCA).

Charter is invoked, that local legislation may modify or exclude any English enactments including Magna Carta.[100]

VI.   Not a Supreme Law

Chapters 1 and 63 of Magna Carta 1215 indicated that the commitments in the Charter were intended to last in perpetuity, but as the five iterations of the Charter in the 13th century show, it was never a static document. Despite 14th-century assertions that amendments contrary to the Charter "shall be holden for none and altogether made void,"[101] the Charter does not have the status of a supreme law. Nor in a legal sense is it the foundation of the written constitution,[102] even if some of its ideas have found their way into the text of the constitution itself. The belief in the fundamental status of Magna Carta confuses the historical origins of an idea with its contemporary juridical foundation. The Charter has often been invoked as if it were a fundamental law that controlled all subsequent statutes or even prevented subsequent laws supposed to be inconsistent with it from being made, and, if made, rendered them invalid. In short the argument was a version of what the Canadian Supreme Court has termed the frozen statute book theory of the law,[103] meaning that the theory that a statute is to be read as its language was originally understood, that the statute does not change through subsequent judicial interpretation, and that all subsequent statutes are subordinate to it.

This argument appears with amazing frequency and is often advanced in submissions by the self-represented in somewhat eccentric and ultimately futile arguments.[104] One Australian litigant in an election case tried to disqualify his rivals by arguing that the payment of a candidate's deposit had to be in coins because Magna Carta made illegal all forms of financial payments such as checks, credit cards, and electronic transfers. Since the other candidates had lodged their deposits in other forms of legal tender, he

---

100. *Baker v New S. Wales Police* [2013] NSWSC 57 [13]–[17]; *R v 7 Named Accused* [2004] PNSC 1 [202]–[206] (Pitcairn Is. SC); *R v Walker* [1989] 2 Qd R 79, 85 (Queensl. CCA); *Silbernagel v Canadian Stevedoring Co. Ltd.* [1997] Canlii 4057 [13] (BC CA).

101. Ordinance of 1311, 5 Edw. II c. 3; 1 Statutes of the Realm 165; Observance of Due Process of Law 1368; 42 Edw. III c. 1; 1 Statutes of the Realm 388.

102. *R v Jebbett* [2003] BCCA 69 [4] (BC CA); *R v Ahmad* (2008) 256 CCC (3d) 552, 567 (Ont. SCJ); *Macdonald v Cnty. Court of Victoria* [2013] VSC 109 [37] (Vict. SC).

103. *Curr. v R* [1972] S.C.R. 889, 903 (SCC).

104. *DADS Transp. Sys. Inc. v MacDonald* [1996] Canlii 566[10] (British Columbia SC); *Priestley v Godwin & Others (No 3)* (2008) 172 FCR 139, 150 [52]–[58] (Austl. Fed. Ct.); *Juries Against Illegal Laws Inc. v Tasmania* [2010] FCA 1277 [14] (Austl. Fed. Ct.); *Middleton v Timaru Dist. Council* [2012] NZHC 3471 [10]–[15], [17].

insisted that they should be disqualified from standing. Not surprisingly the court disagreed, invoking the right of the legislature to pass legislation on legal tender.[105] Although the judge did not refer to the practical implications if such an argument were to succeed, the results are easy to envisage. It would render a modern financial system unworkable. Imagine paying for a house or a car with a truckload of coins. In another case, this time from New Zealand, Magna Carta was invoked to resist the payment of taxes, but the court made it clear that the Charter of 1297 neither prevented taxes from being levied nor invalidated modern income tax legislation by the New Zealand parliament.[106] It is true that chapter 12 of the 1215 version refers to the imposition of scutage or aids with the consent of the common council of the kingdom, but that chapter is not part of New Zealand law and does not appear in a sole chapter of the 1297 version that remains on the New Zealand statute book.[107]

It was laid down early in several jurisdictions that Magna Carta is an ordinary statute that could be altered, repealed, or superseded by later legislation[108] and this was well understood by legislators as well.[109] Indeed, where there is a written constitution, usually described as the supreme law, Magna Carta is subject to that constitution, a point stressed several times in Canadian decisions since the passage of the Canada Act 1982.[110] Because Magna Carta is regarded as an ordinary statute, the legislatures of Commonwealth states are competent to repeal, amend, or supersede the Charter as they could any other statute inherited as part of what was once called imperial law.[111] The formal basis for this principle flows from the doctrine of parliamentary supremacy, which states that no parliament

---

105. *Re Cusack* (1986) 60 ALJR 302, 304 (HCA).

106. *Kaihau v Inland Revenue Dept.* [1990] 3 NZLR 344, 345 (HC); *Shaw v Comm'r of Inland Revenue* [1999] 3 NZLR 1, 157 [14] (CA); *Matahaere v Police* [2012] NZHC 2436 [13]. Canadian and Australian courts have reached the same conclusion. *See, e.g., Re Proteau* [2006] SKQB 324[5] (Saskatchewan QB); *R v Klundert* [2008] ONCA 767 (Canlii) (Ont. CA); *Bishop v Australian Taxation Dept.* (1996) 32 ATR 644, 645 (S. Austl. SC).

107. *Re Shaw* [1997] 3 NZLR 611, 613–14 (HC).

108. *Fenton v Hampton* (1858) 11 Moo PC 347, 352 [14 ER 727, 729] (PC); *Chia Gee v Martin* (1905) 3 CLR 649, 653 (HCA); *Attorney Gen. of British Columbia v Attorney Gen. of Canada* [1914] AC 153, 169–70; (PC) *Shaw v Comm'r of Inland Revenue* [1999] 3 NZLR 154, 157 (CA); *West v Martin* [2001] NZAR 49, 56[26] (CA), *R v Ahmad* (2008) 256 CCC (3d) 552, 567 (Ont. SCJ); *Harper v Atchison* [2011] SKQB 38[10] (Sask. QB).

109. Australia, COMMONWEALTH PARLIAMENTARY DEBATES, HOUSE OF REPRESENTATIVES 231 (Sept. 7, 8, 1939).

110. *R v Demers* [2004] 2 S.C.R. 489, 534 [82] (SCC).

111. *Vincent v Ah Cheung* (1906) 8 WALR 145, 146 (W. Austl. SC).

can bind, i.e., prevent its successors from changing an earlier statute.[112] In the vast majority of Commonwealth states, the argument is that if it was constitutional to pass legislation, it is also constitutionally permissible to repeal the same legislation.[113] The logic of this is clear, since no modern state or legal system could operate if it were limited to the terms of a rather vague 13th-century statute. Several courts have decided that Magna Carta should be regarded less as a statute than as an account of the common law, and as such it could be altered by later enactments on the principle that legislation may alter or even abolish the common law.[114] It also follows that as the courts are free to shape the common law of the jurisdiction, they may alter received common law handed down from the colonial period. As an English court explained in 1920, "Magna Carta has not remained untouched; and like every other law of England, it is not condemned to that immunity from development or improvement which was attributed to the laws of the Medes and the Persians."[115]

VII.   Idea of a Constitutional Presence

All of the aforementioned might suggest that the Charter has no role to play in modern Commonwealth law, but an idea or principle can live on in the law as a presence even if it has little practical utility. Legal arguments need a basis and while normally they are rooted in cases and statutes, constitutional law is a combination of elements of history, statutory interpretation, and political philosophy.[116] The use of the Charter as a starting point for a modern argument is partly about a search for origins, partly about legitimizing a chain of reasoning, and partly a demonstration of the transmutation of an original idea into a modern form embodied in modern legislation.

The salience of the Charter in the popular mind also explains the survival of the Charter. In several English colonies, including those in the Americas, the Charter was published and read.[117] In the 19th century, knowledge of the Charter was part of the education of children in a number of colonies

---

112. *Ellen Estates Ltd. v Minister of Health* [1934] 1 KB 590, 597 (Eng. CA); *S.E. Drainage Bd. (S. Austl.) v Savings Bank of South Australia* (1939) 62 CLR 603, 617 (HCA).

113. *Kartinyeri v Commonwealth* (1998) 195 CLR 337, 356 [14] (HCA).

114. *R v Valentine* (1871) 10 S.C.R. (NSW) 113, 130; *Attorney Gen. for Canada v Attorney Gen. for Quebec* [1921] 1 AC 413, 422 (PC); *R v Wright, ex parte Klar* (1971) 1 SASR 103, 108 (S. Austl. SC); *R v Vollmer* [1996] 1 VR 95, 178 (Vict. SC).

115. *Chester v Bateson* [1920] 1 KB 829, 832 (Eng. KBD) cited in *Murphy v Gardiner* [1951] NZLR 549, 553 (SC).

116. *Shaw v MIMIA* (2003) 218 CLR 28, 37 [12] (HCA).

117. Edwin B. Bronner, *First Printing of Magna Charta in America*, 7 AM. J. LEG. HIST. 189, 189–97 (1963).

where history meant English constitutional history, and it was also part of the education of lawyers since they had to study English constitutional history as a precondition for admission to the legal profession.[118] References to constitutional landmarks such as Magna Carta and England's Habeas Corpus Act 1679 and opposition to arbitrary taxation by John Hampden were also common in the newspapers during the same period.[119]

The Charter was also invoked during the struggle for responsible government or self-government by the colonies as part of the rights of British subjects who were said to carry immemorial rights with them wherever they settled.[120] Magna Carta has also been the subject of a poem by Rudyard Kipling in 1915,[121] a cantata by Henry Coward first created in 1884,[122] and a play by John Arden in 1965.[123] Even modern music has taken on the name. In 1969, a rock group called "Magna Carta" was formed in the United Kingdom and in July 2013 the American singer Jay-Z (Shawn Corey Carter) released an album titled *Magna Carta the Holy Grail* and that same month visited Salisbury Cathedral to see a copy of the 1215 Charter. The Cathedral displayed the album cover alongside the original.[124] In the 1920s and 1940s, the American idea of a Magna Carta day celebrated on the 15th of June spread to Australia and New Zealand.[125] Later Magna Carta even became part of the physical as well as the intellectual landscape. Thus the Australian government bought a copy of the 1297 Charter in 1952[126] and in 2001 a Magna Carta Place was created in Australia's capital city of Canberra.[127] In 1988, the Lincoln Cathedral copy of Magna Carta 1215 was loaned to

---

118. *The Chief Justice's Examination Papers*, [1875] COLONIAL L. J. (NZ) 34–35; Queensland, *Votes and Proceedings of the Legislative Assembly 1880*, REGULAE GENE-RALES, RULE 42 at 490.

119. THE TASMANIAN STRUGGLE, THE REGISTER (ADELAIDE), Sept. 25, 1855, at 2; Clio, *Magna Charta*, THE MERCURY (HOBART), Oct. 28, 1874, at 3; *Liberty of the People*, AUCKLAND STAR (NZ) Aug. 19, 1924, at 7.

120. K.D. McRae, *An Upper Canada Letter of 1829*, 31 CAN. HIST. REV. 288, 293 (1950); Francis Lord, *New Constitution*, SYDNEY MORNING HERALD, Mar. 24, 1848, at 2.

121. *The Reeds of Runnymede*, in RUDYARD KIPLING, RUDYARD KIPLING'S VERSE 719–21 (1940).

122. *Magna Carta*, MARLBOROUGH EXPRESS (NZ), Oct. 26, 1909, at 8.

123. JOHN ARDEN, LEFT-HANDED LIBERTY: A PLAY ABOUT MAGNA CARTA (1965).

124. *See Jay Z Visits U.K.'s Salisbury Cathedral*, BILLBOARD.COM (July 19, 2013), http://www.billboard.com/articles/columns/the-juice/3230991/jay-z-visits-uks-salisbury-cathedral-to-see-the-original-magna.

125. *Magna Carta Day*, EVENING POST (WELLINGTON, NZ), June 16, 1927, at 7; *Magna Carta Day*, THE ARGUS (MELBOURNE), June 8, 1932 at 15; *Magna Carta Day*, SYDNEY MORNING HERALD, June 15, 1944, at 4.

126. Australia, COMMONWEALTH PARLIAMENTARY DEBATES, HOUSE OF REPRESEN-TATIVES 381–82 (Aug. 19, 1952); Australia, SENATE 1280 (Sept. 11, 1952). *See also* Commonwealth of Australia, Senate, *Australia's Magna Carta* 6–19 (2010).

127. COMMONWEALTH OF AUSTRALIA, ANNUAL REPORT OF THE NATIONAL CAPITAL AUTHORITY 1999–2000, at 37 (2001).

Australia for the Expo in Brisbane.[128] In 2010, a stone from Runnymede was given by Queen Elizabeth to the Canadian Human Rights Museum in Winnipeg, while a copy of the 1217 reissue of the Charter was put on display in the legislative building in the same city.[129] This was not the first time the Charter had ventured overseas. The Lincoln Cathedral's Magna Carta was sent to the United States, initially in 1939 for the World's Fair in New York,[130] and then to Fort Knox for safekeeping during the war, after which it was loaned to Congress in 1946 for two years.[131] The American interest in the Charter was reinforced in 1957 when the American Bar Association erected a Magna Carta Memorial at Runnymede.[132] Moreover, as Sandra Day O'Connor pointed out in her address "Magna Carta and the Rule of Law,"[133] there is a marble frieze on the Supreme Court Building in Washington, D.C., of King John holding Magna Carta.

VIII. Adapted to Modern Circumstances

Two of the practical problems with Magna Carta as it has come down to the 21st century are (1) that some chapters are so vague that they require adaption to contemporary circumstances, and (2) that the Charter contains no effective mechanism for its enforcement.[134] The enforcement mechanism in chapter 61 of the Charter of 1215 involved 25 barons who were to maintain "the peace and liberties in the charter." That provision, however, was nullified when the Charter was annulled by the pope in August 1215 and it was not included in the 1216 and subsequent versions of the Charter. Nevertheless there is evidence from the late 13th century through 1476 that efforts were made to enforce the Charter by the issue of patents to deal with complaints "of transgressions against"[135] the Charter.[136] It was only much later that judicial review of administrative action in England emerged

---

128. *Queen to Bring Magna Carta to Expo*, CANBERRA TIMES, Mar. 5, 1988, at 1.

129. *Province of Manitoba: The Magna Carta Comes to Manitoba*, GOV.MB.CA, http://www.gov.mb.ca/magnacarta/index.html (last visited May 19, 2014).

130. Carl L Meyer, *Magna Carta in America*, 26 A.B.A. J. 37, 37 (1940); Nicolas J Cull, *Overture to an Alliance: British Propaganda and the New York World's Fair, 1939–1940*, 36 J. BRIT. STUD. 325, 342–44, 351 (1997).

131. British Museum Act 1946, (UK) § 1.

132. *The Magna Carta Ceremonies* 43 A.B.A. J. 900, 900–07 (1957).

133. SANDRA DAY O'CONNOR, THE MAJESTY OF THE LAW xi, 33 (2003).

134. *Rahey v The Queen* [1987] 1 S.C.R. 588, 634 (SCC).

135. CALENDAR OF THE PATENT ROLLS, EDWARD I, 1292–1301, at 515 (London: HMSO 1895).

136. *Id.*, CALENDAR OF PATENT ROLLS, EDWARD III, 1327–1330, at 150 (London: HMSO 1891); 10 CALENDAR OF PATENT ROLLS, EDWARD III, 1354–1358, at 236, 396 (1909); CALENDAR OF PATENT ROLLS, EDWARD IV, EDWARD V, RICHARD III, 1476–1485, at 23 (London: HMSO, 1901).

to provide for the enforcement of the law. But the very generality of the language of Magna Carta was not necessarily an obstacle, for it provided common law judges with the capacity to craft the language to suit modern conditions.[137] As we saw previously, the courts have held that the legislature is competent to modify ancient statutes, even one that is revered as much as Magna Carta.

The way around the argument that the language of the 13th century is controlling in the courts of the 21st century is to point out that the promise made by the king in chapter 29 of 1297 refers to the law of the land. In the modern courts this means not the law of the land as it stood in the 13th century, but the current law of the land in the jurisdiction concerned.[138] The Charter provided in chapter 29 (1297), for example, that a person would be subject to the "lawful judgment of his peers." In the 13th century, this meant that aristocrats—peers of the realm—would be judged by their fellow peers. That remained the legal position for many centuries,[139] but the special privileges of peers in criminal proceedings in England were abolished in 1948.[140] In societies with no aristocracy, the term "peers" has come to mean fellow citizens. In the 18th century, an English court held that the chapter applied in the case of a trial of a commoner to "a jury of lawful men upon their oaths."[141] In jurisdictions where there is no requirement as to the ethnic or gender composition of a jury, as in England,[142] an accused cannot argue, as one Aboriginal Australian man did, that he was entitled to a jury of persons from his own community. In *R v. Walker*,[143] a Queensland court held that in a modern context, the Magna Carta term "peers"[144] meant fellow citizens. In New Zealand the term "freeman" in chapter 39 of the 1215 version has also been translated as "citizen."[145] Of course, all of this

---

137. *Wilson v Comm'r of Stamp Duties* (1986) 6 NSWLR 410, 415 D–E (SC).

138. *La Trobe Univ. v Robinson & Pola* [1972] VR 883, 891 (Vict. SC); *Handberg v Walter & Registrar of Titles* [2001] VSC 177 [12] (Vict. SC); *Singh v Commonwealth* (2004) 222 CLR 322, 333 [13] (HCA); *Borleis v Wacol Correctional Centre* [2011] QSC 232 (Queensl. SC).

139. *Case of the Duke of Norfolk* (1571), *in* 2 REPORTS FROM THE LOST NOTE-BOOKS OF SIR JAMES DYER 243 (J.H. Baker ed., 1994); *Isobel Countess of Rutland's Case* (1606) 6 Co Rep 52b, [77 ER 332] (Star Chamber); LORD LONGFORD, A HISTORY OF THE HOUSE OF LORDS 158–61 (1988). For the history from oath helpers to a modern jury see *R v J. SM* (2013) 117 SASR 535, 541–47[34]–[52] (S. Austl. CCA).

140. Criminal Justice Act 1948 (UK) § 30(2).

141. *Ashby v White* (1701) 15 Ruling Cases (with American Notes) 52, 77 (Eng. KB).

142. *R v Ford (Royston)* [1989] QB 868 (Eng. CA); *R v Smith* [2003] 1 WLR 2229 (Eng. CA).

143. *R v Walker* [1989] 2 Qd R 79, 85–86 (Queensl. CCA). *See also R v Buzzacott* (2004) 149 A Crim. R. 320, 327 [27] (Austl. Capital Territory SC).

144. *R v Walker* [1989] 2 Qd R 79, 85 (Queensl. CCA).

145. *Kohu v Police* (1989) 5 CRNZ 52, 54 (NZ HC); *Ellis v The Queen* [2011] NZSC 60 [4]; *R v Ellis* [2011] 4 LRC 515, 526 [33]–[34] (NZ CA).

assumes that the trials are of individuals, but where a civil matter arises between corporations it is hard to see how a jury of corporate peers could be constructed, and the courts have adapted the Charter to fit modern trial circumstances.[146]

IX. Origin of a Modern Argument

Although formally Magna Carta does not exist as a specific statute in most Commonwealth jurisdictions, it is nevertheless resorted to as the starting point for modern arguments and is also often deployed to stand for a principle rather than for a formal proposition of law, even if the Charter has now been superseded by modern legislation. One area in Australia, Canada, and New Zealand where Magna Carta is put to a contemporary use is to support arguments for indigenous rights. In Canada, the Royal Proclamation of 1763, which among other things refers to the protection to be given to Indians and to the reservation of their hunting grounds and their lands, is often described as the "Magna Carta of Indian rights."[147] Similarly the Treaty of Waitangi between the indigenous Maori and the British for the cession of New Zealand has been described as the Maori Magna Carta.[148]

Other areas of modern law said to have begun with Magna Carta are the idea of proportionality in punishments[149] and the right to fish in public waters, which it was said could not be limited by the prerogative "or otherwise."[150] Actually the right to fish predates Magna Carta and the Charter is taken to support the proposition that it merely took away from the Crown the right to restrict fishing rights at common law by the prerogative.[151] Even

---

146. *Ins. Comm'r v Australian Associated Motor Insurers Ltd.* (1982) 65 CLR 172, 183–84 (HCA).

147. *R v Marshall* [2005] 2 S.C.R. 220, 257 [86] (SCC). The text of the Royal Proclamation of 1763 appears at 281–84.

148. *Waitangi Treaty*, Evening Post (Wellington, NZ), Aug. 19, 1932 at 7; Paul McHugh, The Maori Magna Carta (1991).

149. *Leung Kwok Hung v HKSAR* [2005] 3 HKLRD 164, 220 [169] (HK Ct of Final Appeal); *Bowe v R* [2006] 1 WLR 1623, 1635 [30] (PC).

150. *Attorney Gen. of British Columbia v Attorney Gen. of Canada* [1914] AC 153, 169–70 (PC); *Waipapakura v Hempton* (1914) 33 NZLR 1065, 1072 (NZ SC); *Minister for Primary Indus. & Energy v Davey* (1993) 47 FCR 151, 168D (Austl. Fed. Ct. FC); *R v Gladstone* [1996] 2 S.C.R. 723, 770 [67] (SCC); *Commonwealth v Yarmirr* (2001) 208 CLR 1, 56 [60] (HCA); *Georgeski v Owners Corp. SP49833* (2004) 62 NSWLR 534, 555 [78] (SC); *Isle of Anglesey Cnty. Council v Welsh Ministers* [2010] QB 163, 175 [35] (Eng. CA); *The United Kingdom Ass'n of Fish Producer Org. v Sec'y of State for Env't* [2013] EWHC 1959 (Admin) [9] (Eng. HC).

151. *Malcomson v O'Dea* (1863) 10 HLC 591, 618–19, [11 ER 1155, 1165–1166], (HL(I)); *Neill v Duke of Devonshire* (1882) 8 App Cas 135, 158 (HL(I)); *Stephens v Snell* [1939] 3 All ER 622 (Eng. Ch. D); *Harper v Minister for Sea Fisheries* (1989) 168 CLR

this view receives little support in the text of the Charter, for chapter 33 of 1215 merely refers to the removal of all fish weirs from the Thames and the Medway and says nothing generally about the right to fish, nor do the statutory versions of Magna Carta support the right to fish per se.[152] The right of the public to fish seems to be an idea attributed to Magna Carta by later commentators. Of course, a legal beginning in the 13th century does not end the matter as in all cases these rights are now governed by contemporary statutes on fishing and conservation.[153] Offices mentioned in chapter 24 such as the coroner are sometimes mentioned in judicial accounts of the office,[154] and even the right to petition is said to have been given its rise in chapter 61 though it more properly was given in Section 5 of the English Bill of Rights, 1688–1689.[155] Thus the Charter is most often cited in Commonwealth legal discourse as the origin either of a specific legal idea or the beginning of a tradition of constitutional government.[156]

X.   Exceptions Made to Magna Carta

While chapter 39 of the Charter forbade exile of a person "except by the lawful judgment of his peers or by the law of the land," these medieval exceptions disappeared and were replaced by broader statements. The long title of the Habeas Corpus Act 1679[157] states that one of the purposes of the act was "for Prevention of Imprisonments beyond the seas." Section 11 of the same act forbade exile to foreign places of subjects of England and Wales save for the exceptions in Sections 13–16, that is, for persons sent abroad as a condition of a contract, transportation of those convicted of a felony, cases occurring before the passage of the act, and persons charged with a capital offense in the overseas territory concerned. At the time, Section 11 was designed to prevent the sending of the English to the colony of Tangier, in particular, a practice that ended with the relinquishment of that territory to the Moors in 1683. Still the idea of prohibiting exile lived on. One of the complaints made by the Americans in the Declaration of Independence was against the British practice of "transporting us beyond Seas to be tried for

---

314, 329–30 (HCA); *Lardil Peoples v Queensland* [2004] FCA 298 [216]–[217] (Austl. Fed. Ct.).

152. As chapter 23 of *Magna Carta* 1297. 25 Edw 1 c 9; 1 Statutes of the Realm 114, 117.

153. *UHA Research Soc'y v Attorney Gen. of Canada* [2013] FC 169 [37]–[40] (Can. Fed. Ct)

154. *Perre v Chivell* (2000) 77 SASR 282, 288 [23] (S. Austl. SC).

155. *Millar v Bornholt* (2009) 177 FCR 67, 76 [24] (Austl. Fed. Ct.).

156. *Ex parte Reid, Re Lynch* (1943) 43 SR (NSW) 207, 223 (SC); *Special reference by Fly River Provincial Executive Council* [2010] PNGSC 3 [252] (Papua N.G. SC).

157. 31 Cha. II c. 2; 5 Statutes of the Realm 935, 937.

pretended offences."[158] But the British still had need of transportation after the conclusion of the Revolutionary War in 1783, and consequently New South Wales was chosen for this purpose and the first prisoners arrived in 1788.[159]

In many colonies, banishment legislation was passed and despite attempts to argue that these enactments were contrary to Magna Carta, these challenges failed.[160] Sometimes executive orders were for a form of internal exile or banishment,[161] while in many cases political prisoner laws operated to send subjects overseas and these statutes existed in colonial territories until the middle of the 1960s.[162] Modern law does not usually contain such statutes and in the case of Section 2(a) of the Canadian Bill of Rights Act 1960, exile is expressly forbidden,[163] but of course all jurisdictions have extradition legislation, which may also apply to citizens, and deportation provisions in immigration statutes that apply to noncitizens. None of this legislation is contrary to the general law and, if there are exceptions to Magna Carta, they are exceptions provided for by the legislature by subsequent legislation. In the case of extradition, it too is regulated by law and is subject to a meaningful judicial process, a requirement said to be as old as Magna Carta.[164]

XI.   Survivals: Chapter 29

Given the retention of chapter 29 of 1297 in several Commonwealth jurisdictions, it is not surprising that its various elements are frequently before the courts. Interestingly, the text of chapter 29 diverges from that of chapter 40 of 1215 since the word "delay" does not appear in Magna Carta 1297. Nevertheless almost all jurisdictions have observed that delay is the natural enemy of justice[165] and that Magna Carta is the origin of

---

158. *Declaration of Independence July 4, 1776, in* The American Reader 40 (Diane Ravitch ed.) (2000).

159. Transportation Act 1784 (UK), 24 Geo. III Sess. 2, c. 56; 9 Statutes at Large 492.

160. *Walker v Hughes* [1839] NSW Sup. Ct. 71 page 6; *In re Lo Tsun Man* (1910) 5 HKLR 166, 179 (Full Ct); *Li Hong Mi v Attorney Gen.* (1918) 18 HKLR 6, 40 (SC).

161. Samoa Amendment Act 1927 (NZ) § 2(3)(b); *Tagaloa v Inspector of Police* [1927] NZLR 883 (SC).

162. David Clark & Gerard McCoy, The Most Fundamental Legal Right: Habeas Corpus in the Commonwealth 49–55 (2000).

163. § 2(a) discussed in *Divito v Canada* [2012] 4 FCR 31 [30] (Can Fed CA).

164. *Ferras v United States* [2006] 2 S.C.R. 77, 89 [19] (SCC); *United States v Dotcom* [2012] NZHC 2076 [76]; *Holt v Hogan* (1993) 44 FCR 572, 574 (Austl. Fed. Ct.).

165. *Hodgson v Amcor Ltd.* (2011) 32 VR 495, 500 [11] (Vict. SC).

the promise not to delay justice,[166] a message one English judge described as "timeless."[167] In many cases the promise made in chapter 29 has been embodied in constitutional provisions requiring a trial within a reasonable time,[168] in contrast to the language of the Sixth Amendment to the United States Constitution, which promises a speedy trial. All jurisdictions, however, have had to face the same problem of how to take vague language and give it greater content. As Justice Lewis Powell pointed out in *Barker v. Wingo*, the right to a speedy trial "is a more vague concept than other procedural rights."[169] Given the slippery nature of the speedy trial right, the court in *Barker* famously set down four criteria as an aid in assessing whether the right had been denied: the length of the delay, the reason for the delay, the defendant's assertion of the right, and the prejudice to the defendant.[170]

Now while the case has been widely cited in Commonwealth decisions,[171] the juridical right to a speedy trial is treated differently in Commonwealth jurisdictions both because the term "speedy trial" does not appear in the statutes and constitutions of Commonwealth states and because the different constitutional context requires a different evaluation of the problem.[172] The delay provision applies not only to the time taken to bring a case to trial but also to delays in the post-conviction appellate process.[173] The law concentrates on elaborating on the sources of delay and the forms it takes as well as on remedies if it is found to occur. This takes us a long way from 1215 and is one of the best illustrations of how a Magna Carta idea has been set free from the circumstances of the 13th century.

In Australia's case, despite a valiant effort on the part of one member of the High Court of Australia to argue for such a right to a speedy trial,[174] the

---

166. *ACT Textiles v Zodhlatis* [1986] 1 CLR 89, 96 (Cyprus SC); *R v Rahey* [1987] 1 S.C.R. 588, 636 (SCC); *R v Hung* [1992] 2 HKCLR 90, 93 (HC).

167. *R (Casey) v Restomel Borough Council* [2007] EWHC 2554 (Admin) [33] (Eng. HC).

168. Canadian Charter of Rights and Freedoms, § 11(b); Constitution of the Solomon Islands, § 10(8); Constitution of Jamaica, § 20(1); Constitution of Samoa, art. 9(1); Constitution of Mauritius, § 10(1); Constitution of the Seychelles, art. 19(1); Constitution of Kenya, § 50(2)(e).

169. Barker v. Wingo, 407 U.S. 514, 521 (1972).

170. *Id.* at 530.

171. *Bell v Dir. of Pub. Prosecutions* [1985] AC 937, 951 (PC); *Mills v R* [1986] 1 S.C.R. 863, 924 (SCC); *Jago v Dist. Court of New South Wales* (1989) 168 CLR 23, 60 (HCA); *Charles v State* [2000] 1 WLR 384, 388 (PC); *Boolell v Mauritius* [2012] 1 WLR 3718, 3724 [23] (PC); *Puni v Attorney Gen.* [2012] WSCA 12[12] (Samoa CA).

172. *R v Morin* [1992] 1 S.C.R. 771, 784 (SCC); *R v Askov* [1990] 2 S.C.R. 1199, 1223–32 (SCC).

173. *Hamilton v The Queen* [2012] 1 WLR 2875, 2883 [18] (PC); *Tapper v Dir. of Pub. Prosecutions of Jamaica* [2012] 1 WLR 2712 (PC).

174. David Clark, *The Icon of Liberty: Magna Carta in Australian and New Zealand Law*, 24 MELBOURNE U. L. REV. 866, 880–82 (2000).

court concluded that there is no such right in Australia; but it did indicate that there is a right to a fair trial and that excessive delay might impinge on this right.[175] Similarly, in England, while the courts have long had an inherent power to protect themselves against abuse of process,[176] the obligation to avoid delay arises out of Article 6(1) of the European Convention on Human Rights to accord a person a fair and public trial within a reasonable time.[177] In India, the Supreme Court has said that the right to a speedy trial is a derivation from a provision of Magna Carta and can be read into Article 21 of the Constitution as one of the facets of a fundamental right to life and liberty.[178]

The decisions of the Canadian Supreme Court have proved to be the most influential in this area since they have been widely cited in other Commonwealth jurisdictions.[179] Starting with the factors identified in *Barker v. Wingo*, the Supreme Court in *R v. Morin*[180] elaborated upon these to include the length of the delay, the waiver of time periods, and the reasons for the delay, including: (a) inherent time requirements of the case; (b) actions of the accused; (c) actions of the Crown; (d) limits on institutional resources; (e) any other reasons for the delay; and (f) prejudice to the accused. In this and other decisions, the Canadian Supreme Court differed from U.S. law in both the elements to be considered and the weight to be given to them.[181]

One feature of the Commonwealth jurisprudence is that the notion of delay must be considered in light of the institutional arrangements in the jurisdiction concerned. As the Court of Appeal of Samoa pointed out in a recent case, the court sits only twice a year since it is staffed by judges from Australia and New Zealand and the court has a small caseload. It follows then that Magna Carta's prohibition on delay can receive only a reasonable response, not an immediate one.[182]

The principle that justice should not be delayed applies to civil (including administrative decisions)[183] as well as to criminal proceedings. The remedies for excessive delay depend upon the type of proceeding and

---

175. *Jago v The Dist. Court of New South Wales* (1989) 168 CLR 23, 59 (HCA).

176. *Connelly v Dir. of Pub. Prosecutions* [1964] AC 1254 (HL(E)).

177. *Dyer v Watson* [2004] 1 AC 379, 420 [124] (PC).

178. *Kartar Singh v Punjab* [1994] INSC 172 [84], [86], [88] (Indian SC); *Ranjan Dwivedi v CBI TR Dir. Gen.* [2012] INSC 454 [14] (Indian SC).

179. *Martin v Tauranga Dist. Court* [1995] 2 NZLR 419, 423 (CA); *Sanderson v Attorney Gen. of the E. Cape* [1998] 2 LRC 543, 554 [25] (S. African Con Ct); *Police v Ropati* [2006] 2 LRC 62, 66 (Samoa SC); *Mbugua v Republic* [2011] 2 LRC 1, 16 (Kenya CA).

180. *R v Morin* [1992] 1 S.C.R. 771, 787–88 (SCC).

181. R v *Rahey* [1987] 1 S.C.R. 588, 608 (SCC).

182. *Police v Ropati* [2006] 2 LRC 62, 75d–e (Samoa SC); *Samoa Party v Attorney Gen.* [2010] WSCA 4 [54].

183. *Blencoe v British Columbia (Human Rights Commission)* [2000] 2 S.C.R. 307, 392 (SCC).

the circumstances. In civil cases, the court may simply dismiss an action for want of prosecution,[184] stay the proceedings,[185] and award costs against the offending party.[186] In criminal cases, depending upon the circumstances, the remedy may be to substitute a fine for a term of imprisonment; as in one case from Mauritius where a man was charged in 1991 but only sentenced in 2003,[187] quash the conviction where the delay lasted 15 years;[188] or remit the matter to a lower court with a recommendation to impose a reduced sentence.[189]

Chapter 40 of the 1215 Magna Carta also refers to the selling of justice and attempts have been made to invoke this as an argument against the imposition of court fees and even charges for court transcripts. These arguments have failed in part because, as one judge explained, chapter 40 "was not intended to apply literally."[190] The gap between 1215 and the present was highlighted in the same case when Lord Justice Stoughton commented:

> If an officious bystander at Runnymede in 1215 had asked the Prince-Bishop of Durham whether a prisoner in his goal was entitled to be transported free of cost to a civil court in London (assuming that the case was not within the local palatinate jurisdiction), I imagine that he would have received a terse and negative reply.[191]

There are within modern legal systems situations where persons are denied access to the seat of justice, such as when a person is declared a vexatious litigant, a situation once described as an exception to Magna Carta.[192]

---

184. *Allen v Sir Alfred McAlpine & Sons Ltd.* [1968] 2 QB 229, 245 (Eng. CA); *Wong Lan & Anor v Sri Haruta Jaya Sdn Bhd & Anor* [1996] MLJ 293 [3] (Kuala Lumpur HC).

185. *Attorney-General's Reference (No 2 of 2001)* [2004] 2 AC 72, 86 [17] (HL(E)); *R v Williams* [2009] 2 NZLR 750, 760 [18] (SC).

186. *Birkett v James* [1978] AC 297, 319–20 (HL(E)); *Atkinson v Namale W. Inc.* [2012] FJHC 1363 [10] (Fiji HC).

187. *Boolell v State* [2007] 2 LRC 483 (PC).

188. *Darmalingum v State* [2000] 1 WLR 2303 (PC).

189. *Rummun v Mauritius* [2013] 1 WLR 598, 604 [21] (PC).

190. *R v Sec'y of State for the Home Dept., ex parte Wynne* [1992] 1 QB 406, 427F (Eng. CA).

191. *Id.* at 427F.

192. *Pountney v Griffiths* [1976] AC 314, 329C (HL(E)).

XII.   Property

The Charter has often been cited as the foundation for the proposition that private property cannot be taken by the government unless authorized by law.[193] The argument is not that Magna Carta prohibits taking by the government, but that the modern law on the subject can be traced back to 1215.[194] Certainly there are modern statutory provisions that protect the taking of property and require that such taking be in accordance with the law.[195] The important related proposition is that if private property is taken, then, in the absence of a provision to the contrary,[196] just compensation must be paid for the property.[197] In some cases, this is a constitutional requirement where just terms are guaranteed if property is appropriated by legislation,[198] but several jurisdictions provide protection through ordinary statutes.[199] If the legislation authorizing the taking of property is silent as to compensation, the presumption is that that compensation is payable.[200] Classes of taking without compensation, which are therefore a departure from the general proposition in chapter 39 of Magna Carta 1215, are, for example, the law authorizing the seizure of criminal assets,[201] the valid

---

193. *Edelsten v Wilcox* (1988) 83 ALR 99, 111 [33] (Austl. Fed. Ct.); *Queensland Maintenance Services Pty Ltd. v Fed. Comm'r of Taxation* (2011) 207 FCR 405, 440 [138] (Austl. Fed. Ct.); *Westco Lagan Ltd. v Attorney Gen.* [2001] 1 NZLR 40, 50–51 [34]–[42] (HC).

194. *Malika Holdings Ltd. v Stretton* (2001) 204 CLR 290, 328 [121] (HCA); *Waitakere City Council v Brunel* [2008] NZHC 1406 [18]–[19].

195. Canadian Bill of Rights, SC 1960, c 44, § 1(a) explained in *Authorson v Canada* [2003] 2 S.C.R. 40, 52 [34] (SCC).

196. *Belfast Corp. v O D Cars Ltd.* [1960] AC 490, 519 (HL (NI)); *Manitoba Fisheries Ltd. v R* [1979] 1 S.C.R. 101, 118 (SCC); *Wells v Newfoundland* [1999] 3 S.C.R. 199, 216 [41] (SCC).

197. *Jaundoo v Attorney Gen. of Guyana* [1971] AC 972, 986–87 (PC); *Attorney Gen. v Antigua Times Ltd.* [1976] AC 16, 28 (PC); *Societé United Docks v Government of Mauritius* [1985] 1 AC 585, 595 (PC); Alberta Pers. Prop. Bill of Rights, RSA 2000, c A-31, § 2; Public Works Act 1981 (NZ) § 60.

198. Commonwealth Constitution (Austl.), § 51(xxxi); *ICM Agriculture Pty Ltd. v Commonwealth* (2009) 240 CLR 140, 209–10 [179]–[181] (HCA), Constitution of Samoa, art. 14; *Penaia v Land & Titles Court* [2012] WSCA 6 [21] (Samoa CA); Constitution of Mauritius, art. 8; Constitution of the Independent State of Papua New Guinea, art. 53(2); Constitution of South Africa, art. 25(2)(b); Constitution of Kenya, art. 40(4); Constitution of Malaysia, art. 13(1); Constitution of St. Christopher and Nevis, § 6.

199. Such as the *Canadian Bill of Rights*, SC 1960, c 44, § 1(a); Alberta Bill of Rights, RSA 2000, c A-14, § 1(a).

200. *Attorney Gen. v De Keyser's Royal Hotel Ltd.* [1920] AC 508 (HL(E)); *Burmah Oil Co. Ltd. v Lord Advocate* [1965] AC 75 (HL(Sc)); *Fazzolari v Parramatta City Council* (2009) 237 CLR 603, 618–20 [40]–[45](HCA).

201. *Westpac Banking Corp.* [2001] WASC 365 [58]–[60] (W. Austrl. SC); *Dir. of Pub. Prosecutions of Mauritius v Bholah* [2012] 1 WLR 1737, 1742–45 [17]–[31] (PC).

levying of taxes,[202] and even the towing of an illegally parked car until an expiation fee is paid.[203] In addition, property may be taken for authorized public purposes such as in the interests of defense, public safety, public health, and town and country planning.[204] All of this illustrates both the initial influence of the Charter, and the ways in which later societies have developed the law, including creating exceptions to the broad statements in the Charter, in order to deal with the complexities of modern life. In this sense, then, Magna Carta has not merely survived eight centuries, it has done so by being constantly adjusted to new circumstances.

XIII. Transformation in Modern Bills of Rights

Of the 53 Commonwealth states, all but New Zealand and the United Kingdom have a written constitution, though both have important constitutional enactments and they also protect human rights through legislation.[205] Thus a Malaysian court contrasted the British and English constitutional arrangements, which it characterized as "bits and pieces in the Magna Carta, the Bills of Rights, the Act of Settlement and a series of parliamentary acts," with the formal constitutional document of that country.[206] Thus the written constitutions of Commonwealth states are said to be based upon four main principles: (1) the rule of law, (2) the separation of powers, (3) the arming of each of the three branches of government with powers to discharge their functions, and (4) the power of the judiciary to judicially review executive and legislative acts.[207]

A typical bill of rights in a Commonwealth jurisdiction protects rights such as freedom of speech, assembly and association, conscience, private and family life, and life, liberty, and property.[208] Many of these rights simply

---

202. *Mutual Pools & Staff Pty Ltd. v Commonwealth* (1994) 179 CLR 155, 187–88 (HCA).

203. *Alleyn-Forte v Attorney Gen. of Trin. & Tobago* [1998] 1 WLR 68, 72C–D (PC).

204. Constitution of Mauritius, § 8; Constitution of Kiribati, § 8(1).

205. Constitution Act 1986 (NZ); Constitutional Reform Act 2005 (UK); New Zealand Bill of Rights Act 1990 (NZ); Human Rights Act 1998 (UK).

206. *Dato' Dr Zambry bin Abd Kadir v Dato' Seri Ir Hj Mohammad Nizar bin Jamaluddin* [2009] 5 MLJ 464, 497–98 [80] (Malay. CA); *Accord Beaureguard v R* [1981] 2 FC 543, 559 (Can. Fed. Ct.); *R (HS2 Action Alliance) v Sec'y of State for Transp.* [2014] 1 WLR 324[207] (SC(E)).

207. *Hinds v The Queen* [1977] AC 195, 213 (PC); *Ahnee v Dir. of Pub. Prosecutions* [1999] 2 AC 294, 303 (PC); *Khan v Trinidad* [2005] 1 AC 374, 383–84 (PC); *Mauritius v Khoyratty* [2007] 1 AC 80, 90–91 (PC).

208. *See, e.g.*, Human Rights Act 1998 (UK) § 1 and sch. 1; Canadian Charter of Rights and Freedoms as Part 1 of the Constitution Act 1982 (Can), §§ 1–31; Constitution of Mauritius, Chapter II, sections 3–16; New Zealand Bill of Rights Act 1990 (NZ) pt. II, §§ 8–18; Constitution of the Republic of Trinidad and Tobago, ch. 1 §§ 4–5; Constitution

did not exist in the 13th century and although they were created in later centuries, nevertheless the imprint of Magna Carta can be seen both in some of the specific provisions and in the general spirit of these modern charters. In many cases the jurisprudence on these modern constitutional provisions refers to the Charter as an historical foundation for the rights in question, as other parts of this chapter show. Thus the modern law has moved well beyond the Charter to create remedies unknown in the 13th century, such as vindicatory damages for breaches of constitutional or human rights.[209] Perhaps the greatest change has been in the creation of new rights unheard of in the 13th century. This may be seen in the rise of statutes to prohibit forms of discrimination that do occur in a modern state and that are protected by specialized human rights agencies.[210]

Of the remaining 51 jurisdictions, only Australia does not have a national bill of rights, though one state[211] and one territory do have a bill of rights,[212] and Canada retains the Canadian Bill of Rights Act 1960 alongside the Charter of Rights and Freedoms 1982.[213] These instruments provide a range of rights for those in custody, for example, the right to be told of the reasons for the arrest or detention, to consult a lawyer, to test the validity of the detention by habeas corpus, to prepare a defense, and to have an interpreter.[214] Traces of the Charter's influence can also be found in criminal procedure statutes and human rights enactments. Thus, it is standard in criminal procedure statutes in Australia, for example, for arrested persons to have an array of rights such as the right to make a telephone call, to have a lawyer present when questioned, to have an interpreter, to remain silent, to be informed of their rights, and to be told that anything taken down may be

---

of the Independent State of Papua New Guinea, §§ 35–37, 42–56; Constitution of South Africa, ch. 2, §§ 7–39; Constitution of Malta, pt. II.

209. *Attorney Gen. of Trin. & Tobago v Ramanoop* [2006] 1 AC 328, 335–36 [18]–[20] (PC); *Attorney Gen. v Taunoa* [2006] 2 NZLR 457, 515–17 [294]–[303] (CA); *R (Lumba) v Sec'y of State for the Home Dept.* [2012] 1 AC 245, 313–14 [214]–[215] (SC(E)).

210. The Saskatchewan Human Rights Code (Statutes of Saskatchewan 1979, ch. S-24.1 (originally 1947); Canadian Human Rights Act, RSC 1985, ch. 6; Human Rights Code, RSO 1990, ch. 19; Charter of Human Rights and Freedoms, RSQ, ch. C-12; Human Rights Act 1993 (NZ); Australian Human Rights Commission Act 1986 (Cth); Human Rights (Parliamentary Scrutiny) Act 2011 (Cth).

211. Charter of Rights and Responsibilities Act 2007 (Vic).

212. Human Rights Act 2004 (ACT).

213. *Authorson v Canada* [2003] 2 S.C.R. 40, 51 (SCC).

214. Canadian Charter of Rights and Freedoms 1982, § 10; New Zealand Bill of Rights Act 1990 (NZ) §§ 23–25.

used in evidence.[215] It is also mandated by statute that all interviews by the police with arrested persons be recorded or videoed.[216]

XIV. Personal Liberty

The courts have long accepted that the personal liberty of the citizen is a "fundamental constitutional principle,"[217] usually sourced to either Magna Carta[218] or to subsequent developments through the writ of habeas corpus.[219] It is also an established principle of statutory interpretation in Commonwealth jurisdictions that statutes be construed in favor of the liberty of the citizen.[220] It remains the starting point in the common law that a person has rights and remedies even when detained by the police, unless such rights are excluded by statute, a position said to have its inspiration in chapter 39 of Magna Carta 1215.[221]

The references to habeas corpus often make the doubtful claim that Magna Carta was the origin of the writ. There are examples of courts and legislators who seem to think that habeas corpus, which in fact predates 1215,[222] was created by the Charter.[223] On the other hand, mythology is corrected by the more historically knowledgeable judges to notice that the main developments that gave habeas corpus its reach occurred in the 17th

---

215. Summary Offences Act 1953 (S. Austl.) § 79A; Criminal Law (Detention and Investigation) Act 1995 (Tas.) §§ 5–9; Criminal Investigation Act 2007 (W. Austl.) § 138.

216. Police Powers and Responsibilities Act 2000 (Qld) §§ 436–38.

217. *Delaney v Delaney* [1996] QB 387, 397 (Eng. CA); *R (Von Brandenburg) v E. London & City Mental Health NHS Trust* [2004] 2 AC 280, 292 [6] (HL(E)); *A v Secr'y of State for the Home Dept.* [2005] 2 AC 68, 107 [36] (HL(E)); *R(M) v Hackney LBC* [2011] 1 WLR 2873, 2884 [33] (Eng. CA); *R (WL(Congo)) v Home Sec'y* [2012] 1 AC 245, 315 [219] (SC(E)); *Re Bolton, ex parte Beane* (1987) 162 CLR 514, 520–21 (HCA).

218. *Makomberedze v Minister of State (Security)* [1987] LRC (Const) 504, 507 (Zimbabwe HC); *Re B (Child Abduction)* [1994] 2 FLR 479, 486F (Eng CA); *Munday v Australian Capital Territory* (1998) 146 FLR 17, 23–24 (Austl. Capital Territory SC); *B v Sec'y of State for Justice* [2012] 1 WLR 2043, 2063 [53] (Eng. CA).

219. *In re SC (Mental Patient: Habeas Corpus)* [1996] QB 599, 603 (Eng. CA); *May v Warden of Ferndale Inst.* [2005] 3 S.C.R. 809, 823[19] (SCC); *R (CHJ by SW) v Cardiff City Council* [2011] EWCA Civ. 1590 [20] (Eng. CA).

220. *Re Stanbridge's Application* (1996) 70 ALJR 640, 642 (HCA).

221. *Groves v Commonwealth* (1982) 150 CLR 113, 126 (HCA); *Lukatela v Birch* (2008) 223 FLR 1, 3 (Austl. Capital Territory SC).

222. *See Baldwin Tyrell's Case 1214, in* 1 SELECT PLEAS OF THE CROWN 67 (F.W. Maitland ed., 1887).

223. *R (Nikonovs) v Governor of Brixton Prison* [2006] 1 WLR 1518, 1522 (QBD) (citing a member of the House of Lords in a debate on an Extradition Bill); New Zealand, PARLIAMENTARY DEBATES 8069 (Feb. 20, 2013) (debate on the Habeas Corpus Amendment Bill 2013).

century.[224] Apart from a constitutional right to apply for habeas corpus, which exists in Canada and in other Commonwealth jurisdictions,[225] several jurisdictions have their own habeas corpus acts while others have passed Liberty of the Subject statutes[226] to accomplish the same result.[227] In those jurisdictions with a bill of rights, the right to seek relief from unlawful detention is guaranteed by the constitution, sometimes explicitly by habeas corpus, though more usually as a general constitutional remedy. Thus, Article 21 of the Constitution of India, for example, provides for the protection of personal liberty and the Supreme Court has given it a wide meaning to include immunity from arrest and detention, and freedom of speech and association,[228] as well as the right to travel abroad.[229] There are, however, restrictions on this right, for the citizen needs a valid passport, and there are laws on unpaid taxes, the repayments of debts, and unpaid child support.[230] In jurisdictions, such as Australia, that lack local habeas corpus legislation, inherited English acts on habeas corpus remain on the local statute book and, of course, as habeas corpus exists at common law it is available from a local supreme court.[231]

XV.   Due Process and Procedural Fairness

It is an ancient principle that a person should not be condemned in either criminal or civil proceedings without first being accorded a fair hearing. Chapter 39 of 1215 stressed this with the words "by the lawful judgment of his peers, or by the law of the land" and this passage is said to be the origin of the modern idea that no person should lose his or her liberty without due

---

224. *R v Halliday* [1917] AC 260, 295 (HL(E)); *In re Storgoff* [1945] S.C.R. 526, 568 (SCC); *Kanu Sanyal v Dist. Magistrate, Darjeeling*, AIR 1973 SC 2684, 2687 (Indian SC); *May v Warden of Ferndale Inst.* [2005] 3 S.C.R. 809, 823 [19] (SCC); *Abdul Ghani Haroon v Ketua Polis Negara* [2001] 2 MLJ 689, 695 [14] (Malaysian HC); Paul D. Halliday, Habeas Corpus: From England to Empire 15–16 (2010).

225. Canadian Charter of Rights and Freedoms 1982, § 10(c); Constitution of Belize, § 5(2)(d).

226. These statutes are in effect habeas corpus acts under another name. Judith Farbey, R.J. Sharpe & Simon Atrill, The Law of Habeas Corpus xlvii (3d ed. 2011).

227. *Id.*

228. *Siddharam Satlingappa Mhetre v Maharashtra* [2010] INSC 1052 [60]–[61] (Indian SC).

229. *Satwant Singh Sawhney v Assistant Passport Officer*, AIR 1967 SC 1836, 1841–42[13] (Indian SC).

230. *Columbia Exp. Packers (HK) Ltd. v McCulloch* [1975] DCLR 108, 117 (HK Dist. Ct).

231. *Antunovic v Dawson* (2010) 30 VR 355, 360–62 [14]–[21] (Vict. SC); David Clark & Gerard McCoy, Habeas Corpus: Australia, New Zealand and the South Pacific ch. 10 (2000).

process.[232] The phrase "due process of law" does not appear in the Charter, however, and only makes its formal appearance in 1354[233] and again in 1368.[234] Of course, in the 14th century the term had a quite different meaning from that of today, as a careful study of the phrase in its original context reveals.[235] In Commonwealth jurisdictions, where the phrase appears in the constitution,[236] due process is in most cases procedural not substantive, unlike in the United States, and in many jurisdictions the term "natural justice"[237] or "procedural fairness" is preferred.[238] Australia considered but rejected in 1898 the inclusion of an American-style due process clause in the draft of what became the Commonwealth Constitution.[239] Although in several Australian states the due process legislation of the 14th century is part of the received law of the jurisdiction, due process has been confined to procedural matters only and the courts have rejected attempts to widen it beyond procedural fairness.[240] Nevertheless, as an element of the principle of legality, there is a presumption in favor of procedural fairness.[241]

A fair process necessarily includes a hearing by a neutral or unbiased judge or decision maker and by courts that are independent of the executive and that act in an impartial manner.[242] In a number of Commonwealth jurisdictions with a constitutional bill of rights, the phrase "due process"

---

232. *Gopalan v State of Madras*, AIR 1950 SC 27, 98 [182] (Indian SC); *Lasalle v Attorney Gen.* (1971) 18 WIR 379, 389 (Trin. & Tobago CA); *R v Doucette* (1985) 23 CCC (3d) 520, 529 (N.S. Provincial Magistrate's Ct); *United States v Ferras* [2006] 2 S.C.R. 77, 89 [19] (SCC).

233. 28 Ed III c. III; 1 Statutes of the Realm 345; *R v MacKellar, ex parte Ratu* (1977) 137 CLR 461, 483 (HCA).

234. 42 Ed III c. I, II; 1 Statutes of the Realm 388.

235. Keith Jurow, *Untimely Thoughts: A Reconsideration of the Origins of Due Process of Law*, 19 AM. J. LEGAL HIST., 265, 265–79 (1975); *Adler v Dist. Court of New S. Wales* (1990) 19 NSWLR 317, 349A (NSW CA).

236. *See, e.g.,* the Constitution of Trinidad and Tobago s 1(a); *Re Application by Bahadur* [1986] LRC (Const) 297, 305 (Trin. & Tobago HC).

237. *Canara Bank v Debassis Das* [2003] INSC 166 [13]–[21] (Indian SC); *Uma Nath Pandey v Uttar Pradesh*, [2009] INSC 535 [8] (Indian SC); *D v Havill* [2009] NZHC 2623 [87]–[109]; *Saeed v Minister for Immigration and Citizenship* (2010) 241 CLR 252, 258–59 [11]–[15] (HCA); *McLaughlan v Cayman Islands Governor* [2007] 1 WLR 2839, 2846 [14] (PC).

238. *R ex parte Hoffmann v Comm'r of Inquiry and Governor of the Turks and Caicos* [2012] UKPC 17 [31]–[32], [36].

239. *Kruger v Commonwealth* (1997) 190 CLR 1, 61 (HCA).

240. *Adler v Dist. Court of New S. Wales* (1990) 19 NSWLR 317, 352C (NSW CA).

241. *R v Sec'y of State for the Home Dept. ex parte Pierson* [1998] AC 539, 589 (HL(E)).

242. *Reliance Petrochemicals Ltd. v Proprietors of Indian Express Newspapers, Bombay Pvt. Ltd.*, AIR 1989 SC 190 [10]; *Ebner v Official Trustee in Bankruptcy* (2000) 205 CLR 337, 343 [3] (HCA); *Ford v Labrador* [2003] 1 WLR 2082, 2087 [16] (PC); *Ferras v United States* [2006] 2 S.C.R. 77, 90–91 [24] (SCC); *R v Adams* [1993] 1 NZLR 443, 448 (HC); *Pakistan v Gilani* [2013] 1 LRC 223, 237–41 (Pakistan SC).

or its equivalent, while it includes natural justice or a fair hearing,[243] also is given a wider meaning. Thus in one appeal from Jamaica a man on death row was obliged to wait 14 years before the execution and this was held to be a denial of due process and a form of inhuman punishment contrary to the constitution.[244] The argument is that due process entails a fair trial and a right to a fair legal system as a whole.[245] This right is not merely confined to the trial itself but extends to preventing external influences, such as unfair pretrial publicity, from undermining a fair trial.[246] The right also includes a fair process when decisions are made by administrative agencies.[247]

Of course, the law is not static. In Canada's case, due process was included in the Canadian Bill of Rights Act 1960 and was, before the adoption of the Charter of Rights and Freedoms in 1982, and even for a time after 1982, given a restrictive meaning. Thus, in a decision made in 1972, the Supreme Court held out the possibility that due process might have a substantive content but nevertheless concluded that it referred to procedural matters only.[248] Subsequent decisions on the meaning of the phrase "principles of fundamental justice"[249] in Section 7 of the Charter of Rights and Freedoms have broadened the notion of process values, though the Supreme Court has been at pains to point out that, unlike the United States constitutional provisions on due process, the Canadian charter operates in a different legal context.[250] It was made clear that section 7 is not confined to natural or procedural justice since different terminology was used.[251] The Canadian courts are also opposed to the simple dichotomy between procedural and substantive justice. The presumption of innocence, for example, may be viewed as a substantive principle of fundamental justice but also necessarily entails procedural elements as well. Thus the rebuttable presumption of fact may be viewed as procedural, going to the allocation of the burden of proof.[252]

---

243. *Naidike v Attorney Gen. of Trin. & Tobago* [2005] 1 AC 538, 555 [53] (PC).

244. *Pratt v Attorney Gen. of Jam.* [1994] 2 AC 1, 27–28 (PC).

245. *Chokolingo v Attorney Gen. of Trin. & Tobago* [1981] 1 WLR 106, 111D (PC); *Thomas v Baptiste* [2000] 2 AC 1, 22 (PC); *Lewis v Attorney Gen. of Jam.* [2001] 2 AC 50, 81H (PC); *Trin. & Tobago v Boyce* [2006] 2 AC 76, 86 [14] (PC).

246. *Boodram v Attorney Gen. of Trin. & Tobago* [1996] AC 842, 854E (PC).

247. *Zhong v Minister of Citizenship & Immigration* [2009] FC 632 [6] (Can Fed Ct); *Re Therrien* [2001] 2 S.C.R. 3, 58 [81] (SCC); Constitution of Kenya, Art 47; Constitution of South Africa, § 33.

248. *Curr v R* [1972] S.C.R. 889, 902 (SCC); *Smith, Kline & French Laboratories v Attorney Gen. of Canada* [1986] 1 FC 274, 302–05 (Can. Fed. Ct. Trial Div.).

249. Canadian Charter of Rights and Freedoms, *supra* note 225.

250. Re British Columbia Motor Vehicle Act, [1985] S.C.R. 486, 498 (SCC).

251. *Id.* at 503, 521, 530.

252. *Id.* at 531.

XVI. Conclusion

While Magna Carta was a medieval document, it was the work of later generations that broke the Charter free of its 13th-century limitations and established legal principles that today are integral to the rule of law. The first and greatest of these principles is that everyone (including the highest in the land) is bound by the law of the land. This principle lies at the heart of constitutional government. The second principle flows from the first, and was also extended by subsequent constitutional developments, namely that legal proceedings are to be conducted in accordance with established laws and these laws are to be consistent with the Constitution. Third, the state cannot interfere with private property except by the law of the land. Fourth, a tradition of liberty emerged that struck a balance between order and freedom under the law.

A tradition, as this chapter has shown, is not static and survives precisely because it is able to change while retaining, in the arresting imagery of a former justice of the High Court of Australia, a skeleton of principle.[253] Although some of the claims about the Charter are mythic, it should be remembered that a tradition can be invented and transformed to fit later circumstances. It is this capacity for renewal that has allowed Magna Carta as an idea to survive in the law and explains why people and lawyers in common law countries continue to refer to it 800 years after it was concluded in a meadow called Runnymede at a time when the countries to which it spread were then unknown in Europe. That this transformation took place in different ways in different places is itself a tribute to the flexible adaption of the law to new circumstances, while retaining a familial resemblance that allows a lawyer from Austin, Brisbane, Christchurch, Edmonton, New Delhi, London, or Port of Spain to meet on common legal ground through a shared constitutional vocabulary.

---

253. *Mabo v Queensland (No 2)* (1992) 175 CLR 1, 43 (HCA).

Chapter 11
Magna Carta, Civil Law, and Canon Law

Thomas J. McSweeney*

I.   Introduction

In the spring of 1215, as King John (r. 1199–1216) and the barons were
negotiating the terms of Magna Carta, bishops, abbots, royal ambassadors,
and an army of advisers, servants, and clerks were preparing for a general
council of the Western Church to be held at the Cathedral of St. John Lateran, in Rome, the following November.[1] Pope Innocent III (r. 1198–1216)
had called them together to make canons for the reform of the Church.[2]
On the agenda were the suppression of heresy, the provision of ministers
who could preach in the language of their people, and the enforcement of
clerical celibacy.[3] The council was the first to require annual confession by
all believers and the first to require Jews and Muslims to wear distinctive
clothing.[4] It was also responsible for certain reforms in the administration of
Church law. It afforded due process before a sentence of excommunication
could be pronounced and established a right of appeal, with the possibility
of damages for an unjust sentence.[5] It required every ecclesiastical judge to
employ a notary to keep a record of his court.[6] It decreed that no defendant
was to be called before a court more than two days' journey from his dio-
cese.[7] The council had an important impact, for good and ill, on Western
Europe for centuries afterward. Some of its ripples are still felt today. And
yet the Fourth Lateran Council is the forgotten event of 1215. It is overshad-
owed by the events that took place at Runnymede.

---

*The author would like to thank Nate Oman, Dick Helmholz, Joel Anderson, and Jason
Taliadoros for their very helpful comments on an earlier draft of this chapter.
    1. Jane Sayers, Innocent III: Leader of Europe 1198–1216 at 96 (1994).
    2. *Id.*
    3. 3 English Historical Documents 645–47, 650, 652–53 (Harry Rothwell
ed., 1975) (canons 3, 9, and 14).
    4. *Id.* at 654–55, 672 (canons 21 and 68).
    5. *Id.* at 663–64 (canon 47).
    6. *Id.* at 660–61 (canon 38).
    7. *Id.* at 660 (canon 37).

The canons of the Fourth Lateran Council became part of the law of the Western Church, a body of law known as canon law. Canon law had been developing for centuries by 1215, but in the 70 or 80 years before Magna Carta, the study of canon law had taken a new turn. Europe's first universities were just starting to come together in the 12th century. The center of learning at Bologna in Italy actually coalesced around the teaching of canon law and its close cousin, Roman law.[8] Romanists and canonists studied each other's laws, borrowed doctrines from each other, and shared a common, dialectical method of scholarship.[9] The two were often referred to by contemporaries as *utrumque ius* ("both laws") or the *ius commune* ("the common law") and were treated by scholars in the universities, by the beginning of the 13th century, as forming a unified system.[10] They were the two universal laws of Latin Christendom, one being the law of the secular power and the other being the law of the Church. The modern civil law—by twists and turns that took it through the age of nation-states and codification—is the descendant of this medieval *ius commune*.

The degree to which Roman and canon law have influenced the Anglo-American common law is a question that common law lawyers have been debating for a long time and, because Magna Carta is an important text of the common law tradition, scholars have naturally turned their attention to the possibility of Roman and canon law influence on Magna Carta. None of the authors who have written about Magna Carta's civilian pedigree have spent much time on the question of the mechanisms by which *ius commune* would have made its way into Magna Carta, however. When historians and legal scholars talk about influence from one system to another, they tend to assume that it occurs through some process of organic osmosis. Scholars have assumed that the people who were drafting Magna Carta saw *ius commune* and common law as parallel and coequal systems of law and would therefore have thought it natural to borrow doctrines from one to insert into the other. This is one possible model of *ius commune* influence and examples of this kind of influence do exist in 12th- and 13th-century English texts. The *Bracton* treatise is examined below as one example. But the *ius commune* influence found in Magna Carta is of a different kind, and a different model for understanding it is required.

---

8. Peter Stein, Roman Law in European History 46–49 (1999); Anders Winroth, The Making of Gratian's Decretum 157–74 (2000).

9. James A. Brundage, The Medieval Origins of the Legal Profession 234 n.55 (2008) (recounting a medieval proverb: "Legista sine canonibus parum valet, canonista sine legibus nihil," or "A Romanist without canon law isn't worth much and a canonist without Roman law is worth nothing at all").

10. Manlio Bellomo, The Common Legal Past of Europe 1000–1800 at 74 (Lydia G. Cochrane trans., 1995).

This chapter looks more closely at those people in England who had been trained in *ius commune* and who had an interest in seeing it in Magna Carta. The central argument of this chapter is that where *ius commune* influence appears in Magna Carta, it is not there because someone in England thought the rules of Roman and canon law should be adopted into or adapted to the needs of the nascent common law. The *ius commune* influence in the text has very little to do with common law. Rather, this chapter considers another way people deployed *ius commune* in England in the 12th and 13th centuries—as a political language that they knew would appeal to the pope—and suggests that *ius commune*'s appeal to an audience in Rome was the main impetus for its inclusion in Magna Carta. Roman and canon law were used offensively and defensively in this period by the major players in England's greatest political battles, such as the Becket dispute of the 1160s and 1170s.[11] The two laws were useful because the pope was often an important figure in these political battles. He was one of the audiences that the various disputing parties were trying to please, and he understood the language of the *ius commune*. Previous scholars have done an admirable job of placing Magna Carta in the context of broader intellectual developments in law in the Middle Ages. To get a better view of how *ius commune* influenced Magna Carta, however, Magna Carta must be placed in the broader context of European politics, in which the fight between John and the barons was a sideshow to a larger story that involved reform of the Western Church. All politics are local, but in the case of Magna Carta, they were also international.

II.   Magna Carta, the *Ius Commune*, and the Historians

R. C. van Caenegem, a Belgian historian of English and Continental European law, was the first scholar to seriously turn his attention to the possibility of *ius commune* influence on Magna Carta.[12] Van Caenegem, whose work has been aimed at placing English common law in the context of the legal developments that were happening everywhere in Europe in the 12th and 13th centuries, suggested that there was some similarity between provisions of Magna Carta and rules of Roman and canon law.[13] Richard Helmholz followed up on Van Caenegem's suggestion in a highly detailed article, in which he examined Magna Carta chapter by chapter in order to make

---

11. BERYL SMALLEY, THE BECKET CONFLICT AND THE SCHOOLS: A STUDY OF INTELLECTUALS IN POLITICS IN THE TWELFTH CENTURY 161–62 (1973).

12. RAOUL VAN CAENEGEM, AN HISTORICAL INTRODUCTION TO PRIVATE LAW 180–81 (1992).

13. *Id.*

the maximum case for *ius commune* influence on Magna Carta.[14] Helmholz argued for the possibility of *ius commune* influence on 34 out of the charter's 63 chapters (chapters 1, 4, 5, 7–12, 14, 20–22, 26–28, 30, 31, 33, 35, 36, 38–42, 45, 52-54, 55, 57, 61, and 63), a substantial portion of the text.[15] The chapters vary considerably, however, in both the degree and the probability of *ius commune* influence. A few (chapters 1, 22, 52, 53, 57, and 63) clearly show the influence of canon law rules.[16] Others merely bear some minimal resemblance to Roman and canon law rules. Helmholz stops short of claiming that all of the chapters he outlines are the result of the influence of the *ius commune* on Magna Carta. Rather, his piece is a building block for further research, making the strongest possible case for *ius commune* influence everywhere he sees a reasonable possibility.

Helmholz's article sparked a lively debate about *ius commune* influence on Magna Carta. Kenneth Pennington built upon Helmholz's analysis of chapter 9 of the text, which dealt with the question of whether a creditor could seek redress against his debtor's sureties if the debtor himself was available and solvent.[17] Pennington bolstered Helmholz's argument that the rule stated in Magna Carta closely tracked the *ius commune* rule with evidence from canon law texts that would have been available in England in 1215.[18] Helmholz's article has also attracted a critical response, however, in the form of John Hudson's article, "Magna Carta, the *Ius Commune*, and English Common Law."[19] Hudson argues that most of the rules in Magna Carta that Helmholz points to as evincing *ius commune* influence have other possible sources, in many cases more likely ones.[20] For instance, Hudson disputes Helmholz's suggestion that chapter 20 of Magna Carta, which essentially says that a fine should be proportional to the gravity of the offense, is a borrowing from the *ius commune*.[21] Helmholz demonstrated that proportionality, as a general principle, appears throughout the *ius commune*.[22] Hudson shows us, however, that the specific rule that a fine should be proportional to the gravity of the offense appears in many English texts, dating back at least to the early 12th century, a time before scholars had thought to combine Roman and canon law into a *ius commune* and before

---

14. R.H. Helmholz, *Magna Carta and the Ius Commune*, 66 U. CHI. L. REV. 297 (1999).

15. *Id.*

16. *Id.* at 311–14, 329–31, 347–50.

17. Kenneth Pennington, *The Ius Commune, Suretyship, and Magna Carta*, 11 RIVISTA INTERNAZIONALE DI DIRITTO COMUNE 255 (2000).

18. *Id.* at 265–67.

19. John Hudson, *Magna Carta, the Ius Commune, and English Common Law, in* MAGNA CARTA AND THE ENGLAND OF KING JOHN 99 (Janet S. Loengard ed., 2010).

20. *Id.*

21. *Id.* at 104–05.

22. Helmholz, *supra* note 14, at 328.

the first teacher of Roman law had arrived in England.[23] The major problem for Helmholz's maximalist case is that the drafters of Magna Carta did not unambiguously borrow any terminology from the *ius commune*, except in chapters 1, 22, 52, 53, 57, and 63, all chapters that deal with issues that implicated canon law, a special case that will be dealt with later in this chapter.[24] The case for *ius commune* influence on the other 28 chapters Helmholz points to thus must be a circumstantial one, based on similarities in the ways rules in Magna Carta and the *ius commune* operate. As Helmholz admitted, "there is no smoking gun."[25]

III. Borrowing Style

Helmholz thought it was possible that "some of the drafters of the Charter . . . desired actively to advance the fortunes of the *ius commune* in England and saw this as an opportunity to promote that goal."[26] This is certainly a possibility. One early 13th-century text demonstrates the deep commitment to the *ius commune* as a system that Helmholz suggests. The treatise, now known as *Bracton*, was written by a succession of royal justices and their clerks. These authors were invested in making the practices of the English king's courts more like those of the *ius commune*. *Bracton* was an attempt to describe the practices of the English king's courts—the procedures that had grown up around the English writs—using the forms and terminology of the two laws.

In previous work, I have argued that *Bracton* evinces the same kind of approach to the *ius commune* that has been described by scholars such as Pennington and Manlio Bellomo in contemporary legal texts from continental Europe.[27] Bellomo, in particular, has argued that even though Roman law was not applied directly as positive law in any court in Europe, it had a heavy influence on the secular legal systems throughout Europe, because there was a normative element to the notion that Roman law was a universal law.[28] If it is a universal law, then the laws of kingdoms and cities should in some way reflect that universal law. Bellomo describes the *ius commune*'s role in medieval Europe in almost Platonic terms: *ius commune* is the ideal form of law, which should be reflected in the law as it is practiced in local

---

23. Hudson, *supra* note 19, at 106.
24. VAN CAENEGEM, *supra* note 12, at 181.
25. Helmholz, *supra* note 14, at 359.
26. *Id.* at 367.
27. BELLOMO, *supra* note 10, at 153–55; Kenneth Pennington, *Learned Law, Droit Savant, Gelehrtes Recht: The Tyranny of a Concept*, 20 SYRACUSE J. INT'L L. & COM. 205 (1994).
28. BELLOMO, *supra* note 10, at 153–55.

courts.[29] There certainly do seem to have been people who believed that, if their local law was to be worthy of the name, it should, in some way, reflect the universal glory of the *ius commune*.[30] The justices who were involved in the writing and revision of *Bracton*—Martin of Pattishall, William of Raleigh, and Henry of Bratton—were committed to the notion that the law of the English king's courts should conform to the *ius commune* to the extent possible. Romanisms appear in the trial records of all three justices, something that was extremely uncommon for the time.[31] In the *Bracton* treatise, which was begun about a decade after the events at Runnymede, these justices were striving to explain the English writ system in terms of the Roman law of property, going to great lengths to make the two compatible even when they had to torture their texts to do so.[32]

A person like Pattishall, Raleigh, or Bratton, committed to the idea that English court practices should in some way reflect the *ius commune*, would have several ways of showing that commitment in a text. Texts can draw their authority, at least partly, from being written in a particular style. The *Bracton* treatise, for instance, is written in a *ius commune* format. It is designed as a *summa*, a type of text that Roman and canon law scholars were writing at the beginning of the 13th century.[33] A drafter of Magna Carta who was thinking like Pattishall or Raleigh might be expected to model the text of Magna Carta on texts that were common in the two laws. Imperial constitutions—the legislative acts issued by the Roman emperors—would have been a reasonable model. This was the model followed 16 years after Magna Carta by Frederick II, the Holy Roman Emperor (r. 1220–1250), when he issued the *Constitutions of Melfi* as a set of laws for his kingdom of Sicily.[34] Although admittedly "not issued on the scale of the Roman codes," but instead designed to "deal with problems specific to a kingdom in urgent need of reconstruction" (much like the provisions of Magna Carta, one might add), the *Constitutions* nevertheless draw on the genres used by Roman emperors to express the imperial will.[35] Magna Carta

---

29. *Id.*

30. *Id.* at 83–111 (discussing examples from Italy, Spain, Germany, and France of local legal texts that are modeled on the *ius commune*).

31. David J. Seipp, *Roman Legal Categories in the Early Common Law*, in Legal Record and Historical Reality, Proceedings of the Eighth British Legal History Conference, Cardiff 1987 at 9, 12 (Thomas G. Watkin ed., 1989).

32. Thomas J. McSweeney, *Property before Property: Romanizing the English Law of Land*, 60 Buff. L. Rev. 1139, 1172–98 (2012).

33. It is probably modeled on the popular *summa* of Azo of Bologna, a civilian who was famous throughout Europe at the turn of the 13th century. *See* Select Passages from the Works of Bracton and Azo (Frederic William Maitland ed., 1895).

34. James M. Powell, *Introduction*, in The Liber Augustalis xx (James M. Powell trans., 1971).

35. David Abulafia, Frederick II: A Medieval Emperor 202–03 (1992).

does not, however, follow the patterns of *ius commune* documents. It is written in the format of a charter of liberties, for which there are ample English antecedents, from the charters that established towns, to rural charters of liberties, to Henry I's (r. 1100–1135) coronation charter. The drafters of Magna Carta would have been familiar with all of these texts, as they drew on them for the substantive provisions of their charter.[36] The charter genre is not a style that anyone would associate specifically with *ius commune*. If, among the drafters of Magna Carta there were any of the *ius commune's* true believers, they did not leave their mark in this way.

We might also expect the drafters of Magna Carta to use *ius commune* terminology in the text, even if only by accident; students of Roman and canon law often memorized large parts of their texts so they could recall them in an instant.[37] Van Caenegem, in stating the problem of finding *ius commune* influence in Magna Carta, put his finger on the primary issue, however, when he said that "it is no doubt significant that Magna Carta, unlike other old English legal texts, contains no Roman terminology."[38] To state the problem a bit more accurately, Magna Carta contains no terminology that unambiguously comes from Roman law[39] and further contains only six chapters (chapters 1, 22, 52, 53, 57, and 63) that draw on canon law terminology, which will be examined in more detail shortly.

Chapter 9 of Magna Carta is a case in point. This chapter—which states that as long as a debtor is capable of paying his debt, his creditors may not seek satisfaction from his pledges (what would today be called sureties)—is one of the best candidates for *ius commune* influence.[40] The rule Magna Carta states was the current rule in Romanist and canonist circles in 1215.[41]

---

36. WILLIAM SHARP MCKECHNIE, MAGNA CARTA: A COMMENTARY ON THE GREAT CHARTER OF KING JOHN 289 (2d ed. 1914) (discussion of borough charters); J.C. HOLT, MAGNA CARTA 67–68 (2d ed. 1992) (1207 charter of Peter de Brus to the freeholders of Langbargh); 1 THE CHARTULARY OF GUISBOROUGH 92–94 (W. Brown ed., 1889) (Latin text of Peter de Brus's charter); HOLT, *supra*, at 36–38, 222–25 (discussion of Henry I's charter as a rallying point for the barons).

37. MARY CARRUTHERS, THE BOOK OF MEMORY: A STUDY OF MEMORY IN MEDIEVAL CULTURE 127 (2d ed. 2008).

38. VAN CAENEGEM, *supra* note 12, at 181.

39. Helmholz suggests that the use of the word "delictum" in chapters 20 and 21 of the charter indicates the drafter was trained in the *ius commune*, as delict is a field of law in Roman and canon law roughly equivalent to the common law's tort. Helmholz, *supra* note 14, at 368. Hudson points out that "delictum" is also the general term for a wrong used in much of the Latin Vulgate version of the Bible. Hudson, *supra* note 19, at 108. Virtually anyone who could read and write Latin in the 13th century would have been familiar with at least parts of the Vulgate, so the use of the word "delictum" does not reveal much more about the person who drafted the charter than we already know, only that he was trained to write in Latin.

40. *1215 Magna Carta ch. 9, in* HOLT, *supra* note 36, at 453.

41. Helmholz, *supra* note 14, at 318–19.

Helmholz pointed out that it was not the rule followed in England before 1215 and it was not even followed in English courts after its inclusion in the 1215, 1216, 1217, and 1225 versions of Magna Carta, making a strong circumstantial case that it ran counter to notions of how debt should be handled in the English royal courts.[42] One way to interpret this evidence is that the rule came from some outside source, such as the *ius commune*. And yet, the text from Justinian's *Novellae* that Helmholz cites as the principal *ius commune* text on the subject contains none of the same language as chapter 9. The text of the Roman novel reads as follows:

> If anyone shall have loaned money and accepted a *fideiussor*, a *mandator*, or a *sponsor* [three different types of surety], he should not first proceed against the *mandator* or *fideiussor*, or *sponsor*, and he should not molest the intercessors of the debtor as a negligent person, but he should come first to him who took the money and contracted the debt.[43]

Magna Carta reads:

> Neither we nor our bailiffs will seize any land or rent in payment of a debt, so long as the chattels of the debtor are sufficient to repay the debt; nor shall the sureties [*plegii*] of the debtor be distrained so long as the debtor himself is capable of paying the debt; and if the principal debtor defaults in the payment of the debt, having nothing wherewith to pay it, the sureties shall be answerable for the debt; and, if they wish, they may have the lands and revenues of the debtor until they receive satisfaction for the debt they paid on his behalf, unless the principal debtor shows that he has discharged his obligation to the sureties.[44]

The only significant word the two texts seem to share is *debitor*, the Latin word for debtor. Nothing else could have been borrowed from the Roman law text. Its format is markedly different. Where the novel is written in the form of a restriction on the creditor, Magna Carta's ninth chapter is written in the form of a promise to the surety. The novel focuses on what a creditor may and may not do to his debtor. The creditor is the subject and the verbs

---

42. *Id.* This chapter does appear in the later reissues of Magna Carta. *1225 Magna Carta ch. 8, in* HOLT, *supra* note 36, at 504.

43. "Si quis igitur crediderit et fideiussorem aut mandatorem aut sponsorem acceperit, is non primum mox adversus mandatorem aut fideiussorem aut sponsorem accedat, neque neglegens debitoris intercessoribus molestus sit, sed veniat primum ad eum, qui aurum accepit debitumque contraxit." Nov.4.1.1. (535) (translation by author).

44. HOLT, *supra* note 36, at 453.

are all in the active voice. Chapter 9 of Magna Carta begins in the active voice, but it states what the king and his bailiffs may not do, with no reference to the creditor. It then shifts into the passive voice, placing its focus on the sureties and what may not *be done* to them. The creditor never becomes a character in Magna Carta as he does in the Justinianic text.

Pennington cites two papal decretals—texts of canon law—circulating in England in the early 13th century that he argues could have supplied the rule. These are difficult to compare to any of the other texts because they are commands to two papal judges—the bishop of Ely and the archbishop of Canterbury—ordering them to proceed in a particular way.[45] These decretals speak in specifics, not in the language of general rules seen in the novel and in Magna Carta. Pennington also cites a treatise that discusses the decretals, however: it is the *Summa* of Bernardus Papiensis, a canon law text that was almost certainly circulating in England in 1215.[46] Like the novel, Bernardus' text focuses on the creditor:

> It should be noted that at one time a creditor could ask either the principal debtor or the surety for payment. Today, if the debtor is present and solvent, the surety [*fideiussor*] cannot be summoned. The debtor is obligated to the surety to free him from his obligation. Or if the surety pays the debt, the debtor is obligated to reimburse the surety for the principal and interest, as in Lucius' decretals.[47]

In this text, the author borrows some of his structure and patterns of thought from Justinian's novel, which, as a scholar of canon law, Bernardus had undoubtedly read since the two laws were so closely related. The text begins by stating what the creditor may and may not do, just like the novel does. Bernardus's explanation does bear one similarity to the text of Magna Carta. In its second sentence it focuses on what may not be done to the surety, in the passive voice. It then shifts to the debtor's obligations, however, which do not appear in Magna Carta. Again, the potential source text bears little resemblance to the text of Magna Carta itself.

It is difficult to believe that, in a world where students of Roman and canon law memorized large portions of their legal texts, a proponent of the *ius commune* would have adopted *ius commune* rules without, at least accidentally, using some of the language and structure of the *ius commune* texts.[48] How would a person trained in *ius commune* adopt a specific rule

---

45. Peter Landau, *Bürgschaft und Darlehen im Dekretalenrecht des 12. Jahrhunderts, in* FESTSCHRIFT FÜR DIETER MEDICUS 297, 314–16 (Volker Beuthien et al. eds. 1999) (text of the decretals).

46. Pennington, *supra* note 17, at 267.

47. *Id.*

48. CARRUTHERS, *supra* note 37, at 127.

from the *ius commune* without thinking about it in the terms in which the *ius commune* presented it? One does not adopt specific rules from a legal system simply because ideas from that system are in the air at the time. There must be some concrete mechanism for the borrowing. If that mechanism involved borrowing from *ius commune* texts, it is likely that the language of those texts would have left some mark upon Magna Carta.

It is of course possible that the drafters had reason to hide the rules' origins. Twenty-one years later, at the council of Merton, the barons would reject the canon law rule for legitimation of a child whose parents married after his birth, saying that they "did not wish the laws of England to change."[49] Later in the century, the justice Roger of Thurkilby would reject canon law influence on the common law, saying, "[B]ehold now the civil court is befouled by the example of the ecclesiastical court and a stream is poisoned by a font of sulphur."[50] It is unlikely that the drafters felt the need to hide *ius commune* origins, however, for the simple reason that, in six chapters of the charter (chapters 1, 22, 52, 53, 57, and 63), they used *ius commune* language explicitly. If there were parties with some animus against *ius commune* at the time, one would expect *ius commune* influence to be hidden in all parts of the charter, not hidden in some parts and explicit in others.

It is useful to compare treatment of the surety in the novel and Magna Carta to the treatment of the same problem in *Bracton*, because *Bracton* treats this issue in a much more Romanesque way. In a passage where he reconciles what appears to be a contradiction in outcomes between two cases that had been heard in the royal courts, one of the *Bracton* authors explains:

> [T]he contradiction is resolved thus, that in the first case, where the prohibition did not lie, the chief and principal debtor was summoned, and in the second the sureties [*fideiussores*] were summoned and impleaded, though the principal debtor was solvent, and where after the prohibition it was adjudged in the secular court that the parson should betake himself to the principal debtor who was solvent, and that the sureties [*fideiussores*] be quit.[51]

---

49. 1 FREDERICK WILLIAM MAITLAND, BRACTON'S NOTE BOOK 115 (1887) (translation by author).

50. "Ecce jam civilis curia exemplo ecclesiasticae coinquinatur, et a sulphureo fonte rivulus intoxicatur." 5 MATTHEW PARIS, CHRONICA MAJORA 211 (Henry Richards Luard ed., 1880) (translation by author).

51. 4 BRACTON ON THE LAWS AND CUSTOMS OF ENGLAND 266–67 (George Woodbine ed. & Samuel E. Thorne trans., 1977).

The difference between this treatment of the issue of the surety and Magna Carta's is striking. The authors of the *Bracton* text, royal justices themselves, were discussing cases that they had heard in the king's courts. But instead of using the language they would have actually been using in the courts to describe what had occurred there, they used the language of Roman and canon law. The *plegii* who appeared in Magna Carta and who would have appeared in the plea roll record of the case become Roman *fideiussores* in the *Bracton* text. This text—like Justinian's novel and the papal decretals, but unlike chapter 9 of Magna Carta—focuses on what the creditor can and cannot do. The *Bracton* authors even adopt styles of textual exposition from texts of Roman and canon law. Placing two authoritative texts beside each other and working out the apparent contradictions between them was a common way to teach in the Roman and canon law faculties of the universities.[52] In other parts of the text, they cite and quote Roman and canon law directly.[53] The justices who wrote *Bracton* wanted the world to know that they were making use of the *ius commune*. This is simply not the case in chapter 9 of Magna Carta. *Bracton* therefore represents the road not taken in Magna Carta. It demonstrates what Magna Carta could have looked like had it been written by the *ius commune*'s true believers.

IV.   Canon Law and the Politics of Church Reform

All six of the chapters that contain express and unequivocal *ius commune* terminology (chapters 1, 22, 52, 53, 57, and 63) involve canon law. These six chapters have little to do with canon law influencing the common law, however. Canon law made its way into these six chapters because the struggle between the king and the barons in 1215 had become entangled with a battle that had been going on in England and the rest of Europe for the previous century and a half on the proper relationship between the Church and the crown: the Gregorian reform movement.[54] The papacy and almost every kingdom in Europe had become involved in it in some way. It was this international dimension to John's fight with the barons that probably led to the inclusion of canon law. As mentioned above, while John and the barons were negotiating Magna Carta, Pope Innocent was preparing a major council of the Church. The canon law in Magna Carta may have been intended to appeal to a pope who was concerned with Church reform.

---

52. Thomas McSweeney, *English Judges and Roman Jurists: The Civilian Learning Behind England's First Case Law*, 84 Temple L. Rev. 847–50 (2012).

53. *See* 2 Bracton on the Laws and Customs of England 182, 427 (George Woodbine ed. & Samuel E. Thorne trans., 1968).

54. Eamon Duffy, Saints and Sinners: A History of the Popes 87–115 (1997).

The first and last chapters of the Charter (chapters 1 and 63), which grant freedom to the Church in perpetuity, are clearly tied to the reform movement. Chapter 1 specifies that this freedom includes the right to free elections, an important topic for Church reformers.[55] In theory, bishops were elected by their cathedral chapters, which were composed of the senior clergy of the cathedral church. Abbots, likewise, were elected by the monks of their houses. In reality, bishops and the most important abbots were often picked by the king, who placed pressure on the electors to accept his candidates.[56] Ecclesiastical elections were a live political issue in 1215. In 1207, the archbishop of Canterbury, Hubert Walter, died. John wanted a reliable supporter in that position, particularly since the archbishop of Canterbury was the most powerful ecclesiastic in England, and the king campaigned to put John de Gray into the post. De Gray was clearly John's man: he had been part of John's household before John was king, had become a chancery clerk under Hubert Walter after John ascended to the throne, and had secured the chancellorship for his nephew on Walter's death.[57] John even pawned the crown jewels to him at one point in exchange for some ready cash.[58] The archbishopric would be both de Gray's reward for a job well done and the king's assurance that the archbishop of Canterbury would not oppose him.

John ran into problems, however. First, the bishops of the province of Canterbury claimed the right to participate in the election of its archbishop.[59] Then the monks at Canterbury, worried that if they did not move quickly to assert their right to elect the archbishop they would lose the right to the bishops or the king, elected their own sub-prior archbishop.[60] In the face of John's wrath at their presumption they agreed to vote again and this time elected de Gray.[61] Many of the monks were unhappy with this result, however, and a group of them appealed the irregular election to Pope Innocent III, who ordered a new election, recommending his old university friend, Stephen Langton, to the electors.[62] The Canterbury chapter obligingly elected Langton in 1207, but he was unacceptable to John. Langton was an English theologian at the University of Paris, which was Latin Christendom's foremost theological center; but Paris was also the capital of John's principal rival, Philip Augustus, the king of France (r. 1180–1223). John saw Langton as too cozy with the French court and refused to allow him to take

---

55. *1215 Magna Carta ch. 1*, in Holt, *supra* note 36, at 448–51.

56. W.L. Warren, King John 159–60 (1961).

57. Roy Martin Haynes, *Gray, John de (d. 1214)*, in Oxford Dictionary of National Biography, http://www.oxforddnb.com/view/article/11541?docPos=4 (last visited May 18, 2014).

58. *Id.*

59. Warren, *supra* note 56, at 161.

60. *Id.*

61. *Id.*

62. *Id.* at 161–62.

up his post.[63] The result was a six-year battle with the papacy.[64] Innocent placed an interdict on England, suspending most sacraments for England's inhabitants, and excommunicated John.[65] This battle ended only in 1213, when John surrendered England to the pope as a papal fief and became his vassal.[66]

The battle between John, on the one hand, and Langton and Innocent on the other, was really part of a much wider struggle that had been going on for over a century. The Gregorian Reform movement, begun in the 11th century, sought to take the Church out from under the thumb of secular rulers. More generally, the Church reformers sought to separate sacred power from secular power. Reformers thought, for instance, that bishops should not be servants of kings. In Germany, the reform movement spawned a battle between the pope and the Holy Roman Emperor over the practice of laymen investing bishops with the symbols of their office.[67] The reformers believed that bishops should not, even symbolically, be beholden to secular rulers for their offices. The reform movement was felt as far away as Iceland where, in the 12th and 13th centuries, reforming bishops attempted, with mixed success, to prevent secular chieftains from becoming priests, on the theory that no one person should wield both secular and sacred power.[68]

In the late 12th century, the reform movement manifested itself in a spectacular seven-year battle between John's father, Henry II (r. 1154–1189), and his archbishop of Canterbury, Thomas Becket. When Henry produced a text called the Constitutions of Clarendon, laying out what Henry claimed were the customs of England concerning the relationship between the Church and the Crown, Becket refused to assent to them.[69] Henry claimed that the Constitutions merely represented the ancient customs of the English Church, but many, including Becket, claimed that they violated the Church's liberties as detailed in canon law. William FitzStephen, one of Becket's legal advisers, wrote during the debate that "Never is the Lord found to have said 'I am the custom'; Rather, he said 'I am the truth,'" and, for William FitzStephen, that truth was expressed by the Church through the medium of canon law.[70]

---

63. *Id.* at 162–63.

64. *Id.* at 164, 208–09.

65. *Id.* at 164–69.

66. *Id.* at 208–09.

67. Barbara H. Rosenwein, A Short History of the Middle Ages 179–81 (2d ed. 2004).

68. Jesse Byock, Viking Age Iceland 326–30 (2001).

69. William Stubbs, Select Charters and Other Illustrations of English Constitutional History 135–40 (6th ed. 1888).

70. Smalley, *supra* note 11, at 128; 3 Materials for the History of Archbishop Thomas Becket 47–48 (J.C. Robertson & J.B. Sheppard eds., 1877) (translation by author).

Canon law came into conflict with Henry's customs in several ways. For example, where contemporary canon law stated that a cleric accused of a crime could be tried only in an ecclesiastical court, the Constitutions insisted that clerical felons were to be tried in the courts of the king.[71] This violated the principle of ecclesiastical liberty espoused by the reformers. After a struggle that included Becket's trial, lengthy exile, and reconciliation with Henry, Becket was murdered in his own cathedral by four knights who thought they were doing Henry's bidding.[72] Although Henry ultimately won on many of the points of law contained in the Constitutions, the Becket affair in many ways was a defining moment for England's Angevin dynasty, a black spot they were never able to wash out completely.

The events of 45 years earlier still loomed large in 1215. Becket was, by then, a saint of international stature; his feast was celebrated as far away as Poland and Hungary.[73] He was a martyr for the liberties of the Church and John's father Henry was painted as an enemy of reform, the villain in a saint's life. Langton was compared to Becket—another archbishop of Canterbury driven into exile—and some propagandists for Church liberties fit the battles between John and Langton into a continuing story of Angevin resistance to the reform movement.[74]

Canon law was an important medium for the reformers. It served as a sort of language of reform. With issues of Church liberty, freedom of elections, and the separation of priestly and secular power still in the air, canon law certainly could have had some influence in the drafting of chapters of Magna Carta that had to do with these issues. It is important to note, however, that a contemporary might not have looked at a provision on Church liberty and immediately identified it with canon law. Certainly canon law had something to say about the liberty of the Church, but Church liberty was also an issue discussed by theologians, like Langton.[75] The average Englishman might, by 1215, have merely thought of Church liberty as a political issue, one of the great debates of the day, rather than associating it specifically with the discourse of canon law, which was only one of many contexts in which it was discussed. Chapters 1 and 63, then, might not owe as much to canon law as they do to the Becket and Langton disputes.

Other sections of Magna Carta that concern Church liberties, like chapter 22, on the amercement of clerics, hearken more directly to canon law. In

---

71. STUBBS, *supra* note 69, at 138.

72. FRANK BARLOW, THOMAS BECKET 235–48 (1986).

73. SMALLEY, *supra* note 11, at 191–92.

74. Langton himself used the imagery of Becket to paint his fight with John as a continuation of Henry's battles with the Church. NICHOLAS VINCENT, MAGNA CARTA: A VERY SHORT INTRODUCTION 51 (2012).

75. Christopher Holdsworth, *Langton, Stephen (d. 1228), in* OXFORD DICTIONARY OF NATIONAL BIOGRAPHY, http://www.oxforddnb.com.proxy.wm.edu/view/article /16044?docPos=10 (last visited May 18, 2014).

the months leading up to the issuance of Magna Carta in June of 1215, the barons were concerned with amercements. One can think of amercements as something akin to modern fines; if a person committed a wrong against the king—which could include anything from breaching the king's peace, to bringing a false claim in court, to cutting down trees in the king's forest— that person was said to be in the king's mercy (*in misericordia*).[76] The king would accept some kind of payment to let the person out of his mercy. For certain wrongs, such as failure to prosecute one's case, the payment was standardized and substantial, but not overwhelming. Half a mark, equivalent to one-third of a pound, was fairly standard.[77] But John was famous for arbitrarily amercing his barons.[78] This, along with John's other arbitrary financial exactions, would have been a major issue for the barons in 1215. Sometime in the period between 1213 and June of 1215, a group of barons issued a list of preliminary demands that are now called the Unknown Charter.[79] The Unknown Charter included a copy of King Henry I's coronation charter, which the barons wanted John to confirm as a statement of the good, old law as it was observed in the time of John's great-grandfather. [80] One chapter of Henry I's coronation charter that appears in the Unknown Charter reads:

> If any baron or man of mine should have committed a wrong he will not give gage in mercy of the whole of his money as used to be done in the time of my father and brother, but according to the manner of the wrong."[81]

Henry I's charter essentially provides that the amercement should fit the crime. A baron should not be amerced for the whole of his fortune for a trivial offense. A more precise statement of this principle appears in the Articles of the Barons, a text produced in the days leading up to Magna Carta as a product of negotiations between the king and the barons, which was probably sealed by John on June 10 as a sign of his good faith: "[The

---

76. 3 CURIA REGIS ROLLS OF THE REIGNS OF RICHARD AND JOHN PRESERVED IN THE PUBLIC RECORD OFFICE: 5–7 JOHN 4 (A.E. Stamp ed., 1926) (example from 1203 of a litigant amerced half a mark for a disseisin).

77. HOLT, *supra* note 36, at 333, n.109.

78. WARREN, *supra* note 56, at 182.

79. RALPH V. TURNER, MAGNA CARTA THROUGH THE AGES 61–62 (2003); HOLT, *supra* note 36, at 420–23.

80. HOLT, *supra* note 36, at 240, 421. The unknown charter seems to have been written by someone with little background in the writing style of the English Chancery; it does not look like John's men were involved in writing it. It uses the third person and first person singular, while Chancery documents used the first person plural, what we would call the "royal we." *Id*. at 419. It was probably drafted entirely within the baronial camp.

81. *Id*. at 426 (translation by author).

King concedes] that a free man is amerced for a small wrong according to
the manner of the wrong, and for a great wrong according to the magnitude
of the wrong."[82] The articles add that a man cannot be amerced to the extent
that it would destroy his livelihood and that the amercement is to be set by
the upright men of the neighborhood.[83] All of these provisions can be found
in earlier charters of liberties, granted to towns and rural communities.[84]
They were fairly common liberties to purchase from one's lord in the period
leading up to 1215.

Chapter 10 of the articles adds something else, however, that was not
included in Henry I's coronation charter and was not commonly found in
charters of the period. It adds that "a cleric is amerced from his lay fee
according to the manner of the others aforesaid, and not according to his
ecclesiastical benefice."[85] This provision, modified slightly, became chapter
22 of Magna Carta. This meant that if a cleric was brought into a secular
court for some reason and was amerced, the amercement could not be levied on the lands owned by the cleric's church, only on those owned by the
cleric as an individual. The cleric's office, called his benefice, would have
lands attached to it, which produced revenue for the support of the parish
and its cleric. Canon law made it clear, however, that the lands belonged to
the benefice, not to the cleric. Gratian's *Decretum*, the standard textbook of
canon law used in the universities and cathedral schools in 1215, summed
up this position in the phrase, "the cleric does not make the fruits of the
benefice his own."[86] The rector merely had use of the rectory's lands while
he was rector, and the permissible uses were limited. Gratian developed this
principle further, arguing specifically that a secular judge could not levy a
judgment on a cleric's benefice because "the delicts of the parson cannot be
converted into an injury to the church."[87]

This was a countercultural position to take in 1215, when titles and secular offices were treated as personal property that could be purchased or
even inherited by one's heirs.[88] Gratian's position was related to the reform
movement. The reformers wanted to make the point that an ecclesiastical
office was not like a secular lordship. Clerics should not be able to create
secular dynasties and treat the Church's wealth as family wealth. Rather,
they should use the Church's wealth for the cure of souls. The Church was

---

82. *Id.* at 431–32; TURNER, *supra* note 79, at 62. *Articles of the Barons ch. 9, in*
HOLT, *supra* note 36, at 434 (translation by author).

83. *Articles of the Barons, in* HOLT, *supra* note 36, at 434.

84. Hudson, *supra* note 19, at 106.

85. *Articles of the Barons ch. 10, in* HOLT, *supra* note 36, at 434 (translation by
author).

86. Helmholz, *supra* note 14, at 331; C.12 q.5 c.4.

87. *Id.* at 330; C.16 q.6 c.3.

88. Scott L. Waugh, *Tenure to Contract: Lordship and Clientage in Thirteenth-Century England*, 101 ENG. HIST. REV. 811, 813 (1986).

fighting established notions of land and service by severing the individual from his office and, perhaps more importantly, severing the lands that belonged to the person from the lands that belonged to the office.[89] Canon law thus spoke specifically to the problem of the amercement of clerics and it is almost certain that the drafters of Magna Carta were taking their lead from the law of the Church when they included chapter 22.

Chapters 1, 22, and 63 of Magna Carta were clearly influenced by the reform movement and are therefore strong candidates for canon law influence. But why are they there? The traditional explanation is that Stephen Langton put them there. There is some support for this theory in the chronology of the drafting. All three chapters entered Magna Carta late in the process. The promise of free elections outlined in chapter 1, in particular, appears to have been an eleventh-hour addition.[90] Langton and the other bishops came to the party late. They would eventually side with the barons, but in the early stages of baronial dissent they appear to have seen themselves as mediators rather than partisans.[91] As the spring wore on, Langton and the bishops were increasingly throwing in their lot with the barons, however.[92] Langton can be placed at Windsor with the king on June 9, the day before the articles of the barons were likely sealed, and, according to one source, he was in conference with the king for the better part of the day.[93] He certainly had a motive to ask for the inclusion of these chapters. It is evident from Langton's theological writings that he had an interest in the reform movement.[94] He was either an old school friend or teacher of the pope, who was a reformer of the most extreme variety.[95] Innocent was not content to simply separate the sacred power from the secular; he wanted to place all secular rulers beneath the pope, who was both king and priest in Innocent's view.[96] In addition, Langton had several canonists in his episcopal household who could have handled the details, although issues of

---

89. Helmholz, *supra* note 14, at 330–31.

90. The promise of free elections appears in neither the unknown charter nor the articles of the barons. *1215 Magna Carta, in* HOLT, *supra* note 36, at 448–51. The author would like to thank John Hudson for pointing this out.

91. *Id.* at 231. Despite Langton's troubles with John between 1207 and 1213, the king seems to have trusted him in 1215. According to a safe conduct John issued on April 23 to the rebels who wished to speak with him, Langton was to lead them to John. *Id.* at 232; 1 ROTULI LITTERARUM PATENTIUM IN TURRI LONDINENSI ASSERVATI 134 (T. Duffus Hardy ed., 1833).

92. On May 27, Langton and Saer de Quincy, who was one of the rebels, received letters of safe conduct from John's chancery so that they could meet with John on the barons' behalf. HOLT, *supra* note 36, at 242. Saer de Quincy was the other baron who received letters of safe conduct.

93. *Id.* at 243.

94. Holdsworth, *supra* note 75.

95. SAYERS, *supra* note 1, at 18–19.

96. *Id.* at 88.

clerical amercement and the freedom of Church elections would not have required much conferral with professional jurists; both were salient issues that any learned cleric would have known about.[97]

Langton had a motive to include canon law, he had the expertise necessary to do it, and his appearance in the negotiations coincides with the inclusion of these three chapters. The evidence does line up well with the hypothesis that Langton was the driving force behind chapters 1, 22, and 63. Langton is not the only possible source for these chapters, however, and other possible sources have not been given their due by historians. Both the barons and King John may have had reasons for including them even in the absence of urging from the clergy. When the charter was issued, the barons and the king were both trying to placate the pope, who must have been a primary audience of the charter. While negotiations were taking place in the spring of 1215, both sides launched appeals to Innocent, as John's overlord, to decide who had the right of it.[98] John, remember, had become a papal vassal. Moreover, even apart from his unique role with respect to England, Innocent had immense prestige and influence within Christendom.

The barons must have been aware that, in order to secure Innocent's support for the charter, they should include elements that would appeal to him. They had already clothed their rebellion in the sanction of the Church; when he assumed command of the rebel army in the spring of 1215, Robert Fitz-Walter named himself "Marshal of the Army of God and the Holy Church" in an attempt to claim that the barons' authority to overthrow John was connected with John's alleged impiety.[99] Adding two sections on the freedom of the Church and one on clerical amercements would not only show that the barons were concerned with things that were dear to the pope, but would also paint John as an impious king who had oppressed the English Church along with the English baronage, and who now had to be prevented from amercing Church property and interfering in Church governance. It would additionally place the conflict between John and his barons in the larger context of the fight between the sacred and secular powers as it was understood by advocates of the reform movement.

After Langton's drawn-out battle with John over his election to Canterbury, which had resulted in an interdict that had deprived the barons, and everyone else in England, of the sacraments for five years, it must have been clear to the barons that the freedom of episcopal elections was a matter of

---

97. Two of Langton's archdeacons, Adam of Tilney and William of Bardney, had canon law training. James Brundage, *The Managerial Revolution in the English Church*, in MAGNA CARTA AND THE ENGLAND OF KING JOHN 83, 96 (Janet S. Loengard ed., 2010).

98. HOLT, *supra* note 36, at 231.

99. Matthew Strickland, *Fitzwalter, Robert (d. 1235)*, in OXFORD DICTIONARY OF NATIONAL BIOGRAPHY, http://www.oxforddnb.com.proxy.wm.edu/view/article/9648?docPos=1 (last visited May 18, 2014).

importance for the pope, and that fighting for free elections would solidify their claim to being "the army of God and the Holy Church."[100] The issue of clerical amercements may not have been as obvious to them, and is more likely to have been suggested by a cleric who was aware that this was something in which the clergy and the reforming papacy had an interest. The barons, however, would have had plenty of learned clerics in their party. In the early 13th century, as barons began to manage their estates personally, rather than placing vassals on them or farming them out, they relied more and more heavily on professional administrators.[101] They often turned to clerics educated in the schools, who could keep written records of their estate management. Several of the barons are known to have had such clerics in their retinues in the rebellions of 1212 and 1215.[102] They would not have necessarily needed to turn to Langton or the bishops for guidance on these issues.

We should also not discount the possibility that chapters 1, 22, and 63 were added by someone in John's party. John had learned how to manipulate the papacy during his extended battle to keep Langton out of the see of Canterbury. John had despoiled the Church during his excommunication and had earned a reputation for impiety.[103] His status as an excommunicate had emboldened his enemies; a Welsh revolt, a plot to murder him, and a planned French invasion, all between the years 1212 and 1213, were justified under the banner of removing an excommunicate king from the throne, even if piety did not provide the initial impetus for any of them.[104] John understood the power of religious rhetoric. In 1213, he was able to reverse the religious rhetoric against him and transform himself from the Church's enemy to its special ward and son. John showed himself to be a savvy politician who knew how to ingratiate himself with the pope. John knew that Innocent, an advocate of the position that the pope should be at the apex of the secular hierarchy as well as the sacred one, would jump at the opportunity to make the English king a vassal.[105] When he surrendered England to Innocent as a papal fief and allowed Langton to take up his see, he forestalled the French invasion; moving against a special son of the papacy was very different from ousting an excommunicate king.[106] Facing a rebellious baronage and an increasingly hostile episcopate, John showed again in 1215 that he knew how to manipulate the pope and prevent his enemies from taking action against him in the name of the Church. In May

---

100. *Id.*
101. Waugh, *supra* note 88, at 813–15.
102. Holt, *supra* note 36, at 283.
103. Warren, *supra* note 56, at 167–68.
104. *Id.* at 202–05.
105. Sayers, *supra* note 1, at 88.
106. *Id.*

of 1215, John took up the crusader's cross.[107] Whether John ever intended to fulfill his crusader's vow and go to the Holy Land is beside the point. In May of 1215, it placed the barons in an awkward position. It was a sin to attack a crusader and John's promise to launch a crusade pleased Innocent a great deal.[108]

The issue of ecclesiastical elections specifically was on John's mind in the months leading up to the issuance of the charter. Even after the Langton affair was over, John and Innocent continued to squabble over ecclesiastical elections, leading John to issue a special charter in November of 1214, a mere seven months before Runnymede, guaranteeing free elections to cathedral churches and monasteries.[109] It does not require a great stretch of the imagination to think that, in June, when John was faced with baronial demands and wanted the pope to declare their rising an illegal act of rebellion, he would confirm the same provisions he had conceded to the pope seven months before. There is actually one bit of canon law in Magna Carta that assuredly was added by John, as it served only his interests. In three chapters (52, 53, and 57) that deal with land that had been unjustly confiscated or afforested by Henry II and Richard I (r. 1189–1199), John promised to make amends, but with a "respite for the usual crusader's term."[110] At canon law, crusaders were immune from suit for a certain period of time.[111] John was using his crusade vow and the canon law related to it as an excuse to delay the implementation of parts of the charter.[112]

---

107. John Gillingham, *John (1167–1216)*, in OXFORD DICTIONARY OF NATIONAL BIOGRAPHY, http://www.oxforddnb.com.proxy.wm.edu/view/article/14841?docPos=2 (last visited May 18, 2014).

108. *Id.* As a sign of how completely John's tactic worked to reverse the papacy's policies against him, by 1219, the pope and his legate were actually supporting John's minor son, Henry III, in his disputes with individual religious houses over Church and crown rights. As a vassal and ward of the papacy, the pope reasoned, the King of England was under his special protection. D.A. CARPENTER, THE MINORITY OF HENRY III 143 (1990).

109. CHRISTOPHER R. CHENEY, POPE INNOCENT III AND ENGLAND 161–62, 168–70 (1976).

110. *1215 Magna Carta chs. 52, 53, 57*, in HOLT, *supra* note 36, at 464–69; Helmholz, *supra* note 14, at 349.

111. Helmholz, *supra* note 14, at 349.

112. It is worth noting that John may have taken this rule from the practices of his own courts rather than canon law. It appears that the royal courts were, by the early 13th century, granting respite to crusaders; *Bracton* allows an essoin, or excuse, to anyone who has gone to the Holy Land and specifically mentions crusaders who have left as part of a general crusade. A crusader is given a year and a day to respond to any writ brought against him while he is away. It is more likely that John drew this rule from canon law, however. At canon law, it was immaterial whether the crusader was present in England or absent. The royal courts' essoin was useful only to the crusader who had actually left for the Holy Land, "beyond the sea of the Greeks." John had not left for his crusade yet and fully expected to receive his respite. 4 BRACTON, *supra* note 51, at 75, 324.

We know Langton could look to the example of Becket and his supporters to find precedent for use of *ius commune* against the king. Becket's episcopal *familia* had used it well.[113] What is less well known is that John had precedents of his own to draw upon. When John's father, Henry II, had put Thomas Becket on trial at Northampton in 1164, he used a Romano-Canonical trial format.[114] This was not the ordinary way to try a recalcitrant subject before the English king. Henry must have known that, in the midst of a debate where the reformist clergy were representing him as a defender of unjust custom against the righteous truth—represented by canon law—he could defuse some of the antiroyal propaganda by turning Becket's own language against him.[115] If Becket was convicted using the forms of the royal court, it would be another sign of the king's injustice. If he was convicted using the forms of the *ius commune*, however, it would be much more difficult to make that argument. Certainly Henry's judicial performance was intended to speak to reforming clergy generally, but the pope, who would ultimately mediate the dispute between Henry and Becket, was likely Henry's primary audience, just as Innocent was an audience for the performances of John, Langton, and the barons. John, like his father, had canonists in his own camp and clearly knew how to draw on canon law to serve his own interests.[116] In the end, John played his cards well. In September of 1215, Innocent not only suspended Stephen Langton from his office, but declared Magna Carta to be "illegal and unjust" and a "shameless presumption," because it was wrung from John's hands under duress.[117] The fact that Innocent ultimately used canon law to justify John's position should give us pause in assigning the canon law influence in the charter to Stephen Langton and the barons.

V. Influence from Legal Practice

Ius commune was a political tool that could be used to reach international audiences,[118] and it was clearly used in this way in Magna Carta. All of the major players had incentives to include it—and to include it explicitly, in language that would be understood by readers as *ius commune*—in certain instances. But what of the many examples Helmholz produces of chapters of Magna Carta that contain the substantive rule of the *ius commune*, but

---

113. Smalley, *supra* note 11, at 160–63.

114. Anne J. Duggan, *Roman, Canon and Common Law in Twelfth-Century England: The Council of Northampton (1164) Re-Examined*, 83 Hist. Res. 379, 386 (2010).

115. *Id.* at 386.

116. Brundage, *supra* note 97, at 96.

117. Warren, *supra* note 56, at 245.

118. Bellomo, *supra* note 10, at 83–111.

adopt none of its language? While I agree with Hudson when he argues that most of these chapters have more plausible explanations that do not involve the *ius commune*, there is another possible route of *ius commune* influence that has been underdeveloped in the literature: legal practice.

Although Pennington and Helmholz do not say so explicitly, they seem to assume that, if there was *ius commune* influence on Magna Carta, it came through texts. The evidence they use for similarities between Magna Carta and the *ius commune* is primarily evidence from the texts of Roman and canon law that were being studied in the universities. But canon law was also practiced in English ecclesiastical courts. Canon law was the law in England and, as late as the 19th century, was a law that the average English-man would come into contact with at some point in his life: issues like marriage formation and probate of personal property were within the exclusive jurisdiction of the ecclesiastical courts.[119] The Church even claimed jurisdiction over contracts sealed by solemn oath.[120] It had its own lawyers, trained separately from the lawyers of the common law courts.[121] Most of the ecclesiastical jurisdiction has been subsumed into the common law in England and its former colonies and its origin in canon law has largely been forgotten. Probate and marriage are now issues for the regular state courts, but in 13th-, 14th-, and 15th-century England, and even much later, there was no such thing as a common law of probate or marriage formation.[122]

As noted above, Pennington discusses two papal decretals that stated the rule on sureties as it was stated in Magna Carta. Decretals were letters that the pope issued as legal rulings in individual cases. When the parties or the judges in an ecclesiastical court were unsure about the relevant law in a case, they could request a decretal on the matter.[123] These decretals were a source of law in the late 12th and early 13th centuries, a type of ecclesiastical case law. They were brought together in decretal collections, which generated their own glosses and commentaries.[124] The two decretals that Pennington cites were both issued in English cases, and both concerned litigation over debts. Pennington draws the potential line of influence from the decretals to Magna Carta through the *Compilatio Prima*, a decretal collection that was circulating in England at the beginning of the 13th century. It is entirely

119. R.H. Helmholz, The Oxford History of the Laws of England, Volume One: The Canon Law and Ecclesiastical Jurisdiction from 597 to the 1640s at 387–89 (2004).

120. *Id.* at 359.

121. *Id.* at 221–26.

122. J.H. Baker, An Introduction to English Legal History 132, 387, 479 (4th ed. 2002).

123. Harry Dondorp & Eltjo J.H. Schrage, *The Sources of Medieval Learned Law, in* The Creation of the Ius Commune: From Casus to Regula 37–38 (John W. Cairns & Paul J. du Plessis eds., 2010).

124. *Id.* at 40–45.

possible that a learned cleric or justice who had read the *Compilatio Prima* or Bernardus' *Summa* was then involved in the negotiations for Magna Carta and wanted to include the canonical rule but, to hide its canonist origin, clothed the rule in an entirely different vocabulary. It requires a much smaller leap of the imagination, however, to posit that the barons had heard about these cases in the ecclesiastical courts, liked their rule better than the one the king's courts were offering, and demanded it in Magna Carta.

The two cases that produced these decretals were probably well known. At least one of them involved prominent litigants. In 1179, Stephen of Tournai stood surety for Peter of Blois for a debt Peter incurred on a visit to the papal court. Peter failed to pay his creditors, who began to hound Stephen for their money. Stephen, knowing that Peter had the means to pay, sued Peter in the archbishop of Canterbury's court and, sometime between 1181 and 1185, the pope issued a decretal siding with Stephen, relying on the Roman law rule that the debtor can recover against the sureties only if the primary debtor is insolvent.[125] It would be surprising if elites in the 1180s were not talking about this case. At the time, Stephen was a canonist of international stature and abbot of the influential monastery of Sainte-Geneviève in Paris.[126] Peter was a popular theologian, a Latin secretary and occasional ambassador for Henry II, and chancellor to the archbishop of Canterbury.[127] He would become archdeacon of Bath during the course of the litigation.[128] This case could have been the means of disseminating the *ius commune* rule that the creditors had to seek out the debtor first without communicating it in the vocabulary of the *ius commune*. People who traveled in the elite circles of late 13th-century England would know the result, but they probably would not have heard it quoted in the language of the decretal. When they told the story, nonclerical elites would likely have spoken about *pleges* in the French and Middle English vernacular spoken by the barons, rather than the Latin *fideiussores*. They would now know that if you stood as a pledge for someone who contracted a debt, the ecclesiastical courts would not force you to pay back the debt unless your debtor was insolvent, while the king's courts would require you to satisfy it even if the debtor had the means to pay. Some barons may even have had experience of their own with debt cases in the ecclesiastical courts. People in 12th- and 13th-century Europe engaged in forum-shopping; when the ecclesiastical courts offered a rule or procedure they preferred, they found

---

125. Pennington, *supra* note 17, at 266.

126. Landau, *supra* note 45, at 304.

127. *Id.* at 304, 315; R.W. Southern, *Blois, Peter of (1125X30–1212), in* OXFORD DICTIONARY OF NATIONAL BIOGRAPHY, http://www.oxforddnb.com.proxy.wm.edu/view /article/22012?docPos=1 (last visited May 18, 2014).

128. *Id.*

ways to get into them.[129] A baron who was creditor to a cleric might sue the cleric or his clerical sureties in the ecclesiastical courts, which had personal jurisdiction over all clerics.[130] Barons hired canon lawyers at times to help them navigate the courts of the Church, and those lawyers would almost certainly have known about the two decretals sent to England that constituted the controlling authority on the matter of sureties.[131] Unfortunately, there are no surviving records from the Church courts of the early 13th century, so one cannot know for sure whether laymen did engage in this kind of litigation.

VI. Conclusion: Canon Law, Common Law, and 1215

Ius commune did leave a mark upon Magna Carta, even if only a very small one. While it is possible that *ius commune* made its way into the text because English legal reformers were looking to the *ius commune* for ideas, there is really very little evidence for this reading of Magna Carta. The evidence more readily supports a conclusion that *ius commune* appears in the text as a political language, a common currency of the political class in the 13th century, forged in the fires of the Becket conflict and the Church reform movement, that certain players in the process could deploy to bring the pope, or the reformist branch of the Church more generally, into the conflict on their side. It was a political and religious language that could be used to give cosmic significance to their parochial concerns. Innocent was concerned with the separation of the sacred from the secular, with placing the papacy on a firmer footing, with the threat posed to him by the political situation in Sicily and the Holy Roman Empire, and with the project of recovering Jerusalem, which had been lost to Saladin 28 years earlier.[132] England's internal politics were of concern to him, but they were not the first thing on his mind. Both sides knew, however, that if England's internal politics could be placed within the context of the reform movement, Innocent might become more inclined to intervene.

To the historian or lawyer who is primarily interested in how the *ius commune*, as one legal system, influenced the common law, as another, the answer that the *ius commune* in Magna Carta is mostly there as political posturing is likely to be unsatisfying. The historical debate about civilian influence on the common law has usually assumed the former kind of influence. Frederick William Maitland—who could rightfully be called the father

---

129. R.H. Helmholz, The Ius Commune in England: Four Studies 359–60 (2001).

130. *Id.* at 188–89.

131. Patricia M. Barnes, *The Anstey Case, in* A Medieval Miscellany for Doris M. Stenton 1, 7 (Patricia M. Barnes & C.F. Slade eds., 1962).

132. Sayers, *supra* note 1, at 63–64, 177.

of the modern, academic study of English legal history—even made the case that the earliest English writs, those little pieces of paper that would become the building blocks for the common law system, were modeled on actions available in the ecclesiastical courts at the same time.[133] Subsequent scholars have followed him in arguing for Roman and canon law precedents for the writs.[134] The question of civil law influence on the common law has been reinvigorated in the past two decades. With globalization, common law and civil law are coming into contact more often and legal systems are drawing closer together. In the European context, the European Union has raised issues of common law and civil law compatibility. In spite of the U.S. Supreme Court's general unwillingness to accept foreign precedents, not even the United States has been fully insulated from this process. Any time an American lawyer needs to deal with Japan, China, continental Europe, or Central or South America, she is dealing with a civilian system. With the systems coming into contact, lawyers and historians have become interested in the historical connections between common law and civil law.

It is only natural that historians would extend their inquiry of civilian influence to Magna Carta, since the history of Magna Carta has been bound together with the history of the common law. When lawyers first started to make collections of English statutes in the late 13th century, usually in the form of small reference books that could be carried around as they followed the king's itinerant courts, Magna Carta was included along with the great statutes of Henry III (r. 1216–1272) and his son, Edward I (r. 1272–1307), even though it was not initially written in the form of a statute and it was not treated as one in 1215.[135] These lawyers established Magna Carta as England's first statute, a place of honor it would hold in all subsequent statute collections.[136] When Sir Edward Coke asserted the common law's independence from the Stuart monarchy in the early 17th century, he turned to Magna Carta to do it, presenting it as a statement of immemorial common law.[137] And when a memorial was built at Runnymede in 1957, it was the

---

133. The assize of novel disseisin was, in Maitland's view, modeled on the ecclesiastical *actio spolii*. 2 Frederick Pollock and Frederic William Maitland, The History of English Law before the Time of Edward I 48 (2d ed. 1905); Donald Sutherland, The Assize of Novel Disseisin 21 (1973). For the contrary view, that the petty assizes have antecedents in longstanding English practices, not in the *ius commune*, see R.C. van Caenegem, The Birth of the English Common Law 44 (2d ed. 1988).

134. Sutherland, *supra* note 133, at 22–24; Mary Cheney, Possessio/proprietas, *Ecclesiastical Courts in Mid-Twelfth Century England, in* Law and Government in Medieval England and Normandy: Essays in Honour of Sir James Holt (George Garnett & John Hudson eds., 1994); Joshua C. Tate, *Ownership and Possession in the Early Common Law*, 48 Am. J. Legal Hist. 281 (2006).

135. *See* Huntington Library MS HM 25782 (late 13th-century statute book).

136. Vincent, *supra* note 74, at 90–91.

137. Turner, *supra* note 79, at 147.

American Bar Association that built it to honor Magna Carta's role in the common law tradition.

In 1215, the idea that Magna Carta was one of the great, foundational texts of the common law was still in the future. Magna Carta started life in 1215 as a peace treaty, and not a very successful one. In fact, at the time Magna Carta was written, no one had yet thought to use the term "common law" to describe the work performed by the king's courts. By 1215, English people were imagining that work as a single legal system for the whole of England; Magna Carta itself uses the terms *lex regni* ("the law of the realm") and *lex terrae* ("the law of the land"), although both usages seem to have been relatively new in 1215, as they are attested in few other documents.[138] The term "common law" would not make its first appearance until the 1240s, and it would not be used regularly to describe the law of the king's courts until the 1270s.[139]

Magna Carta does not supply the kind of civilian influence that common law historians are looking for. It does not show one legal system influencing the reform of another. Additionally, focus on Magna Carta often causes historians to miss the bigger picture with respect to *ius commune* influence on the common law. The *ius commune* has had an influence on English law and did from the very beginning. Canon law was ubiquitous in England in 1215. It was as much the law of England as the nascent common law was. Clerics and laymen alike would have had regular contact with the courts of the Church. Both the royal and ecclesiastical administration employed men trained in Roman and canon law in 1215. Some went as far away as Bologna to be trained in the two laws.[140] Some were teaching it closer to home, at centers like Oxford and Lincoln.[141] One must assume that great value was placed on *ius commune* learning in England if there were people who were prepared to commit several years to its study, possibly in a foreign country.[142]

The ideas these scholars brought back from those periods of study might have had effects on the ways people thought about law and politics in England, even if they were not directly applying *ius commune* doctrine. The elements of *Bracton*, for instance, that had the longest impact on the

---

138. *1215 Magna Carta chs. 39, 42, and 55, in* Holt, *supra* note 36, at 460–03, 466–07.

139. Paul Brand, *Law and Custom in the English Thirteenth Century Common Law*, *in* Custom: The Development and Use of a Legal Concept in the Middle Ages 20–21 (Per Andersen & Mia Münster Swendsen, 2009).

140. Brundage, *supra* note 97, at 224.

141. Peter Landau, *The Origins of Legal Science in England in the Twelfth Century: Lincoln, Oxford, and the Career of Vacarius, in* Readers, Compilers, and Texts in the Early Middle Ages: Studies in Medieval Canon Law in Honour of Linda Fowler-Magerl 165–182 (Martin Brett and Kathleen Cushing eds., 2009).

142. Bellomo, *supra* note 10, at 123–24.

development of the common law were not its Romanist legal doctrines, many of which were actually out of sync with legal practice in the English courts and remained so after the treatise was written. *Bracton*'s influence was more subtle than that but also more fundamental. Roman and canon law gave the authors of *Bracton* a framework for thinking about the work they were doing in the royal courts—which could as easily be described as administrative work—as a coherent legal system held together by a structure of interlocking abstract concepts.[143]

It is possible that *ius commune* had already had similar effects on political thinkers in England by the time Magna Carta was drafted, and a few scholars have pursued this line of research. Cary Nederman, for instance, has suggested that theological and political thought from the schools influenced the way the drafters of Magna Carta thought about liberties. He argues that the concept of Church liberty, as espoused by learned figures like John of Salisbury, was qualitatively different from the contemporary lay concept of liberties as personal privileges that derive from the monarch's will.[144] Jason Taliadoros likewise suggests that *ius commune* concepts of subjective right might have influenced the way the drafters of Magna Carta thought about rights.[145] This kind of influence seems more likely to have occurred by the kind of organic osmosis that historians of the common law usually assume. A person trained in one legal system might be taught to understand a word like "liberty" according to that system's conventions and then carry that understanding over to another system. This subtle form of influence is also more satisfying than the borrowing of doctrine is. Doctrines change over time and most of the doctrines that Helmholz points to as having been borrowed from *ius commune* did not last. General concepts and ways of thinking about law, however, tend to last. Liberty became an important discourse in the Anglo-American legal tradition. If it owes something to canon law, then canon law has touched the common law in a fundamental way.

Oddly enough, one of the most significant elements of the common law, the criminal jury, did come about as a result of canon law influence and as a result of the events of 1215. Chapter 39 of Magna Carta—the famous, "No free man shall be taken or imprisoned or disseised or outlawed or exiled or in any way ruined, nor will we go or send against him, except by the lawful judgment of his peers or by the law of the land"—usually gets credit for the right to trial by jury, but the origins of the criminal jury have nothing to do with Magna Carta.[146] For the origins of the English criminal jury, one must

---

143. McSweeney, *supra* note 32, at 1170–72.

144. Cary J. Nederman, *The Liberty of the Church and the Road to Runnymede: John of Salisbury and the Intellectual Foundations of the Magna Carta*, 43 CANADIAN J. POL. SCI. 457–61 (2010).

145. Jason Taliadoros, *Subjective Rights and Magna Carta* (forthcoming).

146. *1215 Magna Carta, in* HOLT, *supra* note 36, at 461.

go back to the Fourth Lateran Council, because it was the canons of the Fourth Lateran Council and their ban on clerical participation in judicial ordeals that led to the widespread use of criminal juries in England.

Ordeals had been the primary procedure for determining guilt or innocence in criminal trials in the English royal courts up to 1215.[147] The ordeal of iron required the accused to carry a red-hot iron several paces. The burns on his hands were wrapped and then unwrapped several days later. If the wounds had festered, the accused was judged guilty.[148] In the late 12th century there was increasing skepticism about the efficacy of the ordeal, which largely centered on the fact that it was manipulable and forced God to give an answer on command.[149] The Lateran Council, responding to these criticisms, forbade clerical participation in the ordeal. This severely hampered secular courts' ability to hold ordeals; the ordeal required the presence and participation of a priest, who would hear the accused's confession, give him communion, and bless the iron.[150]

After the civil war between John's party and the barons ended in 1217, the new king's regency council prepared to send justices into the counties on eyre circuits, the first regular royal courts to operate since 1215.[151] The regents sent instructions to the justices in 1218 that they could no longer use trial by ordeal because of the canon of the Lateran Council, which they understood to ban ordeals altogether.[152] They did not order the justices to begin using trial by jury, however. They merely instructed them to hold certain accused felons until the king's government figured out what to do with them, and to release others if they could find sureties for their good behavior.[153] The regents—who, it should be noted, had themselves reissued Magna Carta twice already, in 1216 and 1217—did not understand Magna Carta's chapter 39, "no free man shall be taken or imprisoned . . . except by the lawful judgment of his peers or by the law of the land," to require a jury trial.[154] The fact that the chapter contains an "or" itself implies that there were acceptable modes of trial apart from judgment of one's peers. The "or" has had to be ignored or explained away by later generations of

---

147. Roger D. Groot, *The Early Thirteenth-Century Criminal Jury*, in Twelve Good Men and True: The Criminal Trial Jury in England, 1200–1800, at 5–7 (1988).

148. Paul R. Hyams, *Trial By Ordeal: The Key to Proof in the Early Common Law*, in On the Laws and Customs of England: Essays in Honor of Samuel E. Thorne 93–94 (1981).

149. *Id.* at 102–03.

150. *Id.* at 109–10.

151. David Crook, Records of the General Eyre 71 (1982).

152. D.M. Stenton, Rolls of the Justices in Eyre: Being the Rolls of Pleas and Assizes for Yorkshire 3 Henry III (1218–19) xl (1937); Groot, *supra* note 147, at 3–4.

153. Groot, *supra* note 147, at 10; Stenton, *supra* note 152.

154. *1215 Magna Carta*, in Holt, *supra* note 36, at 461.

common-law lawyers who pointed to Magna Carta as the source of the jury right.[155] When the justices began to use the jury as the primary mode of trial for felons, they did so as a matter of expediency, not because they believed that Magna Carta required trial by jury.[156]

The Lateran Council created no right to a trial by jury, but it did make the jury the regular means of trial in the English courts. There would likely have been no jury right if the king's regents had not heeded the commands of canon law. The *ius commune*, that combination of Roman and canon law that is the ancestor of the modern civil law, may not have left a significant mark on Magna Carta, but what little it did leave is useful for showing how *ius commune* was operating in England in 1215. It was certainly the law of the ecclesiastical courts. There were some people who were interested in assimilating English law to the *ius commune*, but to the major players in English politics—the people who drafted Magna Carta—it was primarily a language of political dispute, used to turn their local problems into the pope's problems.

---

155. McKechnie, *supra* note 36, at 381 (arguing that the Latin word "vel" can mean "and").

156. Groot, *supra* note 147, at 12–13, 18–19.

Chapter 12

The Charter of the Forest: Evolving Human Rights in Nature

Nicholas A. Robinson

In 1759, William Blackstone published The Great Charter and the Charter of the Forest, with other Authentic Instruments, to which is Prefixed An Introductory Discourse, containing The History of the Charters.[1] Since then, much has been written about Magna Carta, but little has been written about the companion Forest Charter. This chapter reexamines "these two sacred charters,"[2] focusing upon the "liberties of the forest"[3] that the Forest Charter established, and how they evolved amid the contentious struggles over stewardship of England's forest resources.[4] The Forest Charter both contributed to establishing the rule of law and also launched eight centuries of legislation conserving forest resources and landscapes.

Carta de Foresta, the Charter of the Forest of 1217, is among the first statutes in environmental law of any nation. Crafted to reform patently unjust governance of natural resources in 13th-century England, the Charter of the Forest became a framework through which to reconcile competing environmental claims, then and into the future. The Charter confirmed the rights of "free men."[5] Kings resisted conceding these rights. When confronted with violations of the Charter, barons and royal councils obliged

---

1. WILLIAM BLACKSTONE, THE GREAT CHARTER AND THE CHARTER OF THE FOREST, WITH OTHER AUTHENTIC INSTRUMENTS, TO WHICH IS PREFIXED AN INTRODUCTORY DISCOURSE CONTAINING THE HISTORY OF THE CHARTER (Oxford at the Clarendon Press 1759). References are to the first edition of this elegantly printed work, an outstanding aesthetic and technical achievement. WILFRED PREST, WILLIAM BLACKSTONE: LAWS AND LETTERS IN THE EIGHTEENTH CENTURY 165 (2008).

2. BLACKSTONE, *supra* note 1, at vliv ("sacred charters").

3. *Forest Charter, in* 1 STATUTES OF THE REALM, *Charters of Liberties*, nos. 10 and 12 at ch. 17 (Record Commission 1810–28, Nicholas Robinson trans. 2013).

4. Blackstone recounts how clergy worried that the "generality of the provisions in Magna Carta chap. 48" might endanger the "very being of all forests," and declared that it was not the intention of the parties "to abolish the customs of the forests, without which the forests themselves could not be preserved." They lodged their views in the Tower of London. BLACKSTONE, *supra* note 1, at xx–xxi.

5. *Forest Charter, supra* note 3, at chs. 4, 9, 12 & 17.

kings repeatedly to reissue the Forest Charter and pledge anew to obey its terms. Henry III (r. 1216–1272) did so in 1225 and Edward I (r. 1272–1307) did in 1297 and 1300.[6] More than a century passed before the Crown came to accept that the Forest Charter as a law was binding upon the king.

Thereafter, for the next six centuries the Forest Charter was central to competing claims by England's governments and people to the forest landscapes. During the 16th century and onward, Parliament gradually enacted several hundred separate acts amending different provisions that the Forest Charter originally addressed.[7] Parliament embedded the Charter so deeply in the law of the land that its formalistic repeal in 1971 was anticlimactic.[8] The Forest Charter shaped England's constitution as well as its landscape, and it continues to confer benefits for both law and the biosphere today. Organically, over some 30 generations, humans evolved English law to conserve the oldest national system of protected natural areas in the world.

---

6. The Charter of the Forest of 1217, in Latin, is given the statutory citation as 1 Hen. 3; the second Charter of the Forest in 1225 appears at 9 Hen. 3. William Stubbs records the 32 times after 1217 that the king was obliged to reconfirm the Forest Charter (and Magna Carta), doing so in 1300 in the statute "*Articuli Super Cartas.*" *See* William Stubbs, Select Charters and Other Illustrations of English Constitutional History 490 (Oxford, 9th. ed., 1870). In Article I of his confirmation, King Edward provided in Norman French: "Know ye that we to the honor of God and of holy Church, and to the profit of all our realm, have granted for us and our heirs, that the great charter of Liberties [*la graunt charter des fraunchises*] and the charter of the forest [*la chartres de la foreste*], which were made by common assent of all the realm, in the time of King Henry our father, shall be kept in every point without breach . . . ." While the text of Carta de Foresta as of 1225 became well established, it took more than a century for the Forest Charter to be accepted by the king as binding law. Only in the reigns of Edward III or Richard II were the terms of the Forest Charter being observed by the Crown as law, and there would still be subsequent efforts by kings to undermine or reject its provisions. *See* Ch. Petit-Dutaillis & George Lefebvre, Studies and Notes Supplementary to Stubb's Constitutional History 232 (James Tait trans., 1930).

7. Ninety-four acts related primarily to providing timber from Royal Forests are compiled in Appendix II of N.D.G. James, A History of English Forestry (1981). A total of 185 separate acts on forest wildlife and game relevant to those of the Forest Law appear in the table of statutes of Lawrence Mead, Oke's Game Laws (5th ed., 1912), primarily amending hunting laws. Separate acts exist for each of the Royal Forests, as their uses or ownership were revised; 57 separate acts for different Royal Forests are recorded in the appendix to Raymond K.J. Grant, The Royal Forests of England (1991). A larger body of acts after World War II provide for conservation norms and recreational uses. References to selected acts appear throughout this chapter. No comprehensive set of parliamentary acts elaborating the Forest Charter has been compiled.

8. An Act to Abolish Certain Rights of Her Majesty to Wild Creatures and Certain Related Rights and Franchises, to Abrogate the Forest Law (subject to exceptions), and to Repeal Enactments Relating to those Rights and Franchises and to Forest and the Forest Law, and for Connected Purposes, 1971, c. 47 [hereinafter The Wild Creatures and Forest Laws Act].

As is typical of medieval royal charters, hand-copied on vellum, Carta de Foresta is found in several versions. It was issued in 1217[9] and proclaimed in a definitive text again by Henry III in 1225;[10] thereafter, kings repeatedly decreed it as a Charter or confirmed it in statutes, and it was copied into numerous subsequent collections of laws.[11] The Forest Charter elaborated three chapters regarding the Royal Forests[12] contained in King John's Carta de Libertatis Angliae of 1215. When King John (r. 1199–1216) convinced Pope Innocent III (r. 1198–1216) to annul that Charter, including the chapters of forest promises, in August 1215, his act produced outrage, fueling the civil war against John. Following John's death, the coronation of Henry III led to the reissuance of the Charter in 1216, and then again in 1217, at which time there was a simultaneous proclamation of a detailed and distinct new charter, which elaborated English forest rights in 17 articles. To distinguish the Forest Charter from the 1217 reissue of the much longer

---

9. Blackstone could not find this original version and reported it to have been lost. Nonetheless, he found contemporary reports and copies of its provisions to verify its proclamation. BLACKSTONE, *supra* note 1, at xvii, xxi, xlii.

10. The British Library has placed online the image of the Forest Charter of 1225 (manuscript Add. ch. 24712), with the deeply blue-hued (nearly black) wax seal of Henry III still attached by cords woven into the vellum (three-fourths original wax, the balance one-third side restored). *See* British Library, *Taking Liberties: Laws of Forests*, The British Library, http://www.bl.uk/onlinegallery/takingliberties/staritems/28lawsofforestspic.html (last visited May 20, 2014).

11. The Forest Charter's text, as printed in this book's appendix H, is a translation by Nicholas Robinson of the Latin version as found in 1 STATUTES OF THE REALM (l. y's Printer, 1734), at p. 1s of the Forest71, *Charters of Liberties*, nos. 10 & 12 (Record Commission 1810–28). An original text of the Forest Charter is found compiled in the Lansdowne Manuscript, conserved in the British Library (MS 652/17). Minor variations exist among different extant versions of the Charter. *See* STUBBS, *supra* note 6, at 344 in Part VI as "Charter of the Forest." The Charter's name itself appears in variations: "Charta de Foresta" in JOHN MANWOOD, TREATISE OF THE FOREST LAWS 409 (4th. ed. 1717), *available at* https://archive.org/details/manwoodstreatis00manwgoog; *Charta Foresta, in* THE STATUTES AT LARGE MADE FOR THE PRESERVATION OF GAME 1 (J. Baskett, His Majesty's Printer, 1734); *Carta Forestae,* classical Latin to parallel *Magna Carta*. This chapter follows William Blackstone's usage, as *Carta de Foresta, see* BLACKSTONE, *supra* note 1.

12. Royal Forests were established by William I (the Conqueror) beginning in 1066 to assert the king's demesne and rule over the flora and fauna, in particular deer and other game, of many tracts of lands, including fields, woods, water bodies, and all the natural resources found therein. The king reserved all hunting rights in Royal Forests to the crown. In some instances, prior occupants were evicted. The *Domesday Book* records that villeins and others in Eling were evicted when the New Forest was established. DOMESDAY BOOK I.51–52 (Abraham Farley ed., n.p., 1783) (1086). Kings who succeeded William I expanded the area of Royal Forests. *See* CHARLES COX, THE ROYAL FORESTS OF ENGLAND (1720).

Charter of Liberties, the latter was dubbed the Great Charter, or Magna Charta, which later was changed to Magna Carta.[13]

The histories of these two companion charters are inextricably linked, although the knowledge of Magna Carta has eclipsed memory of Carta de Foresta. In the 21st century, when environmental crises abound, it is instructive to recall anew the remarkable saga of England's Forest Charter.

Tangible legacies of the Forest Charter exist in the governmental stewardship of many of its 129 remnant Royal Forests as protected areas,[14] or in the Ankerwycke Yew (*taxus baccata*) at Runnymede, a tree more than 2,000 years old, which witnessed the negotiation between King John and the barons in 1215. English law today safeguards this sentinel as one of the realm's "very old trees of cultural and/or biological interest."[15] The Forest Charter's intangible legacies inhere in the principles that it—together with Magna Carta—forged to establish. These include establishing the rule of law, and proclaiming the "liberties of the forest,"[16] which shaped foundations for what has become sustainable natural resources law, and in particular regimes for protection of natural areas.[17]

---

13. A.E. Dick Howard, *Magna Carta Celebrates Its 750th Year*, 51 A.B.A. J. 529, 530 (1965).

14. There are 129 forests described in James, *supra* note 7, at ch. 4. *See* Henry Spelman, Glossarium Archiaologicum (1687) (reporting 68 forests, 13 chases). *See* Forestry Commission, *Forestry Statistics*, http://www.forestry.gov.uk/forestry/infd-7aqdgc (last visited May 20, 2014) (providing the Forest Commission's current statistics). One-time Royal Forests now include New Forest, Dean, Epping, Alice Holt Forest (Surrey), Carrods Chasse (Staffordshire), Rockingham Forest (Northamptonshire), and others. *See* *A List of the Royal Forests of England*, *in* Grant, *supra* note 7, at 221–29; *see also* Charles R. Young, The Royal Forests of Medieval England 62–63 (1979).

15. Department of Environment, Food and Rural Affaires and Forestry Commission, Keepers of Time. A Statement of Policy for England's Ancient and Native Woodland 7 (2005), http://www.forestry.gov.uk/pdf/anw-policy.pdf/$file /anw-policy.pdf. The Ankerwycke Yew was placed under an order of protection in April of 1990. *See Six of Britain's Oldest Trees*, Guardian, July 22, 2009, http://www .theguardian.com/environment/gallery/2009/jul/21/oldest-trees-uk (last visited May 20, 2014); Jacob Strutt, *Sylva Britannica* (1826) (the tree is celebrated in the following lines: "What scenes have pass'd, since first this ancient Yew/ In all the strength of youthful beauty grew! /Here patriot Barons might have musing stood, /And plann'd the Charter for their Country's good; /And here, perhaps, from Runnymede retired, /The haughty John, with secret vengeance fired, /Might curse the day which saw his weakness yield / Extorted rights in yonder tented field."). *See Forest Research–Veteran Trees*, Forestry Commission, http://www.forestry.gov.uk/fr/infd-5w2g5b (last visited May 20, 2014) (regarding "veteran tree" designations generally).

16. *Forest Charter*, *supra* note 3, at ch. 17.

17. *See About IUCN*, iucn.org (Jul. 10, 2013), http://www.iucn.org/about/ (last visited May 20, 2014) (The World Commission on Protected Areas of the International Union for the Conservation of Nature & Natural Resource (IUCN) has established standards for protected areas, and every decade it convenes a World Parks Congress to advance national protected-area practices).

Study of the Forest Charter affords a glimpse into the complex relationships in feudal England among commoners, barons, clergy, the king, and his officers. It also provides a lens through which to assess laws and policies about nature and natural resources over the past 800 years. Beyond codifying customary laws associated with the Royal Forest, the Charter consciously designed new legal means to foster justice and sustain relations between the people and the natural resources of the 13th century. In doing so, it became a foundation for an intergenerational struggle toward defining a rule of law for nature.

No comprehensive history of the Forest Charter exists.[18] The American Bar Association has providently elected to restore memory about Carta de Foresta, as an offspring of Magna Carta, during the commemoration of the 800th anniversary of the latter.[19] Each generation has reconceived the Forest Charter's "liberties of the forest"[20] in light of the demands of its times. The perspective of Blackstone's age was celebratory, confirming the sacred charters' contributions to the realm's rule of law and ordered liberties. Today the focus is on the Forest Charter's role in sustaining ecological resilience. Throughout the Forest Charter's legal life, it mediated dynamic tensions between interests competing over forest products and landscapes. In its first 200 years, repeated demands that the Forest Charter's rights be implemented provided occasions to proclaim anew the Forest Charter, together with Magna Carta. The existence of rule of law principles owes an

---

18. Various descriptions of aspects of the Forest Charter exist. Some are references ancillary to accounts of Magna Carta. *See, e.g.*, J.C. HOLT, MAGNA CARTA 338–42, 393–97, and *passim* (2d ed. 1992) and others referenced in the annotations throughout this chapter. No single book or other study devoted solely to the Forest Charter has been found. Legal commentary about the Forest Charter is mentioned in the context of discussing administration of the Royal Forests but is not singled out for specific legal analysis as a legal instrument. *See* YOUNG, *supra* note 14, and GRANT, *supra* note 7. In other studies, the Forest Charter is selectively discussed relevant to their focus. For example, in assessing hunting, *see* EMMA GRIFFIN, BLOOD SPORT: HUNTING IN BRITAIN SINCE 1066, at 36–48 (2008), or in urging a socialist or radical reappraisal of property rights. PETER LINEBAUGH, MAGNA CARTA MANIFESTO: LIBERTIES AND COMMONS FOR ALL (2008). Notwithstanding such diverse studies devoted to objectives other than recounting the special role of the Forest Charter, scholarship has yet to produce any in-depth analysis primarily of the Forest Charter.

19. The ABA Section on International Law's 2013 Fall Meeting was held in London on October 15–19, 2013, and its opening day panel titled "Magna Carta: The Foundation of Freedom and Democracy" included a lecture on the Forest Charter. This lecture may well have been the first lecture delivered in London devoted exclusively to the Carta de Foresta since George Trehern (d. 1526) lectured at Lincoln's Inn in 1520 (the 33 pages recording Trehern's reading are conserved in the British Library, Add Ms 73517), or since Joshua Williams lectured at Gray's Inn in 1877 as noted, *see* HERBERT BROOM & EDWARD A. HADLEY, COMMENTARIES ON THE LAWS OF ENGLAND (London, W. Maxwell, 1869). Records of professional lectures on the Forest Charter are scant.

20. *Forest Charter, supra* note 3, at ch. 17.

early debt to Carta de Foresta. But the Forest Charter also has had a life of its own.

The history of the Forest Charter falls into five distinctive periods. First is the Charter's role in the law and life of those in England in the 13th and 14th centuries. Forests were vital to the economy of this era. Forest struggles were central to the creation of the rule of law.

Second, from the 15th to the 18th centuries, the Charter served each king's quest for revenues or resources, competing with the demands of the governed, who defended their interests by seeking public participation in the Crown's decision making. This period culminates with Parliament gradually assuming authority over the Royal Forests. Forests were essential for producing timber for building ships, and Parliament established the Office of Woods to govern them. The rule of law matured.

Third, from the mid-19th century to World War II, the Forest Charter's environmental content evolved, reflecting (a) new knowledge derived from studies in ecology and other advances in the natural sciences, (b) society's new sensibilities to beauty in nature, and (c) emerging social movements protecting the English countryside in the wake of enclosures (also referred to as "inclosures"; these terms are used interchangeably in this chapter), expanding urbanization, and industrialization. Coincidentally as the 20th century began, legal scholars published translations of the early documents about both Magna Carta and the Forest Charter, enabling renewed study of both charters. Access to the historical record enabled invocations of forest liberties and rights in debates about common access to open space and nature conservation. In this period of rapid social evolution, Parliament transformed the Law of the Forest by establishing the Forest Commission in 1919.

Fourth, in the later 20th century, especially after World War II, spirited debates about the recreation in the countryside and the content of maturing conservation law reshaped public policy. Advances in the still young science of ecology and acceptance of norms for sustainable development progressively prompted changes to Forest Laws. Laws for publicly protected areas consciously emerged as Parliament increasingly amended aspects of the Forest Charter. Ad hoc lawmaking inevitably left vestiges of the medieval Forest Law under the Forest Charter still in force, a handful of incidents once intended to protect commoners still formalistically burdening lands near former Royal Forests.[21] To quiet these legal relics burdening land stewardship, Parliament finally repealed the Forest Charter in 1971. Today,

---

21. For example, until 1971, in the New Forest in order to assert and preserve royal prerogatives on then essentially private land holdings, "keepers entered the ancient assarts and fired a ritual shot to declare the crown's rights each year." Colin R. Tubbs, The New Forest 73 (1986).

governance of the New Forest[22] illustrates how traditional Forest Charter liberties have been integrated with contemporary ecological practices, outdoor recreation, and cultural heritage.

Fifth, the future of the Forest Charter's "liberties" in the 21st century extends into the Anthropocene Epoch,[23] whose rapid environmental changes are altering Earth's natural systems. A well-documented record of legal management of natural resources over ten centuries is rare and merits deeper study. The Forest Charter's resilient past offers insights about stewardship of natural areas in the Anthropocene.

I.   Introduction: The Forest Charter in a Nutshell

An overview of these five periods charts a pathway through the details of the Forest Charter's history, lest a reader miss the forest for the trees. In the 13th century, the Charter of the Forest's legal architecture mediated competing uses of natural resources in and around the Royal Forests. Rudiments of forest governance had existed under Edward the Confessor (r. 1042–1066), before the Norman invasion.[24] After 1066, William I (the Conqueror) (r. 1066–1087) brought to England his Norman concepts to English forests. He set aside Royal Forests, such as the New Forest in 1079, displacing or limiting the customary access of many, including commoners, to forest areas. Popular demands to reaffirm traditional forest uses led to including three chapters in Magna Carta dealing with forest rights. When the Forest Charter was issued on November 6, 1217,[25] it strengthened provisions of chapters 44, 47, and 48 of Magna Carta of 1215. Where once William had held unfettered sway in forest domains, the 150 years following the Forest

---

22. The New Forest includes one of the largest remaining tracts of unenclosed pasture land, heathland, and forest in southern England.

23. The Anthropocene Epoch is the current geological age in which human activity is the dominant influence on the environment, including climate. *See Subcomission on Quaternary Stratigraphy, ICS, Working Groups, Working Group on the "Anthropocene,"* QUARTERNARYSTRATIGRAPHY.ORG (Aug. 1, 2014), http://quaternary.stratigraphy.org /workinggroups/anthropocene/.

24. H.G. RICHARDSON & G.O. SAYLES, THE GOVERNANCE OF MEDIAEVAL ENGLAND FROM CONQUEST TO MAGNA CARTA 22 (1963) (outlining the shift from Old English law to Norman law). *See also* GRANT, *supra* note 7, at 7–8.

25. The Forest Code was issued in the name of the nine-year-old King Henry III, with the Seals of the Papal Legate and Earl of Pembroke William Marshall as regent, because the young king had no seal for the first two years of his reign. G.J. TURNER, SELECT PLEAS OF THE FOREST ix–cxxxiv (1901), *available at* https://archive.org/details /selectpleasoffor00engluoft. Henry III reissued the Forest Charter on February 11, 1225, and confirmed it in 1227 when he became of full age. Edward I reconfirmed Magna Carta and the Forest Charter in 1297. *See* Magna Carta, 1297, 25 Edw., cc. 1, 9, 29, *available at* http://www.legislation.gov.uk/aep/Edw1cc1929/25/9.

Charter established rules binding William's successors to respect others' rights. It guaranteed rights for commoners (free men, *liber homo*), *and* prescribed procedures to ensure the king's continued compliant observance of these "forest liberties."

The Forest Law[26] exclusively served royal prerogatives,[27] governing the king's dominion over deer and other forest resources. Often arbitrary or avaricious enforcement of Forest Law produced fines and payments, which provided the king with significant revenues, and aroused resistance from barons, the Church, and commoners alike. Kings regularly expanded their Royal Forests by adding adjacent lands to them, and then assessing fines and payments for ongoing uses of those lands from nobles, churchmen, and commoners. Simon Shama observes, "It seems like sylvan gangsterism, and so it was."[28] Early Forest Law was characterized by arbitrary and unjust practices. Exactions of fines and rents, retroactively and unfairly, caused widespread civil strife and contributed to civil wars. King John had promised in chapter 48 of Magna Carta to renounce "all evil customs"[29] in governing the Royal Forests, but then he reneged on this pledge. To address this concern, the Forest Charter was issued to reverse the king's aggrandizement of lands and resources and to restore the "ancient" rights. Among other things, the Forest Charter confirmed the rights of commoners to resources associated with the Royal Forests.[30] Commoners would reassert their rights repeatedly in centuries to come, and parliamentary acts confirmed their "forest liberties."

Successive kings resisted the constraints of the Forest Charter, neglecting it or acting as if it had never been issued. The Tudors later would use the Forest Charter proactively to reassert their prerogatives. As Parliament incrementally acquired its lawmaking powers, it removed the king's authority

---

26. He refers to an extensive body of law based on royal edicts and rulings of royal officials and courts devoted exclusively to the administration of the king's Royal Forests. As much as 25 percent of England in the 13th century was governed by Forest Law, as it comprised Royal Forests. The Forest Law was governed in the Royal Forest separately from the common law, with its own elaborate system of officers and courts. The 12th-century royal treasurer Richard FitzNigel described Forest Law as: "The whole organization of the forests, the punishment, pecuniary or corporal, of forest offenses, is outside the jurisdiction of other courts, and solely dependent on the decision of the king or of some officer especially appointed by him." Richard FitzNigel, Dialogue Concerning the Exchequer 60 (Charles Johnson ed. & trans., London 1960) (*circa* 1180).

27. Kings asserted the law of the forest and the Forest Charter in Wales and Scotland, but in ways that differ from England. The Forest Charter's history outside of England is beyond the scope of this chapter.

28. Simon Schama, Landscape and Memory 148 (1995).

29. *1215 Magna Carta ch. 48, in* Holt, *supra* note 18, at 465.

30. The barons had protected their own interests, but more importantly they provided that "[e]qually, all sections of society might benefit from the Charter of the Forest." D.A. Carpenter, The Minority of Henry III 63 (1990).

to govern the Royal Forests. With changing times, Parliament redefined Forest Law to promote timber production, facilitate private game parks, and allow enclosures of open forest countryside. These measures conflicted with commoners' usufructs for three centuries, but commoners continued to practice their rights to agricultural pasturage or recreational activities (e.g., hiking or "rambling") as best they could. Later, usufructuory rights held in common regained ascendancy. By the 21st century, the Charter's recognition of commoner's "forest liberties"[31] became a principal concern of Parliament. Today, Parliament aims to sustain multiple uses for the once Royal Forests, mediating among the still competing users.

Despite its contested existence, throughout its initial two centuries the Forest Charter provided a legal foundation for socioeconomic life in England. The Forest Charter both regulated a principal source of revenue for the Crown, and confirmed core components of the agrarian production for ecclesiastical holdings and baronial manors, as well as for the livelihoods of the people. In order to finance King John's expensive military ventures, the Crusades and wars with the French, Scots, or Welsh, and his civil wars with the barons, the king enforced Forest Law to raise as much income as possible. Resentful of high-handed tactics of the king's forest officers, the barons resisted when they could, and constrained the king through asserting their Forest Charter rights. Throughout these struggles, the *curia regis* of Norman kings, with its churchmen and barons, evolved so that by Henry III's reign it had become an assembly or a *parliamentum* (a gathering for parlay or colloquy) mostly about war and taxation.[32]

Later monarchs, such as the Tudors and Stuarts, would invoke the Forest Charter to reassert royal prerogatives.[33] Yet by the time Henry VIII (r. 1509–1547) created a Royal Forest at Hampton Court in 1540 for his personal hunting, or Charles I (r. 1625–1649) did so with the Forest of Richmond in 1634, both monarchs were obliged to act with the consent of Parliament. Inaugurated by the Forest Charter, a system of "laws not men" had begun to constrain the monarch in the context of forest governance.

---

31. Some contend that the Forest Charter and Magna Carta were not genuinely concerned with the interests of commoners. Both Charters' formations as statutes are explored in a text-based exegesis on analogies between law and music. Desmond Manderson, *Statuta v. Acts: Interpretation, Music, and Early English Legislation*, 7 YALE J. L. & HUMAN. 317, 317 (1995). Manderson deemed that the Charters' texts lacked norms that spoke to the community as a whole. This view, however, is derived primarily from an analysis of the language in the texts, and is not supported by historical scholarship of communities in the 13th century. *See* KATE NORGATE, THE MINORITY OF HENRY III 250 (1912) and CARPENTER, *supra* note 30, at 60–63.

32. MICHAEL PRESTWICH, EDWARD I 466–68 (1997) (1988). *See also* G.W.S. BARROW, FEUDAL BRITAIN—THE COMPLETION OF THE MEDIEVAL KINGDOMS 1066–1314, at 296–309 (1956).

33. *See* GRANT, *supra* note 7, at 181–203.

When royal prerogatives continued to circumscribe rights held in common, the commoners protested, often with riots in the 17th century.[34]

In the 17th century, individuals who received grants of forest lands and rights from the Crown would invoke rights that they derived from the Forest Charter to justify their aristocratic control of game, with parliamentary sanction.[35] In time, resources within Royal Forests would come to serve wider national objectives, rather than generating income for the king. Laws were enacted to provide timber for the royal navy in the 16th and 17th centuries,[36] and once begun, plantations for timber would persist into the 19th and 20th centuries.

In the 18th century, jurists in Great Britain and abroad took note of the Forest Charter anew. They recalled the commentaries about the Forest Charter in Edward Coke's *Institutes* (1641).[37] More important in setting the stage for parliamentary reforms was the definitive republishing of the texts of the Great Charter and the Charter of the Forests by William Blackstone in 1759.[38] Blackstone made the Forest Charter accessible to all those who studied the common law and the Acts of Parliament. When writing his *Institutes* Coke had been "uncritical and unhistorical,"[39] whereas Blackstone was meticulous, seeking out full texts of both Charters, authenticating their terms, and placing them in historical contexts. Lawyers and courts in the

---

34. Lacking resort to forest courts, which were little used in the 17th century, there were riots by commoners in Rockingham Forest in 1607, Leicester Forest in 1627, Gillingham Forest in 1628–1629, Dean Forest in 1632, and Pendall Forest 1633. *See* BUCHANAN SHARP, IN CONTEMPT OF ALL AUTHORITY: RURAL ARTISANS AND RIOTS IN THE WEST OF ENGLAND 1586–1660 (1980).

35. By the Game Law (1671), freeholds valued at 100 pounds were accorded the right to hunt. JOHN WILLIS BUND, OKES HANDY BOOK OF THE GAME LAWS 25–26 (Butterworth ed., 1912) advises that 69 forests allocating Royal Forest rights to hunt granted by the Crown existed by the 19th century. Extensive private property rights to hunting had replaced the regime of the Forest Charter, such as the Game Act, 1831, 1 & 2 Will. 4, c. 32 § 69. The Forestry (Transfer of Woods) Act transferred the remnant Royal Forests to a newly established Forestry Commission. The Forestry (Transfer of Woods) Act, 1923, 13 & 14 Geo. 5, c. 21 [hereinafter Transfer of Woods Act].

36. JAMES, *supra* note 7, at pt. II. SYLVIE NAIL, FOREST POLICIES AND SOCIAL CHANGE IN ENGLAND Section 1.3.3, at 22–23 (2008).

37. EDWARD COKE, THE FOURTH PART OF THE INSTITUTES OF THE LAWS OF ENGLAND ch. 73 (London, 1671) (2009), available at http://books.google.com/books?id=M _bY7-JOMgAC&printsec=frontcover&source=gbs_ge_summary_r&cad=0#v=onepage &q&f=false.

38. BLACKSTONE, *supra* note 1, was originally published in a presentation edition for the Earl of Westmoreland. Reissued by Oxford University Press. The *Carta de Foresta* appears at page 60.

39. WILLIAM S. MCKECHNIE, MAGNA CARTA: A COMMENTARY ON THE GREAT CHARTER OF KING JOHN 178 (2d ed. 1914).

United States relied on Blackstone's commentaries, sometimes citing the Forest Charter.[40]

In the later romantic age of the 19th century, cultural reimagination "recalled" Royal Forests and the Charter as the "greenwood," a place of freedom and chivalry described in Walter Scott's *Ivanhoe*, or the tales of Robin Hood.[41] Living then increasingly in urban settings, people began to visit forests and the countryside for recreation, appreciation of natural beauty, and nature study. By the late 19th and 20th centuries, the "liberties and customs" guaranteed in chapter 17 of the Forest Charter had evolved to encompass norms for conservation of nature and sustaining biological diversity. Formally repealed in 1971,[42] some of the Charter's original provisions and offices, reconstituted by Parliament, operate still today, such as in the New Forest.[43] Concepts originally found in the Forest Charter reappear today worldwide in policy debates about accessing and sharing the benefits of natural resources.[44]

The rule of law is established, strengthened, and observed in the crucible of conflict. Disputes over the forest repeatedly tested the principles of Carta de Foresta and Magna Carta throughout the 13th and 14th centuries. Contests to vindicate the Forest Charter's liberties served to keep Magna Carta alive. Each time the barons forced the king to adhere to the terms of the Forest Charter, the king was obliged to reissue both Charters and to redisseminate them across the realm. The intensity of the forest struggles carried Magna Carta forward in its early years.

If knowledge of the Forest Charter is scant outside of England, it is because Forest Law under the Charter was a body of royal law, which was found essentially only in England. Forest Law was not received, as was common law, into the law of the British colonies. Moreover, rules regarding governance of game or timber emerged independently in the New World, where there was an abundance of natural resources and no tradition of

---

40. *See, e.g.*, State v. Mallory, 73 Ark. 236, 83 S.W. 955 (1904) (citing Blackstone's *Commentaries on the Laws of England*).

41. SCHAMA, *supra* note 28, at 149–53; J.C. HOLT, ROBIN HOOD (1982).

42. The measure was amended gradually, especially in the 18th and 19th centuries, to vest aspects of the Charter in different new statutes. *See* THE WILD CREATURES AND FOREST LAW 1971, c. 47, http://www.legislation.gov.uk/ukpga/1971/47 (last visited May 20, 2014) (formally repealing the Forest Charter). *See also* NAIL, *supra* note 36, at 18.

43. *See* Verderers of the New Forest, *Verderers' Court in the New Forest*, VERD-ERERS.ORG.UK, http://www.verderers.org.uk/court.html (last visited May 20, 2014) (the Verderers' Court for the New Forest is now a National Park).

44. The third objective of the UN Convention on Biological Diversity is the fair and equitable sharing of benefits arising from the use of genetic resources. Issues of access and benefit-sharing (ABS) are hotly contested among and within nations. *See* United Nations Convention on Biological Diversity, art. 1, 2, 15, 16, 19, June 5, 1992, 1760 UNTS 79, ILM 818, http://www.cbd.int/convention/text (last visited May 20, 2014).

commoners' usufructs against the Crown. Courts cited Blackstone on the status of wild animals,[45] and in cases involving taking wild honey bees, a species (*Apis mellifera*) imported to the colonies from England, which escaped to form wild hives, courts adopted the right established in the Forest Charter to allow capture of wild bee hives in forests.[46] When North American governments made decisions about competing uses of natural resources, it was only natural to create rules tailored to the prevailing local environmental conditions. There was little reason to look to how the Forest Charter constrained the king in England's Royal Forests.[47] More significantly, by the time that legislators in the early United States of America enacted their first laws on fish, game, and forests, they had accepted the fundamental legacy of both Magna Carta and the Forest Charter, that *there shall be public participation in governance over natural resources*. The state's sovereignty is not absolute but it embodies fiduciary duties to govern natural resources in the best interests of the people, with the people.[48] Rule of law principles embodied in these two Charters had become second nature.

---

45. *See, e.g.,* Jeffrey Omar Usman, *The Game Is Afoot: Constitutionalizing the Right to Hunt and Fish in the Tennessee Constitution*, 77 Tenn. L. Rev. 57, 57 (2009–2010) (citing William Blackstone and the Forest Charter).

46. *See, e.g.,* Idol v. Jones, 13 N.C. 162 (2 Dev. 1829); Gillet v. Mason, 7 Johns. 16 (N.Y. Sup. Ct. 1810).

47. Linebaugh, *supra* note 18. Linebaugh bemoans neglect of the Forest Charter in the United States, arguing that the Forest Charter's concerns for justice and the rights of the commons entitled it to some deference, which political forces precluded. Linebaugh, however, misapprehends the Forest Charter's bonding with the forest landscape of England, from which it shaped environmental conservation laws. The Forest Charter's indirect impact in the United States was to advance the principles of the rule of law, and to have repeatedly sustained Magna Carta in its roles confirming liberty, and it is ahistorical to contend otherwise.

48. The U.S. Supreme Court, and other courts, often cited and *in dicta*, referenced the Forest Charter, *see, e.g.*, State v. Mallory 73 Ark 236, 83 S.W. 955 (1904). States, sovereign within their own territory, enacted their own statues for forestry and wildlife. The relevance of the Forest Charter was slight. Roscoe Pound references it obliquely: "Except for Coke's exposition of Magna Carta and the legislation of Edward I, there has been little to do in the way of building a system of legal precepts upon a foundation of authoritative texts." Roscoe Pound, The Formative Era of American Law 97 (1939). When Congress allocated public lands, under the U.S. Constitution's property clause, it often granted wide access to pioneers to explore and develop natural resources. By the end of the 19th century, conservation laws began to constrain development, first in eastern states and then in federal law. Article XIV of the 1894 Constitution of New York established the Adirondack and Catskill Forest Preserve as "forever wild forest land," and New York enacted the first comprehensive statutory code, the NYS Conservation Law, in 1911. Roscoe Pound, An Introduction to the Philosophy of Law 198–99 (1922) (noting that government stewardship of wild game, for example, is "a sort of guardianship for social purposes"). National parks were established for public access and enjoyment, and national forests for their multiple uses, including recreation. These

The Forest Charter's resilience across eight centuries provides insights for understanding contemporary environmental law and policy-making about nature and natural resources. The Forest Charter's norms persisted because the Charter embodied both rights *and* a framework of procedures for adjusting the rights equitably over time, in judicial and legislative settings. It provided a context within which a reciprocity or balancing of competing interests could evolve into stable legal patterns for stewardship of nature, especially for areas protected for nature conservation. Despite the intense pressures of the agricultural and industrial revolutions, and rapid urbanization, England's protected former Royal Forests persist, thanks to the dynamics that the Forest Charter launched.

Relations between humans and nature have always been complex. How should the wealth from harvesting nature's bounty be shared? What measures are required to sustain biological yield and not deplete renewable natural resources? How should revenues be raised for the commonwealth? How does the love of nature, in recreation or appreciation of beauty, find a place in utilitarian or mercantile regimes to exploit nature? How does the rule of law sustain principled means to decide such questions, in place of whim or avarice? These issues of law and policy are strands woven through the life of the Forest Charter.

As a legal instrument consciously allocating rights of access to natural resources and determining correlative entitlements to their benefits, the Forest Charter is a classic environmental statute. Its chapters reflected how society valued nature. They confirmed customary, common rights, and ensured their equitable exercise. Abuses of those rights led to prosecutions as well as to appeals when commoners' rights were abridged. In the course of hearing such cases, the early forest courts and royal councils evolved into judicial or legislative bodies. Being in the form of a statute, the Forest Charter was amenable to revision by a parliament, and over time Parliament duly amended it often, reflecting evolving social values.

Values ascribed to forest ecosystems often coexist, overlap, or conflict. For example, these values include harvesting natural forest products, deriving revenues from the wealth of those harvests, hunting for recreation, grubbing new farmlands out of the woods and heaths, establishing plantations to produce commercial timber, appreciating nature's beauty, studying natural history, securing access for hiking across the countryside, extending new roads for motor vehicles or routing pipelines and power grids to traverse the countryside, preserving cultural landscapes for their own sake, sustaining wildlife corridors and biologically significant habitats, curbing excessive use of chemicals affecting the health of nature and people, safeguarding

---

regimes are conceptually like the regulatory antecedents ensuring access for commoners found in the Forest Charter.

habitats for their intrinsic natural integrity, enhancing forest photosynthesis for sequestering carbon within the global carbon cycle, and providing other ecosystem services locally and transnationally. How best may such competing values be accommodated? Magna Carta and the Forest Charter affirm that it is essential to reconcile competing uses in fair and efficient ways, with a neutral process for doing so sustained by the rule of law.

Today environmental rights have become central to legal discourse.[49] It is instructive to recall how the Forest Charter recognized socioeconomic and civil-political rights in the 13th century. Despite the emergence since the 1970s of the field of environmental law, few legal scholars have reflected upon the Forest Charter. Indeed, scholarship of any sort about the Forest Charter is rather scant.[50] This study invites others to fill this lacuna.

II. 13th-Century Society: The Crucible for Forging the Forest Charter

The Forest Charter cannot be understood apart from knowing the socioeconomic, political, legal, and ecological conditions of 13th-century England.[51] Commoners practiced their customary law rights for the use of forest resources long before the appearance of the Forest chapters of Magna Carta or Carta de Foresta. The Charters confirmed these customary law rights. Therefore, to understand the Forest Charter, one needs to become acquainted with the laws and practices of medieval England. The contours of governance in that age may be briefly recounted.

Feudal society in England after the Norman Conquest formed around the king's royal institutions, the Church both in Rome and locally, the barons and their manors, and the emerging trading centers in London and elsewhere, as well as with peasants (free men, villeins, and others) who labored throughout to sustain the economy of those times. The barons owed obligations to the Crown, both to provide military services, and to pay taxes. The king required substantial and steady income to pay for England's constant warfare, with the Scots, the Welsh, or the French.

In 1066, England had 1.2 million people, and some 15 percent of the land was forested.[52] As William the Conqueror confirmed or parceled his

---

49. A total of 147 nations provide for environmental rights in their constitutions. *See* DAVID. R. BOYD, THE ENVIRONMENTAL RIGHTS REVOLUTION (2012).

50. *See, e.g.,* Luis Kutner, *Charter of the Forest: Forgotten Companion of the Magna Carta,* 6(1) THE COMMON LAW LAWYER, 1, 1–8 (Jan/Feb. 1981).

51. *See generally* CHRISTOPHER DYER, MAKING A LIVING IN THE MIDDLE AGES 850–1520 (2002).

52. NAIL, *supra* note 36, at 3, 7–9; GRAME J. WHITE, THE MEDIEVAL ENGLISH LANDSCAPE 1200–1540, at 1–11 (2012).

conquered lands to nobility in manors or to the Church, he left customary uses by commoners largely as they were. His *Domesday Book* (1086) recorded parts of today's 143 extant Forests that William reserved to serve the Crown.[53] William decreed that Royal Forests were subject only to his law. Wherever the king held court in different parts of England, there was always a nearby Royal Forest to serve up assured supplies of venison, forest or farm produce, fuel, and timber for building his castles and other structures. The king also derived vast political power by allocating or withdrawing lands, particularly parts of Royal Forests, among his vassals. The king held about twice the amount of forestland as all others.[54] He received taxes, fees, and fines, but most importantly could sell or seize forestland to aggrandize his income, finance wars, pay for the large body of his forest administrators, allocate sinecures, and generally exercise political will.

While valuable for the king, Royal Forests were essential to baronial manors, church properties, towns, small landowners, and commoners. None could subsist without the produce of the lands and forests. Since the 12th century, Royal Forests consisted not merely of trees, but included meadows, grasslands, heaths, moors, streams, wetlands, and also cultivated fields, gardens, priories and church lands, villages and farms, and the Roman roads and other byways that crossed the lands, along with longstanding commoners' usufructs for pasturage or collecting wood. Forest landscapes exclusively the king's were royal *demesne*, for his deer or boar hunting or timber harvests. Adjacent common usufructs often overlapped with the king's demesne. Substantial legal effort necessarily was devoted to delimiting each of the various uses, a process known as the "Law of the Forest" that continued for centuries.

The designation as a Royal Forest covered much more than woodlands. Lands in Royal Forests were not fenced; animals and people came and went. When peasants expanded their farmland by grubbing out trees and stumps, they often encroached on the king's demesne, and royal officers would fine such conduct and assess annual payments (*assarts*) in return for granting permission to allow the encroachments to continue.[55] Such unauthorized clearings for expanding farming often competed with other commoners'

---

53. YOUNG, *supra* note 14, at 9 (providing a map of William's initial Royal Forests); OLIVER RACKHAM, THE HISTORY OF THE COUNTRYSIDE 75–88 (1986) (estimating the extent of forest cover); STUBBS, *supra* note 6, at 490 (noting that full extent of the Royal Forest only became clear in 1222, when many are listed in the Patent and Close Rolls); GRANT, *supra* note 7, at 221–29 (recording the Royal Forests and their associated acts for disafforestment).

54. RACKHAM, *supra* note 53, at 131. *The Domesday Book* records that six out of ten parishes held forested lands. *See* RICHARD MABEY, THE COMMON GROUND—THE HISTORY, EVOLUTION AND FUTURE OF BRITAIN'S COUNTRYSIDE 52–63 (1980) [hereinafter THE COMMON GROUND].

55. YOUNG, *supra* note 14, at 93, 109, 121–22.

usufructs, depriving some of them of their sources of fuel or pasturage. Royal measures to curb such *peasant irresponsibility* had the beneficial side effect of protecting forest habitats and maintaining the "ecological balance of the countryside."[56]

Economic entitlements in Royal Forests were specifically accorded their appropriate legal status. Hunting deer and most other large animals (e.g., boar) was "the right of *venison*" (the right to take red and fallow deer), and this right belonged exclusively to the king. The unlawful killing of any animal resulted in a coroner's inquest and prosecutions. Beyond royal hunting, the king supplied his court with meat and fuel from his demesne, as well as timber for his buildings.

Customary law usufructs for forest natural resources were shared by many. None but the king had the right of venison. The commoners' use rights, which often extended into Royal Forests, were for the forest's flora, as "rights of *vert*" (the trees, bushes, understory, and other plants). These usufructs included, for example: collecting bracken (*fugerium*); collecting wood (*estover*); coppicing to produce fuel wood (*robara*); cutting heathland turf for fuel (*tubary*); harvesting bark for tanning; gathering wood for making charcoal and operating iron works and smelters; running pigs in forests (*pannage*) to feed on acorns (*mas*) or beech mast; allowing cattle to graze (*pasturage*) in forest clearings; gathering herbs and berries (*herbage*); harvesting timber for bridges and buildings; preparing charcoal; mining and operating forges; and hunting and fishing. Allowing domestic animals to use Royal Forests was regulated and required payment of fees (*agistment*). *Trespasses against venison* (taking deer) originally resulted in corporal punishment, but by the 12th century it would be punished by heavy fines and imprisonment. *Trespasses against vert* (taking biological products, abuse of pasturage, or wood-cutting) resulted in fines (*amercements*) and confiscation of goods. Those who exceeded what was allowed under their customary rights, as in collecting wood from pollards, committed the offense of "waste" (*vastum*). *For committing waste*, whenever the Forest Eyre[57] was held a woodcutter would be amerced (required to pay a fine) until the damaged trees had grown back to their former state.[58]

---

56. Dyer, *supra* note 51, at 162: "Ultimately the arable land would yield badly, as it was poor land at the outset, better suited for pasture, and would be deprived of nutrients by the shortage of grazing for animals by which manure was produced. By their reckless assarting, it could be said, peasants displayed either short-sighted greed, or desperation."

57. The Forest Eyre was a royal court that convened in the countryside to adjudicate charges that someone had transgressed the Forest Law. As Turner explains, "The Forest Eyre was a court called into being by the king's letters patent appointing justices to hear and determine pleas of the forest in a particular county or group of counties." G.J. Turner, *supra* note 25, at l (1899).

58. Petit-Dutaillis & Lefebvre, *supra* note 6, at 157.

When the king allocated his forestlands to barons or church establishments, different legal regimes then governed such non royal places. These lands were known as parks, chases, or warrens.[59] Private owners had to observe duties comparable to those of the king, and they had to ensure that continuing royal rights were observed. Royal officers would inspect these private properties to ensure that they did not encroach on his legal rights, and to regularly and frequently assess fines and collect rents on unauthorized land uses (*assarts*). Disputes about many of the customary uses of lands in the Royal Forests existed since their creation, and would continue to feature in contemporary conservation disputes, as seen in the New Forest today.

Royal governance of such forest uses required a large bureaucracy, some of which existed even before the Norman Conquest under Edward the Confessor. Whenever the king curbed another person's rights to natural resources, disputes arose. Friction between the Crown and forest users was frequent, and measures to clarify correlative legal rights were taken. For example, the Assize of Woodstock (1184)[60] had proclaimed principles of fairness to resolve disputes and avert renewed instances of unjust treatment.

The king's *Justiciar*, sometimes referred to as the chief justice of the forest, was the king's principal minister, a vice-regent. William established the office of Justiciar as he knew it from its use in his provinces in France. Since the king was often abroad, in his French territories or at war, the Justiciar governed for him in England, supplying the king his revenues and other support. The Justiciar's arbitrary acts on behalf of the king often offended baron and commoner alike. (Edward I finally abolished the post, to eliminate an appearance of injustice. He preferred to exercise power through his chancellor.[61]) Unjust, arbitrary, and capricious application of forest rules contributed greatly to the discontent that produced the rebellions against the king in 1215 and 1216–1217, producing Magna Carta and the Forest Charter.

Royal Forests cannot be understood in today's ecological terms. They were special creations of law, not recognitions of natural places. As *engines* of wealth in a pre-industrial and pre-mercantile age, Royal Forests were of paramount value. The pipe rolls and sheepskin membranes, the written records of the administrative process of collecting royal revenues, were

---

59. MANWOOD, *supra* note 11, states definitions for the different types of protected areas: "chase" at 49, "warren" at 368, and "woods" at 370. G.J. TURNER, *supra* note 25, later restates other accepted legal meanings for "chase," at cix, "warren," and "parks," at cxv. Essentially, a "park" is an area enclosed by a fence; a "chase" is an area of protected lands where the wild animals are not reserved and may be hunted; a "warren" is a land where wild animals are found and where the right to hunt has been conferred selectively.

60. STUBBS, *supra* note 6, at 185.

61. *See* ROY MARTIN HAINES, KING EDWARD II: HIS LIFE, HIS REIGN, AND ITS AFTERMATH 1284–1330, at 287 (2003).

carefully maintained.[62] These records reveal that each king extracted as much wealth from the users of the forests as possible. This governance system was resilient, lasting 500 years. In the 17th century, a Restoration aristocrat characterized woodlands as "an excrescence of the earth provided by God for the payment of debts."[63] The need for securing royal revenues produced the records that tell the story of the Forest Charter.

The Forest Charter confirmed and brought within legal constraints the extensive executive and judicial institutions that the Norman kings established to govern their Royal Forests. These regimes persisted strongly through the Tudors, when Forest Law had become a largely settled subject, and bar and bench alike were accustomed to the practice of the law of the forest. Forest Law was administered through a complex regime, which will briefly be described.

To govern the vast royal enterprises of the Royal Forests (*boscus dominicus regis*), under the king, the Justiciar supervised an administrative headquarters system, the *Capitalis Forestarius*.[64] The duties of the *forest justices*, under the Justiciar, were essentially ministerial, or quasi-judicial, with appeals of their decisions or hearings on major matters coming to the Justiciar. The forest justices governed by convening courts in each forest, and through their agents (the wardens) would see to the release on bail for poachers, hold inquisitions on requests for royal grants, and oversee forest governance. In 1236, the chief justice of the forest's functions were divided, north and south of the river Trent. The offices of the two forest justices continued until abolished by the Act of 1817.[65]

A number of courts convened in the forests. For example, some adjudicated charges of crimes, such as the *attachment courts*, meeting routinely about every 40 days, to hear pleas of violations for which arrests (*attachments*) had been made, and to assess fines for violations of rights of *vert* or to punish escapes of domestic animals into the king's demesne. Some courts were quasi-judicial, and some were like boards convened three times a year to address issues for administration of Forest Law. For example, the *swanimotes* convened foresters, Verderers, and agisters together to arrange for the agistment into the woods of the king's demesne, pannage, for example, and assessing the fees for such. Other assemblies were executive conclaves, royal courts. There were *Special Inquests* regarding individual forest venison offenses, which gathered

---

62. *See* Charles R. Young, *The Forest Eyre in England During the Thirteenth Century*, 18 AM. J. LEGAL HIST. 321, n.3 *passim* (1974) (discussing the records for the Forest Eyres).

63. ROGER MILES, FORESTRY IN THE ENGLISH LANDSCAPE 26 (1967).

64. On the king's administration, *see generally* RICHARDSON & SAYLES, *supra* note 24. The seat of governance is referenced in the Forest Charter chapter 16.

65. Abolition of Certain Officer of Royal Forests Act, 1817, 57 Geo. 3, c. 61; *see* GRANT, *supra* note 7, at 88.

evidence to submit to the Forest Eyre, whether by individuals or townships. The high court, or *Justices in Eyre of the Forest* (also known as the justice seat), eventually came to absorb these other courts.

The king appointed justices to the Forest Court, or *Forest Eyre*, to determine pleas of the forest in various counties concerning *purprestures* or encroachments on royal rights, wastes, and trespasses. All earls, barons, and knights who held land in or near the Royal Forests, and all bishops, and other ecclesiastics in the area were summoned to attend the Forest Eyre. The foresters, Verderers, and agisters attended as well. The Forest Eyre reviewed the king's interests, and heard the forest pleas, which were many and varied.[66] For example, under the Forest Charter,[67] high churchmen and nobility could take two deer while passing through a Forest for their food, but exceeding this amount was prosecuted as venison taken without warrant. Attendance of everyone local at a Special Inquisition or Forest Eyre was required, and amercements were collected from those who failed to attend. Those who failed to attend the Forest Eyre were fined.[68] *General Inquisitions* were held when townships did not fully attend, and fines were assessed. Decisions of the Forest Eyres were recorded, doubtless more to oversee revenues due the king than to report adjudications of rights.[69] By the time of Edward I, legal representatives not yet with legal education were representing noble landholders, appearing in these courts to press pleas.[70] Forest Eyres reviewed claims of illegal exactions, encroachments on the king's rights, payments due for assarts, herbage, timber exports, harms from overgrazing of pastures by domestic animals, waste or destruction of forest resources, and the value of windfalls of wood. Forest Eyres were authorized to convene a jury of 12 knights and free men, which Forest Justices consulted to determine fines (*amercements*). The Forest Eyres received pleas complaining of violations of the Forest Charter, which suggests that there was confidence in the adjudicatory process and judges.[71] These courts were also largely the only pathway open to complain and seek relief.

---

66. *See* G.J. TURNER, *supra* note 25, at 1–131 (reprinting the memorials of the deliberations of the forest justices).

67. *See Forest Charter, supra* note 3, at ch. 11.

68. GRANT, *supra* note 7, at 55.

69. Pipe rolls recorded the financial returns by sheriffs, including rents, fees, and the fines and amercements of the Forest courts. *See, e.g.,* D.J. STAGG, A CALENDAR OF NEW FOREST DOCUMENTS 1244–1334 (1979).

70. 4 THE FOREST OF PICKERING, NORTH RIDING OF THE COUNTY OF YORK xli (Robert B. Turton ed., the North Riding Record Society, 1897).

71. Ralph V. Turner, *John and Justice, in* KING JOHN: NEW INTERPRETATIONS 317, 317 (S.D. Church ed., 1999).

In addition to itinerant eyres and other courts held around, in or near Royal Forests, there were officials residing in each Forest.[72] Under the Justiciar, a *warden* governed one or more Forests, and with the consent of the king could assign portions of his wardenship to others for life. They were the king's executive officers in the Forests, and they delivered venison or wood as directed by the king. Some were hereditary offices, and some also were granted special rights, such as for hunting by falconry. A warden would lose his office if found by the Forest Eyre to have abused it.[73]

To check on the wardens, each Forest also had a set of four *Verderers* (*viridarii*), who reported directly to the king, not to the wardens. They were elected in each county and held office for life, or until removal by the king. Verderers were usually landed barons or knights. Their chief work was to attend the forest courts. *Foresters* were appointed by the wardens, and paid by the warden. Usually numbered at five per Forest, each with an *under-forester* or page, they policed the Forest for trespasses of venison or vert, for poaching and timber removals, and they arrested (*attached*) those found violating royal rights of venison or vert. To pay for a forester's services, the king conveyed rights to receive income to each warden. Examples of such entitlement were collecting bark or wood, or charging fees for required services, such as *chiminage* (the escort of persons through the Forest, as when deer were fawning in the fortnights before and after midsummer). However, as payments were often inadequate to meet their needs, foresters extorted their remuneration from inhabitants of the Forests as they could.

Pleas asserting grievances against foresters and wardens were lodged in inquisitions and eyres, which the Justiciar convened either routinely or at special times. Attendance at those courts also was compulsory for local inhabitants. In each Forest the wardens appointed four *agisters*, to collect money from those who had permission to have their cattle and pigs in the king's demesne fields and woods (*agistments*). They counted the animals allowed into and coming out of the pasturage and pannage.

When the king granted lands from the Royal Forest to barons or to the Church for his military retainers (*boscus bara, boscus priori, boscus mili*), these proprietors of lands (thereafter known as parks, chases, or warrens*)* were obliged to have *woodwards* and other officers (e.g., warreners, reeves, beadles) whose jobs were to police the woods and game to ensure that royal rights were not abridged. Providing services analogous to a royal forester, these private officers served the lord who retained them as well as the king;

---

72. MCKECHNIE, *supra* note 39, at 414. The Forest offices are described in detail in MANWOOD, *supra* note 11, and G.J. TURNER, *supra* note 25, at "*Introduction.*" For other legal institutions, *see generally* GEORGE B. ADAMS, COUNCIL AND COURTS IN ANGLO-NORMAN ENGLAND (1926).

73. GRANT, *supra* note 7, at 94.

the lord of each manor presented these woodwards or other private officials to the king's forest justice to swear an oath to protect the king's interests.

Finally, once in three years an inspection of all the metes and bounds of the Royal Forests was to be conducted by the *regarders*. This *regard*, recognized in the Charter of the Forest,[74] took place when the king ordered an eyre convened, and directed that 12 knights be appointed to investigate and answer to a set of interrogatories about the king's demesne and his rights (known as the chapters of the Regard).[75] *Perambulations* of Royal Forests were held to clarify borders of royal demesne. This audit settled disputes, adjusted rights, and appears to have served a purpose not unlike a contemporary fiscal audit by an auditor-general or *cours des comptes*. Failure of the regarders to make their inspections or report to the Forest Eyre resulted in the eyre assessing fines against them.

To sustain such an elaborate regime for governing the Royal Forests, all kings, and particularly King Henry II (r. 1154–1189) and King John, devoted significant personal attention to appointing and supervising the officers chosen for this forest bureaucracy. King John may have been illiterate,[76] and in any event relied on his scribes and officials to administer his Forest Law regime. As Oliver Rackham notes,

> The Forests were of more than merely economic value to the king. Medieval kings were poor, and their authority depended on the power to make gifts of a kind money could not buy, such as deer and giant oaks. The Forest hierarchy gave the king unlimited opportunities to reward those who served him well with honorific sinecures.[77]

For example, in 1204 King John disafforested much of the Dartmoor Royal Forest to the benefit of the Earls of Cornwall and commoners, in order

---

74. *Forest Charter, supra* note 3, at ch. 5.

75. Richard FitzNigel, *Dialogus de Scaccario et Constitutio Domus Regis of 1177, in* THE DIALOGUE OF THE EXCHEQUER AND THE ESTABLISHMENT OF THE ROYAL HOUSE-HOLD 90–91 (Emilie Amt & S.D. Church transl. & eds., 2008): "Indeed, the law of the forest, and the monetary or corporal punishment of those who transgress there, or their absolution, is separate from the rest of the kingdom's judicial system, and is subject to the sole judgment of the king or his especially appointed deputy. For it has its own laws, which are said to be bases on the will of princes, not on the law of the whole kingdom, so that what is done under Forest Law is called just according to Forest Law, rather than absolutely just." It was not just the rights of access that were clarified by the forest per-ambulations and regards, to inspect and make clear the borders, but also which body of justice would apply. *See also* STUBBS, *supra* note 6, at 201.

76. CLAIRE BREAY, MAGNA CARTA: MANUSCRIPTS AND MYTHS 38 (2002).

77. RACKHAM, *supra* note 53, at 138. This process continued into the future. Rack-ham notes: "Was not Chaucer, in the middle of a busy life, made under-Forester of an obscure Somerset Forest?"

to secure funds for his wars with France.[78] Such grants of Royal Forest lands raised funds but also led to expanding of farming and economic production in England. These developments incrementally reduced some forest cover while conserving the rest.

Changes in forest use also often led to new disputes. Incursions into the adjacent Royal Forests were frequent, and often led to fines or were allowed on the condition that annual payments (*assarts*) would be made. Disputes often led to civil unrest and armed conflict, including questions about who should serve in the various Forest offices described above. In the period immediately following the Conquest, Norman *familiares* were unacceptable in some regions, especially in Northern England. Administration of this vast and complex regime was problematic. Kings Henry II and John made governance of their Royal Forests a personal high priority, because their income and power depended upon it.[79]

Until the 19th century, all kings after William the Conqueror expanded the Royal Forest to aggrandize their assets. These expansions of forest boundaries were called "*afforestation*." By expanding the borders of a Royal Forest, land was removed from the common law and placed under the Forest Law, and became the king's royal demesne. The barons and commoners alike resisted afforestation whenever they could. At each coronation, before swearing oaths of fealty, the barons demanded that each new king acknowledge past wrongs under Forest Law, including various afforestations. A Charter of Liberties had been granted by Henry I (r. 1100–1135) on his coronation in 1100, which attests to the early and ongoing political sensitivity associated with unjust management of uses of the Royal Forests. Henry I's Charter of Liberties (also referred to as the Coronation Charter, an English-language translation of which appears in this book as appendix A) had required that the bounds of the Royal Forest be restricted to the Royal Forests' limits as they had been established at the death of his father, William the Conqueror. This test became the benchmark for the legitimate boundaries of Royal Forests. As they assumed the crown, new kings conceded past inequities in governing the Royal Forests and agreed to inspections necessary to undertake "*disafforestation*." Implementing the promise to return to William's limitations on Royal Forests, however, was invariably prolonged and delayed. Meanwhile, the king collected his revenues, and his forest officers conducted business as usual.

Notwithstanding promises to maintain ancient limits to the Royal Forests, Henry II and his successors repeatedly engaged in afforestation, thereby increasing their revenues through additional collections of fees, rents, and fines, or grants of land. A contemporary observer, Radulfi Nigri, recorded

---

78. NAIL, *supra* note 36, at 13.
79. HOLT, *supra* note 18.

that Henry II used his royal powers to amass new sources of income: "His greed was never sated; having abolished the ancient laws, he issued new laws each year, and called them assizes."[80] Significant expansions of the lands held within Royal Forests, and the exactions that forest officers and courts collected, prompted opposition. Barons often invoked their ancient rights demanding disafforestations, citing the Charter of Liberties granted by Henry I. On King John's coronation, the barons invoked Henry I's Charter of Liberties, and John agreed in principle that the boundaries of the Royal Forests would be disafforested and restored to William's forest borders.[81]

In the decades following the reign of William the Conqueror, as the population grew, so did the ranks of forest users, and disputes as well. When the barons would express their own distress, they increasingly were the virtual representatives of all others who used the forests, commons, or church alike. In the 13th century, the well-being of all depended on the yields of agriculture and silvaculture by the commoners and small landholders, as well as villeins on manorial estates. If the king exacted too large a part of the Forest's income, this caused shortfalls in what was available to others.

This entire Royal Forest regime was largely independent of the common law, or of the governance by sheriffs in each shire, or by manorial courts. It was a powerful socioeconomic and political force. It persisted for decades after the Forest Charter was issued, albeit declining in vigor. By 1327, royal acceptance of the Forest Charter's rights had been sufficiently acknowledged such that Forest Eyres and Regards were held less often.[82]

From a social perspective, the customary law usufructs of the commoners, confirmed in the Forest Charter, were of more lasting importance than the king's institutional systems to extract royal revenues. In feudal times, the king's legitimacy formally rested on the papal endorsement of each king's coronation oaths, but the king's temporal power depended on the feudal obligations of "knight service," that is, military service given by his barons, which over time was satisfied by a monetary payment (*scutage*), since increasingly the king hired mercenaries paid using royal income. The economy of the forest was at the foundation of these complex and interrelated aspects of feudal political power. The growth of London, its trade, and the economy of money rather than an economy of feudal services undermined

---

80. RADULFUS, RADULFI NIGRI CHRONICA (THE CHRONICLES OF RALPH NIGER) 13 (Robert Anstruther ed., publications of the Caxton Society 1967) (1851).

81. This Charter abrogates "evil customs" and promises an end to unjust practices. It divided lands for which military service was required from lands that could be taxed. In chapter 10 it provided that "I retain in my hand, by the common consent of my barons, my forests as my father had them." By such an acknowledgment, the barons ensured that King John would not hold greater space. STUBBS, *supra* note 6, at 116.

82. YOUNG, *supra* note 14, at 151. The statute of 1327 was reaffirmed when Richard II (r. 1377–1399) accepted the Royal Forest boundaries of his grandfather in 1383.

medieval obligations of fealty. Commoners' traditional usufructs persisted, grounded as they were in the relationships of humans with the forests.

Norman feudal legal relationships already had changed and had become muddled by the beginning of the 13th century. The mix of Norman laws with older Anglo-Saxon rules and customary practices, together with legal innovations by kings, such as the announcement of new Forest rules for pannage or chiminage at the Eyre of 1198 in the northern counties, led to disagreements about what laws governed conduct in Royal Forests. One contemporary observer bemoaned how the king's need for money for his wars in Normandy depleted everyone's assets, and complained that new rules announced at the Eyre of 1198 were a "torment for the confusion of the men of the realm."[83] Disagreement about the content of the rights in the Royal Forests was widespread.[84]

As the first decade of the 13th century opened, the barons' frustration regarding perceived unjust or arbitrary actions by King John and his forest officers mounted. Several barons were in open rebellion. In a realm accustomed to arguing about laws to justify exercises of power, it is perhaps not surprising that two legal charters would become the tools used to settle the English civil wars of 1214–1217. Carta de Foresta emerged to establish justice.

III.   The Creation of the Forest Charter

What is less predictable is how Magna Carta and the Forest Charter would establish the foundations for the evolution of the social contract in England through the rule of law,[85] or that the Forest Charter would establish norms for just relations between crucial parts of an economy grounded in natural resources. Both Charters protected the rights of commoners and their land holdings,[86] empowering barons and commoners alike in their recurring

---

83. GRANT, *supra* note 7, at 20 (quoting Hoveden, (Rolls Sr.) IV 63–65).

84. These claims to competing authority have been explored in analysis of the languages through which they were asserted. *See* Scott Kleinman, Frid *and* Fredom: *Royal Forests and the English Jurisprudence of Laȝmon's* Brut *and Its Readers*, 109 MODERN PHILOLOGY 17, 17–45 (2011), http://www.jstor.org/stable/10.1086/661955 (last visited May 20, 2014).

85. When Henry III reissued the Forest Charter and Magna Carta in 1225, based on his "spontaneous and free will, he was sealing a contract with society." "[T]he new Charters being part of a mutual bargain between the king and his realm. This was because they had been paid for. As the Charters themselves stated, in return for the concession of liberties, everyone in the kingdom had granted the king a fifteenth of their movable property." CARPENTER, *supra* note 30, at 383.

86. Articles 39 and 40 of Magna Carta provide that no freeman shall lose (be disseized of) his freehold except by due process of law.

disputes with the king. Throughout generations of contested decisions about Royal Forests, the Forest Charter produced the collateral benefit of stabilizing large tracts of forest countryside that have endured for a millennium.

When King John met the rebellious barons at Runnymede, he conceded forest rights in three chapters of Magna Carta.[87] Chapter 44 excused all but the accused from being summoned to attend the Forest Eyres, attendance at which had been mandatory since the Assize of Woodstock. This freed up the time of all and prevented the king from fining those who did not attend court sessions. Chapter 47 provided that all forests made under King John "shall forthwith be disafforested," and that riverbanks placed "in defense" would be made open to public use again. Chapter 48 mandated an inquiry by 12 sworn knights, chosen by honest men in each county, into "all evil customs concerning forests and warrens" and mandated that such evils be abolished within 40 days of the inquest, provided King John would be informed and would be present in England rather than being abroad, as for war or crusade. On the same day that Magna Carta was issued, the barons obliged King John to issue writs to his sheriffs directing them to select knights to hold the local inquiries into evil customs and issues of disafforestation. Some knights began this work.[88]

Once King John left Runnymede, he sought to undo all that he had agreed to do. As noted above, he convinced Pope Innocent III to annul Magna Carta, which occurred on August 24, 1215. (Pope Innocent III also excommunicated the barons and suspended Archbishop Stephen Langton, who had facilitated the agreement on Magna Carta.[89]) Moreover, when Henry III's guardians issued a new version of Magna Carta in 1216, these three chapters on forests were deleted (as were some other chapters). When King John disavowed Magna Carta, including the chapters of forest rights, he signaled his disrespect for the entire pact agreed upon at Runnymede. John called upon loyal barons and his mercenaries to continue his civil war with the rebellious barons. The continuing civil war in England was

---

87. *1215 Magna Carta chs. 44, 47, 48, in* HOLT, *supra* note 18, at 463 and 465.

88. J. C. Holt, among others, surmises that the detail of the provisions of the Forest Charter is evidence that the inquires of at least some of the knights commissioned by Magna Carta to investigate the grievances that arose during the reign of King John had resulted in reports that were reduced to the separate chapters of the Forest Charter. *See, e.g.,* HOLT, *supra* note 18, at 384–85; Holt observes: "The work of the commissions of 1215 must have been even more valuable in compiling the Charter of the Forest." Except for chapter 2 of the Forest Charter, "the rest were new and they carried the regulation of the forest law far beyond anything considered or even suggested in any of the earlier documents."

89. G.W.S. BARROW, FEUDAL BRITAIN 204–09, 258–59 (1956). *See also* G.B. Adams, *Innocent III and the Great Charter, in* MAGNA CARTA COMMEMORATIVE ESSAYS 26 (Henry Elliot Malden, ed., 1917).

complicated in 1216 by the invasion of Prince Louis of France, the future Louis VIII (r. 1223–1226).

King John's unexpected death on October 19, 1216, prompted renewed negotiations between the Crown and the barons. Amidst the continuing civil war and invasion by Louis of France, William Marshal, the Earl of Pembroke, with other barons managed to restore the kingdom's governance. John's nine year-old son, Henry, was crowned king by the papal legate Gaulo (sometimes spelled Gaula). William Marshal became *Rector Regis et Regent*, and managed to reunify the barons who had fought for and against King John. In the name of young Henry III, Marshal reissued a shortened Charter of Liberties (without the forest chapters) over Marshal's own seal and that of Gaulo, to legitimize the new king and win support of barons loyal to John. Louis' invasion was reversed; he lost a significant naval battle and lacked sufficient munitions to continue. In September of 1217, having negotiated the Treaty of Kingston (Lambeth), Marshal and the curia regis, in the presence of Gaulo, agreed with Louis that he would abandon his claim to the English crown and return to France in 1217.[90]

At this point, William Marshal consolidated support for the regency. In 1217, the regency made possible both the reissue of Magna Carta (without the forest provisions, as noted above) and the issuance of the new Carta de Foresta, which expanded the forest rights of commoners and others, in order to end the excesses of the king's administration of Forest Law. As Professor J.C. Holt has observed, the 1215 Magna Carta was the work of King John's enemies, but the 1216 and 1217 Magna Cartas and the Carta de Foresta were the work of King Henry III's friends and supporters.[91]

The barons who had begun to investigate abuses of ancient rights under chapter 48 of Magna Carta had evidently compiled sufficient reports about abuses of rights that these could form the basis for drafting the more detailed rules for the Forest Charter. The barons had drafts of express forest liberties that they wished to confirm and have observed. As Professor Holt notes, "it is unlikely that such lengthy regulations could have been drawn up so soon after the civil war without some kind of documentary preparation."[92] No records have been found to document the actual drafting of the Forest Charter, but its provisions speak for themselves. They are significantly stricter on the king than his three abjured Magna Carta articles.

As regent, just two years before he died, William Marshal arranged for Henry III to proclaim the Forest Charter on November 6, 1217.[93] For the next six years, forest disputes receded as the Crown, the barons, the Church,

---

90. Kate Norgate, The Minority of Henry III 58–60, 279–80 (1912).

91. Holt, *supra* note 18, at 378.

92. *Id.* at 384–85.

93. The history of this era is well documented. *See, e.g.,* Thos. Pitt Taswell-Langmead, English Constitutional History 112–16 (1905).

and the commoners restored post-war relations. Nonetheless, old habits die hard, and the Crown's forest officers engaged in renewed arbitrary actions, and violations of the Forest Charter recurred. The archbishop of Canterbury, with support of the barons, exhorted Henry III to reissue the Forest Charter. When William Briwere, one of the king's counselors, resisted, saying that concessions extorted by force might not be observed, the archbishop replied: "William, if you loved the King you would not disturb the peace of the kingdom."[94] On February 11, 1225, the Forest Charter was reissued, along with Magna Carta, each over Henry III's own seal.

At the time, Henry III had an urgent need for funds to confront French aggression, and he agreed to issue the Charters in return for which the barons agreed to provide the funds he required, a fifteenth of their moveable property. Blackstone cites contemporaneous historical accounts: "Matthew Paris informs us, that an original great charter under seal was sent to every county in England, and to those which had forests within them a charter of the forest was sent also."[95] In fact, the king ordered his sheriffs to proclaim and obey the Charters at the same time that he ordered them to assess and collect the tax. Indeed, crusaders were told that their heirs could not enjoy the liberties of the Charters unless they paid the tax.[96] This became known as the Forest Charter of 1225. It was indeed a social contract.

Yet, no sooner had Henry III reissued the Charters, he and his successor Edward I chose to ignore or renounce them when they thought they could get away with doing so. When Henry became of legal age in 1228, he neglected (some contend he annulled) both the Charters, on the grounds that they had been issued during the regency (even though the 1225 charters had been issued over his own seal), and he also reversed disafforestments made during his minority.[97] Then in 1236, when the Crown again sorely needed funds, the barons prevailed on him to reconfirm the Charters, acknowledging that he did so notwithstanding that they were issued during his minority. This pattern was to recur throughout Henry III's reign, with subsequent confirmations of the Charter issued in 1251, 1253, and 1264, each time largely because the king needed financial support from his barons. Each resulted in royal concessions, including measures for disafforestations. Gradually, the terms of the Forest Charter were becoming well known throughout the realm.

Despite the guarantees of Forest Charter liberties, unjust enforcement of Forest Law produced new conflict in the countryside. To stay the unrest, Edward I reconfirmed the Charter while abroad on November 5, 1297, and

---

94. BOYD C. BARRINGTON, THE MAGNA CARTA AND OTHER CHARTERS OF ENGLAND 165 (1900).

95. *Id.* at xlv.

96. *See* CARPENTER, *supra* note 30, at 383.

97. *Id.* at 392–95.

was forced to do so again in person on his return to England in 1298. He also was compelled to name commissioners and perambulators to inspect the Royal Forest's boundaries.[98] Edward convened a parliament in 1300 to receive his commissioners' report and then once again issued the two Charters. Their legal standing was becoming indisputable, and there was continuing popular intolerance of unjust enforcement of Forest Law or afforestation.

King Edward I reconfirmed the Charter because he needed funds for his battles with France and then the Scots. He had increased taxes on the clergy, merchants of wool and leather, and the barons. The Church joined the barons in their complaints. Edward also revived a tax on towns and those living in royal demesne (*tallage*), and imposed duties on merchants. As he assessed fines and collected taxes, complaints about violations of the Forest Charter escalated.[99] The king resisted the *monstraunces*, or protests, filed by the earls and barons, but in 1297 the Crown published royal letters patent confirming Magna Carta and the Forest Charter "in all points."[100] The Charters were ordered to be read aloud in every cathedral church twice a year.[101] Perambulations undertaken under King Edward I in 1297 brought some relief; they determined, for example, that half of the Forest of Dean was not Royal Forest, and so for Bernwood and elsewhere.[102]

When he died in 1307, Edward's continued confirmation of the Forest Charter had come to be matched by his acceptance of parliamentary assemblies, which met now to "assent and enact" (*consentiendum et faciendum*) the law. In the estimation of Williams Stubbs, the constitutional "machinery" of England was now complete.[103] David Carpenter concurs: by 1225 the king knew he "was subject to the law. It was neither 'fitting nor right' for him to act unjustly."[104] Those governing then knew that Charters would become a permanent feature of English political life, which "laid tracks for the future but also sealed up the divisions of the past."[105] Although still honored too often in the breach, the terms of the Forest Charter of 1225 would stay intact until Parliament would amend them centuries later.

---

98. YOUNG, *supra* note 14, at 124–25, 136–45.

99. *Id.* at 157–59.

100. G.W.S. BARROW, FEUDAL BRITAIN—THE COMPLETION OF THE MEDIEVAL KINGDOMS 1066–1314, at 382 (1956).

101. HOLT, *supra* note 18, at 400–05.

102. Perambulations were repeatedly demanded by barons and acceded to by the king. YOUNG, *supra* note 14, at 135–48. For example, the Forest of Essex benefited from perambulations in 1224, 1225, 1228, 1277, 1298, 1299, 1301, 1333–1335, and thereafter. WILLIAM RICHARD FISHER, THE FORESTS OF ESSEX 18–52 (London, Butterworths 1887), *available at* https://archive.org/details/forestessexitsh00fishgoog.

103. STUBBS, *supra* note 6, at 54–56.

104. CARPENTER, *supra* note 30, at 386.

105. *Id.* at 386, 388.

IV. Substantive Provisions of the Forest Charter

The Forest Charter proclaimed forest *liberties* with such clarity that those holding the rights could assert them through the Forest Eyres. The recurring struggles applying the Charter of the Forest to the king's Forest Law were proving grounds for Magna Carta. Professor Holt observes that issues of disafforestation remained contentious throughout the 12th and 13th centuries: "Indeed, the repeated demand for disafforestation was one of the main reasons for the periodical confirmation of the Charters from 1225 on to the end of the reign of Edward I. The Forest Charter, and the particular issue of disafforestation helped to keep the Magna Carta alive."[106] Ch. Petit-Dutaillis similarly observes, "It was principally the struggle for disafforestment which connected the history of the Forest with the history of the English constitution."[107] In its first 200 years of life, the Forest Charter provided the principal legal framework in which rule of law principles could take shape in practice. In this early period, Magna Carta provided only incidental support for the Forest Charter. Centuries later the relationship of each Charter would reverse.

The two charters were interdependent. Pleas of the forest would invoke Magna Carta as grounds for mitigating enforcement excesses. Forest justices had long assessed the amounts of amercements with regard to the social status and wealth of the offender. Under chapter 20 of Magna Carta, a freeman's fines were to be an amount that he could afford to pay "saving his livelihood."[108] Invoking this provision constrained the Crown's interest in raising as much revenue as it could from pleas heard in a Forest Eyre.[109]

Pleas litigated under the Forest Laws incrementally fostered respect for law by claiming rights under the Charters. The Forest Charter's importance today lies less in its particular provisions than in the fact that it defined the legal space within which competing rights could be contested and through which social order could be sustained. As Professor Holt further observed, "The forest provisions of the Great Charter of 1215 and the Charter of the Forest of 1217 marked an assertion of custom and the establishment of law in a field recognized hitherto as totally dependent on the will of the king."[110] Establishing respect for the rule of law does not happen in the abstract. It occurs and is reaffirmed in context, when concrete adverse interests can apply existing law to settle ongoing disputes. It depends on knowing one's

---

106. HOLT, *supra* note 18, at 386.

107. PETIT-DUTAILLIS & LEFEBVRE, *supra* note 6, at vol. II, chs. 6,7,8.

108. *1215 Magna Carta ch. 20, in* HOLT, *supra* note 18, at 457.

109. *See* Young, *supra* note 62, at 327–28.

110. HOLT, *supra* note 18, at 53. *Accord* FITZNIGEL, *supra* note 26, at 60 (confirming that the Forest Laws were not based on or governed by Common Law but were exclusively at the will of the king).

rights. The provisions of the Forest Charter and Magna Carta were well known, since both were repeatedly copied, sent throughout the realm, and read aloud together.[111] Adjudicating the pleas of the forest bred respect for commoner's rights and forged foundations for the rule of law.

The text of the Forest Charter is extraordinary because it speaks to the rights and interests of the people more than those of the Crown, the law-giver. A chance occurrence made this politically possible. The sudden death of King John, and the succession of nine-year old Henry to the throne, provided the collective leadership of the regency with the opportunity to legislate terms to settle the raging forest disputes through proclaiming the new Forest Charter. Henry's Regent, William Marshal, Earl of Pembroke, had been with the barons at Runnymede. At and after Henry's coronation, he administered the realm to bring the Crown and barons into accord on what rights and liberties could avoid the injustices experienced under Forest Law. By 1225, when Henry III reissued the Forest Charter *spontanea et bona voluntate nostra*, the Forest Charter had become an acknowledged legal bond between the Crown and the barons.[112]

The Forest Charter consists of 17 chapters addressed to two groups: (a) those who hold and use lands subject to the Forest Law (i.e., the archbishops, bishops, abbots, priors, earls, and barons); and (b) those officers whose discretion is now fettered by the restrictions of the Forest Charter, as the Charter's salutation recites the justiciars, foresters, sheriffs, reeves, ministers, "*et omnibus ballivis et fidelibus suis.*"[113] The terms of the Forest Charter of 1217 restricted the king more severely than had the three forest chapters of Magna Carta in 1215. Only one forest provision from Magna Carta (chapter 44) was carried over into the Forest Charter: in chapter 2. All the rest of the Forest Charter was new, and it confirmed customary law rights against rights of the Crown. Through the Forest Charter, the king pardoned past offenses and reversed the assarts and purprestures on private properties since Henry II's reign,[114] and assured the rights of those with legal usufructs in the Royal Forests.[115] Most significantly, the Forest Charter immediately decreed disafforestment of the lands added to Royal Forests by Kings Richard I (r. 1189–1199) and John beyond the boundaries of the Royal Forests of 1087, when William the Conqueror died. To implement this disafforestment, the Forest Charter

---

111. Faith Thompson, The First Century of Magna Carta 63 (1925).

112. Henry III also "put on record the grant of a fifteenth of moveables made to him in return for this 'concession and donation' on his part." Kate Norgate, The Minority of Henry III 250 (1912). The barons would not make the payments the king needed without the issuance again of the Forest Charter and Magna Carta.

113. *Forest Charter, supra* note 3, at salutation ("to all bailiffs and our other faithful subjects.").

114. *Id.* at chs. 4 and 15.

115. *Id.* at chs. 9, 12, 13, and 17.

required an inquest "by good and lawfull men"[116] of the afforestments of Henry II, to determine which were to be disafforested. Only William's demesne was to remain Royal Forest. Whereas Magna Carta in 1215 had deferred disafforestments of areas acquired by Henry II and Richard I, the 1217 Charter decreed immediate disafforestment and enabled many future perambulations that were to restore rights upon which kings had encroached. A procedure to enforce Forest Charter rights existed, and would be used repeatedly.

The Forest Charter's separate articles, or chapters, may be restated from their Latin text and summarized, in plain English with chapter numbers added for easier reference, as follows:[117]

1. The common right of gathering herbs and berries in the forests (*herbage*) is preserved, even in the king's Royal Forest domain (*demesne*), and all Henry II's expansions of his Royal Forest domain (*afforestations*) are to be reversed following an independent inspection.

2. Those who live in or near the Forests no longer must attend sessions of the Forest Courts (*eyres*) when these itinerant courts come to their area, unless they have been charged with an offense or are sureties for those charged. This frees all from the threat of being fined (*amerced*) for failure to appear, and frees up significant amounts of time.

3. All expansions of Royal Forests (*afforestations*) under Kings Richard and John are reversed immediately. Existing procedures for the physical inspections of Royal Forest boundaries (*perambulations*) provided a means to enforce this provision, and restore lands that had been unjustly taken.

4. All holdings by ecclesiastic, noble, and free holders (*libere tenentes*), as they were at the time of the coronation of Henry are to be restored, and any fines, rents, and fees assessed on these lands are forgiven; unauthorized land uses (*purprestures*), degradation of resources (*wastes*), and compulsory payments, like rents (*assarts*) required for those uses, as they were in existence from the second year after Henry III's coronation, are to be assessed and paid. This set limits on what the Crown could claim for revenues.

5. Inspections of the Royal Forests (*regards*) are to be held in accordance with the practices as prescribed at the time of the coronation of Henry II, every three years regularly. This restores traditionally accepted procedures, and restricts the king to follow only this procedure.

---

116. *Id.* at ch. 1.
117. *Id.* (in its entirety).

6. Formal investigations (*inquiry*) to determine who possesses dogs near Royal Forests is constrained, and the practice of removing the toes of dogs ("lawing"), ostensibly to keep them from chasing and killing the king's deer is curbed, and allowed only where the practice was in force as of the coronation of Henry II, and when a dog is found the cutting is limited to three toes cut from the front foot. The fine for having dogs whose toes have not been removed (unlawed) is set at three shillings, and no longer may an ox be taken for the lawing of a dog. Hunting or traveling through Royal Forest with dogs remains banned.

7. Foresters may not collect exactions of grains or sheep or pigs. The number of foresters is to be determined by the 12 knights chosen for conducting investigations (*regarders*) during their inspections of Royal Forests.

8. Councils to supervise the introduction of domestic animals into the forests [*Swanimote* courts, from an old Anglo-Saxon word, "swainmote," meaning a meeting of swineherders] are to be held regularly three times a year, to arrange for the counting (*agistment*) of the pigs that enter the Royal Forest for eating mast and acorns (*pannage*), or to manage commoners' usufructs to ensure no disturbance of allowing for mating and fawning of deer. Foresters and Verderers are to meet every 40 days to deal with arrests for offenses of killing or hunting deer (trespasses of *venison*) or harvesting vegetation without authority (trespasses of *vert*).

9. Every free man (*liber homo*) can let his animals use (*agist*) his own forestlands located within Royal Forests at will, and can drive his pigs through the Royal Forest to allow them to reach places to eat acorns (*pannage*), and if a pig strays into the Royal Forest for a night, it shall not be an offense.

10. No one shall lose life or suffer loss of limbs as punishment for killing a deer. [The old penalty, still allowed in 1198, had been loss of eyes and testicles, but in place of dismemberment, severe fines had become preferred in the 13th century.[118]] The person who kills a deer shall be fined and if he cannot pay a fine, he shall be imprisoned for a year and a day. He can then be released, if he posts sureties, but if he cannot do so then he is to be exiled.

11. Archbishops, bishops, earls, and barons traversing Royal Forests may take one or two deer, in view of the foresters, for their own use, and may blow horns to scare up deer or show when they are not hunting.

12. On his own land and with his own access to water within a Royal Forest, every freeman (*liber homo*) can make a mill, fishpond, dam,

118. *See* Griffin, *supra* note 18, at 16.

marsh pit, or dike, or reclaim arable ground, without danger of constituting an offense under the Forest Law, so long as it is not a nuisance to any of his neighbors.

13. Within his own lands located in Royal Forests, every free man (*liber homo*) can have eyries and nests of hawks, and other birds, and may take any honey from wild bee trees discovered in the forest.

14. Only a forester who holds his office by hereditary right (*forester in fee*) can escort persons through a Royal Forest and take a fee for doing so (*cheminage*) or collect a toll, which is set for carriage by a cart at two pence per half year, and for a horse a half penny per half year. Persons carrying their brush or bark or charcoal on their backs shall pay no fee (*cheminage*), unless they are removing it from the king's domain in a Royal Forest (*demesne*).

15. All offenses committed during the time of Henry II to the coronation of Henry III are pardoned, but those pardoned must find sureties to pledge that they shall not commit new violations.

16. Procedures for handling offenses are regularized. No warden of a castle may hold a court to enforce Forest Law or to hear pleas of the Forest, and foresters who make arrests (*attachments*) must present them to the Verederes, who will make a record and present them to the forest justices when Royal Forest Courts (*Eyres*) are held to determine forest pleas.

17. These liberties of the forest (*libertates de forestis*) and free customs traditionally had (*consuetudines predictas et libertates*), both within and without the Royal Forests, are granted to ecclesiastics, nobles, freeholders, and all in our realm (*omnes de regno nostro*), in short to everyone. Everyone is also obliged to observe the liberties and customs granted in the Forest Charter.

With these 17 specific, succinct, and clear provisions, the Forest Charter established the terms for a just society in the critical context of forest governance in 13th-century England. These terms would remain intact for the next 500 years and more. The Charter's requirements that the afforestations of Kings Henry II, Richard I, and John be disafforested meant that these lands would be removed from under the Forest Law and returned to the realm of the common law, and to their prior proprietors.[119] Previous royal grants of privileges for clergy and nobles were confirmed.[120] Past injustices were erased when amercements for offenses in the reign of Henry II were remitted and amnesties granted.[121] Prospectively, restrictions on the

---

119. *Forest Charter, supra* note 3, at chs. 1, 3.
120. *Id.* at ch. 17.
121. *Id.* at chs. 4, 15.

use of the forest's produce were reformed.[122] Very limited hunting rights were accorded to landed nobility.[123] Rules for Forest Court proceedings were regularized[124] and penalties clarified.[125] Unlawful exactions and other evils and malpractices of foresters were prohibited.[126]

The Forest Charter's provisions for commoners hold continuing importance. The Charter made numerous references to customary rights of commoners, such as herbage, estover, pannage, pasturage, and other usufructs. When the barons insisted on confirming rights that would benefit all of the people in the 13th century, they set society on a path for ensuring public rights generally. Parliament's later mandate to represent the people is forecast in chapters of the Forest Charter privileging commoners. When the Forest Charter established liberties of the forest for all, rights that sustain their economic and social lives, the Charter also anticipated what today is expressed in human rights instruments.[127] The open-ended provision of chapter 17 in the Forest Charter, guaranteeing the "liberties of the forest" and "free customs," allowed future generations to elaborate and evolve new definitions of these liberties and shared rights.

Important also was that the Forest Charter acknowledges the legitimacy of the king's demesne, his core holdings in the Royal Forests. There is a reciprocity between the king and the people. The Forest Charter insists that its terms be observed by the people, as well as by the Crown. King Henry III used this duty to resist disafforestments that encroached on his demesne. Moreover, by appearing to defend the rights of commoners, the Crown "could hope to win favour of sections of society below the magnates."[128]

Because the Forest Charter confirmed that the king's Royal Forests were his legitimate sovereign estate, these forest areas were protected against development. The environmental stewardship implicit in this has not been acknowledged, but it should be. In retrospect, this acknowledgment has been fundamental over the centuries in stabilizing the Royal Forests as what we now call protected areas. They were largely removed from what became a marketplace in land (except for the Crown's own disafforestments), and everyone regarded them as being set aside under a special governance regime.

In 1225, the Forest Charter's recognition of Royal Forests was also a concession to the king's ancient rights, legitimizing the Royal Forests with the borders that William the Conqueror had established. Once the ancient

---

122. *Id.* at chs. 9, 12, 13.
123. *Id.* at ch. 11.
124. *Id.* at chs. 2, 8, 16.
125. *Id.* at ch. 10.
126. *Id.* at chs. 5, 7, 14.
127. Guarantees of economic and social rights, as human rights, are today found in the Universal Declaration on Human Rights, and the two Covenants bring these rights into public international law.
128. CARPENTER, *supra* note 30, at 386–87.

metes and bounds of the king's demesne were confirmed, Carta de Foresta provided that the king had to observe customary law usufructs therein. Chapter 1 recites that, although the king's demesne is acknowledged, existing common rights of herbage, and other uses in the forest, are secured. These rights of "free men" persist to the present, as is seen today in the New Forest.

Finally, the terms of the Forest Charter are prescient in the ways that they linked rights to procedure for vindicating those rights. When kings resisted observing Forest Charter rights, recourse to these procedures provided avenues to seek justice. Although often ineffective, by repeatedly invoking their rights through available procedures, commoners and barons over time won the Crown's observance of their Forest Charter "liberties." Disafforestations were implemented following perambulations; the adjudication of the rights following disafforestation led to hearings of competing claims, settled by laws rather than resort to arms. The open proceedings of the Forest Eyres allowed predictable and fairly transparent decision making, while affording the right of a hearing. The pleas of the forest were procedural means to invoke and apply rights of the Forest Charter in specific instances. The Charter's clear articulation of specific rights, correlated with known procedures and designated royal officers to administer them, is among the Forest Charter's most significant features. The Charter provided rights with remedies.

The Forest Charter bolstered the economy of its time, providing a more secure and stable setting for agriculture and silvaculture. The Charter's provisions in chapter 14 about the role of charcoal production and trade anticipate roles that Royal Forests would come to play in the 16th and 17th centuries. Additional uses beyond customary law usufructs already had appeared by 1217, and further new uses of forest resources would emerge. While sustaining traditional forest usufructs was the Charter's immediate focus, by leaving the scope of forest "liberties" open-ended, the Charter allowed for their evolution in later ages. The Forest Charter would accommodate remarkable adaptations in centuries to come.

V. Evolution: A Forest Charter for Each Generation

Over the next 500 years, each generation shaped the Charter of the Forest to serve its own interests. The unique Law of the Forest, so ably set forth by John Manwood for the times of Queen Elizabeth I (r. 1558–1603),[129] gradually evolved into a regime for commercial timber and subsequently into the conservation law regime under Queen Elizabeth II (r. 1952–present).[130]

---

129. MANWOOD, *supra* note 11.

130. *See, e.g.*, the 20 conservation areas in the New Forest National Park, "of which three straddle the boundary between the Park and New Forest District Council's area." *Conservation Areas—New Forest National Park Authority*, NEWFORESTNPA.GOV.UK,

The intervening years endowed the Forest Charter with attributes sought by each prevailing social order. The Forest Charter itself became the focus of new appeals to tradition, just as in the 13th century advocates for Royal Forest rights invoked the Charter of Liberties of Henry I. Eventually, English common law eclipsed the Law of the Forest, and Parliamentary statutes absorbed, revised, and elaborated provisions of the Forest Charter.[131] The four next stages of this social evolution offer insights about both the rule of law and environmental conservation.

A.   The Forest Charter from 1400 to 1850

The social history of how English society regarded nature, particularly in each of the Royal Forests, is a task beyond the scope of this chapter. Suffice it to say that each generation's perceptions of the law of the land reflected prevailing perceptions of nature. Recalling the highlights of these social changes over four centuries sets the stage for examining the contemporary relevance of the Forest Charter on the eve of its 800th anniversary.

During the 14th and 15th centuries, the Forest Charter was no longer at the center of governmental decision making. Society endured the turmoil of extensive and deep loss of life caused by the Black Death in 1349, by civil strife including the Peasants' Revolt of 1381, and by the War of the Roses, which weakened the barons. Repeatedly, kings raised revenues through grants of forest tracts to others. By the 17th century, private wooded parks, chases, and warrens were widespread, and their proprietors tended to their natural resources more assiduously than the Crown did for the largely untended Royal Forests. Commoners expanded their uses of forest resources in Royal Forests. Forest Courts continued in some places to mediate disputes. Urban centers and trade grew more powerful, with wool farmers, manufacturers, and merchants gaining wealth and influence.[132]

---

http://www.newforestnpa.gov.uk/info/20044/building_conservation/27/conservation
_areas#.U16qBCjmKBg (last visited May 20, 2014). Queen Elizabeth II visited the New Forest at the conclusion of her Diamond Jubilee. *See Diamond Jubilee: Queen Visits Cowes and New Forest on Final Day*, BBC NEWS, Jul. 25, 2012, http://www.bbc.com /news/uk-england-hampshire-18971802.

131. During the reign of Henry III, several authors compiled the treatise. *See* HENRY OF BRATTON, DE LEGIBUS ET CONSUETUDINIBUS ANGLIAE: ON THE LAWS AND CUSTOMS OF ENGLAND (1235). This text elaborates legal practices of land tenures and other provisions of what would become common law, but makes slight mention of Magna Carta and omits the Forest Charter, probably because Henry III did not wish to acknowledge that his Forest Law prerogatives were restrained by the Forest Charter. *See* Harvard Law School, *Bracton Online Home Page*, BRACTON.LAW (Apr. 2003), http://bracton.law .harvard.edu (last visited May 20, 2014).

132. *See generally*, EILEEN POWER, THE WOOL GRADE IN ENGLISH MEDIEVAL HISTORY (1941).

Parliament's authority also was growing. In 1407, Henry IV (r. 1399–1413) recognized Parliament's decision-making roles regarding taxation and spending.[133] Legislation shaped law consciously, rather than relying on custom or judge-made common law. The struggles and bargaining between the Crown and the barons was absorbed into an emerging parliamentary system.

Types of forest uses also changed. By 1476, the printing press had been developed in England, and millions of tons of wood were harvested per year to produce paper.[134] Renewable timber production became a priority. Timber was also needed to build the ships for the Royal Navy and merchant marine. Parliament began enacting legislation in 1482 through the 17th century to facilitate converting forests into timber plantations.[135]

The Tudors used the Forest Charter when it suited them. Georges Ferrers published an English translation of the Great Charter of Liberties and the Forest Charter in 1534,[136] and went on to advise King Henry VIII (r. 1509–1547), who invoked the Forest Charter to revive royal forest prerogatives.[137] Henry VIII incurred large debts. Seeking to increase royal income independently from Parliament, he allocated Royal Forest lands to secure wealth, political support, and services, and seized Catholic Church assets in 1536 when he broke with Rome.[138] Henry collectively governed

---

133. Douglas Biggs, *An Ill and Infirm King: Henry IV, Health and the Gloucester Parliament of 1407*, *in* THE REIGN OF HENRY IV: REBELLION AND SURVIVAL 1403–1413, at 180 (Gwilyn Dodd & Douglas Biggs eds., 2008). The long Parliament of 1406 from March and to the end of December met and granted taxes only after securing major reforms, including an audit of the new land tax passed at Coventry in 1404, and reforms of the Council (Councilors had to swear not to take anything but their official salaries).

134. HENRY R. PLOMER, A SHORT HISTORY OF ENGLISH PRINTING 1476–1900 (1900).

135. Legislation to encourage the production of timber included the following: An Act for Inclosing of Woods in Forests, Chases and Purlieus, 1482, 22 Edw. 4, c. 7; An Act for the Preservation of Woods, 1543, 35 Hen. 8, c. 39; The Delimitation of Forests Act, 1640, 16 Car. 1, c. 16; and An Act for the Punishment of Unlawful Cutting or Steeling or Spoiling of Wood and Under-Wood and Destroyers of Young Timber-Trees, 1663, 15 Car. 2, c. 2. *See* JAMES, *supra* note 7, at 139–88.

136. "The Great Charter called in laytn Magna Carta with divers olde statutes whole titles appere in the next leafe newly corrected [. . . translated out of Latyn and Frenche into Englysshe by George Ferrers], Imprynted at London, in Paules church yerde at the signe of the Maydens heed by Thomas Petyt, 1542." GEORGES FERRERS, DIVERSE OLDE STATUTES (1534).

137. "Henry VIII, for instance, who hunted deer with passion, was the last king to create a Royal Forest, the forest of Honour at Hampton Court in 1539." NAIL, *supra* note 36, at 14–15. "[T]he structure in Epping Forest now misnamed 'Queen Elizabeth's Hunting Lodge' is really a 'standing,' or observation tower for ceremonial hunts, built by Henry VIII in the 1540s when he tried to make a part in part of the Forest of which he had confiscated the land from Waltham Abby." RACKHAM, *supra* note 53, at 138.

138. Henry VIII's Statute of Enrolments recorded land tenures. *See* 27 Hen. 8, c. 16.

all the Church and Royal Forests in the Crown Estate, first in 1547 under a Court of Augmentations with two masters and two surveyors-general, and subsequently directly under the exchequer.[139] Administrative surveys replaced the perambulations. The king also sold Royal Forest lands and harvested timber to build ships and run forges. Elizabeth I followed this path. In her reign, John Manwood first published his *Treatise of the Forest*, definitively accounting for the Charter of the Forest and Forest Law.[140]

King James I (r. 1603–1625) sought to restore control over Royal Forests to enhance his revenues. He announced he would enforce the Forest Laws "which were as ancient and authentic as the Great Charter."[141] Disingenuously, he omitted any reference to the Forest Charter. In 1661, his grandson, Charles II (r. 1660–1685), cut down 1,800 oaks in the New Forest for building ships for his Royal Navy.[142] Forest symbols would come to be synonymous with the king's power, foremost the oak tree. James launched inspections of assarts in Royal Forests, raising £25,000 by compounding the fixed payments due that were applied to those occupying royal lands.[143]

King Charles I (r. 1625–1649) continued to disafforest and sell Royal Forests, such as in Dean.[144] Again needing funds to deal with the French, Charles returned to afforestment, enlarging the Royal Forests, and then selling off the parts he had seized. Royal commissioners were sent to perambulate the Forests and reclaim lands. Landholders were required to pay substantial sums to have the land they wished to have disafforested. The Crown imposed the heavy royal penalties of the Forest Law widely.[145] Around 1635, Charles reestablished Forest Eyres.[146] His afforestations caused riots, the "Western Rising," in West Country forests, including Gillingham, Braydon, Dean, and Feckenham.[147] Charles I's offensive personal rule over Royal Forests contributed to the discontent that ended his reign. The Grand Remonstrance of 1641 protested "enlargements of forests, contrary to *Carta de Foresta*," and the king's "destruction of the Forest in Dean, [which was]

---

139. *See generally* WALTER C. RICHARDSON, HISTORY OF THE COURT OF AUGMENTATIONS (1961). An Act for the Preservation of Woods, *supra* note 135, established woodland management rules to increase timber production. These rules were applied to both Royal Forests and the woods taken from the Church; the Crown's principal interest was in increasing revenues, not in silvaculture.

140. *See* MANWOOD, *supra* note 11.

141. GRANT, *supra* note 7, at 187.

142. NAIL, *supra* note 36, at 23.

143. GRANT, *supra* note 7, at 186–88.

144. SCHAMA, *supra* note 28, at 156; *see also* J.P. Sommerville, *The Personal Rule of Charles I*, FACULTY.HISTORY.WISC.EDU, http://faculty.history.wisc.edu/sommerville /123/123%20303%20Personal%20Rule.htm (last visited May 20, 2014).

145. *Id.*

146. *Id.*

147. SHARP, *supra* note 34.

sold to Papists," and demanded enactment of a "good law" to reduce forests "to their rightful bounds."[148]

New uses also came to the Royal Forests. The Royal Forest of Dean expanded its provision of charcoal for the forges for making iron there.[149] Forges were situated within the Dean Forest from 1612 until about 1670. Iron making was the subject of a parliamentary Reafforestation Act in 1667.[150] Forest Courts were held to regulate the activities of the Free Miners in Dean. Dean continued to be a source of wood for producing charcoal in the late 18th century, and the Free Miners of the Forest of Dean continue their practices to this day, under an Act of Parliament.[151]

The leading jurist in the 17th century, Edward Coke described the Forest Charter and law of the forest in the fourth part (chapter 73) of his *Institutes of the Laws of England* (1671).[152] This publication shaped the knowledge of the Forest Charter for generations. Coke, when asserting the rule of law against James I, was removed as chief justice, was for a time detained in the Tower of London, and helped prepare the Petition of Right of 1628. His *Institutes*, published posthumously, described the Forest Charter and argued that the Law of the Forest was constrained by common law. However, it was to be Parliament, not common law judges, that revised the Forest Charter as a statute.[153]

Needing additional funds from Parliament for his struggles with France, Charles I convened Parliament in 1628. In its deliberations over whether to provide funds for the Crown, Parliament secured the king's consent to the Petition of Right, which formally provided for no taxation without

---

148. *Gardiner: Constitutional Documents of the Puritan Revolution, 43. The Grand Remonstrance, with the Petition Accompanying it,* CONSTITUTION.ORG, http://www.constitution.org/eng/conpur043.htm (last visited May 20, 2014).

149. YOUNG, *supra* note 14, at 132–33; Mary Ley Bazeley, *The Forest of Dean in Its Relations with the Crown During the Twelfth and Thirteenth Centuries,* 33 TRANSACTIONS OF THE BRISTOL & GLOUCESTERSHIRE ARCHAEOLOGICAL SOC'Y 153, 153–285 (1910). *See* SARA MAITLAND, GOSSIP FROM THE FOREST: THE TANGLED ROOTS OF OUR FORESTS AND FAIRYTALES 171–88 (2012).

150. The Dean Forest (Reafforestation) Act, 1668, 20 Car. 2, c. 3. *See* ANDREW RICHARD WARMINGTOIN, CIVIL WAR, INTERREGNUM & RESTORATION IN GLOUCESTERSHIRE 1640–1672 (1997).

151. The Dean Forest (Mine) Act, 1838, 1 & 2 Vict., c. 43.

152. COKE, *supra* note 37, at ch. 73.

153. The Forest Charter was not subject to interpretation by the common law courts. The analogous courts of the forest, the eyres, applied and enforced the Forest Law, but did not change its terms through case law. As Parliament assumed authority to enact statutes, over time it selectively revised the Forest Charter's provisions. See references at *supra* note 7. For example, in the 19th century, "[t]he game laws eroded the principles of the Forest Charter. Where the Charter had proudly restated the right of all to hunt wild animals on their own land, the game laws removed that right." GRIFFIN, *supra* note 18, at 62. Finally in 1971 they saw no need for the residue of the ancient Charter, repealing even that, *supra* note 8.

consent of Parliament, along with ensuring other rights, such as no arbitrary imprisonment. This was the most important royal concession of rights to the people since the confirmation of the Forest Charter and Magna Carta in 1297. The Petition of Right, in principle, resolved in the people's favor the recurring struggle about the Crown's renewing its promise to adhere to the Charters when in need of new revenues.

Nonetheless, in 1640, Charles I again needed funding and convened Parliament. Complaints about administration of the Forest Law had continued. Upset with the Crown's practice of using the courts to collect revenues through fines, Parliament passed legislation curbing abusive royal practices in Royal Forests.[154] Thereafter, concerns about the Forest Charter again receded with the social discord that accompanied the English Civil War. Oliver Cromwell prevailed and Charles I was executed. By 1653, Parliament had granted its powers over to Cromwell, and Cromwell annulled the Forest Charter and took Royal Forests into his power.[155] His acts, however, would prove ephemeral. After Cromwell's death in 1659, the army and barons recalled the former Parliament, which invited Charles II to return to England from his exile abroad. The Royal Forests and Charter were restored, whereupon Charles II continued to sell off parts of the Royal Forests to finance his regime.

In the Restoration, the Crown reverted to treating Royal Forests as revenue, and commoners' rights suffered. The king's policy toward Royal Forests shifted to favoring timber production. In 1664, John Evelyn published *Silva, or A Discourse of Forest Trees and the Propagation of Timber in His Majesty's Dominions*, in print through a fifth edition in 1729.[156] Evelyn makes no mention of the Forest Charter and essentially dismissed commoners' rights to their forest usufructs. Allowing commoners' usufructs hindered the silvaculture that Evelyn espoused. His work promoted forest management for timber production, and provided justifications for the Crown's restoring its rule in Forests in order to produce timber, primarily for ships. Reflecting the influence of *Silva*, the Forest Courts took decisions to preserve and advance the production of timber for the Royal Navy.[157] Now

---

154. 1640, 16 Car. 1, c. 16, *supra* note 135.

155. *See, e.g.*, Cromwell's actions with regard to the Forest of Needwood. JOHN CHARLES COX, THE ROYAL FOREST OF ENGLAND 142 (1905).

156. JOHN EVELYN, SILVA: OR, A DISCOURSE OF FOREST TREES AND THE PROPAGATION OF TIMBER IN HIS MAJESTY'S DOMINIONS, AS IT WAS DELIVERED IN THE ROYAL SOCIETY IN 1662 (1st ed. 1664), *available at* https://archive.org/details/silvaordiscourse 01evel (last visited May 20, 2014).

157. France pursued forest timber policies akin to those in England. *See* JEAN-BAPTISTE COLBERT, ORDONNANCE DE SAINT GERMAIN EN LAYE (n.p. 1669).

the national defense required timber production. Inclosures were ordered to protect tree plantations from deer or intrusions by commoners.[158]

James II (r. 1685–1688) followed Charles II and was displaced in favor of William III (r. 1689–1702) and Mary II (r. 1689–1694) in 1689.[159] Thereafter Parliament's enactment of statutes began to reshape elements of the Forest Charter, Forest Law, and Magna Carta. In January of 1689, Parliament enacted the Declaration of Rights,[160] strengthening civil and political rights, but weakening the collective, common rights accorded in the Forest Charter. Landed property owners were redefining forest uses through their influence in Parliament. These private parks were often enclosed, and commoners excluded, in disregard of their common law usufructory rights or the Forest Charter's provisions. The Game Law of 1671[161] confirmed that hunting was a privilege of freehold property owners. Poaching was made a felony. This regime for hunting and fishing continued until 1831. Enclosures on forested private parks and chases, with deer farms, transformed hunting by gentry and kings alike into a restricted, legal privilege. Management of these privately protected areas also privileged conservation of nature, to enhance deer forest habitat.[162]

The Enclosure Acts allowed private landowners to exclude both commoners and the king from forestlands.[163] English imports of wood from its colonies and the expanse of trade generally reduced demand for wood products from Royal Forests, which also facilitated conversion of once Royal Forests into private preserves. For example, Royal Forests disafforested, sold, and enclosed included Enfield Chases (Middlesex) in 1877, Needwood Forest (Staffordshire) in 1801, Windsor Forest in 1817, and Wynchwood Forest in 1857.[164] Oliver Rackham notes, "When a Forest was enclosed its

---

158. CHRISTOPHER JESSEL, A LEGAL HISTORY OF THE ENGLISH LANDSCAPE 129–38 (2011) ("Enclosures and Inclosure"). *See generally* JAMES, *supra* note 7, at 3 and app. II with a roster of the Acts of Parliament from 1184 to 1971 relating to forests and forestry.

159. The Stuarts, History of the Monarchy, ROYAL.GOV.UK, http://www.royal.gov.uk /HistoryoftheMonarchy/KingsandQueensoftheUnitedKingdom/TheStuarts/TheStuarts .aspx (last visited May 20, 2014).

160. This instrument, also termed the "Bill of Rights," is a statutory enactment on December 16, 1689, of the "Declaration of Right," which Parliament presented to William and Mary in March of 1689. An Act Declaring the Rights and Liberties of the Subject and Settling the Succession of the Crown, 1688, 1 W. & M. c. 2, sess. 2.

161. An Act for the Better Preservation of Game, and for Securing Warrens Not Inclosed, and the Severall Fishings of This Realme, 1671, 22 & 23 Car. 2, c. 25, *in* 5 STATUTES OF THE REALM 1628–1680, at 745–46 (1891), *available at* http://www.british-history .ac.uk/report.aspx?compid=47447 (last visited May 20, 2014), *discussed in* P.B. MUNSCHE, GENTLEMEN AND POACHERS: THE ENGLISH GAME LAWS 1671–1831 (1981).

162. JESSEL, *supra* note 158, at 115–28 ("Ch. 11: Landed Estates").

163. Extensive inclosures occurred in 1760–1780 and 1800–1815. See JESSEL, *supra* note 158, at ch. 12 ("Enclosures and Inclosures 1660–1900").

164. RACKHAM, *supra* note 53, at 139. *See also* JAMES, *supra* note 7, at 167 (1981).

wood-pasture, heath, etc., passed to private owners who, with rare exceptions, instantly destroyed them."[165] The enclosures were inimical to the multiple-use approach that the Forest Charter had sanctioned.

Enclosures were not always peaceful. Disafforestation and enclosures excluded commoners from their pasturage, pannage, and other usufructs. Commoners protested. Riots took place at Feckenham Forest (Worcestershire) in 1631–1632, and took place also from time to time elsewhere.[166] Riots at Dean occurred as late as 1831.[167]

Some Forest Eyres continued to be held, for example, one was held for the New Forest in 1670. However, the role of forest courts was declining. The system of eyres and perambulations was replaced in 1715 when Parliament formally established the Office of Surveyor.[168] Royal Forests remained part of the Crown estate. The rights of freeholders, landed gentry, and customary forest users with their commoners' rights of grazing, and timber resources of the nation, were now a major focus of the Crown's attention.

In 1787 and 1793, the Royal Commission on Crown Woods and Forests reported about neglect and decline of the Royal Forests and other government forest lands, particularly in Sherwood Forest, New Forest, and three others in Hampshire; Windsor Forest in Berkshire; the Forest of Dean in Gloucestershire; Waltham or Epping Forest in Essex; three forests in Northamptonshire; and Wychwood in Oxfordshire. While swanimote courts still administered some of the Forests locally, Crown supervision was lacking. The Royal Commission's report favored continued use of Royal Forests for timber production.[169]

The Crown's administrative governance of Royal Forests developed slowly in the 19th century. In 1810, the surveyors-general, who had reported to the auditors of Land Revenue, were replaced by a Commission of Woods, Forests, and Land Revenues.[170] The Commission's forest duties were diluted between 1832 and 1851, as responsibilities for *Works and Buildings* were assigned to it.[171] But by 1851, the Commission's duties again were focused

---

165. Rackham, *supra* note 53, at 139.

166. Grant, *supra* note 7, at 189–90; Sharp, *supra* note 34, at 143–68.

167. Nail, *supra* note 36, at 18, *citing* P. Large, *From Swanimote to Disafforestation: Feckenham Forest in the Early Seventeenth Century*, in The Estates of the English Crown 1558–1640 (R. Hoyle ed. 2002).

168. The surveyor general of woods, forests, parks, and chases oversaw the management of Royal Forests and their revenues. In 1810, the office was subsumed within the Surveyor General of Land Revenues. An Act for Uniting the Offices of the Surveyor General of the Land Revenues of the Crown and Surveyor General of His Majesties Woods, Forests, Parks and Chases, 1810, 50 Geo. 3, c. 65, *amended* 10 Geo. 4, c. 50.

169. James, *supra* note 7, at 179–181.

170. 1810, 50 Geo. 3, c. 65, *supra* note 168.

171. James, *supra* note 7, at 184.

on woods, forests, and revenue.[172] The Office of Woods came to exercise governmental authority over Royal Forests, emphasizing timber production and enhancing revenues for the Crown. By now the Royal Navy's fleet was built of steel and its demand for wood had receded.

Inclosure acts[173] and forest plantations continued to induce opposition from commoners, frustrated with the Crown's disregard of their ancient Forest Charter rights. Emerging social values competed with tree plantations. Controversies between the Crown and the public varied from forest to forest. Examples in four Royal Forests illustrate trends defining new forest "liberties" despite each Royal Forest's distinctively local history.

In New Forest, tree plantations emerged with an Act of Parliament of 1698,[174] and timber production from the New Forest was extensive. In 1851, Parliament adopted the Deer Removal Act[175] to remove deer from the New Forest, facilitating its further use for tree plantations and not as a deer farm for the king. This act produced strong opposition. Besides commoners, new stakeholders sought to protect the New Forest. In 1863, John Wise published his book *The New Forest, Its History and Scenery*, and in 1867 the New Forest Association was formed to protect common rights in the New Forest. In 1871, the Crown's Office of Woods proposed a bill in Parliament that would have removed all forest rights to enable conversion to plantation wood production. Opposition from civic groups prevented the bill's adoption. After the bill failed, in 1877, Parliament passed the New Forest Act,[176] which recognized the rights of commoners and provided that the Court of Verderers would administer and manage those rights.

In Epping Forest, a different path appears. A Royal Forest since Henry I, commoners had enjoyed their usufructs for generations. Throughout the 18th century, they resisted inclosures, which accelerated with expansion of agricultural lands in the 19th century. In 1851, Hainault Forest adjacent to Epping had been disafforested, its trees removed and replaced with plowed and fenced fields. In 1866, commoners sued in Chancery to challenge enclosures that denied them their Forest Charter rights. They were joined by the Corporation of the City of London, which wished to save Epping for the health and recreation of the residents of London. Courts held that

---

172. *Id.*

173. JESSEL, *supra* note 158, at 134–36.

174. *See* An Act for the Increase and Preservation of Timber in New Forest in the County of Southampton, 1698, 9 & 10 Will. 3, c. 36.

175. An Act to Extinguish the Right of the Crown to Deer in the New Forest, and to Give Compensation in Lieu Thereof, and for Other Purposes Relating to the Said Forest, 1851, 40 & 41 Vict., c. 121 [commonly referred to as the "Deer Removal Act"]. *See* COLIN R. TUBBS, THE NEW FOREST 76–77 (1986).

176. An Act to Amend the Administration of the Law Relating to the New Forest in the County of Southampton, and for Other Purposes, 1877, 40 & 41 Vict. c. 121 [hereinafter The New Forest Act 1877].

commoners could not have consented to enclosures by purchase, because "it would be impossible for the landowners to demonstrate that every single entitled commoner had given consent and been compensated, and that since the right was individual rather than collective, each and every commoner had the right to veto the change."[177] Enclosures in Epping Forest were thus unlawful. In the wake of this ruling, in 1878, the city acquired 3,500 acres of forest, and then secured Parliament's adoption of the Epping Forest Act, making London the Conservator of the Forest. When Queen Victoria inaugurated Epping Forest as a place for public recreation, it marked a new conception of the "liberties of the forest."[178] Under the Epping Forest Act 1878, conservators were "at all times as far as possible [to] preserve the natural aspect of the Forests . . . protect the timber and other trees, pollards, shrubs, underwood, heather, gorse, turf and herbage."[179] The documented rights of commoners were to continue unchanged, and Verderers were to be selected to defend the interests of commoners. Initially lacking scientific capacity to guide preservation, it took time to build a nature conservation theme at Epping. Oliver Rackham worried that Epping "is well on the way of becoming just another Chiltern-type beech-wood."[180] Notwithstanding Rackham's concern, two-thirds of Epping have been designated as Sites of Special Scientific Interest[181] and English Nature identifies Epping's biodiversity as "outstanding."[182] The City of London saved Epping from becoming a plantation for timber. Epping today hosts numerous recreational facilities.

In the Forest of Dean, established by William the Conqueror for its large oak forests, Parliament enacted individual laws also. Dean's rich oak resources had built the Cathedral in York and the Tower of London. It was a great source of revenue for the Crown.[183] In the 1850s, deer were ordered

---

177. Maitland, *supra* note 149, at 92 (the account of Epping).

178. *Forest Charter*, *supra* note 3, at ch. 17. *See generally* Alfred Qvist, Epping Forest (1958).

179. The Common Ground, *supra* note 54, at 136.

180. Rackham, *supra* note 53, at 150.

181. Sites of Special Scientific Interest (SSSIs) began as an inventory of sites, and became a network of natural areas, initially designated by the Council of the Nature Conservancy, an agency established by the National Parks and Access to the Countryside Act of 1949. National Parks and Access to the Countryside Act, 1949, 12, 13 & 14 Geo. 6, c. 97, http://www.legislation.gov.uk/ukpga/1949/97/pdfs/ukpga_19490097_en.pdf [hereinafter Access to the Countryside Act]. More than 344 SSSIs are situated in Crown Forests. *See* David Evans, A History of Nature Conservation in Britain 202–03 (1992).

182. *See Biodiversity Action Plan—Epping Forest District Council*, epping forest dc.gov.uk, http://www.eppingforestdc.gov.uk/index.php/residents/your-home/285-out-and-about/our-countryside/countrycare/biodiversity/676-the-epping-forest-biodiversity-action-plan (last visited May 20, 2014).

183. The annual income from this one forest in 1195–1232 equaled the annual revenue of Henry II and more than half that of Henry III. Young, *supra* note 14, at 131.

removed from Dean to further plantations, and in five years all were elim-inated.[184] By the 19th century, it was a significant source of timber for the navy. By 1809, four-fifths of Dean was enclosed for plantations, which coex-isted with ironworks dating from Roman and medieval periods. Miners had been granted royal charters by Edward I, and in 1838 Parliament confirmed their rights. "There are around 150 Free Miners alive today"[185] in Dean. Dean illustrates a mixed-use approach today. The Forestry Commission now administers Dean, which hosts small herds of fallow deer along with camping and other recreational facilities. The Verderers court administers access to the commons and a "Speech Court" is held every 40 days.[186] Dean too has been reinvented.

Exmoor Forest was afforested by King John but restored to its original boundaries under the Forest Charter, and the boundaries were enforced by perambulations in 1279, 1298, and 1651.[187] Exmoor had little oak wood, but ample deer for royal hunting.[188] Numerous streams and rivers traverse Exmoor. Parliament disafforested Exmoor in 1851 and a portion of Crown lands was sold to John Knight in 1818.[189] The Knight family designed the landscape of Exmoor, planting woodlands and enclosing farmlands (only 14 percent is now enclosed).[190] Exmoor's mixed uses include farming, raising sheep, forestry, recreation, and scientific pursuits.[191] Situated along the Bris-tol Channel, Exmoor is removed from major population centers. Exmoor was proposed for status as a National Park in 1945, and designated one in 1954. The Forestry Commission and two County Committees and a Joint Advisory Committee govern Exmoor. The history of Exmoor is more respect-ful of commoners' interests. It accommodates private agricultural proper-ties, customary usufructs, aesthetic amenities, recreation, timber production, and the harvesting of other natural resources. Exmoor's patterns of land use appear to have entailed less conflict than in other former Royal Forests. Exmoor appears well suited to the national park planning regimes.[192]

These four different administrative patterns for protection of common and public interest in Royal Forests developed partially in reaction to the Industrial Revolution in England. The Industrial Revolution shifted demands away from wood to coal and coke for industrial production. Parliament enacted legislation for new roads, canals, and railways. As

---

184. GRANT, *supra* note 7, at 212.
185. MAITLAND, *supra* note 149, at 180.
186. GRANT, *supra* note 7, at 214–16.
187. *Id.* at 155, 159; *see also* JAMES, *supra* note 7, at 923–93.
188. JAMES, *supra* note 7, at 34, 133.
189. *Id.* at 93.
190. C.S. ORWIN, THE RECLAMATION OF EXMOOR FOREST (1929).
191. ROGER MILLS, FORESTRY IN THE ENGLISH LANDSCAPE 139–70 (1967).
192. *Id.* at 135–242; *see also* Home Page, EXMOOR NATIONAL PARK, http://www .exmoor-nationalpark.gov.uk (last visited May 20, 2014).

demands for timber fell in the late 19th century, the Crown's Office of Woods was less assiduous in promoting forest productivity. Laws promoted industrialization, mining, and new financing systems, which were needed for economic development. As industrial pollution burgeoned, Parliament enacted the Alkali Acts (1863)[193] and the Public Health Act (1875),[194] and unpolluted forests beckoned. Railways allowed urban dwellers easy access to the countryside. The population of England shifted from being largely rural in 1800 to doubling in size and becoming increasingly urban by the 1850s. England's population nearly doubled again by 1900, with most people living in urban settings. Urban congestion and slums emerged; as open space and public gardens in cities disappeared, public demands grew for access to natural areas. Trevelyan notes that: "[I]t was characteristic of the altered balance of society that enclosure of commons was ultimately stopped in the decade between 1865 and 1875 by the protest not of the rural peasantry, but of the urban populations, who objected to exclusion from its holiday playgrounds and rural breathing spaces."[195] Parliament responded. "Liberties of the Forest" were now espoused in new ways.

The late 19th century also ushered in a new sensibility toward nature. Reacting to the excesses of the Industrial Revolution, the Romantic movement emerged in aesthetics, literature, and art.[196] Appreciation of natural beauty became a popular priority, infusing renewed interest in the once Royal Forests, as is illustrated in the many organizations celebrating the Lake District. The Commons, Open Spaces and Footpaths Preservation Society was established in 1865. In 1895, the National Trust for Places of Historic Interest or Natural Beauty was founded. These trends bred conflicts with the prevailing policies of the Office of Woods.

Timber operations expanded to serve needs in World War I. Forest lands accounted for some 5 percent of England's landscape in 1914. In 1919, Parliament established the Forestry Commission, and in 1924 transferred authority for the Royal Forests to the new Commission, setting the stage again for conflicts between the Crown's interests in timber and the commoners' rights and the new public stakeholders with their amenity, aesthetic, recreational or scientific values.

Two significant advances in knowledge stimulated new values regarding Royal Forests in the late 19th and early 20th century. Both would refocus English attitudes toward Royal Forests and the Forest Charter. First was the scientific revolution associated with the discoveries of Charles Darwin

---

193. Evans, *supra* note 181, at 56.
194. Public Health Act, 1875, 38 & 39 Vict., c. 55.
195. G.M. Trevelyan, English Social History 537 (1942).
196. *See, e.g.,* the works of William Wordsworth (literature), John Ruskin (aesthetics), and John Constable or J.M.W. Turner (landscape painting).

and the birth of the science of ecology. Second was the publication of forest courts' records, enabling legal scholarship to rediscover the importance of the Forest Charter. Both deserve to be recalled, for both quietly influenced the "liberties of the forest."

B. Evolution and Ecology: The Science and Ethics of Nature Conservation

Commoners' rights under the Forest Charter persisted both in law and practice, although royal grants alienating lands and allowing governmental inclosures and private enclosures often excluded commoners. In the 18th and 19th centuries, new commonly held interests in the nature of the forest countryside were emerging. This was the study of natural history. Widening economic prosperity in England led to a flowering of natural history studies. Works like Gilbert White's *The Natural History and Antiquities of Selborne* (1788) reflected and inspired a growing interest in the flora, fauna, and geography of England.[197] Natural history societies emerged to foster collections and classifications of the variety of natural life, and by 1851 Cambridge University launched a degree in natural science.[198]

When Charles Darwin published *The Origin of Species* (1859), and the *Descent of Man* (1871), his theories of natural selection were a scientific revolution in biology, with profound implications for all scientific inquiry. The Education Act of 1870[199] required, for the first time, the teaching of elementary science in all government schools. The public explored the countryside to study geological and biological phenomena.

A public informed about natural science emerged. The expansion of railways, provided ready access to the countryside, for appreciation and study of nature. Enclosures restricted access to natural areas, and opposition to enclosures emerged. In 1865, John Stuart Mill and others founded the Commons Preservation Society, which won open space access for Epping Forest, Blackheath, Hampstead Heath, Wandsworth Common, Wimbledon Common, and elsewhere.[200] Similarly, civic conservation societies emerged,

---

197. RICHARD MABEY, GILBERT WHITE: A BIOGRAPHY OF THE AUTHOR OF THE NATURAL HISTORY OF SELBORNE 1–13 (1986). The edition of White's *Natural History of Selborne* published in 1827 by William Jardine led to a wider readership, including the young Charles Darwin.

198. DAVID ELLISTON ALLEN, THE NATURALIST IN BRITAIN—A SOCIAL HISTORY 162 (1976).

199. The Elementary Education Act, 1870, 33 & 34 Vict., c.75, *available at* http://www.educationengland.org.uk/documents/acts/1870-elementary-education-act.html.

200. The Open Spaces Society (OSS) continues this movement, and OSS provides a history of the movement. *Open Spaces Society*, OSS.ORG, www.oss.org.uk/ (last visited May 20, 2014).

such as the Royal Society for the Protection of Birds. In 1895, the National Trust for England and Wales was created, leading to the enactment of the National Trust Act (1907).[201] The Society for the Promotion of Nature Reserves was founded in 1912, later becoming the Royal Society for Nature Conservation. Advocates for nature conservation were becoming a political force. New uses for the forests had emerged.

While social movements for conservation grew, scientists tested and refined knowledge of ecology as the 19th century concluded. The Oxford ecologist A.G. Tansley and others founded the world's first Ecological Society in 1913.[202] The science of ecology rapidly matured, although it was set back when a generation of young scientists was killed in World War I.[203] Stewardship of land increasingly came to be measured by norms based on ecological relationships. The ecological approach would reverberate back to stimulate reforms in management of the governments' timber plantations and remnant Royal Forests.

As public concern grew about the loss of species and habitats, Parliament enacted further laws for nature conservation, such as The Wild Birds Protection Act (1880).[204] Local lands were set aside and opened for public access. Nature conservation was often congruent with commoners' usufructuary rights, since both relied on stable and healthy

---

A succinct history of the OSS movement:

Lord Eversley, the former Liberal MP and minister, founded the Commons Preservation Society in 1865. The aim of the society was to save London commons for the enjoyment and recreation of the public. Its committee members included such important figures as Octavia Hill, the social reformer, Sir Robert Hunter, solicitor and later co-founder of the National Trust, Professor Huxley, and the MPs, Sir Charles Dilke and James Bryce. Most of the society's members initially came from the south east, so their interests focused on London.

In 1899 the Commons Preservation Society amalgamated with the National Footpaths Society, adopting the title Commons Open Spaces and Footpath Preservation Society. The shortened name, Open Spaces Society was adopted in the 1980s. The society promoted important pieces of legislation, including the Commons Acts of 1876 and 1899.

Open Spaces Society—University of Reading, The Museum of English Rural Life, reading. ac.uk, http://www.reading.ac.uk/merl/collections/Archives_A_to_Z/merl-SR_OSS.aspx (last visited May 20, 2014).

201. An Act to Incorporate and Confer Powers Upon the National Trust for Places of Historic Interest or Natural Beauty, 1907, 7 Edw. 7, c. 136.

202. The British Ecological Society grew out of the 1904 Committee for the Study of British Vegetation. Evans, supra note 181, at 53.

203. Donald Worster, Nature's Economy—A History of Ecological Ideas 205–42 (1977).

204. The Preservation of Wild Fowl Act of 1876 was soon replaced by An Act to Amend the Laws Relating to the Protection of Wild Birds. See the Preservation of Wild Fowl Act, 1876, 39 & 40 Vict., c. 29; the Wild Birds Protection Act, 1880, 43 & 44 Vict., c. 35. See Mead, supra note 7, at 208.

natural habitats. The mix of values supporting forests and countryside embraced new objectives: restoring and safeguarding species, habitats, ecosystems, landscapes, and aesthetic values. Legal reforms would gradually accommodate new uses of once Royal Forests: for rambling hikes, nature study, and environmental conservation.[205] These practices were reasserting common rights. Rediscovery of the Forest Charter's rights could complement them.

C. The Forest Charter Reemerges:
The Selden Society and Legal Historians

While scientific knowledge about nature (and humans) was evolving, legal and historical knowledge about humans (and nature) rediscovered the Forest Charter. Law, as a learned profession, investigated its medieval roots. Scholars probed behind the text of the Forest Charter. Blackstone had reconciled the various original versions of the Forest Charter, providing an authoritative text.[206] His commentary reported about the Charter, rather than evaluating its legal process. Blackstone relied on few primary sources, largely limited to extant copies of the Charters and the writings of Matthew Paris. In his 1759 work, Blackstone wrote that "The charter of the forest . . . is printed from an original in the archives of the cathedral at Durham; the seal whereof, being of green wax, is still perfect, but the body of the charter has been unfortunately gnawn by rats, which has occasioned pretty great mutilations."[207] Blackstone inspected other extant variants of the Forest Charter and also the enrollments of the Charters in the Tower of London, and supplied the words that the rats left missing in the Durham Charter. He set the stage for subsequent legal scholarship about the Forest Charter to search where he left off.

Whig interpretations of history had projected a progressive and felicitous chain of governmental development from ancient traditions of the English nation to its celebrated unwritten constitution. These perceptions are belied by the tortuous and troubled history of the Forest Charter. The story of the Forest Charter in the 20th century was profoundly influenced by the unearthing in the late 19th century of the documentary history of the Forest Law and Carta de Foresta. While the Justiciars of old, and their successors, had required the keeping of careful records of royal revenues and adjudications of disputes, these documents lay unread in libraries, unrecalled. Translating Latin and Norman French texts written on sheepskin into English, scholars made this trove of materials accessible. Their work transformed knowledge

---

205. MILES, *supra* note 63, at 53–58; Philippa Bassett, *A Brief History of the Ramblers Association, in* LIST OF HISTORICAL RECORDS OF THE RAMBLERS ASSOCIATION (1980).
206. PREST, *supra* note 1.
207. BLACKSTONE, *supra* note 1, at l.

of the 13th century, inspiring new studies about how its events reverberated in later eras.

In 1882, the William Salt Society printed two rolls of proceedings before the justices in Staffordshire in 1199 and 1203.[208] The Pipe Roll Society was established in 1883 to publish all unprinted records before the year 1200.[209] Building on such studies, knowledge of the Forest Courts under Kings Richard I and John was further advanced when Francis Palgrave published *Rotuli Curiae Regis*,[210] and Frederic Maitland edited, and the Selden Society published, the first volume of the *Select Pleas of the Crown* in 1887.[211] Maitland edited a number of Selden Society volumes. The Selden Society's contribution to understanding the Forest Charter and Magna Carta cannot be underestimated. Without Turner's *Introduction* and the documents that he edited for *Select Pleas of the Forest* (1901),[212] there would be little contemporary understanding of the origins and the extraordinary role of the Forest Charter in the 13th century. Reviewing Turner's work upon its publication, the *Harvard Law Review* noted, "Heretofore Manwood's Laws of the Forest and Coke's Fourth Institute, chapter 73, have been the chief authorities on the subject."[213] The *Harvard Law Review* welcomed the lively new understanding of law in the 13th century.

The scholarship that followed refreshed knowledge of both the Forest Charter and Magna Carta. With Frederick Pollock, Frederic William Maitland wrote the *History of English Law Before the Time of Edward I* in 1895, with a second edition in 1898. William Sharp McKechnie published his *Magna Carta: A Commentary on the Great Charter of King John* in 1905, with a second augmented edition in 1914.

Legal scholarship refreshed the memory of the Forest Charter, restoring it to public policy discourse. The Charter could now feature in debates about nature conservation, ecology, biodiversity, land use, and heritage cultural values. The Forest Charter's new relevance was also possible because Magna Carta's principles for the rule of law guaranteed that appeals to legal

---

208. The William Salt Archaeological Society, now the Staffordshire Record Society, published these documents in Volume I, First Series (1879). *See The Staffordshire Record Society Publications First Series*, S-H-C.ORG.UK, http://www.s-h-c.org.uk/Publications %20first%20series.html (last visited May 20, 2014).

209. *See The Pipe Roll Society—Home*, PIPE ROLL SOCIETY, http://www.piperollsociety .co.uk/index.htm (last visited May 20, 2014).

210. FRANCIS PALGRAVE, ROTULI CURIAE REGIS: ROLLS AND RECORDS OF THE COURT HELD BEFORE THE KING'S JUSTICIARS OR JUSTICES (1835).

211. ENGLAND CURIA REGIS, 1 SELECT PLEAS OF THE CROWN: A.D. 1200–1225 (Frederic W. Maitland ed., London, Selden Society 1887).

212. William Turner wrote a lengthy *Introduction* to SELECT PLEAS OF THE FOREST, *supra* note 25.

213. Books & Periodicals Review, 15 HARV. L. REV. 421, 421–22 (1901), reviewing SELECT PLEAS OF THE FOREST (G.J. Turner ed., 1901).

norms, like those of the Forest Charter, would have a receptive audience in Parliament.

D. Forest Charter "Liberties" in the 20th Century

The administrative law systems of the modern state emerged in the 1900s, especially after World War II. In the 20th century, conservationists brought scientific reassessments of nature in England to the attention of Parliament. Where each Royal Forest once reflected more or less the same application of Forest Law, or of the Crown's regimes for timber plantations, each now tended to evolve its own separate stewardship regime, reflecting local contexts and stakeholders. Intellectual and social changes redefined competing forest values. Through uniquely English appeals to tradition, some former Royal Forests retained institutions of Forest Law, such as Verderers, retooling them to serve new functions and meshing their mandates with those of new administrative agencies. While two world wars and the Great Depression suppressed reforms of forest governance, pressures persisted from holders of commoners' usufructs, and from advocates of countryside protection and nature conservation. The question remained: What should the Crown do about forests, the Royal Forests, and the Forest Charter? Age-old debates about common forest rights versus the Crown's search for revenues recurred anew.

Meanwhile, utilitarian mandates to promote timber production advanced on their own separate pathways. In 1919, Parliament enacted the Forestry Act.[214] Forest Commissioners were granted full authority to develop timber resources and buy or sell lands, and exercise eminent domain to take lands.[215] In 1924, the Royal Forests were transferred to a newly established Forestry Commission.[216] By 1939, the Commissioners had bought 172,000 hectares for new forest plantations.[217] Critics found the plantations impoverished the landscape's beauty and ecological richness.[218]

To ameliorate public concerns, Forestry Commissioners set up forest parks, including one in the Forest of Dean.[219] Nonetheless, public debates about reconciling nature conservation and resource exploitation grew. For example, on August 26, 1936, the Forest Commissioners published a

---

214. An Act for Establishing a Forestry Commission for the United Kingdom, and Promoting Afforestation and the Production and Supply of Timber Therein, and for Purposes in Connexion Therewith, 1919, 9 & 10 Geo., c. 58.

215. *Id.* at § 7.

216. The Transfer of Woods Act, *supra* note 35, at § 1, transferred the Crown interest in Royal Forests to the Forestry Commission.

217. MILES, *supra* note 63, at 207–58.

218. THE COMMON GROUND, *supra* note 54, at 47, 73–80 (1980).

219. EVANS, *supra* note 181, at 171; for earlier analogous uses of the Forest of Dean in 1946, *see* MILES, *supra* note 63, at 239.

white paper proposing expanded tree plantations for the Lake District. The Council for the Preservation of Rural England, Ramblers Federation, Friends of the Lake District, and others protested against the loss of native hardwood ecology and traditional landscape aesthetics.[220] The Commission argued that its afforestation increased timber production and created jobs. Opponents cited losses of sheep pastures and their jobs. Above all, however, opponents urged protection for common rights of access to open space and aesthetics. Their vision was clear: "The ideal for the Lake District is a national park, not a national forest."[221]

Competition and conflict between forest *users* of nature conservation for species or open-space landscape versus timber production grew sharper. After 1945, the Forestry Commission acquired new lands, and then poisoned or rooted out native vegetation to replace it, usually with conifer plantations.[222] Oliver Rackham notes that "for its first twenty-five years the Forestry Commission had little direct impact on woodland,"[223] but the Commission's post-war expansion was more intense.

> This was justified by a crude sort of cost-benefit analysis, which treated a plantation as if it were an investment in Government stock, and tried to set off hoped-for income against present expenditure by a discounting procedure . . . As much ancient woodland was destroyed in twenty-eight years as in the previous 400 years; the rate of destruction in the 1950s and 1960s was without parallel in history.[224]

Protests persisted.

In the Forestry Act (1951), Parliament directed the Forestry Commission to respect the amenity value of lands that it purchased for plantations.[225] In the 1960s, the Commissioners began to provide picnic areas, trails, and other recreational facilities.[226] By 1965, the Forestry Commission had

---

220. Opposing the cost-benefit analysis of the Forestry Commission, Symonds argued inter alia that "Beauty as a whole, one and indivisible. And it has an absolute claim. You cannot measure it in statistics, or plot its benefits in a curve, as men live by it, and much as by bread or wood-pulp: It has a final value." H.H. Symonds, Afforestation in the Lake District 13 (1936).

221. Symonds, *supra* note 220, at 67.

222. Rackham, *supra* note 53, at 93.

223. *Id.*

224. Rackham, *supra* note 53, at 97.

225. An Act to Provide for the Maintenance of Reserves of Growing Trees in Great Britain and to Regulate the Felling of Trees, to Amend the Procedure Applicable to Compulsory Purchase Orders under the Forestry Act, 1945, and for Purposes Connected with the Matter Aforesaid, 1951, 14 & 15 Geo. 6, c. 61.

226. This did not always satisfy commoners whose land uses would be affected by afforestation. The Royal Commission on Common Land in 1955 recommended full access to all commons lands. Act to Provide for the Registration of Common Land and

adopted policies to conserve and manage wildlife since forests were "acting as a wildlife reservoir."[227] It created a Conservation and Recreation Branch in 1970, and designated its own forest nature reserves.[228]

The battles like those with the Forestry Commission arose in other sectors. World War II–era England had few laws governing land use.[229] In 1925, Parliament modernized its laws on sales and transfers of private property.[230] The stage was set for suburban real estate development. As automobiles enabled strip development along roads, in 1935 Parliament found the need to enact the Ribbon Development Act.[231] While town and country development land planning was still in its infancy, Parliament also enacted statutes facilitating designation of nature reserves in many locations. By 1943, 61 reserves had been established by non-governmental organizations or governmental units.[232] Nonetheless, areas around former Royal Forests faced growing development pressures.

The second half of the 20th century witnessed enactment of stronger land use controls in the wake of rapid post-war real estate development. Government control of land began when the War Ministry ruled that lands were needed for the war effort. To guide post-war recovery, Parliament enacted the Town & Country Planning Act of 1947.[233] Local authorities assumed control over new land. Real estate development flourished, and public debates over competing land uses ensued.

Responding to growing demands for access to open space and strong nature conservation, Parliament withdrew support for treating forests as primarily sources for timber and revenue, and it enacted new laws defining and protecting public interests in forests and countryside. In 1949, Parliament adopted the National Parks and Access to Countryside Act,

---

Town or Village Greens, to Amend the Law as to Prescriptive Claims to Rights of Common, and for Purposes Connected Therewith, 1965, c. 64 (Eng.) (provided for a registration of all commons, but did not provide for how this was to occur) [hereinafter the Commons Registration Act].

227. Forestry Commission, *State Forest Memorandum* of June 1965, *cited in* Evans, *supra* note 181, at 12.

228. MILES, *supra* note 63, at 116–17, 129–32.

229. *See, e.g.*, The Housing and Town Planning Act, 1909, 9 Edw. 7, c. 44; JESSEL, *supra* note 158, at 172–76.

230. JESSEL, *supra* note 158, at 172 (observes that "In 1926 there was, for lawyers, an English revolution. . . . The property legislation of 1922 to 1925 [Notably, the Law of Property Acts of 1922 and 1925, the Settled Land Act 1925 and the Land Registration Act 1925], came into force on the first day of the new year. It did away with many of the ancient laws.").

231. The Restriction of Ribbon Development Act, 1935, 25 & 26 Geo. 5, c. 47.

232. EVANS, *supra* note 181, at 68–69.

233. Town and Country Planning Act, 1947, 10 & 11 Geo. 6, c. 51 [hereinafter the Town and Country Planning Act].

authorizing nature reserves.[234] To help resolve the controversies that raged when commoners' customary rights interfered with new land development, Parliament adopted the Commons Registration Act of 1965,[235] revised again in the Commons Act of 2006.[236] Rules for tree preservation orders were added to the Town & Country Planning Act.[237] Permits to cut down trees were established in the Forestry Act of 1967.[238] Nature reserves were more systematically provided for in the Countryside Act of 1968.[239] The Wildlife & Countryside Act of 1981[240] authorized designation of Sites of Special Scientific Interest (SSSIs) on public and private lands; despite having been designated, SSSIs have sustained damage estimated annually at 5 to 10 percent of sites.[241] SSSI nature reserves were identified in some Royal Forests, such as the New Forest's heaths and mores. While these Acts privileged scientific preservation over other values, such as aesthetics or recreation, Parliament separately acknowledged these forest uses also. In contrast, Areas of Outstanding National Beauty (AONB) were designated

---

234. Access to the Countryside Act, *supra* note 181, at § 15, http://www.legislation .gov.uk/ukpga/Geo6/12-13-14/97. The Act defined nature reserves for (a) "the study of, and research into, matters relating to fauna and flora of Great Britain and the physical conditions in which they live, and for the study of geological and physiographical features of special interest in the area, or (b) of preserving flora, fauna or geological and physio- graphical features of special interest in the area, or for both these purposes."

235. The Commons Registration Act, *supra* note 226.

236. The Commons Act, 2006, c. 26.

237. The Town and Country Planning (Environmental Impact Assessment) Reg- ulations, 2011, S.I. 1824 (U.K.), http://www.legislation.gov.uk/uksi/2011/1824/pdfs /uksi_20111824_en.pdf.

238. An Act to Consolidate the Forestry Acts 1919 to 1963 with Corrections and Improvements Made Under the Consolidation of Enactments (Procedure) Act, 1949 (also known as Forestry Act 1967). The Forestry Act, 1967, c. 10, http://faolex.fao.org/docs /pdf/gbr18985.pdf.

239. An Act to Enlarge the Functions of the Commission Established Under the National Parks and Access to the Countryside Act 1949, to Confer New Powers on Local Authorities and Other Bodies for the Conservation and Enhancement of Natural Beauty and for the Benefit of those Resorting to the Countryside and to Make Other Provision for the Matters Dealt with in the Act of 1949 and Generally as Respects the Country- side, and to Amend the Law about Trees and Woodlands, and Footpaths and Bridleways, and Other Public Paths, 968 c. 41, http://www.legislation.gov.uk/ukpga/1968/41/pdfs /ukpga_19680041_en.pdf (amended in 1973) [hereinafter the Countryside Act].

240. An Act to Repeal and Re-Enact with Amendments the Protection of Birds Acts 1954 to 1967 and the Conservation of Wild Creatures and Wild Plants Act 1975, to Prohibit Certain Methods of Killing or Taking Wild Animals, to Amend the Law Relating to Protection of Certain Mammals, to Restrict the Introduction of Certain Animals and Plants, to Amend the Endangered Species (Import and Export) Act 1976, to Amend the Law Relating to Nature Conservation, the Countryside and National Parks and to Make Provision with Respect to the Countryside Commission, to Amend the Law Relating to Public Rights of Way, and for Connected Purposes, 1981 c. 69.

241. Peter Marren, *Appendix B*, *in* THE COMMON GROUND, *supra* note 54, at 210 (1980).

separately.[242] Hikers, walkers, and ramblers won statutes confirming rights of way across private lands for footpaths. In 2000, the Countryside and Rights of Way Act[243] established rights of access on commons and open space, as did the Marine and Coastal Access Act in 2009.[244]

Statutes also specifically protected species. For example, the Protection of Birds Act (1954)[245] protected wild birds and their nests and eggs, imposing criminal sanctions for violations. Parliament mandated that boards and ministers "take into account any effect which their undertakings could have on 'the natural beauty of the countryside' or flora, fauna or features."[246]

The laws for recreation, aesthetics, science, and conservation often operated independently of each other. Procedures to integrate these various laws in the context of approving new developments were adopted.[247] Laws for environmental impact assessment (EIA) were enacted in response to the 1985 Directive of the European Union.[248] Too often, however, the EIA provisions were applied with a narrow focus. Little effective integration of these various laws was achieved.

In the Wildlife and Countryside (Amendment) Act of 1985, Parliament directed the Forestry Commission to strike a reasonable balance between forestry and the environment.[249] The Commission began to diversify its plantings to include broad-leafed and deciduous trees. In 1991, the Forestry Commission was split into the Forestry Authority, to administer grants and licenses to cut trees on private woodlands, and the Forestry Enterprise, to manage the Forestry estate.[250] The Forestry Enterprise was mandated to protect and enhance the environment and provide recreational facilities. The Commission agreed to manage many SSSI sites. This evolution of the Forestry Commission's work is significant because the Forestry Commission

---

242. EVANS, *supra* note 181, at 80, 82–85. Areas of outstanding natural beauty are designated under the National Parks and Access to the Countryside Act of 1949, but any protection accorded to these areas is provided by local authorities.

243. The Countryside and Rights of Way Act, 2000, c. 37.

244. The Marine and Coastal Access Act, 2009, c. 23.

245. An Act to Amend the Law Relating to the Protection of Birds (also known as Protection of Birds Act), 1954, 2 & 3 Eliz. 2, c. 30, http://www.legislation.gov.uk /ukpga/1954/30/pdfs/ukpga_19540030_en.pdf.

246. Evans, *supra* note 181, at 104.

247. *See, e.g.*, the environmental impact assessment procedures for forestry projects: Forestry Commission, *Environmental Impact Assessment (EIA) (England)*, Forestry Gov UK, http://www.forestry.gov.uk/england-eia (last visited May 20, 2014).

248. Council Directive 85/337/EEC.

249. The Wildlife and Countryside (Amendment) Act, 1985, c. 31.

250. The Forestry Enterprise (FEE) became an executive agency of the Forestry Commission. Forestry Commission, *Forest Enterprise, Local Offices (England)*, FORESTRY Gov UK, http://www.forestry.gov.uk/forestry/HCOU-4U4HZV.

not only governed much land in the former Royal Forests, but it had become the largest landowner in Britain, holding 6 percent of its lands in 1987.[251]

The transformation of the Forestry Commission shadowed an evolving debate over National Parks. Public advocacy for national parks was growing throughout England, not just in the Lake District. Since 1926, the Council for the Preservation of Rural England had been promoting policies to stabilize landscapes and combat the effects of suburban sprawl. In response to public pressure from nature conservationists in 1929, Prime Minister Ramsay MacDonald established a commission to study ways to preserve natural landscapes and wildlife. In 1931, the Addison Commission endorsed creation of national parks in England, but the government delayed responding.[252] Parliament enacted a modest land use planning law, the Town and Country Planning Act of 1932,[253] but it did not stem new land developmental incursions into the countryside, nor did it address past problems. Public protests against past enclosures grew, accompanied by civil disobedience.[254] "Trespass hikes" were held, with landowners complaining and police making arrests.[255] Civil discord marked the renewed fight for "forest liberties," albeit now liberties that were not recognized at the time of the Forest Charter.

After World War II, renewed pressure for establishing a system of national parks emerged. Because the Town and Country Planning Act of 1947[256] empowered local county councils to control land development, local government defended its prerogatives and now opposed ceding authority to any national park agency. Despite its name, the National Parks and Access to the Countryside Act 1949[257] modestly authorized only providing scientific advice about conservation and managing nature reserves. County councils were authorized to provide public access to protected areas and private properties (a response to the unlawful mass trespasses). The Act allowed the term "national park" to be applied to areas that were essentially regional parks for recreation, with various provisions for nature protection while allowing for various roads, farms, and buildings. The Countryside Act of 1968 extended the definition of wild landscapes in national parks to include woodlands.[258] National Parks today cover 9 percent of England and

---

251. Evans, *supra* note 181, at 201.

252. On the Addison Report on National Parks (1931), *see* Miles, *supra* note 63, at 68.

253. The Town and Country Planning Act, 1932, 22 & 23 Geo. 5, c. 48, http://www.legislation.gov.uk/ukpga/1932/48/pdfs/ukpga_19320048_en.pdf.

254. Evans, *supra* note 181, at 62–64.

255. *Id.*

256. The Town and Country Planning Act, *supra* note 233.

257. Access to the Countryside Act, *supra* note 181.

258. The Countryside Act, *supra* note 239.

Wales.[259] The designations overlap with nature reserves and various other environmental conservation categories.

Gradually, as Parliament reshaped England's laws for governing forests and fostering environmental conservation, it supplanted the original statutory provisions of the Forest Charter. New statutes had so often replaced the Charter that its final repeal in 1971 was formalistic and anticlimactic. The interests of commoners, so evident in Forest Charter, were now reflected throughout many Acts of Parliament. The public's "forest liberties" had been redefined.

VI. A Case Study of the New Forest: Contemporary "Liberties of the Forest"

The New Forest is a living synthesis of legal reforms reiterated over many years. It was William the Conqueror's first Royal Forest (1079); today the rule of law mediates competing interests. Carta de Foresta was proclaimed to bring the rule of law to the king's command of the Royal Forests and secure the rights of commoners, whose welfare depended on access to the fields, forests, and waters. The Charter's legacy is reflected in the New Forest's landscape with its once-medieval forest officers, who today serve the rights of commoners to pasturage and herbage and advance the wider public's enjoyment of nature conservation, recreation, and beauty.

New Forest consists of heaths, bogs, and grazed forests, mingled with villages and historic buildings, crossed by lanes and roads and walking paths.[260] Sustaining vast and diverse habitats, New Forest wildlife is exceptional. Inclosures are found there, the result of the Forestry Commission's 40 years of afforestations begun in the 1960s, renewing timber operations in prior eras. Enclosures are found where private estate owners secured leave to remove commoners' rights from their land. Private land owners usually enclose farm or lands planted for wood. Some original heathland is also enclosed and left undeveloped.[261]

Where once perambulations under the Forest Charter set borders, now Acts of Parliament do so.[262] Of the 37,907 hectares within the New

---

259. National Parks include some former Royal Forests, such as Exmoor and New Forest. *See National Parks UK: National Parks UK*, NATIONAL PARKS.GOV.UK, www .nationalparks.gov.uk (last visited May 20, 2014).

260. CLIVE CHATTERS & MIKE READ, NEW FOREST NATIONAL PARK (2009).

261. *See id.*

262. An Act to Alter Perambulations for the New Forest, to Make Further Provisions for the New Forest, to Amend the New Forests Acts 1877 to 1949, and for Purposes Connected with the Matters Aforesaid, 1964, Eliz. 2, c. 83, http://www.legislation.gov.uk /ukpga/1964/83/pdfs/ukpga_19640083_en.pdf [hereinafter New Forest Act 1964].

Forest, portions are owned by Parish Councils, Hampshire County Council, and private owners. Commoners' rights of pasturage cut across all these holdings. An Atlas of Commons Rights (such as for *pasturage* and *pannage*, or rights to collect firewood or turf) are recorded in the Verderers' Court. Animals roaming freely are branded to identify their owner, and marking fees are assessed.

Efforts by the Office of Woods to expand inclosures for plantations in the New Forest, facilitated by the Deer Removal Act of 1851,[263] stimulated intense opposition from commoners and freeholders. Parliament then enacted the New Forest Act of 1871, reinventing the court of Verderers, as a "special board of commons conservators,"[264] whose loyalties were to the Forest itself and the usufructs it supported, not to the Crown or its revenues. Because timber operations under the Crown's Office of Woods conflicted with the usufructs of commoners, this Act also restored powers to the court of Verderers, limited the Crown's right to inclose, and regulated commoners' rights. The court's regulations still guide its administrative and judicial proceedings.[265]

Throughout the 19th century, Verderers opposed legislation requested by the Office of Woods that would authorize expanding inclosures for timber plantations, expanding drainage of wetlands, allowing open burning and clearing, and promoting other projects. As the 20th century opened, the Verderers and commoners were in a "perpetual state of conflict with the Crown."[266] The House of Commons' Select Committee of 1912 reviewed all the "controversies that had plagued the Forest since 1877."[267] World War I interrupted any efforts to resolve disputes, and necessitated military use of parts of the New Forest, with again constraints on the exercise of the rights of commoners. Between the world wars, old tensions resurfaced and new ones emerged. In 1916, the Verderers arranged for insurance for commoners' stock because of increasing numbers of motor vehicle road accidents with commonable animals.[268] World War II brought two airfields and bombing ranges and timbering to the New Forest, leaving it in "a physical and

---

263. An Act to Authorize the Right of the Crown to Deer in the New Forest, and to Give Compensation in Lieu Thereof; and for Other Purposes Relating to the Said Forest, 1851, 14 & 15 Vict. c. 76.

264. ANTHONY PASMORE, VERDERERS OF THE NEW FOREST—A HISTORY OF THE NEW FOREST 1877–1977, at 2 (1976).

265. The New Forest Act 1877, *supra* note 176, at § 24. *See Verderers' Court in the New Forest*, VERDERERS.ORG.UK, *The History of the Verderers*, http://www.verderers.org.uk/court.html (last visited May 20, 2014).

266. PASMORE, *supra* note 264, at 79.

267. *Id.* at 121.

268. *Id.* at 148.

administrative mess."[269] In the post-war years, Parliament adopted statutes for New Forest in 1949 and 1964.[270] Competition intensified between commoners' usufructs, recreational activities, siting of new highways or utility lines, and projects of the Forestry Commission. Verderers fought efforts by the Forestry Commission to sell off open forest without even consulting the Verderers.[271] Verderers opposed commercial expansion of timberlands and urged the Forestry Commission to plant diverse woods, with more broad-leafed trees. Verderers also won an end to unrestrained camping in open forest in 1971.[272] The disputes led Parliament to enact legislation to resolve disputes, and coincidently in 1971 led to the formal repeal of the Forest Charter and remnant incidental duties of the Forest Law.[273]

The New Forest Act of 1949[274] had increased the number of Verderers to nine (five elected, one of whom is the Official Verderer, and four appointed). The Act also authorized the Verderers to adopt bylaws. Today the Verderers exercise powers conferred under the Countryside Act of 1968 (sec. 23),[275] as well as under the New Forest Acts of 1877, 1879, 1949, 1964, and 1970.[276] The court's bylaws[277] specify forest rights of common pasture (ponies, cattle, donkeys, and mules in the Open Forest), common pasture for sheep, a common of *mas* (pigs in the fall devouring acorns), *estovers* for fuel wood, a common of *marl* (the right to dig clay), and a common of *turbary* (the right to cut peat turves). These rights of commoners, confirmed by the Forest Charter, have been practiced in the New Forest since the 11th century. A registry of these rights is published in the Atlas of Forest Rights.[278]

---

269. JAMES, *supra* note 7, at 226–37; F. E. KENCHINGTON, THE COMMONERS' NEW FOREST 144–52 (1944).

270. An Act to Make Further Provisions as Respects the New Forest in the County of Southampton, 1949, 12, 13 &14 Geo. 6, c. 69, http://www.legislation.gov.uk/ukpga /1949/69/pdfs/ukpga_19490069_en.pdf [hereinafter the New Forest Act 1949]; the New Forest Act 1964, *supra* note 262.

271. PASMORE, *supra* note 264, at 220–221.

272. *Id.*

273. The Wild Creatures & Forest Laws Act, *supra* note 8.

274. The New Forest Act, 1949, *supra* note 270.

275. The Countryside Act, *supra* note 239, at § 23.

276. The New Forest Act 1877, *supra* note 176; An Act to Amend the New Forest Act, 1879, 42 & 43 Vict., c. 194; New Forest Act 1949, *supra* note 270; the New Forest Act 1964, *supra* note 262; An Act to Make Further Provision for the New Forest, 1970, c. 21, http://www.legislation.gov.uk/ukpga/1970/21/pdfs/ukpga_19700021_en.pdf?timeline =true.

277. *Policies and Byelaws of the New Forest and Verderers*, VERDERERS.ORG.UK, *Bye-laws*, http://www.verderers.org.uk/policies.html#byelaws (last visited May 20, 2014).

278. For access to the Atlas of Rights, *see Forest Rights in the New Forest*, VERDERERS.ORG.UK, *Byelaws*, http://www.verderers.org.uk/rights.html (last visited May 20, 2014). The New Forest has provisions for registering common rights apart from the Commons Registration Act of 1965.

The Verderers employ agisters to oversee the management of the commoner's stock in the Forest, who inform Verderers of breaches of the bylaws, attend to automobile accidents involving animals and deal with injured animals, and manage the fall roundups of ponies and cattle. The Verderers' court is formally the Courts of Attachment and Swainmote, and it hears presentments from forest residents about issues affecting the environment and the various uses made of the Forest. While the Verderers' court can prosecute criminal offenses of protected forest interests, these today are usually handled by the Magistrate's Court in Lyndhurst or Southampton. Many "pleas of the forest" today involve charges of automobiles driving through the New Forest colliding with free-ranging animals.[279]

Today the New Forest is a biologically diverse place, with an amalgam of overlapping laws and institutions. The forest regime accommodates commoners' rights to access forest assets, respect for local villages and their land development roles, nature protection, recreation and public access, sustainable forestry practices, and yield revenues. It is a regime adapting to new technologies and times, and perhaps its whole is greater than the sum of its parts. Sylvie Nail observes,

> A study of landscape preservation campaigns at the turn of the 20th century devotes a passage to the New Forest in the 1890s, and the arguments used are worth noting, all the more so as the New Forest represents the Royal Forest *par excellence*. They refer mostly, not to the landscape or amenity value of the site, but to the historical and heritage value of the Forest, stating that the New Forest provided a glimpse of "the England that was and ceased to be," the "England of the outlaw, or the singer of ballads, of the lover of the greenwood life." This vision of the New Forest as a "national inheritance," providing a "connection with the Saxon origins of modern England" . . . .[280]

To all other forest uses, cultural heritage now is added. Cultural memory is a principal reason given for preserving New Forest as a national park. The New Forest National Park was established in 2005, the first to be designated after Northumberland National Park was named in 1956, and the smallest to have been designated.[281]

---

279. Annually between 1955 and 1975, between 170 and 349 motor vehicle accidents with commonable stock took place on roads traversing the New Forest. *See* Passmore, *supra* note 264, at app. IV, at 278.

280. Nail, *supra* note 36, at 18 (citing Paul Readman, *Landscape Preservation, "Advertising Disfigurement" and English National Identity c. 1890–1914*, 12 Rural Hist: Econ. Soc'y, Culture 61, 61–83 (2001)). A number of articles and books about New Forest exist. *See, e.g.*, Sarah Nield, Forest Law and the Verderers of the New Forest (2005).

281. *Id.*

The Verderers court's roles overlap with other authorities in the New Forest. Jurisdictional conflicts among authorities are resolved largely by negotiations through various planning systems. The Verderers and the Forestry Commission have a Memorandum of Understanding[282] regarding the exercise of their respective responsibilities within the Forest. The Forestry Commission's duties to provide recreation, including appropriating land in the New Forest for recreation, involve operating camping, sporting, and other recreational activities. Tensions still exist between competing uses and safeguarding the remnant primeval ecological niches, SSIS sites, and heritage areas. The Forestry Commission has its own planning procedures.[283] The Verderers also have their own guidelines for the competing interests found in the New Forest: "precious wilderness or suburban park?"[284] There is also the Master Plan (2010–2015) of the National Park Authority, which is a branch of local government, representing local councils, the Crown, and the public.[285]

Numerous additional layers of law also exist to confirm the stewardship of nature in New Forest. The European Union's Wild Birds and Habitats directives apply.[286] New Forest's wetlands are registered under the Ramsar Convention on Wetlands of International Importance.[287] New Forest is also a UNESCO World Heritage Site.[288]

---

282. *Verderers' Court in the New Forest, supra* note 43; MEMORANDUM OF UNDERSTANDING BETWEEN THE FORESTRY COMMISSIONERS AND THE VERDERERS OF THE NEW FOREST (2002), http://www.verderers.org.uk/mou.pdf.

283. *Forestry Commission Homepage,* FORESTRY.GOV.UK, http://www.forestry.gov.uk (last visited May 20, 2014).

284. THE VERDERERS OF THE NEW FOREST, THE NEW FOREST: PRECIOUS WILDERNESS OR SUBURBAN PARK? (2007), http://www.verderers.org.uk/wilderness_park.pdf.

285. *See New Forest National Park Authority Homepage,* NEWFORESTNPA, http://www.newforestnpa.gov.uk (last visited May 20, 2014).

286. Council Directive 2009/147/EC of the European Parliament and of the Council of 30 Nov. 2009 on the Conservation of Wild Birds, 2009 O.J. (L 20) (EU), http://eur-lex.europa.eu/legal-content/EN/TXT/PDF/?uri=CELEX:32009L0147&from=EN (also known as "The Wild Birds Directive"); Council Directive 92/43/EEC of 21 May 1992 on the Conservation of Natural Habitats and of Wild Fauna and Flora, 1992 O.J. (L 206) (EC), http://eur-lex.europa.eu/legal-content/EN/TXT/PDF/?uri=CELEX:31992L0043&from=EN (also known as "Habitats Directive"). For guidance on the application of article 6(4) in England see, DEPARTMENT FOR ENVIRONMENT, FOOD & RURAL AFFAIRS, HABITATS AND WILD BIRDS DIRECTIVES: GUIDANCE ON THE APPLICATION OF ARTICLE 6(4) (2012), https://www.gov.uk/government/uploads/system/uploads/attachment_data/file/69622/pb13840-habitats-iropi-guide-20121211.pdf.

287. Convention on Wetlands of International Importance Especially as Waterfowl Habitat, Feb. 2, 1971, T.I.A.S. 11084, 996 U.N.T.S. 245, *amended by* the Paris Protocol, Dec. 3, 1982, *and* Regina Amendments, May 28, 1987, http://www.ramsar.org/cda/en/ramsar-documents-texts-convention-on/main/ramsar/1-31-38%5E20671_4000_0__.

288. United Nations Educational, Scientific and Cultural Organization, Convention Concerning the Protection of the World Cultural and Natural Heritage, Nov. 16, 1972,

Major threats to New Forest arise from increasing demands from urban and suburban populations located nearby. Some 24 million visitors and tourists use New Forest for recreation every year. The need to produce revenues to manage the various recreation and conservation programs is ongoing. At the same time, New Forest finds it must cope with the rise in sea level on its coasts and the changes that new weather patterns bring.

The accretion of legal stewardship regimes in the New Forest complicates how such new problems will be addressed. National Park planning procedures guide negotiations about the future administration of New Forest. Environmental laws, mandating protection for nature, constrain new human endeavors. Just as the Forest Charter once constrained the king, now Parliamentary Acts constrain all to conserve biological features. The bogs, downs and other heaths, ponds, woods, rivers, fields, coastal wetlands, eelgrass, lagoons, and foreshores are protected for themselves.

VII.   Conclusion: The Once and Future "Liberties of the Forest"

If the history of the Forest Charter demonstrates nothing else, it is that human management of forests is controversial. This is so not just in England but in all countries. The United Nations Earth Summit in 1992 agreed on a great deal about sustainable development, but it could not agree on a treaty about forests.[289] The eight centuries of policy changes, political jockeying, and legal decision making with respect to Carta de Foresta and Royal Forests in England are remarkable in providing a well-documented record of cultural evolution. By privileging extensive forest biomes with legal protection, the law ensured their continuity for both humans and nature. The Royal Forests were the subject of many disputes and even warfare over conflicting uses of the same natural resources, but because the Crown initially had set each forest aside, their essential biological, hydrologic, and other natural systems were allowed to function overtime without irreversible human interruption. The legal (*de jure*) protection afforded by the initial Royal Forest designation,

---

1037 U.N.T.S. 151; 27 UST 37, http://whc.unesco.org/archive/convention-en.pdf (commonly referred to as the World Heritage Convention).

289. In 1992, the United Nations Conference on Environment and Development (UNCED) in Rio de Janeiro agreed on recommendations for combating deforestation in Chapter 11 of *Agenda 21*, but rather than negotiate an international agreement on forests as International Union for Conservation of Nature and others had urged, UNCED adopted a statement titled the "Non-legally Binding Authoritative Statement of Principles For A Global Consensus on the Management, Conservation and Sustainable Development of all Types of Forests." *See* N.A. ROBINSON, AGENDA 21: EARTH'S ACTION PLAN 666 (1993) (reprinting the Statement of Principles).

coupled with the rights later accorded by the Forest Charter, had the *de facto* consequence of inducing most development, urbanization, industrialization, and other activities destructive of forests, to locate elsewhere.

England's intergenerational record of sustaining large natural areas may serve humans and nature well in the future. Sustaining extensive natural areas is important in the era of climate change. The Anthropocene Epoch disrupts human development and transforms landscapes.[290] Where natural systems are robust, ecology teaches that they can reset, adapt, and persist.[291] Where they are degraded, or fragile, or managed for an exclusive, single purpose, they may be lost. The size of the intact biological area is important in this respect. The history of the Forest Charter offers guidance for human stewardship necessary to conserve large natural areas to allow for their evolution in Earth's new climatic conditions.

There are at least five dimensions of the Forest Charter's legacy that deserve further study. First, human society's stewardship to sustain ecosystems depends upon having a just stewardship framework that understands and values the way nature provides services to humans, and therefore acts to conserve nature. Humans can understand the reciprocity involved in enabling nature to thrive in order to provide for human needs.

Second, justice is an innate requirement of stable human stewardship regimes, and depends on the rule of law. Without the rule of law, there is neither sustainable development nor a peaceful social order. The gradual evolution of parliamentary acts and judicial decisions from the early forest councils and eyres built an expectation that law could ensure exercise of forest rights. The settlement of the many incidents of injustice in administration of the Royal Forests over time built institutions and norms that respected the rule of law.

Third, "forests" cannot be reduced to a single definition or purpose, such as being dedicated solely for producing timber or hunting deer. "Forests" are nested richly in layers of relationships with many species and systems, such as the Earth's hydrologic or carbon cycles. This complex of forest ecosystems in turn is networked into a great variety of human expectations and needs. Deer hunting and autumnal pannage for pigs can coexist with plant photosynthesis and aquifer recharge through wetlands. Stewardship of natural resources entails diffuse complexes of land uses, claims, and entitlements, and rights about the same natural places, and their ecosystem

---

290. *See* Will Steffen et al., *The Anthropocene: Are Humans Now Overwhelming the Great Forces of Nature?* 36 AMBIO 614, 614–21 (Dec, 2007).

291. B. WALKER & D. SALT, RESILIENCE THINKING: SUSTAINING ECOSYSTEMS & PEOPLE IN A CHANGING WORLD (2006). For the studies at the Stockholm Resilience Center, *see Stockholm Resilience Center*, STOCKHOLMRESILIENCE, *Sustainability Science for Biosphere Stewardship*, http://www.stockholmresilience.org (last visited May 20, 2014).

services and functions. A sustainable legal regime, as has evolved in the New Forest, recognizes and accommodates these competing interests.

Fourth, the efficacy of nature conservation depends on the multilayered legal regime that emerges from respecting a community of values and expectations, such as has grown up about each of the former Royal Forests, as well as the involvement of civil society. When forest rights of commoners were threatened by either the king, landed gentry asserting exclusivity of hunting rights, or the Office of Woods or Forestry Commission planning inclosures for timber plantations, the responses were protests, riots, civil disobedience, and demands for law reforms. Ultimately the curia regis and eventually Parliament would reassert a balance among competing rights. Overlapping or competing forest rights produce messy politics, but they can induce dispute-resolution systems, reaffirming the rule of law and sustaining the ecosystems without which no forest rights would exist.

Fifth, legal regimes that accommodate this sort of competition end up promoting cooperation, as planning systems at work in the New Forest illustrate. Disputes are not eliminated but are channeled into regimes for collaboration, which result in sustaining the natural resource. All stakeholders need a seat at the table.

Where these five dimensions of ecological stewardship are found, natural systems tend to be sustained, maintaining their benefits to humans. Reciprocal rights and responsibilities produce dynamic interactions that maintain a balance of human uses, as is evident in England's Royal Forests today. Encroachments, or overreaching by any one interest, produces reactions by other adversely affected interests. When competing forest users are aware of each other, expectations about how to behave are shared, and accommodation of other interests is possible.[292] As the case study of New Forest illustrates, when disruptions emerge, there is a struggle to reset the balance of relationships. This resilience merits wider analysis.

The Forest Charter embedded in the culture of the English people an expectation that they possessed "liberties of the forest" worth defending. Were it not for the Forest Charter, England would have conserved fewer of its large Royal Forest natural areas.

The Forest Charter has wider legacies as well. English biologists and lawyers have been leaders in expanding protected areas around the world, through the International Union for the Conservation of Nature (IUCN).[293] Large areas conserve biological diversity[294] and sustain photosynthesis

---

292. These dynamics are found in academic studies of forest governance in places other than England. *See, e.g.*, Ryan C.L. Bullock & Kevin S. Hanna, Community Forestry 1–42 (2012).

293. Martin Holdgate, The Green Web (1999); Evans, *supra* note 181.

294. Convention on Biological Diversity, *supra* note 44.

services that remove carbon dioxide from the atmosphere.[295] Through the United Kingdom's membership in the European Union, English law implements the Habitats Directive,[296] the Wild Birds Directive,[297] and the UNESCO 1972 Convention Concerning Protection of the World Cultural and Natural Heritage.[298] Internationally, both the Forest Charter and Magna Carta repeatedly inspire the adoption of new charters to further the rule of law. The United Nations General Assembly adopted the World Charter for Nature,[299] whose principles are incorporated into the Convention on Biological Diversity. An Earth Charter is promoted by civil society and some governments.[300] Multilateral environmental agreements are evolving a complex system of laws to protect the biosphere.[301]

These intergovernmental laws now also serve former Royal Forests. The complexity of the interrelated laws protecting the many stakeholder interests in the New Forest only make it more likely to be sustained. Where too few laws exist to protect a site, what scant legal protection exists can be stripped away, with rapid and irreversible loss to ecosystems. Ecosystem complexity is matched by the legal complexity of statutes and customs that align the laws of humans with the laws of nature.

It is possible that law and ecology have combined in this felicitous manner not merely by coincidence. The biologist Edward O. Wilson has posited that humans have an instinct to protect nature, which he terms "biophilia."[302] The history of the Forest Charter and England's Royal Forests lends support to his hypothesis.[303] Humans saved English forest areas since the 12th century not only because they depended on them for survival, but also because they had an affinity for these natural areas. Their *evolved norms* became customary law and eventually statutory law, replete with administrative implementation.[304]

---

295. See IUCN, LEGAL FRAMEWORKS FOR REDD: DESIGN & IMPLEMENTATION AT THE NATIONAL LEVEL 3–11 (John Costenbader ed., 2009), https://portals.iucn.org /library/efiles/documents/EPLP-077.pdf (REDD stands for reducing emissions from deforestation and degradation).

296. See 92/43/EEC, *supra* note 286.

297. Council Directive 79/409/EEC.

298. See Convention Concerning the Protection of the World Cultural and Natural Heritage, Nov. 23 1972, 27 U.S.T. 37, 1037 U.N.T.S. 151, http://whc.unesco.org/archive /convention-en.pdf.

299. G.A. Res. 37/7, U.N. Doc. A/RES/37/7 (Oct. 28, 1982).

300. The Earth Charter, Earth Charter Commission (2000), http://www.earthcharter inaction.org/invent/images/uploads/echarter_english.pdf.

301. MANUAL ON INTERNATIONAL ENVIRONMENTAL LAW (L. Kurukulasuriya & N.A. Robinson eds., 2006).

302. E.O. WILSON, BIOPHILIA: THE HUMAN BOND WITH OTHER SPECIES (1984).

303. STEPHEN R. KELLER & EDWARD O. WILSON, THE BIOPHILIA HYPOTHESIS (1993).

304. Nicholas A. Robinson, *Evolved Norms: A Canon for the Anthropocene, in* CHRISTINA VOIGT, RULE OF LAW FOR NATURE: NEW DIMENSIONS AND IDEAS IN ENVIRONMENTAL LAW 46–72 (2013).

The history of the Forest Charter also offers insights about how property law works. Exclusivity of title is a fragile way to sustain nature. Instead, recognizing multiple rights and shared uses of the same natural system is more robust, and fosters resilience. Stakeholders act to conserve the resources upon which they mutually depend. The history of the Forest Charter teaches that shared rights can be sustained over time, even in the face of efforts by persons in power to rescind or restrict those rights. Common property rights, exercised locally, have as much or more staying capacity than do private property rights. They require legal recognition and the legal means by which they can be asserted, and vindicated. Guided by the Forest Charter, England's system of Forest Law legitimized common rights, often seemingly against all odds. Comparable dynamics are at work in contemporary forest struggles, as is evident in applying the environmental rights accorded by Article 225 of the Constitution of Brazil to administration of Brazil's Forest Code in the Amazon.[305]

Finally, at a time when many nations have yet to embrace the rule of law, the history of the Forest Charter offers lessons for resolving conflicts over natural resources and suggests ways to foster the rule of law. The elements of the Forest Charter's effectiveness can be applied to the work of conservationists elsewhere. In Russia, conservationists have repeatedly won battles to conserve Lake Baikal. China has established pervasive nature conservation programs in Yunnan Province and elsewhere. In central Africa, customary law together with national park designations sustains ecological systems, against all odds.

Where environmental laws lack the resilience of the Forest Charter, it may be because they are not grounded in a specific forest or for a particular species, or because the political system does not allow expression and resolution of opposing views. For example, hunting or endangered species laws are effective because they target specific species and specify unjust behavior.[306] The survival of Royal Forests suggests that legal systems work robustly when law is connected to nature, and where those who seek to vindicate the law have access to a relatively balanced and neutral system for resolving competing demands.

Sharing a common birth, Magna Carta and Carta de Foresta are foundations for the principle and practice of the rule of law. This alone

---

305. Nicholas S. Bryner, *Brazil's Green Court: Environmental Law in the Superior Tribunal de Justiça (High Court of Brazil)*, 29 PACE ENVT'L L. REV. 441, 470–537 (2012).

306. Compare the current smuggling and unlawful trade in endangered species today, under the Convention on the International Trade in Endangered Species, with the unlawful taking of game in the Royal Forests. *See* Convention on the International Trade in Endangered Species, Mar. 3, 1973, 27 U.S.T. 1087, 993 U.N.T.S. 243, http://www.cites.org/sites/default/files/eng/disc/E-Text.pdf; ARTHUR L. CROSS, EIGHTEENTH CENTURY DOCUMENTS IN RELATION TO THE ROYAL FORESTS—THE SHERIFFS AND SMUGGLING (1928).

is sufficient reason to celebrate the Forest Charter after almost 800 years. Yet today the history of the Forest Charter resonates also for what it teaches about how society values and conserves nature. The history of the Forest Charter invites new inquiries into how law shapes nature that in turn nurtures the well-being of humans. Both Charters hold transcendent importance in society's adaptations to changing climatic conditions, Magna Carta for bolstering the rule of law in troubled times, and Carta de Foresta for stimulating resilient norms for stewardship of nature. As it was for past generations, the wider value of the Forest Charter is to serve the next generation.

APPENDIX A
Coronation Charter of Henry I*

Henry, king of the English, to Bishop Samson and Urso de Abetot and all his barons and faithful, both French and English, of Worcestershire,[1] greeting.

[1] Know that by the mercy of God and the common Counsel of the barons of the whole kingdom of England I have been crowned king of said kingdom; and because the kingdom had been oppressed by unjust exactions, I, through fear of God and the love which I have toward you all, in the first place make the holy church of God free, so that I will neither sell nor put to farm [sic], nor on the death of archbishop or bishop or abbot will I take anything from the church's demesne or from its men until the successor shall enter it. And I take away all the bad customs by which the kingdom of England was unjustly oppressed; which bad customs I here set down in part:

[2] If any of my barons, earls, or others who hold of me shall have died, his heir shall not buy back his land as he used to do in the time of my brother, but he shall relieve it by a just and lawful relief. Likewise also the men of my barons shall relieve their lands from their lords by a just and lawful relief.

[3] And if any of my barons or other men should wish to give his daughter, sister, niece, or kinswoman in marriage, let him speak with me about it; but I will neither take anything from him for this permission nor prevent his giving her unless he should be minded to join her to my enemy. And if, upon the death of a baron or other of my men, a daughter is left as heir, I will give her with her land by the advice of my barons. And if, on the death of her husband, the wife is left and without children, she shall have her dowry and right of marriage, and I will not give her to a husband unless according to her will.

[4] But if a wife be left with children, she shall indeed have her dowry and right of marriage so long as she shall keep her body lawfully, and I will not give her unless according to her will. And the guardian of the land and

---

*Latin text *in* WILLIAM STUBBS, SELECT CHARTERS 117–19 (9th ed. 1913). The translation reproduced here was found in ALBERT BEEBE WHITE & WALLACE NOTESTEIN, SOURCE PROBLEMS IN ENGLISH HISTORY 367–70 (1915).

Note: All footnotes are from the translation.

1. Copies were sent to all the shires.

children shall be either the wife or another of the relatives who more justly ought to be. And I command that my barons restrain themselves similarly in dealing with the sons and daughters or wives of their men.

[5] The common seigniorage, which has been taken through the cities and counties, but which was not taken in the time of King Edward, I absolutely forbid henceforth. If any one, whether a moneyer or other, be taken with false money, let due justice be done for it.

[6] I remit all pleas and all debts which were owing to my brother, except my lawful fixed revenues and except those amounts which had been agreed upon for the inheritances of others or for things which more justly concerned others. And if any one had pledged anything for his own inheritance, I remit it; also all reliefs which had been agreed upon for just inheritances.

[7] And if any of my barons or men shall grow feeble, as he shall give or arrange to give his money, I grant that it be so given. But if, prevented by arms or sickness, he shall not have given or arranged to give his money, his wife, children, relatives, or lawful men shall distribute it for the good of his soul as shall seem best to them.

[8] If any of my barons or men commit a crime, he shall not bind himself to a payment at the king's mercy as he has been doing in the time of my father or my brother; but he shall make amends according to the extent of the crime as he would have done before the time of my father in the time of my other predecessors. But if he be convicted of treachery or heinous crime, he shall make amends as is just.

[9] I forgive all murders committed before the day I was crowned king; and those which shall be committed in the future shall be justly compensated according to the law of King Edward.

[10] By the common consent of my barons I have kept in my hands the forests as my father had them.

[11] To those knights who render military service for their lands I grant of my own gift that the lands of their demesne ploughs be free from all payments and all labor, so that, having been released from so great a burden, they may equip themselves well with horses and arms and be fully prepared for my service and the defense of my kingdom.

[12] I impose a strict peace upon my whole kingdom and command that it be maintained henceforth.

[13] I restore to you the law of King Edward with those amendments introduced into it by my father with the advice of his barons.

[14] If any one, since the death of King William my brother, has taken anything belonging to me or to any one else, the whole is to be quickly

restored without fine; but if any one keep anything of it, he upon whom it shall be found shall pay me a heavy fine.

Witnesses Maurice bishop of London, and William bishop elect of Winchester, and Gerard bishop of Hereford, and earl Henry, and earl Simon, and Walter Giffard, and Robert de Montfort, and Roger Bigot, and Eudo the steward, and Robert son of Hamo, and Robert Malet. At London when I was crowned. Farewell.

APPENDIX B
Articles of the Barons*

[1] After the death of their predecessors, heirs of full age are to have their inheritance by the ancient relief to be set out in the charter.

[2] Heirs who are under age and in wardship are when they come of age to have their inheritance without relief or fine.

[3] The guardian of an heir's land is to take reasonable issues, customs and services, without destruction and waste of his men and goods, and if the guardian of the land inflicts destruction and waste, he is to lose the wardship. And the guardian is to maintain buildings, parks, fishponds, pools, mills and other things pertaining to that land, out of the issues of the same. And heirs are to be so married that they are not disparaged, and this by the counsel of their near kinsmen.

[4] No widow is to give anything for her dower or marriage portion after the death of her husband, but she may remain in his house for forty days after his death, and her dower is to be assigned to her within that period; and she is to have her marriage portion and her inheritance immediately.

[5] Neither the king nor his bailiff are to seize any land for debt while the debtor's chattels suffice; nor are the debtor's pledges to be distrained, while the principal debtor has enough to make payment; if indeed the principal debtor defaults on his payment, the pledges are, if they wish, to have the debtor's lands until the debt is fully paid, unless the principal debtor can show that he is quit with regard to the pledges.

[6] The king is not to grant to any baron the right to take an aid from his free men, except to ransom his person, to knight his first-born son, and to marry, once, his first-born daughter, and he is to do this by way of a reasonable aid.

[7] No-one is to do more service for a knight's fee than is owed for it.

[8] Common pleas are not to follow the king's court, but are to be appointed to some fixed place. And recognitions are to be held in the same

---

*Latin text *in* WILLIAM STUBBS, SELECT CHARTERS 285–91 (9th ed. 1913). The translation reproduced here was prepared by Dr. Henry Summerson in 2012 for the AHRC Magna Carta Project. From: *The Magna Carta Project, The Articles of the Barons,* THE MAGNA CARTA PROJECT (2012), http://magnacarta.cmp.uea.ac.uk/read/articles _of_barons/!all.

counties, in this manner: the king is to send two justices four times in the year, who with four knights of the same county, chosen by the county court, are to take assizes of novel disseisin, mort d'ancestor and darrein present-ment, nor is anyone to be summoned on account of this except the jurors and the two parties.

[9] A free man is to be amerced for a small offence in proportion to the nature of the offence, and for a great offence in accordance with its mag-nitude, saving to him his livelihood; the villein is also to be amerced in the same way, saving to him his crops under cultivation; and the merchant in the same way, saving to him his stock in trade, by oath of trustworthy men of the vicinity.

[10] A cleric is to be amerced in respect of his lay fee in the same manner as the aforesaid, and without regard to his ecclesiastical benefice.

[11] No township is to be amerced for making bridges over rivers, unless they used rightfully to be there of old.

[12] The measure of corn and wine, and the widths of cloths and other things, are to be reformed; and weights likewise.

[13] Assizes of novel disseisin and mort d'ancestor are to be expedited, and other assizes likewise.

[14] No sheriff is to involve himself in pleas pertaining to the crown without the coroners; and counties and hundreds are to be at their old farms without any increment, except for the king's demesne manors.

[15] If anyone holding from the king dies, it is to be lawful for the sheriff or other royal bailiff to seize and record his chattels by the view of law-abiding men, as long as none of them are removed, until it is more fully known whether he owes any clear debt to the king; and then when the debt to the king is paid, the residue is to be relinquished to the executors to perform the testament of the deceased; and if nothing is owing to the king then all the chattels are to go to the deceased.

[16] If any free man dies intestate, his goods are to be distributed by the hand of his nearest kinsmen on both sides of his family, under the supervi-sion of the church.

[17] Widows are not to be distrained to marry, when they wish to live without a husband, as long as they give security that they will not marry without the consent of the king, if they hold of him, or the consent of their lords of whom they hold.

[18] No constable or other bailiff is to take corn or other chattels, unless he pays cash for them immediately, (or) unless he has respite with the con-sent of the seller.

[19] No constable is to distrain any knight to give money instead of castle-guard, if he is willing to perform that guard in person or, if he is unable to do it for a satisfactory reason, through another reliable man; and if the king takes him in the army, he is to be quit of castle-guard in proportion to the amount of time [away].

[20] No sheriff or royal bailiff, or anyone else, is to take any free man's horses or carts for transporting things, except with his consent.

[21] Neither the king nor his bailiff is to take another man's wood to his castles or on other of his business, except with the consent of the person whose wood it is.

[22] The king is not to hold the land of those who have been convicted of felony except for a year and a day, and then it is to be surrendered to the lord of the fee.

[23] All fish-weirs are in future to be entirely removed from the Thames and Medway, and throughout the whole of England.

[24] The writ called praecipe is not in future to be issued to anyone for any tenement in respect of which a free man could lose his court.

[25] If anyone has been disseised or dispossessed without judgment by the king of lands, liberties and his right, it is to be restored to him immediately; and if a dispute arises about this, it is to be settled by judgment of the twenty-five barons; and those who were disseised by the king's father or brother are to have their right without delay by judgment of their peers in the king's court; and the archbishop and bishops are to deliver judgment at a specific day, without the possibility of an appeal, as to whether the king ought to have the term [of exemption] of other crusaders.

[26] Nothing is to be given for a writ for an inquest concerning life or members, but it is to be granted without payment and not denied.

[27] If anyone holds of the king by fee-farm, socage or burgage, and of someone else by knight service, the king is not to have the wardship of the knights of another man's fee by reason of the burgage or socage, nor is he to have the wardship of the burgage, socage or fee-farm. And no free man is to lose his knights by reason of petty serjeanties, like those who hold a tenement by rendering knives or arrows or suchlike.

[28] No bailiff is to put anyone to law by his accusation alone, without trustworthy witnesses.

[29] The body of a free man is not to be arrested, or imprisoned, or disseised, or outlawed, or exiled, or in any way ruined, nor is the king to go against him or send forcibly against him, except by judgment of his peers or by the law of the land.

[30] Right is not to be sold or delayed or withheld.

[31] Merchants are to have safe conduct to go and come to buy and sell, without any evil exactions but paying only the old and rightful customs.

[32] No scutage or aid is to be imposed in the kingdom except by the common counsel of the kingdom, unless for ransoming the person of the king, and knighting his first-born son, and marrying, once, his first-born daughter, and for this a reasonable aid is to be taken. Tallages and aids on the city of London, and on other cities which have such liberties, are to be taken in like manner. And the city of London is to have in full its ancient liberties and free customs, both by water and by land.

[33] It is to be lawful for each man to leave the kingdom and return to it, saving his allegiance to the king, except in time of war for some short time, for the sake of the common utility of the kingdom.

[34] If anyone has taken a loan from Jews, great or small, and dies before the debt is paid, the debt is not to incur interest as long as the heir is under age, whoever he may hold from. And if the debt falls into the hand of the king, he is to take only the principal recorded in the charter.

[35] If anyone dies and is indebted to Jews, let his wife have her dower. And if there are surviving children, let their needs be met from the property, and let the debt be paid from the residue, saving the service of the lords. And let other debts be dealt with in like manner. And let the keeper of the land surrender to the heir, when he comes of age, his land stocked with what the issues of the land can reasonably provide by way of ploughs and other necessary implements.

[36] If anyone holds of an escheat, as of the honour(s) of Wallingford, Nottingham, Boulogne and Lancaster, or of other escheats which are in the king's hand and are baronies, and dies, his heir will not give a relief or perform any service to the king other than he would to the baron; and the king is to hold it in the same manner in which the baron held it.

[37] Fines made for dowers, marriages, inheritances and amercements, unjustly and against the law of the land, are to be entirely remitted; or they are to be dealt with by judgment of the twenty-five barons, or by judgment of the greater part of them, together with the archbishop and others whom he wishes to convoke to act with him. On condition that if any or some of the twenty-five are in such an action, they are to be removed and others substituted in their place by the rest of the twenty-five.

[38] Hostages and bonds which were surrendered to the king as security are to be restored.

[39] Those who have been outside the forest are not to come before the forest justices on the grounds of common summonses, unless they are involved

in pleadings or [are] pledges. And the evil customs of forests and foresters, of warrens, and sheriffs, and rivers, are to be put right by twelve knights of each county, who should be chosen by the good men of that county.

[40] Let the king remove entirely from office the kinsmen and whole brood of Gerard d'Athée, so that they may not hold office in future: namely, Engelard, Andrew, Peter and Guy de Chanceaux, Guy de Cigogné, Matthew de Martigny and his brothers; and his nephew Geoffrey, and Philip Mark.

[41] And let the king remove the foreign knights, mercenaries, crossbowmen, routiers and serjeants who come with horses and arms to the detriment of the realm.

[42] And let the king make justices, constables, sheriffs and bailiffs from those who know the law of the land and are willing to keep it well.

[43] Let barons who have founded abbeys, for which they have royal charters or ancient tenure, have the custody of them when they are vacant.

[44] If the king has disseised or dispossessed Welshmen of their lands, liberties or anything else in England or, in Wales, they are to be given back to them immediately, without any legal proceedings. And if they were disseised or dispossessed of their English tenements by the king's father or brother without judgment of their peers, the king will without delay do them justice, in the same way that he is to do justice to Englishmen, for tenements in England according to the law of England, for tenements in Wales according to the law of Wales, and for tenements in the march according to the law of the march. Let the Welsh do the same for the king and his men.

[45] Let the king give back the son of Llywelyn, and also other hostages from Wales, and the bonds which were handed over to him as security for peace, unless things should be otherwise under the charters which the king has, by judgment of the archbishop and such others as he wishes to convoke to act with him.

[46] Let the king deal with the king of Scots for the returning of hostages, and over his liberties and right, in accordance with the terms he comes to with the barons of England, unless it should be otherwise under the charters which the king has, by judgment of the archbishop and such others as he wishes to convoke to act with him.

[47] And all the forests which have been afforested by the king during his reign are to be disafforested, and let the same be done with regard to the rivers which are game reserves by this king's doing.

[48] What is more, all these customs and liberties which the king has granted to the realm, to be observed on his own account with regard to his own men, all the men of the realm, both clergy and laity, will observe on their own account with regard to their own men.

APPENDIX C
1215 Magna Carta[*]

John by God's grace king of England, lord of Ireland, duke of Normandy and Aquitaine, count of Anjou, to his archbishops, bishops, abbots, earls, barons, justices, foresters, sheriffs, reeves, officers and all bailiffs and subjects, greeting. Know that for the sake of God and for the salvation of our soul and the souls of all our forebears and heirs, to the honour of God and the advancement of [the] holy church, and the reform of our kingdom, by the counsel of our venerable fathers Stephen, archbishop of Canterbury, primate of all England and cardinal of the holy Roman church; Henry, archbishop of Dublin; Bishops William of London, Peter of Winchester, Joscelin of Bath and Glastonbury, Hugh of Lincoln, Walter of Worcester, William of Coventry and Benedict of Rochester; Master Pandulf, subdeacon and confidant of the lord pope, Brother Eymeric, master of the Knights Templar in England; and the noble men William Marshal, earl of Pembroke, William, earl of Salisbury, William, earl of Warenne, William, earl of Arundel, Alan of Galloway, constable of Scotland, Warin fitzGerold, Peter fitzHerbert, Hubert de Burgh, seneschal of Poitou, Hugh de Neville, Matthew fitzHerbert, Thomas Basset, Alan Basset, Philip d'Aubigny, Robert of Ropsley, John Marshal, John fitzHugh, and others of our subjects:

[1] We have first of all granted to God, and by this our present charter confirmed, for ourselves and our heirs in perpetuity, that the English Church is to be free, and to have its full rights and its liberties intact, and we wish this to be observed accordingly, as may appear from our having of our true and unconstrained volition, before discord arose between us and our barons, granted, and by our charter confirmed, the freedom of elections which is deemed to be the English Church's very greatest want, and obtained its

---

[*]Latin text *in* WILLIAM STUBBS, SELECT CHARTERS 292–302 (9th ed. 1913). The translation reproduced here was prepared by Dr. Henry Summerson in 2012 for the AHRC Magna Carta Project. From: *The Magna Carta Project, Magna Carta 1215*, THE MAGNA CARTA PROJECT (2012), http://magnacarta.cmp.uea.ac.uk/read/magna_carta_1215/!all.

Note: The British Library provides a translation to the 1215 Magna Carta with annotations to all clauses removed thereafter. The translation also provides which 1215 clauses are valid under the 1225 version. British Library, *Treasures in Full: Magna Carta, Translation*, BL.UK, http://www.bl.uk/treasures/magnacarta/translation/mc_trans.html (last visited May 30, 2014).

confirmation by the lord pope Innocent III; which we will ourselves observe and wish to be observed by our heirs in good faith in perpetuity. And we have also granted to all the free men of our kingdom, for ourselves and our heirs in perpetuity, all the following liberties, for them and their heirs to have and to hold of us and our heirs.

[2] If any of our earls or barons, or others holding in chief of us by knight service, shall die and his heir at his decease shall be of full age and owes a relief, he is to have his inheritance by the old relief: that is, for the heir or heirs of an earl £100 for the whole barony of the earl; the heir or heirs of a baron £100 for the whole barony; the heir or heirs of a knight 100 shillings at the most for a whole knight's fee; and anyone owing less is to give less according to the ancient custom of fees.

[3] If, however, the heir of any of the above shall be under age and in wardship, when he comes of age he is to have his inheritance without a relief and without a fine.

[4] The guardian of the land of such an heir who is under age is not to take from the heir's land more than reasonable issues, customs and services, and this without destruction and waste of either men or goods. And if we have committed the wardship of any such land to a sheriff or anyone else who ought to answer to us for its issues, and he shall inflict destruction or waste upon the wardship, we will take amends from him, and the land is to be entrusted to two law-abiding and discreet men of that fee, who are to answer for the issues to us or to the person to whom we have assigned them; and if we have given or sold to anyone the wardship of any such land, and he has destroyed or wasted it, he is to lose that wardship, which is to be entrusted to two law-abiding and discreet men of that fee, who likewise are to answer to us as aforesaid.

[5] But as long as the guardian has the wardship of the land he is to maintain buildings, parks, fishponds, pools, mills and other things appertaining to the land, out of the issues of the same; and when the heir comes of age, he is to hand all his land over to him, stocked with ploughs and growing crops, according to what the agricultural season requires and the issues of the land can reasonably sustain.

[6] Heirs are to be married without disparagement, provided that before the marriage is agreed upon the heir's near kin are informed.

[7] After the death of her husband a widow is to have her marriage portion and inheritance immediately and without difficulty, nor is she to give anything for her dower, or for her marriage portion, or for the inheritance which she and her husband held on the day of his death, and she may remain in her husband's house for forty days after his death, during which she is to be assigned her dower.

[8] No widow is to be distrained to marry while she wishes to live without a husband, as long as she gives security that she will not marry without our consent, if she holds of us, or without the consent of her lord of whom she holds, if she holds of someone else.

[9] Neither we nor our bailiffs are to seize any land or rent for any debt, as long as the debtor's chattels suffice to pay the debt. Nor are the debtor's pledges to be distrained as long as the principal debtor has enough to pay the debt. And if the principal debtor defaults on the payment of the debt, not having the means to pay it, the pledges are to answer for it, and if they wish they are to have the debtor's lands and rents until they have been satisfied for the debt which they previously paid for him, unless the principal debtor shows that he is quit with regard to the pledges.

[10] If anyone has taken a loan from Jews, great or small, and dies before the debt is paid, the debt is not to incur interest for as long as the heir is under age, whoever he may hold from. And if the debt comes into our hands, we will take only the principal recorded in the charter.

[11] And if anyone dies, and owes a debt to Jews, his wife is to have her dower and pay nothing towards that debt. And if there are surviving children of the deceased who are under age, their needs are to be provided for them in proportion to the dead man's tenement, and the debt is to be paid from the residue, saving the service owed to the lords. Debts owed to others besides Jews are to be dealt with in like manner.

[12] No scutage or aid is to be imposed in our kingdom except by the common counsel of our kingdom, unless for the ransoming of our person, and knighting of our first-born son, and for marrying, once, our first-born daughter, and for these only a reasonable aid is to be taken. Aids from the city of London are to be treated in like manner.

[13] And the city of London is to have all its ancient liberties and free customs, both on land and water. Moreover we wish and grant that all other cities, boroughs, towns and ports are to have all their liberties and free customs.

[14] And in order to have the common counsel of the kingdom for the levying of an aid, other than in the three instances aforesaid, or for the levying of scutage, we are to cause the archbishops, bishops, abbots, earls and greater barons to be summoned individually by our letters; and moreover we are to have a general summons made, through our sheriffs and bailiffs, of all who hold in chief of us; for a fixed day, at least forty days thence, and at a fixed place. And in all the letters of summons we are to set out its cause. And after the summons has thus been made the business is to go forward on the appointed day according to the counsel of those present, even if not all those summoned have come.

[15] We are not to grant in future that anyone may take an aid from his free men, except for the ransoming of his person, and the knighting of his first-born son, and the marrying, once, of his first-born daughter, and for these there is to be only a reasonable aid.

[16] No person is to be distrained to do more service for a knight's fee, or for another free tenement, than is owed for it.

[17] Common pleas are not to follow our court but are to be held in some fixed place.

[18] Recognitions of novel disseisin, mort d'ancestor and darrein presentment are not to [be] held except in the counties concerned, and in this manner: we, or our chief justiciar if we are outside the kingdom, are to send two justices through every county four times in the year, who with four knights of each county chosen by that county court, are to hear those assizes in the county court, and on the day and at the place of the meeting of the county court.

[19] And if those assizes cannot be held on the day of the county court, as many knights and free tenants are to remain out of those who were present on that day of the county court [as are needed] for the sufficient making of judgments, according to whether the business is great or small.

[20] A free man is not to be amerced for a small offence except in proportion to the nature of the offence, and for a great offence he is to be amerced in accordance with its magnitude, saving to him his livelihood, and a merchant in the same manner, saving to him his stock in trade, and a villein is to be amerced in the same manner, saving to him his growing crops, if they fall into our mercy. And none of the aforesaid amercements is to be imposed except by the oath of trustworthy men of the vicinity.

[21] Earls and barons are not to be amerced except by their peers, and not except in proportion to the nature of the offence.

[22] No cleric is to be amerced in respect of his free lay tenement, except in the same way as the others aforesaid, and without regard to the value of his ecclesiastical benefice.

[23] Neither township nor man is to be distrained to make bridges over rivers, except those who should of old and rightfully do so.

[24] No sheriff[s], constable[s], coroners or other of our bailiffs are to hold the pleas of our crown.

[25] All counties, hundreds, wapentakes and ridings are to be at their old farms, without any increment, except for our demesne manors.

[26] If anyone holding a lay fee of us dies, and the sheriff or a bailiff of ours shows our letters patent of summons for a debt which the dead man

owed us, it is to be lawful for the sheriff or our bailiff to attach and record the chattels of the deceased found on the lay fee to the value of the debt, by the view of law-abiding men, so that nothing is to be removed thence, until the clear debt is paid to us; and the residue is to be relinquished to the executors to carry out the testament of the deceased; and if nothing is owed us by him, all the chattels are to go to the deceased, but reserving their rightful shares to his wife and children.

[27] If any free man shall die intestate, his chattels are to be distributed by his nearest kinsmen on both sides of his family, under the supervision of the church, but saving to everyone the debts which the dead man owed him.

[28] No constable or other bailiff of ours is to take anyone's corn or other chattels, unless he pays cash for them immediately, or obtains respite of payment with the consent of the seller.

[29] No constable is to distrain any knight to give money instead of performing castle-guard, if he is willing to perform that guard in person, or, if he is unable to do it for a satisfactory reason, through another reliable man. And if we have led or sent him in the army, he is to be quit of castle-guard in proportion to the time he is in the army at our behest.

[30] No sheriff, or bailiff of ours, or anyone else is to take any free man's horses or carts for transporting things, except with the free man's consent.

[31] Neither we nor our bailiffs are to take another man's wood to a castle, or on other business of ours, except with the consent of the person whose wood it is.

[32] We will hold the lands of those convicted of felony for only a year and a day, and then the lands are to be surrendered to the lords of the fees.

[33] All fish-weirs are in future to be entirely removed from the Thames and the Medway, and throughout the whole of England, except on the sea-coast.

[34] The writ called Praecipe is not in future to be issued to anyone for any tenement in respect of which a free man could lose his court.

[35] There is to be one measure of wine throughout our kingdom, and one measure of ale, and one measure of corn, namely the quarter of London, and one breadth of dyed, russet and haberget cloths, that is, two ells within the borders; and let weights be dealt with as with measures.

[36] Nothing is to be given or taken in future for a writ for an inquest concerning life or members, but it is to be given without payment and not denied.

[37] If anyone holds of us by fee-farm, socage or burgage, and holds of someone else by knight service, we will not have the wardship of his heir,

or of the land which forms part of the other man's fee, by reason of that fee-farm, socage or burgage; nor will we have the wardship of that fee-farm, socage or burgage, unless the fee-farm owes knight service. We will not have the wardship of the heir, or of anyone's land which he holds of someone else by knight service, by reason of some petty serjeanty which he holds of us by the service of rendering us knives or arrows and the like.

[38] No bailiff is in future to put anyone to law by his accusation alone, without trustworthy witnesses being brought in for this.

[39] No free man is to be arrested, or imprisoned, or disseised, or outlawed, or exiled, or in any other way ruined, nor will we go against him or send against him, except by the lawful judgment of his peers or by the law of the land.

[40] We will not sell, or deny, or delay right or justice to anyone.

[41] All merchants are to be safe and secure in departing from and coming to England, and in their residing and movements in England, by both land and water, for buying and selling, without any evil exactions but only paying the ancient and rightful customs, except in time of war and if they come from the land against us in war. And if the latter are found in our land at the outbreak of war, they are to be attached without harm to their bodies and goods, until we or our chief justiciar know how merchants of our own land, who are then found in the land against us in war; are being treated, and if ours are safe there, the others are to be safe in our land.

[42] It is to be lawful in future for every man to depart from our kingdom, and to return to it, safely and securely, by land and water, saving our allegiance, except in time of war for some short time, for the sake of the common utility of the kingdom, [and] excepting those imprisoned and outlawed according to the law of the kingdom, and people from the land against us in war, and merchants who are to be dealt with as aforesaid.

[43] If anyone dies who held of any escheat, like the honour(s) of Wallingford, Nottingham, Boulogne, Lancaster, or of other escheats which are in our hand and are baronies, his heir is not to give any other relief, or to do us any other service, than he would have done to the baron if the barony was in the baron's hand; and we will hold it in the same manner that the baron held it.

[44] Men who reside outside the forest are not in future to come before our forest justices upon common summonses, unless they are involved in pleadings, or are the pledges of a person or persons who have been attached for forest business.

[45] We will not appoint justices, constables, sheriffs or bailiffs except from such as know the law of the kingdom and are willing to keep it well.

[46] All barons who have founded abbeys for which they have charters of the kings of England, or ancient tenure, are to have the custody of them when they are vacant, as they should have.

[47] All the forests which have been afforested during our reign are to be disafforested immediately, and the same is to be done with regard to rivers which have been fenced off by us in our time.

[48] All the evil customs relating to forests and warrens, foresters and warreners, sheriffs and their officers, rivers and their keepers, are to be immediately investigated in each county by twelve sworn knights of the same county, who should be chosen by upright men of the same county, and within forty days of the investigation being made, they are to be completely abolished by them, never to be revived, as long as we, or our justiciar if we are not in England, know about it beforehand.

[49] We will immediately surrender all hostages and charters which have been handed over to us by Englishmen as security for peace or loyal service.

[50] We will remove entirely the kinsmen of Gerard d'Athée from their bailiwicks, so that in future they may hold no bailiwick in England, [namely] Engelard de Cigogné, Peter, Guy and Andrew de Chanceaux, Guy de Cigogné, Geoffrey de Martigny and his brothers, Philip Marc, his brothers, and Geoffrey his nephew, and the whole of their brood.

[51] And immediately after the restoration of peace we will remove from the kingdom all foreign knights, crossbowmen, serjeants and mercenaries, who have come with horses and arms to the detriment of the kingdom.

[52] If anyone has been disseised or dispossessed by us, without lawful judgment of his peers, of lands, castles, liberties, or of his right, we will restore them to him immediately. And if dispute should arise concerning this, then it is to be dealt with by judgment of the twenty-five barons named below in the security for peace. But concerning all those things of which anyone was disseised or dispossessed, without lawful judgment of his peers, by King Henry our father or King Richard our brother, which we have in our hand, or which others hold and which we ought to warrant, we will have respite during the usual crusader's term [of exemption], except for those matters over which a plea was begun or an inquest held on our orders before our taking of the cross. But when we have returned from our crusade, or if perchance we have stayed at home without going on crusade, we will then at once do full justice in such cases.

[53] We will have the same respite, and in the same fashion, for doing justice concerning the disafforestation or retention of forests which Henry our father or Richard our brother afforested, and concerning wardships of lands which are part of another fee, wardships which up till now we have had by

reason of a fee which someone held of us by knight tenure, and concerning abbeys which were founded on a fee other than our own, in which the lord of the fee has claimed his right. And when we have returned, or if we stay at home without going on our crusade, we will at once do full justice to those complaining of these things.

[54] No man is to be arrested or imprisoned on account of a woman's appeal for the death of anyone other than her own husband.

[55] All fines which have been made with us unjustly and against the law of the land, and all amercements made unjustly and against the law of the land, are to be completely remitted, or dealt with by judgment of the twenty-five barons named below in the security for peace, or by judgment of the greater part of them, together with Stephen, archbishop of Canterbury, if he can attend, and others whom he may wish to convoke to act with him in this. And if he cannot attend, let the business nonetheless proceed without him. On condition, however, that if one or some of the aforesaid twenty-five barons are involved in such a plea, they are to be removed in respect of this judgment, and others chosen and sworn by the rest of the twenty-five to act in their place in this case only.

[56] If we have disseised or dispossessed Welshmen of lands or liberties or anything else, without lawful judgment of their peers, in England or in Wales, they are to be returned to them at once. And if a dispute arises about this, then it is to be dealt with on the March by judgment of their peers—for English tenements according to the law of England, for Welsh tenements according to the law of Wales, for tenements in the March according to the law of the March. And the Welsh are to do the same for us and our men.

[57] With regard, however, to all those possessions of which any Welshman was disseised or dispossessed without lawful judgment of his peers by King Henry our father or King Richard our brother, and which we have in our hand, or which others hold and which we ought to warrant, we will have a respite during the usual term [of exemption] of crusaders, except for those matters over which a plea was begun or an inquest held on our order before our taking the cross. But when we have returned, or if perchance we have stayed at home without going on crusade, then we will at once do full justice according to the law of Wales and of the parts aforesaid.

[58] We will at once surrender the son of Llywelyn and all hostages from Wales, and the charters which were handed over to us as security for peace.

[59] We will deal with Alexander, king of Scots, concerning the return of his sisters and hostages, and his liberties and right, in the same manner in which we deal with our other barons of England, unless it should be otherwise under the charters which we have from his father William, former king of Scots. And this will be by judgment of his peers in our court.

[60] Moreover, all the aforesaid customs and liberties, which we have granted to be maintained in our kingdom as far as we are concerned with regard to our own men, all the men of our kingdom, both clergy and laity, are also to observe as far as they are concerned them with regard to their own men.

[61] Moreover, since we have granted all these things aforesaid for the sake of God, and for the reform of our kingdom, and the better to still the discord arisen between us and our barons, wishing that these things be enjoyed with a whole and constant stability in perpetuity, we make and grant them the following security: to wit, that the barons are to choose twenty-five barons of the kingdom, whoever they wish, who should with all their strength observe, hold and cause to be observed the peace and liberties which we have granted them, and by this our present charter confirmed, so that if we, or our justiciar, or our bailiffs, or any of our officers shall in any way offend against anyone, or transgress against any of the articles of peace or security, and the offence has been shown to four of the aforesaid twenty-five barons, those four are to go to us, or to our justiciar if we shall be out of the kingdom, setting forth the transgression, and demand that we have it reformed without delay. And if we do not have the transgression rectified, or, if we are out of the kingdom, our justiciar has not done so, within the space of forty days, counting from the time it was shown to us, or to our justiciar if we were out of the kingdom, the four barons aforesaid are to refer the case to the rest of the twenty-five barons, and those twenty-five barons and the commune of the whole land will distrain and afflict us by every means possible, by taking castles, lands and possessions and in any other ways they can, until it is rectified in accordance with their judgment, albeit sparing our own person and the persons of our queen and children. And once the matter has been redressed let them submit to our authority as they did before. And whosoever of the land so wishes is to swear that as to executing all the above he will obey the orders of the twenty-five barons aforesaid, and that with them he will afflict us to the best of his ability, and we openly and freely give permission to swear to whoever wishes to do so, and we will never forbid anyone to swear. But all those of the land who are unwilling to swear individually and voluntarily to the twenty-five barons, to distrain and afflict us with them, we will make them swear by our order as aforesaid. And if any of the twenty-five barons dies, or departs from the land, or is prevented in any other way from being able to act as aforesaid, the remainder of the twenty-five are to choose another man in his place, as they see fit, who will be sworn in like manner as the rest. Moreover in everything which shall be entrusted to the twenty-five barons to carry out, if perchance the twenty-five are present and disagree among themselves over anything, or if any of them, being summoned, will not or cannot attend, what the majority of those who are present shall provide or instruct is to be

deemed as determined and binding, as if all twenty-five had agreed to it. And the aforesaid twenty-five will swear that they will faithfully comply with all the aforesaid, and cause it to be upheld to the best of their ability. And we will seek to obtain nothing from anyone, in our own person or through someone else, whereby any of these grants or liberties may be revoked or diminished, and if any such thing be obtained, let it be void and invalid, and we will never make use of it, in our own person or through someone else.

[62] And we have fully remitted and pardoned everyone all the ill will, indignation and resentment which has arisen between us and our men, clergy and laity, in the time of discord. Moreover we have fully remitted to all men, clergy and laity, and in so far as we are concerned fully pardoned, all the trespasses committed as a result of that discord from Easter in the sixteenth year of our reign until the reestablishment of peace. And moreover we have had letters patent made by Lord Stephen, archbishop of Canterbury, Lord Henry, archbishop of Dublin, the aforesaid bishops, and Master Pandulf, testifying to this security and the aforesaid grants.

[63] Wherefore we wish and firmly command that the English church be free, and that the men in our kingdom have and hold all the liberties, rights and grants aforesaid, well and in peace, freely and quietly, for themselves and their heirs, of us and our heirs, in all things and places, in perpetuity, as aforesaid. This has been sworn to both on our behalf and on that of the barons, that all these things named above will be observed in good faith and without evil intent. Witnesses as aforesaid, with many others. Given by our hand in the meadow called Runnymede, between Windsor and Staines, on the fifteenth day of June in the seventeenth year of our reign.

APPENDIX D
King's Writ[*]

John, by the grace of God king of England, lord of Ireland, duke of Normandy [and] Aquitaine, and count of Anjou, [sends] greeting to the sheriff of Gloucester, [and] the foresters, warreners, keepers of the riverbanks and all his bailiffs in that same county. Know that through God's grace a firm peace has been re-established between us and the barons and freemen of our kingdom, as you may hear and see through our charter which we have caused to be made concerning this peace, and which we have also ordered to be read out publicly throughout your whole jurisdiction and to be firmly kept. We wish and sternly command that you, O sheriff, in accordance with the form of the aforesaid charter, make all from your jurisdiction swear to the Twenty-Five Barons mentioned in the charter, at their command—or at the command of the majority of them, in the presence of these barons or in the presence of those whom these barons shall attorn[1] for this matter through their letters patent—both on the day and at the place which the aforesaid barons or their attorneys shall fix to do this. We also wish and order that twelve knights from your county—who shall be elected by that county in the first county court that is held after the receipt of those letters in your region—shall swear to inquire into the evil customs of the sheriffs as well as of their officials, of forests, foresters, warrens and warreners, and of riverbanks and their keepers, and to abolish these [evil customs], just as it is contained in that charter. Therefore, as you love us and our honour and the peace of our realm, you shall both observe inviolably everything contained in that charter, and make everyone observe it, lest—may God avert it—because of your neglect or through your transgression the peace of our realm comes to be disturbed once more. And you, O sheriff, are to have our peace proclaimed throughout your jurisdiction, and you are to order it to be firmly kept. And in testimony of this matter, we are sending you our letters patent in respect thereof. Witnessed by me at Runnymede, on 20 June in the 17th year of our reign [1215].

---

*Latin text *in* Hereford, Hereford Cathedral Archives no. 2256. The translation reproduced here was prepared by Professor Daniel Power, Swansea University (UK) 2014.

Note: All footnotes are from the translation.

   1 *I.e.*, appointed in their place.

APPENDIX E
Pope Innocent III: Papal Bull Declaring That Magna Carta Is Null & Void*

Innocent, bishop, servant of the servants of God, to all the faithful of Christ who will see this document, greeting and apostolic benediction.

ALTHOUGH OUR WELL-BELOVED son in Christ, John illustrious king of the English, grievously offended God and the Church—in consequence of which we excommunicated him and put his kingdom under ecclesiastical interdict—yet, by the merciful inspiration of Him who desireth not the death of a sinner but rather that he should turn from his wickedness and live, the king at length returned to his senses, and humbly made to God and the Church such complete amends that he not only paid compensation for losses and restored property wrongfully seized, but also conferred full liberty on the English church; and further, on the relaxation of the two sentences, he yielded his kingdom of England and of Ireland to St. Peter and the Roman Church, and received it from us again as fief under an annual payment of one thousand marks, having sworn an oath of fealty to us, as is clearly stated in his privilege furnished with a golden seal; and desiring still further to please Almighty God, he reverently assumed the badge of the life-giving Cross, intending to go to the relief of the Holy Land—a project for which he was splendidly preparing. But the enemy of the human race, who always hates good impulses, by his cunning wiles stirred up against him the barons of England so that, with a wicked inconsistency, the men who supported him when injuring the Church rebelled against him when he turned from his sin and made amends to the Church. A matter of dispute had arisen between them: several days had been fixed for the parties to discuss a settlement: meanwhile, formal envoys had been sent to us: with them we conferred diligently, and after full deliberation we sent letters by them to the archbishop and the English bishops, charging and commanding them to devote earnest attention and effective effort to restoring a genuine and full agreement between the two sides; by apostolic authority they were to denounce as void my leagues and conspiracies which might have been formed after the outbreak of trouble between the kingdom and the priesthood: they were

---

* Latin text *in* British Museum, Cotton MS Cleopatra E. I. fo. 155.

1 REGESTA PONTIFICUM ROMANORUM 4990 (August Potthast ed., Berlin, 1874).

401

to prohibit, under sentence of excommunication, any attempt to form such leagues in future: and they were prudently to admonish the magnates and nobles of England, and strongly to enjoin on them, to strive to conciliate the king by manifest proofs of loyalty and submission; and then, if they should decide to make a demand of him, to implore it respectfully and not arrogantly, maintaining his royal honour and rendering the customary services which they and their predecessors paid to him and his predecessors (since the king ought not to lose these services without a judicial decision), that in this way they might the more easily gain their object. For we in our letters, and equally through the archbishop and bishops, have asked and advised the king, enjoining it on him as he hopes to have his sins remitted, to treat these magnates and nobles kindly and to hear their just petitions graciously, so that they too might recognise with gladness how by divine grace he had had a change of heart, and that thereby they and their heirs should serve him and his heirs readily and loyally; and we also asked him to grant them full safeconduct for the outward and homeward journey and the time between, so that if they could not arrive at agreement the dispute might be decided in his court by their peers according to the laws and customs of the kingdom. But before the envoys bearing this wise and just mandate had reached England, the barons threw over their oath of fealty; and though, even if the king had wrongfully oppressed them they should not have proceeded against him by constituting themselves both judges and executors of the judgment in their own suit, yet, openly conspiring as vassals against their lord and as knights against their king, they leagued themselves with his acknowledged enemies as well as with others, and dared to make war on him, occupying and devastating his territory and even seizing the city of London, the capital of the kingdom, which had been treacherously surrendered to them. Meantime the aforesaid envoys returned to England and the king offered, in accordance with the terms of our mandate, to grant the barons full justice. This they altogether rejected and began to stretch forth their hands to deeds still worse. So the king, appealing to our tribunal, offered to grant them justice before us to whom the decision of this suit belonged by reason of our lordship: but this they utterly rejected. Then he offered that four discreet men chosen by him and four more chosen by themselves should, together with us, end the dispute, and he promised that, first in his reforms, he would repeal all abuses introduced into England in his reign: but this also they contemptuously refused. Finally, the king declared to them that, since the lordship of the kingdom belonged to the Roman Church, he neither could nor should, without our special mandate, make any change in it to our prejudice: and so he again appealed to our tribunal, placing under apostolic protection both himself and his kingdom with all his honour and rights. But making no progress by any method, he asked the archbishop and the bishops to execute our mandate, to defend the rights of the Roman

Church, and to protect himself in accordance with the form of the privilege granted to Crusaders. When the archbishop and bishops would not take any action, seeing himself bereft of almost all counsel and help, he did not dare to refuse what the barons had dared to demand. And so by such violence and fear as might affect the most courageous of men he was forced to accept an agreement which is not only shameful and demeaning but also illegal and unjust, thereby lessening unduly and impairing his royal rights and dignity.

But because the Lord has said to us by the prophet Jeremiah, "I have set thee over the nations and over the kingdoms, to root out, and to destroy, to build and to plant," and also by Isaiah, "Loose the bands of wickedness, undo the heavy burdens," we refuse to ignore such shameless presumption, for thereby the Apostolic See would be dishonoured, the king's rights injured, the English nation shamed, and the whole plan for a Crusade seriously endangered; and as this danger would be imminent if concessions, thus extorted from a great prince who has taken the cross, were not cancelled by our authority, even though he himself should prefer them to be upheld, on behalf of Almighty God, Father, Son, and Holy Spirit, and by the authority of SS Peter and Paul His apostles, and by our own authority, acting on the general advice of our brethren, we utterly reject and condemn this settlement, and under threat of excommunication we order that the king should not dare to observe it and that the barons and their associates should not require it to be observed: the charter, with all undertakings and guarantees whether confirming it or resulting from it, we declare to be null, and void of all validity for ever. Wherefore, let no man deem it lawful to infringe this document of our annulment and prohibition, or presume to oppose it. If anyone should presume to do so, let him know that he will incur the anger of Almighty God and of SS Peter and Paul His apostles.

Anagni, the 24th of August, in the eighteenth year of our Pontificate (August 24, 1215).

APPENDIX F
1216 Magna Carta*

[That the changes made in reissuing the charter shall be clear, the text is given in full with the differences shown—alterations and additions by italics,[1] omissions by footnotes. Only a few verbal or stylistic changes affecting neither the sense nor the translation have been ignored.]

Henry, by the grace of God king of England, lord of Ireland, duke of Normandy and Aquitaine, and count of Anjou, to the archbishops, bishops, abbots, earls, barons, justiciars, foresters, sheriffs, stewards, servants, bailiffs and to all his faithful subjects, greeting. Know that we, out of reverence for God and for the salvation of our soul and those of all our ancestors and *successors*, for the honour of God and the exaltation of holy church, and for the reform of our realm, on the advice of our venerable fathers, the *Lord Gualo, cardinal priest of St Martin, legate of the apostolic see, Peter of Winchester, R. of St Asaph, J. of Bath and Glastonbury, S. of Exeter, R. of Chichester, W. of Coventry, B. of Rochester, H. of Llandaff, — of St David's, — of Bangor and S. of Worcester*, bishops, and of the noble men *William Marshal earl of Pembroke, Ranulf earl of Chester, William de Ferrers earl of Derby, William count of Aumale, Hubert de Burgh our justiciar, Savari de Mauléon, William Brewer the father, William Brewer the son, Robert de Courtenay, Fawkes de Breauté, Reynold de Vautort, Walter de Lacy, Hugh de Mortimer, John of Monmouth, Walter de Beauchamp, Walter de Clifford, Roger de Clifford, Robert de Mortimer, William de Cantilupe, Matthew fitz Herbert, John Marshal, Alan Basset, Philip de Aubeney, John Lestrange* and others, our faithful subjects:

[1] In the first place have granted to God, and by this our present charter confirmed for us and our heirs for ever, that the English church shall be free, and shall have its rights undiminished and its liberties unimpaired.[2] We have

---

* Latin text *in* 1 STATUTES OF THE REALM 14–16 (1810). The translation reproduced here is from: 3 ENGLISH HISTORICAL DOCUMENTS 327–32 (Harry Rothwell ed., Eyre & Spottiswoode 1975). Reproduced by permission of Taylor & Francis Books UK.

Note: All footnotes are from the translation. Annex C: "Magna Carta 1215" is translated by a different translator than 1216, 1217, and 1225.

1. Thus, Latin terms (regularly printed in italics) here revert to roman. *See also* Annex G 1217 Magna Carta, Annex I 1225 Magna Carta.

2. The rest of the sentence of 1215 Magna Carta ("and it is our will . . . good faith for ever") is omitted.

also granted to all free men of our kingdom, for ourselves and our heirs for ever, all the liberties written below, to be had and held by them and their heirs of us and our heirs. [1215, ch.1]

[2] If any of our earls or barons or others holding of us in chief by knight service dies, and at his death his heir be of full age and owe relief he shall have his inheritance on payment of the old relief, namely the heir or heirs of an earl ££100 for a whole earl's barony, the heir or heirs of a baron ££100 for a whole barony, the heir or heirs of a knight 100s, at most, for a whole knight's fee; and he who owes less shall give less according to the ancient usage of fiefs. [1215, ch. 2]

[3] If, however, the heir of any such be under age, *his lord shall not have wardship of him, nor of his land, before he has received his homage; and after being a ward such an heir* shall have his inheritance when he comes of age, *that is of twenty-one years*, without paying relief and without fine, *so, however, that if he is made a knight while still under age, the land nevertheless shall remain in his lord's wardship for the full term.* [1215, ch. 3]

[4] The guardian of the land of such an heir who is under age shall take from the land of the heir no more than reasonable revenues, reasonable customary dues and reasonable services, and that without destruction and waste of men or goods; and if we commit the wardship of the land of any such to a sheriff, or to any other who is answerable to us for the revenues of that land, and he destroys or wastes what he has wardship of, we will take compensation from him and the land shall be committed to two lawful and discreet men of that fief, who shall be answerable for the revenues to us or to him to whom we have assigned them; and if we give or sell to anyone the wardship of any such land and he causes destruction or waste therein, he shall lose that wardship and it shall be transferred to two lawful and discreet men of that fief, who shall similarly be answerable to us as is aforesaid. [1215, ch. 4]

[5] Moreover, so long as he has the wardship of the land, the guardian shall keep in repair the houses, parks, preserves, ponds, mills, and other things pertaining to the land out of the revenues from it; and he shall restore to the heir when he comes of age his land fully stocked with ploughs and *all other things in at least the measure he received. All these things shall be observed in the case of warships of vacant archbishoprics, bishoprics, abbeys, priories, churches and dignities, except that wardships of this kind may not be sold.* [1215, ch. 5]

[6] Heirs shall be married without disparagement.[3] [1215, ch. 6]

---

3. The rest of 1215, ch. 6, is omitted.

[7] A widow shall have her marriage portion and inheritance forthwith and without *any* difficulty after the death of her husband; nor shall she pay anything to have her dower or her marriage portion or the inheritance which she and her husband held on the day of her husband's death; and she may remain in her husband's house for forty days after his death, within which time her dower shall be assigned to her, *unless it has already been assigned to her or unless the house is a castle; and if she leaves the castle, a suitable house shall be immediately provided for her in which she can stay honourably until her dower is assigned to her in accordance with what is aforesaid.* [1215, ch. 7]

[8] No widow shall be forced to marry so long as she wishes to live without a husband, provided that she gives security not to marry without our consent if she holds of us, or without the consent of her lord[4] if she holds of another. [1215, ch. 8]

[9] *We or our bailiffs* will not seize for any debt any land or rent, so long as the *available* chattels of the debtors are sufficient to repay the debt *and the debtor himself is prepared to have it paid therefrom*; nor will those who have gone surety for the debtor be distrained so long as the principal debtor is himself able to pay the debt; and if the principal debtor fails to pay the debt, having nothing wherewith to pay it *or is able but unwilling to pay*, then shall the sureties answer for the debt; and they shall, if they wish, have the lands and rents of the debtor until they are reimbursed for the debt which they had paid for him, unless the principal debtor can show that he has discharged his obligation in the matter to the said sureties. [1215, ch. 9][5]

[10] The city of London shall have all its ancient liberties and free customs.[6] Furthermore, we will and grant that all other cities, boroughs, towns, *the barons of the Cinque Ports* and *all ports* shall have all their liberties and free customs. [1215, ch. 13][7]

[11] No one shall be compelled to do greater service for a knight's fee or for any other free holding than is due from it. [1215, ch. 16]

[12] Common pleas shall not follow our court, but shall be held in some fixed place. [1215, ch. 17]

[13] Recognitions of novel disseisin, of mort d'ancestor, and of darrein presentment, shall not be held elsewhere than in the counties to which they relate, and in this manner—we, or, if we should be out of the realm, our

4. The "of whom she holds" of 1215, ch. 8, is omitted.
5. Chapters 10–12 of 1215 Magna Carta are omitted.
6. In 1215 Magna Carta this sentence begins with "And" and ends with "as well by land as by water."
7. Chapters 14–15 of 1215 Magna Carta are omitted.

chief justiciar, will send two justices through each county four times a year, who, with four knights of each county chosen by the county, shall hold said assizes in the county and on the day and in the place of meeting of the county court. [1215, ch. 18]

[14] And if the said assizes cannot all be held on the day of the county court, there shall stay behind as many the knights and freeholders who were present at the county court on that day as are necessary for the sufficient making of judgments, according to the amount of business to be done. [1215, ch. 19]

[15] A free man shall not be amerced for a trivial offence except in accordance with the degree of the offence, and for a grave offence[8] in accordance with its gravity, yet saving his way of living; and a merchant in the same way, saying his means of livelihood; if *he has* fallen into our mercy: and none of the aforesaid amercements shall be imposed except by the oath of good *and law-worthy* men of the neighbourhood. [1215, ch. 20]

[16] Earls and barons shall not be amerced except by their peers, and only in accordance with the degree of the offence. [1215, ch. 21]

[17] No clerk shall be amerced[9] except after the fashion of the aforesaid and not according to the amount of his ecclesiastical benefice. [1215, ch. 22]

[18] No vill or individual shall be compelled to make bridges at river banks, except *one* who from of old *is* legally bound to do so. [1215, ch. 23]

[19] No sheriff, constable, coroners, or others of our bailiffs shall hold pleas of our crown. [1215, ch. 24][10]

[20] If anyone holding a lay fief of us dies and our sheriff or bailiff shows our letters patent of summons for a debt that the deceased owed us, it shall be lawful for our sheriff or bailiff to attach and make a list of chattels of the deceased found upon the lay fief to the value of that debt under supervision of law-worthy men, provided that none of the chattels shall be removed until the debt which is manifest has been paid to us in full; and the residue shall be left to the executors for carrying out the will of the deceased. And if nothing is owing to us from him, all the chattels shall accrue to the deceased, saving to his wife and *his* children their reasonable shares. [1215, ch. 26][11]

[21] No constable or *his bailiff* shall take the corn or other chattels of anyone *who is not of the vill where the castle is situated* unless he pays on the spot in cash for them or can delay payment by arrangement with the

---

8. The "he shall he amerced" of 1215, ch. 20, is omitted.
9. The "in respect of his lay holding" of 1215, ch. 22, is omitted.
10. Chapter 25 of 1215 is omitted.
11. Chapter 27 of 1215 is omitted.

seller; *if the seller is of the vill, he shall be bound to pay within three weeks.* [1215, ch. 28]

[22] No constable shall compel any knight to give money instead of castle-guard if he is willing to do *it* himself or through another good man, if for some good reason he cannot do it himself; and if we lead or send him on military service, he shall be excused guard in proportion to the time that because of us he has been on service. [1215, ch. 29]

[23] No sheriff, or bailiff of ours, or *other person* shall take *anyone's* horses or carts for transport work unless *he pays for them at the old-established rates, namely at ten pence a day for a cart with two horses and fourteen pence a day for a cart with three horses.* [1215, ch. 30]

[24] Neither we nor our bailiffs will take, for castles or other works of ours, timber which is not ours, except with the agreement of him whose timber it is. [1215, ch. 31]

[25] We will not hold for more than a year and a day the lands of those convicted of felony, and then the lands shall be handed over to the lords of the fiefs. [1215, ch. 32]

[26] Henceforth all fish-weirs shall be cleared completely from the Thames and the Medway and throughout all England, except along the sea coast. [1215, ch. 33]

[27] The writ called Praecipe shall not in future be issued to anyone in respect of any holding whereby a free man may lose his court. [1215, ch. 34]

[28] Let there be one measure for wine throughout our kingdom, and one measure for ale, and one measure for corn, namely "the London's quarter"; and one width for clothes whether dyed, russet or halberget, namely two ells within the selvedges. Let it be the same with weights as with measures. [1215, ch. 35]

[29] Nothing shall be given[12] in future for the writ of inquisition of life or limbs: instead, it shall be granted free of charge and not refused. [1215, ch. 36]

[30] If anyone holds of us by fee-farm, by socage, or by burgage, and holds land of another by knight service, we will not, by reason of that fee-farm, socage, or burgage, have the wardship of his heir or of land of his that is of the fief of the other; nor will we have custody of the fee-farm, socage, or burgage, unless such fee-farm owes knight service. We will not have custody of anyone's heir or land which he holds of another by knight service by reason of any petty serjeanty which he holds of us by the service of rendering to us knives or arrows or the like. [1215, ch. 37]

---

12. The "or taken" of 1215, ch. 36, is omitted.

[31] No bailiff shall in future put anyone to trial upon his own bare word without reliable witnesses produced for this purpose. [1215, ch. 38]

[32] No free man shall be arrested or imprisoned or disseised or outlawed or exiled or victimised in any *other* way, neither will we attack him or send anyone to attack him, except by the lawful judgment of his peers or by the law of the land. [1215, ch. 39]

[33] To no one will we sell, to no one will we refuse or delay right or justice. [1215, ch. 40]

[34] All merchants, *unless they have been publicly prohibited beforehand*, shall be able to go out of and come into England safely and securely and stay and travel throughout England, as well by land as by water, for buying and selling by the ancient and right customs free from all evil tolls, except in time of war and if they are of the land that is at war with us. And if such are found in our land at the beginning of a war, they shall be attached, without injury to their persons or goods, until we, or our chief justiciar, know how merchants of our land are treated who were found in the land at war with us when war broke out; and if ours are safe there, the others shall be safe in our land. [1215, ch. 41][13]

[35] If anyone who holds of some escheat such as the honour of Wallingford, Nottingham, Boulogne, Lancaster, or of other escheats which are in our hand and are baronies dies, his heir shall give no other relief and do no other relief and do no other service to us than he would have done to the baron if that *land* had been in the baron's hands; and we will hold it in the same manner in which the barons held it. [1215, ch. 43]

[36] Men who live outside the forest need not henceforth come before our justices of the forest upon a general summons, unless they are impleaded or are sureties for any person or persons who are attached for forest offences. [1215, ch. 44][14]

[37] All barons who have founded abbeys for which they have charters of the kings of England or ancient tenure shall have the custody of them during vacancies, as they ought to have *and as it is made clear above.*[15] [1215, ch. 46]

[38] All forests that were made forest in the time of *king John, our father,* shall be immediately disafforsted; and so be it done with river-banks that were made preserves by *the same J. in his* time. [1215, ch. 47][16]

---

13. Chapter 42 of 1215 is omitted.
14. Chapter 45 of 1215 is omitted.
15. Chapter 5.
16. Chapters 48–53 of 1215 are omitted.

[39] No one shall be arrested or imprisoned upon the appeal of a woman for the death of anyone except her husband. [1215, ch. 54][17]

[40] *And if king J. our father* disseised or kept out Welshmen from lands or liberties or other things without the legal judgment of their peers in England or in Wales, they shall be immediately restored to them; and if a dispute arises over this, then let it be decided in the March by the judgment of their peers—for holdings in England according to the law of England, for holdings in Wales according to the law of Wales, and for holdings in the March according to the law of the March. Welshmen shall do the same to us and ours. [1215, ch. 56][18]

[41] All these aforesaid customs and liberties which we have granted to be observed in our kingdom as far as it pertains to us towards our men, all of our kingdom, clerks as well as laymen, shall observe as far as it pertains to them towards their men. [1215, ch. 60][19]

[42] *However, because there were certain [chapters] contained in the former charter which seemed important yet doubtful, namely On the assessing of scutage and aids,* [20] *On debts of Jews and others,*[21] *On freedom to leave and return to our kingdom,*[22] *On forests and foresters, warrens and warreners,*[23] *On the customs of counties,*[24] *and On river-banks and their wardens,*[25] *the above-mentioned prelates and magnates have agreed to these being deferred until we have fuller counsel, when we will, most fully in these as well as other matters that have to be amended, do what is for the common good*[26] *and the peace and estate*[27] *of ourselves and our kingdom. Because we have not yet a seal, we have had the present charter sealed with the seals of our venerable father, the lord Gualo cardinal priest of St Martin, legate of the apostolic see, and William Marshal earl of Pembroke, ruler of us and of our kingdom. Witness all the aforementioned and many others. Given by the hands of the aforesaid lord, the legate, and William Marshal earl of Pembroke at Bristol on the twelfth day of November in the first year of our reign.*

---

17. Chapter 55 of 1215 is omitted.
18. Chapters 57–59 of 1215 are omitted.
19. All the rest of 1215 (i.e., chapters 61–63) is omitted and the following new chapter (42) substituted.
20. Magna Carta 1215, chs. 12, 14, and 15.
21. Magna Carta 1215, chs. 10, 11, and 27.
22. Magna Carta 1215, ch. 42.
23. Magna Carta 1215, ch. 48.
24. Magna Carta 1215, chs. 25 and 45.
25. Magna Carta 1215, ch. 48.
26. *Ad communem omnium utilitatem.*
27. *Statum.*

APPENDIX G
1217 Magna Carta[*]

[The further changes made in the charter in this reissue compared with that of 1216 are shown in the same way that the differences of 1216 from 1215 were shown.]

Henry, by the grace of God king of England, lord of Ireland, duke of Normandy, Aquitaine, and count of Anjou, to the archbishops, bishops, abbots, *priors*, earls, barons,[1] sheriffs, stewards, servants and to all his bailiffs and faithful subjects *who shall look at the present charter*, greeting. Know that out of reverence for God and for the salvation of our soul and the souls of[2] our ancestors and successors, for[3] the exaltation of holy church and the reform of our realm, *we have granted and by this present charter confirmed for us and our heirs for ever*, on the advice of our venerable *father, the lord Gualo, cardinal priest of St Martin and legate of the apostolic see; of the lord Walter archbishop of York, William bishop of London and the other bishops of England* and of[4] *William Marshal earl of Pembroke, ruler of us and of our kingdom, and our faithful earls and barons of England, these liberties written below to be held in our kingdom of England for ever.*

[1] In the first place *we* have granted to God, and by this our present charter confirmed for us and our heirs for ever, that the English church shall be free and shall have its rights undiminished and its liberties unimpaired. We have also granted to all free men of our kingdom, for ourselves and our heirs for ever, all the liberties written below, to be[5] held by them and their heirs of us and our heirs. [1216, ch. 1]

[2] If any of our earls or barons or others holding of us in chief by knight service dies, and at his death his heir be of full age and owe relief he shall have his inheritance on payment of the old relief, namely the heir or heirs of

---

* Latin text *in* 1 STATUTES OF THE REALM 17–19 (1810). The translation reproduced here is from 3 ENGLISH HISTORICAL DOCUMENTS 332–37 (Harry Rothwell ed., Eyre & Spottiswoode 1975). Reproduced by permission of Taylor & Francis Books UK.

Note: All footnotes are from the translation. Annex C: "Magna Carta 1215" is translated by a different translator than 1216, 1217, and 1225.

1. The "justiciars, foresters" of 1216 is omitted.
2. The "all" of 1216 is omitted.
3. Here "the honour of God and" of 1216 is omitted.
4. Here "the noble men" of 1216 is omitted.
5. The "had and" of 1216 is omitted.

an earl ££100 for a whole earl's barony, the heir or heirs of a baron ££100 for a whole barony, the heir or heirs of a knight 100s, at most, for a whole knight's fee; and he who owes less shall give less according to the ancient usage of fiefs. [1216, ch. 2]

[3] If, however, the heir of any such be under age, his lord shall not have wardship of him, nor of his land, before he has received his homage; and after being a ward such an heir shall have his inheritance when he comes of age, that is of twenty-one years, without paying relief and without fine, so, however, that if he is made a knight while[6] still under age, the land nevertheless shall remain of his *lords* for the full term. [1216, ch. 3]

[4] The guardian of the land of such an heir who is under age shall take from the land of the heir no more than reasonable revenues, reasonable customary dues and reasonable services, and that without destruction and waste of men or goods; and if we commit the wardship of the land of any such to a sheriff, or to any other who is answerable to us for the revenues of that land, and he destroys or wastes what he has wardship of, we will take compensation from him and the land shall be committed to two lawful and discreet men of that fief, who shall be answerable for the revenues to us or to him to whom we have assigned them; and if we give or sell to anyone the wardship of any such land and he causes destruction or waste therein, he shall lose that wardship and it shall be transferred to two lawful and discreet men of that fief, who shall similarly be answerable to us as is aforesaid. [1216, ch. 4]

[5] Moreover, so long as he has the wardship of the land, the guardian shall keep in repair the houses, parks, preserves, ponds, mills, and other things pertaining to the land out of the revenues from it; and he shall restore to the heir when he comes of age his land fully stocked with ploughs and all other things in at least the measure he received. All these things shall be observed in the case of warships of vacant archbishoprics, bishoprics, abbeys, priories, churches and dignities *that pertain to us* except that wardships of this kind may not be sold. [1216, ch. 5]

[6] Heirs shall be married without disparagement. [1216, ch. 6]

[7] A widow shall have her marriage portion and inheritance forthwith and without any difficulty after the death of her husband; nor shall she pay anything to have her dower or her marriage portion or the inheritance which she and her husband held on the day of her husband's death; and she may remain in *chief* house of her husband for forty days after his death, within which time her dower shall be assigned to her, unless it has already been assigned to her or unless the house is a castle; and if she leaves the

---

6. Here "while" is wanting, but its omission would appear to be no more than accidental and Magna Carta 1225 restores it.

castle, a suitable house shall be immediately provided for her in which she can stay honourably until her dower is assigned to her in accordance with what is aforesaid, *and she shall have meanwhile her reasonable estover of common.*[7] *There shall be assigned to her for her dower a third of all her husband's land which was his in his lifetime, unless a smaller share was given her at the church door.*[8] [1216, ch. 7]

[8] No widow shall be forced to marry so long as she wishes to live without a husband, provided that she gives security not to marry without our consent if she holds of us, or without the consent of her lord if she holds of another. [1216, ch. 8]

[9] We or our bailiffs will not seize for any debt any land or rent, so long as the available chattels of the debtor are sufficient to repay the debt and the debtor himself is prepared to have it paid therefrom; nor will those who have gone surety for the debtor be distrained so long as the principal debtor is himself able to pay the debt; and if the principal debtor fails to pay the debt, having nothing wherewith to pay it or is able but unwilling to pay, then shall the sureties answer for the debt; and they shall, if they wish, have the lands and rents of the debtor until they are reimbursed for the debt which they have paid for him, unless the principal debtor can show that he has discharged his obligation in the matter to the said sureties. [1216, ch. 9]

[10] The city of London shall have all its ancient liberties and free customs. Furthermore, we will and grant that all other cities, boroughs, towns, the barons of the Cinque Ports, and all ports shall have all their liberties and free customs. [1216, ch. 10]

[11] No one shall be compelled to do greater service for a knight's fee or for any other free holding than is due from it. [1216, ch. 11]

[12] Common pleas shall not follow our court, but shall be held in some fixed place. [1216, ch. 12]

[13] Recognitions of novel disseisin, of mort d'ancestor[9] shall not be held elsewhere than in the counties to which they relate, and in this manner—we, or, if we should be out of the realm, our chief justiciar, will *send justices through each county once a year, who with knights of the counties shall hold the said assizes in the counties.* [1216, chs. 13–14]

[14] *And those which cannot on that visit be determined in the county to which they relate by the said justices sent to hold the said assizes shall*

---

7. *I.e.*, reasonable allowances from the estate of things necessary to maintain her pending provision out of it of the dower.

8. The amount of dower was usually arranged at the church door at the time of the marriage.

9. The "and of darrein presentment" of 1216 is omitted; the resulting rough edge is smoothed in 1225 by the insertion of "and" before "of mort d'ancester."

be determined by them elsewhere on their circuit, and those which can-
not be determined by them because of difficulty over certain articles shall
be referred to our justices of the bench and determined there. [1216, chs. 13–14]

[15] *Assizes of darrein presentment shall always be held before the jus-*
tices of the bench and determined there. [1216, chs. 13–14]

[16] A free man shall not be amerced for a trivial offence except in accordance with the degree of the offence and for a grave offence in accordance
with its gravity, yet saving his way of living; and a merchant in the same
way, saving stock-in-trade; and a villein *other than one of our own* shall
be amerced in the same way, saving his means of livelihood; if he has fallen
into our mercy: and none of the aforesaid amercements shall be imposed
except by the *oaths* of good and law-worthy men of the neighbourhood.
[1216, ch. 15]

[17] Earls and barons shall not be amerced except by their peers, and
only in accordance with the degree of the offence. [1216, ch. 16]

[18] No *ecclesiastical person* shall be amerced *according to the amount*
of his ecclesiastical benefice but in accordance with his lay holding and in
accordance with the degree of the offence. [1216, ch. 17]

[19] No vill or individual shall be compelled to make bridges at river
banks, except one who from of old is legally bound to do so. [1216, ch. 18]

[20] *No river bank shall henceforth be made a preserve, except those*
which were preserves *in the time of king Henry, our grandfather, in the same*
places and for the same periods as they used to be in his day. [1216, ch. 38][10]

[21] No sheriff, constable, coroners, or others of our bailiffs shall hold
pleas of our crown. [1216, ch. 19]

[22] If anyone holding a lay fief of us dies and our sheriff or bailiff shows
our letters patent of summons for a debt that the deceased owed us, it shall
be lawful for our sheriff or bailiff to attach and make a list of chattels of the
deceased found upon the lay fief to the value of that debt under supervision
of law-worthy men, provided that none of the chattels shall be removed
until the debt which is manifest has been paid to us in full; and the residue
shall be left to the executors for carrying out the will of the deceased. And if
nothing is owing to us from him, all the chattels shall accrue to the deceased,
saving to his wife[11] and their reasonable shares. [1216, ch. 20]

---

10. The residue of 1216, ch. 38 after the forest part had been transferred to the
separate Charter of the Forest: it is not promoted to bring it and chapter 19 of Magna
Carta 1217 together.

11. Here the "and his children" of 1216 is omitted, but quite obviously from the
plural ("their reasonable shares") unintentionally, and Magna Carta 1225 restores it.

[23] No constable or his bailiff shall take the corn or other chattels of anyone who is not of the vill where the castle is situated unless he pays on the spot in cash for them or can delay payment by arrangement with the seller; if the seller is of *that* vill and he *shall pay* within *forty days.* [1216, ch. 21]

[24] No constable shall compel any knight to give money instead of castle-guard if he is willing to do it himself or through another good man, if for some good reason he cannot do it himself; and if we lead or send him on military service, he shall be excused guard in respect *of the fief for which he did service in the army* in proportion to the time that because of us he has been on service. [1216, ch. 22]

[25] No sheriff, or bailiff of ours, or other person shall take anyone's horses or carts for transport work unless he pays for them at the old-established rates, namely at ten pence a day for a cart with two horses and fourteen pence a day for a cart with three horses. [1216, ch. 23]

[26] *No demesne cart of any ecclesiastical person or knight or of any lady shall be taken by the aforesaid bailiffs.*

[27] Neither we nor our bailiffs *nor others* will take, for castles or other works of ours, timber which is not ours, except with the agreement of him whose timber it is. [1216, ch. 24]

[28] We will not hold for more than a year and a day the lands of those convicted of felony, and then the lands shall be handed over to the lords of the fiefs. [1216, ch. 25]

[29] Henceforth all fish-weirs shall be cleared completely from the Thames and the Medway and throughout all England, except along the sea coast. [1216, ch. 26]

[30] The writ called Praecipe shall not in future be issued to anyone in respect of any holding whereby a free man may lose his court. [1216, ch. 27]

[31] Let there be one measure for wine throughout our kingdom, and one measure for ale, and one measure for corn, namely "the London quarter"; and one width for cloths whether dyed, russet or halberget, namely two ells within the selvedges. Let it be the same with weights as with measures. [1216, ch. 28]

[32] Nothing shall be given in future for the writ of inquisition *by him who seeks an inquisition* of life or limbs: instead, it shall be granted free of charge and not refused. [1216, ch. 29]

[33] If anyone holds of us by fee-farm, by socage, or by burgage, and holds land of another by knight service, we will not, by reason of that fee-farm, socage or burgage, have the wardship of his heir or of land of his that is of the fief of the other; nor will we have custody of the fee-farm, socage, or

burgage, unless such fee-farm owes knight service. We will not have custody of anyone's heir or land which he holds of another by knight service by reason of any petty serjeanty which he holds of us by the service of rendering[12] knives or arrows or the like. [1216, ch. 30]

[34] No bailiff shall in future put anyone to *manifest* trial or *to oath* upon his own bare word without reliable witnesses produced for this purpose. [1216, ch. 31]

[35] No free man shall be arrested or imprisoned or disseised *of his freehold, liberties or free customs,* or outlawed or exiled or victimised in any other way, neither will we attack him or send anyone to attack him, except by the lawful judgment of his peers or by the law of the land. [1216, ch. 32]

[36] To no one will we sell, to no one will we refuse or delay right or justice. [1216, ch. 33]

[37] All merchants, unless they have been publicly prohibited beforehand, shall be able to go out of and come into England safely and securely[13] and stay and travel throughout England, as well by land as by water, for buying and selling by the ancient and right customs free from all evil tolls, except in time of war and if they are of the land that is at war with us. And if such are found in our land at the beginning of a war, they shall be attached without injury to their persons or goods, until we, or our chief justiciar, know how merchants of our land are treated who were found in the land at war with us when war broke out; and if ours are safe there, the others shall be safe in our land. [1216, ch. 34]

[38] If anyone who holds of some escheat such as the honour of Wallingford, Boulogne, Nottingham, Lancaster, or of other escheats which are in our hands and are baronies dies, his heir shall give no other relief and do no other service to us than he would have done to the baron if that[14] had been in the baron's hands; and we will hold it in the same manner in which the baron held it. *Nor will we by reason of such a barony or escheat have any escheat or wardship of any men of ours unless he who held the barony or escheat held in chief of us elsewhere.* [1216, ch. 35][15]

---

12. The "to us" of 1216 is omitted (but restored in 1225).

13. The text as printed in STATUTES OF THE REALM, "conduct" is given (*salvum et securum conductum exire*). There is no warrant for it in the 1215, 1216, or the 1225 issues and it is scarcely explicable save as an interpolation. It should be added that *conductum* is given in the text, which was confirmed by inspeximus in 1297 and 1300 (1 STATUTES OF THE REALM 33, 38, and 144 (1810)).

14. The "land" of 1216 is omitted.

15. Chapter 36 of 1216 (on the forest) is omitted, being transferred to the separate charter on forest matters (Charter of the Forest, 1217, ch. 2) and replaced as chapter 39 here by a new chapter on alienation.

[39] *No free man shall henceforth give or sell to anyone more of his land than will leave enough for the full service due from the fief to be rendered to the lord of the fief.*

[40] All *patrons* of abbeys *who have charters of advowson* of the kings of England or ancient *tenure or possession* shall have the custody of them during vacancies, as they ought to have and as is made clear above.[16] [1216, ch. 37][17]

[41] No one shall be arrested or imprisoned upon the appeal of a woman for the death of anyone except her husband. [1216, ch. 39][18]

[42] *No county shall in future be held more often than once a month and where a greater interval has been customary let it be greater. Nor shall any sheriff or his bailiff make his tourn through the hundred save twice a year (and then only in the due and accustomed place), that is to say, once after Easter and again after Michaelmas. And view of frankpledge shall be held then at the Michaelmas term without interference,[19] that is to say, so that each has his liberties which he had and was accustomed to have in the time of king Henry our grandfather or which he has since acquired. View of frankpledge shall be held in this manner, namely, that our peace be kept, that a tithing be kept full as it used to be, and that the sheriff shall not look for opportunities for exactions,[20] but be satisfied with what a sheriff used to get from holding his view in the time of king Henry our grandfather.*

[43] *It shall not in future be lawful for anyone to give land of his to any religious house in such a way that he gets it back again as a tenant of that house. Nor shall it be lawful for any religious house to receive anyone's land to hand it back to him as a tenant. And if in future anyone does give land of his in this way to any religious house and he is convicted of it, his gift shall be utterly quashed and the land shall be forfeit to the lord of the fief concerned.*

[44] *Scutage shall be taken in future as it used to be taken in the time of king Henry our grandfather.*

---

16. Chapter 5 above.
17. Chapter 38 of 1216 is omitted and divided, the forest part being taken into the new Charter of the Forest, and the residue about river banks becoming a chapter in its own right as chapter 20 above.
18. Chapter 40 of 1216 is omitted, but before continuing with chapter 41 of 1216 three new chapters are introduced, presumably so as to have them too covered by chapter 41 (which becomes ch. 45 below). Of the new chapters (chs. 42–44 below), two, 42 and 44, in fact reintroduce matters deferred by 1216; *see* ch. 42, for further consideration. Chapter 43 is entirely new.
19. *Sine occasione.*
20. *Non querat occasions.*

[45] All these aforesaid customs and liberties which we have granted to be observed in our kingdom as far as it pertains to us towards our men, all of our kingdom, clerks as well as laymen, shall observe as far as it pertains to them towards their men. [1216, ch. 41][21]

[46] Saving[22] to archbishops, bishops, abbots, priors, Templars, Hospitallers, earls, barons and all other persons, ecclesiastical and secular, the liberties and free customs they had previously.

[47] We have also with the common counsel of our whole realm decreed that all adulterine castles, that is to say, those built or rebuilt since the beginning of the war between the lord John our father and his barons of England, shall be destroyed immediately. Because we have not yet a seal, we have had this [charter] sealed with the seals of the aforesaid lord legate and the earl W. Marshal, ruler of us and of our kingdom.

---

21. All the rest of Magna Carta 1216 (ch. 42, including the final protocol) is omitted and the following (chapters 46–47) substituted.

22. In the Latin this article is not a sentence but an ablative absolute. Both the construction and the context are changed in the 1225 reissue (1225, ch. 37).

1217 Carta de Foresta (Charter of the Forest)*

[1] The common right of gathering herbs and berries in the forests (*herbage*) is preserved, even in the King's Royal Forest domain (*demesne*), and all Henry II's expansions of his Royal forest domain (*afforestations*) are to be reversed following an independent inspection.

[2] Those who live in or near the Forests no longer must attend sessions of the Forest Courts (*eyres*) when these itinerant courts come to their area, unless they have been charged with an offence or are sureties for those charged. This frees all from the threat of being fined (*amerced*) for failure to appear, and frees up significant amounts of time.

[3] All expansions of Royal Forests (*afforestations*) under Kings Richard and John are reversed immediately. Existing procedures for the physical inspections of Royal Forest boundaries (*perambulations*) provided a means to enforce this provision, and restore lands that had been unjustly taken.

[4] All holdings by ecclesiastic, noble and free holders (*libere tenentes*), as they were at the time of the coronation of Henry are to be restored, and any fines, rents and fees assessed on these lands are forgiven; unauthorized land uses (*purprestures*), degradation of resources (*wastes*) and compulsory payments, like rents (*assarts*) required for those uses, as they were in existence from the second year after Henry III's coronation, are to be assessed and paid. This set limits on what the Crown could claim for revenues.

[5] Inspections of the Royal Forests (*regards*) are to be held in accordance with the practices as prescribed at the time of the coronation of Henry II, every three years regularly. This restores traditionally accepted procedures, and restricts the King to follow only this procedure.

[6] Formal investigations (*inquiry*) to determine who possesses dogs near Royal Forests is constrained, and the practice of removing the toes of dogs ("lawing"), ostensibly to keep them from chasing and killing the King's deer

---

* Latin text *in* 1 STATUTES OF THE REALM 20–21 (1810). The translation reproduced here was prepared by Professor Nicholas Robinson, Pace University and Professor Adjunct, Yale University School of Forestry & Environmental Studies.

Note: All footnotes are from the translation.

is curbed, and allowed only where the practice was in force as of the coronation of Henry II, and when a dog is found the cutting is limited to three toes cut from the front foot. The fine for having dogs whose toes have not been removed (unlawed) is set at 3 shillings, and no longer may an ox be taken for the lawing of a dog. Hunting or travelling through Royal Forest with dogs remains banned.

[7] Foresters may not collect exactions of grains or sheep or pigs. The number of foresters is to be determined by the twelve knights chosen for conducting investigations (regarders) during their inspections of Royal Forests.

[8] Councils to supervise the introduction of domestic animals into the forests[1] are to be held regularly three times a year, to arrange for the counting (agistment) of the pigs that enter the Royal Forest for eating mast and acorns (pannage), or to manage commoners' usufructs to ensure no disturbance of allowing for mating and fawning of deer. Foresters and verderers are to meet every 40 days to deal with arrests for offenses of killing or hunting deer (trespasses of venison) or harvesting vegetation without authority (trespasses of vert).

[9] Every free man (liber homo) can let his animals use (agist) his own forests lands located within Royal Forests at will, and can drive his pigs through the Royal Forest to allow them to reach places to eat acorns (pannage), and if a pig strays into the Royal Forest for a night, it shall not be an offense.

[10] No one shall lose life or suffer loss of limbs as punishment for killing a deer.[2] The person who kills a deer shall be fined and if he cannot pay a fine, he shall be imprisoned for a year and a day. He can then be released, if he posts sureties, but if he cannot do so then he is to be exiled.

[11] Archbishops, Bishops, Earls and Barons traversing Royal Forests may take one or two deer, in view of the foresters, for their own use, and may blow horns to scare up deer or show when they are not hunting.

[12] On his own land and with his own access to water within a Royal Forest, every freeman (liber homo) can make a mill, fishpond, dam, marsh pit or dike, or reclaim arable ground, without danger of constituting an offense under the Forest Law, so long as it is not a nuisance to any of his neighbors.

---

1. Swanimote courts, from an old Anglo-Saxon word, "swainmote," meaning a meeting of swineherders.
2. The old penalty, still allowed in 1198, had been loss of eyes and testicles, but in place of dismemberment, severe fines had become preferred in the 13th century.

[13] Within his own lands located in Royal Forests, every free man (*liber homo*) can have eyries and nests of hawks, and other birds, and may take any honey from wild bee trees discovered in the forest.

[14] Only a forester who holds his office by hereditary right (*forester in fee*) can escort persons through a Royal Forest and take a fee for doing so (*cheminage*) or collect a toll, which is set for carriage by a cart at 2 pence per half year, and for a horse a half penny per half year. Persons carrying their brush or bark or charcoal on their backs shall pay no fee (*cheminage*), unless they are removing it from the King's domain in a Royal Forest (*demesne*).

[15] All offenses committed during the time of Henry II to the coronation of Henry III are pardoned, but those pardoned must find sureties to pledge that they shall not commit new violations.

[16] Procedures for handling offenses are regularized. No warden of a castle may hold a court to enforce Forest Law or to hear pleas of the Forest, and foresters who make arrests (*attachments*) must present them to the verederes, who will make a record and present them to the Forest Justices when Royal Forest Courts (*Eyres*) are held to determine forest pleas.

[17] These liberties of the forest (*libertates de forestis*) and free customs traditionally had (*consuetudines predictas et libertates*), both within and without the Royal Forests, are granted to ecclesiastics, nobles, freeholders, and all in our realm (*omnes de regno nostro*), in short to everyone. Everyone is also obliged to observe the liberties and customs granted in the Forest Charter.

APPENDIX I

1225 Magna Carta[*]

[The further changes made in this reissue of the Charter compared with that of 1217 are shown in the same way as the differences between previous reissues. The modern editorial division of the text into chapters is again preserved, not because it is in this case the best possible, but because it is by now conventional and therefore necessary for ease of reference.]

Henry by the grace of God, king of England, lord of Ireland, duke of Normandy, Aquitaine, and count of Anjou, to the archbishops, bishops, abbots, priors, earls, barons, sheriffs, stewards, servants and to all his bailiffs and faithful subjects who shall look at the present charter, greeting. Know that we, out of reverence for God and for the salvation of our soul and the souls of our ancestors and successors, for the exaltation of holy church and the reform of our realm, have *of our own spontaneous goodwill given and granted to the archbishops, bishops, abbots, priors, earls, barons and all of our realm* these liberties written below to be held in our kingdom of England for ever.

[1] In the first place we have granted to God, and by this our present charter confirmed for us and our heirs for ever, that the English church shall be free and shall have *all* its rights undiminished and its liberties unimpaired. We have also granted to all free men of our kingdom, for ourselves and our heirs for ever, all the liberties written below to be *had and*[1] held by them and their heirs of us and our heirs *for ever.* [1217, ch. 1]

[2] If any of our earls or barons or others holding of us in chief by knight service dies, and at his death his heir be of full age and owe relief he shall have his inheritance on payment of the old relief, namely the heir or heirs of an earl ££100 for a whole earl's barony, the heir or heirs of a baron ££100 for a whole barony, the heir or heirs of a knight 100*s*, at most, for a whole knight's fee; and he who owes less shall give less according to the ancient usage of fiefs. [1217, ch. 2]

* Latin text *in* 1 STATUTES OF THE REALM 22–25 (1810). The translation reproduced here is from 3 ENGLISH HISTORICAL DOCUMENTS 341–46 (Harry Rothwell ed., Eyre & Spottiswoode 1975). Reproduced by permission of Taylor & Francis Books UK.

Note: All footnotes are from the translation. Annex C: "Magna Carta 1215" is translated by a different translator than 1216, 1217, and 1225.

    1. The "had and" omitted in 1217 is restored.

[3] If, however, the heir of any such be under age, his lord shall not have wardship of him, nor of his land, before he has received his homage; and after being a ward such an heir shall have his inheritance when he comes of age, that is of twenty-one years, without paying relief and without making fine, so, however, that if he is made a knight *while*[2] still under age, the land nevertheless shall remain in the wardship of his lords for the full term. [1217, ch. 3]

[4] The guardian of the land of such an heir who is under age shall take from the land of the heir no more than reasonable revenues, reasonable customary dues and reasonable services, and that without destruction and waste of men or goods; and if we commit the wardship of the land of any such to a sheriff, or to any other who is answerable to us for the revenues of that land, and he destroys or wastes what he has wardship of, we will take compensation from him and the land shall be committed to two lawful and discreet men of that fief, who shall be answerable for the revenues to us or to him to whom we have assigned them; and if we give or sell to anyone the wardship of any such land and he causes destruction or waste therein, he shall lose that wardship and it shall be transferred to two lawful and discreet men of that fief, who shall similarly be answerable to us as is aforesaid. [1217, ch. 4]

[5] Moreover, so long as he has the wardship of the land, the guardian shall keep in repair the houses, parks, preserves, ponds, mills, and other things pertaining to the land out of the revenues from it; and he shall restore to the heir when he comes of age his land fully stocked with ploughs and all other things in at least the measure he received. All these things shall be observed in the case of warships of vacant archbishoprics, bishoprics, abbeys, priories, churches and dignities that pertain to us except that wardships of this kind may not be sold. [1217, ch. 5]

[6] Heirs shall be married without disparagement. [1217, ch. 6]

[7] A widow shall have her marriage portion and inheritance forthwith and without any difficulty after the death of her husband; nor shall she pay anything to have her dower or her marriage portion or the inheritance which she and her husband held on the day of her husband's death; and she may remain in chief house of her husband for forty days after his death, within which time her dower shall be assigned to her, unless it has already been assigned to her or unless the house is a castle; and if she leaves the castle, a suitable house shall be immediately provided for her in which she can stay honourably until her dower is assigned to her in accordance with what is aforesaid, and she shall have meanwhile her reasonable estover of common. There shall be assigned to her for her dower a third of all her

---

2. The "while" omitted in 1217 is restored.

husband's land which was his in his lifetime, unless a smaller share was given her at the church door. No widow shall be forced to marry so long as she wishes to live without a husband, provided that she gives security not to marry without our consent if she holds of us, or without the consent of her lord if she holds of another. [1217, chs. 7–8]

[8] We or our bailiffs will not seize for any debt any land or rent, so long as the available chattels of the debtor are sufficient to repay the debt and the debtor himself is prepared to have it paid therefrom; nor will those who have gone surety for the debtor be distrained so long as the principal debtor is himself able to pay the debt; and if the principal debtor fails to pay the debt, having nothing wherewith to pay it or is able but unwilling to pay, then shall the sureties answer for the debt; and they shall, if they wish, have the lands and rents of the debtor until they are reimbursed for the debt which they have paid for him, unless the principal debtor can show that he has discharged his obligation in the matter to the said sureties. [1217, ch. 9]

[9] The city of London shall have all its ancient liberties and free customs. Furthermore, we will and grant that all other cities, boroughs, towns, the barons of the Cinque Ports, and all ports shall have all their liberties and free customs. [1217, ch. 10]

[10] No one shall be compelled to do greater service for a knight's fee or for any other free holding than is due from it. [1217, ch. 11]

[11] Common pleas shall not follow our court, but shall be held in some fixed place. [1217, ch. 12]

[12] Recognitions of novel disseisin *and*[3] of mort d'ancestor shall not be held elsewhere than in the counties to which they relate, and in this manner—we, or, if we should be out of the realm, our chief justiciar, will send justices through each county once a year, who with knights of the counties shall hold said assizes in the counties, and those which cannot on that visit be determined in the county to which they relate by the said justices sent to hold the said assizes shall be determined by them elsewhere on their circuit, and those which cannot be determined by them because of difficulty over certain articles shall be referred to our justices of the bench and determined there. [1217, chs. 13–14]

[13] Assizes of darrein presentment shall always be held before the justices of the bench and determined there. [1217, ch. 15]

[14] A free man shall not be amerced for a trivial offence except in accordance with the degree of the offence and for a grave offence in accordance with its gravity, yet saving his way of living; and a merchant in the same way, saving his stock-in-trade; and a villein other than one of our own shall

---

3. The rough edge smoothed. *See* 1217, ch. 13, n. 9.

be amerced in the same way, saving his means of livelihood; if he has fallen into our mercy: and none of the aforesaid amercements shall be imposed except by the *oaths* of good and law-worthy men of the neighbourhood. Earls and barons shall not be amerced except by their peers, and only in accordance with the degree of the offence. No ecclesiastical person shall be amerced according to the amount of his ecclesiastical benefice but in accordance with his lay holding and in accordance with the degree of the offence. [1217, chs. 16-18]

[15] No vill or individual shall be compelled to make bridges at river banks, except one who from of old is legally bound to do so. [1217, ch. 19]

[16] No river bank shall henceforth be made a preserve, except those which were preserves in the time of king Henry, our grandfather, in the same places and for the same periods as they used to be in his day. [1217, ch. 20]

[17] No sheriff, constable, coroners, or others of our bailiffs shall hold pleas of our crown. [1217, ch. 21]

[18] If anyone holding a lay fief of us dies and our sheriff or bailiff shows our letters patent of summons for a debt that the deceased owed us, it shall be lawful for our sheriff or bailiff to attach and make a list of chattels of the deceased found upon the lay fief to the value of that debt under supervision of law-worthy men, provided that none of the chattels shall be removed until the debt which is manifest has been paid to us in full; and the residue shall be left to the executors for carrying out the will of the deceased. And if nothing is owing to us from him, all the chattels shall accrue to the deceased, saving to his wife *and his children*[4] their reasonable shares. [1217, ch. 22]

[19] No constable or his bailiff shall take the corn or other chattels of anyone who is not of the vill where the castle is situated unless he pays on the spot in cash for them or can delay payment by arrangement with the seller; if the seller is of that vill and he shall pay within forty days. [1217, ch. 23]

[20] No constable shall compel any knight to give money instead of castle-guard he is willing to do it himself or through another good man, if for some good reason he cannot do it himself; and if we lead or send him on military service, he shall be excused guard in respect of the fief for which he did service in the army in proportion to the time that because of us he has been on service. [1217, ch. 24]

[21] No sheriff, or bailiff of ours, or other person shall take anyone's horses or carts for transport work unless he pays for them at the old-established rates, namely at ten pence a day for a cart with two horses and fourteen pence a day for a cart with three horses. No demesne cart of any

---

4. The "and his children" omitted in 1217 is restored.

ecclesiastical person or knight or of any lady shall be taken by the aforesaid bailiffs. Neither we nor our bailiffs nor others will take, for castles or other works of ours, timber which is not ours, except with the agreement of him whose timber it is. [1217, chs. 25–27]

[22] We will not hold for more than a year and a day the lands of those convicted of felony, and then the lands shall be handed over to the lords of the fiefs. [1217, ch. 28]

[23] Henceforth all fish-weirs shall be cleared completely from the Thames and the Medway and throughout all England, except along the sea coast. [1217, ch. 29]

[24] The writ called Praecipe shall not in future be issued to anyone in respect of any holding whereby a free man may lose his court. [1217, ch. 30]

[25] Let there be one measure for wine throughout our kingdom, and one measure for ale, and one measure for corn, namely "the London quarter"; and one width for cloths whether dyed, russet or halberget, namely two ells within the selvedges. Let it be the same with weights as with measures. [1217, ch. 31]

[26] Nothing shall be given in future for the writ of inquisition by him who seeks an inquisition of life or limbs: instead, it shall be granted free of charge and not refused. [1217, ch. 32]

[27] If anyone holds of us by fee-farm, by socage, or by burgage, and holds land of another by knight service, we will not, by reason of that fee-farm, socage or burgage, have the wardship of his heir or of land of his that is of the fief of the other; nor will we have custody of the fee-farm, socage, or burgage, unless such fee-farm owes knight service. We will not have custody of anyone's heir or land which he holds of another by knight service by reason of any petty serjeanty which he holds of us by the service of rendering *to us*[5] knives or arrows or the like. [1217, ch. 33]

[28] No bailiff shall in future put anyone to manifest trial or to oath upon his own bare word without reliable witnesses produced for this purpose. [1217, ch. 34]

[29] No free man shall *in future* be arrested or imprisoned or disseised of his freehold, liberties or free customs, or outlawed or exiled or victimised in any other way, neither will we attack him or send anyone to attack him, except by the lawful judgment of his peers or by the law of the land. To no one will we sell, to no one will we refuse or delay right or justice. [1217, chs. 35–36]

---

5. The "to us" omitted in 1217 is restored.

[30] All merchants, unless they have been publicly prohibited beforehand, shall be able to go out of and come into England safely and securely and stay and travel throughout England, as well by land as by water, for buying and selling by the ancient and right customs free from all evil tolls, except in time of war and if they are of the land that is at war with us. And if such are found in our land at the beginning of a war, they shall be attached without injury to their persons or goods, until we, or our chief justiciar, know how merchants of our land are treated who were found in the land at war with us when war broke out; and if ours are safe there, the others shall be safe in our land. [1217, ch. 37]

[31] If anyone who holds of some escheat such as the honour of Wallingford, Boulogne, Nottingham, Lancaster, or of other escheats which are in our hands and are baronies dies, his heir shall give no other relief and do no other service to us than he would have done to the baron if that[6] had been in the baron's hands; and we will hold it in the same manner in which the barons held it. Nor will we by reason of such a barony or escheat have any escheat or wardship of any men of ours unless he who held the barony or escheat held in chief of us elsewhere. [1217, ch. 38]

[32] No free man shall henceforth give or sell to anyone more of his land than will leave enough for the full service due from the fief to be rendered to the lord of the fief. [1217, ch. 39]

[33] All patrons of abbeys who have charters of advowson of the kings of England or ancient tenure or possession shall have the custody of them during vacancies, as they ought to have and as is made clear above. [1217, ch. 40]

[34] No one shall be arrested or imprisoned upon the appeal of a woman for the death of anyone except her husband. [1217, ch. 41]

[35] No county shall in future be held more often than once a month and where a greater interval has been customary let it be greater. Nor shall any sheriff or[7] his bailiff make his tourn through the hundred save twice a year (and then only in the due and accustomed place), that is to say, once after Easter and again after Michaelmas. And view of frankpledge shall be held then at the Michaelmas term without interference, that is to say, so that each has his liberties which he had and was accustomed to have in the time of king Henry our grandfather or which he has since acquired. View of frankpledge shall be held in this manner, namely, that our peace be kept, that a tithing be kept full as it used to be, and that the sheriff shall not look

---

6. For "that" 1225 gives "ipsa" instead of the "illa" of 1217, but (curiously, in view of the other omissions by 1217 which are restored) 1225 restores neither the "land" of 1216 (ch. 35) nor the "barony" of 1215 (ch. 43).

7. The "his" of 1217, ch. 42, is omitted.

for opportunities for exactions but be satisfied with what a sheriff used to get from holding his view in the time of king Henry our grandfather. [1217, ch. 42]

[36] It shall not in future be lawful for anyone to give land of his to any religious house in such a way that he gets it back again as a tenant of that house. Nor shall it be lawful for any religious house to receive anyone's land to hand it back to him as a tenant. And if in future anyone does give land of his in this way to any religious house and he is convicted of it, his gift shall be utterly quashed and the land shall be forfeit to the lord of the fief concerned. [1217, ch. 43]

[37] Scutage shall be taken in future as it used to be taken in the time of king Henry our grandfather. *And let there be saved*[8] to archbishops, bishops, abbots, priors, Templars, Hospitallers, earls, barons and all other persons, ecclesiastical and secular, the liberties and free customs they had previously. All these aforesaid customs and liberties which we have granted to be observed in our kingdom as far as it pertains to us towards our men, all of our kingdom, clerks as well as laymen, shall observe as far as it pertains to them towards their men. *In return for this grant and gift of these liberties and of the other liberties contained in our charter on the liberties of the forest, the archbishops, bishops, abbots, priors, earls, barons, knights, freeholders and all of our realm have given us a fifteenth part of all their movables. We have also granted to them for us and our heirs that neither we nor our heirs will procure anything whereby the liberties contained in the charter shall be infringed or weakened; and if anything contrary to this is procured from anyone, it shall avail nothing and be held for nought. These being witness: the lord S. archbishop of Canterbury, E. of London, J. of Bath, P. of Winchester, H. of Lincoln, R. of Salisbury, B. of Rochester, W. of Worcester, J. of Ely, H. of Herefold, R. of Chichester and W. of Exeter, bishops; the abbot of St Albans, the abbot of Bury St Edmunds, the abbot of Battle, the abbot St Augustine's, Canterbury, the abbot of Evesham, the abbot of Westminster, the abbot of Peterborough, the abbot of Reading, the abbot of Abingdon, the abbot of Malmesbury, the abbot of Winchcombe, the abbot of Hyde, the abbot of Chertsey, the abbot of Sherborne, the abbot of Cerne, the abbot of Abbotsbury, the abbot of Milton, the abbot of Selby, the abbot of Whitby, the abbot of Cirenester, H. de Burgh the justiciar, R. earl of Chester and Lincoln, W. earl of Salisbury, W. earl of Warenne, G. de Clare earl of Gloucester and Hertford, W. de Ferrers earl of Derby, W. de Mandeville earl of Essex, H. le Bigod earl of Norfolk, W. count of Aumale, H. earl of Hereford, John the constable of Chester, Robert de Ros, Robert fitz Walter, Robert de Vipont, William Brewer, Richard de Munfichet, Peter fitz Herbert, Matthew fitz Herbert, William de Aubeney, Robert Grelley,*

---

8. *See* 1217, ch. 46, n. 22.

Reginald de Braose, John of Monmouth, John fitz Alan, Hugh de Mortimer, Walter de Beauchamp, William of St John, Peter de Mauley, Brain de Lisle, Thomas of Moulton, Richard de Argentein, Geoffrey de Neville, William Mauduit, John de Balun. Given at Westminster on the eleventh day of February in the ninth year of our reign.[9]

---

9. Chapter 37 gives chapters 44, 46, and 45 of 1217 (in that order), omits 47 and, instead, concludes the charter with "In return . . . year of our reign." This writes into the charter the fact that the fifteenth was a *quid pro quo*, restores the dropped provision of 1215 (chapter 61) that any attempt to annul the charter shall itself be null, and substitutes for 1217's rather perfunctory ending a full final protocol in proper charter form.

APPENDIX J
Confirmatio Cartarum 1297
(Confirmation of the Charters)*

[1] Edward, by the grace of God king of England, lord of Ireland and duke of Aquitaine, to all those who see or hear these present letters, greeting. Know that we, to the honour of God and of holy church and for the benefit of our whole realm, have granted for us and our heirs that the great charter of liberties and the forest charter which were made by common assent of all the realm in the time of king Henry, our father, be kept in all their points without any impediment to their working. And we will that these same charters be sent under our seal to our justices (to those of the forest as well as to the others), to all sheriffs of counties, and to all our other officials, and to all our cities throughout the land, together with our writs, in which it shall be contained that they cause the aforesaid charters to be published and have it declared to the people that we have granted they be kept in all their points; and to our justices, sheriffs, mayors and other officials, who have to administer under us and for us the law of the land, to have these same charters allowed in all their points in pleadings before them and in judgments—the greater charter of liberties, that is, as common law and the forest charter in accordance with the assize of the forest—for the betterment of our people.

[2] And we will that if any judgments are given henceforth contrary to the points of the aforesaid charters by justices or by other officials of ours who hold pleas before them contrary to the points of the charters, they shall be undone and held for nought.

[3] And we will that these same charters be sent under our seal to cathedral churches throughout our realm and remain there, and be read before the people twice a year.

[4] And that archbishops and bishops pronounce sentences of greater excommunication against all those who contravene the aforesaid charters

---

* French text *in* W. STUBBS, SELECT CHARTERS & OTHER ILLUSTRATIONS OF ENGLISH CONSTITUTIONAL HISTORY 490–91 (H.W.C. Davis ed., 9th ed. 1913). The translation reproduced here is from 3 ENGLISH HISTORICAL DOCUMENTS 485–86 (Harry Rothwell ed., Eyre & Spottiswoode 1975). Reproduced by permission of Taylor & Francis Books UK.

Note: All footnotes are from the translation.

(whether of their own doing or by assisting or advising) or infringe or contravene any point of them. And that these sentences be pronounced and published twice a year by the aforesaid prelates. And if the same prelates, the bishops, or any of them are negligent over making the abovesaid denunciation, let them be reprimanded by the archbishops of Canterbury and York for the time being, as is proper, and be compelled to make this same denunciation in the form aforesaid.

[5] And because some people of our realm fear that the aids and contributions[1] they have furnished us with of their own granting and their goodwill before now for our wars and other needs in whatever way they were done could lead to bondage for them and their heirs because another time they might be found enrolled, and likewise the prises which have been taken throughout the realm by our officials in our name, we have granted for us and our heirs that henceforth we will not make a precedent of[2] such aids, mises or prises for anything that may have been done or that could be found out from a roll or in any other way.

[6] And we have likewise granted for us and our heirs to the archbishops, bishops, abbots, priors and other folk of holy church, and to the earls and barons and all the community of the land that for no need will we take such manner of aids, mises or prises from our realm henceforth except with the common assent of all the realm and for the common profit of the same realm, saving the ancient aids and prises due and accustomed.

[7] And because by far the greater part of the community of the realm feel themselves greatly burdened by the maltote on wool, namely 40 shillings on each sack of wool, and have entreated us to be good enough to relieve them, we at their request have completely relieved them and have granted that we will not take this or any other in future without their common assent and their goodwill, saving for us and our heirs the custom on wool, skins and leathers granted earlier by the community of the aforesaid realm. In witness of which things we have had these our letters patent made. Given at Ghent, the fifth day of November in the twenty-fifth year of our reign [5 November 1297, Ghent].

---

1. *Mises*
2. Literally "draw into a custom." It was a medieval saying that "twice makes a custom."

APPENDIX K
United States Constitution*

We the People of the United States, in Order to form a more perfect Union, establish Justice, insure domestic Tranquility, provide for the common defence, promote the general Welfare, and secure the Blessings of Liberty to ourselves and our Posterity, do ordain and establish this Constitution for the United States of America.

Article I

Section 1

All legislative powers herein granted shall be vested in a congress of the United States, which shall consist of a senate and house of representatives.

Section 2

The House of Representatives shall be composed of Members chosen every second Year by the People of the several States, and the Electors in each State shall have the Qualifications requisite for Electors of the most numerous Branch of the State Legislature.

No Person shall be a Representative who shall not have attained to the Age of twenty five Years, and been seven Years a Citizen of the United States, and who shall not, when elected, be an Inhabitant of that State in which he shall be chosen.

Representatives and direct Taxes shall be apportioned among the several States which may be included within this Union, according to their respective Numbers, which shall be determined by adding to the whole Number of free Persons, including those bound to Service for a Term of Years, and excluding Indians not taxed, three fifths of all other Persons. The actual Enumeration shall be made within three Years after the first Meeting of the Congress of the United States, and within every subsequent Term of ten Years, in such Manner as they shall by Law direct. The Number of Representatives shall

* Source: U.S. National Archives, *available at* http://www.archives.gov/exhibits /charters/print_friendly.html?page=constitution_transcript_content.html&title=The%20 Constitution%20of%20the%20United%20States%3A%20A%20Transcription.

not exceed one for every thirty Thousand, but each State shall have at Least one Representative; and until such enumeration shall be made, the State of New Hampshire shall be entitled to chuse three, Massachusetts eight, Rhode-Island and Providence Plantations one, Connecticut five, New-York six, New Jersey four, Pennsylvania eight, Delaware one, Maryland six, Virginia ten, North Carolina five, South Carolina five, and Georgia three.

When vacancies happen in the Representation from any State, the Executive Authority thereof shall issue Writs of Election to fill such Vacancies.

The House of Representatives shall chuse their Speaker and other Officers; and shall have the sole Power of Impeachment.

Section 3

The Senate of the United States shall be composed of two Senators from each State, chosen by the Legislature thereof for six Years; and each Senator shall have one Vote.

Immediately after they shall be assembled in Consequence of the first Election, they shall be divided as equally as may be into three Classes. The Seats of the Senators of the first Class shall be vacated at the Expiration of the second Year, of the second Class at the Expiration of the fourth Year, and of the third Class at the Expiration of the sixth Year, so that one third may be chosen every second Year; and if Vacancies happen by Resignation, or otherwise, during the Recess of the Legislature of any State, the Executive thereof may make temporary Appointments until the next Meeting of the Legislature, which shall then fill such Vacancies.

No Person shall be a Senator who shall not have attained to the Age of thirty Years, and been nine Years a Citizen of the United States, and who shall not, when elected, be an Inhabitant of that State for which he shall be chosen.

The Vice President of the United States shall be President of the Senate, but shall have no Vote, unless they be equally divided.

The Senate shall chuse their other Officers, and also a President pro tempore, in the Absence of the Vice President, or when he shall exercise the Office of President of the United States.

The Senate shall have the sole Power to try all Impeachments. When sitting for that Purpose, they shall be on Oath or Affirmation. When the President of the United States is tried, the Chief Justice shall preside: And no Person shall be convicted without the Concurrence of two thirds of the Members present.

Judgment in Cases of Impeachment shall not extend further than to removal from Office, and disqualification to hold and enjoy any Office of honor, Trust or Profit under the United States: but the Party convicted shall nevertheless be liable and subject to Indictment, Trial, Judgment and Punishment, according to Law.

Section 4

The Times, Places and Manner of holding Elections for Senators and Representatives, shall be prescribed in each State by the Legislature thereof; but the Congress may at any time by Law make or alter such Regulations, except as to the Places of chusing Senators.

The Congress shall assemble at least once in every Year, and such Meeting shall be on the first Monday in December, unless they shall by Law appoint a different Day.

Section 5

Each House shall be the Judge of the Elections, Returns and Qualifications of its own Members, and a Majority of each shall constitute a Quorum to do Business; but a smaller Number may adjourn from day to day, and may be authorized to compel the Attendance of absent Members, in such Manner, and under such Penalties as each House may provide.

Each House may determine the Rules of its Proceedings, punish its Members for disorderly Behaviour, and, with the Concurrence of two thirds, expel a Member.

Each House shall keep a Journal of its Proceedings, and from time to time publish the same, excepting such Parts as may in their Judgment require Secrecy; and the Yeas and Nays of the Members of either House on any question shall, at the Desire of one fifth of those Present, be entered on the Journal.

Neither House, during the Session of Congress, shall, without the Consent of the other, adjourn for more than three days, nor to any other Place than that in which the two Houses shall be sitting.

Section 6

The Senators and Representatives shall receive a Compensation for their Services, to be ascertained by Law, and paid out of the Treasury of the United States. They shall in all Cases, except Treason, Felony and Breach of the Peace, be privileged from Arrest during their Attendance at the Session of their respective Houses, and in going to and returning from the same; and for any Speech or Debate in either House, they shall not be questioned in any other Place.

No Senator or Representative shall, during the Time for which he was elected, be appointed to any civil Office under the Authority of the United States, which shall have been created, or the Emoluments whereof shall have been encreased during such time; and no Person holding any Office under the United States, shall be a Member of either House during his Continuance in Office.

Section 7

All Bills for raising Revenue shall originate in the House of Representatives; but the Senate may propose or concur with Amendments as on other Bills.

Every Bill which shall have passed the House of Representatives and the Senate, shall, before it become a Law, be presented to the President of the United States: If he approve he shall sign it, but if not he shall return it, with his Objections to that House in which it shall have originated, who shall enter the Objections at large on their Journal, and proceed to reconsider it. If after such Reconsideration two thirds of that House shall agree to pass the Bill, it shall be sent, together with the Objections, to the other House, by which it shall likewise be reconsidered, and if approved by two thirds of that House, it shall become a Law. But in all such Cases the Votes of both Houses shall be determined by yeas and Nays, and the Names of the Persons voting for and against the Bill shall be entered on the Journal of each House respectively. If any Bill shall not be returned by the President within ten Days (Sundays excepted) after it shall have been presented to him, the Same shall be a Law, in like Manner as if he had signed it, unless the Congress by their Adjournment prevent its Return, in which Case it shall not be a Law.

Every Order, Resolution, or Vote to which the Concurrence of the Senate and House of Representatives may be necessary (except on a question of Adjournment) shall be presented to the President of the United States; and before the Same shall take Effect, shall be approved by him, or being disapproved by him, shall be repassed by two thirds of the Senate and House of Representatives, according to the Rules and Limitations prescribed in the Case of a Bill.

Section 8

The Congress shall have Power To lay and collect Taxes, Duties, Imposts and Excises, to pay the Debts and provide for the common Defence and general Welfare of the United States; but all Duties, Imposts and Excises shall be uniform throughout the United States;

To borrow Money on the credit of the United States;

To regulate Commerce with foreign Nations, and among the several States, and with the Indian Tribes;

To establish an uniform Rule of Naturalization, and uniform Laws on the subject of Bankruptcies throughout the United States;

To coin Money, regulate the Value thereof, and of foreign Coin, and fix the Standard of Weights and Measures;

To provide for the Punishment of counterfeiting the Securities and current Coin of the United States;

To establish Post Offices and post Roads;

To promote the Progress of Science and useful Arts, by securing for limited Times to Authors and Inventors the exclusive Right to their respective Writings and Discoveries;

To constitute Tribunals inferior to the supreme Court;

To define and punish Piracies and Felonies committed on the high Seas, and Offences against the Law of Nations;

To declare War, grant Letters of Marque and Reprisal, and make Rules concerning Captures on Land and Water;

To raise and support Armies, but no Appropriation of Money to that Use shall be for a longer Term than two Years;

To provide and maintain a Navy;

To make Rules for the Government and Regulation of the land and naval Forces;

To provide for calling forth the Militia to execute the Laws of the Union, suppress Insurrections and repel Invasions;

To provide for organizing, arming, and disciplining, the Militia, and for governing such Part of them as may be employed in the Service of the United States, reserving to the States respectively, the Appointment of the Officers, and the Authority of training the Militia according to the discipline prescribed by Congress;

To exercise exclusive Legislation in all Cases whatsoever, over such District (not exceeding ten Miles square) as may, by Cession of particular States, and the Acceptance of Congress, become the Seat of the Government of the United States, and to exercise like Authority over all Places purchased by the Consent of the Legislature of the State in which the Same shall be, for the Erection of Forts, Magazines, Arsenals, dock-Yards, and other needful Buildings;—And

To make all Laws which shall be necessary and proper for carrying into Execution the foregoing Powers, and all other Powers vested by this Constitution in the Government of the United States, or in any Department or Officer thereof.

Section 9

The Migration or Importation of such Persons as any of the States now existing shall think proper to admit, shall not be prohibited by the Congress prior to the Year one thousand eight hundred and eight, but a Tax or duty may be imposed on such Importation, not exceeding ten dollars for each Person.

The Privilege of the Writ of Habeas Corpus shall not be suspended, unless when in Cases of Rebellion or Invasion the public Safety may require it.

No Bill of Attainder or ex post facto Law shall be passed.

No Capitation, or other direct, Tax shall be laid, unless in Proportion to the Census or enumeration herein before directed to be taken.

No Tax or Duty shall be laid on Articles exported from any State.

No Preference shall be given by any Regulation of Commerce or Revenue to the Ports of one State over those of another; nor shall Vessels bound to, or from, one State, be obliged to enter, clear, or pay Duties in another.

No Money shall be drawn from the Treasury, but in Consequence of Appropriations made by Law; and a regular Statement and Account of the Receipts and Expenditures of all public Money shall be published from time to time.

No Title of Nobility shall be granted by the United States: And no Person holding any Office of Profit or Trust under them, shall, without the Consent of the Congress, accept of any present, Emolument, Office, or Title, of any kind whatever, from any King, Prince, or foreign State.

Section 10

No State shall enter into any Treaty, Alliance, or Confederation; grant Letters of Marque and Reprisal; coin Money; emit Bills of Credit; make any Thing but gold and silver Coin a Tender in Payment of Debts; pass any Bill of Attainder, ex post facto Law, or Law impairing the Obligation of Contracts, or grant any Title of Nobility.

No State shall, without the Consent of the Congress, lay any Imposts or Duties on Imports or Exports, except what may be absolutely necessary for executing it's inspection Laws: and the net Produce of all Duties and Imposts, laid by any State on Imports or Exports, shall be for the Use of the Treasury of the United States; and all such Laws shall be subject to the Revision and Controul of the Congress.

No State shall, without the Consent of Congress, lay any Duty of Tonnage, keep Troops, or Ships of War in time of Peace, enter into any Agreement or Compact with another State, or with a foreign Power, or engage in War, unless actually invaded, or in such imminent Danger as will not admit of delay.

Article II

Section 1

The executive Power shall be vested in a President of the United States of America. He shall hold his Office during the Term of four Years, and, together with the Vice President, chosen for the same Term, be elected, as follows:

Each State shall appoint, in such Manner as the Legislature thereof may direct, a Number of Electors, equal to the whole Number of Senators and Representatives to which the State may be entitled in the Congress: but no Senator or Representative, or Person holding an Office of Trust or Profit under the United States, shall be appointed an Elector.

The Electors shall meet in their respective States, and vote by Ballot for two Persons, of whom one at least shall not be an Inhabitant of the same State with themselves. And they shall make a List of all the Persons voted for, and of the Number of Votes for each; which List they shall sign and certify, and transmit sealed to the Seat of the Government of the United States, directed to the President of the Senate. The President of the Senate shall, in the Presence of the Senate and House of Representatives, open all the Certificates, and the Votes shall then be counted. The Person having the greatest Number of Votes shall be the President, if such Number be a Majority of the whole Number of Electors appointed; and if there be more than one who have such Majority, and have an equal Number of Votes, then the House of Representatives shall immediately chuse by Ballot one of them for President; and if no Person have a Majority, then from the five highest on the List the said House shall in like Manner chuse the President. But in chusing the President, the Votes shall be taken by States, the Representation from each State having one Vote; A quorum for this purpose shall consist of a Member or Members from two thirds of the States, and a Majority of all the States shall be necessary to a Choice. In every Case, after the Choice of the President, the Person having the greatest Number of Votes of the Electors shall be the Vice President. But if there should remain two or more who have equal Votes, the Senate shall chuse from them by Ballot the Vice President.

The Congress may determine the Time of chusing the Electors, and the Day on which they shall give their Votes; which Day shall be the same throughout the United States.

No Person except a natural born Citizen, or a Citizen of the United States, at the time of the Adoption of this Constitution, shall be eligible to the Office of President; neither shall any Person be eligible to that Office who shall not have attained to the Age of thirty five Years, and been fourteen Years a Resident within the United States.

In Case of the Removal of the President from Office, or of his Death, Resignation, or Inability to discharge the Powers and Duties of the said Office, the Same shall devolve on the Vice President, and the Congress may by Law provide for the Case of Removal, Death, Resignation or Inability, both of the President and Vice President, declaring what Officer shall then act as President, and such Officer shall act accordingly, until the Disability be removed, or a President shall be elected.

The President shall, at stated Times, receive for his Services, a Compensation, which shall neither be increased nor diminished during the Period for which he shall have been elected, and he shall not receive within that Period any other Emolument from the United States, or any of them.

Before he enter on the Execution of his Office, he shall take the following Oath or Affirmation:—"I do solemnly swear (or affirm) that I will faithfully execute the Office of President of the United States, and will to the best of my Ability, preserve, protect and defend the Constitution of the United States."

Section 2

The President shall be Commander in Chief of the Army and Navy of the United States, and of the Militia of the several States, when called into the actual Service of the United States; he may require the Opinion, in writing, of the principal Officer in each of the executive Departments, upon any Subject relating to the Duties of their respective Offices, and he shall have Power to grant Reprieves and Pardons for Offences against the United States, except in Cases of Impeachment.

He shall have Power, by and with the Advice and Consent of the Senate, to make Treaties, provided two thirds of the Senators present concur; and he shall nominate, and by and with the Advice and Consent of the Senate, shall appoint Ambassadors, other public Ministers and Consuls, Judges of the supreme Court, and all other Officers of the United States, whose Appointments are not herein otherwise provided for, and which shall be established by Law: but the Congress may by Law vest the Appointment of such inferior Officers, as they think proper, in the President alone, in the Courts of Law, or in the Heads of Departments.

The President shall have Power to fill up all Vacancies that may happen during the Recess of the Senate, by granting Commissions which shall expire at the End of their next Session.

Section 3

He shall from time to time give to the Congress Information of the State of the Union, and recommend to their Consideration such Measures as he shall judge necessary and expedient; he may, on extraordinary Occasions, convene both Houses, or either of them, and in Case of Disagreement between them, with Respect to the Time of Adjournment, he may adjourn them to such Time as he shall think proper; he shall receive Ambassadors and other public Ministers; he shall take Care that the Laws be faithfully executed, and shall Commission all the Officers of the United States.

Section 4

The President, Vice President and all civil Officers of the United States, shall be removed from Office on Impeachment for, and Conviction of, Treason, Bribery, or other high Crimes and Misdemeanors.

Article III

Section 1

The judicial Power of the United States shall be vested in one supreme Court, and in such inferior Courts as the Congress may from time to time ordain and establish. The Judges, both of the supreme and inferior Courts, shall hold their Offices during good Behaviour, and shall, at stated Times, receive for their Services a Compensation, which shall not be diminished during their Continuance in Office.

Section 2

The judicial Power shall extend to all Cases, in Law and Equity, arising under this Constitution, the Laws of the United States, and Treaties made, or which shall be made, under their Authority;—to all Cases affecting Ambassadors, other public Ministers and Consuls;—to all Cases of admiralty and maritime Jurisdiction;—to Controversies to which the United States shall be a Party;—to Controversies between two or more States;—between a State and Citizens of another State,—between Citizens of different States,—between Citizens of the same State claiming Lands under Grants of different States, and between a State, or the Citizens thereof, and foreign States, Citizens or Subjects.

In all Cases affecting Ambassadors, other public Ministers and Consuls, and those in which a State shall be Party, the supreme Court shall have original Jurisdiction. In all the other Cases before mentioned, the supreme Court shall have appellate Jurisdiction, both as to Law and Fact, with such Exceptions, and under such Regulations as the Congress shall make.

The Trial of all Crimes, except in Cases of Impeachment, shall be by Jury; and such Trial shall be held in the State where the said Crimes shall have been committed; but when not committed within any State, the Trial shall be at such Place or Places as the Congress may by Law have directed.

Section 3

Treason against the United States, shall consist only in levying War against them, or in adhering to their Enemies, giving them Aid and Comfort.

No Person shall be convicted of Treason unless on the Testimony of two Witnesses to the same overt Act, or on Confession in open Court.

The Congress shall have Power to declare the Punishment of Treason, but no Attainder of Treason shall work Corruption of Blood, or Forfeiture except during the Life of the Person attainted.

Article IV

Section 1

Full Faith and Credit shall be given in each State to the public Acts, Records, and judicial Proceedings of every other State. And the Congress may by general Laws prescribe the Manner in which such Acts, Records and Proceedings shall be proved, and the Effect thereof.

Section 2

The Citizens of each State shall be entitled to all Privileges and Immunities of Citizens in the several States.

A Person charged in any State with Treason, Felony, or other Crime, who shall flee from Justice, and be found in another State, shall on Demand of the executive Authority of the State from which he fled, be delivered up, to be removed to the State having Jurisdiction of the Crime.

No Person held to Service or Labour in one State, under the Laws thereof, escaping into another, shall, in Consequence of any Law or Regulation therein, be discharged from such Service or Labour, but shall be delivered up on Claim of the Party to whom such Service or Labour may be due.

Section 3

New States may be admitted by the Congress into this Union; but no new State shall be formed or erected within the Jurisdiction of any other State; nor any State be formed by the Junction of two or more States, or Parts of States, without the Consent of the Legislatures of the States concerned as well as of the Congress.

The Congress shall have Power to dispose of and make all needful Rules and Regulations respecting the Territory or other Property belonging to the United States; and nothing in this Constitution shall be so construed as to Prejudice any Claims of the United States, or of any particular State.

Section 4

The United States shall guarantee to every State in this Union a Republican Form of Government, and shall protect each of them against Invasion;

and on Application of the Legislature, or of the Executive (when the Legislature cannot be convened), against domestic Violence.

Article V

The Congress, whenever two thirds of both Houses shall deem it necessary, shall propose Amendments to this Constitution, or, on the Application of the Legislatures of two thirds of the several States, shall call a Convention for proposing Amendments, which, in either Case, shall be valid to all Intents and Purposes, as Part of this Constitution, when ratified by the Legislatures of three fourths of the several States, or by Conventions in three fourths thereof, as the one or the other Mode of Ratification may be proposed by the Congress; Provided that no Amendment which may be made prior to the Year One thousand eight hundred and eight shall in any Manner affect the first and fourth Clauses in the Ninth Section of the first Article; and that no State, without its Consent, shall be deprived of its equal Suffrage in the Senate.

Article VI

All Debts contracted and Engagements entered into, before the Adoption of this Constitution, shall be as valid against the United States under this Constitution, as under the Confederation.

This Constitution, and the Laws of the United States which shall be made in Pursuance thereof; and all Treaties made, or which shall be made, under the Authority of the United States, shall be the supreme Law of the Land; and the Judges in every State shall be bound thereby, any Thing in the Constitution or Laws of any State to the Contrary notwithstanding.

The Senators and Representatives before mentioned, and the Members of the several State Legislatures, and all executive and judicial Officers, both of the United States and of the several States, shall be bound by Oath or Affirmation, to support this Constitution; but no religious Test shall ever be required as a Qualification to any Office or public Trust under the United States.

Article VII

The Ratification of the Conventions of nine States, shall be sufficient for the Establishment of this Constitution between the States so ratifying the Same.

The Word, "the," being interlined between the seventh and eighth Lines of the first Page, the Word "Thirty" being partly written on an Erazure in the fifteenth Line of the first Page, The Words "is tried" being interlined between the thirty second and thirty third Lines of the first Page and the Word "the" being interlined between the forty third and forty fourth Lines of the second Page.

Attest William Jackson Secretary

done in Convention by the Unanimous Consent of the States present the Seventeenth Day of September in the Year of our Lord one thousand seven hundred and Eighty seven and of the Independance of the United States of America the Twelfth In witness whereof We have hereunto subscribed our Names,

(names omitted)

APPENDIX L
United States Bill of Rights*

The Preamble to The Bill of Rights

Congress of the United States begun and held at the City of New-York, on Wednesday the fourth of March, one thousand seven hundred and eighty nine.

THE conventions of a number of the states, having at the time of their adopting the constitution, expressed a desire, in order to prevent misconstruction or abuse of its powers, that further declaratory and restrictive clauses should be added: and as extending the ground of public confidence in the government, will best ensure the beneficent ends of its institution.

RESOLVED by the Senate and House of Representatives of the United States of America, in Congress assembled, two thirds of both Houses concurring, that the following Articles be proposed to the Legislatures of the several States, as amendments to the Constitution of the United States, all, or any of which Articles, when ratified by three fourths of the said Legislatures, to be valid to all intents and purposes, as part of the said Constitution; viz.

ARTICLES in addition to, and Amendment of the Constitution of the United States of America, proposed by Congress, and ratified by the Legislatures of the several States, pursuant to the fifth Article of the original Constitution.

---

* Source: U.S. National Archives, *available at* http://www.archives.gov/exhibits/charters/bill_of_rights_transcript.html.

Note: This text is a transcription of the first ten amendments to the Constitution in their original form. These amendments were ratified December 15, 1791, and from what is known as the "Bill of the Rights." The capitalization and punctuation in this version is from the enrolled original of the Joint Resolution of Congress proposing the Bill of Rights, which is on permanent display in the Rotunda of the National Archives Building, Washington, D.C.

Amendment I

Congress shall make no law respecting an establishment of religion, or prohibiting the free exercise thereof; or abridging the freedom of speech, or of the press; or the right of the people peaceably to assemble, and to petition the Government for a redress of grievances.

Amendment II

A well regulated Militia, being necessary to the security of a free State, the right of the people to keep and bear Arms, shall not be infringed.

Amendment III

No Soldier shall, in time of peace be quartered in any house, without the consent of the Owner, nor in time of war, but in a manner to be prescribed by law.

Amendment IV

The right of the people to be secure in their persons, houses, papers, and effects, against unreasonable searches and seizures, shall not be violated, and no Warrants shall issue, but upon probable cause, supported by Oath or affirmation, and particularly describing the place to be searched, and the persons or things to be seized.

Amendment V

No person shall be held to answer for a capital, or otherwise infamous crime, unless on a presentment or indictment of a Grand Jury, except in cases arising in the land or naval forces, or in the Militia, when in actual service in time of War or public danger; nor shall any person be subject for the same offence to be twice put in jeopardy of life or limb; nor shall be compelled in any criminal case to be a witness against himself, nor be deprived of life, liberty, or property, without due process of law; nor shall private property be taken for public use, without just compensation.

Amendment VI

In all criminal prosecutions, the accused shall enjoy the right to a speedy and public trial, by an impartial jury of the State and district wherein the crime shall have been committed, which district shall have been previously ascertained by law, and to be informed of the nature and cause of the accusation; to be confronted with the witnesses against him; to have compulsory process for obtaining witnesses in his favor, and to have the Assistance of Counsel for his defence.

Amendment VII

In Suits at common law, where the value in controversy shall exceed twenty dollars, the right of trial by jury shall be preserved, and no fact tried by a jury, shall be otherwise re-examined in any Court of the United States, than according to the rules of the common law.

Amendment VIII

Excessive bail shall not be required, nor excessive fines imposed, nor cruel and unusual punishments inflicted.

Amendment IX

The enumeration in the Constitution, of certain rights, shall not be construed to deny or disparage others retained by the people.

Amendment X

The powers not delegated to the United States by the Constitution, nor prohibited by it to the States, are reserved to the States respectively, or to the people.

APPENDIX M
Chronology of Magna Carta and Related Events

August 5, 1100	Henry I issues Coronation Charter with many of the same provisions as would later appear in the 1215 Magna Carta.
January 8, 1198	Elevation of Pope Innocent III.
May 27, 1199	Accession of King John; no coronation charter is issued.
1199	First recorded reference to habeas corpus.
June 1207	Innocent III selects Stephen Langton to be Archbishop of Canterbury despite King John's objections.
March 24, 1208	England is placed under papal interdict by Pope Innocent III, prohibiting priests from conducting many religious ceremonies.
November 8, 1209	Innocent III excommunicates King John.
June 1, 1213	King John agrees to Langton as Archbishop of Canterbury.
July 1213	King John's excommunication is lifted.
April 21, 1214	King John cedes England to Pope Innocent III in exchange for removal of papal interdict, thus gaining the king a powerful ally.
July 27, 1214	France defeats England at the Battle of Bouvines, politically weakening King John.
May 5, 1215	Rebellious barons withdraw their allegiance from King John.
May 17, 1215	Rebellious barons secure control over London.
June 10, 1215	Rebellious barons and King John meet at Runnymede.
June 15, 1215	King John agrees to Magna Carta.
June 19, 1215	King John receives renewed oaths of fealty from the barons, thus making peace.
June 20, 1215	King John issues the King's Writ announcing Magna Carta and instructing each sheriff to have it read publicly and to ensure that its terms are honored.
June 24, 1215	The initial seven exemplifications of Magna Carta are distributed, dated June 15, 1215.
June 27, 1215	Translation of the Magna Carta in the vernacular Anglo-Norman French is prepared for knights.

July, 1215	Innocent III excommunicates the rebel barons, followed not long afterward by renewed fighting between the barons and King John.
August 24, 1215	Pope Innocent III annuls Magna Carta on grounds of coercion through a papal bull (the papal bull reaches England in September 1215).
May 22, 1216	The military forces of Prince Louis of France land in England.
July 16, 1216	Pope Innocent III dies.
October 18/19, 1216	King John dies and is succeeded by his nine-year-old son, Henry III.
November 12, 1216	A second iteration of Magna Carta is promulgated over the seals of royal regent, William Marshall, and papal legate, Guala Bicchieri. Several chapters are deleted.
November 6, 1217	A third iteration of Magna Carta is promulgated, again over the seals of Marshall and the papal legate, with further changes. Carta de Foresta (also known as Charter of the Forest), which includes some clauses formerly in Magna Carta, is promulgated for the first time.
1221	First known legal citation to Magna Carta is made by a private litigant.
February 11, 1225	King Henry III, now 18, promulgates a fourth iteration of Magna Carta; this will turn out to be the most commonly cited version. Carta de Foresta is also reissued.
1297	King Edward I reissues the two Charters of 1225. Soon afterward, the reissued text of Magna Carta is included in the first English statute roll. He also issues *confirmatio cartarum* confirming both Magna Carta and Carta de Foresta.
1305	The *confirmatio cartarum* is voided by Pope Clement V.
1331–1369	"The Six Statutes" are enacted, recasting certain parts of the Charters. The third statute, adopted in 1354, redefines chapter 39/29, "free man" becoming "no man, of whatever estate or condition he may be," and the phrase "due process of law" replacing "lawful judgement of his peers or the law of the land."
14th century	Magna Carta is reaffirmed on more than 30 occasions.
15th century	Magna Carta is reaffirmed on eight occasions.
17th century	Colonial charters in North America draw upon concepts derived from Magna Carta.
Early 17th century	Sir Edward Coke, John Selden, John Hampden, and others argue effectively, if inaccurately, that Magna Carta reflects the "ancient constitution" of England. They also contend that the document runs counter to the absolutist pretensions of the early Stuart kings.

1627	Selden makes the novel argument in *Darnel's case* that habeas corpus is tied to Magna Carta, contending that the Charter's due process provisions preclude summary detention by the Crown.
June 1628	Parliament passes the Petition of Right. During the debate, Coke, the primary drafter, argues that chapter 39/29 meant that no one could be imprisoned without due process of law.
1670	The independence of juries is bolstered through legal argument made by William Penn citing Magna Carta.
May 27, 1679	The Habeas Corpus Act is enacted in England, reinforcing the traditional common law writ.
December 16, 1689	The English Bill of Rights is adopted, building on the spirit of Magna Carta.
1765–1769	William Blackstone publishes his widely read *Commentaries on the Laws of England*, which discusses Magna Carta and distinguishes between the original Charter and later reissues.
1770s–1780s	New state constitutions in the United States draw upon concepts derived from Magna Carta.
September 17, 1787	The drafting of the U.S. Constitution is completed.
December 15, 1791	The American Bill of Rights is adopted which draws upon principles derived from Magna Carta.
19th and 20th centuries	All but three and a half Magna Carta provisions are repealed in Britain.
1957	The Magna Carta memorial at Runnymede is donated by the American Bar Association.
2015	The 800th Anniversary of Magna Carta is commemorated around the world.

Glossary

Advowson—The authority to recommend or appoint an individual to an open benefice.

Afforestation—Enlargement of Royal Forest domain and jurisdiction.

Agist—To permit cattle to graze for a fee.

Agistment—The proceeds of pasturage in the Royal Forests.

Aids—A grant of funds owed to a lord by a tenant during highly trying or disruptive times.

Amercements—Fines imposed at the discretion of a royal official.

Assarts—Mandatory payments, e.g., rent.

Assize—A judicial or council session.

Assize of darrein presentment—A writ permitting a jury to decide who has proper right of advowson over a benefice.

Attachments—Arrests.

Balivus—Bailiff. In Magna Carta, it likely refers to all governmental officials.

Benefice—An ecclesiastical appointment to conduct pastoral duties that include the receipt of property and income.

Boscus dominicus regis—Royal Forests.

Burgage—A type of landholding within a town or borough whereby property was held in exchange for rent to a lord.

Cheminage—The authority to charge fees to escort people through a Royal Forest.

Common of marl—The right to extract clay or other marl.

Common of turbary—The right to cut peat or turf, typically used for fuel, on another's property or on common land.

Curia regis—The King's court or council.

Demesne—In the context of the Forest Charter, the domain of the Royal Forest.

Disafforestation—To reduce the Royal Forest domain and free land from its jurisdiction.

Ells—A unit of measure roughly approximating a yard.

Enumerated power—Power expressly provided by the Constitution to a branch of government.

Escheat—Reversion of land to the king or lord upon the death of an heirless landowner.

Estover—The right to collect wood.

Fee-farm—Fee-simple property that is assessed a fixed amount of rent.

Fideiussor—Under Roman law, a guarantor.

Fish-weirs—Barriers inserted into a river to trap or direct fish.

Forest Eyre—Proceedings of the Royal Forest Courts.

Forester in fee—A forester who inherits his office.

Fugerium—The right to collect bracken.

Herbage—The right to gather berries and herbs.

Implied power—Power not expressly granted in the Constitution but that may be reasonably inferred to exist to carry out the stated powers of a branch of government.

Inherent power—Power not expressly granted or implied in the Constitution but that is thought to be part of the very nature of a particular branch of government.

Ius commune or jus commune—A medieval legal system composed of a combination of canon law and Roman law that is the precursor of today's civil law.

Jus cogens—Under international law, peremptory principles and norms.

Jus sanguine—The law where an individual's parents were from.

Jus soli—The law where an individual was born.

Justiciar—A royal official who presided over judicial proceedings, e.g., proceedings regarding forest law.

Lawing—The act of removing dogs' toes to prevent them from hunting deer or other animals of the Royal Forest.

Legate—Papal envoy or representative.

Legem terrae—"Law of the land"; today also read as "due process of law."

Liber homo—A free man.

Libere tenentes—Land held by the church, nobles, and free holders.

Libertates de forestis—Liberties of the forest.

Maltote—A tax placed on wool.

Marl— An earthy mixture of fine-grained minerals, which range widely in composition; calcium-containing marl is referred to as clay.

Mas—Acorns or beech mast.

Mesne—In feudal society, an individual who ranked between a tenant and the lord.

Mises—The issue to be determined in a writ of right (a legal action brought to reclaim property possessed by another).

Moneyer—one who lends money or mints currency.

Monstrans de droit—A method of obtaining redress from the king.

Monstraunces—Grievances.

Mort d'ancestor— An action to recover a person's lands after being deprived of them by another after the passing of an ancestor.

Nonrefoulement—A principle of international law that refugees should not be returned to countries where their basic rights to life or liberty are likely to be violated.

Novel disseisin—An action to recover lands of which the claimant had been dispossessed.

Omnes de regno nostro—Everyone in the kingdom.

Pannage—Releasing domestic pigs in a forest to feed.

Pasturage—The right permitting cattle to graze.

Perambulation—The act of inspecting the boundaries of a holding, such as a Royal Forest.

Prises—Seized property.

Purprestures—Encroachments or enclosures on royal land rights through unauthorized use.

Regard—Inspections or oversight of the Royal Forests.

Regarders—Twelve knights responsible for conducting investigations of the Royal Forests.

Right of venison—The king's right to hunt deer, boar, and most other large animals in Royal Forests.

Right of vert—The right to take or use trees, bushes, understory, and other flora.

Robara—Cutting back a tree or shrub to produce fuel wood.

Routier—A mercenary.

Royal Forests—Land and natural resources under the dominion of the king.

Salvific knowledge—A body of beliefs related to salvation.

Scutage—A monetary payment in place of providing military service to the king by the barons.

Selvedge—The edge of a part of fabric.

Serjeanties—A type of feudal obligation that could only be granted to the king.

Socage—The holding of land in return for nonmilitary service.

Swainmote—A gathering of pig herders.

Swanimotes—Councils (foresters, verderers, and agisters) to supervise the introduction of domestic animals into the forests.

Tallage—A land tax or toll typically assessed on those who lived in towns and royal demesne.

Trespasses of venison—The unlawful hunting of deer.

Trespasses of vert—The unlawful harvesting of vegetation.

Turbary—The right to extract heathland turf for fuel.

Utrumque ius—Used interchangeably with *ius commune*.

Vastum—Waste; collecting more than the allowed right, resulting in a degradation of resources.

Verderer—An elected official responsible for the Royal Forest and removable by the king.

Villein—A partially free man with rights against all except his lord.

Wapentakes— An administrative subdivision within a shire or county.

Woodward—An official whose responsibility was to ensure that royal rights in the forest were not encroached upon.

Writ of praecipe—A writ instructing an individual to take a certain action or appear in court and demonstrate why he should not have to take such action.

Index